STARTING THE DIALOGUE

M000099295

PERSPECTIVES ON TECHNOLOGY & SOCIETY
SECOND EDITION

Kendall Hunt
publishing company

Cover images © Shutterstock, Inc.

Kendall Hunt
publishing company

www.kendallhunt.com
Send all inquiries to:
4050 Westmark Drive
Dubuque, IA 52004-1840

Contents

Acknowledgments

We extend thanks to the editors and staff at Kendall-Hunt Publishers, in particular Sara McGovern and Katie Wendler, for their support for this project and for their patience; to our colleague Brian Raichle, who collaborated on the first edition of this book; and to our students in the Department of Sustainable Technology & the Built Environment at Appalachian State University, whose passion and commitment to a sustainable future provide inspiration to us all.

Authors' Note

All royalties from sales of this textbook at Appalachian State University are placed in a foundation account established to support student projects and activities within the Department of Sustainable Technology & the Built Environment.

Preface

Introduction

The idea for this book has percolated for several years, during which time we have both taught university courses focusing on the interactions between technology and society. Part of the joy in teaching these courses has been the opportunity to introduce our students to the wealth of excellent books, articles, and other media that delve into the issues surrounding the development and use of technology. These resources range from very philosophical examinations of technology as an expression of human creativity to very technical treatments of specific technologies, and everything in between. To borrow a distinction made by a former colleague, we can talk about "big T" technology, meaning the *phenomenon* of technological activity and its implications; or we can talk about "little t" technology, meaning the myriad specific tools, objects, systems, and processes that comprise the human-made world. This book strives to provide a mix of these two perspectives, using articles and excerpts that have been specifically chosen for their capacity to illustrate—and spur discussions on—societal issues associated with technology.

For readers unfamiliar with the interdisciplinary field of the study of technology, a definition is in order. Specifically, we define technology as the artifacts and processes that make up the human-made world. From an academic perspective, one could say that technology is *the study of* those artifacts and processes. Most importantly, we wish for readers of this book to view technology from the broad range of human technological activity, rather than from the narrowly constrained view of computer technologies often intended when the word "technology" appears in common usage. In addition, readers are encouraged to remember that they use and interact daily with these technological artifacts and systems, and that understanding these technologies will benefit them personally, and society collectively.

A number of books have been published that are similar in structure to this one; these edited compilations are evidence of the broad literature on, and growing interest in, society and technology interactions. We have used and appreciated these edited volumes, but over the years continued to believe that there was room for another text that offers a broader mix of topical readings, including some with a heavier technical emphasis and with a particular emphasis on sustainability. In addition, we have provided background information on each topic, discussion questions, and suggestions for activities and additional resources, all of which we hope will make for a very user-friendly, and useful, book.

This is a far-ranging book in the sense that we have selected a diverse set of examples to illustrate the many technological choices we face on a daily basis. The key word is *choice*; all of us make daily decisions about which technologies we will use, buy, promote, support, and/or ignore. Sometimes, these decisions are thrust upon us as we react to the negative impacts of a particular technology; sometimes, our choices are very constrained. No matter the case, we believe that all of us share a responsibility for becoming as informed as possible about technologies and their impacts, both good and bad.

The Structure of This Book

For the second edition of this book, we have selected a number of new readings and replaced others that were part of the first edition. All of the section introductions have been significantly revised and updated, and the supporting activities and additional resources sections have similarly been revised. As in the first edition, the book is divided into 10 thematic sections. We encourage readers to read the section introductions before reading any of the excerpts, because these introductions provide contextual information that helps to frame the readings contained in each section. Similarly, we hope that you'll read the excerpt introductions, which provide background information about the topic and about the authors.

Section One discusses the reasons for and importance of treating technology studies as a much-needed and legitimate academic discipline. It also offers a more comprehensive exploration of the definition of technology and an introduction to the philosophy of technology so as to provide a framework for discussing the topical issues covered in the remainder of the book. The excerpt by technology historian Melvin Kranzberg outlines six basic laws of technology to help readers develop a perspective on the broad and largely unstudied field of technology. Kranzberg acknowledges the compelling ability of technology to shape society and be self-perpetuating, but ultimately feels we have the ability to control and remake our world through knowledge of technology's interactions with culture and society. Professor Bryan Pfaffenburger wants to persuade his colleagues in anthropology to study technology and conversely to bring anthropological theory to technology studies. Pfaffenburger's *Social Anthropology of Technology,* the second excerpt in Section One, attempts to unite these two fields of study. Both of these articles explore the importance of

technology studies and allow us to identify some of the fundamental arguments surrounding the interplay of technology and society.

Section Two extends the discussion started in the first section by illustrating technological factors that shape society and how those interactions affect technological choice. Beginning the section is an excerpt from the book *The Whale and the Reactor* by Langdon Winner, which explores specifically how our technologies necessarily create systems that affect the ways we must behave in order for the system to function, thereby influencing our relationships with one another and the larger society. The following excerpt by Evan and Manion explores quantitative means of assessing the effects of technology. They describe some of the accepted strategies for calculating costs, benefits, and risks associated with new technologies. Although risk assessment and cost/benefit analysis are important components of the decision-making process, as these authors point out our ability to identify (let alone quantify) risks in complex systems is limited at best. Malcolm Gladwell, who in his role as a staff writer at *The New Yorker* has written very accessible and entertaining case studies about technological decision-making, uses the example of choice related to the personal automobile. Through this example we see that decisions about technology are sometimes based more on *perceptions* of the way things are than they are on more factual information, and thus are not always well reasoned. Finally, we include an excerpt from the book *The Hockey Stick and the Climate Wars,* by climatologist Michael Mann, which explores how societal forces shape debates about scientific and technological issues. Important policy decisions concerning technology are not just based on the merit of sound science and engineering, but also on economic, cultural, and political realities. Like other complex phenomena, it's impossible to document or to predict with 100% accuracy the likely trajectory of climate change, particularly when the effects are at a global scale. Those with an interest in discounting or denying climate change exploit these complexities and uncertainties to undermine the weight of evidence that supports the scientific community's predictions. Through the examples in this section, we hope that readers will understand that technology has a profound effect on the society we live in, but predicting or understanding those effects is a difficult task, and the ability of society to control technological choice is a complicated issue impacted by multiple cultural, scientific, and political forces.

In Section Three, we start our exploration of specific technologies with those that address our most fundamental needs of food, water, and shelter. Out of all the technological dilemmas we face, those associated with meeting these basic needs are, surprisingly, often the least widely discussed. The section starts with a declaration delivered by Newton Crain Blanchard, the governor of the State of Louisiana in 1908 at the first Conference of the National Governors Association, which was convened by President Theodore Roosevelt. It serves to show that we in the United States have long officially considered the conservation of our natural resources as a national duty and priority (even if our policy has not always reflected that). Fred Pearce offers some sobering statistics about water usage worldwide, and describes several large-scale projects designed to meet the growing demand for fresh water for irrigation and residential and commercial use. Access to fresh water is increasingly being understood as the global crisis it may soon become, and efforts to exploit existing freshwater resources can often lead to massive environmental and cultural disruptions. Gay Daly describes another concern associated with pollutants in our water and air supplies: the growing body of evidence that ubiquitous human-made chemical compounds

may in fact be disrupting the reproductive capacity of animals, including humans. On a more positive note, the section moves on to some articles that highlight new approaches to the design of buildings, detailing the many elements of structures that can lead to a healthier, more efficient built environment while conserving both material and energy resources. Finally, Michael Bomford makes the link between energy consumption and food production. Industrial agriculture has helped to feed billions; however, it has led to excessive water use, energy consumption, and pollution from fertilizers and pesticides. Bomford explores the possibilities of a more sustainable food production system. The writings in this section illustrate how all the systems that provide us food, water, and shelter are interconnected, and the sustainable use of these resources will involve changes in all three.

Section Four focuses on the resource that fuels all of human technology: energy. More specifically, the excerpts in this section examine the variety of energy resources upon which we rely as well as some of the issues related to energy utilization. Generally, when we speak of energy within these excerpts we are actually referring to two aspects of energy: the conversion technologies that bring us electricity in usable forms to power our appliances, lights, and machines; and petroleum products that provide the liquid fuel to power our automobiles and other transport devices. The first excerpt of this section establishes the essential rationale for resource conservation. E.F Schumacher explains that our natural resources are the capital upon which our industrial system relies, and yet we mistakenly treat these resources like income. He states that this is a fundamentally tragic error since a business can only survive if it conserves its capital and develops its income, so it is imperative for the enterprise of industrial society to conserve its natural capital such as fossil fuels and develop its income fuels like solar and hydro power. The subsequent writings explore our stewardship of this natural capital. Maryanne Vollers provides a poignant look at the way our appetite for coal-based electricity has affected the rural communities of Appalachia. Heinberg tackles the problem of oil and challenges notions about supplies by explaining in careful detail the concept of "peak oil" and its ramifications for a society that is so dependent on this fuel source. Amory Lovins demonstrates in some detail that our most effective energy resource is actually energy efficiency. Nevertheless, the last selection by Edwin Dobb shows that for all the lip service we may give to conservation and protecting our natural resources, when there is money to be made we push the pedal to the metal (mistakenly treating our capital as if it is income).

Sections Five through Nine are linked conceptually in that each of these sections offers selected perspectives on different technological contexts, including transportation technologies, communication technologies, biological and medical technologies, military technologies, and workplace technologies. Each of these sections includes readings that highlight the social, cultural, environmental, or economic questions posed by various technologies, and the questions raised provide opportunities for further study and discussion about technology's effects. The readings included here were selected because they offer interesting cases through which both the technical details associated with the technology and the explorations of the larger contexts in which the technologies are used can be examined. For example, in *Surveillance Nation* Farmer and Mann describe the tools being used to monitor public spaces, but the larger topics this leads to include privacy,

government policy, and the implications of widespread use of surveillance tools.

We complete the book in Section Ten with two book excerpts that illustrate the perspectives on technology introduced in Section One, but with an eye toward the future. Science fiction novels, television dramas, and movies have long painted visions of what our technological future might look like, and these visions generally share some common features: we'll be smarter; own more labor-saving devices; and be able to further overcome the constraints of space, time, and biological heritage, or we will all die in a dystopian hell hole. If you could design the technological future, what would it look like? Susan Greenfield looks into the future, noting that the scientific breakthroughs of the twenty-first century will lead to higher levels of technical feasibility, but also reminding us of the hard-earned lessons of the past: that technological advancement comes at a price. Section One emphasized the importance of studying and understanding technology in order to make sound decisions about the future of our technological society. To drive this point home one last time, our final excerpt asks: are we sleepwalking into the future? James Howard Kunstler takes a hard look at a post-oil world, and sees a dystopian future. Will the transition be as traumatic as he predicts? The answer to that question is as difficult as all the other questions regarding technological choices we have explored in this book. But studying and attempting to understand the technological system and how it is integrated with society helps us to understand what the issues, challenges, and realities will be, and forces us to reflect upon possibilities, rather than just "sleepwalking into the future."

Defining Technology And Its Role

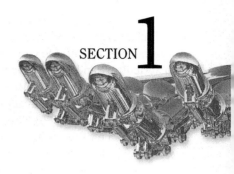

Technological Literacy

Any examination of the relationship between society and technology must start by establishing a context that helps frame the nature of that examination. Much has been written and said about the nature and impacts of technology, although curiously the formal study of this field has gained only modest traction in traditional academic circles. The French writer Jacques Ellul, whose work *The Technological Society* has been one of the most influential in the genre, stated four decades ago: "No social, human, or spiritual fact is so important as the fact of technique in the modern world. And yet no subject is so little understood" (Ellul, 1964, p. 5). The situation is little changed today.

Why is this so? We could point to any number of reasons, but will highlight just a few. First, technology encompasses such a vast array of human activity that its scope is difficult to grasp. If technology represents the totality of the tools and systems that make up the human-made environment, it's difficult to place technology within the disciplinary boundaries that often define our formal educational institutions. Second, for many who adhere to the purity of what might be called a "classical" education, technology is often dismissed as an "applied science," the study of which is the provenance of mechanics, engineers, or technicians. Third, even among those who do

focus their attention on the phenomenon of technology, some are more drawn to the details of the tools and techniques, while others are more inclined to theorize about the social and environmental impacts of technology and care less about technical details. Few of us have, in other words, all the information necessary for a comprehensive understanding of technology.

Nevertheless, there is a growing belief that all members of modern society, dependent as we are on technological tools and systems, must achieve what has been termed *technological literacy*. The characteristics of this literacy include knowing about the concepts, benefits, and risks associated with technology; exhibiting a willingness to learn about new technologies; participating in decision-making about technology; and having the capabilities to use, design, and evaluate technologies. The benefits of technological literacy to the individual include the ability to make better-informed choices, to become a more actively engaged citizen, to contribute to the workforce, and to function more effectively in society (National Academy of Engineering, 2002).

There is yet another reason to promote the goal of technological literacy for all, having to do with the changing nature of our technological development. From an evolutionary perspective, one does not have to look too far into our past to find a time when the technological tools and systems we employed were relatively simple and relatively small-scale. As recently as 1900, for example, 41% of U.S. citizens were employed in agriculture and 60% of the population lived in rural areas; by 2000 less than 2% of the U.S. workforce was employed in agriculture (Dmitri, Effland, & Conklin, 2005). This is just one piece of evidence pointing to an overall shift in our technological development. While agrarian activity decreased in importance, industrial activity, with its associated resource implications, advanced. According to Paul DeVore, the types of changes that took place in society as the result of industrialization were important in three ways (DeVore, 1980). Because industrial activity is so capital and resource intensive, it requires a hierarchical organizational structure. Furthermore, industrialization "presupposes mass consumption," rapidly altering the size of the production system and the scope of its reach (presaging globalization). Finally, production of this size and scope demands an emphasis on production *efficiency*. Whereas once we toiled with simple tools to produce food, shelter, and basic amenities for the survival of ourselves and our families, today we engage in increasingly specialized work with highly evolved tools to create and manage complex, often centralized systems of manufacturing, energy production, transportation, communication, and beyond. The key characteristics of this technological evolution, for purposes of this discussion, are two: technologies have become harder to understand (and thus to evaluate and control); and the potential reach of these technologies has expanded far beyond the level of local impact to, in some cases, *global* impact. Tools of war and global climate change represent just two examples of this characteristic.

These last points are worthy of some additional examination. With regard to the first—the greater complexity and the emphasis on

hierarchical, centralized organizational structures associated with modern technology—there is a subtle side effect that results. In order to participate in the benefits of the complex system, and sometimes even in spite of a conscious desire to avoid the system, we must accept the confines and dictates of the system—we must play by the rules. In this way, the system itself begins to exert control over those who created and use it. For example, air travel requires an enormous infrastructure of schedules, baggage handling, people movers, and systems for ticketing and planning. Individuals who wish to travel by air have to conform to specific ways of acting and moving in order to take advantage of the system, even when this conformity is inconvenient, unhelpful, or unpleasant.

With regard to the second point—the reach of modern technology—there is an important, related issue. The reach of technology can extend in two kinds of ways. One way has to do with the power of an individual technology; the nuclear bomb, for example, is a single artifact whose reach when detonated can potentially harm millions of people and destroy entire ecosystems. The second way the reach of technology can extend is a function of population. If one person dumps sewage into the river its effect will be minimal; if a city of a million people does the same, the effects can be catastrophic.

Toward a Philosophy and Definition of Technology

Defining technology may seem like strictly an academic exercise. And yet, how can one discuss an undefined subject? Often people chafe at the inability to settle on a singular definition of technology. However, the root of "define" is the Latin *difinire* (to set boundaries), so the mere discussion of a definition helps the process of setting the boundaries of the subject. Indeed, the varying definitions of technology often set the parameters for debate about technology and its effects. For instance, according to Robert Wauzzinski (2001), in his book *Discerning Prometheus: The Cry for Wisdom in Our Technological Society*, if one defines technologies as merely tools one is more inclined to see technology as being neutral. However, if one's definition includes systems (both physical and intellectual), then the argument for the non-neutrality of technology is more compelling. Wauzzinski pointed out that systems create structures that we must live within and rules that we must adhere to if the systems are going to function. Indeed, if systems define technology it is difficult to make the argument for the autonomy of humanity from technology. People do not have a choice about the system they are born into, and it is the nature of those systems and the technologies they contain that often dictate the behaviors that we must practice.

Seen in that light, the effects of technology hardly seem neutral, or even anything that a single individual has much control over. Langdon Winner (1986) devoted an entire essay to this concept in his book *The Whale and the Reactor: A Search for Limits in an Age of High Technology* when he explored "Technologies as Forms of Life." Contrary to what the title suggests, Winner was not implying that technologies are life forms, but rather that they create the structures in which we must live; he stated that in modern society "technologies are not merely aids to human activity, but also powerful forces acting to reshape that activity and its meaning" (p. 6). One might ask, as Winner did, "as 'we make things work,' what kind of world are we making?" (p. 17). Adherents of this view of technology, shared by the father of the appropriate technology movement E.F. Schumacher in his seminal book *Small is Beautiful: Economics as if People Mattered* (1973), are often

referred to as Structuralists. Wauzzinski characterized structuralists as the type of individual who believes technological development must be guided by rules and principles that do not assume the autonomy of people from technology. The most important question for a stucturalist is the proper place that technology occupies in our lives. A more extreme version of this type is a Technological Determinist, who contends that humanity has little, if any, control over technology, and that in reality technology and the resources at hand have more to do with determining human culture and civilization than does any specific human intention. Jared Diamond is often cited as one of the foremost contemporary adherents of this philosophy. In his Pulitzer Prize-winning book *Guns, Germs and Steel: The Fate of Human Societies* (1999) he argued that some societies advanced technologically and others did not based primarily on the luck of their particular geography and whether it was conducive to the development of an agriculture that could lead to food surpluses.

Other types of philosophical views of technology commonly listed are Optimists (a.k.a. Cornucopians), Pessimists, and Realists. Optimists assume technology is value-free, accept the autonomy of humanity, and see technology as a universal liberator of humanity. Buckminster Fuller, twentieth-century philosopher, scientist, and inventor, is often given as an example of such a type. Fuller wrote in *Grunch of Giants* (1983):

> I do know that technologically humanity now has the opportunity, for the first time in its history, to operate our planet in such a manner as to support and accommodate all humanity at a substantially more advanced standard of living than any humans have ever experienced. (p. xx)

Pessimists largely see the negative impacts of technology and liken it to Frankenstein's monster: it is our own creation yet we cannot control it and it will ultimately destroy us. The term *Luddite* is sometimes applied to technological pessimists. The name derives from Ned Ludd, the mythical leader of nineteenth-century textile workers in England who resisted the mechanization of the textile trade and who sabotaged machines to protest low wages and poor working conditions. Realists believe technology has both positives and negatives that can be determined scientifically through risk assessment, and that humans are ultimately utility maximizers. Such an outlook has bred the cost-benefit analysis, one important method of assessing the value of technology today.

Of course, all of these typologies are stereotypes that attempt to capture the essence of a particular viewpoint. In reality, few people adhere completely to one type or the other. Most of us can identify elements of all these perspectives in our own views of technology. They are merely a way of organizing the debate, which is the function of philosophy. The concept of autonomy often lies at the heart of any debate about technology. Do we have dominion over our technology (realists, optimists), or is pursuit of technology so ingrained within our nature that we have as little control over it as we do our emotions (pessimists, determinists)? Therefore, how we define technology is fundamental to our understanding of it and its effect on our lives (structuralists).

One approach to definition is to look at the etymology, or origin, of the word. The word *technology* itself comes from two Greek words, transliterated: *techne* and *logos*. *Techne* means art or skill, as evidenced in our understanding of the word *technique*, and *logos* refers to understanding something through reason, or the study of the thing—for example, biology is the study of life, and anthropology the study of humans. Purely through transliteration, technology would mean the study of the skilled arts and crafts, or technique. Jacques Ellul (1964)

reflected this definition of technology when he wrote, "no social, human, or spiritual fact is so important as the fact of technique in the modern world (p. 3)." The first book in English where the word *technology* actually appeared was Bigelow's (1831) *Elements of Technology*. He stated, "technology consists of the principles, processes, and nomenclatures of the most conspicuous arts, particularly those which involve applications of science" (p. *v*). These early definitions and uses of the word seem to reflect its etymology, but differ from the more contemporary use of the word, which applies more to the physical objects of our creation rather than to the processes, or techniques, that create them.

Val Dusek (2006), in his book *Philosophy of Technology: An Introduction,* presented the following guidelines for a definition:

1. A definition should not be too broad or narrow. (That is, the definition should not include things we would not designate by the word we are defining, and the definition should not be so restricted as to exclude things that should fall under the term defined.)
2. A definition should not be circular. (For instance, we shouldn't define "technology" as "anything technological" and then define "technological" as "anything pertaining to technology.")
3. A definition should not use figurative language or metaphors.
4. A definition should not be solely negative but should be in positive terms. (A purely negative definition in most cases would not sufficiently limit the range of application of the term). (p. 30)

As the root of definition (*difinire*) suggests, due to the broad nature of technology it might be best to approach its definition by identifying what is not technology. Obviously, not *everything* can be technology; if so, the word loses all meaning. To mean everything is to mean nothing. So what is *not* technology? Is a tree technology? A bone? What if that bone is wielded by a hominid to dig a hole? Why is an unutilized bone not technology, but if it is utilized for a particular end it becomes technology? This hints at a fundamental character of technology. But what is it? How can it be expressed? The test of a definition is that you can think of no example that is not covered by the definition. Dusek (2006) suggested four definitions of technology that cover most of the concepts ordinarily found in the literature of technology.

The first definition views technology as hardware, tools and machines. The second defines technology as rules, or patterns of means-and-end relationships. A third definition views technology as a system. This approach states that artifacts need to be considered within the context of their use. The fourth definition views technology as applied science, which can be misleading, according to Dusek. Science, or the combination of controlled experiments and mathematical laws of nature, is only about 400 years old, and arguably technology has existed since that first hominid picked up the first bone to be used as a tool. Dusek contended that discoveries and innovations are often not the result of straightforward application of scientific theory. Even recently, many inventors have not known the laws of science that applied to their inventions, undermining the notion that technology is simply applied science. For instance, Thomas Edison did not know the electromagnetic theory of Maxwell, and Louis Pasteur knew nothing of germs until he saw them in the microscope. Pasteur described the effect of science on technology and innovation as "chance favors the prepared mind."

4 definitions

1. hardware → computers, etc.
2. rules → means-+-ends relationships
3. system → context of use
4. applied science → technology as science
   ↳ misleading b/c tech. came before science.

Kranzberg's Laws

Melvin Kranzberg is an historian of technology. Brian Arthur (2009) wrote, in *The Nature of Technology: What it is and How it Evolves,* that as he perused the literature about technology he found "historians of all people had the most to say about the ways and essence of technology and its innovation" (p. 4). In this excerpt from 1986, Kranzberg stated in his fifth law that "all history is relevant, but the history of technology is most relevant" (p. 553). He based that claim on his belief in the fundamentally technological nature of humanity. If those in highly technological societies want to better understand their society, how it came into being, and what are the best ways forward, Kranzberg believed it is imperative for them to understand the history of the technologies that brought them to the present moment.

Kranzberg outlined six basic laws of technology, not as commandments but as truisms, that he felt can help us develop some perspective on the broad, largely unstudied field of technology. His desire to create these laws was driven primarily over a concern about what he considered the cliché of our age, that we do not control technology, but rather it controls us: the deterministic viewpoint. He claimed that we may never reach an agreement on this issue, but "there are several things that we do know" (p. 545). He summed those things up in *Kranzberg's Laws.* The essence of the argument that runs through all his laws is that although technology is not neutral and its internal mechanisms do tend to breed new technologies and innovation, it is also not completely deterministic. Other factors besides technology itself, such as environmental concerns and other social factors, affect its adoption and innovation.

As much as Kranzberg recognized the compelling ability of technology to shape society and be self-perpetuating, he ultimately felt we have the ability to control and remake our world, particularly through "a knowledge of the development of technology and of its interactions with culture and society" (p. 559).

Melvin Kranzberg was the Callaway Professor of the History of Technology at the Georgia Institute of Technology, and the founding editor of the journal *Technology and Culture.* He was a recipient of the Society for the History of Technology's (SHOT) Leonardo da Vinci Medal, and later served as president of SHOT. Kranzberg died in 1995.

Presidential Address
Technology and History: "Kranzberg's Laws"

Melvin Kranzberg

A few months ago I received a note from a long-time collaborator in building the Society for the History of Technology, Eugene S. Ferguson, in which he wrote, "Each of us has only one message to convey." Ferguson was being typically modest in referring to an article of his in a French journal[1] emphasizing the hands-on, design component of technical development, and

DR. KRANZBERG, Callaway Professor of the History of Technology at the Georgia Institute of Technology, was the founding editor of *Technology and Culture,* the recipient of the Society for the History of Technology's Leonardo da Vinci Medal in 1967, and president of SHOT in 1983–84. He presented this presidential address on October 19, 1985, at the Henry Ford Museum in Dearborn, Michigan.

Kranzberg, Melvin. "Technology and History: 'Kranzberg's Laws.'" Technology and Culture 27:3 (1986), 544-560. © 1986 by the Society for the History of Technology. Reprinted with permission of Johns Hopkins University Press.

he claimed that he had been making exactly the same point in his many other writings. True, but he has also given us many other messages over the years.

However, Ferguson's statement of "only one message" might indeed be true in my case. For I have been conveying basically the same message for over thirty years, namely, the significance in human affairs of the history of technology and the value of the contextual approach in understanding technical developments.

Because I have repeated that same message so often, utilizing various examples or stressing certain elements to accord with the interests of the different audiences I was attempting to reach, my thoughts have jelled into what have been called "Kranzberg's Laws." These are not laws in the sense of commandments but rather a series of truisms deriving from a longtime immersion in the study of the development of technology and its interactions with sociocultural change.

We historians tend to think of historical change in terms of cause and effect and of means and ends. Although it is not always easy to find causative elements and to distinguish ends from means in the interactions between technology and society, that has not kept scholars from trying to do so.

Indeed one of the intellectual clichés of our time, whose scholarly statement is embodied in the writings of Jacques Ellul and Langdon Winner, is that technology is pursued for its own sake and without regard to human need.[2] Technology, it is said, has become autonomous and has outrun human control; in a startling reversal, the machines have become the masters of man. Such arguments frequently result in the philosophical doctrine of technological determinism, namely, that technology is the prime factor in shaping our life-styles, values, institutions, and other elements of our society.

Not all scholars accept this version of technological omnipotence. Lynn White, jr., has said that a technical device "merely opens a door, it does not compel one to enter."[3] In this view, technology might be regarded as simply a means that humans are free to employ or not, as they see fit—and White recognizes that many nontechnical factors might affect that decision. Nevertheless, several questions do arise. True, one is not compelled to enter White's open door, but an open door is an invitation. Besides, who decides which doors to open—and, once one has entered the door, are not one's future directions guided by the contours of the corridor or chamber into which one has stepped? Equally important, once one has crossed the threshold, can one turn back?

Frankly, we historians do not know the answer to this question of technological determinism. Ours is a new discipline; we are still working on the problem, and we might never reach agreement on an answer—which means that it will provide employment for historians of technology for decades to come. Yet there are several things that we do know, and that I summarize under the label of Kranzberg's First Law.

Kranzberg's First Law reads as follows: Technology is neither good nor bad; nor is it neutral.

By that I mean that technology's interaction with the social ecology is such that technical developments frequently have environmental, social, and human consequences that go far beyond the immediate purposes of the technical devices and practices themselves, and the same technology can have quite different results when introduced into different contexts or under different circumstances.

Many of our technology-related problems arise because of the unforeseen consequences when apparently benign technologies are employed on a massive scale. Hence many technical applications that seemed a boon to mankind when first introduced became threats when their use became widespread. For example, DDT was employed to raise agricultural productivity and to eliminate disease-carrying pests. Then we discovered that DDT not only did that but also threatened ecological systems, including the food chain of birds, fishes, and eventually man. So the Western industrialized nations banned DDT. They could afford to do so, because their high technological level enabled them to use alternative means of pest control to achieve the same results at a slightly higher cost.

But India continued to employ DDT, despite the possibility of environmental damage, because it was not economically feasible to change to less persistent insecticides—and because, to India, the use of DDT in agriculture was secondary to its role in disease prevention. According to the World Health Organization, the use of DDT in the 1950s and 1960s in India cut the incidence of malaria in that country from 100 million cases a year to only 15,000, and the death toll from 750,000 to 1,500 a year. Is it surprising that the Indians viewed DDT differently from us, welcoming it rather than banning it? The point is that the same technology can answer questions differently, depending on the context into which it is introduced and the problem it is designed to solve.

Thus while some American scholars point to the dehumanizing character of work in a modern factory,[4] D. S. Naipaul, the great Indian author, assesses it differently from the standpoint of his culture, saying, "Indian poverty is more dehumanizing than any machine."[5] Hence in judging the efficacy of technological development, we historians must take cognizance of varying social contexts.

It is also imperative that we compare short-range and long-range impacts. In the 19th century, Romantic writers and social critics condemned industrial technology for the harsh conditions under which the mill workers and coal miners labored. Yet, according to Fernand Braudel, conditions on the medieval manor were even worse.[6] Certain economic historians have pointed out that, although the conditions of the early factory workers left much to be desired, in the long run the worker's living standards improved as industrialization brought forth a torrent of goods that were made available to an ever-wider public.[7] Of course, those long-run benefits were small comfort to those who suffered in the short run; yet it is the duty of the historian to show the differences between the immediate and long-range implications of technological developments.

Although our technological advances have yielded manifold benefits in increasing food supply, in providing a deluge of material goods, and in prolonging human life, people do not always appreciate technology's contributions to their lives and comfort. Nicholas Rescher, citing statistical data on the way people perceive their conditions, explains their dissatisfaction on the paradoxical ground that technical progress inflates their expectations faster than it can actually meet them.[8]

Of course, the public's perception of technological advantages can change over time. A century ago, smoke from industrial smokestacks was regarded as a sign of a region's prosperity; only later was it recognized that the smoke was despoiling the environment. There were "technological fixes," of course. Thus, one of the aims of the Clean Air Act of 1972 was to prevent the harmful particulates emitted by smokestacks from falling on nearby communities. One way to do away with this problem was to build the smokestacks hundreds of feet high; then a few years later we discovered that the sulfur dioxide and other oxides, when sent high into the air, combined with water vapor to shower the earth with acid rain that has polluted lakes and caused forests to die hundreds of miles away.

Unforeseen "dis-benefits" can thus arise from presumably beneficent technologies. For example, although advances in medical technology and water and sewage treatment have freed millions of people from disease and plague and have lowered infant mortality, these have also brought the possibility of overcrowding the earth and producing, from other causes, human suffering on a vast scale. Similarly, nuclear technology offers the prospect of unlimited energy resources, but it has also brought the possibility of worldwide destruction.

That is why I think that my first law—Technology is neither good nor bad; nor is it neutral—should constantly remind us that it is the historian's duty to compare short-term versus long-term results, the utopian hopes versus the spotted actuality, the what-might-have-been against what actually happened, and the trade-offs among various "goods" and possible "bads." All of this can be done only by seeing how technology interacts in different ways with different values and institutions, indeed, with the entire sociocultural milieu.[9]

Whereas my first law stresses the interactions between technology and society, my second law starts with internalist elements in technology and then stretches to include many nontechnical factors. Kranzberg's Second Law can be simply stated: Invention is the mother of necessity.

Every technical innovation seems to require additional technical advances in order to make it fully effective. If one invents a lathe that can cut metal faster than existing machines, this necessitates improvements in the lubricating system to keep the mechanism running efficiently, improved grinding materials to stand up under the enhanced speed, and new means of taking away quickly the waste material from the item being turned.

Many major innovations have required further inventions to make them completely effective. Thus, Alexander Graham Bell's telephone spawned a variety of technical improvements, ranging from Edison's carbon-granule microphone to central-switching mechanisms. A variation on this same theme is described in Hugh Aitken's book on the origins of radio, in which he indicates the various innovative steps whereby the spark technology that produced radio waves was tuned into harmony (syntonized) with the receiver.[10] In more recent times, the design of a more powerful rocket, giving greater thrust, necessitates innovation in chemical engineering to produce the thrust, in materials to withstand the blast, in electronic control mechanisms, and the like.

A good case of invention mothering necessity can be seen in the landmark textile inventions of the 18th century. Kay's "flying shuttle" wove so quickly that it upset the usual ratio of four spinners to one weaver; either there had to be many more spinners or else spinning had to be similarly quickened by application of machinery. Thereupon Hargreaves, Cartwright, and Crompton improved the spinning process; then Cartwright set about further mechanizing the weaving operation in order to take full advantage of the now-abundant yarn produced by the new spinning machines.

Thomas P. Hughes would refer to the phenomenon that I have just described as a "reverse salient";[11] but I prefer to call it a "technological imbalance," a situation in which an improvement in one machine upsets the previous balance and necessitates an effort to right the balance by means of a new innovation. No matter what one calls it, Hughes and I are talking about the same thing. Indeed, Hughes has gone further in discussing technological systems, for he shows how, as a system grows, it generates new properties and new problems, which in turn necessitate further changes.

The automobile is a prime example of how a successful technology requires auxiliary technologies to make it fully effective, for it brought whole new industries into being and turned existing industries in new directions by its need for rubber tires, petroleum products, and new tools and materials. Furthermore, large-scale use of the auto demanded a host of auxiliary technological activities—roads and highways, garages and parking lots, traffic signals, and parking meters.

While it might be said that each of these other developments occurred in response to a specific need, I claim that it was the original invention that mothered that necessity. If we look into the internal history of any mechanical device, we find that the basic invention required other innovative changes to make it fully effective and that the completed mechanism in turn necessitated changes in auxiliary and supporting technological systems, which, taken all together, brought many changes in economic and sociocultural patterns.

What I have just said is virtually a statement of my Third Law: Technology comes in packages, big and small.

The fact is that today's complex mechanisms usually involve several processes and components. Radar, for example, is a very complicated system, requiring specialized materials, power sources, and intricate devices to send out waves of the proper frequency, detect them when they bounce off an object, and then interpret them and place the results on a screen.

That might explain why so many different people have laid claim to inventing radar. Each is perfectly right in pointing out that he provided an element essential to the final product, but that final product is composed of many separate elements brought together in a system that could not function without every single one of the components. Thus radar is the product of a packaging process, bringing together elements of different technologies into a single device.

In his fascinating account of the development of mass production, David A. Hounshell tells how many different experiments and techniques were employed in bringing Ford's assembly line into being.[12] Although many of the component elements were already in existence, Ford put these together into a comprehensive system—but not without having to develop additional technical capabilities, such as conveyor lines, to make the assembly process more effective.

My third law has been extended even further by Thomas P. Hughes's 1985 Dexter Prize-winning book *Networks of Power*. What I call "packages" Hughes more precisely and accurately calls "systems," which he defines as coherent structures composed of interacting, interconnected components.[13] When one component changes, other parts of the system must undergo transformations so that the system might continue to function. Hence the parts of a system cannot be viewed in isolation but must be studied in terms of their interrelations with the other parts.

Although Hughes concentrates on electric power systems, what he provides is a paradigm that is applicable to other systems—transportation, water supply, communications, and the like. And because entire systems interact with other systems, a system cannot be studied in isolation any more than can its component parts; hence one must also look at the interaction of these systems with the entire social, political, economic, and cultural environment. Hughes's book thus provides excellent case studies proving the validity of the first three of Kranzberg's Laws, and also of my fourth dictum.

Unfortunately, Kranzberg's Fourth Law cannot be stated so pithily as the first three. It reads as follows: Although technology might be a prime element in many public issues, nontechnical factors take precedence in technology-policy decisions.

Engineers claim that their solutions to technical problems are not based on mushy social considerations; instead, they boast that their decisions depend on the hard and measurable facts of technical efficiency, which they define in terms of input-output factors such as cost of resources, power, and labor. However, as Edward Constant has shown in studying the Kuhnian paradigm's applicability to technological developments, many complicated sociocultural factors, especially human elements, are involved, even in what might seem to be "purely technical" decisions.[14]

Besides, engineers do not always agree with one another; different fields of engineering might have different solutions to the same problem, and even within the same field they might disagree on what weight to assign to different trade-off factors. Indeed, as Stuart W. Leslie demonstrated in his Usher Prize article on "Charles F. Kettering and the Copper-cooled Engine,"[15] the most efficient device does not always win out even in what we might regard as a narrowly technical decision within a single industrial corporation. Although Kettering regarded his copper-cooled engine as a technical success, it never went into production. Why not? True, it had some technical "bugs," but these could not be successfully ironed out because of divisions between the research engineers and the production people—and because of the overall decision that the copper-cooled engine could not meet the corporate demand for immediate profit. So technical worth, or at least potential technical capability and efficiency, was not the decisive element in halting the copper-cooled engine.

In *Networks of Power* Hughes likewise demonstrates how nontechnical factors affected the efficient growth of electrical networks by comparing developments in Chicago, Berlin, and London. Private enterprise in Chicago, in the person of Samuel Insull, followed the path of the most efficient technology in seeking economies of scale. In Berlin and London, however, municipal governments were more concerned about their own authority than about technical efficiency, and political infighting meant that they lagged behind in developing the most economical power networks.

Technologically "sweet" solutions do not always triumph over political and social forces.[16] The debate a dozen years ago over the supersonic transport (SST) provides an example. Although the SST offered potential advantages, its development to the point where its feasibility and desirability could be properly determined was never allowed to take place. Economic factors might have underlain the decision to cut R&D funds for the SST, but the public decision seems also to have been based on a fear of the environmental hazards posed by the supersonic aircraft in commercial aviation.

Environmental concerns have indeed assumed a major place in public decisions regarding technical initiatives. These concerns are not groundless, for we have seen how certain technologies, employed without awareness of potential environmental effects, have boomeranged to present hazardous problems, despite their early beneficial effects. Many engineers believe that hysterical fear about technological development has so gripped our nation that people overlook the benefits provided by technology and concentrate on the dangers presented either by ill-conceived technological applications or by human error or oversight in technical operations. But who can blame the public, with Love Canal and Bhopal crowding the headlines?[17]

American politics has now become the battleground of special-interest groups, and few of these groups are willing to make the trade-offs required in many engineering decisions. In the case of potential environmental hazards, Daniel

A. Koshland has stated that we can satisfy one or the other of the different groups, but only at a cost of something undesirable to the others.[18]

Especially politicized has been the question of nuclear power. The nuclear industry itself has been partly to blame for technological deficiencies, but the presumption of risk by the public, especially following the Three Mile Island and Chernobyl accidents, has affected the future of what was once regarded as a safe and inexhaustible source of power. The public fears possible catastrophic consequences from nuclear generators.

Yet the historical fact is that no one has been killed by commercial nuclear power accidents in this country. Contrast this with the 50,000 Americans killed each year by automobiles. But although antinuclear protestors picket nuclear power plants under construction, we never see any demonstrators bearing signs saying "Ban the Buick"!

Partly this is due to the public's perception of risk, rather than to the actual risks themselves.[19] People seek a zero-risk society. But as Aaron Wildavsky has so aptly put it, "No risk is the highest risk of all."[20] For it would not only petrify our technology but also stultify developmental growth in society along any lines.

Nevertheless, the fact that political considerations take precedence over purely technical considerations should not alarm us. In a democracy, that is as it should be. To deal with questions involving the interactions between technology and the ecology, both natural and social, we have devised new social instruments, such as "technology assessment," to evaluate the possible consequences of the applications of technologies before they are applied.

Of course, political considerations often continue to take precedence over the common-sensible results of comprehensive and impartial technological assessments. But at least there is the recognition that technological developments frequently have social, human, and environmental implications that go far beyond the intention of the original technology itself.

The fact that historians of technology must be aware of outside forces and factors affecting technology—from the human personality of the inventor to the larger social, economic, political, and cultural milieu—has led me to Kranzberg's Fifth Law: All history is relevant, but the history of technology is the most relevant.

In her presidential address to the Organization of American Historians several years ago, Gerda Lerner pointed out how history satisfies a variety of human needs, serving as a cultural tradition that gives us personal identity in the continuum of the past and future of the human enterprise.[21] Other apologists for the profession point out that history is one of the fundamental liberal arts and is essential as a key to an understanding of the future.

No one would quarrel with such worthy sentiments, but, to repeat questions raised by Eugene D. Genovese, "If so, how can we explain the dangerous decline in the teaching of history in our schools; the cynical taunt, 'What is history good for anyway?'"[22] Although historians might write loftily of the importance of historical understanding by civilized people and citizens, many of today's students simply do not see the relevance of history to the present or to their future. I suggest that this is because most history, as it is currently taught, ignores the technological element.

Two centuries ago the great German philosopher Immanuel Kant stated that the two great questions in life are (1) What can I know? and (2) What ought I do?

To answer Kant's first question, we can learn the history of the past. I look on history as a series of questions that we ask of the past in order to find out how our present world came into being. We call ours a "technological age." How did it get to be that way? That indeed is the major question that the history of technology attempts to answer. Our students know that they live in a technological age, but any history that ignores the technological factor in societal development does little to enable them to comprehend how their world came into being.

True, economic and business historians have perforce taken cognizance of those technological elements that had a mighty effect on their subject matter. Similarly, social historians of the *Annales* school have stressed how technology set the patterns of daily life for the vast majority of people throughout history, and Brooke Hindle, in a fine historiographical article, has indicated how some of our fellow historians have begun to see how technology impinges on their special fields of study.[23] But for the most part, social, political, and intellectual historians have been oblivious to the technological parameters of their own subjects.

Perhaps most guilty of neglecting technology are those concerned with the history of the arts and with the entire panoply of humanistic concerns. Indeed, in many cases they are disdainful of technology, regarding it as somehow opposed to the humanities. This might be because they regard technology solely in terms of mechanical devices and do not even begin to comprehend the complex nature of technological developments and their direct influences on the arts, to say nothing of their indirect influence on mankind's humanistic endeavors.

Yet anyone familiar with Cyril Stanley Smith's writings would be aware of the importance of the aesthetic impulse in technical accomplishments and of how these in turn amplified the materials and techniques available for artistic expression.[24] And any historian of art or of the Renaissance should perceive that such artistic masters as Leonardo and Michelangelo were also great engineers. That relationship continues today, as David Billington has shown in stressing the relationship of structural design and art.[25]

Today's technological age provides new technical capabilities to enlarge the horizons and means of expression for artists in every field. Advances in musical instruments have given larger scope to the imagination of composers and to musical interpretation by performers. The advent of photography, the phonograph, radio, movies, and television have not only given artists, composers, and dramatists new tools with which to exercise their vision and talents but have also enlarged the audience for music, drama, and the whole panoply of the arts. They also extend our audio and visual memory, enabling us to see, hear, and preserve the great works of the past and present.

In the field of learning and education, there is little point in belaboring the impact of writing tools, paper, the printing press, and, nowadays, radio and TV. But there is also an indirect influence of technology on education, one that makes it more possible than ever before in human history for larger numbers of people in the industrialized nations to take advantage of formal schooling.

Let me give a brief example drawn from American history. Thomas Jefferson was very proud of the educational system that he devised for the state of Virginia. But in his educational scheme, only a very small percentage could ever hope to ascend to the heights of a university education.

This is not because Jefferson was an elitist. Far from it! But the fact is that the agrarian technology of his time was not productive enough to allow large numbers of youth to participate in the educational process. From a very early age, children worked in the fields alongside their parents or, if they were town dwellers, were apprenticed to craftsmen. Only when great increases in agricultural and industrial productivity were made possible by revolutionary developments in technology did society acquire sufficient wealth to keep children out of the work force and enable them to attend school. As the 19th century progressed, first elementary education was made compulsory, then secondary education, and by the mid-20th century, America had grown so wealthy that it could afford a college education for all its citizens. True, some students drop out of high school before completing it, and not everyone going to college takes full advantage of the educational opportunities. But the fact is that the majority of Americans today have the equivalent education of the small segment of the upper-class elite in preindustrial society. In brief, technology has been a significant factor, not only in the pattern of our daily lives and in our workaday world, but also in democratizing education and the intellectual realm of the arts and humanities.

However, such vast generalizations might do little to convince the public of the wisdom of Stanley N. Katz's vision of scholars participating "in public discourse in order to recover the traditional role of the humanist as a public figure."[26] But the relevance of the history of technology to today's world can be spelled out in very specific terms. For example, because we live in a "global village," made so by technological developments, we are conscious of the need to transfer technological expertise to our less fortunate brethren in the less developed nations. And the history of technology has a great deal to say about the conditions, complexities, and problems of technology transfer.

Likewise, we are faced with public decisions regarding global strategy, environmental concerns, educational directions, and the ratio of resources to the world's burgeoning population. Technological history can cast light on many parameters of these very specific problems confronting us now and in the future—and that is why I say that the history of technology is more relevant than other histories.

One proof of this is that the outside world, especially the political community, is becoming increasingly cognizant of the contributions that historians of technology can make to public concerns. Whereas several decades ago historians were rarely called on to provide information to Congress on matters other than historical archives, memorials, and national celebrations, nowadays it is almost commonplace for historians of technology to testify before congressional committees dealing with scientific and technological expenditures, aerospace developments, transportation, water supplies, and other problems having a technological component. Congressmen obviously think that the information provided by historians of technology is relevant to coping with the problems of today and tomorrow.

Leaders in all fields are increasingly turning to historians of technology for expertise regarding the nature of the sociotechnical problems facing them. Let me give a few more specific examples. SHOT is an affiliate of the American Association for the Advancement of Science (AAAS), and there was a time when historians of technology appeared only on the program sessions of Section L of the AAAS, the History and Philosophy of Science. But historians of technology also have important things to say to a public larger than that composed of their historical colleagues. Hence it was a source of great personal pride to me—almost paternal pride—when, at the 1985 AAAS meeting, Carroll Pursell appeared on a program session with a congressman and a former assistant secretary of commerce; the program dealt with certain social and economic problems affecting the United States today, and Pursell's historical account of the technological parameters was truly germane to the thrust of the discussion. Similarly, at a recent conference, at my own Georgia Tech, on the problems expected to affect the workplace in the future, David Hounshell provided a meaningful technological historical context for a discussion that involved top labor leaders, political figures, and corporate executives. (I took family pride in that too!)

I regard this entrance of historians of technology into the public arena as empirical evidence of the true relevance of the history of technology to the worlds of today and tomorrow. To reiterate, all history is relevant, but the history of technology is most relevant. The rest of the world realizes that, and SHOT is working to make our historical colleagues from other fields recognize it too.

This brings me to my final law, Kranzberg's Sixth Law: Technology is a very human activity—and so is the history of technology.

Anthropologists and archaeologists studying primate evolution tell us of the importance of purposive toolmaking in the formation of *Homo sapiens*. The physical development of our species is apparently inextricably bound up with cultural developments, so that technology is classed as one of the earliest and most basic of human cultural characteristics, one helping to develop language and abstract thinking. Or, to put it another way, man could not have become *Homo sapiens*, "man the thinker," had he not at the same time been *Homo faber*, "man the maker."

Man is a constituent element of the technical process. Machines are made and used by human beings. Behind every machine, I see a face—indeed, many faces: the engineer, the worker, the businessman or businesswoman, and, sometimes, the general and admiral. Furthermore, the function of the technology is its use by human beings—and sometimes, alas, its abuse and misuse.

To those who identify technology simply with the machines themselves, I use the computer as a metaphor to show the importance of the interaction of human and social factors with the technical elements—for computers require both the mechanical element, the "hardware," and the human element, the "software"; without the software, the machine is simply an inert device, but without the hardware, the software is meaningless. We need both, the human and the purely technical components, in order to make the computer a usable and useful piece of technology.

Those of you who were at our Silver Anniversary meeting in 1983 will recall that I told an anecdote, which I sometimes use to quiet my most voluble antitechnological humanistic colleagues. A lady came up to the great violinist Fritz Kreisler after a concert and gushed, "Maestro, your violin makes such beautiful music." Kreisler held his violin up to his ear and said, "I don't hear any music coming out of it."

You see, the instrument, the hardware, the violin itself, was of no use without the human element. But then again, without the instrument, Kreisler would not have been able to make music. The history of technology is the story of man and tool—hand and mind—working together. If the hardware is faulty or if the software is deficient, the sounds that emerge will be discordant; but when man and machine work together, they can make some beautiful music.

People sometimes speak of the "technological imperative," meaning that technology rules our lives. Indeed, they can point to many technical elements, such as the clock, that determine the character and pace of our daily existence. Likewise, the automobile determines where and how we Americans live, work, think, play, and pray.

But this does not necessarily mean that the "technological imperative," usually based on efficiency or economy, necessarily directs all our thoughts and actions. We can point to many technical devices that would make life simpler or easier for us but which our social values and human sensibilities simply reject. Thus, for example, Ruth Schwartz Cowan has shown in her Dexter Prize–winning book, *More Work for Mother,* how communal kitchens would be feasible and save the mother from much drudgery of food preparation. But our adherence to the concept of the home has made that technical solution unworkable; instead, we have turned to other technologies to ease the housework and cooking chores, albeit requiring more time and attention from mother.[27]

In other words, technological capabilities do not necessarily determine our actions. Indeed, how else can we explain why we have spent billions of dollars on nuclear power plants that we have had to abandon before they were completed? Obviously, other human factors proved more powerful than the combined technical and economic pressures.

Our reluctance to bow to the "technological imperative" is shown by the great efforts to make machines "user friendly"— and we are also embarking on the task of making humans "machine friendly" through educational programs in "technological literacy" and through the work of our SHOT special-interest groups to reach out to a wider public.

One final note on this point. Today's technology makes possible teleconferencing. Hence it would be cheaper to stay at home and have the papers and discussions of the SHOT meeting brought to us by telecommunication devices. But here we are, gathered together in Dearborn, Michigan, because we recognize that there is more to be derived from a SHOT meeting than the fine scholarly papers. There is the stimulation and camaraderie of being together and bouncing our ideas off one another in a face-to-face context. SHOT meetings are notable for their collegial atmosphere. Perhaps it is because we are still a relatively young discipline, so that the average age of historians of technology is probably younger than that of those in other, older fields. Or perhaps it is because we have very efficient program and local arrangements committees, which tend to our needs and provide the wherewithal for our conviviality.

All that is so, but I also believe that SHOT meetings are so friendly and wonderful because we are united in our pursuit of knowledge. Surely we sometimes disagree in our interpretations of the historical facts; we would be less than human if we did not, and we would not be doing our proper job as scholars if we accepted unquestioningly everything our colleagues said.

But more important, we are united in our concern to understand the past—and also look at the future. Remember that I pointed out earlier that Immanuel Kant said that the two great questions in life are, first, What can I know? and, second, What ought I do?

What we can know is how our present world came to be, and that requires a knowledge of the development of technology and of its interactions with culture and society—the very things for which we stand. But we also have a mission in relation to the second of Kant's great questions—What ought we do with our knowledge?— for we possess special capabilities because of our growing knowledge and understanding of technological developments and their varying interactions with the sociocultural milieu.

After all, we call ours a man-made world. And it is that, because mankind, with the aid of its technology, has fashioned our physical and social environment, our institutions, and other accoutrements of our society. But if ours is truly a man-made world, I claim that mankind can *re*-make it. And in that remaking process, the history of technology can play a very important role in enabling us to meet the challenges besetting mankind now and in the future.

That might seem a vain, utopian ideal. But historians of technology who have studied the great triumphs of the human mind and ingenuity embodied in mankind's technological accomplishments (and also mankind's failures) throughout the ages—such historians can indeed "dare to dream" of remaking ours into a better world.

Social Anthropology of Technology

At the onset of the twentieth century, the study of technology and material culture by anthropologists was largely abandoned to focus on humanitarian subjects such as art and social organization, due to a concern among social scientists about "the tendency to study artifacts without regard for their social and cultural context" (Pfaffenberger, 1992, p. 491). Because of this, Pfaffenberger's stated goal was to persuade his colleagues in anthropology to study technology, and to bring anthropological theory to technology studies. In this excerpt he described an approach to unite the two fields of study.

According to Pfaffenberger, the study of the connections between technology and culture was returning in the nonanthropological field known as science and technology studies (STS). Emerging from social and historical studies, STS advances the sociotechnical system concept that emphasizes the social nature of human technological activity. STS explores questions about the relationship between technological development and cultural evolution and what kind of cultural meaning is embodied in technological artifacts. Pfaffenberger argued that STS could help resolve key controversies within anthropology.

Like Lewis Mumford (1968) before him in *Technics and the Nature of Man*, Pfaffenberger challenged the "Standard View" that technology's main purpose is assisting humanity in its struggle for survival against the forces of nature, and that necessity is the mother of invention. He lamented that the social nature of technology has been diminished by these limited doctrines of necessity and function.

> Against the Standard View's exaggerated picture of technological evolution from simple tools to complex machines, the sociotechnical system concept puts forward a universal conception of human technological activity, in which complex social structures, nonverbal activity systems, advanced linguistic communication, the ritual coordination of labor, advanced artifact manufacture, the linkage of phenomenally diverse social and nonsocial actors, and the social use of diverse artifacts are all recognized as parts of a single complex that is simultaneously adaptive and expressive. (p. 513)

Pfaffenberger hoped that such an approach would allow us to view technology in a way that links all human cultures regardless of their level of technological development, permitting us to see, "what is distinctly human about activities as diverse as making stone tools and launching space vehicles" (p. 513).

Bryan Pfaffenberger is a professor in the Department of Science, Technology, and Society at the University of Virginia, and is the managing editor of STS Wiki, which he conceived and developed. He has published broadly on STS topics, including the 1990 book *Democratizing Information: Online Databases and the Rise of End-User Searching*.

Social Anthropology of Technology
Bryan Pfaffenberger

Division of Humanities, School of Engineering and Applied Science, University of Virginia, Charlottesville, Virginia 22901

KEYWORDS: activity systems, technological change, sociotechnical systems, ritual, artifacts

At the onset of the 20th century, anthropologists such as Balfour, Marett, and Haddon could readily identify three spheres of strength in anthropological research: material culture, social organization, and physical anthropology (49). The study of technology and material culture, however, was about to be jettisoned, and with stunning finality. By 1914, Wissler (103:447) complained that the study of these subjects "has been quite out of fashion." Researchers were giving their attention to "language, art, ceremonies, and social organization" in place of the former almost obsessive concentration on the minute description of techniques and artifacts, and on the tendency to study artifacts without regard for their social and cultural context. As I aim to show in this chapter, the anthropological study of technology and material culture is poised, finally, for a comeback, if in a different guise. Its findings may significantly alter the way anthropologists analyze everyday life, cultural reproduction, and human evolution.

If this all-but-forgotten field is to play such a role, it must overcome nearly a century of peripheral status. In anthropology's quest for professionalism, material-culture studies came to stand for all that was academically embarrassing: extreme and conjectural forms of diffusionist and evolutionist explanation, armchair anthropology, "field work" undertaken by amateurs on collecting holidays, and the simplistic interpretation of artifacts shorn of their social and cultural context. Malinowski, for instance, condemned the "purely technological enthusiasms" of material culture ethnologists and adopted an "intransigent position" that the study of "technology alone" is "scientifically sterile" (69:460). The study of technology and material culture, a topic that was (and is still) perceived as "dry, even intellectually arid and boring" (92, 5), was relegated to museums, where—out of contact with developments in social anthropology and deprived of

ethnographic experience—museum scholars lacked the resources to advance the field. For their part, cultural anthropologists argued that studying techniques and artifacts could only deflect anthropologists from their proper role—that is, from studying culture. Kroeber & Kluckhohn, for example, dismissed the term *material culture* out of hand, arguing that "what is culture is the *idea* behind the artifact" (55:65). "Accordingly," Kroeber argued, "we may forget about this distinction between material and nonmaterial culture, except as a literal difference, that is sometimes of practical convenience to observe" (54:296). For anthropology, jettisoning material culture studies was a necessary step in establishing the scientific basis, the intellectual appeal, and the distinctive subject matter of the discipline.

Periodic attempts have been made to revive the seriously ill patient (e.g. 21, 34, 49, 59, 65, 66, 85, and 88), with their pace quickening in the 1980s (43, 44, 62, 63, 72, 73, 84, 92, 96). Yet, arguably, no real resuscitation has taken place, owing largely to the continued insouciance with which Anglo-American anthropologists regard the study of material culture and technology. In a recent restatement of the Kroeber & Kluckhohn view, Bouquet (13:352) condemns the "recent bids to reinstate the 'materiality' of material culture," as if such bids stemmed from some Philistine conspiracy, against which she prefers recognition of the "hegemony of linguistic approaches to the object world." Noting that the excesses of early material-culture scholars were rightly pilloried, Sillitoe laments that the "mud seems to have stuck more to artifacts and their study . . . than to the [evolutionists'] wild-guess theories," which have themselves enjoyed a modest comeback (92, p. 6). As it stands, a topic with which anthropology was once closely identified—the cross-cultural study of technology and material culture—has been largely taken up by scholars working in other fields, such as the history of technology and the interdisciplinary field known as science and technology studies (STS), or by anthropologists with marginal appointments in museums or in the general studies divisions of engineering and technical colleges.

Despite the peripheral status of the anthropology of technology and material culture, compelling questions remain: What is technology? Is technology a human universal? What is the relationship between technological development and cultural evolution? Are there common themes in the appropriation of artifacts that bridge capitalist and precapitalist societies? How do people employ artifacts to accomplish social purposes in the course of everyday life? What kind of cultural meaning is embodied in technological artifacts? How does culture influence technological innovation—and how does technological innovation influence culture?

These questions are far from trivial—and, arguably, only anthropology can answer them. No other discipline offers sufficient comparative depth or appropriate methodologies. The challenge still remains, as Malinowski himself put it, to understand the role of technology as "an indispensable means of approach to economic and sociological activities and to what might be called native science" (69:460). And the challenge is even greater now that scholars generally concede that language, tool use, and social behavior evolved in a process of complex mutual interaction and feedback. Summing up the consensus of a conference titled "Tools, Language, and Intelligence: Evolutionary Implications," Gibson concludes that "We need to know more about the ways in which speaking, tool-using, and sociality are interwoven into the texture of everyday life in contemporary human groups" (29:263).

In this chapter, I argue that social anthropology has already discovered a great deal about human technological activity—especially when anthropological findings are interpreted in the context of recent, stunning advances in the sociology of scientific knowledge (11), the history and sociology of technology, and the emergent field known as science and technology studies (STS). Collectively, these fields, without much anthropological involvement, have developed a concept, the *sociotechnical system* concept (48), that refuses to deny the *sociality* of human technological activity. Developed mainly in social and historical studies of industrial societies, the sociotechnical system concept, I seek to show, serves fruitfully to integrate anthropological findings about *pre*industrial societies into a coherent picture of the universals of human technology and material culture. The central objective of this review, then, is to convey the sociotechnical system concept to an anthropological audience, and to show how it resolves key controversies within anthropology. The results should prove of interest to anthropologists working in fields as diverse as cultural ecology, ritual, symbolic anthropology, ethnoarchaeology, archaeology, and human evolution studies.

One reason for the rapid advance of STS is its refusal to accept the myths of science and technology at face value. Mulkay (74), for example, shows that sociology's refusal to develop a sociological analysis of scientific knowledge stems from sociologists' uncritical acceptance of a mythic Standard View of science. I suggest that the achievement of a truly *social* anthropology of technology likewise requires extending anthropology's recent productive venture into reflexivity (18, 70)— specifically, by making the mythic Standard View of technology explicit, and resolutely questioning its implications. For this reason, this essay begins with the Standard View of technology, and although its purpose is to present the sociotechnical system concept and explore its implications for anthropology, it is organized as a series of attacks on the implications of the Standard View.

The Standard View of Technology

Like the Standard View of science (74: 19–21), the Standard View of technology underlies much scholarly as well as popular thinking. A master narrative of modern culture, the Standard View of technology could be elicited, more or less intact, from any undergraduate class. Occasionally, it is made explicit in anthropological writings (e.g. 39). By suggesting that such a Standard View exists, I do not mean to imply that every scholar who has advanced some part of it necessarily endorses the rest. In what follows, I deliberately use the masculine pronoun to stand for humankind; to do otherwise would strip the Standard View of its gender ideology.

Necessity is the mother of invention. As Man has been faced with severe survival challenges, certain extraordinary individuals have seen, often in a brilliant flash of inspiration, how to address the challenge of Need by applying the forces, potentialities, and affordances of Nature to the fabrication of tools and material artifacts. The power of Nature is there, waiting to be harnessed, to the extent that the inventor can clear away the cobwebs of culture to see the world from a purely utilitarian standpoint. In this we see Man's thirst for Progress.

Form follows function. To be sure, Man decorates his tools and artifacts, but artifacts are adopted to the extent that their form shows a clear and rational relationship to the artifacts' intended function—that is, its ability to satisfy the need that was the raison d'être of the artifact's creation. Thus, a society's material culture becomes a physical record of its characteristic survival adaptation; material culture is the primary means by which society effects its reproduction. The meaning of human artifacts is a surface matter of style, of surface burnish or minor symbolization.

By viewing the material record of Man's technological achievements, one can directly perceive the challenges Man faced in the past, and how he met these challenges. This record shows a unilinear progression over time, because technology is cumulative. Each new level of penetration into Nature's secrets builds on the previous one, producing ever more powerful inventions. The digging stick had to precede the plough. Those inventions that significantly increase Man's reach bring about revolutionary changes in social organization and subsistence. Accordingly, the ages of Man can be expressed in terms of technological stages, such as the Stone Age, the Iron Age, the Bronze Age, and so on. Our age is the Information Age, brought on by the invention of the computer. Overall, the movement is from very simple tools to very complex machines. It was also a movement from primitive sensorimotor skills (techniques) to highly elaborate systems of objective, linguistically encoded knowledge about Nature and its potential (technology).

Now, we live in a material world. The result of the explosion of technological knowledge has been a massive expansion of Man's reach, but with lamentable and unavoidable social, environmental, and cultural consequences: We live in a fabricated environment, mediated by machines. Technology was more authentic when we used tools, because we could control them. Machines, in contrast, control us. Thus one can identify a Great Divide or Rupture when Man lost his authenticity as a cultural creature, his Faustian depth as a being living in a world of cultural meaning, and gave himself over to a world ruled by instrumentalism and superficiality. This Rupture was the Industrial Revolution, which launched the Age of the Machine. As the primacy of function over aesthetics rips through culture, we increasingly live in a homogenous world of functionally driven design coherence. Our culture has become an inauthentic one in which reified images of technology predominate. We can define ourselves only by purchasing plastic, ersatz artifacts made far away. To retain some measure of authenticity the young must be brought into direct contact with the great works of art and literature.

The Standard View of technology appears to be a pillar of Modernism, a cultural, literary, and artistic period noted for its extreme ambivalence toward technology. According to most scholars (e.g. 40), Modernism reached its apex between the two World Wars. In essence, Modernism represents a struggle to find a stable ground of being within the promise and peril of science and technological development. Like Siva in Hindu iconography, technology is seen through the Modernist lens as both creator and destroyer, an agent both of future promise and of culture's destruction. Echoed perfectly in the Standard View of technology, Modernism amounts to

> an extraordinary compound of the futurist and the nihilistic, the revolutionary and the conservative, the romantic and the classical. It was the celebration of a technological age and a condemnation of it; an excited acceptance of the belief that the old regimes of culture were over, and a deep despairing in the face of that fear (15:46).

Modernism is an almost unavoidable response, as Bradbury & McFarlane put it, to the "scenario of our chaos" (15:27). Accordingly, any attempt to grasp the role of human technological activity must begin by questioning the Standard View's assumptions, which could, if left unexamined, color anthropological thought.

"Necessity is the Mother of Invention"

The Standard View puts forth a commonsense view of technology and material culture that accords perfectly with our everyday understanding. All around us are artifacts originally developed to fulfill a specific need—juicers, word processors, vacuum cleaners, and telephones; and apart from artifacts that are decorative or symbolic, the most useful artifacts—the ones that increase our fitness or efficiency in dealing with everyday life—are associated each with a specific Master Function, given by the physical or technological properties of the object itself. Extending this commonsense view one quickly arrives at a theory of technological evolution (parodied by 4:6): People need water, "so they dig wells, dam rivers and streams, and develop hydraulic technology. They need shelter and defense, so they build houses, forts, cities, and military machines. . . . They need to move through the environment with ease, so they invent ships, chariots, charts, carriages, bicycles, automobiles, airplanes, and spacecraft."

The New Archaeology, which sought to put archaeology on a firm modernist footing, puts forward a view of technology and artifacts firmly in accord with the Standard View and its presumption of need-driven technological evolution. Culture, according to Binford (7), is an "extrasomatic means of adaptation"; thus technology and material culture form the primary means by which people establish their viability, given the constraints imposed upon them by their environment and the demands of social integration. It follows, as Binford argued in 1965 (8), that every artifact has two dimensions, the primary, referring to the instrumental dimension related to the artifact's function, and the secondary, related to the artifact's social meaning and symbolism. Echoing this view, Dunnell makes explicit the connection that is assumed between an artifact's function and group survival: The artifact's function is that which "directly enhances the Darwinian fitness of the populations in which they occur" (23:199). Style, in contrast, is something added on the surface, a burnish or decoration, that might play some useful role in symbolizing group solidarity but is decidedly secondary. In the Modernist view, there are universal human needs, and for each of these there is an ideal artifact. For the primitive technologist, discovering such an artifact is like discovering

America: It was there before the explorers finally found it—and to the extent that anyone bothers to look, it will be found, and inevitably adopted (although it might be resisted for a time). The tale of Man's rise, then, is the story of increasing technological prowess, as digging sticks develop into ploughs, drums into telephones, carts into cars.

The Standard View of technology offers a seemingly "hard" or "tough-minded" view of artifacts and technological evolution, but there is ample evidence that its "hardness" dissolves when examined critically. What seems to us an incontrovertible need, for which there is an ideal artifact, may well be generated by our own culture's fixations. Basalla (4:7–11) demonstrates this point forcefully with respect to the wheel. First used for ceremonial purposes in the Near East, the wheel took on military applications before finally finding transport applications. In Mesoamerica, the wheel was never adopted for transport functions, given the constraints of terrain and the lack of draught animals. Even in the Near East, where the wheel was first invented, it was gradually given up in favor of camels. Basalla comments, "A bias for the wheel led Western scholars to underrate the utility of pack animals and overestimate the contribution made by wheeled vehicles in the years before the camel replaced the wheel" (4:11). Against all Modernist bias, Basalla's view echoes the findings of recent social anthropologists who have argued that it is impossible to identify a class of "authentic" artifacts that directly and rationally address "real" needs (2, 22:72; 87). Culture, not nature, defines necessity. One could reassert that a "hard" or "tough-minded" approach requires the recognition, after all, that people must eat, and so on, but it is abundantly evident that a huge variety of techniques and artifacts can be chosen to accomplish any given utilitarian objective (91).

The supposed functions of artifacts, then, do not provide a clear portrait of a human culture's needs (38), and what is more, one cannot unambiguously infer from them precisely which challenges a human population has faced. The natives of chilly Tierra del Fuego, after all, were content to do without clothing. Accordingly, some archaeologists and social anthropologists would break radically with the Standard View in asserting that material culture does not play a decisive role in shaping a human group's adaptation to its environment. Golson (32) notes that a basic stone toolkit survives intact through "revolutionary" changes in subsistence in both the classic Old World sites and in the New Guinea highlands. A survey of the New Guinea tools, Golson concludes, "revealed none that is indispensable to any form, from the simplest to the most complex, of Highlands agricultural practice, except the stone axe or adze and the digging stick which are not only common to all but also serviceable in other than agricultural contexts" (32:161). Summarizing the evidence from social anthropology, Sahlins (86:81) puts this point well: "For the greater part of human history, labor has been more significant than tools, the intelligent efforts of the producer more significant than his simple equipment." Sahlins' view is echoed by Lemonnier (62:151), who notes that the "search for correspondences between technical level and 'stage' of economic organization does not seem likely to lead to a theory of the relation between technical systems and society, other than one so over-simplified and general that it quickly loses all interest." Material culture alone provides only a shadowy picture of human adaptations.

If techniques and artifacts are not the linchpins of human adaptation, as is so often surmised, then radical redefinitions are in order. It is not mere technology, but technology in concert with the social coordination of labor, that constitutes a human population's adaptation to its environment. In most prein-dustrial societies, technology plays second fiddle to the human capacity to invent and deploy fab-ulously complex and variable social arrange-ments. How, then, should we define technology? Spier (93:2), for instance, defines technology as the means by which "man seeks to modify or control his natural environment." This defini-tion is clearly unsatisfactory. It assumes, a pri-ori, that Man's inherent aim is domination or control of nature; and, anyway, it is wrong, since (as has just been argued) techniques and artifacts are secondary to the social coordina-tion of labor in shaping human adaptations. One could broaden the definition of technology to include the social dimension. But because the term "technology" so easily conjures up "merely technical" activity shorn of its social context (77), I believe it preferable to employ two definitions, the one more restricted, and the other more inclusive. *Technique* (following 62, 63) refers to the system of material re-sources, tools, operational sequences and skills, verbal and nonverbal knowledge, and *specific* modes of work coordination that come into play in the fabrication of material artifacts. *Socio-technical system,* in contrast, refers to the dis-tinctive technological activity that stems from the linkage of techniques and material culture to the social coordination of labor. The proper and indispensable subjects of a social anthropol-ogy of technology, therefore, include all three: techniques, sociotechnical systems, and mate-rial culture.

The sociotechnical system concept stems from the work of Thomas Hughes on the rise of modern electrical power systems (45, 46; for applications of the concept, see 68, 81). Accord-ing to Hughes, those who seek to develop new technologies must concern themselves not only with techniques and artifacts; they must also engineer the social, economic, legal, scien-tific, and political context of the technology.

A successful technological innovation occurs only when all the elements of the system, the social as well as the technological, have been modified so that they work together effectively. Hughes (45) shows how Edison sought to sup-ply electric lighting at a price competitive with natural gas (economic), to obtain the support of key politicians (political), to cut down the cost of transmitting power (technical), and to find a bulb filament of sufficiently high resis-tance (scientific). In a successful sociotechnical system, such as the electric lighting industry founded by Edison, the "web is seamless": "the social is indissolubly linked with the techno-logical and the economic" (60:112). In short, sociotechnical systems are heterogeneous con-structs that stem from the successful modifica-tion of social and nonsocial actors so that they work together harmoniously—that is, so that they resist dissociation (60:166–17)— i.e. resist dissolving or failing in the face of the system's adversaries. One or more sociotechnical sys-tems may be found in a given human society, each devoted to a productive goal.

Extending Hughes's concept, Law (60) and Latour (57) emphasize the difficulty of creating a system capable of resisting dissociation. A sys-tem builder is faced with natural and social ad-versaries, each of which must be controlled and modified if the system is to work. Some of them are more obdurate, and some of them more malleable, than others. In illustrating this point, Law shows that the sociotechnical system con-cept applies fruitfully to the study of preindus-trial technology, in this case the rise of the Por-tuguese mixed-rigged vessels in the 14th and early 15th centuries. The real achievement, ar-gues Law, was not merely the creation of the mixed-rigged vessel, with its increased cargo capacity and storm stability. Equally important was the magnetic compass, which allowed a consistent heading in the absence of clear skies; the simplification of the astrolabe, such that even semieducated mariners could determine their latitude; exploration that was specifically intended to produce tables of data, against which position could be judged; and an understanding of Atlantic trade winds, which allowed ships to go forth in one season and come back in another. To achieve the necessary integration of all these factors, the system builders had to get mariners, ship builders, kings, merchants, winds, sails, wood, instruments, and measurements to work together harmoniously. The system they created resisted dissociation; they were able to sail out beyond the Pillars of Hercules, down the coast of Africa, and soon around the globe.

Although it is no easy trick to construct a system resistant to dissociation, sociotechnical systems are not inevitable responses to immutable constraints; they do not provide the only way to get the job done. People unfamiliar with technology usually gravely understate the degrees of latitude and choice open to innovators as they seek to solve technical problems (48). More commonly, one sees a range of options, each with its tradeoffs, and it is far from obvious which, if any, is superior. In virtually every technical area, there is substantial latitude for choice. For instance, Lemonnier (62) points to the apparently arbitrary variation of techniques as one moves across the New Guinea highlands; such variation is to be found, Lemonnier notes, even among those "functional" (as opposed to "stylistic") aspects of a tool that are directly implicated in its action upon material (62:160). It would be wrong to attribute a system's "success" (i.e. in resisting dissociation) to the choice of the "correct" technique or social-coordination method.

By analogy to the sociology of scientific knowledge (11), this point can be formulated as a *principle of symmetry*. In the sociology of scientific knowledge, this principle countered an older sociology of science that explained the

success of a theory by its conformity to the Truth, while ascribing the failure of another theory to social factors (bias, influence, "interests," etc). The principle of symmetry calls for precisely the same kind of social explanation to be used in accounting for the success as well as the failure of a theory—or, by extension, of a sociotechnical system. Accordingly, it would violate the principle of symmetry to argue that one system succeeds because its builders chose the "right" techniques, the ones that really "work." Of apparently successful systems, we can say only that the system builders have apparently succeeded in bringing to life one out of a range of possible systems that could achieve its goal (e.g. trapping wild pigs, growing rice, or sailing down the coast of Africa). Such a system could be viewed as an adaptation, in line with cultural ecology, but only by abandoning the *post hoc, ergo propter hoc* fallacy of functionalism. That a sociotechnical system develops does not imply that it is the logical system, or the only possible system, that could have developed under the circumstances; social choice, tactics, alternative techniques, and the social redefinition of needs and aspirations all play a role in the rise of sociotechnical systems.

An additional example, south Indian temple irrigation, should help to clarify the sociotechnical system concept and its implications. A marked characteristic of agriculture in medieval south India was the royal donation of wastelands to communities of Brahmans, who in turn were encouraged to organize and supervise agricultural production. They did so by investing the lands in newly constructed temples, which provided a locus of managerial control for the construction, maintenance, and management of complex irrigation systems (42, 67) that successfully resisted drought and led to a majestic efflorescence of south Indian Hindu culture. The heterogeneous quality of such a system is immediately evident. The system linked into a cohesive, successful system actors such as kings, canal-digging techniques, dams, flowing water, modes of coordinating labor for rice production, agricultural rituals, deities, notions of social rank and authority, conceptions of merit flowing from donations, conceptions of caste relations and occupations, conceptions of socially differentiated space, religious notions of the salutary effect of temples on the fertility of the earth, economic relations (land entitlements), trade, temple architecture, and knowledge of astrological and astronomic cycles (used to coordinate agricultural activities). A human sociotechnical system links a fabulous diversity of social and nonsocial actors into a seamless web (47).

Any sociotechnical system shows the imprint of the context from which it arose, since system builders must draw on existing social and cultural resources. But it is important to stress that every sociotechnical system is in principle a de novo construct; to make the system work, system builders draw from existing resources but modify them to make them function within the system. In this sense, sociotechnical-system building is almost inevitably *sociogenic* (56): Society is the result of sociotechnical-system building. The distinctive social formation of medieval south India, for instance, is in almost every instance attributable to the achievement of the sociotechnical system of temple irrigation. The system of temple irrigation draws on old ideas of gods, kings, water, dams, castes, gifts, and all the rest, but it transforms every one of these ideas in important ways. In this sense, the sociotechnical system concept is in accord with the structuration theory of Giddens (30): People construct their social world using the social resources and structures at hand, but their activities modify the structures even as they are reproduced.

A sociotechnical system, then, is one of the chief means by which humans produce their social world. Yet sociotechnical systems are all but invisible through the lenses provided by Western economic, political, and social theory, as Lansing (56) discovered in his study of Balinese irrigation. From the standpoint of Western theory, irrigation is organized either by the despotic state, as Wittfogel argued, or by autonomous village communities, as anthropologists argued in reply. Invisible within this discourse, Lansing found, was the Balinese water temple, a key component in a *regional* sociotechnical system devoted to the coordination of irrigation. Lansing discovered that the rites in these Balinese water temples define the rights and responsibilities of subsidiary shrines (and with them, the *subaks,* or local rice-growing collectivities, that line the watershed) through offerings and libations of holy water. By symbolically embedding each local group's quest for water within the supra-local compass of temple ritual, water temples encourage the cooperation necessary to ensure not only the equitable distribution of water but also the regulated flow of inundation and fallowing that proves vital for pest control and fertility. Tellingly, the solidarity that is created is not political; the king has obvious interests in promoting this kind of solidarity but does not actively intervene within it. And neither is this solidarity purely economic; it crosscuts other arenas of economic integration. A sociotechnical system engenders a distinctive form of social solidarity that is neither economic nor political (47); that is why it took so long for these systems to be "discovered" by anthropologists indoctrinated with classical social theory.

Sociotechnical systems have remained equally invisible through the lens provided by the Standard View of technology, which refuses to deal with the ritual dimension of technical activity. According to the Standard View, and to virtually every anthropological definition of technology, a technique is an *effective* act

(62:154, citing 71), as opposed to magic or religion. Spier makes this commonsense assumption explicit in excluding from "technology" any "magico-religious means" by which people seek to control nature (93:2). Such a view forestalls any consideration of the crucial role that ritual institutions play in the coordination of labor and the network's legitimation (24, 35, 83, 95), a point that should already be apparent from the south Indian and Balinese examples already discussed. Among the Montagnards of highland Vietnam (19), agriculture is no mere matter of material culture and manual labor. On the contrary, ritual is a key component of agricultural work; the rites call forth social groups to engage in specific activities, and they provide a metacommentary on the entire productive process. Sociotechnical systems may very well include ritual components with explicit productive goals that we find "false," such as enhancing the fertility of the earth; but to ignore them is to miss the crucial role they play in the coordination of labor. I would therefore argue that the social anthropology of technology, against all common sense, should adopt a principle of absolute impartiality with respect to whether a given activity "works" (i.e. is "technical") or "doesn't work" (i.e. is "magico-religious"); only if we adopt such impartiality do the social dimensions of sociotechnical activity come to the fore (80).

The labor-coordination role of ritual is surprisingly widespread, and for good reason: Ritual works surpassingly well to coordinate labor under conditions of statelessness or local autonomy. Among the Piaroa of lowland south America, for example, shamanic rituals employ scarce mystical knowledge to transfer mystical powers of fertility and increase to people who feel themselves in need of such powers; Granero views such rituals as an *"essential part of the productive practices of Piaroa society"* (35:665, Granero's emphasis). Given their access to what Granero tellingly calls the "mystical means of

reproduction," shamans legitimately claim the right to solicit and coordinate agricultural labor, as well as organize trade (1986). Under stateless or locally autonomous conditions, rituals provide the ideal medium for the coordination of labor in that they virtually rule out dissent (9): "you cannot argue with a song." In Sri Lanka, 19th-century civil servants meticulously recorded the rites of the threshing floor, which required economically significant transactions to be conducted with a superstitious scrupulousness of detail, and a special, virtually incomprehensible language. This ritual language required participants to adopt an "odd shibboleth," as one observer termed it, for these vital economic transactions; the limited vocabulary sharply constrained what could be said (79). Thus another key feature of sociotechnical systems is their *silence,* the relatively insignificant role played by human language as against nonverbal communication in ritual (28) as a coordinator of technical activities. Here we see yet another reason for the invisibility of such systems within the compass of Western social theory, which excessively privileges language over nonverbal cognition and behavior (10).

A successful sociotechnical system achieves a stable integration of social and nonsocial actors, but it is no static thing: Keeping the network functioning requires constant vigilance, and it may also require additional technical or social modification. Every sociotechnical system must cope with what Hughes calls *reverse salients,* areas of obduracy or resistance that prevent the system from expanding or threaten it with dissociation. On reaching the Indies, the Portuguese found that Muslims had monopolized the trade with Hindu princes; the Portuguese response was to work a good deal to make the cannon lighter and more powerful (60:127–28). Sociotechnical systems also betray a characteristic life cycle (46) as they grow from invention, small-scale innovation, growth and development, and a climax of maximum elaboration and scope, followed by senescence and decay, until the system disappears or is replaced by a competing system. Such life cycles may be visible in the myriad cycles of innovation, growth, efflorescence, and decay that characterize the archaeological record.

The sociotechnical system concept, in sum, suggests that mere necessity is by no means the mother of invention, just as production alone is by no means the sole rationale for the astonishing linkages that occur in sociotechnical systems (cf 5). To be sure, sociotechnical-system builders react to perceived needs, as their culture defines them. But we see in their activities the essentially creative spirit that underlies sociogenesis, which is surely among the supreme modes of human cultural expression. Basalla (4:14) puts this point well: A human technology is a "material manifestation of the various ways men and women throughout time have chosen to define and pursue existence. Seen in this light, the history of technology is part of the much broader history of human aspirations, and the plethora of made things are a product of human minds replete with fantasies, longings, wants, and desires." Basalla's point suggests that no account of technology can be complete that does not consider fully the *meaning* of sociotechnical activities, and in particular, the non-productive roles of technical activities in the ongoing, pragmatic constitution of human polities and subjective selves. Sociotechnical systems can be understood, as I argue in the next section, only by acknowledging that they produce power and meaning as well as goods.

"The Meaning of an Artifact is a Surface Matter of Style"

The commonsense Modernism of the Standard View desocializes human technological activity, as has just been argued, by reducing the creativity of sociotechnical-system building to the doctrine of Necessity. In precisely the same way, the Standard View desocializes the meaning of technological artifacts by reducing this meaning to the artifact's alleged function, with a residual and secondary role left for the relatively superficial matter (it is claimed) of style. To recapture the sociality of human artifacts, it is necessary to turn this distinction upside down. I begin, therefore, by arguing that the supposedly "hard" part of the artifact, its function, is in reality the "softest," the one that is most subject to cultural definition.

Archaeologists commonly distinguish function and style, as has already been noted. But as Shanks & Tilley argue,

> It is impossible to separate out style and the function [for instance] in either vessel shape or projectile point morphology. There is no way in which we can meaningfully measure and determine what proportion of a vessel's shape performs some utilitarian end, the remainder being assigned to the domain of style. To take a chair—what proportion of this is functional as opposed to stylistic? No answer can be given; the style inheres in the function and vice versa. Furthermore, ascribing any specific or strictly delimited function to an object is in many, if not all cases, an extremely dubious exercise. A chair may be to sit on, it nominally fulfills this function, but chairs can also be used for standing on, or for knocking people over the head with, as pendulums, rulers, or almost anything else. This is not to deny the banal point that objects have uses and may normally be used in just one way, but it is to suggest that such a position represents, at best, a starting point rather than an end point for archaeological analysis (91:92).

The views of Shanks & Tilley are echoed by Norman (75:9), who calls attention to an artifact's *affordances*. An affordance is a perceived property of an artifact that suggests how it should be used. Affordances are inherently multiple: Differing perceptions lead to different uses. You can drink water from a cup to quench thirst, but you can also use a cup to show you are well bred, to emphasize your taste in choosing decor, or to hold model airplane parts. But is not such a point just so much strained, special pleading? Everyone knows that chairs are *primarily* for sitting in; despite "minor" variations associated with specific historical styles and tastes, isn't the chair's function the pre-eminent matter? Such a distinction between function and style is common sense only to the extent that we ignore a key component of technology, ritual. In the preceding section I stressed ritual's prominent role in coordinating labor in sociotechnical systems. Here, I emphasize the equally prominent role of ritual in defining the function of material culture.

To illustrate this point with a convenient and simple example, I draw on the work of K. L. Ames on Victorian hallway furnishings (1). Ames notes that the hallway was the only space in the Victorian house likely to be used by both masters and servants. Masters and visitors of the masters' class would pass through the hall, while servants and tradesmen would be asked to sit there and wait. Ames calls attention to the contradictory character of these artifacts: They had to be visually appealing to the master class as they passed through the hall; but if they included seats, they had to be austere, without upholstery, and uncomfortable, befitting the lower social status of the messenger boys, book agents, census personnel, and soap-sellers who were made to wait there. Plain and uncomfortable, the bench echoed the design of servants' furnishings, which resembled (in the words of a servant quoted by Ames) the furnishings of a penal colony. With such constant reminders of their status, the servants would have no occasion to compare their status favorably with that of their master and mistress. Peers and people

of higher status, Ames notes, were shown past the bench and directly into the house. In short, the Victorian hallway is a special space devoted to the enactment of entry rituals.

As the Victorian hallway bench suggests, style and function cannot be distinguished as easily as the Standard View would claim. What appears in a naive analysis to be the superficial matter of "style" (the bench's austerity) turns out, thanks to Ames' deeper contextual reading of hallway artifacts, to be the very "function" of the artifact (to remind servants of their status)! Note that here the function of the artifact (to be attractive to masters and remind servants of their station) can be known only by comprehending the perceived social role that the artifact is designed to fulfill; this perceived social role, in turn, can be known only from a contextual analysis that fully explores the dimensions of Victorian class sensibilities. I do not mean that the flatness and discomfort of the Victorian hallway bench were intended merely to "reflect" Victorian class sensibilities. When employed in a ritual context, the bench was obviously intended to *construct* Victorian statuses in ways not obvious outside the ritual context. With this analysis in view, one can argue that the dimension of an artifact identified by archaeologists, historians, and collectors as "style" once formed part of a now lost ritual system, and for that reason now stands out oddly and mysteriously against the artifact's supposed "function." In short, the distinction between "function" and "style" is a product of the *decontextualization and dehistoricization of artifacts* (see 43:107–20 for an excellent illustration of this point).

Daniel Miller's work among south Indian potters (72) demonstrates that artifacts play key roles in *framing* ritual activities—that is, in providing cues that establish the cultural significance of the events taking place. In a little-understood process that is unconscious and nonverbal, frames—though inconspicuous—play an important social role, establishing the context within which social action takes on meaning. For Miller artifacts are on the one hand extremely visible and omnipresent; yet on the other hand, they operate silently and invisibly (73:109). As many anthropologists have discovered, people find it difficult and pointless to talk about the meaning of artifacts: When pressed, informants resort to their last-ditch tactic, "Our ancestors did it this way" (62:165). Once again we meet a familiar theme: the silence of human technological activity and its invisibility within the compass of theories that assign excessive privilege to speech and writing.

Miller's work among south Indian potters shows the cross-cultural relevance of my point about Victorian hallway artifacts—namely, that the "style" of an artifact, when restored fully to its cultural context, turns out to be its "function." But what is even more important, Miller's work suggests that this "function" of artifacts may inspire artifact diversity, a key feature of human technology. When many versions of an artifact are available, they can play many roles in social life. Miller concludes: "Technology could be analyzed as the *systematic exploitation of the range of methods used in order to produce patterned variation* (72:201, my emphasis). Pushing this point further, one can argue that a major rationale for the creation of sociotechnical systems, beyond mere Necessity, is the elaboration of the material symbols that are indispensable for the conduct of everyday life. And one can identify here another form of linkage, as yet unexplored: the linkage between the rituals that coordinate labor and the rituals that frame human social behavior by employing material artifacts as cues. It seems likely that such linkages amount to a formidable apparatus of domination, even under conditions of statelessness, thus belying the mythos of egalitarianism in stateless societies.

If no form of domination goes unresisted, then one would expect artifacts to be employed in redressive rituals that are specifically designed to mute or counter the invidious status implications of the dominant ritual system. I therefore see the social use of artifacts, paraphrasing Richard Brown (12:129), as a process of nonverbal communication. In this process, each new act of ritual framing is a statement in an ongoing dialogue of ritual statements and counterstatements. In the counterstatements, people whose status is adversely affected by rituals try to obtain or modify valued artifacts, in an attempt to blunt or subvert the dominant rituals' implications. These statements, and their subsequent *counterstatements,* help to constitute social relations as a *polity.* I therefore call attention to *redressive* technological activities, which are interpretive responses to technological domination, to highlight the political dimension of technology. I call this polity-building process a *technological drama.*

A technological drama (78, 82) is a discourse of technological "statements" and "counterstatements" in which there are three recognizable processes: *technological regularization, technological adjustment,* and *technological reconstitution.* A technological drama begins with technological regularization. In this process, a design constituency creates, appropriates, or modifies a technological production process, artifact, user activity, or system in such a way that some of its technical features embody a political aim—that is, an intention to alter the allocation of power, prestige, or wealth (57). Because a sociotechnical system is so closely embedded in ritual and mythic narrative, the technological processes or objects that embody these aims can easily be cloaked in myths of unusual power. Ford's assembly line, for example, was cloaked in the myth that it was the most efficient method of assembling automobiles—a myth indeed, since Norwegian and Swedish experiments have shown that team assembly and worker empowerment are just as efficient.

The myth masked a political aim: Ford saw the rigid and repetitive work roles as a way of domesticating and controlling the potentially chaotic and disruptive workforce of Southern and Eastern European immigrants (94:153). The stratifying role of the Victorian hallway bench, to cite another example, was cloaked in a myth of hygiene, which ascribed its plainness to its function in seating those who had recently sojourned in the filthy streets (1, 27).

Like texts, the technological processes and artifacts generated by technological regularization are subject to multiple interpretations, in which the dominating discourse may be challenged tacitly or openly. I call such challenges *technological adjustment* or *technological reconstitution*. In technological adjustment, impact constituencies—the people who lose when a new production process or artifact is introduced—engage in strategies to compensate the loss of self-esteem, social prestige, and social power caused by the technology. In this process they make use of contradictions, ambiguities, and inconsistencies within the hegemonic frame of meaning as they try to validate their actions. They try to control and alter the discourse that affects them so invidiously, and they try to alter the discursively regulated social contexts that regularization creates. Police whose movements are tracked by surveillance systems, for example, become adept at finding bridges and hills that break the surveillance system's tracking signal. They can then grab a burger or chat with another cop without having their location logged. Adjustment strategies include appropriation, in which the impact constituency tries to gain access to a process or artifact from which it has been excluded (e.g. 17). Before the personal computer, computer enthusiasts and hobbyists learned how to hack their way into mainframe systems—as did the youthful Bill Gates (now the CEO of Microsoft Corporation), who was reputed to have hacked his way into

systems widely thought to be impregnable. In technological reconstitution, impact constituencies try to reverse the implications of a technology through a symbolic inversion process I call *antisignification*. Reconstitution can lead to the fabrication of counterartifacts (e.g. 51), such as the personal computer or "appropriate technology," which embody features believed to negate or reverse the political implications of the dominant system.

Following Victor Turner (97:91–94, 98:32), I choose the metaphor of "drama" to describe these processes. A technological drama's statements and counterstatements draw upon a culture's root paradigms, its axioms about social life; in consequence, technological activities bring entrenched moral imperatives into prominence. To create the personal computer, for example, was not only to create new production processes and artifacts, but also to bring computational power to the People, to deal the Establishment a blow by appropriating its military-derived tools, and to restore the political autonomy of the household vis-à -vis the Corporation. Here we see the dimension of desire that Basalla (4) emphasizes: To construct a sociotechnical system is not merely to engage in some creative or productive activity. It is to bring to life a deeply desired vision of social life, often with a degree of fervor that can only be termed millenarian.

In any explanation of the motivations underlying sociotechnical-system building and artifact appropriation the role of such activities in the subjective processes of self-definition deserves emphasis (22). In the grip of what Miller calls the mass culture critique, we tend to treat contemporary acts of artifact appropriation in capitalist society "as so tainted, superficial, and trite that they could not possibly be worth investigating." Materialistc people, in addition, are seen as "superficial and deluded, and are unable to comprehend their position" (73:166). Yet, as

Miller stresses (73:86–108) there are good grounds for arguing that artifacts play a key role cross-culturally in the formation of the self: Artifact manipulation and play, for example, provide the conceptual groundwork for the later acquisition of language (100). We learn early, argues Miller (73:215), that artifacts play key roles in a "process of social self-creation" in which artifacts are "directly constitutive of our understanding of ourselves and others." In this sense contemporary societies, despite the rise of the Consumer Culture, possess much in common with preindustrial societies (2, c.f. 14:228–9): Artifacts are multiplied, elaborated, appropriated, and employed in framing activities as a form of self-knowledge and self-definition, a contention supported by the dizzying and unfathomable array of spectacular artifacts now collecting dust in ethnological museums. Miller's point leads directly to a consideration of a third contention of the Standard View, the doctrine that technological evolution has proceeded from simple to complex, and has deprived modern Man of his authenticity.

"A Unilinear Progression . . . From Simple Tools To Complex Machines"

It would be idiotic to deny that contemporary humans know a great deal more about technology than did our predecessors. History shows cumulative trends in virtually every field of technological endeavor. But the sociotechnical system concept leads to the equally inescapable conclusion that an enormous amount of human knowledge about building sociotechnical systems has been utterly and irretrievably lost. I argue here that the extent of this loss can be appreciated only by understanding the heterogeneous nature of sociotechnical systems and by radically questioning the Standard View's assumption that the evolution of technology may be described as the shift from Tool to

Machine. Such an analysis will raise equally radical questions about the Standard View's notion of Rupture.

In a preindustrial society, people do not often talk about the technical knowledge they possess. In studying weavers in Ghana, for instance, Goody was surprised by the insignificant role of questioning and answering in the teaching of apprentices (33). Although highly elaborate systems of ethnobotanical classification may play key roles in subsistence systems, an enormous amount of technological knowledge is learned, stored, and transmitted by experiential learning, visual/spatial thinking, and analogical reasoning. Bloch (10:187) describes the nonlinguistic learning that takes place, a form of learning very incompletely understood in the cognitive sciences:. . .

> Imagine a Malagasy shifting cultivator with a fairly clear, yet supple mental model, perhaps we could say a script, stored in long-term memory, of what a 'good swidden' is like; and that this model is partly visual, partly analytical (though not necessarily in a sentential logical way), partly welded to a series of procedures about what you should do to make and maintain a swidden. This Malagasy is going through the forest with a friend who says to him, 'Look over there at that bit of forest, that would make a good swidden.' What happens then is that, after a rapid conceptualization of the bit of forest, the model of 'the good swidden' is mentally matched with the conceptualized area of forest, and then a new but related model, 'this particular place as a potential swidden,' is established and stored in long-term memory.

Bloch argues that the linguistically derived theory of human cognition is insufficient because it cannot account for the speed with which we perform daily tasks such as identifying a 'good swidden.' It cannot account, as Miller notes (73:102), for our ability to absorb almost instantly the social implications of a furnished interior "consisting of a combination which is not only almost certainly in some degree unique, but some of whose basic elements may also be new to us." As we use technology for practical and social purposes, then, we draw on a nonverbal form of human cognition whose capabilities clearly form an enormous, but heretofore little recognized, component of our species' everyday intelligence. The portion of technical knowledge that people can verbalize represents only the tip of the iceberg.

The notion that technology is applied science—that it represents the practical use of logically-formulated, linguistically-encoded knowledge—is very misleading. A sociotechnical system is much better described as an *activity system*, a domain of purposive, goal-oriented action in which knowledge and behavior are reciprocally constituted by social, individual, and material phenomena (64, 102). As Janet and Charles Keller have emphasized, and as Bloch's example so tellingly illustrates, an activity system constantly fluxes between being and becoming: "Action has an emergent quality which results from the continual feedback from external events to internal representations and from the internal representations back to enactment" (52:2). Crucial to this process is an equally flexible cycling among alternative cognitive modes, including visual/spatial thinking and linguistic/classificatory thinking (53). Visual/spatial thinking is widespread in all technological activity systems, including today's high technology (25, 26, 101, 99). But visual/spatial thinking is silent. Competent producers and users rarely mention it. This kind of knowledge is lost, sometimes irretrievably, in the wake of technological "progress." Recreation of a system that has been lost is virtually impossible. We have no idea how some preindustrial artifacts were made, let alone how highly effective activity systems were so successfully coordinated under preindustrial conditions.

When one views a sociotechnical system as a complex heterogeneous linkage of knowledge, ritual, artifacts, techniques, and activity, it is apparent that much more than visual/spatial knowledge about manufacture can be lost when a system dissociates. A human sociotechnical system involves the coordination of a massively complex network; in the case of Portuguese naval expansion this network consisted of such entities as kings and queens, ships, crews, winds, cannons, maps, sails, astrolabes, Muslims, and gold. Viewed as an activity system, a sociotechnical system must include all the conceptual, visual, experiential, tactile, and intuitive knowledge necessary to modify these diverse elements so that they work together harmoniously. Even in the most "primitive" sociotechnical systems, such as those of contemporary hunters and gatherers living in marginal environments (e.g. 61), the scope of knowledge integration involved is phenomenal. The complexity of any human sociotechnical system is belied by the simplicity of its tools (32).

All human sociotechnical systems, whether "primitive" or "preindustrial," are enormously complex and inherently heterogeneous. Through recognition of this fact one can begin a critique of the notion of Rupture that figures so prominently in the Standard View. According to the Standard view, tool use is *authentic* and fosters *autonomy;* one owns and controls one's own tools and isn't dependent on or exploited by others. When we use machines, in contrast, we must work at rhythms not of our own making, and we become ensnared in the supralocal relations necessary for their production, distribution, and maintenance. To the extent that we become dependent on machines we do not own, the stage is set for exploitation. We become divorced from nature, and our conceptions of the world become pathological, through a process called *reification* (a malady frequently asserted to occur only in industrial societies). According to the doctrine of Rupture, reification occurs because we employ objects as a means of knowing ourselves. When these objects are no longer our own authentic products, as is the case with industrially produced artifacts, our attention is deflected from critical self-awareness to the incompletely understood Other who generates the artifact (73:44).

The concept of sociotechnical systems enables us to see to what degree the doctrine of Rupture overstates the consequences of the transition from Tool to Machine. Although one would be foolish to deny the significant consequences of the machine's rise, preindustrial sociotechnical systems were themselves complex and exploitive—frequently more so than the Standard View acknowledges. A preindustrial sociotechnical system unifies material, ritual, and social resources in a comprehensive strategy for societal reproduction. In the course of participation in such a system, many if not most individuals find themselves playing dependent and exploited roles. By no means is reification restricted to industrial technology. As Lansing notes for Bali,

> Water temples establish connections between productive groups and the components of the natural landscape that they seek to control. The natural world surrounding each village is not a wilderness but an engineered landscape of rice terraces, gardens, and aqueducts created by the coordinated labor of generations. Anthropomorphic deities evoke this residual human presence in an engineered landscape. . . . Each wier is the origin of an irrigation system, which has both physical and social components. The concept of the deity of the wier evokes the collective social presence at the weir, where free-flowing river water becomes controlled irrigation water (56:128).

It would appear, then, that preindustrial sociotechnical systems have much in common with today's machine-based technological systems: Both rely extensively on nonverbal cognition, both show enormous complexity and elaboration, and both seem to generate reified notions rather than "authentic" self-awareness. Moreover, the conditions of freedom in preindustrial societies are falsely represented by focusing on the allegedly nonconstraining nature of tool (as opposed to machine) use. Any sociotechnical system, ancient or modern, primitive or industrialized, stems from the efforts of system builders who attempt to create a network capable of resisting dissociation. As previously argued, the use of ritual to coordinate productive activity in preindustrial sociotechnical systems amounts to a form of domination and control, even under stateless conditions. One can suggest, in fact, that both modern devices and preindustrial systems of ritual coordination are machines, as Latour (57:129) defines the term: "A machine, as the name implies, is first of all a machination, a stratagem, a kind of cunning, where borrowed forces keep one another in check so that none can fly apart from the group." Latour refers here to the role that machines play in uniting the constituent elements of modern sociotechnical systems: Machines tie the assembled forces to one another in a sustainable network (see 57:103–44 for telling discussions of the diesel engine, the Kodak camera, and the telephone). To argue thus is not to deny that the rise of the machine has brought about important, if as yet incompletely understood, alterations in human sociotechnical activity. It is to stress that the Standard View, with its division of human history into the Age of the Tool and the Age of the Machine, substantially overstates the political and subjective implications of the rise of machines (50:174).

What can the sociotechnical systems concept tell us about another kind of rupture, the kind produced when a modern industrial technology or artifact is adopted by a "traditional" society? A variant of the Standard View, perfectly expressed in the film "The Gods Must Be Crazy," alleges that the world-wide distribution of industrial artifacts will inevitably tear out the foundations of "authentic" traditional cultures and draw all the peoples in the world within the grip of consumer ideology. Implicit in this view is a strong version of technological determinism, the doctrine that because there is only one way to make or use a material artifact, every culture that adopts it will be forced to develop the same social and labor relations. Because social information is so crudely encoded in artifacts, however, it is extremely unlikely that a transferred artifact will succeed in bringing with it the ideological structure that produced it. For example, Hebdige (41) shows how motor scooters were deliberately developed in Italy to signify the feminine as opposed to the masculine motorbike: The motor was covered and quiet, the curves were soft and the shapes rounded, and so on. In Britain in the 1960s, however, the motor scooter was adopted by Mods, male and female, for whom it signified a European ("soft") image, as against the Rockers, who appropriated the motorcycle to signify an American ("hard") image.

Thus the "recipient" (appropriating) culture can reinterpret the transferred artifact as it sees fit. No less should be expected of people in so-called "traditional societies." According to the sociotechnical systems model, no such thing as a "traditional society" exists. Every human society is a world in the process of becoming, in which people are engaged in the active technological elaboration, appropriation, and modification of artifacts as the means of coming to know themselves and of coordinating labor to sustain their lives. New resources are unlikely to be ignored if they can be woven into an existing or new activity system. An artifact's determinative implications for labor in one context may be nullified if it is adopted to fulfill an essentially expressive function, as is the case for

many "showpiece" industrial installations in Third World countries.

In a recent important essay, Schaniel (89) has stressed that the adoption of artifacts does not necessarily imply the adoption of the system of logic that produced the technology. Schaniel illustrates this point by discussing the history of Maori appropriation of iron artifacts. In the first phase, the Maori ignored the artifacts, seeing little or no value in them. After some experimentation, the Maori found that hoes and spades could be worked into their indigenous system of agriculture. European observers were shocked to find that the Maori bound their hoes to short handles and used this implement from the squatting position. The favorite implement for levering up the ground remained the digging stick. The Maori later modified the digging stick by affixing to it a short piece of straight iron (89:496). Schaniel concludes that "the process of adopting and adapting introduced technology . . . does not imply that introduced technology does not lead to change, but the change is not pre-ordained by the technology adapted. . . . The process of technological adaptation is one where the introduced technology is adopted to the social processes of the adopting society, and not vice-versa" (89:496–98).

That said, the appropriation of modern technology, whether for productive or symbolic purposes, may bring with it what Pelto calls "de-localization," the irreversible growth of dependence on nonlocal sources of energy (76:166–68). As Pelto's study of the snowmobile in Lapland suggests, de-localization may expand the geographical scope within which people actively appropriate artifacts, with extensive implications for social and cultural change. It would be wrong, however, to try to predict the trajectory of such change from a technical analysis of the transferred technology, as the extensive literature on the social impact of the Green Revolution attests. According to some studies (36, 37), the Green Revolution invariably leads to "techno-economic differentiation" and the growth of a pauper class because rich farmers disproportionately benefit from the extra-local resources (high-yielding varieties, pesticides, herbicides, and fertilizers). Other studies report that Green Revolution technology does not necessarily produce socioeconomic differentiation, so long as countervailing customs assure the equitable use of agricultural inputs (3, 20, 31). In assessing the social and cultural impact of de-localization, however, it is important to bear in mind that assuming technological determinism is much easier than conducting a fully contextual study in which people are shown to be the active appropriators, rather than the passive victims, of transferred technology (79).

Sharp's famous analysis of steel axes among "stone-age" Australians illustrates the peril of reading too much technological determinism into a single case. Sharp showed how missionaries, by providing stone axes to women and young men, whose status had previously been defined by having to ask tribal elders for these artifacts, brought down a precariously legitimated stratification system. However, any status differentiation system that depends on sumptuary regulations, rules that deny certain artifacts to those deemed low in status, is vulnerable to furious adjustment strategies if such artifacts suddenly become widely available; culture contact and technology transfer are by no means required to set such processes in motion. The process Sharp described is not constitutive of technology transfer per se; a clear analogue is the erosion of the medieval aristocracy's status as peasants freed themselves from sumptuary regulations and acquired high-status artifacts (73:135–36).

Where technological change has apparently disrupted so-called "traditional societies," the villain is much more likely to be colonialism than technology. Colonialism disrupts indigenous political, legal, and ritual systems, and in so doing, may seriously degrade the capacity of local system-builders to function effectively within indigenous activity systems. In colonial Sri Lanka, the liberal British government was obsessed with the eradication of multiple claims to land, which were perceived to discourage investment and social progress. The legal eradication of such claims destroyed the ability of native headmen to adjust holdings to changing water supply levels and undermined the traditional basis by which labor was coordinated for the repair of dams and irrigation canals. Village tanks and canals fell into disrepair as impecunious villagers allowed their lands to be taken over by village boutique owners and moneylenders (79). This example suggests that it is not transferred technology, but rather the imposition of an alien and hegemonic legal and political ideology—arguably, technicism, but not technology—that effects disastrous social change in colonized countries.

It is when sociotechnical systems come into direct competition, as is the case in advanced technological diffusion, that spectacular disintegrations of indigenous systems can occur. The sudden deployment of a competing system may outstrip the capacity of indigenous system participants to conceptualize their circumstances and make the necessary adjustments; their mode of deploying resources, material and human, no longer works. Latour (58:32) comments:

> The huge iron and steel plants of Lorraine are rusting away, no matter how many elements they tied together, because the world [their builders] were supposing to hold has changed. They are much like these beautiful words Scrabble players love to compose but which they do not know how to place on the board because the shape of the board has been modified by other players.

Conclusions

Against the Standard View's exaggerated picture of technological evolution from simple tools to complex machines, the sociotechnical system concept puts forward a universal conception of human technological activity, in which complex social structures, nonverbal activity systems, advanced linguistic communication, the ritual coordination of labor, advanced artifact manufacture, the linkage of phenomenally diverse social and nonsocial actors, and the social use of diverse artifacts are all recognized as parts of a single complex that is simultaneously adaptive and expressive.

The sociotechnical systems of the Machine Age do differ from their preindustrial predecessors, but the Standard View grossly exaggerates these differences. For example, most modern definitions of technology assert that, unlike their preindustrial predecessors, modern technological systems are systems for the application of science, drawing their productive power from objective, linguistically encoded knowledge (e.g. 16). But on closer examination we see here the influence of Standard View mythology. Historians of technology tell us that virtually none of the technologies that structure our current social landscape were produced by the application of science; on the contrary, science and organized objective knowledge are more commonly the *result* of technology. The principles of thermodynamics, for example, were discovered as scientists sought to determine how devices actually worked and what their operating parameters were (26). The notion that modern technology is efffective because it is founded in objective, "true" knowledge violates the principle of symmetry advanced earlier in this essay, even as it denigrates the achievements of preindustrial sociotechnical systems. As Lansing notes (56), Balinese water temples were more effective managers of irrigation than the all-but-disastrous Green Revolution techniques have been.

By jettisoning material-culture studies in the early 20th century, anthropology lost one means of developing a holistic, multi-disciplinary approach to culture. By reinstating the social anthropology of technology and material culture, we lay the foundation once again for fruitful communication among social anthropologists, ethnoarchaeologists, archaeologists, and students of human evolution. Besides challenging certain myths about technology that social anthropologists often take for granted, I hope this essay helps to raise the level of such interdisciplinary discourse. For example, efforts are now underway to comprehend human evolution in terms of the complex interplay among "tools, language, and intelligence" (29). From the perspective of this essay, such an effort is misconceived: It overprivileges tools and language, and disguises the truly significant phenomena—namely, sociotechnical systems and nonverbal cognition. To grasp the evolutionary significance of human technological activity, I suggest that anthropologists lay aside the myths of the Standard View ("necessity is the mother of invention," "the meaning of an artifact is a surface matter of style," and "the history of technology is a unilinear progression from tools to machines"), and view human technological activity using the concept of the sociotechnical system. Once we do so, we can begin to construct hypotheses about the *universals* of human technology—universals that highlight what is distinctly *human* about activities as diverse as making stone tools and launching space vehicles.

Literature Cited

1. Ames, K. 1978. Meaning in artefacts: hall furnishings in Victorian America. *J. Interdis. Hist.* 9:19–46
2. Appadurai, A. 1986. Introduction: commodites and the politics of value. In *The Social Life of Things: Commodities in Cultural Perspective,*

ed. A. Appadurai, pp. 3–61. Cambridge: Cambridge Univ. Press

3. Attwood, D. 1979. Why some of the poor get richer: economic change and mobility in rural Western India. *Curr. Anthropol.* 20:495–514

4. Basalla, G. 1988. *The Evolution of Technology.* Cambridge: Cambridge Univ. Press

5. Baudrillard, J. 1975. *The Mirror of Production,* transl. M. Poster. St. Louis: Telos Press

6. Bijker, W., Hughes, T., Pinch, T., eds. 1987. *The Social Construction of Technological Systems: New Directions in the Sociology and History of Technology.* Cambridge: MIT Press

7. Binford, L. 1962. Archaeology as anthropology. *Am. Antiq.* 28:217–25

8. Binford, L. 1965. Archaeological systematics and the study of culture process. *Am. Antiq.* 31:203–10

9. Bloch, M. 1974. Symbol, song, dance, and the features of articulation. *Eur. J. Sociol.* 15:55–81.

10. Bloch, M. 1991. Language, anthropology, and cognitive science. *Man* 26:183–98

11. Bloor, D. 1991. *Knowledge and Social Imagery.* Chicago: Univ. Chicago Press. 2nd. ed.

12. Brown, R. 1987. *Society as Text: Essays on Rhetoric, Reason, and Reality.* Chicago: Univ. Chicago Press

13. Bouquet, M. 1991. Images of artefacts. *Crit. Anthropol.* 11:333–56

14. Bourdieu, P. 1984. *Distinction: A social Critique of the Judgement of Taste.* London: Routledge and Kegan Paul.

15. Bradbury, M., McFarlane, J. 1976. The name and nature of modernism. In *Modernism,* ed. M. Bradbury, J. McFarlane, pp. 19–55. Harmondsworth: Penguin

16. Bruzina, R. 1982. Art and architecture, ancient and modern. *Res. Philos. Technol.* 5:163–87

17. Burke, P. 1978. *Popular Culture in Early Modern Europe.* London: Temple Smith

18. Clifford, J., Marcus, G., eds. 1986. *Writing Culture: The Poetics and Politics of Ethnography.* Berkeley: Univ. Calif. Press.

19. Condominas, G. 1986. Ritual technology in swidden agriculture. In *Rice Societies: Asian Problems and Prospects,* ed. I. Norlund, S. Cederroth, I. Gerden. pp. 29–37. Riverdale: Curzon Press

20. Coward, E. 1979. Principles of social organization in an indigenous irrigation system. *Hum. Organ.* 38:35–43

21. Digard, J.-P. 1979. La technologie en anthropologie: fin de parcours ou nouveau souffle? *L'Homme* 19:105–40

22. Douglas, M., Isherwood, B. 1979. *The World of Goods.* New York: Basic Books

23. Dunnell, R. 1978. Style and function: a fundamental dichotomy. *Am. Antiq.* 43:192–202

24. Flannery, K. V., Marcus, J. 1976. Formative Oaxaca and the Zapotec cosmos. *Am. Sci.* 64:374–83

25. Ferguson, E. S. 1977. The mind's eye: nonverbal thought in technology. *Science* 197:827–36

26. Fores, M. 1982. Technological change and the "technology" myth. *Scand. Econ. Hist. Rev.* 30:167–88

27. Forty, A. 1986. *Objects of Desire.* New York: Pantheon

28. Gell, A. 1975. *Metamorphosis of the Cassowaries.* London: Athlone Press

29. Gibson, K. 1991. Tools, language, and intelligence: evolutionary implications. *Man* 26:255–64

30. Giddens, A. 1979. *Central Problems in Social Theory.* London: MacMillan

31. Goldman, H., Squire, L. 1982. Technical change, labor use, and income distribution in the Muda irrigation project. *Econ. Dev. Cult. Change* 30:753–76

32. Golson, J. 1977. Simple tools and complex technology. In *Stone Tools as Cultural Markers: Change, Evolution, and Complexity,* ed. R. Wright, pp. 154–161. Canberra: Australian Inst. Aborig. Stud.

33. Goody, E. 1978. Toward a theory of questions. In *Questions and Politeness: Strategies in Social Interaction,* ed. E. Goody. Cambridge: Cambridge Univ. Press

34. Gould, R. 1968. Living archaeology: the Ngatatjara of Western Australia. *Southwest. J. Anthropol.* 24:101–22

35. Granero, F. 1986. Power, ideology, and the ritual of production in lowland south America. *Man* 21:657–79

36. Griffin, K. 1974. *The Political Economy of Agrarian Change: An Essay on the Green Revolution.* Cambridge: Harvard Univ. Press

37. Grotsch, K. 1972. Technical change and the destruction of income in rural areas. *Am. J. Agric. Econ.* 54:326–41

38. Hally, D. 1985. The identification of vessel function: a case study from northwest Georgia. *Am. Antiq.* 51:267–95

39. Harris, M. 1968. *The Rise of Anthropological Theory.* New York: Crowell
40. Harvey, D. 1989. *The Condition of Post-modernity: An Enquiry into the Origins of Cultural Change.* Oxford: Blackwell
41. Hebdige, D. 1981. Object as image: the Italian scooter cycle. *Block* 4:39–56
42. Heitzman, E. 1987. Temple urbanism in medieval south India. *J. Asian Stud.* 46:791–826
43. Hodder, I. 1985. *Reading the Past: Current Approaches to Interpretation in Archaeology.* Cambridge: Cambridge Univ. Press
44. Hodder, I., ed. 1989. *The Meaning of Things: Material Culture and Symbolic Expression.* London: Unwin Hyman
45. Hughes, T. 1983. *Networks of Power: Electrification in Western Society, 1880–1930.* Baltimore: Johns Hopkins Univ. Press
46. Hughes, T. 1987. The evolution of large technological systems. See Ref. 6, pp. 51–82
47. Hughes, T. 1989. *American Genesis: A Century of Innovation and Technological Enthusiasm, 1870–1970.* New York: Penguin
48. Hughes, T. 1990. From deterministic dynamos to seamless-web systems. In *Engineering as a Social Enterprise,* ed. H. Sladovich, pp. 7–25. Washington: Natl. Acad. Press
49. Hutton, J. H. 1944. The place of material culture in the study of anthropology. *J. Roy. Anthropol. Inst.* 74:1–6
50. Ingold, T. 1988. Tools, minds, and machines: an excursion into the philosophy of technology. *Techniques et Cultures* 12:151–76
51. James, S. 1979. Confections, concoctions, and conceptions. *J. Anthropol. Soc. Oxford* 10:83–95
52. Keller, C., Keller, J. 1991a. *Thinking and Acting with Iron.* Urbana: Beckman Inst.
53. Keller, C., Keller, J. 1991b. Imaging in iron or thought is not inner speech. Presented at Wenner-Gren Found. Anthropol. Res. Symp. No. 112, Rethinking Linguistic Relativity
54. Kroeber, A. L. 1948. *Anthropology.* New York: Harcourt & Brace
55. Kroeber, A., Kluckhohn, C. 1952. *Culture: A Critical Review of Concepts and Definitions.* Cambridge: Harvard Univ. Press
56. Lansing, S. 1991. *Priests and Programmers: Technologies of Power in the Engineered Lanscape of Bali.* Princeton: Princeton Univ. Press
57. Latour, B. 1987. *Science in Action: How to Follow Scientists and Engineers Through Society.* Cambridge: Harvard Univ. Press
58. Latour, B. 1986. The Prince for machines as well as for machinations. Paper read at the Seminar on Technology and Social Change, Univ. of Edinburgh (June 12–13, 1986)
59. Lauer, P., ed. 1974. *Readings in Material Culture.* Brisbane: Queensland Univ. Anthropol. Mus.
60. Law, J. 1987. Technology and heterogeneous engineering: the case of Portuguese expansion. See Ref. 6, pp. 111–34
61. Lee, R. 1979. *The !Kung San: Men, Women, and Work in a Foraging Society.* Cambridge: Cambridge Univ. Press
62. Lemonnier, P. 1986. The study of material culture today: toward an anthropology of technical systems. *J. Anthropol. Archaeol.* 5:147–86
63. Lemonnier, P. 1989. Bark capes, arrowheads, and Concorde: on social representations of technology. See Ref. 44, pp. 156–71
64. Leont'ev, A. 1981. The problem of activity in psychology. See Ref. 102, pp. 37–71
65. Leroi-Gourhan, A. 1943. *Evolution et techniques. L'homme et la matière.* Paris: Albin Michel
66. Leroi-Gourhan, A. 1945. *Evolution et techniques. Milieu et techniques.* Paris: Albin Michel
67. Ludden, D. 1985. *Peasant Society in South India.* Princeton: Princeton Univ. Press
68. MacKenzie, D. 1987. Missile accuracy: a case study in the social processes of technological change. See Ref 6, pp. 195–222
69. Malinowski, B. 1935. *Coral Gardens and Their Magic.* London: Routledge
70. Marcus, G., Fischer, M. 1986. *Anthropology as Cultural Critique: An Experimental Moment in the Human Sciences.* Chicago: Univ. Chicago Press.
71. Mauss, M. 1983. *Sociologie et anthropologie.* Paris: Presses Universitaires de France
72. Miller, D., ed. 1983. Things ain't what they used to be." *Roy. Anthropol. Inst. News* 59:5–16
73. Miller, D. 1987. *Material Culture and Mass Consumption.* London: Basil Black-well
74. Mulkay, M. 1978. *Science and the Sociology of Knowledge.* London: George Allen and Unwin
75. Norman, D. 1988. *The Psychology of Everyday Things.* New York: Basic Books

76. Pelto, P. 1973. *The Snowmobile Revolution: Technology and Social Change in the Arctic.* Menlo Park, CA: Benjamin Cummings

77. Pfaffenberger, B. 1988. Festishized objects and humanized nature: toward an anthropology of technology. *Man* 23:236–52

78. Pfaffenberger, B. 1988. The social meaning of the personal computer, or, why the personal computer revolution was no revolution. *Anthropol. Q.* 61:39–47

79. Pfaffenberger, B. 1990. The harsh facts of hydraulics: technology and society in Sri Lanka's colonization schemes. *Technol. Cult.* 31:361–97

80. Pfaffenberger, B. 1990. The Hindu temple as a machine, or the Western machine as a temple. *Techniques et Cultures* (16):183–202

81. Pfaffenberger, B. 1990. *Democratizing Information: Online Databases and the Rise of End-User Searching.* Boston: G. K. Hall

82. Pfaffenberger, B. 1992. Technological dramas. *Sci., Technol., Human Values* 17. In press

83. Rappaport, R. A. 1971. Ritual, sanctity, and cybernetics. *Am. Anthropol.* 73:59–76

84. Reynolds, B. 1983. The relevance of material culture to anthropology. *J. Anthropol. Soc. Oxford* 14:209–17

85. Richardson, M., ed. 1974. *The Human Mirror: Material and Spatial Images of Man.* Baton Rouge: Louisiana State Univ. Press

86. Sahlins, M. 1972. *Stone Age Economics.* Chicago: Aldine

87. Sahlins, M. 1976. *Culture and Practical Reason.* Chicago: Univ. Chicago Press

88. Sayce, R. 1933. *Primitive Arts and Crafts: An Introduction to the Study of Material Culture.* Cambridge: Cambridge Univ. Press

89. Schaniel, W. 1988. New technology and cultural change in traditional societies. *J. Econ. Issues* 22:493–98

90. Scheffler, I. 1967. *Science and Subjectivity.* New York: Knopf

91. Shanks, M., Tilley, C. 1987. *Social Theory and Archaeology.* Albuquerque: Univ. New Mexico Press

92. Sillitoe, P. 1988. *Made in Niugini: Technology in the Highlands of Papua New Guinea.* London: Brit. Mus.

93. Spier, R. 1970. *From the Hand of Man: Primitive and Preindustrial Technologies.* Boston: Houghton-Mifflin

94. Staudenmaier, J. 1989. The politics of successful technologies. In *In Context: History and the History of Technology,* ed. H. Cutliffe, R. Post, pp. 150–71. Bethlehem: Lehigh Univ. Press

95. Tennekoon, S. 1988. Rituals of development: the accelerated Mahaweli development program of Sri Lanka. *Am. Ethnol.* 15:294–310

96. Tilley, C. 1990. *Reading Material Culture.* Oxford: Blackwell

97. Turner, V. 1957. *Schism and Continuity in an African Society: A Study of Ndembu Village Life.* Manchester: Manchester Univ. Press

98. Turner, V. 1974. *Dramas, Fields, and Metaphors: Symbolic Action in Human Society.* Ithaca: Cornell Univ. Press

99. Vicente, W. 1984. Technological knowledge without science: the innovation of flush riveting in American airplanes, ca. 1930–1950. *Technol. Cult.* 25:540–76.

100. Vygotsky, L. 1978. *Mind in Society.* Cambridge: Harvard Univ. Press

101. Wallace, A. 1978. *Rockdale: The Growth of an American Village in the Early Industrial Revolution.* New York: Alfred A. Knopf

102. Wertsch, J., ed. 1981. *The Concept of Activity in Soviet Psychology.* Armonk, NY: M. E. Sharpe

103. Wissler, C. 1914. Material cultures of the North American Indians. *Am. Anthropol.* 16:447–505

Discussion Questions

1. What is technological literacy? Why is it important?
2. Pfaffenberger questions the Standard View of technology that "necessity is the mother of invention." Kranzberg's second law is that "invention is the mother of necessity." In what ways are the perspectives of these two authors similar? What does Kranzberg's second law mean to you?
3. The introduction to Section One describes four prevailing perspectives of technology. With which of these perspectives do you most strongly align, and why?
4. Kranzberg considers the autonomy of humanity from technology as one of the great unresolved questions of technology. Do we control technology or does technology control us? In spite of considering this an open question, Kranzberg's first law is that technology is not neutral. Pfaffenberger questions the tendency to think of tools as merely functional artifacts, but believes they have embedded culture. What do you think of these concepts? How do they bear on important societal debates about technologies like guns, nuclear power, computers, and so on?
5. These authors (and many others) have noted that technology's effects can vary from one person or group to the next: in other words, a technology can benefit some while harming others. Give an example from your own experience to illustrate this point. Propose a strategy that could be used by policy makers to resolve this dilemma.

 Supporting Activities

Note: the supporting activities included in this section are designed to be adapted for use with any section in the book.

1. Talk to five friends or family members to find out how they define *technology*. If you can, determine what their dominant perspective about technological progress is. Are they technological optimists? Pessimists? Realists? Structuralists? Or are they largely unconcerned or uninterested in technology? Contrast this with your response to Question 3 above.
2. Generate a list of popular movies (recent or older; there are a lot!) that explore themes associated with the impacts of technology (titles might include *2001: A Space Odyssey, Apollo 13, Gattica, Fat Man and Little Boy, Mad Max, The Island, Blade Runner, The Postman,* and *Her,* to name just a few). Watch the movie, and then write a review of the movie that provides a synopsis of the plot and a discussion of how the movie addresses class discussions.
3. Find and report on a current event that in your view illustrates some aspect of the relationship between society and technology. Describe why you selected the event and why you think it's interesting and/or important.
4. Identify technology policy issues that are currently being discussed at the local, national, or international level and conduct a classroom debate. Examples of topics include labeling on genetically modified food products, increasing federal support for public transit systems, use of national identity cards, and installation of utility-scale wind farms. Divide into opposing pairs or teams, research the facts and opinions on both sides of the argument, and conduct an oral debate in class. An excellent resource for this activity is the International Debate Education Association web site: http://www.idebate.org/.

Additional Resources

1. Watch the 1996 video about R. Buckminster Fuller, *Thinking Out Loud*, available on YouTube: https://www.youtube.com/watch?v=_8NGNhDxzzw.
2. The International Technology and Engineering Educators Association *Standards for Technological Literacy,* published in 2000, outlines the knowledge and skills necessary for technological literacy. They can be viewed online at: http://www.iteaconnect.org/TAA/Publications/TAA_Publications.html.
3. The Society for the History of Technology (SHOT) has published the quarterly journal *Technology and Culture* for over fifty years. An index to all volumes, and electronic access to all articles published since 1998, can be found at: http://etc.technologyandculture.net/about/.
4. There are a number of scholarly and popular journals that regularly publish articles dealing with technology and society. Notable titles include *Technology Review*, *Wired*, *National Geographic*, and *Scientific American*.
5. Bryan Pfaffenberger's wiki contains a page with biographical information about the author that includes links to the full text of many of his articles: http://www.stswiki.org/index.php?title=User:Bryan.

 References

Arthur, W. B. (2009). *The nature of technology: What it is and how it evolves.* New York, NY: Free Press.

Bigelow, J. (1831). *Elements of technology.* Boston, MA: Hilliard, Gray, Little and Wilkins.

DeVore, P. (1980). *Technology: An introduction.* Worcester, MA: Davis Publications, Inc.

Diamond, J. (1999). *Guns, germs and steel: The fate of human societies.* New York, NY: W. W. Norton & Company, Inc.

Dimitri, C., Effland, A., & Conklin, N. (2005). *The 20th century transformation of U.S. agriculture and farm policy.* United States Department of Agriculture Economic Research Service. Retrieved from http://www.ers.usda.gov/publications/EIB3/eib3.pdf.

Dusek, V. (2006). *Philosophy of technology: An Introduction.* Malden, MA: Blackwell Publishing.

Ellul, J. (English language copyright, 1964). *The technological society.* New York, NY: Alfred A. Knopf, Inc.

Fuller, R.B. (1983). *Grunch of giants.* New York, NY: St. Martin's Press.

Mumford, L. (1968). Technics and the nature of man. In C. Mitcham & R. Mackey (Eds.), *Philosophy and technology: Readings in the philosophical problems of technology* (pp. 77–85). New York, NY: Free Press.

National Academy of Engineering and National Research Council, Committee on Technological Literacy. (2002). *Technically speaking: Why all Americans need to know more about technology.* Washington, DC: National Academies Press.

Schumacher, E.F. (1973). *Small is beautiful: A study of economics as if people mattered.* London: Blond & Briggs.

Wauzzinski, R. (2001). *Discerning Prometheus: The cry for wisdom in our technological society.* Cranbury, NJ: Rosemont Printing & Publishing Corporation.

Winner, L. (1986). *The whale and the reactor: A search for limits in an age of high technology.* Chicago, IL: The University of Chicago Press.

 **Endnotes**

1. Eugene S. Ferguson, "La Fondation des machines modernes: des dessins," *Culture technique* 14 (June 1985): 182–207. *Culture technique* is the publication of the Centre de Recherche sur la Culture Technique, located in Paris under the direction of Jocelyn de Noblet. The June 1983 edition of *Culture technique,* dedicated to *Technology and Culture,* contained French translations of a number of articles from the SHOT journal.

2. Jacques Ellul, *The Technological Society* (New York, 1964), and Langdon Winner, *Autonomous Technology: Technics Out-of-Control as a Theme in Political History* (Cambridge, Mass., 1977).

3. Lynn White, jr., *Medieval Technology and Social Change* (Oxford, 1962), p. 28.

4. E.g., Christopher Lasch, *The Minimal Self: Psychic Survival in Troubled Times* (New York, 1984).

5. Quoted in Dennis H. Wrong, "The Case against Modernity," *New York Times Book Review,* October 28, 1984, p. 7.

6. Fernand Braudel, *The Structures of Everyday Life,* vol. 1 of *Civilization and Capitalism, 15th–18th Century*
(New York, 1981).

7. E.g., T. S. Ashton, *The Industrial Revolution, 1760–1830* (Oxford, 1948), and David S. Landes, *The Unbound Prometheus: Technological Change and Industrial Development in Western Europe from 1750 to the Present* (Cambridge, 1969).

8. Nicholas Rescher, *Unpopular Essays on Technological Progress* (Pittsburgh, 1980).

9. The "New Directions" program session at the 1985 SHOT annual meeting indicated that historians of technology are continuing to broaden their concerns and are indeed investigating new areas of the sociocultural context in relation to technological developments.

10. Hugh G. J. Aitken, *Syntony and Spark: The Origins of Radio* (New York, 1976).

11. Thomas P. Hughes, "Inventors: The Problems They Choose, the Ideas They Have, and the Inventions They Make," in *Technological Innovation: A Critical Review of Current Knowledge,* ed. Patrick Kelly and Melvin Kranzberg (San Francisco, 1978), pp. 166–82.

12. David A. Hounshell, *From the American System to Mass Production 1800–1932: The Development of Manufacturing Technology in the United States* (Baltimore, 1984), chap. 6.

13. Thomas P. Hughes, *Networks of Power: Electrification in Western Society, 1880–1930* (Baltimore, 1983), p. ix.

14. Edward W. Constant, *The Origins of the Turbojet Revolution* (Baltimore, 1980). This book was awarded the Dexter Prize by SHOT in 1982.

15. Stuart W. Leslie, "Charles F. Kettering and the Copper-cooled Engine," *Technology and Culture* 20 (October 1979): 752–76.

16. Eugene B. Skolnikoff states, "Technology alters the physical reality, but is not the key determinant of the political changes that ensue," in *The International Imperatives of Technology: Technological Development and the International Political System* (Berkeley, Calif.: University of California Institute of International Studies, n.d.), p. 2.

17. Speaking of the Bhopal tragedy, President John S. Morris of Union College has said: "Methyl isocyanate makes it possible to grow good crops and feed millions of people, but it also involves risks. And analyzing risks is not a simple matter" (*New York Times,* April 14, 1985).

18. Daniel A. Koshland, "The Undesirability Principle," *Science* 229 (July 5, 1985): 9.

19. See Dorothy Nelkin, ed., *Controversy: The Politics of Ethical Decisions* (Santa Monica, Calif., 1984).

20. Aaron Wildavsky, "No Risk Is the Highest Risk of All," *American Scientist* 67 (1979): 32–37.

21. Gerda Lerner, "The Necessity of History and the Professional Historian," *Journal of American History* 69 (June 1982): 7–20.

22. Eugene D. Genovese, "To Celebrate a Life—Biography as History," *Humanities* 1 (January–February 1980): 6. An analysis of today's low state of the history profession is to be found in Richard O. Curry and Lawrence D. Goodheart, "Encounters with Clio: The Evolution of Modern American Historical Writing," *OAH Newsletter* 12 (May 1984): 28–32.

23. Brooke Hindle, "'The Exhilaration of Early American Technology': A New Look," in *The History of American Technology: Exhilaration or Discontent?* ed. David A. Hounshell (Wilmington, Del., 1984).

24. See especially Cyril Stanley Smith's Usher Prize article, "Art, Technology, and Science: Notes on Their Historical Interaction," *Technology and Culture* 11 (October 1970): 493–549.

25. See David Billington's Dexter Prize–winning book, *Robert Maillart's Bridges: The Art of Engineering* (Princeton, N.J., 1979), and "Bridges and the New Art of Structural Engineering," *American Scientist* 72 (January-February 1984): 22–31.

26. Stanley N. Katz, "The Scholar and the Public," *Humanities* 6 (June 1985): 14–15.

27. Ruth S. Cowan, *More Work for Mother: The Ironies of Household Technology from the Open Hearth to the Microwave* (New York, 1983), chap. 5.

Technological Decision-Making

A major argument made in the publication *Technically Speaking: Why All Americans Need to Know More About Technology* (National Academy of Engineering, 2002) is that technological literacy is necessary so that as citizens we can make personal decisions about which technologies to adopt, and so that we can be active participants in establishing technology policy. As a society we will ideally make decisions about which technologies to support, what criteria we want to apply to the design of those technologies, and how their use should be regulated, if at all. Federal and state governments play a leading role in these decisions.

How do policy makers reach decisions about technologies? The federal government and most state governments have in place science and technology policy offices. For example, between the years 1972 and 1995, the Office of Technology Assessment (OTA), which served the members of the U.S. Congress, conducted bipartisan analyses of emerging technological trends at the behest of members of Congress. During the 23-year existence of the OTA, over 700 comprehensive reports and case studies were prepared.[1] In 2008 the Senate Committee on Appropriations recommended establishment of a technology assessment function within the Government Accountability Office (GAO).[2] The executive branch is advised by the Office of Science and Technology Policy (OSTP), which was established by Congress in 1976 with the mandate to advise the President and others about the effects of science and technology on domestic and international affairs.[3] Each president since 1933 has convened policy boards of scientists, engineers, and health professionals, including the current President's Council of Advisors on Science and Technology (PCAST), whose role is to make "policy recommendations in the many areas where understanding of science, technology, and innovation is key to strengthening our economy and forming policy that works for the American people" (OSTP, 2015, para. 1).

The OSTP has counterparts in many state government offices nationwide. These often take a decidedly pro-development stance, such as the North Carolina Board of Science, Technology, and Innovation,[4] whose mission is "to improve the economic well-being and quality of life for all North Carolinians through advancing science, technology, and innovation" (NC Department of Commerce, 2015, para. 1). New York has the Empire State Development Division of Science, Technology, and Innovation, whose mission focuses exclusively on "accelerat[ing] the growth of New York State's high-tech economy" (Empire State Development, 2010, para. 1). Generally speaking, much of the science and technology policy effort at the state level is focused on research and development (R&D), innovation, and economic development.[5]

A variation on the practice of maintaining a science and technology policy board is to establish independent, often multinational, boards that are charged with investigating a single issue of broad importance. The Intergovernmental Panel on Climate Change (IPCC) is an excellent example. The IPCC is a large-scale body set up by the United Nations Environment Programme (UNEP) and the World Meteorological Organization (WMO) and is open to membership from all member countries of the WMO and UNEP. It was established not to perform research or monitor climate data, but rather to conduct objective and comprehensive assessments of the *existing* scientific, technical, and socio-economic research being conducted worldwide regarding climate change, and to make those assessments widely available. Its series of climate change reports is considered by many to be the authoritative source for current information on climate change.[6]

Another avenue for input on technology policy is through expert testimony. Numerous nongovernmental think tanks such as the Brookings Institute have as one of their primary activities the role of providing expert testimony on topics related to the core missions of the supporting organizations.[7] Inclusion of such testimony is routine practice during policy debates in Congress as well as during legal debates within the judicial branch.[8] As we see in the excerpt by Michael Mann about what might be termed the politics of climate change, however, "expert" testimony is not always what it seems, and may in fact employ misinformation tools in deliberate attempts to undermine the work of others. Thus, expert testimony is an important and useful source of information but it can also be fraught with bias, and accurate representation of the issues is not assured.

A third important source of input for policy makers is public comment, both formal and informal. This can occur through forums set up by government agencies expressly for the purpose of public input, or can happen through individual or group mail, phone, or e-mail campaigns on particular issues. Increasingly, online media such as blogs, Facebook, and Twitter play a role in communicating public opinion about science and technology issues. A good example is the "USA Freedom Act" recently passed by Congress, which significantly reduces the ability of the National Security Agency (NSA) to conduct surveillance activities, including tapping phone records of citizens. Advocates on both side of the surveillance debate used social media to make their cases.

The challenges of establishing responsible science and technology policy are many. As we see from the excerpt by William Evan and Mark Manion, even systematic approaches to gather objective data for decision-making have significant flaws. This is primarily due to the fact that technological systems must not only satisfy the immediate *technical* challenges of functionality, but are also inextricably linked to the socio-cultural, political, environmental, and economic contexts in which they are created and used. Technologies, by definition, are systems created to serve humankind; challenges can arise in determining exactly who is to be served, how, and at what cost. This is at the heart of theory of technological politics discussed in the excerpt by Langdon Winner: he argues that we must go beyond simply acknowledging that technologies are embedded in social and economic systems, but must understand that the very design and function of a technological system can impose ways of being that might be inconsistent with our social or moral ideals. By structuring a system to conform to a technological need we may, intentionally or unintentionally, adopt systems that convey differential levels of power, benefit, or harm to members of society.

The dilemma of competing priorities is further compounded by the fact that the data do not always provide clear-cut solution pathways. As we see in the excerpt by Michael Mann some problems, such as climate change, confront considerable resistance from those who have a vested interest in the status quo, and it is understandable that many policy makers are loathe to act when uncertainties exist (or when they are led to believe uncertainties exist). Addressing climate change will also require massive alterations in our transportation and energy infrastructures, so it's hard to know which steps to take and how to prioritize them, and harder still to reach consensus on those actions.

Another important challenge with regard to technology policy is that as technological systems become ever more complex they become harder to understand. Thus, fewer and fewer people (including policy makers) have the capability to engage in debate about technologies at more than a superficial level, if at all. Complex systems are also subject to what has been termed *normal accidents*, defined as malfunctions that will inevitably occur due simply to the fact of the system's complexity. In short, these accidents are "normal" because they are unavoidable in our current mode of risk analysis and response (Perrow, 1999). In other words, their complexity means there is no way to anticipate all the ways that a system might malfunction, and thus no way to engineer a foolproof system.

Finally, it is clear that neither technology policy nor individual decisions about technologies are always based on sound judgment, or even an accurate interpretation of data. As we see in the article by Malcolm Gladwell, human decision makers can sometimes revert to a more primal logic when perceptions and emotions gain the upper hand. Thus, even with the most powerful modeling and data collection tools, there is no guarantee that we will make the "right" choices.

From a policy standpoint, once a decision *is* made, for better or worse, there are a variety of mechanisms for shaping human behavior relative to a technology. One method is to mandate or to *legislate* that behavior. For example, most states now have seat belt laws that require all persons riding in automobiles to use seat belts. Another method is to provide *incentives* to encourage a particular action. For example, many states have offered tax breaks to individuals and businesses that install renewable energy systems on their homes or buildings. A third method is to put in place *disincentives* that will have the effect of deterring a course of action. Charging higher rates for water users who exceed an established limit is a disincentive. Yet another mechanism for shaping behavior is to *educate* users about more attractive or desirable alternatives. A fifth mechanism, which is somewhat less direct than the other four mentioned, is to make available reasonable or attractive alternatives. For example, although many individuals might have wished to reduce the amount of gasoline they used, until affordable alternatives in the form of low-maintenance hybrid cars became widely available, their options were relatively limited.

Not mentioned yet is the one decision-making approach that is perhaps the most widely used of all: the decision to do nothing. In the face of uncertainties it is certainly much easier to let technological development proceed unchecked, following the whims and wishes of individual developers or according to its own imperatives. We become passive users or bystanders, potentially affected in both direct and indirect ways, but without the benefit of analysis or of a chance for input. As should be clear from Section One and the sections that follow, we advocate instead for informed participation, and argue that the responsibility for technological literacy lies with us all.

Do Artifacts Have Politics?

In order to fully grasp the underlying message in this excerpt from the book *The Whale and the Reactor*, readers must look beyond the prima facie use of the word "political" to understand its full meaning in this context. Winner's perspective may best be summed up by this quote: "The physical arrangements of industrial production, warfare, communications, and the like have fundamentally changed the exercise of power and the experience of citizenship." It is naïve and insufficient to consider technologies as merely neutral tools whose only effects are determined by the uses to which humans put them. By simply accepting certain technologies into our society we can allow the practical necessities of managing the system to dictate hierarchies of control (for reasons of safety, efficiency, cost, and more); to affect the ways we move and act; and to influence our relationships with one another and the larger society. This is an underlying theme that readers are challenged to identify throughout the excerpts contained in this book: in what ways have we (individually or societally) been willing to make changes in the way we live to "accommodate the technological innovation?" An objective consideration of this question will yield examples from nearly every facet of our lives.

The practical realities of attempting a deep analysis of all the technologies we use and rely on are prohibitive. Many—probably most—individuals neither care to scrutinize the technologies they use nor have the ability to do so. This places an even bigger burden on the technologists, scientists, engineers, and entrepreneurs who develop new technologies to engage in integrated design thinking that considers the full context in which the technology will be used. A more sophisticated approach to technological development may lead to systems designed to function well and to better meet our societal goals.

Langdon Winner is the Thomas Phelan Chair of Humanities and Social Sciences at Rensselaer Polytechnic Institute in Troy, New York, where he has taught since 1985. Winner holds three degrees in Political Science from UC Berkeley. Best known for his books *Autonomous Technology: Technics-out-of-Control as a Theme in Political Thought* (1977) and *The Whale and the Reactor: A Search for Limits in an Age of High Technology* (1986; excerpted here), Winner has written and lectured widely on the topic of technological politics. Throughout his published works, Winner has conveyed a consistent message, supported by historical and current examples: "that we pay attention to the characteristics of technical objects and the meaning of those characteristics."

Do Artifacts Have Politics?

No idea is more provocative in controversies about technology and society than the notion that technical things have political qualities. At issue is the claim that the machines, structures, and systems of modern material culture can be accurately judged not only for their contributions to efficiency and productivity and their positive and negative environmental side effects, but also for the ways in which they can embody specific forms of power and authority. Since ideas of this kind are a persistent and troubling presence in discussions about the meaning of technology, they deserve explicit attention.

Writing in the early 1960s, Lewis Mumford gave classic statement to one version of the theme, arguing that "from late neolithic times in the Near East, right down to our own day, two technologies have recurrently existed side by side: one authoritarian, the other democratic, the first system-centered, immensely powerful, but inherently unstable, the other man-centered, relatively weak, but resourceful and durable." This thesis stands at the heart of Mumford's studies of the city, architecture, and history of technics, and mirrors concerns voiced earlier in the works of Peter Kropotkin, William Morris, and other nineteenth-century critics of industrialism. During the 1970s, antinuclear and pro-solar energy movements in Europe and the United States adopted a similar notion as the centerpiece of their arguments. According to environmentalist Denis Hayes, "The increased deployment of nuclear power facilities must lead society toward authoritarianism. Indeed, safe reliance upon nuclear power as the principal source of energy may be possible only in a totalitarian state." Echoing the views of many proponents of appropriate technology and the soft energy path, Hayes contends that "dispersed solar sources are more compatible than centralized technologies with social equity, freedom and cultural pluralism."

An eagerness to interpret technical artifacts in political language is by no means the exclusive property of critics of large-scale, high-technology systems. A long lineage of boosters has insisted that the biggest and best that science and industry made available were the best guarantees of democracy, freedom, and social justice. The factory system, automobile, telephone, radio, television, space program, and of course nuclear power have all at one time or another been described as democratizing, liberating forces. David Lillienthal's *T.V.A.: Democracy on the March*, for example, found this promise in the phosphate fertilizers and electricity that technical progress was bringing to rural Americans during the 1940s. Three decades later Daniel Boorstin's *The Republic of Technology* extolled television for "its power to disband armies, to cashier presidents, to create a whole new democratic world—democratic in ways never before imagined, even in America." Scarcely a new invention comes along that someone doesn't proclaim it as the salvation of a free society.

It is no surprise to learn that technical systems of various kinds are deeply interwoven in the conditions of modern politics. The physical arrangements of industrial production, warfare, communications, and the like have fundamentally changed the exercise of power and the experience of citizenship. But to go beyond this obvious fact and to argue that certain technologies *in themselves* have political properties seems, at first glance, completely mistaken. We all know that people have politics; things do not. To discover either virtues or evils in aggregates of steel, plastic, transistors, integrated circuits, chemicals, and the like seems just plain wrong, a way of mystifying human artifice and of avoiding the true sources, the human sources of freedom and oppression, justice and injustice. Blaming the hardware appears even more foolish than blaming the victims when it comes to judging conditions of public life.

Hence, the stern advice commonly given those who flirt with the notion that technical artifacts have political qualities: What matters is not technology itself, but the social or economic system in which it is embedded. This maxim, which in a number of variations is the central premise of a theory that can be called the social determination of technology, has an obvious wisdom. It serves as a needed corrective to those who focus uncritically upon such things as "the computer and its social impacts" but who fail to look behind technical devices to see the social circumstances of their development, deployment, and use. This view provides an antidote to naive technological determinism—the idea that technology develops as the sole result of an internal dynamic and then, unmediated by any other influence, molds society to fit its patterns. Those who have not recognized the ways in which technologies are shaped by social and economic forces have not gotten very far.

But the corrective has its own shortcomings; taken literally, it suggests that technical *things* do not matter at all. Once one has done the detective work necessary to reveal the social origins—power holders behind a particular instance of technological change—one will have explained everything of importance. This conclusion offers comfort to social scientists. It validates what they had always suspected, namely, that there is nothing distinctive about the study of technology in the first place. Hence, they can return to their standard models of social power—those of interest-group politics, bureaucratic politics, Marxist models of class struggle, and the like—and have everything they need. The social determination of technology is, in this view, essentially no different from the social determination of, say, welfare policy or taxation.

There are, however, good reasons to believe that technology is politically significant in its own right, good reasons why the standard models of social science only go so far in accounting for what is most interesting and troublesome about the subject. Much of modern social and political thought contains recurring statements of what can be called a theory of technological politics, an odd mongrel of notions often crossbred with orthodox liberal, conservative, and socialist philosophies. The theory of technological politics draws attention to the momentum of large-scale sociotechnical systems, to the response of modern societies to certain technological imperatives, and to the ways human ends are powerfully transformed as they are adapted to technical means. This perspective offers a novel framework of interpretation and explanation for some of the more puzzling patterns that have taken shape in and around the growth of modern material culture. Its starting point is a decision to take technical artifacts seriously. Rather than insist that we immediately reduce everything to the interplay of social forces, the theory of technological politics

suggests that we pay attention to the characteristics of technical objects and the meaning of those characteristics. A necessary complement to, rather than a replacement for, theories of the social determination of technology, this approach identifies certain technologies as political phenomena in their own right. It points us back, to borrow Edmund Husserl's philosophical injunction, *to the things themselves.*

In what follows I will outline and illustrate two ways in which artifacts can contain political properties. First are instances in which the invention, design, or arrangement of a specific technical device or system becomes a way of settling an issue in the affairs of a particular community. Seen in the proper light, examples of this kind are fairly straightforward and easily understood. Second are cases of what can be called "inherently political technologies," manmade systems that appear to require or to be strongly compatible with particular kinds of political relationships. Arguments about cases of this kind are much more troublesome and closer to the heart of the matter. By the term "politics" I mean arrangements of power and authority in human associations as well as the activities that take place within those arrangements. For my purposes here, the term "technology" is understood to mean all of modern practical artifice, but to avoid confusion I prefer to speak of "technologies" plural, smaller or larger pieces or systems of hardware of a specific kind. My intention is not to settle any of the issues here once and for all, but to indicate their general dimensions and significance.

Technical Arrangements and Social Order

ANYONE WHO has traveled the highways of America and has gotten used to the normal height of overpasses may well find something a little odd about some of the bridges over the parkways on Long Island, New York. Many of the overpasses are extraordinarily low, having as little as nine feet of clearance at the curb. Even those who happened to notice this structural peculiarity would not be inclined to attach any special meaning to it. In our accustomed way of looking at things such as roads and bridges, we see the details of form as innocuous and seldom give them a second thought.

It turns out, however, that some two hundred or so low-hanging overpasses on Long Island are there for a reason. They were deliberately designed and built that way by someone who wanted to achieve a particular social effect. Robert Moses, the master builder of roads, parks, bridges, and other public works of the 1920s to the 1970s in New York, built his overpasses according to specifications that would discourage the presence of buses on his parkways. According to evidence provided by Moses' biographer, Robert A. Caro, the reasons reflect Moses' social class bias and racial prejudice. Automobile-owning whites of "upper" and "comfortable middle" classes, as he called them, would be free to use the parkways for recreation and commuting. Poor people and blacks, who normally used public transit, were kept off the roads because the twelve-foot tall buses could not handle the overpasses. One consequence was to limit access of racial minorities and low-income groups to Jones Beach, Moses' widely acclaimed public park. Moses made doubly sure of this result by vetoing a proposed extension of the Long Island Railroad to Jones Beach.

Robert Moses' life is a fascinating story in recent U.S. political history. His dealings with mayors, governors, and presidents; his careful manipulation of legislatures, banks, labor unions, the press, and public opinion could be studied by political scientists for years. But the most important and enduring results of his work are his technologies, the vast engineering projects that give New York much of its present

form. For generations after Moses' death and the alliances he forged have fallen apart, his public works, especially the highways and bridges he built to favor the use of the automobile over the development of mass transit, will continue to shape that city. Many of his monumental structures of concrete and steel embody a systematic social inequality, a way of engineering relationships among people that, after a time, became just another part of the landscape. As New York planner Lee Koppleman told Caro about the low bridges on Wantagh Parkway, "The old son of a gun had made sure that buses would *never* be able to use his goddamned parkways."

Histories of architecture, city planning, and public works contain many examples of physical arrangements with explicit or implicit political purposes. One can point to Baron Haussmann's broad Parisian thoroughfares, engineered at Louis Napoleon's direction to prevent any recurrence of street fighting of the kind that took place during the revolution of 1848. Or one can visit any number of grotesque concrete buildings and huge plazas constructed on university campuses in the United States during the late 1960s and early 1970s to defuse student demonstrations. Studies of industrial machines and instruments also turn up interesting political stories, including some that violate our normal expectations about why technological innovations are made in the first place. If we suppose that new technologies are introduced to achieve increased efficiency, the history of technology shows that we will sometimes be disappointed. Technological change expresses a panoply of human motives, not the least of which is the desire of some to have dominion over others even though it may require an occasional sacrifice of cost savings and some violation of the normal standard of trying to get more from less.

One poignant illustration can be found in the history of nineteenth-century industrial mechanization. At Cyrus McCormick's reaper manufacturing plant in Chicago in the middle 1880s, pneumatic molding machines, a new and largely untested innovation, were added to the foundry at an estimated cost of $500,000. The standard economic interpretation would lead us to expect that this step was taken to modernize the plant and achieve the kind of efficiencies that mechanization brings. But historian Robert Ozanne has put the development in a broader context. At the time, Cyrus McCormick II was engaged in a battle with the National Union of Iron Molders. He saw the addition of the new machines as a way to "weed out the bad element among the men," namely, the skilled workers who had organized the union local in Chicago. The new machines, manned by unskilled laborers, actually produced inferior castings at a higher cost than the earlier process. After three years of use the machines were, in fact, abandoned, but by that time they had served their purpose—the destruction of the union. Thus, the story of these technical developments at the McCormick factory cannot be adequately understood outside the record of workers' attempts to organize, police repression of the labor movement in Chicago during that period, and the events surrounding the bombing at Haymarket Square. Technological history and U.S. political history were at that moment deeply intertwined.

In the examples of Moses' low bridges and McCormick's molding machines, one sees the importance of technical arrangements that precede the *use* of the things in question. It is obvious that technologies can be used in ways that enhance the power, authority, and privilege of some over others, for example, the use of television to sell a candidate. In our accustomed way of thinking technologies are seen as neutral tools that can be used well or poorly, for good, evil, or something in between. But we usually do not stop to inquire whether a given device might have been designed and built in such a way that it produces a set of consequences logically and temporally *prior to any of its professed uses*. Robert Moses' bridges, after all, were used to carry automobiles from one point to another; McCormick's machines were used to make metal castings; both technologies, however, encompassed purposes far beyond their immediate use. If our moral and political language for evaluating technology includes only categories having to do with tools and uses, if it does not include attention to the meaning of the designs and arrangements of our artifacts, then we will be blinded to much that is intellectually and practically crucial.

Because the point is most easily understood in the light of particular intentions embodied in physical form, I have so far offered illustrations that seem almost conspiratorial. But to recognize the political dimensions in the shapes of technology does not require that we look for conscious conspiracies or malicious intentions. The organized movement of handicapped people in the United States during the 1970s pointed out the countless ways in which machines, instruments, and structures of common use—buses, buildings, sidewalks, plumbing fixtures, and so forth—made it impossible for many handicapped persons to move freely about, a condition that systematically excluded them from public life. It is safe to say that designs unsuited for the handicapped arose more from long-standing neglect than from anyone's active intention. But once the issue was brought to public attention, it became evident that justice required a remedy. A whole range of artifacts have been redesigned and rebuilt to accommodate this minority.

Indeed, many of the most important examples of technologies that have political consequences are those that transcend the simple categories "intended" and "unintended" altogether. These are instances in which the very process of technical development is so thoroughly biased in a particular direction that it regularly produces results heralded as wonderful breakthroughs by some social interests and crushing setbacks by others. In such cases it is neither correct nor insightful to say, "Someone intended to do somebody else harm." Rather one must say that the technological deck has been stacked in advance to favor certain social interests and that some people were bound to receive a better hand than others.

The mechanical tomato harvester, a remarkable device perfected by researchers at the University of California from the late 1940s to the present offers an illustrative tale. The machine is able to harvest tomatoes in a single pass through a row, cutting the plants from the ground, shaking the fruit loose, and (in the newest models) sorting the tomatoes electronically into large plastic gondolas that hold up to twenty-five tons of produce headed for canning factories. To accommodate the rough motion of these harvesters in the field, agricultural researchers have bred new varieties of tomatoes that are hardier, sturdier, and less tasty than those previously grown. The harvesters replace the system of handpicking in which crews of farm workers would pass through the fields three or four times, putting ripe tomatoes in lug boxes and saving immature fruit for later harvest.[9] Studies in California indicate that the use of the machine reduces costs by approximately five to seven dollars per ton as compared to hand harvesting. But the benefits are by no means equally divided in the agricultural economy. In fact, the machine in the garden has in this instance been the occasion for a thorough reshaping of social relationships involved in tomato production in rural California.

By virtue of their very size and cost of more than $50,000 each, the machines are compatible only with a highly concentrated form of tomato growing. With the introduction of this new method of harvesting, the number of tomato growers declined from approximately 4,000 in the early 1960s to about 600 in 1973, and yet there was a substantial increase in tons of tomatoes produced. By the late 1970s an estimated 32,000 jobs in the tomato industry had been eliminated as a direct consequence of mechanization. Thus, a jump in productivity to the benefit of very large growers has occurred at the sacrifice of other rural agricultural communities.

The University of California's research on and development of agricultural machines such as the tomato harvester eventually became the subject of a lawsuit filed by attorneys for California Rural Legal Assistance, an organization representing a group of farm workers and other interested parties. The suit charged that university officials are spending tax monies on projects that benefit a handful of private interests to the detriment of farm workers, small farmers, consumers, and rural California generally and asks for a court injunction to stop the practice. The university denied these charges, arguing that to accept them "would require elimination of all research with any potential practical application."

As far as I know, no one argued that the development of the tomato harvester was the result of a plot. Two students of the controversy, William Friedland and Amy Barton, specifically exonerate the original developers of the machine and the hard tomato from any desire to facilitate economic concentration in that industry. What we see here instead is an ongoing social process in which scientific knowledge, technological invention, and corporate profit reinforce each other in deeply entrenched patterns, patterns that bear the unmistakable stamp of political and economic power. Over many decades agricultural research and development in U.S. land-grant colleges and universities has tended to favor the interests of large agribusiness concerns. It is in the face of such subtly ingrained patterns that opponents of innovations such as the tomato harvester are made to seem "antitechnology" or "antiprogress." For the harvester is not merely the symbol of a social order that rewards some while punishing others; it is in a true sense an embodiment of that order.

Within a given category of technological change there are, roughly speaking, two kinds of choices that can affect the relative distribution of power, authority, and privilege in a community. Often the crucial decision is a simple "yes or no" choice—are we going to develop and adopt the thing or not? In recent years many local, national, and international disputes about technology have centered on "yes or no" judgments about such things as food additives, pesticides, the building of highways, nuclear reactors, dam projects, and proposed high-tech weapons. The fundamental choice about an antiballistic missile or supersonic transport is whether or not the thing is going to join society as a piece of its operating equipment. Reasons given for and against are frequently as important as those concerning the adoption of an important new law.

A second range of choices, equally critical in many instances, has to do with specific features in the design or arrangement of a technical system after the decision to go ahead with it has already been made. Even after a utility company wins permission to build a large electric power line, important controversies can remain with respect to the placement of its route and the design of its towers; even after an organization has decided to institute a system of computers, controversies can still arise with regard to the kinds of components, programs, modes of access, and other specific features the system will include. Once the mechanical tomato harvester had been developed in its basic form, a design alteration of critical social significance—the addition of electronic sorters, for example—changed the character of the machine's effects upon the balance of wealth and power in California agriculture. Some of the most interesting research on technology and politics at present focuses upon the attempt to demonstrate in a detailed, concrete fashion how seemingly innocuous design features in mass transit systems, water projects, industrial machinery, and other technologies actually mask social choices of profound significance. Historian David Noble has studied two kinds of automated machine tool systems that have different implications for the relative power of management and labor in the industries that might employ them. He has shown that although the basic electronic and mechanical components of the record/playback and numerical control systems are similar, the choice of one design over another has crucial consequences for social struggles on the shop floor. To see the matter solely in terms of cost cutting, efficiency, or the modernization of equipment is to miss a decisive element in the story.

From such examples I would offer some general conclusions. These correspond to the interpretation of technologies as "forms of life" presented in the previous chapter, filling in the explicitly political dimensions of that point of view.

The things we call "technologies" are ways of building order in our world. Many technical devices and systems important in everyday life contain possibilities for many different ways of ordering human activity. Consciously or unconsciously, deliberately or inadvertently, societies choose structures for technologies that influence how people are going to work, communicate, travel, consume, and so forth over a very long time. In the processes by which structuring decisions are made, different people are situated differently and possess unequal degrees of power as well as unequal levels of awareness. By far the greatest latitude of choice exists the very first time a particular instrument, system, or technique is introduced. Because choices tend to become strongly fixed in material equipment, economic investment, and social habit, the original flexibility vanishes for all practical purposes once the initial commitments are made. In that sense technological innovations are similar to legislative acts or political foundings that establish a framework for public order that will endure over many generations. For that reason the same careful attention one would give to the rules, roles, and relationships of politics must also be given to such things as the building of highways, the creation of television networks, and the tailoring of seemingly insignificant features on new machines. The issues that divide or unite people in society are settled not only in the institutions and practices of politics proper, but also, and less obviously, in tangible arrangements of steel and concrete, wires and semiconductors, nuts and bolts.

Inherently Political Technologies

NONE OF the arguments and examples considered thus far addresses a stronger, more troubling claim often made in writings about technology and society—the belief that some technologies are by their very nature political in a specific way. According to this view, the adoption of a given technical system unavoidably brings with it conditions for human relationships that have a distinctive political cast—for example, centralized or decentralized, egalitarian or inegalitarian, repressive or liberating. This is ultimately what is at stake in assertions such as those of Lewis Mumford that two traditions of technology, one authoritarian, the other democratic, exist side by side in Western history. In all the cases cited above the technologies are relatively flexible in design and arrangement and variable in their effects. Although one can recognize a particular result produced in a particular setting, one can also easily imagine how a roughly similar device or system might have been built or situated with very much different political consequences. The idea we must now examine and evaluate is that certain kinds of technology do not allow such flexibility, and

that to choose them is to choose unalterably a particular form of political life.

A remarkably forceful statement of one version of this argument appears in Friedrich Engels's little essay "On Authority" written in 1872. Answering anarchists who believed that authority is an evil that ought to be abolished altogether, Engels launches into a panegyric for authoritarianism, maintaining, among other things, that strong authority is a necessary condition in modern industry. To advance his case in the strongest possible way, he asks his readers to imagine that the revolution has already occurred. "Supposing a social revolution dethroned the capitalists, who now exercise their authority over the production and circulation of wealth. Supposing, to adopt entirely the point of view of the anti-authoritarians, that the land and the instruments of labour had become the collective property of the workers who use them. Will authority have disappeared or will it have only changed its form?"

His answer draws upon lessons from three sociotechnical systems of his day, cotton-spinning mills, railways, and ships at sea. He observes that on its way to becoming finished thread, cotton moves through a number of different operations at different locations in the factory. The workers perform a wide variety of tasks, from running the steam engine to carrying the products from one room to another. Because these tasks must be coordinated and because the timing of the work is "fixed by the authority of the steam," laborers must learn to accept a rigid discipline. They must, according to Engels, work at regular hours and agree to subordinate their individual wills to the persons in charge of factory operations. If they fail to do so, they risk the horrifying possibility that production will come to a grinding halt. Engels pulls no punches. "The automatic machinery of a big factory," he writes, "is much more despotic than the small capitalists who employ workers ever have been."

Similar lessons are adduced in Engels's analysis of the necessary operating conditions for railways and ships at sea. Both require the subordination of workers to an "imperious authority" that sees to it that things run according to plan. Engels finds that far from being an idiosyncrasy of capitalist social organization, relationships of authority and subordination arise "independently of all social organization, [and] are imposed upon us together with the material conditions under which we produce and make products circulate." Again, he intends this to be stern advice to the anarchists who, according to Engels, thought it possible simply to eradicate subordination and superordination at a single stroke. All such schemes are nonsense. The roots of unavoidable authoritarianism are, he argues, deeply implanted in the human involvement with science and technology. "If man, by dint of his knowledge and inventive genius, has subdued the forces of nature, the latter avenge themselves upon him by subjecting him, insofar as he employs them, to a veritable despotism independent of all social organization."

Attempts to justify strong authority on the basis of supposedly necessary conditions of technical practice have an ancient history. A pivotal theme in the *Republic* is Plato's quest to borrow the authority of *technē* and employ it by analogy to buttress his argument in favor of authority in the state. Among the illustrations he chooses, like Engels, is that of a ship on the high seas. Because large sailing vessels by their very nature need to be steered with a firm hand, sailors must yield to their captain's commands; no reasonable person believes that ships can be run democratically. Plato goes on to suggest that governing a state is rather like being captain of a ship or like practicing medicine as a physician. Much the same conditions that require central rule and decisive action in organized technical activity also create this need in government.

In Engels's argument, and arguments like it, the justification for authority is no longer made by Plato's classic analogy, but rather directly with reference to technology itself. If the basic case is as compelling as Engels believed it to be, one would expect that as a society adopted increasingly complicated technical systems as its material basis, the prospects for authoritarian ways of life would be greatly enhanced. Central control by knowledgeable people acting at the top of a rigid social hierarchy would seem increasingly prudent. In this respect his stand in "On Authority" appears to be at variance with Karl Marx's position in Volume I of *Capital*. Marx tries to show that increasing mechanization will render obsolete the hierarchical division of labor and the relationships of subordination that, in his view, were necessary during the early stages of modern manufacturing. "Modern Industry," he writes, "sweeps away by technical means the manufacturing division of labor, under which each man is bound hand and foot for life to a single detail operation. At the same time, the capitalistic form of that industry reproduces this same division of labour in a still more monstrous shape; in the factory proper, by converting the workman into a living appendage of the machine." In Marx's view the conditions that will eventually dissolve the capitalist division of labor and facilitate proletarian revolution are conditions latent in industrial technology itself. The differences between Marx's position in *Capital* and Engels's in his essay raise an important question for socialism: What, after all, does modern technology make possible or necessary in political life? The theoretical tension we see here mirrors many troubles in the practice of freedom and authority that had muddied the tracks of socialist revolution.

Arguments to the effect that technologies are in some sense inherently political have been advanced in a wide variety of contexts, far too many to summarize here. My reading of such notions, however, reveals there are two basic ways of stating the case. One version claims that the adoption of a given technical system actually requires the creation and maintenance of a particular set of social conditions as the operating environment of that system. Engels's position is of this kind. A similar view is offered by a contemporary writer who holds that "if you accept nuclear power plants, you also accept a techno-scientific-industrial-military elite. Without these people in charge, you could not have nuclear power." In this conception some kinds of technology require their social environments to be structured in a particular way in much the same sense that an automobile requires wheels in order to move. The thing could not exist as an effective operating entity unless certain social as well as material conditions were met. The meaning of "required" here is that of practical (rather than logical) necessity. Thus, Plato thought it a practical necessity that a ship at sea have one captain and an unquestionably obedient crew.

A second, somewhat weaker, version of the argument holds that a given kind of technology is strongly compatible with, but does not strictly require, social and political relationships of a particular stripe. Many advocates of solar energy have argued that technologies of that variety are more compatible with a democratic, egalitarian society than energy systems based on coal, oil, and nuclear power; at the same time they do not maintain that anything about solar energy requires democracy. Their case is, briefly, that solar energy is decentralizing in both a technical and political sense: technically speaking, it is vastly more reasonable to build solar systems in a disaggregated, widely distributed manner than in large-scale centralized plants; politically speaking, solar energy accommodates the attempts of individuals and local communities to manage their affairs effectively because they are dealing with systems that are more accessible, comprehensible, and controlla-ble than huge centralized sources. In this view solar energy is desirable not only for its economic and environmental benefits, but also for the salutary institutions it is likely to permit in other areas of public life.

Within both versions of the argument there is a further distinction to be made between conditions that are internal to the workings of a given technical system and those that are external to it. Engels's thesis concerns internal social relations said to be required within cotton factories and railways, for example; what such relationships mean for the condition of society at large is, for him, a separate question. In contrast, the solar advocate's belief that solar technologies are compatible with democracy pertains to the way they complement aspects of society removed from the organization of those technologies as such.

There are, then, several different directions that arguments of this kind can follow. Are the social conditions predicated said to be required by, or strongly compatible with, the workings of a given technical system? Are those conditions internal to that system or external to it (or both)? Although writings that address such questions are often unclear about what is being asserted, arguments in this general category are an important part of modern political discourse. They enter into many attempts to explain how changes in social life take place in the wake of technological innovation. More important, they are often used to buttress attempts to justify or criticize proposed courses of action involving new technology. By offering distinctly political reasons for or against the adoption of a particular technology, arguments of this kind stand apart from more commonly employed, more easily quantifiable claims about economic costs and benefits, environmental impacts, and possible risks to public health and safety that technical systems may involve. The issue here does not concern how many jobs will be created, how much income generated, how many pollutants added, or how many cancers produced. Rather, the issue has to do with ways in which choices about technology have important consequences for the form and quality of human associations.

If we examine social patterns that characterize the environments of technical systems, we find certain devices and systems almost invariably linked to specific ways of organizing power and authority. The important question is: Does this state of affairs derive from an unavoidable social response to intractable properties in the things themselves, or is it instead a pattern imposed independently by a governing body, ruling class, or some other social or cultural institution to further its own purposes?

Taking the most obvious example, the atom bomb is an inherently political artifact. As long as it exists at all, its lethal properties demand that it be controlled by a centralized, rigidly hierarchical chain of command closed to all influences that might make its workings unpredictable. The internal social system of the bomb must be authoritarian; there is no other way. The state of affairs stands as a practical necessity independent of any larger political system in which the bomb is embedded, independent of the type of regime or character of its rulers. Indeed, democratic states must try to find ways to ensure that the social structures and mentality that characterize the management of nuclear weapons do not "spin off" or "spill over" into the polity as a whole.

The bomb is, of course, a special case. The reasons very rigid relationships of authority are necessary in its immediate presence should be clear to anyone. If, however, we look for other instances in which particular varieties of technology are widely perceived to need the maintenance of a special pattern of power and authority, modern technical history contains a wealth of examples.

Alfred D. Chandler in *The Visible Hand,* a monumental study of modern business enterprise, presents impressive documentation to defend the hypothesis that the construction and day-to-day operation of many systems of production, transportation, and communication in the nineteenth and twentieth centuries require the development of particular social form—a large-scale centralized, hierarchical organization administered by highly skilled managers. Typical of Chandler's reasoning is his analysis of the growth of the railroads.

> *Technology made possible fast, all-weather transportation; but safe, regular, reliable movement of goods and passengers, as well as the continuing maintenance and repair of locomotives, rolling stock, and track, roadbed, stations, roundhouses, and other equipment, required the creation of a sizable administrative organization. It meant the employment of a set of managers to supervise these functional activities over an extensive geographical area; and the appointment of an administrative command of middle and top executives to monitor, evaluate, and coordinate the work of managers responsible for the day-to-day operations.*

Throughout his book Chandler points to ways in which technologies used in the production and distribution of electricity, chemicals, and a wide range of industrial goods "demanded" or "required" this form of human association. "Hence, the operational requirements of railroads demanded the creation of the first administrative hierarchies in American business."

Were there other conceivable ways of organizing these aggregates of people and apparatus? Chandler shows that a previously dominant social form, the small traditional family firm, simply could not handle the task in most cases. Although he does not speculate further, it is clear that he believes there is, to be realistic, very little latitude in the forms of power and authority appropriate within modern sociotechnical systems. The properties of many modern technologies—oil pipelines and refineries, for example—are such that overwhelmingly impressive economies of scale and speed are possible. If such systems are to work effectively, efficiently, quickly, and safely, certain requirements of internal social organization have to be fulfilled; the material possibilities that modern technologies make available could not be exploited otherwise. Chandler acknowledges that as one compares sociotechnical institutions of different nations, one sees "ways in which cultural attitudes, values, ideologies, political systems, and social structure affect these imperatives." But the weight of argument and empirical evidence in *The Visible Hand* suggests that any significant departure from the basic pattern would be, at best, highly unlikely.

It may be that other conceivable arrangements of power and authority, for example, those of decentralized, democratic worker self-management, could prove capable of administering factories, refineries, communications systems, and railroads as well as or better than the organizations Chandler describes. Evidence from automobile assembly teams in Sweden and worker-managed plants in Yugoslavia and other countries is often presented to salvage these possibilities. Unable to settle controversies over this matter here, I merely point to what I consider to be their bone of contention. The available evidence tends to show that many large, sophisticated technological systems are in fact highly compatible with centralized, hierarchical managerial control. The interesting question, however, has to do with whether or not this pattern is in any sense a requirement of such systems, a question that is not solely empirical. The matter ultimately rests on our judgments about what steps, if any, are practically necessary in the workings of particular kinds of technology and what, if anything, such measures require of the structure of human associations. Was Plato right in saying that a ship at sea needs steering by a decisive hand and that this could only be accomplished by a single captain and an obedi-

ent crew? Is Chandler correct in saying that the properties of large-scale systems require centralized, hierarchical managerial control?

To answer such questions, we would have to examine in some detail the moral claims of practical necessity (including those advocated in the doctrines of economics) and weigh them against moral claims of other sorts, for example, the notion that it is good for sailors to participate in the command of a ship or that workers have a right to be involved in making and administering decisions in a factory. It is characteristic of societies based on large, complex technological systems, however, that moral reasons other than those of practical necessity appear increasingly obsolete, "idealistic," and irrelevant. Whatever claims one may wish to make on behalf of liberty, justice, or equality can be immediately neutralized when confronted with arguments to the effect, "Fine, but that's no way to run a railroad" (or steel mill, or airline, or communication system, and so on). Here we encounter an important quality in modern political discourse and in the way people commonly think about what measures are justified in response to the possibilities technologies make available. In many instances, to say that some technologies are inherently political is to say that certain widely accepted reasons of practical necessity—especially the need to maintain crucial technological systems as smoothly working entities—have tended to eclipse other sorts of moral and political reasoning.

One attempt to salvage the autonomy of politics from the bind of practical necessity involves the notion that conditions of human association found in the internal workings of technological systems can easily be kept separate from the polity as a whole. Americans have long rested content in the belief that arrangements of power and authority inside industrial corporations, public utilities, and the like have little bearing on public institutions, practices, and ideas at large. That "democracy stops at the factory gates" was taken as a fact of life that had nothing to do with the practice of political freedom. But can the internal politics of technology and the politics of the whole community be so easily separated? A recent study of business leaders in the United States, contemporary exemplars of Chandler's "visible hand of management," found them remarkably impatient with such democratic scruples as "one man, one vote." If democracy doesn't work for the firm, the most critical institution in all of society, American executives ask, how well can it be expected to work for the government of a nation—particularly when that government attempts to interfere with the achievements of the firm? The authors of the report observe that patterns of authority that work effectively in the corporation become for businessmen "the desirable model against which to compare political and economic relationships in the rest of society." While such findings are far from conclusive, they do reflect a sentiment increasingly common in the land: what dilemmas such as the energy crisis require is not a redistribution of wealth or broader public participation but, rather, stronger, centralized public and private management.

An especially vivid case in which the operational requirements of a technical system might influence the quality of public life is the debates about the risks of nuclear power. As the supply of uranium for nuclear reactors runs out, a proposed alternative fuel is the plutonium generated as a by-product in reactor cores. Well-known objections to plutonium recycling focus on its unacceptable economic costs, its risks of environmental contamination, and its dangers in regard to the international proliferation of nuclear weapons. Beyond these concerns, however, stands another less widely appreciated set of hazards—those that involve the sacrifice of civil liberties. The widespread use of plutonium as a fuel increases the chance that this toxic substance might be stolen by terrorists, orga-

nized crime, or other persons. This raises the prospect, and not a trivial one, that extraordinary measures would have to be taken to safeguard plutonium from theft and to recover it should the substance be stolen. Workers in the nuclear industry as well as ordinary citizens outside could well become subject to background security checks, covert surveillance, wiretapping, informers, and even emergency measures under martial law—all justified by the need to safeguard plutonium.

Russell W. Ayres's study of the legal ramifications of plutonium recycling concludes: "With the passage of time and the increase in the quantity of plutonium in existence will come pressure to eliminate the traditional checks the courts and legislatures place on the activities of the executive and to develop a powerful central authority better able to enforce strict safeguards." He avers that "once a quantity of plutonium had been stolen, the case for literally turning the country upside down to get it back would be overwhelming." Ayres anticipates and worries about the kinds of thinking that, I have argued, characterize inherently political technologies. It is still true that in a world in which human beings make and maintain artificial systems nothing is "required" in an absolute sense. Nevertheless, once a course of action is under way, once artifacts such as nuclear power plants have been built and put in operation, the kinds of reasoning that justify the adaptation of social life to technical requirements pop up as spontaneously as flowers in the spring. In Ayres's words, "Once recycling begins and the risks of plutonium theft become real rather than hypothetical, the case for governmental infringement of protected rights will seem compelling." After a certain point, those who cannot accept the hard requirements and imperatives will be dismissed as dreamers and fools.

The two varieties of interpretation I have outlined indicate how artifacts can have political qualities. In the first instance we noticed ways in which specific features in the design or arrangement of a device or system could provide a convenient means of establishing patterns of power and authority in a given setting. Technologies of this kind have a range of flexibility in the dimensions of their material form. It is precisely because they are flexible that their consequences for society must be understood with reference to the social actors able to influence which designs and arrangements are chosen. In the second instance we examined ways in which the intractable properties of certain kinds of technology are strongly, perhaps unavoidably, linked to particular institutionalized patterns of power and authority. Here the initial choice about whether or not to adopt something is decisive in regard to its consequences. There are no alternative physical designs or arrangements that would make a significant difference; there are, furthermore, no genuine possibilities for creative intervention by different social systems—capitalist or socialist—that could change the intractability of the entity or significantly alter the quality of its political effects.

To know which variety of interpretation is applicable in a given case is often what is at stake in disputes, some of them passionate ones, about the meaning of technology for how we live. I have argued a "both/and" position here, for it seems to me that both kinds of understanding are applicable in different circumstances. Indeed, it can happen that within a particular complex of technology—a system of communication or transportation, for example—some aspects may be flexible in their possibilities for society, while other aspects may be (for better or worse) completely intractable. The two varieties of interpretation I have examined here can overlap and intersect at many points.

These are, of course, issues on which people can disagree. Thus, some proponents of energy from renewable resources now believe they have at last discovered a set of intrinsically democratic, egalitarian, communitarian technologies. In my best estimation, however, the social consequences of building renewable energy systems will surely depend on the specific configurations of both hardware and the social institutions created to bring that energy to us. It may be that we will find ways to turn this silk purse into a sow's ear. By comparison, advocates of the further development of nuclear power seem to believe that they are working on a rather flexible technology whose adverse social effects can be fixed by changing the design parameters of reactors and nuclear waste disposal systems. For reasons indicated above, I believe them to be dead wrong in that faith. Yes, we may be able to manage some of the "risks" to public health and safety that nuclear power brings. But as society adapts to the more dangerous and apparently indelible features of nuclear power, what will be the long-range toll in human freedom?

My belief that we ought to attend more closely to technical objects themselves is not to say that we can ignore the contexts in which those objects are situated. A ship at sea may well require, as Plato and Engels insisted, a single captain and obedient crew. But a ship out of service, parked at the dock, needs only a caretaker. To understand which technologies and which contexts are important to us, and why, is an enterprise that must involve both the study of specific technical systems and their history as well as a thorough grasp of the concepts and controversies of political theory. In our times people are often willing to make drastic changes in the way they live to accommodate technological innovation while at the same time resisting similar kinds of changes justified on political grounds. If for no other reason than that, it is important for us to achieve a clearer view of these matters than has been our habit so far.

Discussion Questions

1. What does Winner's "theory of technological politics" mean to you? What rationale would you provide in support of this theory, or in opposition to this theory?
2. Many of the examples provided by Winner to support his claims about the political qualities of technology address the "patterns of power and authority" that the design or structure of the technology requires. Are there other goals or values that can be influenced by the specific features of technological systems or devices?
3. Which of the historical examples of the political qualities of technology provided by Winner did you find most illuminating or helpful, and why?
4. In the summary of this chapter, Winner states: "In our times people are often willing to make drastic changes in the way they live to accommodate technological innovation while at the same time resisting similar kinds of changes justified on political grounds." Identify and briefly describe a set of current or recent examples that illustrate this point.

 Supporting Activities

1. Select, read, and report on some of the entries to Langdon Winner's blog, *Technopolis*, at http://technopolis.blogspot.com/.
2. The book *Capital in the Twenty-First Century* (English edition, 2014) by French economist Thomas Piketty received a lot of attention when published. Piketty makes the case that income inequality is growing as a result of unchecked capitalism and, in the absence of intervention by governments, this inequality will undermine our democratic institutions. Consider how technology may lead to income inequality, and conversely how income inequality might influence technological decision-making, whether in the political or the personal realm, and what the outcomes of this might be.

 Additional Resources

1. Although dated, Langdon Winner's web site at Rensselaer Polytechnic Institute provides lists of Winner's publications, biographical information, and links worth exploring: http://homepages.rpi.edu/~winner/.

Assessing the Risks of Technology

What might at first seem like a strictly technical examination of two analytical tools—probabilistic risk assessment and risk-cost-benefit analysis—is at its core a cogent argument for a technology assessment strategy that looks broadly at social impacts and policy implications. Evan and Manion reinforced this point by describing in detail the shortcomings of more conventional analytical approaches that focus on quantitative measures.

The analytical tools described by these authors are part of an overall approach to assessing systems that can be broadly categorized as risk management. These tools are designed to try to predict either system failure or the likelihood of negative outcomes such as damage or loss of life or property. Tools like probabilistic risk assessment have most commonly been applied to hazardous undertakings such as nuclear power plants or oil rigs. They provide information that can help system designers anticipate, and manage, risks associated with these systems. In spite of their usefulness, these and similar tools have significant shortcomings that reduce their utility as decision-making tools. Nevertheless, they are an important part of our decision-making approach and over time they can be refined to better overcome these shortcomings.

William M. Evan retired from the University of Pennsylvania, where he taught from 1966–1993, as Professor Emeritus of Sociology and Management. He was the author of over 100 articles for various professional journals and 14 books, including *Nuclear Proliferation and the Legality of Nuclear Weapons* (1995), *War and Peace in an Age of Terrorism* (2005), and *Knowledge and Power in a Global Society* (1981). Evan died in 2009. Mark Manion is a former faculty member in the Department of English and Philosophy at Drexel University, where he taught courses in business and organizational ethics and in the philosophy of technology.

Assessing the Risks of Technology

By William M. Evan and Mark Manion

"In all traditional cultures . . . human beings worried about the risks coming from external nature . . . very recently . . . we started worrying less about what nature can do to us, and more about what we have done to nature. This marks the transition from the predominance of external risk to that of manufactured risk."—ANTHONY GIDDENS

The prevalence of technological disasters points to deficiencies in the way technology is assessed—the way technologies are determined to be or not to be risky. In this chapter we focus on two prominent methods for assessing risk: probabilistic risk assessment (PRA) and risk-cost-benefit analysis (RCBA). If we find the standard methods deficient, then it should not be surprising that we have more disasters than we can expect. The overall lesson is that, if we want to reduce the number and magnitude of technological disasters, we must reform our methods of evaluating the potential impacts of technology—PRA and RCBA—and develop more effective methods.

Experts attempt to separate risk assessment techniques into two independent procedures—the risk identification or risk estimation level, which is supposedly factual, scientific, objective, and value-neutral, and the risk assessment or risk management level—which is supposedly normative, political, subjective, and value-laden (Humphreys, 1987). This rigid demarcation into the "factual" or scientific measurement of risks vs. the "normative" management of the social acceptability of risks is thought to secure for risk assessors a level of scientific objectivity and value neutrality.

We will argue, however, that the factual/normative split is no longer adequate for the proper identification, assessment, and management of technological risk. Consequently, the so-called objective activities of risk identification or risk estimation need to be integrated with the normative and evaluative aspects of risk evaluation and risk management.

Probabilistic Risk Assessment

Probabilistic risk assessment (PRA), or quantitative risk assessment (QRA), attempts to provide a model of the causal interactions of the technological system under study. The goal of PRA is to supply a mathematical technique for estimating the probability of events that cause physical damage or loss of life (Thompson, 1982; 114). A comprehensive probabilistic risk assessment involves three steps: (1) the identification of events that lead to, or initiate, unwanted consequences; (2) the modeling of identified event sequences with respect to probabilities and consequences; and (3) the determination of the magnitude of risks and harms involved (Bier, 1997).

PRA has become one of the standard methods used by engineers for determining the likelihood of an industrial accident or a technological disaster. This method makes use of technical

procedures called *fault-tree analysis* and *event-tree analysis*. Fault-trees and event-trees generate diagrams that trace out the possible ways a malfunction can occur in complex technological systems. They enable design engineers to analyze in a systematic fashion the various failure modes associated with a potential engineering design (Henley and Kumamoto, 1981: 24–28). Failure modes are the ways in which a structure, mechanism, or process can malfunction.

In an event-tree analysis one begins with an initial event—such as a loss of electrical power to a nuclear power plant—and, using inductive logic, reasons *forward,* trying to determine the state of the system to which the event can lead (Henley and Kumamoto, 1981, 24–28). Figure 1 illustrates an event-tree analysis of the probability of radiation release from a standard nuclear power plant. The diagram is based on the authoritative reactor safety study, WASH 1400, the so-called "Rasmussen Report," commissioned by the U.S. government in 1975 (*Reactor Safety Study,* 1975).

The Reactor Safety Study was performed to determine the public risks associated with existing and planned nuclear power plants. The simplified event tree begins with a definite accident-initiating event and tries to identify all the safety systems that can be called upon to mitigate the consequences. The study determined that the failure of the reactor cooling system is the most critical component that could lead to a radiation release. The analysis therefore begins with the initiating event that a (coolant) pipe might break. If the pipe breaks, without any other system failing at the same time, then the probability that there would be a radiation release is P_A, a very small release, as shown in Figure 1. Possible failures are next defined for each system; and accident sequences are constructed, consisting of the initiating event with specific systems failing and specific systems

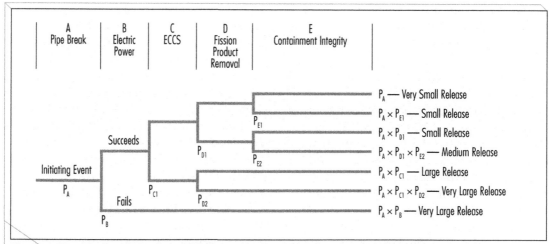

Figure 1. Event-tree analysis of a possible fission product release from a nuclear power plant.

Source: Henley, Ernest and Kumamoto, Hiromitsu (1981). *Reliability engineering and risk assessment*. Englewood Cliffs, NJ: Prentice Hall: 25.

succeeding. For example, the probability of both a pipe breaking and a corresponding loss of electrical power to the plant ($P_A \times P_B$), would lead to a very large release of radiation. Keep in mind that a probability of 1 means that an event is certain to happen. Therefore, the probability that P_A occurs is less than one. In fact, all of the assigned probabilities will be less than 1, and, as the probabilities are multiplied, the total probability will diminish. For example, if the probability of P_A occurring is 0.01 and the probability of P_B occurring is 0.001, then the overall probability that a pipe will break per day and the electrical power will fail is 0.01×0.001, which equals 0.00001 or one in 100,000 events. Even though the probability of a pipe breaking at the same time as the electrical system failing is rather low, the potential consequences are very high.

If electric power does not fail during the pipe break, the analysis moves to determining the relationship between the breaking pipe and the emergency core coolant system (ECCS). The ECCS could either succeed or fail. The probability that ECCS fails at the same time that a

pipe breaks would lead to a large release, namely, ($P_A \times P_{C1}$). If the ECCS succeeds, then the probability that the fission product removal is inhibited and that a pipe breaks would lead to a small release, namely, ($P_A \times P_{D1}$). Likewise, the probability of a pipe breaking and a failure of the ECCS as well as the fission product removal being inhibited would lead to a very large release, namely, ($P_A \times P_{C2} \times P_{D2}$). In the end, each possible system state (failure or success) is connected through a branching logic to give all the specific accident sequences that can arise. The event tree is particularly useful when many individual systems and subsystems interact.

In a fault-tree study, the analyst begins with a hypothetical undesirable event, then, using deductive logic, reasons *backwards* to determine what might have led to the event. Fault-trees follow a cause-and-effect model and can be used whenever hypothetical events can be resolved into more basic, discrete units for which failure data exist or for which failure probabilities are generally easily calculable. Figure 2 illustrates a fault tree for analyzing the possible causes of why a car would not start. For example, a good mechanic would, more than likely, already be aware of all of the possible reasons of why a car will not start. The mechanic would then construct a fault tree as illustrated in Figure 2, checking each subsystem as a possible cause of why the car will not start. An insufficient battery charge is the most likely cause of a car not starting, so the mechanic would begin there and proceed to check whether there was a faulty ground connection, the battery terminals were loose or corroded, or the battery charge was weak, etc. If, for example, it is determined that the terminals are not loose or corroded or the battery charge was not weak, then the mechanic would check to see if there was rust on the ground connections, the connections were corroded or otherwise dirty, or the ground connections were loose. If the battery checks out,

the mechanic would move to an analysis of the starter system, checking each related subsystem. If this checks out, then the mechanic would move to the fuel system and each of the other related subsystems. The mechanic reasons step-by-step through the fault tree until the cause of the car not starting is identified.

Since the first comprehensive application of probabilistic risk assessment in 1975—the U.S. Reactor Safety Study—more than 15 large-scale PRAs have been carried out for nuclear power plants in the United States. In addition, large-scale PRAs have been carried out in Sweden and West Germany and have also been used in determining levels of safety in such varied industries as chemical production, liquid gas transport and storage, oil-drilling rigs, transport of toxic chemicals, and the aerospace and nuclear

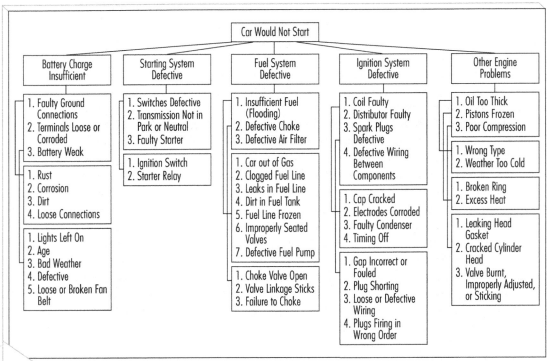

Figure 2. Fault-tree analysis of the failure of an automobile to start.

Source: Fischoff, B., Slovick, P., & Lichtenstein, S.A. (1978). Fault trees: Sensitivity and estimated failure problem representation. *Journal of Experimental Psychology: Human Perception and Performance, 4.* Reprinted with permission.

industries (Linnerooth-Bayer and Wahlstrom, 1991: 240). Even though PRA has been used extensively, there are substantial methodological problems, some of which we will now consider.

The first set of methodological problems in PRA arises when experts attempt to determine which factors to include and which to exclude. The second set of problems arises when scientific uncertainties appear in the modeling process (Rowe, 1994). Thirdly, there are reservations about the adequacy of the method due to uncertainties that arise in attempting to trace out unknown cause-and-effect relationships. A fourth deficiency of the method is its inability to account for uncertainties that inevitably arise due to operator error and other human factors. Fifth, the very complexity of many large-scale technologies renders the PRA method inadequate as the sole source of assessing risks and adequate safety levels. Table 1 lists the five problems pertaining to PRA and the associated issues that arise with each problem.

Given the methodological deficiencies of PRA discussed above, it is safe to assume that technical methods alone, no matter how sophisticated, cannot be the only way to assess the benefits and burdens of technology. Moreover, exclusive focus on probabilities leads analysts to ignore *low-probability but high-consequence events*. In other words, PRA often ignores the category of "catastrophe," because catastrophes entail low-probability, high-consequence events. Ignoring low-probability, high-consequence events is unwise, given the immense complexity of many technologies, especially large-scale sociotechnical systems. No matter how detailed a fault-tree or an event-tree analysis may be, the methodology simply cannot begin to capture all of the common mode failure events that are possible. The inadequacy of PRA in treating low-probability, high-consequence events is glaringly evident in the Three Mile Island, Chernobyl, Challenger, and Bhopal cases. As Lanthrop puts it, "deciding that, say, a nuclear power plant is safe because it is only expected to fail once in every 10,000 successful usages does not rule out that a catastrophe may happen tomorrow, or next year, or the next" (Lanthrop, 1982: 171). This is exactly the kind of assessment failure that happened in the Three Mile Island case.

Even if PRA were an effective method for determining the risks of technology, which it is

Table 1. Problems and Issues with Probabilistic Risk Assessment

Problems	Issues
1. Problems of identifying all potential risk factors	1. Uncertainties arise when experts attempt to anticipate all of the mechanical, physical, electrical, and/or chemical factors to be included in a fault-tree or an event-tree analysis.
2. Problems with uncertainties in the modeling of systems	2. Uncertainties arise from the failure to incorporate in the model important characteristics of the process under investigation.
3. Problems associated with determining cause-and-effect relationships	3. Direct cause-and-effect relationships between potential hazards and consequent harms are often not demonstrable.
4. Uncertainties due to human factors	4. Potential errors are associated with human operators, which often cannot be "modeled" and hence are rarely anticipatable.
5. Problems of complexity and coupling	5. Tight coupling and interactive complexity between system components disallow any complete modeling of potential system failures.

not, it would not be enough in any event. As we have seen in numerous cases discussed previously, beyond technical factors, human, organizational, and socio-cultural factors are often at the root of technological disasters.

Risk-Cost-Benefit Analysis

Along with PRA, cost-benefit analysis (CBA) and risk-cost-benefit analysis (RCBA) arose as the preeminent methods of assessing the risks of technology during the late 1960s and early 1970s, as Congress began to enact legislation on the regulation and monitoring of technology and its social and environmental impacts. RCBA is a variant of CBA in which human health and welfare are brought into the equations, along with the material costs and benefits of a proposed technology.

Comprehensive statutes such as the National Environmental Policy Act of 1970 (NEPA), the Federal Water Pollution Control Act Amendments of 1972, the Consumer Protection Act, and the Clean Air and Clean Water Acts require a government agency to consider technical and economic feasibility characteristics and health and environmental effects when contemplating a technological intervention. In order to accomplish these goals, organizations turned, and continue to turn, to CBA and RCBA in an effort to comply with statutory and judicial requirements (Baram, 1977). The National Aeronautics and Space Administration (NASA) uses RCBA in its feasibility and safety studies. The Nuclear Regulatory Commission (NRC) has followed NASA's lead in employing RCBA almost exclusively in setting "acceptable" radiation standards and in decisions concerning the licensing of nuclear facility construction and operation (Kneese, Ben-David, and Schultze, 1983: 60–61).

RCBA has also been the leading method used by experts as a basis for policy choices concerning controversial problems surrounding the storage and disposal of nuclear waste (Grossman and Cassedy, 1985). In addition, RCBA is utilized frequently in medical economics for assessments of medical interventions and other health-care contexts (Gewirth, 1990: 222). RCBA is also used widely in analysis of and policy making concerning environmental toxins (Baram, 1976). Finally, RCBA is used frequently in large-scale water and waste management technologies.

In order to set up a risk-cost-benefit analysis, one begins by trying to enumerate all adverse consequences that might arise from the implementation of a given technology. Next, one attempts to estimate the probability that each of these adverse consequences will occur. The third step is to estimate the cost or loss to social and individual health and well-being should any or all of the projected adverse consequences come to pass. Fourth, one tries to calculate the expected loss from each possible consequence. Finally, one attempts to compute the total expected losses from the proposed project by summing the expected losses for each of the various possible consequences. One follows a similar procedure to calculate the benefits. In the end, one subtracts the overall costs from the overall benefits. If the benefits outweigh the costs, the project is generally described as feasible.

However, there are significant methodological deficiencies in the RCBA method, especially those that raise ethical problems. Our analysis has identified five methodological deficiencies. They are: (1) problems of identification, (2) the value-of-life problem, (3) the commensurability problem, (4) problems associated with values and market mechanisms, and (5) problems of social and ecological justice. These problems and associated issues are listed in Table 2.

The first methodological problem associated with RCBA is the unquestioned assumption

Table 2. Problems and Issues with Risk-Cost-Benefit Analysis

Problems	Issues
1. Problems of identification	1. It is almost impossible to arrive at a complete enumeration of *all* risks and benefits because one can never know all of the variables that need be assigned diagnostic values, let alone be able to calculate all the costs and benefits.
2. The value-of-life problem	2. A fundamental moral problem arises in assigning a monetary value to human life, a necessary requirement of RCBA.
3. The commensurability problem	3. The erroneous assumption that disparate costs and benefits are quantifiable according to an identical metric leads analysts to believe that all values are commensurable with one another.
4. Human values and market mechanisms	4. Utility maximizations fail to provide satisfaction for all crucial human needs and values.
5. Problems of social and ecological justice	5. RCBA fails to take into account issues of fairness in the distribution of risks and harms across social groups, between different generations, and throughout the natural environment.

that *all* significant consequences can be enumerated in advance. The assumption is that all of the costs and benefits of a particular implementation of a new technology or extension of a "known" technology can be clearly identified and catalogued, that meaningful probability, cost, and benefit values can be obtained and assigned to them, and that often disparate costs and benefits can somehow be made comparable to one another. Such judgments are grounded in unrealistic assumptions about the availability of the data needed to complete the analysis.

As with probabilistic risk assessment, not all of the crucial questions regarding the nature, estimation, or acceptability of the risks, costs, and benefits can be answered with quantitative analysis alone. Conscious normative judgments arise in determining what will be included and what will be excluded. In other words, at least as far as the "problems of identification" are concerned, the same problems associated with PRA also arise with RCBA (or CBA). As Martin (1982) points out:

> PRA and CBA are different techniques, but they have important similarities. Both attempt to translate seemingly incomparable sorts of considerations into a quantifiable common denominator of some sort (whether dollars or mathematical formulae), then tallying up the results for various options, and finally presenting this information in a form that can be readily digested by decision makers . . . [However] . . . cost-benefit analyses, as well as probabilistic risk assessment are value-laden, both in what they count out (usually, for example, considerations of rights and justice) and in what they count in (for example, assumptions about what sorts of things constitute costs and benefits, whose costs and benefits are to be weighed, and how relative values are to be assigned to them). (p. 147)

Uncertainties as to how one should define "harm" or "risk" of a particular action force analysts to make judgments that are value-laden. For example, one contested assumption of both PRA and RCBA is that mortality rates—ignoring morbidity rates—are usually chosen as the focus of analysis.

The second methodological problem with RCBA is a hotly debated issue: the assignment of a monetary value to human life, a necessary requirement of a robust risk-cost-benefit analysis (Byrne, 1988; Kahn, 1986; MacKinnon, 1986; Rescher, 1987). As MacKinnon puts it, "of all the difficulties that surround the attempt to calculate the economic 'value of a life' one of the thorniest is a moral one, namely whether it is morally permissible to place any 'price' on a human life" (MacKinnon, 1986: 29).

Of course, certain practices are used by insurance companies, economists, and risk assessors that demonstrate that society does place some implicit monetary value on human lives (VOL). As one philosopher argues, "If it is permissible to forego life-saving treatment due to its cost, life has a monetary price" (Bayless, 1978: 29). On the other hand, there is a long and venerable tradition in our philosophical attitudes toward the VOL problem, perhaps best articulated by the Enlightenment philosopher Immanuel Kant (1785), when he wrote:

> In the realm of ends everything has either a price or a dignity. Whatever has a price can be replaced by something else as its equivalent; on the other hand, whatever is above all price, and therefore admits of no equivalent, has a dignity.

Of course for Kant, human persons are such creatures who exhibit "dignity." As Rescher puts it "How much is it worth to prevent the death of a person? . . . the question has no answer . . . it assumes that 'life' and 'risk to life' is some measurable quantity that actually exists in a stable and determinable way" (Rescher, 1987: 226). But, since this is false, Rescher concludes: "The question of value of life pushes beyond the proper limits of cost-benefit analysis in its insistence on quantifying something that is inherently unquantifiable" (Rescher, 1987: 226).

Byrne's analysis reveals three general methods to assess the value of life that are used in RCBAs: insurance-based, earnings-related, and willingness-to-pay (WTP) strategies (Byrne, 1988). Unsurprisingly, each one of these methods has serious limitations and deficiencies.

Rescher (1987) points out the limitations of the earnings-related method. As he puts it:

> One study that examined salary as a function of occupational risk concluded that a premium of about $200 per year (1986) was sufficient to induce workers in risky occupations to accept an increase of 0.001 in their annual probability of accidental death, a finding that was interpreted to indicate a life-valuation of around $200,000. . . . The linearity assumption involved in such calculations is questionable—the man who accepts a 1% chance of death for $10,000 may well balk at accepting $1,000,000 for certain death. (p. 227)

In other words, the supposedly higher or lower wages people accept for different types of hazardous jobs are interpreted as a valid measure of the cash value people are thought to place on their own lives. All too frequently, however, when lives are valued based on such criteria as economic worth or expected earnings, this turns into "life is cheap" in poorer neighborhoods or less developed nations. This issue is clearly illustrated in the Bhopal case. Life in Bhopal was implicitly valued less than life in the United States. Therefore, the safety equipment and emergency preparedness at the Bhopal plant in India were far less adequate than those at a similar plant operated by Union Carbide in Institute, West Virginia.

Barbour (1980) states the consequences of following the valuation of life principle to its logical conclusion:

> If applied consistently, the method would require that the lives of the elderly would be valueless. If future earnings are discounted, a child's life would be worth much less than an adult's. . . . I would maintain that there are distinctive characteristics of human life that should make us hesitant to treat it as if it were a commodity on the market. Life cannot be transferred and its loss to a person is irreversible and irreplaceable. (p. 73)

The third methodological problem of RCBA is how to deduce the value attribution of all the identified risks, costs, and benefits. Analysts automatically assume that often disparate costs and benefits can somehow be compared with another—that is, that all values are commensurable and can be fully quantified to reasonably determine whether the benefits of the proposed technological intervention or policy do, in fact, outweigh the risks and costs. Such calculations are necessary for RCBA so that disparate values can be compared and traded off, one against the other. Money becomes the common metric so that "goods" and "bads" can be compared with one another, and price becomes the medium through which all alternatives are evaluated, even those that are not normally perceived to have a market value (Kelman, 1981). This is evident in the "willingness-to-pay" criterion of a free-market economy: what a willing buyer will pay a willing seller. Take, for example, our aesthetic relationship to nature. How much is a beautiful view worth in monetary terms? How much is a landscape worth? A sunset? How much would someone be willing to pay to avoid having a toxic waste dump, a power plant, or an oil refinery built in his or her community?

The fourth methodological deficiency of RCBA becomes visible when one begins to probe the unquestioned assumption that market values provide the best opportunities for human beings to advance their life goals (Kelman, 1981). In other words, an RCBA methodology makes the assumption that the decisions people make in the marketplace are rational with regard to price, needs, and wants. However, it must be admitted that even in the open market the notion of utility maximization does not fully satisfy the variety of human needs and purposes. Notions such as freedom, equality, justice, and aesthetics also matter (Hausman and McPhearson, 1996: 77). In other words, one cannot always trust the market to satisfy all of our preferences

and sustain all of our values. This became all too evident in the case of the Ford Pinto. The public was outraged when they were informed, perhaps for the first time, as to how decisions like this are made. In the end, the problem is that:

> By regarding human happiness, human well-being, human life, and non-human life as mere commodities, cost-benefit analysis ignores the non-market value of these things and the central role they should play in public policy. (Anderson, 1993: 190)

These sentiments are reflected in a sign that Albert Einstein is reported to have had hanging in his office. The sign read: "Not everything that counts can be counted, and not everything that can be counted, counts" (Diwan, 2000). After everything is said, Einstein's aphorism perhaps best sums up the problems that beset using risk-cost-benefit analysis as the preeminent method for assessing the risks of technology. The aphorism also points to why risk-cost-benefit analysis fails as the sole method of determining the appropriate and equitable level of acceptability of those risks. This is no more evident than in RCBA's neglect of social values that contribute to our idea of justice, qualities that one can be sure Einstein would consider among those things that "count, but cannot be counted."

The fifth set of problems that beset the RCBA method are the well-known criticisms that RCBA fails to address adequately issues of fairness associated with the equitable distributions of risks and harms. For one thing, RCBA places exclusive focus on aggregate benefits and cannot address the ways in which those benefits are distributed. It is *not* designed to pay attention to the ethically crucial question: "Who pays the costs, and who gets the benefits?" Typically, such analysis reaches its "bottom line" by aggregating all costs, all risks, and all benefits.

Its goal is to determine, within its limited definition of the goods and harms involved, the *net* good, or harm that a technological intervention will produce. In other words, risk-benefit analysis is concerned only with the amounts of "goods" and "bads" in society, not with their fair or equitable distribution. For example, if the oil refinery in a neighborhood can be calculated to allow millions of distant persons to benefit from the gasoline and other products of that refinery, this can be multiplied into a major benefit. On the other hand, if the refinery results in higher cancer rates, greater medical costs, and residential property devaluation in the immediate neighborhood, this can also be calculated as part of the net costs, or harms, and subtracted from the "greater good." Although the net benefit may greatly outweigh the overall costs, the distribution of goods and harms may not be fair, because as Ferre (1995) puts it: "the principle of beneficence, to create greater good, is satisfied, but the principle of justice has been overlooked" (p. 83).

Justice across geographical, economic, and social space is one crucial set of values that RCBA leaves out of its calculations and equations. In addition, justice across time is almost totally neglected. Since RCBA is geared toward favoring short-range exploitation of opportunities and resources, it tends to ignore what Barbour (1980) calls "intergenerational justice" (p. 173). In other words, RCBA fails to address questions about the duties, obligations, and responsibilities one generation has to the next. Given recent concern over questions of ecological sustainability, resource depletion, and harm to future generations, this constitutes a major ethical flaw in the RCBA method of risk assessment.

In addition to overlooking questions about our duties and obligations to future generations, economists and policy makers seem to either ignore or deny that the market process

in general, and cost- and risk-benefit analysis in particular, systematically undervalue irreplaceable natural assets. RCBA tends to ignore considerations of what Ferre (1995) calls "ecological justice" (p. 84). The scarcity of nonrenewable resources, the irreversibility of habitat and land destruction, the extinction of endangered species, the depletion of the ozone layer, global warming, etc., are all pressing concerns that RCBA fails to address.

Technology Assessment

PRA and RCBA are not the only ways to assess the risks and harms of technology. Another approach is called *technology assessment* (TA). As originally conceived, TA was sensitive to the problems and issues previously discussed. Take, for example, the definition of TA given by one early theorist:

> Technology assessment is the process of taking a purposeful look at the consequences of technological change. It includes the primary cost-benefit balance of short-term localized market-place economics, but particularly goes beyond these to identify affected parties and unanticipated impacts in as broad and long-range fashion as is possible . . . both 'good' and 'bad' side-effects are investigated since a missed opportunity for benefit may be detrimental to society just as an unexpected hazard. (Coates, 1976: 141)

This definition introduces two ideas: the first points to a feasibility analysis performed so as to determine whether a proposed technology would maximize public utility. The second idea calls for mechanisms that focus on second- and higher-order (noneconomic) consequences, which are to be balanced against first-order (economic) benefits. Only with the aid of such an analysis is it possible to take account of unanticipated impacts of technology and also identify how they affect different stakeholders or constituencies. These two different but complementary concerns give voice to two general models, a "narrow" and a "broad" definition of technology assessment.

The narrow definition tends to restrict the meaning of TA to basically an operational analysis of particular technologies defined as concretely as possible (as in PRA):

> Technology assessment is viewed as a systematic planning and forecasting process which encompasses an analysis of a given production method or a line of products . . . it may be considered as a natural follow-up to systems engineering . . . (Coates, 1976: 142)

The broad definition, on the other hand, tends to consider technology assessment as a framework for societal analysis. This requires a systematic and interdisciplinary analysis of the impacts of technological innovation on the social, political, ethical, and medical aspects of life.

Conclusion

To enhance our capacity to prevent technological disasters, a broad concept of technology assessment is in order, the features of which are as follows:

1. *Social impacts.* TA should be concerned with second-, third-, and higher-order impacts such as impacts on human health, society, and the environment, as distinguished from economic utility of exclusively first-order concerns.
2. *Multi-disciplinary analysis.* TA should require that all pertinent aspects—economic, social, ethical, cultural, environmental, and political—be taken into account. Diverse methodologies and inputs from all disciplines are to be employed.

3. *Multi-constituency impacts.* TA should consider the widest range of stakeholders that may be affected by the proposed technology. Comprehensive TAs should require the informed consent of all affected stakeholders, inviting their active participation in the decision-making process.
4. *Policy-making tool.* TA should not be concerned with just technical expertise but, more essentially, with the socio-political problems associated with the impacts and consequences of a proposed technological innovation.

Such principles for a broad technology assessment can only be realized if risk assessment becomes a democratic process rather than one that is dominated by a technocratic and power elite. This critical issue will be the subject of our final chapter.

Author Citations

Anderson, Elizabeth. (1993). *Value in ethics and economics.* Cambridge, MA: Harvard University Press.

Baram, Michael. (1976). "Regulation of environmental carcinogens: Why cost-benefit analysis may be harmful to your health," *Technology Review,* July/August; 78: 40–42.

Baram, Michael. (1977). "An assessment of the use of cost-benefit analysis." In Joel Tarr (Ed.), *Retrospective technology assessment.* San Francisco, CA: San Francisco Press: 15–30.

Barbour, Ian. (1980). *Technology, environment, and human values.* New York: Praeger.

Bayless, Michael. (1978). "The price of life," *Ethics* 89 (1): 28–39.

Bier, Vicki. (1997). "An overview of probabilistic risk analysis for complex engineered systems." In Vlasta Molak (Ed.), *Fundamentals of risk analysis and risk management.* Boston, MA: Lewis Publishers: 67–85.

Bougumil, R.J. (1986). "Limitations of probabilistic assessment," *IEEE Technology and Society Magazine* 24 (8): 24–27.

Byrne, L.J. (1988). "The value of life: The state of the art." In Larry Martin (Ed.), *Risk assessment and management: Emergency planning perspectives.* Waterloo, Canada: University of Waterloo Press: 79–101.

Coates, Joseph. (1976). "The role of formal models in technology assessment," *Technological Forecasting and Social Change* 9: 140–146.

Diwan, Romesh. (2000). "Relational wealth and the quality of life," *The Journal of Social Economics* 29 (4): 305–322.

Ferre, Frederick. (1995). *Philosophy of technology.* Athens, GA: University of Georgia Press.

Gewirth, Alan. (1990). "Two types of cost-benefit analysis." In Donald Scherer (Ed.), *Upstream/ downstream: Issues in environmental ethics.* Philadelphia: Temple University Press: 205–232.

Greenberg, Michael, and Goldberg, Laura. (1994). "Ethical challenges to risk scientist exploratory analysis of survey data," *Science, Technology, and Human Values* 19 (2): 223–241.

Grossman, P.Z., and Cassedy, E.S. (1985). "Cost-benefit analysis of nuclear waste disposal: Accounting for safeguards," *Science, Technology, and Human Values* 10 (4): 47–54.

Haimes, Yacov. (1998). *Risk modeling, assessment, and management.* New York: John Wiley & Sons.

Harris, Charles E., Pritchard, Michael S., and Rabins, Michael J. (2000). *Engineering ethics: Concepts and cases.* Belmont, CA: Wadsworth.

Hausman, Daniel, and McPhearson, Michael. (1996). *Economic analysis and moral philosophy.* London: Cambridge University Press.

Henley, Ernest, and Kumamoto, Hiromitsu. (1981). *Reliability engineering and risk assessment.* Englewood Cliffs, NJ: Prentice Hall.

Humphreys, Paul. (1987). "Philosophical issues in the scientific basis of quantitative risk analyses." In James Humber and Robert Almeder (Eds.), *Quantitative risk assessment: Biomedical ethics reviews.* Clifton, NJ: Humana Press: 205–223.

Kahn, Shulamit. (1986). "Economic estimates of the value of life," *IEEE Technology and Society Magazine*, June: 24–29.

Kant, Immanuel. (1785). *Groundwork for the metaphysics of morals.* Translated by James W. Ellington. (1981). Indianapolis, IN: Hackett Publishing Company.

Kelman, Stephen. (1981). "Cost benefit analysis: An ethical critique." Reprinted in Thomas Donaldson and Patricia Werhane (Eds.), *Ethical issues in business* (5th ed.). Upper Saddle River, NJ: Prentice Hall.

Kneese, Allen, Ben-David, Shaul, and Schultze, William. (1983). "The ethical foundations of cost-benefit analysis." In Douglas MacLean and Peter Brown (Eds.), *Energy and the future.* Totowa, NJ: Rowman and Littlefield: 59–74.

Lanthrop, John. (1982). "Evaluating technological risk: Prescriptive and descriptive perspectives." In Howard Kunreuther and Eryl Levy (Eds.), *The risk analysis controversy: An institutional perspective.* Heidelberg, Germany: Springer-Verlag: 165–180.

Linnerooth-Bayer, Joanne, and Wahlstrom, Bjorn. (1991). "Applications of probabilistic risk assessments: The selection of appropriate tools," *Risk Analysis* 11 (2): 239–248.

MacKinnon, Barbara. (1986). "Pricing human life," *Science, Technology, and Human Values* 11 (2): 29–39.

Martin, Mike. (1982). "Comments on Levy and Copp and Thompson." In Vivian Weil (Ed.), *Beyond whistleblowing: Defining engineers' responsibilities.* Chicago: Center for the Study of Ethics in the Profession, Illinois Institute of Technology: 146–152.

Reactor safety study—An assessment of accident risks in U.S. commercial nuclear power plants. WASH-1400, NUREG-75/014, October 1975. Washington, DC: U.S. Nuclear Regulatory Commission, 1974.

Rescher, Nicholas. (1987). "Risk and the social value of a life." In James Humber and Robert Almeder (Eds.), *Quantitative risk assessment: Biomedical ethics reviews.* Clifton, NJ: Humana Press: 225–237.

Rowe, William. (1994). "Understanding uncertainty," *Risk Analysis* 14 (5): 743–750.

Thompson, Paul. (1982). "Ethics and probabilistic risk assessment." In Vivian Weil (Ed.), *Beyond whistleblowing: Defining engineers' responsibilities.* Chicago: Center for the Study of Ethics in the Profession, Illinois Institute of Technology: 114–126.

Discussion Questions

1. What are the basic features of probabilistic risk assessment? What are the problems or short-comings of probabilistic risk assessment, as enumerated by Evan and Manion?
2. The authors identify and describe five methodological deficiencies of RCBA. What are they? Give an example to illustrate each of these deficiencies.
3. Why is it difficult for tools such as probabilistic risk assessment to adequately assess low-probability, high-consequence events such as Chernobyl?
4. One of the reasons why intangible goals such as environmental health and social equity are often not factored into cost-benefit analyses is that they are extremely difficult to quantify. If they are considered, how are such intangibles factored in? What are the shortcomings of attempts to quantify such factors?

 Supporting Activities

1. Evan and Manion note that "in order to set up a risk-cost-benefit analysis, one begins by trying to enumerate all the adverse consequences that might arise from the implementation of a given technology." Select a technological development that you have recently read about, or one that is under discussion in your community or state, and try to brainstorm all of the potential consequences that might emerge. Try to identify primary, secondary, and even tertiary impacts. It can sometimes be helpful to create a web diagram that shows primary outcomes and the secondary and tertiary outcomes that stem from them.
2. Learn more about the concept of *intergenerational equity* and discuss it from an economic, environmental, and social standpoint. Should intergenerational equity be addressed in decision-making? If so, how should this be accomplished? What principles should apply?
3. Carry out a simple cost-benefit analysis of a selected technology as a small group or class project. The MindTools web site provides a very basic example for how to carry out a CBA, and introduces some related concepts. Instructions can be found at: http://www.mindtools.com/pages/article/newTED_08.htm.

 Additional Resources

1. Review the Endnotes listed for this section for more information about the Office of Science and Technology Policy and the Office of Technology Assessment.
2. For a short but interesting discussion of risk management strategies as applied to the 2012 Olympic Games, see: Jennings, W. (2012). The Olympics as a story of risk management. *Harvard Business Review.* Available: https://hbr.org/2012/08/the-olympics-as-a-story-of-ris.

Big and Bad

If you're an SUV owner you might feel a sense of annoyance or even anger at some of the claims made in this article. Gladwell related information that systematically refutes the notion that sport utility vehicles are safer than passenger cars. If you *are* inclined toward anger, hold off for a minute. A main function of this article was not to insult SUV owners, but rather to call into question the reasoning that we sometimes use with relation to safety and management of risk.

The popularity of SUVs, in spite of the accumulated data about their safety relative to passenger vehicles, provides clear evidence of two things: one, that the "reptilian" response is often stronger than more rational responses[9]; and two, that consumers of a technology are not necessarily well informed about its functions and behaviors. Of all the reasons why an individual might choose to own an SUV, safety should not be at the top of the list. (Although one might try, it's difficult to argue with the laws of physics.) The case of the SUV illustrates that we sometimes make decisions based purely on perception, superstition, or emotion; however, if we're serious about reducing the risks associated with technology, we should probably rely on more objective data.

Malcolm Gladwell has been a staff writer at *The New Yorker* magazine since 1996 and is the author of the bestselling books *The Tipping Point: How Little Things Make a Big Difference* (2000); *Blink: The Power of Thinking Without Thinking* (2005); *Outliers: The Story of Success* (2008); *What the Dog Saw* (2009); and *David and Goliath: Underdogs, Misfits, and Battling Giants* (2013). Gladwell also served as a reporter for the *Washington Post* for nine years, where he reported on business and science. In 2005, he was named one of *Time* magazine's 100 Most Influential People.

Big and Bad
How the S.U.V. Ran Over Automotive Safety

By Malcolm Gladwell

In the summer of 1996, the Ford Motor Company began building the Expedition, its new, full-sized S.U.V., at the Michigan Truck Plant, in the Detroit suburb of Wayne. The Expedition was essentially the F-150 pickup truck with an extra set of doors and two more rows of seats—and the fact that it was a truck was critical. Cars have to meet stringent fuel-efficiency regulations. Trucks don't. The handling and suspension and braking of cars have to be built to the demanding standards of drivers and passengers. Trucks only have to handle like, well, trucks. Cars are built with what is called unit-body construction. To be light enough to meet fuel standards and safe enough to meet safety standards, they have expensive and elaborately engineered steel skeletons, with built-in crumple zones to absorb the impact of a crash. Making a truck is a lot more rudimentary. You build a rectangular steel frame. The engine gets bolted to the front. The seats get bolted to the middle. The body gets lowered over the top. The result is heavy and rigid and not particularly safe. But it's an awfully inexpensive way to build an automobile. Ford had planned to sell the Expedition for thirty-six thousand dollars, and its best estimate was that it could build one for twenty-four thousand—which, in the automotive industry, is a terrifically high profit margin. Sales, the company predicted, weren't going to be huge. After all, how many Americans could reasonably be expected to pay a twelve-thousand-dollar premium for what was essentially a dressed-up truck? But Ford executives decided that the Expedition would be a highly profitable niche product. They were half right. The "highly profitable" part turned out to be true. Yet, almost from the moment Ford's big new S.U.V.s rolled off the assembly line in Wayne, there was nothing "niche" about the Expedition.

Ford had intended to split the assembly line at the Michigan Truck Plant between the Expedition and the Ford F-150 pickup. But, when the first flood of orders started coming in for the Expedition, the factory was entirely given over to S.U.V.s. The orders kept mounting. Assembly-line workers were put on sixty- and seventy-hour weeks. Another night shift was added. The plant was now running twenty-four hours a day, six days a week. Ford executives decided to build a luxury version of the Expedition, the Lincoln Navigator. They bolted a new grille on the Expedition, changed a few body panels, added some sound insulation, took a deep breath, and charged forty-five thousand dollars—and soon Navigators were flying out the door nearly as fast as Expeditions. Before long, the Michigan Truck Plant was the most profitable of Ford's fifty-three assembly plants. By the late nineteen-nineties, it had become the most profitable factory of any industry in the world. In 1998, the Michigan Truck Plant grossed eleven billion dollars, almost as much as McDonald's made that year. Profits were $3.7 billion. Some factory workers, with overtime, were making two hundred thousand dollars a year. The demand for Expeditions and Navigators was so insatiable that even when a blizzard hit the Detroit region in January of 1999—burying

the city in snow, paralyzing the airport, and stranding hundreds of cars on the freeway— Ford officials got on their radios and commandeered parts bound for other factories so that the Michigan Truck Plant assembly line wouldn't slow for a moment. The factory that had begun as just another assembly plant had become the company's crown jewel.

In the history of the automotive industry, few things have been quite as unexpected as the rise of the S.U.V. Detroit is a town of engineers, and engineers like to believe that there is some connection between the success of a vehicle and its technical merits. But the S.U.V. boom was like Apple's bringing back the Macintosh, dressing it up in colorful plastic, and suddenly creating a new market. It made no sense to them. Consumers said they liked four-wheel drive. But the overwhelming majority of consumers don't need four-wheel drive. S.U.V. buyers said they liked the elevated driving position. But when, in focus groups, industry marketers probed further, they heard things that left them rolling their eyes. As Keith Bradsher writes in "High and Mighty"—perhaps the most important book about Detroit since Ralph Nader's "Unsafe at Any Speed"—what consumers said was "If the vehicle is up high, it's easier to see if something is hiding underneath or lurking behind it." Bradsher brilliantly captures the mixture of bafflement and contempt that many auto executives feel toward the customers who buy their S.U.V.s. Fred J. Schaafsma, a top engineer for General Motors, says, "Sport-utility owners tend to be more like 'I wonder how people view me,' and are more willing to trade off flexibility or functionality to get that." According to Bradsher, internal industry market research concluded that S.U.V.s tend to be bought by people who are insecure, vain, self-centered, and self-absorbed, who are frequently nervous about their marriages, and who lack confidence in their driving skills. Ford's S.U.V. designers took their cues from seeing "fashionably dressed women wearing hiking boots or even work boots while walking through expensive malls." Toyota's top marketing executive in the United States, Bradsher writes, loves to tell the story of how at a focus group in Los Angeles "an elegant woman in the group said that she needed her full-sized Lexus LX 470 to drive up over the curb and onto lawns to park at large parties in Beverly Hills." One of Ford's senior marketing executives was even blunter: "The only time those S.U.V.s are going to be off-road is when they miss the driveway at 3 a.m."

The truth, underneath all the rationalizations, seemed to be that S.U.V. buyers thought of big, heavy vehicles as safe: they found comfort in being surrounded by so much rubber and steel. To the engineers, of course, that didn't make any sense, either: if consumers really wanted something that was big and heavy and comforting, they ought to buy minivans, since minivans, with their unit-body construction, do much better in accidents than S.U.V.s. (In a thirty-five m.p.h. crash test, for instance, the driver of a Cadillac Escalade—the G.M. counterpart to the Lincoln Navigator—has a sixteen-per-cent chance of a life-threatening head injury, a twenty percent chance of a life-threatening chest injury, and a thirty-five-per-cent chance of a leg injury. The same numbers in a Ford Windstar minivan—a vehicle engineered from the ground up, as opposed to simply being bolted onto a pickup-truck frame—are, respectively, two percent, four percent, and one percent.) But this desire for safety wasn't a rational calculation. It was a *feeling*. Over the past decade, a number of major automakers in America have relied on the services of a French-born cultural anthropologist, G. Clotaire Rapaille, whose speciality is getting beyond the rational—what he calls "cortex"—impressions of consumers and tapping into their deeper, "reptilian" responses. And what Rapaille concluded

from countless, intensive sessions with car buyers was that when S.U.V. buyers thought about safety they were thinking about something that reached into their deepest unconscious. "The No. 1 feeling is that everything surrounding you should be round and soft, and should give," Rapaille told me. "There should be air bags everywhere. Then there's this notion that you need to be up high. That's a contradiction, because the people who buy these S.U.V.s know at the cortex level that if you are high there is more chance of a rollover. But at the reptilian level they think that if I am bigger and taller I'm safer. You feel secure because you are higher and dominate and look down. That you can look down is psychologically a very powerful notion. And what was the key element of safety when you were a child? It was that your mother fed you, and there was warm liquid. That's why cupholders are absolutely crucial for safety. If there is a car that has no cupholder, it is not safe. If I can put my coffee there, if I can have my food, if everything is round, if it's soft, and if I'm high, then I feel safe. It's amazing that intelligent, educated women will look at a car and the first thing they will look at is how many cupholders it has." During the design of Chrysler's PT Cruiser, one of the things Rapaille learned was that car buyers felt unsafe when they thought that an outsider could easily see inside their vehicles. So Chrysler made the back window of the PT Cruiser smaller. Of course, making windows smaller—and thereby reducing visibility—makes driving *more* dangerous, not less so. But that's the puzzle of what has happened to the automobile world: feeling safe has become more important than actually being safe.

One day this fall, I visited the automobile-testing center of Consumers Union, the organization that publishes *Consumer Reports*. It is tucked away in the woods, in south-central Connecticut, on the site of the old Connecticut

Speedway. The facility has two skid pads to measure cornering, a long straightaway for braking tests, a meandering "handling" course that winds around the back side of the track, and an accident-avoidance obstacle course made out of a row of orange cones. It is headed by a trim, white-haired Englishman named David Champion, who previously worked as an engineer with Land Rover and with Nissan. On the day of my visit, Champion set aside two vehicles: a silver 2003 Chevrolet TrailBlazer—an enormous five-thousand-pound S.U.V.—and a shiny blue two-seater Porsche Boxster convertible.

We started with the TrailBlazer. Champion warmed up the Chevrolet with a few quick circuits of the track, and then drove it hard through the twists and turns of the handling course. He sat in the bucket seat with his back straight and his arms almost fully extended, and drove with practiced grace: every movement smooth and relaxed and unhurried. Champion, as an engineer, did not much like the TrailBlazer. "Cheap interior, cheap plastic," he said, batting the dashboard with his hand. "It's a little bit heavy, cumbersome. Quiet. Bit wallowy, side to side. Doesn't feel that secure. Accelerates heavily. Once it gets going, it's got decent power. Brakes feel a bit spongy." He turned onto the straightaway and stopped a few hundred yards from the obstacle course.

Measuring accident avoidance is a key part of the Consumers Union evaluation. It's a simple setup. The driver has to navigate his vehicle through two rows of cones eight feet wide and sixty feet long. Then he has to steer hard to the left, guiding the vehicle through a gate set off to the side, and immediately swerve hard back to the right, and enter a second sixty-foot corridor of cones that are parallel to the first set. The idea is to see how fast you can drive through the course without knocking over any cones. "It's like you're driving down a road in suburbia," Champion said. "Suddenly, a kid on a bicycle

veers out in front of you. You have to do whatever it takes to avoid the kid. But there's a tractor-trailer coming toward you in the other lane, so you've got to swing back into your own lane as quickly as possible. That's the scenario."

Champion and I put on helmets. He accelerated toward the entrance to the obstacle course. "We do the test without brakes or throttle, so we can just look at handling," Champion said. "I actually take my foot right off the pedals." The car was now moving at forty m.p.h. At that speed, on the smooth tarmac of the raceway, the TrailBlazer was very quiet, and we were seated so high that the road seemed somehow remote. Champion entered the first row of cones. His arms tensed. He jerked the car to the left. The TrailBlazer's tires squealed. I was thrown toward the passenger-side door as the truck's body rolled, then thrown toward Champion as he jerked the TrailBlazer back to the right. My tape recorder went skittering across the cabin. The whole maneuver had taken no more than a few seconds, but it felt as if we had been sailing into a squall. Champion brought the car to a stop. We both looked back: the TrailBlazer had hit the cone at the gate. The kid on the bicycle was probably dead. Champion shook his head. "It's very rubbery. It slides a lot. I'm not getting much communication back from the steering wheel. It feels really ponderous, clumsy. I felt a little bit of tail swing."

I drove the obstacle course next. I started at the conservative speed of thirty-five m.p.h. I got through cleanly. I tried again, this time at thirty-eight m.p.h., and that small increment of speed made a dramatic difference. I made the first left, avoiding the kid on the bicycle. But, when it came time to swerve back to avoid the hypothetical oncoming eighteen-wheeler, I found that I was wrestling with the car. The protests of the tires were jarring. I stopped, shaken. "It wasn't going where you wanted it to go, was it?" Champion said. "Did you feel the weight pulling you sideways? That's what the extra weight that S.U.V.s have tends to do. It pulls you in the wrong direction." Behind us was a string of toppled cones. Getting the TrailBlazer to travel in a straight line, after that sudden diversion, hadn't been easy. "I think you took out a few pedestrians," Champion said with a faint smile.

Next up was the Boxster. The top was down. The sun was warm on my forehead. The car was low to the ground; I had the sense that if I dangled my arm out the window my knuckles would scrape on the tarmac. Standing still, the Boxster didn't feel safe: I could have been sitting in a go-cart. But when I ran it through the handling course I felt that I was in perfect control. On the straightaway, I steadied the Boxster at forty-five m.p.h., and ran it through the obstacle course. I could have balanced a teacup on my knee. At fifty m.p.h., I navigated the left and right turns with what seemed like a twitch of the steering wheel. The tires didn't squeal. The car stayed level. I pushed the Porsche up into the mid-fifties. Every cone was untouched. "Walk in the park!" Champion exclaimed as we pulled to a stop.

Most of us think that S.U.V.s are much safer than sports cars. If you asked the young parents of America whether they would rather strap their infant child in the back seat of the TrailBlazer or the passenger seat of the Boxster, they would choose the TrailBlazer. We feel that way because in the TrailBlazer our chances of surviving a collision with a hypothetical tractor-trailer in the other lane are greater than they are in the Porsche. What we forget, though, is that in the TrailBlazer you're also much more likely to hit the tractor-trailer because you can't get out of the way in time. In the parlance of the automobile world, the TrailBlazer is better at "passive safety." The Boxster is better when it comes to "active safety," which is every bit as important.

Consider the set of safety statistics compiled by Tom Wenzel, a scientist at Lawrence Berkeley National Laboratory, in California, and Marc Ross, a physicist at the University of Michigan. The numbers are expressed in fatalities per million cars, both for drivers of particular models and for the drivers of the cars they hit. (For example, in the first case, for every million Toyota Avalons on the road, forty Avalon drivers die in car accidents every year, and twenty people die in accidents involving Toyota Avalons.) The numbers below have been rounded:

Make/Model	Type	Driver Deaths	Other Deaths	Total
Toyota Avalon	large	40	20	60
Chrysler Town & Country	minivan	31	36	67
Toyota Camry	mid-size	41	29	70
Volkswagen Jetta	subcompact	47	23	70
Ford Windstar	minivan	37	35	72
Nissan Maxima	mid-size	53	26	79
Honda Accord	mid-size	54	27	82
Chevrolet Venture	minivan	51	34	85
Buick Century	mid-size	70	23	93
Subaru Legacy/Outback	compact	74	24	98
Mazda 626	compact	70	29	99
Chevrolet Malibu	mid-size	71	34	105
Chevrolet Suburban	S.U.V.	46	59	105
Jeep Grand Cherokee	S.U.V.	61	44	106
Honda Civic	subcompact	84	25	109
Toyota Corolla	subcompact	81	29	110
Ford Expedition	S.U.V.	55	57	112
GMC Jimmy	S.U.V.	76	39	114
Ford Taurus	mid-size	78	39	117
Nissan Altima	compact	72	49	121
Mercury Marquis	large	80	43	123
Nissan Sentra	subcompact	95	34	129
Toyota 4Runner	S.U.V.	94	43	137
Chevrolet Tahoe	S.U.V.	68	74	141
Dodge Stratus	mid-size	103	40	143
Lincoln Town Car	large	100	47	147

Ford Explorer	S.U.V.	88	60	148
Pontiac Grand Am	compact	118	39	157
Toyota Tacoma	pickup	111	59	171
Chevrolet Cavalier	subcompact	146	41	186
Dodge Neon	subcompact	161	39	199
Pontiac Sunfire	subcompact	158	44	202
Ford F-Series	pickup	110	128	238

Are the best performers the biggest and heaviest vehicles on the road? Not at all. Among the safest cars are the midsize imports, like the Toyota Camry and the Honda Accord. Or consider the extraordinary performance of some subcompacts, like the Volkswagen Jetta. Drivers of the tiny Jetta die at a rate of just forty-seven per million, which is in the same range as drivers of the five-thousand-pound Chevrolet Suburban and almost half that of popular S.U.V. models like the Ford Explorer or the GMC Jimmy. In a head-on crash, an Explorer or a Suburban would crush a Jetta or a Camry. But, clearly, the drivers of Camrys and Jettas are finding a way to avoid head-on crashes with Explorers and Suburbans. The benefits of being nimble—of being in an automobile that's capable of staying out of trouble—are in many cases greater than the benefits of being big.

I had another lesson in active safety at the test track when I got in the TrailBlazer with another Consumers Union engineer, and we did three emergency-stopping tests, taking the Chevrolet up to sixty m.p.h. and then slamming on the brakes. It was not a pleasant exercise. Bringing five thousand pounds of rubber and steel to a sudden stop involves lots of lurching, screeching, and protesting. The first time, the TrailBlazer took 146.2 feet to come to a halt, the second time 151.6 feet, and the third time 153.4 feet. The Boxster can come to a complete stop from sixty m.p.h. in about 124 feet. That's a difference of about two car lengths, and it isn't hard to imagine any number of scenarios where

two car lengths could mean the difference between life and death.

The S.U.V. boom represents, then, a shift in how we conceive of safety—from active to passive. It's what happens when a larger number of drivers conclude, consciously or otherwise, that the extra thirty feet that the TrailBlazer takes to come to a stop don't really matter, that the tractor-trailer will hit them anyway, and that they are better off treating accidents as inevitable rather than avoidable. "The metric that people use is size," says Stephen Popiel, a vice-president of Millward Brown Goldfarb, in Toronto, one of the leading automotive market-research firms. "The bigger something is, the safer it is. In the consumer's mind, the basic equation is, If I were to take this vehicle and drive it into this brick wall, the more metal there is in front of me the better off I'll be."

This is a new idea, and one largely confined to North America. In Europe and Japan, people think of a safe car as a nimble car. That's why they build cars like the Jetta and the Camry, which are designed to carry out the driver's wishes as directly and efficiently as possible. In the Jetta, the engine is clearly audible. The steering is light and precise. The brakes are crisp. The wheelbase is short enough that the car picks up the undulations of the road. The car is so small and close to the ground, and so dwarfed by other cars on the road, that an intelligent driver is constantly reminded of the necessity of driving safely and defensively. An S.U.V. embodies the opposite logic. The driver is seated as high and far from the road as possible. The vehicle is designed to overcome its environment, not to respond to it. Even four-wheel drive, seemingly the most beneficial feature of the S.U.V., serves to reinforce this isolation. Having the engine provide power to all four wheels, safety experts point out, does nothing to improve braking, although many S.U.V.

owners erroneously believe this to be the case. Nor does the feature necessarily make it safer to turn across a slippery surface: that is largely a function of how much friction is generated by the vehicle's tires. All it really does is improve what engineers call tracking—that is, the ability to accelerate without slipping in perilous conditions or in deep snow or mud. Champion says that one of the occasions when he came closest to death was a snowy day, many years ago, just after he had bought a new Range Rover. "Everyone around me was slipping, and I was thinking, *Yeahhh*. And I came to a stop sign on a major road, and I was driving probably twice as fast as I should have been, because I could. I had traction. But I also weighed probably twice as much as most cars. And I still had only four brakes and four tires on the road. I slid right across a four-lane road." Four-wheel drive robs the driver of feedback. "The car driver whose wheels spin once or twice while backing out of the driveway knows that the road is slippery," Bradsher writes. "The SUV driver who navigates the driveway and street without difficulty until she tries to brake may not find out that the road is slippery until it is too late." Jettas are safe because they make their drivers feel unsafe. S.U.V.s are unsafe because they make their drivers feel safe. That feeling of safety isn't the solution; it's the problem.

Perhaps the most troublesome aspect of S.U.V. culture is its attitude toward risk. "Safety, for most automotive consumers, has to do with the notion that they aren't in complete control," Popiel says. "There are unexpected events that at any moment in time can come out and impact them—an oil patch up ahead, an eighteen-wheeler turning over, something falling down. People feel that the elements of the world out of their control are the ones that are going to cause them distress."

Of course, those things really aren't outside a driver's control: an alert driver, in the right kind of vehicle, can navigate the oil patch, avoid the truck, and swerve around the thing that's falling down. Traffic-fatality rates vary strongly with driver behavior. Drunks are 7.6 times more likely to die in accidents than non-drinkers. People who wear their seat belts are almost half as likely to die as those who don't buckle up. Forty-year-olds are ten times less likely to get into accidents than sixteen-year-olds. Drivers of minivans, Wenzel and Ross's statistics tell us, die at a fraction of the rate of drivers of pickup trucks. That's clearly because minivans are family cars, and parents with children in the back seat are less likely to get into accidents. Frank McKenna, a safety expert at the University of Reading, in England, has done experiments where he shows drivers a series of videotaped scenarios—a child running out the front door of his house and onto the street, for example, or a car approaching an intersection at too great a speed to stop at the red light—and asks people to press a button the minute they become aware of the potential for an accident. Experienced drivers press the button between half a second and a second faster than new drivers, which, given that car accidents are events measured in milliseconds, is a significant difference. McKenna's work shows that, with experience, we all learn how to exert some degree of control over what might otherwise appear to be uncontrollable events. Any conception of safety that revolves entirely around the vehicle, then, is incomplete. Is the Boxster safer than the TrailBlazer? It depends on who's behind the wheel. In the hands of, say, my very respectable and prudent middle-aged mother, the Boxster is by far the safer car. In my hands, it probably isn't. On the open road, my reaction to the Porsche's extraordinary road manners and the sweet, irresistible wail of its engine would be to drive much faster than I should. (At the end of my day at Consumers Union, I parked the Boxster, and immediately got into my own car to drive home. In my mind, I was still at the wheel of the Boxster. Within twenty minutes, I had a two-hundred-and-seventy-one-dollar speeding ticket.) The trouble with the S.U.V. ascendancy is that it excludes the really critical component of safety: the driver.

In psychology, there is a concept called learned helplessness, which arose from a series of animal experiments in the nineteen-sixties at the University of Pennsylvania. Dogs were restrained by a harness, so that they couldn't move, and then repeatedly subjected to a series of electrical shocks. Then the same dogs were shocked again, only this time they could easily escape by jumping over a low hurdle. But most of them didn't; they just huddled in the corner, no longer believing that there was anything they could do to influence their own fate. Learned helplessness is now thought to play a role in such phenomena as depression and the failure of battered women to leave their husbands, but one could easily apply it more widely. We live in an age, after all, that is strangely fixated on the idea of helplessness: we're fascinated by hurricanes and terrorist acts and epidemics like SARS—situations in which we feel powerless to affect our own destiny. In fact, the risks posed to life and limb by forces outside our control are dwarfed by the factors we can control. Our fixation with helplessness distorts our perceptions of risk. "When you feel safe, you can be passive," Rapaille says of the fundamental appeal of the S.U.V. "Safe means I can sleep. I can give up control. I can relax. I can take off my shoes. I can listen to music." For years, we've all made fun of the middle-aged man who suddenly trades in his sedate family sedan for a shiny red sports car. That's called a midlife crisis. But at least it involves some degree of engagement with the act of driving. The man who gives up his sedate family sedan for an S.U.V. is saying something far more troubling—that he finds the demands of the road to be overwhelming. Is acting out really worse than giving up?

On August 9, 2000, the Bridgestone Firestone tire company announced one of the largest product recalls in American history. Because of mounting concerns about safety, the company said, it was replacing some fourteen million tires that had been used primarily on the Ford Explorer S.U.V. The cost of the recall—and of a follow-up replacement program initiated by Ford a year later—ran into billions of dollars. Millions more were spent by both companies on fighting and settling lawsuits from Explorer owners, who alleged that their tires had come apart and caused their S.U.V.s to roll over. In the fall of that year, senior executives from both companies were called to Capitol Hill, where they were publicly berated. It was the biggest scandal to hit the automobile industry in years. It was also one of the strangest. According to federal records, the number of fatalities resulting from the failure of a Firestone tire on a Ford Explorer S.U.V., as of September, 2001, was two hundred and seventy-one. That sounds like a lot, until you remember that the total number of tires supplied by Firestone to the Explorer from the moment the S.U.V. was introduced by Ford, in 1990, was fourteen million, and that the average life span of a tire is forty-five thousand miles. The allegation against Firestone amounts to the claim that its tires failed, with fatal results, two hundred and seventy-one times in the course of six hundred and thirty billion vehicle miles. Manufacturers usually win prizes for failure rates that low. It's also worth remembering that during that same ten-year span almost half a million Americans died in traffic accidents. In other words, during the nineteen-nineties hundreds of thousands of people were killed on the roads because they drove too fast or ran red lights or drank too much. And, of those, a fair proportion involved people in S.U.V.s who were lulled by their four-wheel drive into driving recklessly on slick roads, who drove aggressively because they felt invulnerable, who disproportionately killed those they hit because they chose to drive trucks with inflexible steel-frame architecture, and who crashed because they couldn't bring their five-thousand-pound vehicles to a halt in time. Yet, out of all those fatalities, regulators, the legal profession, Congress, and the media

chose to highlight the .0005 percent that could be linked to an alleged defect in the vehicle.

But should that come as a surprise? In the age of the S.U.V., this is what people worry about when they worry about safety—not risks, however commonplace, involving their own behavior but risks, however rare, involving some unexpected event. The Explorer was big and imposing. It was high above the ground. You could look down on other drivers. You could see if someone was lurking behind or beneath it. You could drive it up on someone's lawn with impunity. Didn't it seem like the safest vehicle in the world?

Discussion Questions

1. Why were auto manufacturers in the United States surprised by the success of the SUV? From a marketing standpoint, why are SUVs appealing to manufacturers? To consumers?
2. Based on the statistics provided, can you draw any conclusions about safety and the size of a vehicle? What factors appear to make the biggest difference in automotive safety?
3. Gladwell states that with regard to driving safety we have shifted from an active to a passive conception of safety, and that we worry more about external elements that we perceive to be beyond our control. What does he mean by these statements? Do you agree with these ideas?

 Supporting Activities

1. If you carry automobile or other forms of insurance, you have been impacted by the work of an actuary. Actuaries are people who calculate the financial impacts of risk and uncertainty. For one of the best overviews of what actuaries do, visit Wikipedia: http://en.wikipedia.org/wiki/Actuary.
2. Read the full text of the report by Ross and Wenzel: Ross, M.; & Wenzel, T. (March 2002). *An analysis of traffic deaths by vehicle type and model, report number T021*. Washington, DC: American Council for an Energy-Efficient Economy. http://www2.lbl.gov/Science-Articles/Archive/assets/images/2002/Aug-26-2002/SUV-report.pdf.
3. Research the safety ratings for the car you drive. These data are available through the Insurance Institute for Highway Safety and through automobile pricing sites like Kelley Blue Book.

 Additional Resources

1. Visit Malcolm Gladwell's web site (http://www.gladwell.com), where you can view the full text of his articles in *The New Yorker*, including his January 22, 1996 article about risk theory, titled "Blowup." The site also includes pieces Gladwell has written for the online magazine *Slate*.
2. The book *The Struggle for Auto Safety* (1990) by Jerry Mashaw and David Harfst (Cambridge, MA: Harvard University Press) describes the history of legislation and efforts to regulate automotive safety in the United States.
3. For a glimpse at the book that brought automobile safety squarely into the consumer protection limelight, see Ralph Nader's 1965 *Unsafe at Any Speed: The Designed-In Dangers of the American Automobile* in which he details the known safety hazards of the Chevrolet Corvair. In 2011 *Time* magazine called this book one of the "100 best and most influential" English-language books since 1923.

Origins of Denial

Climate change is one of the defining issues of this age. Although there is compelling evidence indicating the likely causes and effects of global climate change it remains a hotly contested phenomenon (no pun intended). Like other complex phenomena, it is impossible to document or to predict with 100% accuracy the likely trajectory of climate change, particularly when the effects are at a global scale. Those with an interest in discounting or denying climate change can exploit these complexities and uncertainties to undermine the weight of evidence that supports the scientific community's predictions. According to the NASA web site, "ninety-seven percent of climate scientists agree that climate-warming trends over the past century are very likely due to human activities, and most of the leading scientific organizations worldwide have issued public statements endorsing this position" (NASA, 2015). Yet in spite of this "unequivocal" scientific consensus, the systematic efforts on the part of climate deniers have stalled adoption of any meaningful governmental policies to address the problem.

In this chapter, excerpted from his book *The Hockey Stick and the Climate Wars,* climatologist Michael Mann describes the strategies being used to attack climate science and scientists. These are not new strategies. Mann describes efforts used against Rachel Carson in the early 1960s when her book *Silent Spring* uncovered the environmental damage being caused by widespread use of synthetic pesticides. In effect, marketing strategies are used to shape the media message and to influence public opinion in ways that seem to legitimize the "controversy" over climate change, even in the face of established scientific findings. Social media and the Internet are used to amplify the campaign of misinformation, and erroneous messages get repeated with little regard to the accuracy of the original source.

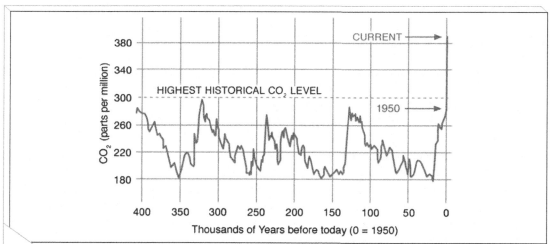

Figure 1. According to ice core data compiled by the National Oceanic & Atmospheric Administration (NOAA), atmospheric CO_2 levels have never been above 300 ppm before 1950 (NASA, 2015, p. 1). In 2015, global CO_2 levels surpassed 400 ppm.

Michael E. Mann is a climatologist and Distinguished Professor of Meteorology and Director of the Earth System Science Center at Penn State University. He is a Fellow of both the American Meteorological Society and the American Geophysical Union. Author of over 180 peer-reviewed and edited publications, Mann was also a lead author of the *Observed Climate Variability and Change* chapter in the IPCC's Third Scientific Assessment Report in 2001 and, along with other IPCC authors was awarded the 2007 Nobel Peace Prize. In 2012 he received the Hans Oeschger Medal of the European Geosciences Union and has been recognized by *Scientific American*, NOAA, the National Wildlife Federation, and the National Center for Science Education, among others. Mann was cofounder of the award-winning website www.RealClimate.org. In addition to the book from which this chapter is excerpted, Mann wrote the 2008 book *Dire Predictions: Understanding Global Warming.*

The Origins of Denial

> *Doubt is our product since it is the best means of competing with the "body of fact" that exists in the mind of the general public.*
> —UNNAMED TOBACCO EXECUTIVE, BROWN & WILLIAMSON (1969)

In the 1990s, as the scientific evidence for human-caused global warming grew stronger and calls for action to curtail greenhouse gas emissions grew louder, fossil fuel industry executives made a critical decision. Rather than concede the potential threat climate change posed and the necessity of ultimately reducing fossil fuel use, they would instead engage in a massive, media-savvy public relations campaign. The strategy was simple: While presenting a seemingly forward-thinking, pro-environmental public face, oil companies and allied economic and political interests would, behind the scenes, use various means to sow doubt about the validity of the underlying science on climate change. It was a finely tuned balancing act intended to forestall any governmental policy action to regulate greenhouse gas emissions while seeking to maintain a positive corporate image.

Doubt Is Their Product

The source of the chapter's opening quote is David Michaels's *Doubt Is Their Product*.[1] The book describes the corporate public relations campaigns that the tobacco and other industries used for decades to discredit research

demonstrating adverse health impacts of their products—a campaign that was successfully satirized in the 2005 movie *Thank You for Smoking*. The striking similarity with the tactics of climate change denial did not go unnoticed by former *Science* magazine editor-in-chief Donald Kennedy, who commented on the book's jacket, "if you're worried about climate change, keep worrying, because the same program is underway there."

In *The Republican War on Science*, Chris Mooney argues that the corporate-funded public relations campaigns of recent decades aimed at discrediting the science behind policies designed to protect our environment and health arose from conservative distaste of governmental regulation.[2] Those campaigns came to a head, he suggests, in the extreme antiregulatory atmosphere of the George W. Bush administration of 2000–2008. Legislation such as the Data Quality Act of 2001 saddled government agencies with onerous requirements on how they must respond to demands and complaints from industry groups regarding any data or scientific studies used in establishing government policy. It was, in Mooney's words, "a science abuser's dream come true," and it signaled the increasing politicization of science at the very time the hockey stick was coming to prominence.

Industry groups sought to frame the public discourse by constructing, to use the characterization of Naomi Oreskes and Erik Conway in *Merchants of Doubt*,[3] a virtual Potemkin village of pseudoscience institutions—think tanks, journals, news sites, and even a cadre of supposed experts, ideally with prestigious affiliations—to promote their own scientific (or, more aptly, antiscientific) messaging. These professed experts were used to promote industry-favorable views in the framing of policy-relevant matters of science, to manufacture doubt about mainstream scientific findings disadvantageous to their client, and to generate pseudoscientific sound bites that could be presented to the public under the auspices of neutral-sounding groups.[4] Using this tactic, industry advocates have, in the words of famed Stanford environmental scientists Paul and Anne Ehrlich, "sowed doubt among journalists, policymakers, and the public at large about the reality and importance" of an array of societal and environmental threats.[5] The Ehrlichs coined the term *brownlash* to characterize this orchestrated backlash against "green" policies.

The choice of language employed in antiscientific attacks is worthy of particular attention, as it has been exploited by purveyors of disinformation in a distinctly Orwellian manner, often to great effect in the public discourse. Their lexicon features simple, pithy terms like "sound science" that are repeated as mantras. Who, after all, could be against sound science? Implicit in this motif, however, is the notion—wholly inconsistent with the way science actually works—that the scientific enterprise must offer absolute proof if it is to be used to inform policy. Like a defense lawyer, industry special interests seek to introduce some measure of doubt into the public mindset. The demand for sound

science is made for a curiously selective array of findings, be they the ozone-depleting properties of the chlorofluorocarbons (CFCs) once used in spray cans, or the adverse health effects of industrial mercury pollution. The true metric applied by industry special interests is, of course, not the actual quality of the underlying science, but simply this: Are the scientific findings in some way inconvenient to their clients (the health insurance industry, the pharmaceutical industry, the chemical industry, the fast food industry, or, of course, the fossil fuel industry)?

If so, those findings are quickly labeled "junk science" and are purported to represent the flawed or even fraudulent claims advanced by a cabal of ostensibly corrupt university professors, scientists, journal editors, and governmental science funding agencies. Mooney notes that, from the language being used, "you would think that environmental science, as conducted by America's leading universities, suffers from endemic corruption on a scale reminiscent of Tammany Hall."[6] The effort seeks simultaneously to paint scientists as enemies of the people and to spread doubt and confusion about established scientific findings. Meanwhile, it encourages educators to "teach the controversy"[7] when—scientifically speaking—there is none.

There is rich irony here, as the clearest cases of true junk science seem to have resulted from the corruptive influence of industry itself. Particularly striking examples can be found in the area of biomedical science and pharmaceuticals, where there have been numerous high-profile scandals involving companies that either ghostwrote articles for scientific journals singing the praises of their particular pharmaceutical product[8] or suppressed, through threat of litigation, scientific publications damaging to the credibility of their advertised claims.[9]

The attacks are typically carried out by organizations and groups with names like

"Citizens for a Sound Economy" that masquerade as grassroots entities but in reality represent powerful industries, and have hence been termed "Astroturf" organizations. These groups employ ideologically aligned media outlets and a network of lawyers, lobbyists, and politicians to advance their message. Their efforts are aided by honest citizens, and sometimes even by mainstream media outlets, who are taken in and exploited, often unwittingly, to create an echo chamber of mass disinformation that permeates our airwaves and television screens and the Internet.

A central focus of many of these campaigns in recent years has, of course, been the discourse over global warming and climate change. For more than a decade, the scientific community, in its effort to communicate the threat of climate change, has had to fight against the headwind of this industry-funded disinformation effort. The collective battles are what I term the "climate wars."

The Climate Wars

The evidence for a well-organized, well-funded, and orchestrated climate change disinformation campaign has been laid out in detail on public interest group Web sites,[10] in articles in popular magazines,[11] and by an increasingly rich array of scrupulously researched books on the topic.[12] The campaign has its roots in the larger industry-funded public relations efforts that emerged during the 1970s and 1980s over acid rain, ozone depletion, missile defense, stem cell research, biodiversity loss, and a host of other issues.[13] Foreshadowing the climate change denying tactics outlined in the 2002 Luntz memo were the activities of the Global Climate Coalition (GCC). Formed in the late 1980s, the GCC was a consortium of more than fifty companies and trade associations representing chemical, mining, automotive, transportation, fossil fuel,

shipping, farming, power, defense, pharmaceutical, and manufacturing industries with the purpose of funding and organizing opposition to emerging policy efforts aimed at greenhouse gas emission reductions. They played a critical role, it may be recalled, in the attacks on Ben Santer, accusing him of "political tampering" and "scientific cleansing" following publication of the IPCC Second Assessment Report.

In April 1998, just days after the publication of our original hockey stick article, new revelations surfaced about a prominent GCC member, the American Petroleum Institute (API). Internal documents leaked to the *New York Times* showed it was hatching a plan to "recruit a cadre of scientists who share the industry's views of climate science and to train them in public relations so they can help convince journalists, politicians and the public that the risk of global warming is too uncertain to justify controls on greenhouse gases."[14] The GCC itself was disbanded in 2001 following the defection of prominent members such as British Petroleum that—with some irony, in retrospect—were concerned about the negative public relations of being associated with an anti-environmental agenda.[15] While the GCC no longer itself exists, the denialist campaigns continued unabated. Other fossil fuel interests—oil giant ExxonMobil being a big player among them—have continued to fund groups spreading climate change disinformation for years.

Wealthy privately held corporations and foundations with close interests in, or ties to, the fossil fuel industry, such as Koch Industries[16] and the Scaife Foundations,[17] have become increasingly active funders of the climate change denial campaign in recent years. Unlike publicly traded companies such as ExxonMobil, these private outfits can hide their finances from public view, and they remain largely invulnerable to outside pressure. In recent years, as ExxonMobil has been pressured by politicians on both sides of the aisle to withdraw from funding the climate change denial movement,[18] Koch and Scaife have stepped up, contributing millions of dollars to the effort.

Many organizations have settled in the Potemkin village of climate change denial. Among them are the American Enterprise Institute, Americans for Prosperity, Advancement of Sound Science Center, Competitive Enterprise Institute, Cato Institute, Hudson Institute, George C. Marshall Institute, Fraser Institute, Heartland Institute, Alexis de Tocqueville Institution, Media Research Center, National Center for Policy Analysis, and Citizens for a Sound Economy (better known now as Freedomworks). There are literally dozens of others.[19]

Among the willing accomplices in the campaign of deceit are the various media outlets that often propagate climate change disinformation in their editorial and opinion pages. These venues include newspapers such as the *National Post* and *Financial Post* in Canada; the *Daily Telegraph, Times,* and *Spectator* in the United Kingdom; and U.S. newspapers such as the *Washington Times* and the various outlets of the Murdoch, Scaife, and Anschutz conservative media empires, which include not only prominent outlets such as Fox News and the *Wall Street Journal,* but syndicates such as the regional Examiner.com network and Web sites like Newsbusters.

Agents of Denial

Not only are there connections between the current campaign to attack the science of climate change and past industry-funded campaigns to deny other industrial health and environmental threats such as the dangers of smoking tobacco and of acid rain, environmental mercury contamination, and ozone depletion. Some of the very same scientists have been employed as advocates for not just one or two, but many of these issues. Think of them as all-purpose deniers.

The grandfather of all-purpose denial was Frederick Seitz, a solid-state physicist possessing impressive scientific credentials. Seitz was a former head of the U.S. National Academy of Sciences and in 1973 was awarded the prestigious Presidential Medal of Science. Seitz found common cause with two other similarly minded physicists—Robert Jastrow, founder of the NASA Goddard Institute for Space Studies (GISS) laboratory now directed by James Hansen, and Nicholas Nierenberg, one-time director of the Scripps Institution for Oceanography—in supporting and advocating for President Ronald Reagan's 1980s missile defense program.[20] The Strategic Defense Initiative was controversial enough that the issue of whether it was wise, let alone efficacious, divided the physics department faculty at UC Berkeley where I was doing my degree at the time.[21]

In 1984, the three scientists joined together to form the George C. Marshall Institute—a conservative think tank that *Newsweek* magazine called a "central cog in the denial machine."[22] Their chief mission was to combat efforts by Cornell University planetary scientist Carl Sagan and others who sought to raise awareness about the potential threat of "nuclear winter." The massive detonation of nuclear warheads during a thermonuclear war, Sagan and others hypothesized, might produce a global dust cloud as devastating for humanity as the asteroid-induced global dust storm that ended the reign of the dinosaurs. The concept had even penetrated into popular culture with the 1983 song "Walking in Your Footsteps" by the Police.[23] That nuclear winter projections were based on climate models brought climate modeling onto the radar screen of Seitz, Jastrow, and Nierenberg, and it set the stage for their later role as key climate change deniers.

Upon retirement from academia in the late 1970s, Seitz worked for the tobacco giant R.J. Reynolds for roughly a decade. In this capacity, he accepted more than half a million dollars while lending his scientific credibility to advocacy efforts aimed at downplaying the health threats posed by the smoking of tobacco.[24] In the early 1990s, Seitz went on to chair the George C. Marshall Institute full time, where he campaigned against the reality of global warming and the threat CFCs posed to the ozone layer.[25]

In 1998, in conjunction with yet another climate change denial group, the Oregon Institute of Science and Medicine, Seitz spearheaded a petition drive opposing the Kyoto Protocol to limit greenhouse emissions, mailing the petition with a cover letter and an article attacking the science of climate change to a broad list of recipients. He portrayed these materials as having the imprimatur of the National Academy of Science (NAS) by formatting the article— "Environmental Effects of Increased Atmospheric Carbon Dioxide" by Arthur B. Robinson, Noah E. Robinson, and Willie Soon—as if it had been published in the prestigious *Proceedings of the National Academy of Science (PNAS)*, which it definitely had not been. Seitz even signed the enclosed letter using his past affiliation as NAS president. The NAS took the extraordinary step of publicly denouncing Seitz's efforts as a deliberate deception, noting that its official position on the science was the opposite of that expressed in Seitz's letter. The matter, coincidentally enough, played out just days before the publication of our 1998 hockey stick article in *Nature*.[26]

The "Oregon petition," with thirty-one thousand nominal "scientist" signatories, has often been touted as evidence of widespread scientific opposition to the science underlying human-caused climate change. However, a subsequent analysis by *Scientific American* found that few of the signatories were even scientists

(the list included the names Geri Halliwell, one of the Spice Girls; and B. J. Hunnicutt, a character from the TV series MASH).[27]

Questionable petitions, misleading articles, and, as we'll see, even one-sided conferences constitute key *modi operandi* in the world of climate change denial. There was indeed a distinct feeling of déjà vu in fall 2007, when I, and many other scientists and engineers, received a packet in the mail consisting of an updated "article" by several of the same authors promoting the same myths and half-truths (e.g., the medieval warm period was warmer than today, the Sun is driving observed temperature changes, and so on). This article, too, was formatted to look as if it had been published as a peer-reviewed journal article,[28] and yet again was accompanied by a petition demanding the United States not sign the Kyoto Protocol. The origin of these materials was, once again, the Oregon Institute of Science and Medicine.

That group's activities seemed to be part of a coordinated effort. One year earlier, Kenneth Green of the American Enterprise Institute (AEI) was implicated in what at least appeared to be an attempt to solicit pieces from climate scientists critical of a recently published IPCC report in return for a cash award of $10,000.[29] In addition, in recent years, the Heartland Institute, a group that has been funded by both tobacco (Philip Morris) and fossil fuel (Exxon, Koch, Scaife) interests, has financed a series of one-sided conferences on climate change, featuring a slate of climate change deniers, many with no discernible scientific credentials, and most with financial connections of one sort or another to the fossil fuel industry or groups they fund.[30]

S. Fred Singer, whom we met in previous chapters, followed in Seitz's footsteps. Like Seitz, Singer's origins were as an academic and a scientist, and like Seitz, he left the academic world in the early 1990s[31] to advocate against what he called the "junk science" of ozone depletion, climate change, tobacco dangers, and a litany of other environmental and health threats.[32] He founded an entity in 1990 called the Science and Environmental Policy Project (SEPP)[33] that he used to launch his attacks and has also received considerable industry funding for his efforts.[34] Singer was the principal behind the denialist response to the IPCC Fourth Assessment Report, the so-called Nongovernmental International Panel on Climate Change (NIPCC) funded by the aforementioned Heartland Institute, and characterized by ABC News as "fabricated nonsense."[35]

Singer, like Seitz, has been accused of having engaged in serious misrepresentation, in this case involving the great scientist Roger Revelle.[36] Revelle was instrumental in our early understanding of human-caused global warming and the potential threat of continued fossil fuel burning. He is also credited with having inspired many of today's leading climate scientists and is cited by former U.S. vice president Al Gore as the origin for his concern about climate change. In 1991, shortly before Revelle's death, Singer added Revelle as a coauthor to a paper he published in the Cosmos Club journal *Cosmos*. The paper attacked the science of climate change and was nearly identical in both title and content to a paper that Singer had previously authored alone.[37] Reports from both Revelle's personal secretary and his former graduate student Justin Lancaster suggest that Revelle was deeply uncomfortable with the manuscript, and that the more dismissive statements in the paper were added after Revelle—who was gravely ill at the time and died just months after the paper's publication—had an opportunity to review it.[38]

While Seitz and Singer may have been the most prolific and versatile of the denialists, other scientists have served as specialists in the climate change denial movement. Frequently,

though not always, they do so with either direct or indirect financial compensation and support from the fossil fuel industry.[39] Many write op-eds and opinion pieces for conservative-leaning newspapers or outlets supported by industry, such as TechCentralStation. Often they are sponsored to go out on the climate change denial lecture circuit, or they write books that are promoted, marketed, and even published by fossil-fuel friendly groups.

One of the more formidable among them is Richard Lindzen. His credentials, like those of Seitz, are impressive; he is a chaired professor at MIT and a member of the National Academy of Sciences. Lindzen—who also has received money from fossil fuel interests[40]—is perhaps best known for his controversial views that climate models grossly overestimate the warming effect of increasing greenhouse gas concentrations. It all has to do with the issue of climate feedbacks. Feedbacks, as we have seen, are mechanisms within the climate system that can act either to amplify (positive feedback) or diminish (negative feedback) the warming expected from increasing greenhouse gas concentrations. If a climate scientist has spent a career looking for missing feedbacks in climate models that are always of the same sign (positive for a "true believer" and negative for a "denier"), one might reasonably suspect that the endeavor has not been entirely objective. (Ironically, the one missing feedback I've argued for in the climate system is a negative one[41]—a rather inconvenient fact for those who would like to label me a "climate change alarmist.")

Lindzen has made a career of searching for missing feedbacks, but apparently only negative ones. Indeed, it seems as if he has never met a negative feedback he didn't like. And he has been quick to trumpet his claims of newly found negative feedbacks in op-eds, opinion pieces, and public testimony,[42] arguing time and again that his findings point to an overestimation of warming by models and are an indication that climate change is an overblown problem. Yet each of his past claims has evaporated under further scrutiny.

For years, Lindzen has argued that hypothesized but as yet un-established negative feedbacks in the climate system will offset the very large positive feedbacks arising from increased evaporation of water into the atmosphere and melting of snow and ice associated with global warming. He has argued that a doubling of CO_2 concentrations will consequently only raise global average temperatures by roughly 1°C (and with zero uncertainty!). Yet the diversity of evidence from the paleoclimate and modern climate record suggests that less than 2°C warming for CO_2 doubling is highly unlikely.[43]

In 1990, Lindzen argued that a drying and cooling of the upper troposphere would mitigate global warming,[44] but later in effect conceded that further work had demonstrated that the mechanism he had proposed was not viable.[45] In 2001 he promoted a new hypothesis, the so-called "iris" effect,[46] in which warming ocean temperatures would supposedly lead to fewer high clouds, causing surface temperatures to cool down.[47] Once again, this hypothesis didn't hold up under scrutiny by other scientists.[48]

Undeterred, Lindzen claimed to find evidence for an additional, new negative cloud feedback, this time based on a putative statistical relationship between tropical sea surface temperatures and satellite measurements of the radiation escaping to space.[49] He claimed that when the tropics warm up, there are more low reflective clouds, causing more solar radiation to be returned to space, thus tending to cool the surface. When climate researcher Kevin Trenberth of the National Center for Atmospheric Research (NCAR) and his collaborators examined Lindzen's claims closely,[50] however, they found the data points Lindzen had chosen to be curiously selective, and the claimed relationship not supported when a more objectively chosen sample was used.[51] A subsequent analysis by other researchers concluded that the available data may actually support a positive overall cloud feedback, not a negative one.[52]

Pros and Amateurs

People like Seitz, Singer, and Lindzen have been in the front lines of professional climate change denial. But others have participated as well. There is a whole corps of columnists and commentators who help promote climate change disinformation. In the United States, they include prominent radio and TV commentators such as Rush Limbaugh, Glenn Beck, and Sean Hannity, as well as many other lesser known, but similarly active and effective protagonists. Some, such as Bret Stephens of the *Wall Street Journal* and Debra Saunders of the *San Francisco Chronicle*, also operate with the imprimatur of ostensibly mainstream news organizations.

The boundaries between journalist, commentator, and paid industry advocate have become increasingly blurred with the development of the new media. Consider in the United States, for example, individuals such as Christopher Horner of the Competitive Enterprise Institute and James Taylor (no, not the singer-songwriter made famous by "Fire and Rain" and "Sweet Baby James") of the Heartland Institute. Though employed as lobbyists or lawyers by the industry-funded Competitive Enterprise Institute, they are regularly granted a forum by conservative news outlets to pen pieces attacking climate science and climate scientists. Tobacco and fossil fuel industry lobbyist Steven J. Milloy sometimes appears as a "junk science expert" on Fox News.[53] He runs a site called junkscience.org, billing himself, with no apparent sense of irony, as the "junk man." In the

United Kingdom, Christopher Booker of the *Telegraph* has such a biased record of reporting on environmental issues that it has earned him the title of "patron saint of charlatans" from award-winning *Guardian* journalist George Monbiot.[54]

Video also has played an increasingly important role in climate change denial. Martin Durkin of the United Kingdom produced the ironically entitled documentary "The Great Global Warming Swindle." British media regulator Ofcom found that the film "did not fulfill obligations to be impartial and to reflect a range of views on controversial issues" and that it "treated interviewees unfairly."[55] This problem was particularly evident in Durkin's interview of MIT physical oceanographer Carl Wunsch, who was upset by the way his words were edited to imply a contrarian viewpoint very much at odds with his actual views.[56]

Then there is the recently deceased science fiction writer Michael Crichton. One of Crichton's last novels, *State of Fear*, was a thinly veiled climate change denialist polemic masquerading as an action adventure novel. Crichton even was invited as a witness in a U.S. Senate committee hearing held by Senator James Inhofe (R-OK) to sow doubt on the reality of climate change. It is telling that Inhofe had to turn to a science fiction novelist to make his case.

The United Kingdom has produced some of the more colorful climate change deniers. Christopher Monckton, the third viscount Monckton of Brenchley, has emerged on the denial scene in recent years. He claims to be an expert on climate change, though he has no formal scientific training. Richard Littlemore of the fossil fuel industry watchdog group DeSmog-Blog tells us that Monckton has been caught on several occasions "indulging in deliberate manipulation of scientific data to arrive at misleading conclusions about climate science."[57] Monckton's assertions aren't confined to science; he

has even claimed, falsely, to have won the Nobel Prize.[58] After he had repeatedly represented himself publicly as a member of the House of Lords, the clerk of Parliament took the unprecedented step of publicly demanding he cease and desist making this false claim.[59]

Then there are the amateurs down in the trenches who execute the ground game in the climate wars. Many of these individuals are simply ill informed, and are no doubt acting in good faith in expressing what they believe to be honest skepticism. But strident claims without substance abound, as do absurd accusations against others. Some of the amateurs are more than willing to engage in some degree of mischief, whether it be taking advantage of the IPCC open review process by flooding its authors with countless frivolous comments (each of which must be responded to, according to IPCC rules) or exploiting the Freedom of Information Act (FOIA) and related laws to launch frivolous requests for documents and private correspondence of scientists. A since deceased Tasmanian named John Daly, with his Web site "Still Waiting for Greenhouse," provided an early proof-of-concept for how a single individual with nothing more than a Web site could battle mainstream climate science by peddling contrarian views and maligning the work of dedicated scientists.

Today, much of the trench warfare takes place on the Internet. Former mining industry consultant Stephen McIntyre is especially well known for his broadsides against established climate science. McIntyre frequently uses his Web site climateaudit to launch attacks against climate scientists themselves, often leveling thinly veiled accusations of fraud and incompetence—once, for example, titling a post about a highly respected NASA climate scientist with the rhetorical question "Is Gavin Schmidt Honest?"[60]

Since then, a number of other amateur climate change denial bloggers have arrived on the scene. Most prominent among them is Anthony Watts, a meteorologist for a Fox News AM radio affiliate in Chico, California, and founder of the site "Watts Up with That?" which has overtaken climateaudit as the leading climate change denial blog. Watts also started the Web site SurfaceStations.org, which purported to identify poorly sited meteorological stations in the United States in an effort to demonstrate that the instrumental record of warming temperatures is hopelessly compromised by instrumental measurement biases. With the assistance of the Heartland Institute, Watts published a glossy, very official-looking report about the project, showing lots of photos of ostensibly badly sited meteorological stations, with plots of the supposedly compromised records.[61]

Curiously absent from that report, however, was any direct comparison showing what the surface temperature record looks like both with and without the sites that Watts deemed unworthy. Scientists at the National Oceanic and Atmospheric Administration (NOAA) went ahead and calculated it themselves, producing versions of the continental U.S. average temperature curve both with and without the records in question. You can probably anticipate the result: It was difficult to distinguish the "with" and "without" versions within the thickness of the plot curves. Eliminating the "suspect" data made virtually no difference at all; in fact, the small bias that was found was of the opposite sign. The "corrected" record showed slightly more warming![62] This is just one example of a favored *modus operandi* among climate change contrarians: hyping real or imagined errors that make no difference to any significant scientific conclusions—the scientific equivalent of identifying a typo in a report.

Finally, there is the front line of the climate change denial ground attack. It consists of anti-climate-science activists and conspiracy theorists who operate largely under the radar

screen but nonetheless play an essential role in the denial agenda. Their primary tool is the "cut-and-paste," the repetition of contrarian talking points in arguments with friends, neighbors, relatives, and coworkers; in letters to editors of local newspapers; in online newsgroups; in comments sections of Internet news articles; and on blogs. Their role is not to be underestimated, as false statements repeated often enough help create the echo chamber of climate change disinformation.

Not all "amateurs" are what they appear to be. A primary goal of the disinformation machine is to manufacture an illusion of grass-roots support. This can be achieved by hiring ringers to pose as ordinary citizens, posting standard contrarian talking points and responses in online news threads, blogs, and the like. Prominent climate change deniers have occasionally been identified making use of a so-called sock-puppet (a "fake online identity to praise, defend or create the illusion of support for one's self, allies or company"[63]). Stephen McIntyre, for example, was found leveling online attacks hiding behind the sock-puppet "Nigel Persaud," while Michael Fumento of the Hudson Institute, perhaps best known for his attacks on environmental activist turned cinematic heroine Erin Brockovich, was once discovered posting self-supporting comments as "Tracy Spencer."[64]

Swiftboating Comes to Climate Change

One of the more unseemly features of the climate change denial campaign has been its use of character assassination as a tool for discrediting climate science itself. It is the art of the smear campaign that has come to be known as "swiftboating." The connection with the term is in fact remarkably direct.

Marc Morano got his start working for radio commentator Rush Limbaugh before moving on to work for the ExxonMobil and Scaife-financed Conservative News Service (now Cybercast News Service).[65] There, Morano was directly implicated in the original swiftboat attack on presidential candidate Senator John Kerry in the run-up to the 2004 presidential election.[66] That attack had taken one of Kerry's greatest strengths—he had been awarded three Purple Hearts for his service in Vietnam, while his opponent, George W. Bush, had avoided active duty—and, through a perversion of revisionist history, turned it instead into a perceived weakness.

Morano went on to become the pit bull of the climate change denial movement, launching swiftboat-like attacks as before, but this time directed against climate science and climate scientists. Among his many unsavory aspersions, he called NASA's James Hansen a "wannabe Unabomber" (suggesting it may be "time for meds").[67] I too have been at the receiving end of Morano's smears, having been called a "charlatan" responsible for "the best science that politics can manufacture."[68]

Beginning in 2006, Morano's efforts were funded on the taxpayer dime: He became a paid staff member on the Senate Environment and Public Works (EPW) Committee for Senate climate change denier Senator James Inhofe. From this perch, Morano promoted climate change denial talking points and launched attacks against climate scientists on the EPW Web site and through an e-mail listserv reaching large numbers of journalists and politicos. Undaunted after his position with Inhofe was terminated in 2009,[69] Morano headed back through the revolving door, this time hired by a Scaife- and ExxonMobil-funded[70] entity known as the Committee for a Constructive Tomorrow (CFACT) to run a new Web site called Climate-Depot.com. The site, which bills itself as "the Senate EPW website on steroids,"[71] provides Morano with a platform from which he can

continue his barrage against the climate science community. In 2010, for example, he proclaimed that climate researchers "deserve to be publicly flogged" for speaking out on the threat of human-caused climate change.[72]

Shoot the Messenger

While the tactic of swiftboating or "shoot the messenger" may have been honed by people like Marc Morano, it has a deeper history when it comes to environmental science in America. Rachel Carson, whose book *Silent Spring*[73] in the early 1960s exposed the environmental threats from widespread use of the pesticide DDT, was the first to experience the wrath of industry-funded smear campaigns. The president of Monsanto Corporation, the largest producer of DDT, for example, called her "a fanatic defender of the cult of the balance of nature."[74] Despite the fact that her scientific findings have stood the test of time, attacks against Carson continue to this day. The Competitive Enterprise Institute boasts a Web site, rachelwaswrong.org, aimed solely at discrediting Carson's legacy. The thinking seems to be, if they can bring down Rachel Carson, they can bring down the entire environmental movement.

Then there was Paul Ehrlich, with his *The Population Bomb* in the late 1960s, which introduced the public to the notion that our patterns of consumption and population increase were on a collision course with environmental sustainability. Among the many others who denounced Ehrlich as an alarmist purveyor of doom and gloom was Julian Simon of the Cato Institute, who accused Ehrlich of having led a "juggernaut of environmentalist hysteria."[75] Yet Ehrlich's early warning has ultimately proven prophetic. In the 1990s, a group of more than fifteen hundred of the world's leading scientists, including half of the living Nobel Prize winners at the time, concluded that "Human beings and the natural world are on a collision course," inflicting "harsh and often irreversible damage on the environment and on critical resources."[76] The major national academies of the world have issued similar joint statements.[77]

A similar story holds for Herbert Needleman—like Rachel Carson, a fellow Pennsylvanian. Needleman's research in the 1970s identified a link between environmental lead contamination and the impairment of childhood brain development. Lead industry-funded scientists accused him of misconduct in his analysis of data.[78] He was ultimately exonerated after a thorough investigation by the National Institutes of Health, and his research findings have been validated by numerous independent studies over the decades.

Each of these scientists helped instill a wider recognition of the dangers posed by unprecedented, uncontrolled, and unchecked human alteration—be it biological, chemical, or physical—of our environment. Carson, Ehrlich, and Needleman were the forerunners of the climate scientists who would be similarly denounced for their inconvenient findings.

Stanford University's Stephen Schneider was among the most articulate scientific voices in the climate change debate from the 1970s through his untimely passing in 2010. He was particularly effective in the way he confronted specious claims by climate change deniers with humor and his own brand of pithy witticisms.[79] A respected scientist and member of the National Academy of Sciences, Schneider made seminal early contributions to the science of modeling Earth's climate system and performed some of the key early climate change experiments. Later in his career, he spearheaded efforts in interdisciplinary climate science, such as integrated assessment—coupling projections of climate change and its potential effects with economic models in order to inform real-world decision making. He was a leading voice in the public discourse over what actions we must take to mitigate potentially devastating future changes in our climate.

Needless to say, Schneider was a target. In the early 1970s, when it was still unclear[80] as to whether the warming effect of human-generated greenhouse gases or the cooling effect of sulfate aerosols would predominate, S. Ichtiaque Rasool and Schneider speculated, quite reasonably, that the latter might indeed win out if emissions of aerosols continued to accelerate.[81] As it turns out, the world's nations chose to follow a scenario in which the greenhouse warming would instead win out, an unintended consequence of the passage of clean air acts in the United States, Europe, and other industrial nations that required aerosols to be "scrubbed" from smokestacks prior to emission, primarily to solve the acid rain problem. But it easily could have turned out otherwise. The Rasool and Schneider paper nevertheless remains the source of the favorite contrarian talking point that goes something like: "Back in the 1970s, Steve Schneider was warning the world about global *cooling!*"

The attacks against Schneider didn't stop with the global cooling myth. One of the most persistent smears relates to a statement he gave in a 1989 interview with *Discover* magazine:

> *On the one hand, as scientists we are ethically bound to the scientific method, in effect promising to tell the truth, the whole truth, and nothing but—which means that we must include all the doubts, the caveats, the ifs, ands, and buts. On the other hand, we are not just scientists but human beings as well. And like most people we'd like to see the world a better place, which in this context translates into our working to reduce the risk of potentially disastrous climatic change. To do that we need to get some broad-based support, to capture the public's imagination. That, of course, entails getting loads of media coverage. So we have to offer up scary*

scenarios, make simplified, dramatic statements, and make little mention of any doubts we might have. This "double ethical bind" we frequently find ourselves in cannot be solved by any formula. Each of us has to decide what the right balance is between being effective and being honest. I hope that means being both.[82]

Contrarians, like Martin Durkin in his "The Global Warming Swindle" polemic, are fond of editing Schneider down to the misleading snippet "we have to offer up scary scenarios, make simplified, dramatic statements, and make little mention of any doubts we might have" without the critical context, including the three sentences that followed it.

James Hansen was the first scientist to publicly testify to Congress that greenhouse warming was indeed upon us. In a sweltering Senate hall in the hot dry summer of 1988, Hansen asserted that "It is time to stop waffling . . . . the evidence is pretty strong that the [anthropogenic] greenhouse effect is here."[83] Though he has been criticized for that statement, in hindsight it appears that Hansen may have been correct that the signal of human-caused climate change had already emerged, albeit only weakly, by the late 1980s. The Reagan administration appeared to be unhappy with Hansen's public testimonies; as a NASA civil servant, he was not immune from their efforts to control his message. Representatives from the Office of Management and Budget repeatedly edited the drafts of his written congressional testimonies. Finally, in 1989, he'd had enough, and in bombshell testimony revealed that his words had been altered by the Bush administration.[84]

As Hansen has grown increasingly outspoken in recent years, the attacks against him by climate change deniers have grown more vicious. Critics have attempted to impugn his science by implying that he supplants objective scientific inquiry with political ideology. Among the baseless accusations have been that he received money from progressive activist George Soros and that he is secretly a Democratic Party operative because he received the Heinz Award in the Environment (in reality, Hansen has been a lifelong Republican, and the award was established to honor the memory of Republican politician John Heinz III, a Pennsylvania congressman who placed great value on environmental stewardship). The politically motivated attacks against Hansen over the years have been so extensive and profound that a separate book has been written on the topic.[85] But this is to get ahead of the story.

In chapter 1 we saw an early instance of an assault on climate scientists in the attack on Ben Santer for his groundbreaking work in the mid-1990s that helped establish a "discernible human influence on climate." He saw his integrity impugned as part of an industry-funded smear campaign, and his job and even his life were at times threatened.[86] The attacks against Santer were a sign of what was to come—for me. As Santer himself put it in an interview with the *New Scientist* a decade later, "There are people who believe that if they bring down Mike Mann, they can bring down the IPCC."[87]

1. David Michaels, *Doubt Is Their Product* (New York, Oxford University Press, 2008).
2. Chris Mooney, *The Republican War on Science* (New York, Basic Books, 2005).
3. Naomi Oreskes and Erik M. Conway, *Merchants of Doubt* (New York, Bloomsbury Press, 2010).
4. This tactic is described by Philip Mirowski in "The Rise of the Dedicated Natural Science Think Tank," *Social Science Research Council*, July 2008. According to Mirowski, "The key tenets were to promote otherwise isolated scientific spokespersons (from gold plated universities, if possible) who would take the industry side in the debate, manufacture uncertainty about the existing scientific literature, launder information through seemingly neutral third party fronts, and wherever possible recast the

debate by moving it away from aspects of the science which it would seem otherwise impossible to challenge" (3).

5. Paul R. Ehrlich and Anne H. Ehrlich, *Betrayal of Science and Reason: How Anti-environmental Rhetoric Threatens Our Future* (Washington, DC, Island Press, 1996), 1.

6. See Mooney, *The Republican War on Science*, 6.

7. This particular phrase was emphasized by the Discovery Institute, a conservative think tank, in its campaign to convince educators to offer the pseudoscientific concept of intelligent design as a credible scientific alternative to the theory of evolution.

8. See, e.g., Elizabeth Lopatto, Jef Feeley, and Margaret Cronin Fisk, "Eli Lilly 'Ghostwrote' Articles to Market Zyprexa, Files Show," *Bloomberg News*, June 12, 2009; Stephanie Saul, "Merck Wrote Drug Studies for Doctors," *New York Times*, April 16, 2008.

9. See, e.g., the discussion of Knoll Pharmaceuticals in Sheldon Krimsky, "Threats to the Integrity of Biomedical Research," in Wendy Wagner and Rena Steinzor, eds., *Rescuing Science from Politics* (New York, Cambridge University Press, 2006), 77. In this example, a peer-reviewed publication presenting damaging findings with regard to one of Knoll's new drugs was retracted by the author after threats of legal action by Knoll.

10. See, e.g., SourceWatch.org and exxonsecrets.org.

11. See, e.g., Chris Mooney, "Some Like It Hot," *Mother Jones*, May/June 2005; Sharon Begley, "The Truth About Denial," *Newsweek*, August 13, 2007; Jane Mayer, "Covert Operations: The Billionaire Brothers Who Are Waging a War Against Obama," *New Yorker*, August 30, 2010.

12. Ehrlich and Ehrlich, *Betrayal of Science and Reason*; Ross Gelbspan, *The Heat Is On* (New York, Basic Books, 1997) and *Boiling Point* (New York, Basic Books, 2004); and more recently James Hoggan and Richard Littlemore, *Climate Cover-Up* (Vancouver, BC, Greystone Books, 2009); Stephen Schneider, *Science as a Contact Sport* (Washington DC, National Geographic, 2009); Oreskes and Conway, *Merchants of Doubt*.

13. Oreskes and Conway in *Merchants of Doubt* provide an especially lucid account of the origins of the climate change denial campaign. They describe how the campaign can be traced back to Cold War hawks' distrust of scientists who questioned the efficacy and appropriateness of developing missile defense systems like the Reagan administrations' Strategic Defense Initiative (popularly known as "Star Wars") in the 1980s.

14. John H. Cushman Jr., "Industrial Group Plans to Battle Climate Treaty," *New York Times*, April 26, 1998.

15. Prior to the April 2010 Deepwater Horizon spill in the Gulf of Mexico— by most standards the worst oil spill disaster in history, BP had cultivated a reputation as one of the more forward-thinking fossil fuel companies, its advertising motto being *"Beyond* Petroleum."

16. See Greenpeace USA, "Koch Industries: Secretly Funding the Climate Denial Machine," March 2010. The report outlines how brothers Charles G. Koch and David H. Koch, who own and control Koch Industries, an oil corporation that is the second largest privately held company in the United States, have, along with family members and their employees, "directed a web of financing that supports conservative special interest groups and think-tanks, with a strong focus on fighting environmental regulation, opposing clean energy legislation, and easing limits on industrial pollution." Greenpeace notes that the money "is typically funneled through one of three 'charitable' foundations the Kochs have set up: the Claude R. Lambe Foundation; the Charles G. Koch Foundation; and the David H. Koch Foundation." See also Mayer, "Covert Operations."

17. The Scaife Foundations comprise the Sarah Mellon Scaife Foundation, the Carthage Foundation, the Allegheny Foundation, and the Scaife Family Foundation. Through these foundations, Richard Mellon Scaife, whose wealth was inherited from the Mellon industrial, oil, mining, and banking fortune, has financed numerous right-wing groups involved in the climate change denial campaign. According to Sourcewatch.org (accessed April 13, 2011), between 1985 and 2001 he donated $15,860,000 to the Heritage Foundation, $4,411,000 to the American Enterprise Institute, $2,575,000 to the Manhattan Institute for Policy Research, $1,855,000 to the George C. Marshall Institute, $1,808,000 to the Hudson Institute, and $1,697,000 to the Cato Institute.

18. In October 2006, Senators Olympia Snowe (R-ME) and Jay Rockefeller (D-WV) publicly demanded that ExxonMobil "end any further financial assistance" to groups "whose public advocacy has contributed to the small but unfortunately effective climate change denial myth." A July 19, 2010, investigative report in the *Times* of London revealed that despite the company's promise in 2007 that "In 2008, we will discontinue contributions to several public policy groups, whose position on climate change could divert attention from the important discussion on how the world will secure energy required for economic growth in a responsible manner," ExxonMobil continued to fund climate change deniers through at least 2009. The *Times* article quotes Bob Ward, policy director at the London School of Economics Grantham Research Institute: "Exxon has engaged in a public relations campaign to convince the world that it has stopped funding climate sceptic groups. But this has turned out to be pure greenwash. Exxon has continued to provide financial support for many groups that are engaged in activities to persuade the public and policy-makers into wrongly believing that climate change is a hoax." The *Guardian* more recently reported that ExxonMobil continued to fund at least one climate change contrarian through at least 2010. John Vidal, "Climate Sceptic Willie Soon Received $1m from Oil Companies, Papers Show," *Guardian*, June 28, 2011.

19. Evidence of fossil fuel industry funding of climate change denial by each of these (in particular, by Koch Industries and ExxonMobil) and numerous other groups can be found, for example, in the following sources: Greenpeace USA, "Koch Industries Secret Funding the Climate Denial Machine," March 2010; Gelbspan, *Boiling Point*; Oreskes and Conway, *Merchants of Doubt*; James Powell, *The Inquisition of Climate Science* (New York, Columbia University Press, 2011).

20. In *Merchants of Doubt*, Oreskes and Conway give a detailed account of these individuals, including their backgrounds and the history of how they became involved in industry-funded public relations campaigns including climate change denial.

21. The physics faculty included Edward Teller, commonly considered the Father of the Hydrogen Bomb for his role in the Manhattan Project in the 1940s, who was one of the most prominent advocates for the Star Wars program, and Charles Schwartz, who staunchly opposed the program. An excellent account of the conflict between the two is provided by Darwin Bondgraham, Nicholas Robinson, and Will Parrish, "California's Nuclear Nexus: A Faux Disarmament Plan Has Roots in the Golden State's Pro-Nuclear Lobby," *Z Magazine*, December 2009.

22. Begley, "The Truth About Denial."

23. The song included the lines "Hey there mighty brontosaurus, / Don't you have a lesson for us. / You thought your rule would always last. / There were no lessons in your past" (Walking in Your Footsteps," Music and Lyrics by Sting, ©1983 G. M. SUMNER, administered by EMI MUSIC PUBLISHING LIMITED. All Rights Reserved, International Copyright Secured. Used by Permission. *Reprinted by Permission of Hal Leonard Corporation*).

24. See Mark Hertsgaard, "While Washington Slept," *Vanity Fair*, May 2006; PBS Frontline, "Hot Politics," April 3, 2006, www.pbs.org/wgbh/pages/frontline/hotpolitics/interviews/seitz.html; Union of Concerned Scientists, "Smoke, Mirrors and Hot Air: How ExxonMobil Uses Big Tobacco's Tactics to 'Manufacture Uncertainty' on Climate Change," January 2007.

25. See, e.g., Hertsgaard, "While Washington Slept."

26. "Statement by the Council of the National Academy of Sciences Regarding Global Change Petition," April 20, 1998, www.nationalacademies.org/onpinews/newsitem.aspx?RecordID=s04201998.

27. "Skepticism About Skeptics," *Scientific American*, October 16, 2001.

28. See "Oregon Institute of Science and Malarkey," RealClimate.org, October 10 2007.

29. The story was reported by Ian Sample, "Scientists Offered Cash to Dispute Climate Study," *Guardian*, February 2, 2007. However, the issue came to light earlier still, in July 2006 when a colleague, Andrew Dressler, scanned and posted on his blog the letter two climate scientists at Texas A&M University had received. The letter begins "The American Enterprise Institute is launching a major project to produce a review and policy critique of the forthcoming Fourth Assessment Report (FAR)."

30. Amusingly, some token mainstream climate scientists, myself included, have been invited by

the organizers to participate in such meetings, presumably in the hope that our attendance might grant these PR events scientific credibility.

31. Singer took leave as a faculty member of the Department of Environmental Sciences at the University of Virginia in the early 1990s to spend full time on advocacy activities, formally retiring from his university position in 1994.

32. *Rolling Stone* magazine had this to say about Singer: "A former mouthpiece for the tobacco industry, the 85-year-old Singer is the granddaddy of fake 'science' designed to debunk global warming. The retired physicist—who also tried to downplay the danger of the hole in the ozone layer—is still wheeled out as an authority by big polluters determined to kill climate legislation. For years, Singer steadfastly denied that the world is heating up: Citing satellite data that has since been discredited, he even made the unhinged claim that 'the climate has been cooling just slightly.' Last year, Singer served as a lead author of 'Climate Change Reconsidered'—an 880-page report by the right-wing Heartland Institute that was laughably presented as a counterweight to the Intergovernmental Panel on Climate Change, the world's scientific authority on global warming. Singer concludes that the unchecked growth of climate-cooking pollution is 'unequivocally good news.' Why? Because 'rising CO2 levels increase plant growth and make plants more resistant to drought and pests.' Small wonder that Heartland's climate work has long been funded by the likes of Exxon and reactionary energy barons like Charles Koch and Richard Mellon Scaife." Tim Dickinson, "The Climate Killers: Meet the 17 Polluters and Deniers Who Are Derailing Efforts to Curb Global Warming," *Rolling Stone*, January 6, 2010.

33. Oreskes and Conway, *Merchants of Doubt*, 129–130.

34. For further information about Singer's funding by industry special interest groups, see Gelbspan, *The Heat Is On*, 46–47; Hoggan and Littlemore, *Climate Cover-Up*, 30, 80, 138–140, 156–157.

35. Dan Harris, Felicia Biberica, Elizabeth Stuart, and Nils Kongshaug, "Global Warming Denier: Fraud or 'Realist'?" ABC News, March 23, 2008.

36. The episode in question is detailed in Hoggan and Littlemore, *Climate Cover-Up*, 135–138.

37. According to Revelle's former colleague, the distinguished oceanographer Walter Munk, "Singer wrote the paper and, as a courtesy, added Roger as a co-author based upon his willingness to review the manuscript and advise on aspects relating to sea-level rise." See Oreskes and Conway, *Merchants of Doubt*, 195.

38. Richard Littlemore, "The Deniers? The World Renowned Scientist Who Got Al Gore Started," DeSmogBlog, April 16, 2008, www.desmogblog.com/the-deniers-the-world-renowned-scientist-who-got-al-gore-started.

39. The widespread funding of climate change contrarians by industry and industry-funded front groups is detailed in books such as Oreskes and Conway, *Merchants of Doubt*; Hoggan and Littlemore, *Climate Cover-Up*; Gelbspan, *Boiling Point*; and others. Useful online sources are the Web sites Sourcewatch.org and ExxonSecrets.org, which provide details regarding the ties between various professional climate change deniers and fossil fuel industry interests and their front groups.

40. In *The Heat Is On*, Ross Gelbspan reports an interview he conducted with Lindzen in which Lindzen admits to receiving (as of 1995) roughly $10,000 per year from fossil fuel industry consulting alone. In "The Heat Is On: The Warming of the World's Climate Sparks a Blaze of Denial," *Harper's*, December 1995, Ross Gelbspan noted, again based on his own interview, that Lindzen "charges oil and coal interests $2,500 a day for his consulting services; his 1991 trip to testify before a Senate committee was paid for by Western Fuels, and a speech he wrote, entitled 'Global Warming: The Origin and Nature of Alleged Scientific Consensus,' was underwritten by OPEC." Lindzen currently lists himself as a member of the Science, Health, and Economic Advisory Council of the Annapolis Center on his curriculum vitae (www-eaps.mit.edu/faculty/lindzen/CV.pdf, July 3, 2011). This organization has been funded by ExxonMobil at least as recently as 2009 (Exxon Mobil Corporation 2009 Worldwide Contributions and Community Investments, www.exxonmobil.com/Corporate/files/gcr_contributions_pub-policy09.pdf).

41. The negative feedback in question relates to the so-called tropical Pacific thermostat mechanism. This mechanism implies a counterintuitive La

Niña-like response to increased greenhouse gas concentrations that leads to less warming or even cooling of sea surface temperatures in the eastern and central tropical Pacific.

42. See, e.g., "Why So Gloomy," *Newsweek*, April 16, 2007; Richard Lindzen, "Climate of Fear," *Wall Street Journal*, April 12, 2006; Lindzen's UK House of Lords testimony on January 25, 2005, www.publications.parliament.uk/pa/ld200506/ldselect/ldeconaf/12/5012501.htm.

43. See, e.g., the discussion in James Hansen, Makiko Sato, Reto Ruedy, Ken Lo, David W. Lea, and Martin Medina-Elizade, "Global Temperature Change," *Proceedings of the National Academy of Science*, 103 (2006): 14288–14293.

44. Richard S. Lindzen, "Some Coolness Concerning Global Warming," *Bulletin of the American Meteorology Society*, 71 (March 1990): 288–299.

45. In Global Climate Coalition, "Primer on Climate Change Science," January 18, 1996, obtained as part of a court action against the automobile industry, the following is stated: "Lindzen's hypothesis that any warming would create more rain which would cool and dry the upper troposphere did offer a mechanism for balancing the effect of increased greenhouse gases. However, the data supporting this hypothesis is weak, and even Lindzen has stopped presenting it as an alternative to the conventional model of climate change."

46. R. S. Lindzen, M.-D. Chou, and A. Y. Hou, "Does the Earth Have an Adaptive Infrared Iris?" *Bulletin of the American Meteorological Society*, 82 (2001): 417–432.

47. Unlike low clouds, high clouds such as cirrus clouds typically have a warming influence on the surface as they block the escape of infrared radiation to space.

48. As summarized in the IPCC's Fourth Assessment Report (2007), "numerous objections have been raised about various aspects of the observational evidence provided so far [for Lindzen's iris hypothesis]." D. A. Randall, R. A. Wood, S. Bony, R. Colman, T. Fichefet, J. Fyfe, V. Kattsov, A. Pitman, J. Shukla, J. Srinivasan, R. J. Stouffer, A. Sumi, and K. E. Taylor, "Climate Models and Their Evaluation," in S. Solomon, D. Qin, M. Manning, Z. Chen, M. Marquis, K. B. Averyt, M. Tignor, and H. L. Miller, eds., *Climate Change 2007: The Physical Science Basis: Contribution of Working Group I to the Fourth Assessment Report of the Intergovernmental Panel on Climate Change* (Cambridge, UK, and New York, Cambridge University Press, 2007). Some authors found no evidence that warming ocean surface temperatures would influence cirrus clouds; D. L. Hartman and M. L. Michelsen, "No Evidence for Iris," *Bulletin of the American Meteorology Society*, 83 (2002): 249–254; while others argued there would actually be more cirrus clouds, therefore favoring instead a positive feedback; Q. Fu, M. Baker, and D. L. Hartman, "Tropical Cirrus and Water Vapor: An Effective Earth Infrared Iris Feedback?" *Atmospheric Chemistry and Physics*, 2 (2002): 31–37; B. Lin, B. Wielicki, L. Chambers, Y. Hu, and K.-M. Xu, "The Iris Hypothesis: A Negative or Positive Cloud Feedback?" *Journal of Climate*, 15 (2002): 3–7.

49. R. S. Lindzen and Y.-S. Choi, "On the Determination of Climate Feedbacks from ERBE Data," *Geophysical Research Letters*, 36 (2009): L16705, doi:10.1029/2009GL039628, www.agu.org/pubs/crossref/2009/2009GL039628.shtml.

50. K. E. Trenberth, J. T. Fasullo, Chris O'Dell, and T. Wong, "Relationships Between Tropical Sea Surface Temperature and Top-of-Atmosphere Radiation," *Geophysical Research Letters*, 37 (2010): L03702, doi:10.1029/2009GL042314. See also the commentary by Fasullo, Trenberth, and O'Dell, "Lindzen and Choi Unraveled," RealClimate, January 8, 2010, www.realclimate.org/index.php/ar chives/2010/01/lindzen-and-choi-unraveled/.

51. Trenberth and colleagues pointed out that the study also fundamentally misinterpreted the observations by assuming that any changes in cloud distribution automatically reflected a response to changes in sea surface temperature.

52. A. E. Dessler, "A Determination of the Cloud Feedback from Climate Variations Over the Past Decade," *Science*, 330 (2010): 1523–1527.

53. Journalist Paul Thacker reported in the January 2006 issue of the *New Republic* that Milloy had received substantial payments from big tobacco (Phillip Morris, specifically) for nearly two decades, as well as substantial money from Exxon-Mobil, while presenting himself as an independent expert. (According to Thacker's article, Fox News claimed to be unaware of Milloy's financial ties to Philip Morris, admitting that "any affiliation he had should have been disclosed.")

Industry funding of Milloy's organization, the Advancement of Sound Science Coalition, is discussed, for example, by Mooney in *Republican War Against Science*, 67–68.

54. The title was "awarded" in George Monbiot, "The Patron Saint of Charlatans," *Guardian*, September 23, 2008.

55. Richard Black, "Climate Documentary 'Broke Rules,'" British Broadcasting Corporation, July 21, 2008, http://news.bbc.co.uk/2/hi/7517509.stm.

56. Wunsch's expression of these opinions is described in the BBC piece cited in the preceding note. Wunsch is a skeptic, as all practicing scientists should be. It was Wunsch, for example, who correctly anticipated—as we will see later—that the claims by one research team of a dramatically weakening conveyor belt ocean circulation were premature. He is not, as the film seemed to imply, a denialist, however.

57. See, e.g., Richard Littlemore, "Pompous Prat Alert!" DeSmogBlog, April 4, 2009, www.desmogblog.com/pompous-prat-alert-viscount-monckton-tour.

58. In an open letter from Christopher Monckton to Senator John McCain (R-AZ), Monckton states in his biographical sketch that "his contribution to the IPCC's Fourth Assessment Report in 2007…earned him the status of Nobel Peace Laureate" (http://scienceandpublicpolicy.org/images/stories/papers/reprint/Letter_to_McCain.pdf, accessed August 11, 2011). As Littlemore notes in "Pompous Prat Alert!" ibid., "Monckton claimed to also be a Nobel winner because he had done such good work trying to undermine their effort. He even got a friend to melt down an old science experiment so they could fashion a little Nobel Prize pin, later presented to Monckton in a highly unofficial ceremony. (For the record, Monckton claims he deserves the accolade because he was a 'reviewer' of the IPCC report. The IPCC accepts reviews, unsolicited, from all parties…)."

59. See Leo Hickman, "Christopher Monckton Told to Stop Claiming He Is a Member of the Lords," *Guardian*, August 11, 2010, http://scienceblogs.com/deltoid/2008/10/monckton_has_a_gold_nobel_priz.php.

60. Stephen McIntyre, "Is Gavin Schmidt Honest?" climateaudit, October 29, 2005.

61. The report, entitled "Is the Surface Temperature Record Reliable," was published by the Heart-land Institute in March 2009 and is available electronically at http://wattsupwiththat.files.wordpress.com/2009/05/surfacestationsreport_spring09.pdf.

62. Matthew J. Menne, Claude N. Williams Jr., and Michael A. Palecki, "On the Reliability of the U.S. Surface Temperature Record," *Journal of Geophysical Research*, 115 (2010): D11108, doi:10.1029/2009JD013094, www1.ncdc.noaa.gov/pub/data/ushcn/v2/monthly/menne-etal2010.pdf. The summary conclusion by the authors was "we find no evidence that the CONUS [Continental U.S.] average temperature trends are inflated due to poor station siting."

63. Brad Stone, "The Hand That Controls the Sock Puppet Could Get Slapped," *New York Times*, July 16, 2007.

64. See, e.g., Tim Lambert, "Sock Puppet Guide," Deltoid, http://science blogs.com/deltoid/2005/08/sockpuppets.php; with regard to Fumento, see his "Fumento's Sidekick," http://scienceblogs.com/deltoid/2005/12/fumentosside-kick.php.

65. See, e.g., Hoggan and Littlemore, *Climate Cover-Up*, 96. Cybercast News Service is a project of the Media Research Center (MRC), which received over $400,000 from ExxonMobil between 1998 and 2009 (www.exxonse crets.org/html/orgfactsheet.php?id=110, accessed July 16, 2011). According to *Media Transparency*, it has received over $3 million from the Sarah Scaife foundation between 1998 and 2009 (http://mediamattersaction.org/transparency/organization/Media_Research_Center/funders, accessed July 16, 2011).

66. See "Kerry 'Unfit to Be Commander-in-Chief,' Say Former Military Colleagues," CNS, May 3, 2004.

67. ClimateDepot.com, July 13, 2010, "Climate Depot's Morano calls NASA's Hansen a 'wannabe Unabomber' for endorsing book urging 'ridding the world of industrial civilization' and 'razing cities' and 'blowing up dams,'" www.climatedepot.com/a/7355/a/4993/Time-for-Meds-NASA-scientist-James-Hansen-endorses-book-which-calls-for-ridding-the-world-of-Industrial-Civilization-ndash-Hansen-declares-author-has-it-rightthe-system-is-the -problem.

68. Clive Hamilton, "Silencing the Scientists: The Rise of Right-Wing Populism," *Our World*, March 2, 2011, http://ourworld.unu.edu/en/

silencing-the-scientists-the-rise-of-right-wing-
populism/#authordata.

69. Morano's position on the EPW staff was termi-
    nated in spring 2009 for reasons that have not
    been made public.

70. See the Sourcewatch.org pages on Committee
    for a Constructive Tomorrow, archived May 3,
    2011, www.sourcewatch.org/index.php?title=-
    Committee_for_a_Constructive_Tomorrow; and
    Climate Depot, archived May 3, 2011, www.
    sourcewatch.org/index.php?title=ClimateDepot.
    com.

71. Marc Morano, "ClimateDepot.com Launch Aims
    to Redefine Global Warming Reporting: Climate
    Clearinghouse to Challenge Mainstream Media's
    Eco-Reporting," ClimateDepot.com, April 6,
    2009.

72. Douglas Fisher and the Daily Climate, "Cyber
    Bullying Intensifies as Climate Data Ques-
    tioned," *Scientific American*, March 1, 2010.

73. Rachel Carson, *Silent Spring* (New York, Hough-
    ton Mifflin, 1962).

74. Christopher J. Bosso, *Pesticides and Politics:
    The Life Cycle of a Public Issue* (Pittsburgh,
    University of Pittsburgh Press, 1987), 116.

75. Ed Regis, "The Doomslayer," *Wired*, February
    1997.

76. World Scientists' Warning to Humanity, Union
    of Concerned Scientists, 1993.

77. For example, a joint statement of fifty-eight of
    the world's academies of science, including the
    United States and United Kingdom, concluded
    that "As human numbers further increase, the
    potential for irreversible changes of far-reaching
    magnitude also increases." "A Joint Statement
    by Fifty-Eight of the World's Scientific Acade-
    mies," *Population Summit of the World's Scien-
    tific Academies*, 1993, available through
    National Academies Press, www.nap.edu/open-
    book.php?record_id=9148&page=R2.

78. Joseph Palca, "Get-the-Lead-Out Guru Chal-
    lenged," *Science*, 253 (1991): 842–844.

79. A personal favorite of mine was his quip with
    regard to the plethora of climate change deniers
    in the petroleum geology industry: A "petroleum
    geologist's opinion on climate science is as good
    as a climate scientist's opinion on oil reserves."

80. U.S. National Academy of Sciences, "Understand-
    ing Climate Change: A Program for Action," The
    1975 US National Academy of Sciences/National
    Research Council Report; Thomas Peterson,
    William Connolley, and John Fleck, "The Myth
    of the 1970s Global Cooling Scientific Consen-
    sus," Bulletin of the American Meteorological
    Society, 89 (2008): 1325–1337.

81. S. I. Rasool and S. H. Schneider, "Atmospheric
    Carbon Dioxide and Aerosols: Effects of Large
    Increases on Global Climate," *Science*, 173
    (1971): 138–141, doi:10.1126/
    science.173.3992.138.

82. *Discover*, October 1989, 45–48.

83. Philip Shabecoff, "Global Warming Has Begun,
    Expert Tells Senate," *New York Times*, June 24,
    1988.

84. See Mark Bowen, *Censoring Science: Inside the
    Political Attack on Dr. James Hansen and the
    Truth of Global Warming* (New York, Dutton,
    2007).

85. Ibid.

86. Conservative Southern California congressman
    Dana Rohrabacher tried to pressure his em-
    ployer to fire him based on the specious allega-
    tions made by the GCC. He was at the receiving
    end of death threats credible enough that law
    enforcement was forced to step in.

87. Fred Pearce, "Climate Change Special: State of
    Denial," *New Scientist*, November 2006.

Discussion Questions

1. The issue of global climate change is championed by many and aggressively challenged by others. Why do you think this issue is so divisive? What are the primary arguments or data used by each side? Which data do you believe are most compelling, and why?
2. Some scientists have warned about human-induced global climate change for many years, and fear that our "window of opportunity" to effectively counteract this effect may have passed. What does this mean? What evidence points to this possibility?
3. What does the term "brownlash," coined by scientists Anne and Paul Erhlich, refer to? What example(s) of brownlash can you find?
4. Mann notes that one strategy of climate deniers is to encourage educators to "teach the controversy"—that is, to present the claims made on both sides of the issue. We see a similar approach taken by those who argue the theory of evolution. Do you think this strategy is appropriate? What are some of the potential negative impacts of this approach?

 Supporting Activities

1. Visit Michael Mann's web site (http://www.meteo.psu.edu/holocene/public_html/Mann/articles/articles.php) and select and read another of his articles on climate change.
2. Review comments or position papers regarding climate change from your congressional representatives in the House and Senate. What official stances, if any, have they taken on this topic?
3. Have members of your class conduct research on some of the various climate change "think tanks" that exist, including those listed within the Mann excerpt. What language is used? What scientific evidence is presented? What do you perceive to be the goals of the organization?
4. Look at the resources on NASA's Global Climate Change web site: http://climate.nasa.gov/. In particular, look at the Evidence categories under the "Facts" tab, and at the Interactive Features under the "Explore" tab.

 Additional Resources

1. *The Guardian* has published an excellent list of the top ten arguments made by global warming skeptics, along with concise responses to each argument. For a clear and easy-to-understand overview of the issues, see: http://www.theguardian.com/environment/climate-consensus-97-per-cent/2014/may/06/top-ten-global-warming-skeptic-arguments-debunked.
2. Watch the movie *An Inconvenient Truth*, for which former Vice-President Al Gore earned an Academy Award for Best Documentary in 2007. For contrast, read and view some of the many attempts to "debunk" climate change claims made in this film.
3. Learn more about the Kyoto Protocol on the United Nations Framework Convention on Climate Change site at: http://unfccc.int/kyoto_protocol/items/2830.php.
4. Watch the movie *Chasing Ice* (2013), winner of multiple awards, including an Emmy Award in 2014 (http://chasingice.com/). Using revolutionary time-lapse photography, the filmmakers were able to capture multiyear changes in the world's glaciers.

 **References**

Empire State Development. (2010). *NYSTAR*. Retrieved from http://esd.ny.gov/nystar/.

National Academy of Engineering and National Research Council, Committee on Technological Literacy. (2002). *Technically speaking: Why all Americans need to know more about technology*. Washington, DC: National Academies Press.

National Aeronautic and Space Administration (NASA). (2015). *Climate change: How do we know?* Retrieved from http://climate.nasa.gov/evidence/.

North Carolina Department of Commerce. (2015). *Board of science, technology, and innovation*. Retrieved from https://www.nccommerce.com/sti/board-of-science-technology-innovation.

Office of Science and Technology Policy (OSTP). (2015). *About PCAST*. Retrieved from https://www.whitehouse.gov/administration/eop/ostp/pcast/about.

Perrow, C. (1999). *Normal accidents: Living with high-risk technologies*. Princeton, NJ: Princeton University Press.

 Endnotes

1. The Office of Technology Assessment was a casualty of the "Contract with America" spearheaded by then-congressman Newt Gingrich (R-GA), which led to the discontinuance of a number of programs in an effort to cut government spending. All of the OTA reports, as well as historical information about the OTA, are available through a site maintained at Princeton University (http://www.princeton.edu/~ota/).

2. Technology assessment reports developed through the GAO's Center for Science, Technology, and Engineering are available through the U.S. Government Accountability Office web site: http://www.gao.gov/technology_assessment/key_reports.

3. Read more about the history and current initiatives of the Office of Science and Technology Policy at: http://www.ostp.gov/.

4. The North Carolina Office of Science, Technology & Innovation is housed within the state's Department of Commerce. More information about the NCSTI and its programs can be found at: https://www.nccommerce.com/sti/.

5. See, for example, the report *State Science and Technology Policy Advice: Issues, Opportunities, and Challenges: Summary of a National Convocation* (2008) published by the National Academies Press and available at: http://books.nap.edu/catalog.php?record_id=12160.

6. More information about the IPCC and full text of the IPCC reports are available online at: http://www.ipcc.ch/index.htm.

7. Browse by topic and read the transcripts of expert testimony provided by Brookings Institute experts at: http://www.brookings.edu/research/testimony. For another example from among the many organizations that conduct similar work, see the National Council for Science and the Environment site: http://www.ncseonline.org/.

8. National Research Council. (2002). *The age of expert testimony: Science in the courtroom*. Washington, DC: National Academies Press. Available: http://www.nap.edu/catalog/10272/the-age-of-expert-testimony-science-in-the-courtroom-report.

9. *Frontline:* "Interview with Clotaire Rapaille." (November 9, 2004). Available: http://www.pbs.org/wgbh/pages/frontline/shows/persuaders/interviews/rapaille.html.

Basic Human Needs: Rethinking Food, Water, and Shelter

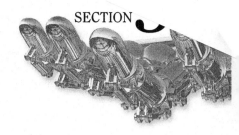

If you were asked what technologies have most affected your life, what would your answer be? Many of us give little thought to the technologies that are associated with food, water, and sanitation unless the work we do is related to providing those necessities. The technologies that enable us to have food, water, and shelter are largely invisible: running underground, tucked out of range of sight and smell, the hidden backdrop to the attractive displays of food on grocery store shelves. We forget or don't need to pay attention to the fact that these technologies are fundamental to existence as we know it. Access to clean water, sewage treatment, and improved living conditions are generally agreed to have resulted in greater reductions in mortality rates in the early part of the twentieth century than any other technology. These benefits are not universal, however. According to World Health Organization/UNICEF Joint Monitoring Programme statistics, over 2.5 billion people worldwide still lack access to improved sanitation facilities, and although safe drinking water is more accessible than ever before in history, there are still over 750 million people worldwide who don't have access to improved drinking water supplies (World Health Organization and UNICEF, 2014), with the largest percentages in sub-Saharan Africa and South Asia. The statistics on world hunger levels are just as staggering: the World Food Programme estimates that over 805 million people worldwide lack sufficient food to lead a healthy, active life—fully one in nine people on earth, including two-thirds of people in Asia. Children are particularly hard hit, with malnutrition causing 45% of deaths in children under five years of age, or some 3.1 million children each year (World Food Programme, 2015).

The problems of unsafe drinking water supplies and malnutrition may be challenging to contemplate from the relative comfort of our living and working conditions in the developed world. It's far easier to put these issues out of mind and get on to the business of our everyday lives. But the problems being experienced in many parts of the developing world may be closer to us than we think; recent articles highlight what may represent looming crises in water supplies and food production capacity that could affect developed and developing nations alike. For example, in California, which produces much of the nation's fruit, nut, and vegetable supply, a multiyear drought has resulted in heavier reliance on groundwater, a practice that is viewed as unsustainable (Gillis & Richter, 2015). By 2050 two factors are expected to exacerbate the environmental challenges presented by agriculture: a world population of nine billion people, and an overall higher level of prosperity that will drive an increased demand for meat and dairy products, coupled with greater use of food crops as energy feedstocks. Currently, about 55% of global food calories are used to directly feed humans, and 45% are used for animal feed and fuel. In the U.S. this ratio is 18% to 82%, respectively (Foley, 2015). The caloric value of grains allocated to animal feed and fuel has a very low return compared to the value of humans consuming the grains directly. For example, 100 calories of grain fed to animals yields just 12 calories of chicken and 3 calories of beef (Foley, 2015). When one considers the soil, water, fuel, and labor inputs required to grow the grain it becomes clear that this is a relatively unproductive use of food.

Population levels play an integral role in the broader problems of pollution and resource depletion, and all of these factors contribute to the increasing uncertainties about water, mineral, and food supplies. Simply put, the more of us there are, the more pollution and resource use results. Most of us are familiar with the fundamental principles of population growth, which often progresses exponentially, resulting in accelerating increases in population. In 1900, world population was estimated at 1.6 billion; by 1950 it had climbed to 2.5 billion, and in the 65-year span to 2015 world population nearly tripled, to 7.25 billion and counting.[1] Projections for the future vary, but U.S. Census Bureau data suggest a world population of nine billion by 2040 (Figure 1), in spite of the fact that overall population growth *rates* are declining (Figure 2). In addition, although consumption levels remain highly disproportionate across developed and developing nations, overall resource consumption per capita is growing. The United Nations predicts that total extraction of minerals, ores, fossil fuels, and biomass worldwide will more than double between 2015 and 2050 as a result of both population growth and increased prosperity (United Nations Environment Programme [UNEP], 2011). To achieve more sustainable levels of growth,

the UNEP promotes the concept of "decoupling" resource use from economic growth—in other words, increasing the rate of resource productivity, or doing more with less. There are a variety of ways this could be approached, including relying on technologies that function more efficiently.

In the early 1970s, scientists Paul Ehrlich, John Holdren, and Barry Commoner developed the so-called IPAT formula (Dimick, 2014) for measuring human impact on the environment, which states:

$$(I)mpact = (P)opulation \times (A)ffluence \times (T)echnology$$

This insightful formula, although difficult to quantify, nevertheless illustrates the multiplying effect of greater wealth, which is usually associated with greater consumption levels, and of technology. It also suggests the tempering effect that technology might have, if it is applied to the task of increasing resource productivity and/or to reducing environmental impacts of human activity. In fact, some authors suggest that the IPAT formula does not adequately capture the relationship between technology and the environment (Goklany, 2007).

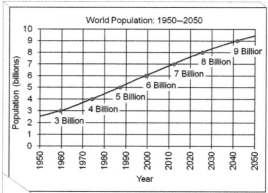

Figure 1. Population growth trends and predictions, 1950–2050 (U.S. Census Bureau, 2011).

Source: U.S. Census Bureau, International Data Base. June 2011 Update.

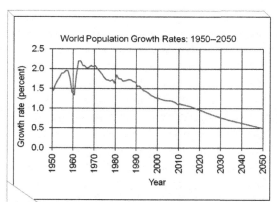

Figure 2. Population growth rates, 1950–2050 (U.S. Census Bureau, 2011).

Source: U.S. Census Bureau, International Data Base. June 2011 Update.

There are three main reactions to evidence about environmental crises linked to human technological activity. One reaction is to simply deny that the evidence (and, therefore, the problem) exists.[2] A second reaction is to look for technological solutions that apply human ingenuity to find ways around constraints or problems.[3] From this vantage point (a technocratic view), humans will always be able to devise strategies to address problems, given enough time, money, or attention. The third type of reaction calls for drastic changes in how we live, including doing without some of the amenities to which we have grown accustomed. As described in Section One of this book, the best-reasoned reaction is likely to be one that searches for multipronged responses by collecting data and then looking for both social *and* technical solutions to the documented problems. For example, the U.S. Geological Survey is currently monitoring water levels throughout the Ogallala High Plains Aquifer, a 174,000 sq mi underground reservoir in the middle section of the United States that is used to irrigate large swaths of productive farm land from South Dakota to Texas. It also supplies drinking water to over 80% of the people living within that region. Monitoring suggests that this water is being drawn (or *discharged*) at levels far higher than are capable of being recharged, with some estimates showing the reservoir depleted in as little as 25 years. With this knowledge in hand, policies can be adopted to better conserve water use in the region, and new technologies can be developed that enable significant reductions in the amount of water used for irrigation, commercial, and home use.

The technology of shelter is another area in which significant reductions in water, material, and energy use can be realized. Approaches to building design and construction vary considerably around the world, from thatched earthen huts to wood cottages to brick mansions, and everything in between. In the United States, the average size of homes has grown by a factor of 1.5 in the past 65 years, from less than 1,000 ft^2 in 1950 to nearly 2,600 ft^2 today (Adler, 2006; Podmolik, 2014). This has occurred even as the average family size has decreased. And although the buildings' *share* (residential and commercial structures combined) of total energy consumption in the United States has decreased in the past 30 years, it still represents approximately 40% of *total* national energy use (U.S. Department of Energy, 2015). This share is projected to increase as relative energy consumption in the industrial sector declines. Space heating, cooling, and ventilation make up approximately half of energy used in buildings (see Figure 3). Over the past decade, the share of energy used for space cooling, lighting, and refrigeration has dropped as a result of enhanced efficiencies in these technologies.

A growing number of standards, codes, and guidelines have emerged in the past 15 years that attempt to identify and promote the so-called "green" building strategies. These include the U.S. EPA ENERGY STAR New Homes standards, the Green Building Council's Leadership in Energy Efficient Design (LEED) standards, and

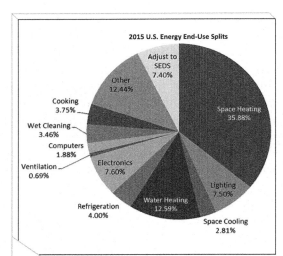

Figure 3. Breakdown of energy use in U.S. buildings. "Wet clean" includes dishwashers and washing machines; "Adjust" percentage accounts for discrepancies between data sources.

Source: Adapted from the U.S. Department of Energy, 2015.

efforts to reduce the overall size of homes.[4] An investigation into any of the green building standards reveals that they focus on sustainable use of materials; incorporating water saving measures; landscaping to enhance cooling and to prevent the need for irrigation; as well as measures to reduce energy use such as low-emissivity windows, insulation, and passive solar siting. The same strategies have been applied to commercial buildings as well, including the use of automated controls for lighting, heating, and cooling.

Clearly, the technologies associated with food, water, and shelter can and will play a tremendous role in determining the environmental footprint of an expanding number of humans on earth. As you read these selections we hope you gain a new appreciation for the technologies that help us meet our basic needs, and identify ways that the basic needs of the world's citizens can be met more efficiently and effectively.

1908 Presidential Address by Newton C. Blanchard

The 1908 Conference of the National Governors Association (NGA) was the first of its kind, called by then-president Theodore Roosevelt on the advice of the Inland Waterways Commission. The Conference was attended by members of Congress, the Supreme Court, conservation experts, federal officials, and all but twelve governors. At the time there were 46 states and 2 territories (Arizona and New Mexico, which became states in 1912). The full title for the meeting was the Conference on the Conservation of Natural Resources. In his opening address, Roosevelt talked about conservation as a national duty. The 3-day meeting included sessions on mineral, land, and water resources.

In 1935, Congress passed Public Law 74–46, stating "the wastage of soil and moisture resources on farm, grazing, and forest lands . . . is a menace to the national welfare," and directing the Secretary of Agriculture to establish the Soil Conservation Service (SCS) as a permanent component of the United States Department of Agriculture (USDA). Congress changed the name to the Natural Resources Conservation Service (NRCS) in 1994 to more accurately reflect the expanded scope of the agency (USDA, 2015, para. 2). The policy recommendations made by the governors at the 1908 Conference were that each state should appoint a commission on the conservation of natural resources and that every state should establish an office of the NRCS, in addition to departments of natural resources or similar agencies.

Newton Crain Blanchard was a Democratic governor of the State of Louisiana from 1904 to 1908. He earned a law degree from Tulane University in 1870, and entered local politics in 1876. His political career included serving as a member of the U.S. House of Representatives from 1881 to 1894; as a U.S. Senator from 1893 to 1897; and as an associate justice of the Louisiana Supreme Court from 1897 to 1903. At the 1908 conference, Blanchard was chosen as chairman of the committee of governors, which included the other signatories to this presidential address.

Fifth Session

The Fifth Session of the Conference was called to order at 10 o'clock a.m. on May 15, 1908, in the East Room of the White House, by the President of the United States.

Governor BLANCHARD: On behalf of the Committee on Resolutions I have a report to make, and with your permission, Mr. President, I will make it from the platform.

The PRESIDENT: Kindly step to the platform, Governor.

Governor BLANCHARD: Mr. President, inasmuch as I am the organ of a Committee of this Conference I trust the bell—the bell calling time on speakers—invisible to the sense of sight, but manifesting itself always to the sense of hearing, will be held in reserve while I present the report of the Committee, and while I am giving the reasons of the Committee for their action.

The PRESIDENT: If not held in reserve you may disregard it.

Governor BLANCHARD: Mr. President, and Gentlemen of the Conference, on behalf of your Committee on Resolutions I beg to present the following declaration of views and recommendations:

Declaration

We, the Governors of the States and Territories of the United States of America, in Conference assembled, do hereby declare the conviction that the great prosperity of our country rests upon the abundant resources of the land chosen by our forefathers for their homes and where they laid the foundation of this great Nation.

We look upon these resources as a heritage to be made use of in establishing and promoting the comfort, prosperity, and happiness of the American People, but not to be wasted, deteriorated, or needlessly destroyed.

We agree that our country's future is involved in this; that the great natural resources supply the material basis on which our civilization must continue to depend, and on which the pertuity of the Nation itself rests.

We agree, in the light of facts brought to our knowledge and from information received from sources which we can not doubt, that this material basis is threatened with exhaustion. Even as each succeeding generation from the birth of the Nation has performed its part in promoting the progress and development of the Republic, so de we in this generation recognize it as a high duty to perform our part; and this duty in large degree lies in the adoption of measures for the conservation of the natural wealth of the country. [Applause]

We declare our firm conviction that this conservation of our natural resources is a subject of transcendent importance, which should engage unremittingly the attention of the Nation, the States, and the People in earnest cooperation. These natural resources include the land on which we live and which yields our food; the living waters which fertilize the soil, supply power, and form great avenues of commerce; the forests which yield the materials for our homes, prevent erosion of the soil, and conserve the navigation and other uses of our steams; and the minerals which form the basis of our industrial life, and supply us with heat, light, and power.

We agree that the land should be so used that erosion and soil-wash shall cease; that

there should be reclamation of arid and semi-arid regions by means of irrigation, and of swamp and overflowed regions by means of drainage; that the waters should be so conserved and used as to promote navigation, to enable the arid regions to be reclaimed by irrigation, and to develop power in the interests of the People; that the forests which regulate our rivers, support our industries, and promote the fertility and productiveness of the soil should be preserved and perpetuated; that the minerals found so abundantly beneath the surface should be so used as to prolong their utility; that the beauty, healthfulness, and habitability of our country should be preserved and increased; that the sources of national wealth exist for the benefit of the People, and that monopoly thereof should not be tolerated. [Applause]

We commend the wise forethought of the President in sounding the note of warning as to the waste and exhaustion of the natural resources of the country, and signify our high appreciation of his action in calling this Conference to consider the same and to seek remedies therefor through cooperation of the Nation and the States. [Applause]

We agree that this cooperation should find expression in suitable action by the Congress within the limits of and coextensive with the national jurisdiction of the subject, and, complementary thereto, by the legislatures of the several States within the limits of and coextensive with their jurisdiction.

We declare the conviction that in the use of the natural resources our independent States are interdependent and bound together by ties of mutual benefits, responsibilities and duties. [Applause]

We agree in the wisdom of future conferences between the President, Members of Congress, and the Governors of States on the conservation of our natural resources with a view of continued cooperation and action on the lines suggested; and to this end we advise that from time to time, as in his judgment may seem wise, the President call the Governors of the States and Members of Congress and other into conference.

We agree that further action is advisable to ascertain the present condition of our natural resources and to promote the conservation of the same; and to that end we recommend the appointment by each State of Commission on the Conservation of Natural Resources, to cooperate with each other and with any similar commission of the Federal Government. [Great applause]

We urge the continuation and extension of forest policies adapted to secure the husbanding and renewal of our diminishing timber supply, the prevention of soil erosion, the protection of headwaters, and the maintenance of the purity and navigability of our streams. We recognize that the private ownership of forest lands entails responsibilities in the interests of all the People, and we favor the enactment of laws of looking to the protection and replacement of privately owned forests. [Applause]

We recognize in our waters a most valuable asset of the People of the United States, and we recommend the enactment of laws looking to the conservation of water resources for irrigation, water supply, power, and navigation, to the end that navigable and source streams may be brought under complete control and fully utilized for every purpose. We especially urge on the Federal Congress the immediate adoption of a wise, active, and thorough waterway policy, providing for the prompt improvement of our streams and the conservation of their watersheds required for the uses of commerce and the protection of the interests of our People. [Applause]

We recommend the enactment of laws looking to the prevention of waste in the mining and extraction of coal, oil, gas, and other minerals with a view to their wise conservation for the use of the People, and to the protection of human life in the mines. [Applause]

Let us conserve the foundations of our prosperity. [Great applause]

Respectfully submitted,
NEWTON C. BLANCHARD, Louisiana, Chairman
JOHN F. FORT, New Jersey
J. O. DAVIDSON, Wisconsin
JOHN C. CUTLER, Utah
M. F. ANSEL, South Carolina

Attest:

W J McGEE, Secretary Inland Waterways Commission, Recording Secretary of the Conference

Statement by Governor Blanchard

Mr. President, it has been observed, doubtless, that the paper submitted by the Committee on Resolutions, as the result of its labors, is general in character, as broad, liberal, and catholic as it was possible to make it, and of a scope purely national.

The Essential Documents of American History was compiled by Norman P. Desmarais and James H. McGovern of Providence College.

Discussion Questions

1. Are you surprised to learn that in 1908 these governors stated that our natural resources were "threatened with exhaustion?"
2. What did the governors mean when they declared that "monopoly [of our natural resources] should not be tolerated?"
3. The governors' address included a recommendation that arid lands should be reclaimed by means of irrigation, and swamps by means of drainage. For what reasons might these recommendations be eschewed today?

 Supporting Activities

1. Read the opening address made by President Roosevelt at the 1908 conference, available in full text at: http://www.nga.org/files/live/sites/NGA/files/pdf/PS1908Roosevelt.pdf.
2. If possible, find examples of statements made by your state's current governor that address conservation or natural resource preservation. Contrast the language used with that contained in the 1908 address.

 Additional Resources

1. Look at the goals, function, and programs of the U.S. Bureau of Land Management (BLM). What can you learn about current policies related to land, minerals, and water on federal lands?
2. Visit the web site of the Nature Conservancy (http://www.nature.org/) to learn more about the conservation actions being taken by this international nongovernmental organization (NGO).

When the Rivers Run Dry

Water use is one of the hidden impacts of globalization. As author Fred Pearce pointed out in this excerpt, when you purchase a shirt made of cotton grown in Pakistan you are unwittingly influencing the hydrology of the Pakistani region. Water used to grow or manufacture goods in one area that are then exported to another area has been termed "virtual water," because although the water itself is not transferred, its use as embodied in the goods that are exported has the same effect. The United States is the biggest "exporter" of virtual water; countries in the Middle East are among the major importers of virtual water.

As knowledge about the importance of better management of our freshwater supplies grows, many individuals have instituted water-saving measures in their homes and communities have enacted water conservation policies. Although helpful and important, conservation in homes and businesses pales in comparison to water use for irrigation; the volume of water needed for the production of crops is staggering, as Pearce noted. To meet the need for water to irrigate and to supply municipalities, local, and federal governments pursue new and larger water projects, generally drawn from existing surface water sources such as rivers and lakes. Several large-scale projects underway or proposed in China, India, Russia, and Canada are described in this excerpt.

Large-scale water projects such as these illustrate the "technological hubris" that underlies some of the most extravagant of the technological optimists' utopian solutions. With a selective myopia that is often typical of the technocratic approach, the attention in these projects is focused simply on moving water, without considering the potential ecological impacts of large-scale changes to the natural systems. Beyond the sheer costs and engineering challenges posed by these projects are the unknown effects of, for instance, intermingling sewage supplies across regions or decreasing water levels in existing waterways. Furthermore, with the potential for meteorological changes in the amount of natural precipitation received due to global climate change, the long-term viability of these engineered waterways is uncertain. Recent photos of California's large lakes, including Shasta, Oroville, Folsom, and Mead, illustrate the plight of large-scale water systems in the face of prolonged drought.[5]

Linked to the issue of water use is the problem of how we handle human organic waste. Incredibly, in many parts of the world we pull water for our domestic use, including drinking water, from the same surface waters into which we then discharge treated and untreated sewage waste. For example, in what it hailed as a "landmark settlement," the USEPA in 2007 reached an agreement with the Allegheny County (PA) Sanitary Authority to reduce the amount of raw sewage that was flowing into surface waterways from Pittsburgh, Pennsylvania and 82 surrounding municipalities. The multiyear plan to upgrade sewage treatment facilities that was part of that settlement was designed to reduce the estimated 22 *billion* gallons of raw sewage that were being discharged annually into Pittsburgh area waterways.[6]

Fred Pearce, who calls water "the defining crisis of the twenty-first century," is a science writer who was born and educated in the United Kingdom. He is the author of fourteen books focused on environmental topics, including *The Land Grabbers: The New Fight over Who Owns the Earth* (2014), *Confessions of an Eco-Sinner: Tracking Down the Sources of My Stuff* (2008) and *With Speed and Violence: Why Scientists Fear Tipping Points in Climate Change* (2007). Pearce has served as an environmental consultant for the magazine *New Scientist* and has written for a number of other publications, including *Time* and *Popular Science*.

The Human Sponge

By Fred Pearce

Few of us realize how much water it takes to get us through the day. On average, we drink no more than a gallon and a half of the stuff. Including water for washing and for flushing the toilet, we use only about 40 gallons each. In some countries suburban lawn sprinklers, swimming pools, and sundry outdoor uses can double that figure. Typical per capita water use in suburban Australia is about 90 gallons, and in the United States around 100 gallons. There are exceptions, though. One suburban household in Orange County, Florida, was billed for 4.1 million gallons in a single year, or more than 10,400 gallons a day. Nobody knows how they got through that much.

We can all save water in the home. But as laudable as it is to take a shower rather than a bath and turn off the faucet while brushing our teeth, we shouldn't get hold of the idea that regular domestic water use is what is really emptying the world's rivers. Manufacturing the goods that we fill our homes with consumes a certain amount, but that's not the real story either. It is only when we add in the water needed to grow what we eat and drink that the numbers really begin to soar.

Get your head around a few of these numbers, if you can. They are mind-boggling. It takes between 250 and 650 gallons of water to grow a pound of rice. That is more water than many households use in a week. For just a bag of rice. Keep going. It takes 130 gallons to grow a pound of wheat and 65 gallons for a pound of potatoes. And when you start feeding grain to livestock for animal products such as meat and milk, the numbers become yet more startling. It takes 3000 gallons to grow the feed for enough cow to make a quarter-pound hamburger, and between 500 and 1000 gallons for that cow to fill its udders with a quart of milk. Cheese? That takes about 650 gallons for a pound of cheddar or brie or camembert.

And if you think your shopping cart is getting a little bulky at this point, maybe you should leave that 1-pound box of sugar on the shelf. It took up to 400 gallons to produce. And the 1-pound jar of coffee tips the scales at 2650 gallons—or 10 tons—of water. Imagine taking *that* home from the store.

Turn these statistics into meal portions and you come up with more than 25 gallons for a portion of rice, 40 gallons for the bread in a sandwich or a serving of toast, 130 gallons for a two-egg omelet or a mixed salad, 265 gallons for a glass of milk, 400 gallons for an ice cream, 530 gallons for a pork chop, 800 gallons for a hamburger, and 1320 gallons for a small steak. And if you have a sweet tooth, so much the worse: every teaspoonful of sugar in your coffee requires 50 cups of water to grow. Which is a lot, but not as much as the 37 gallons of water (or 592 cups) needed to grow the coffee itself. Prefer alcohol? A glass of wine or beer with dinner requires another 66 gallons, and a glass of brandy afterward takes a staggering 530 gallons.

We are all used to reading detailed technical information about the nutritional content of most food. Maybe it is time that we were given some clues as to how much water it took to grow and process the food. As the world's rivers run dry, it matters.

I figure that as a typical meat-eating, beer-swilling, milk-guzzling Westerner, I consume as much as a hundred times my own weight in water every day. Hats off, then, to my vegetarian daughter, who gets by with about half that. It's time, surely, to go out and preach the gospel of water conservation. But don't buy one of those jokey T-shirts advertised on the Internet with slogans like "Save water, bathe with a friend." Good message, but you could fill roughly twenty-five bathtubs with the water needed to grow the 9 ounces of cotton needed to make the shirt. It gives a whole new meaning to the wet T-shirt contest.

Let's do the annual audit. I probably drink only about 265 gallons of water—that's one ton or 1.3 cubic yards—in a whole year. Around the home I probably use between 50 and 100 tons. But growing the crops to feed and clothe me for a year must take between 1500 and 2000 tons—more than half the contents of an Olympic-size swimming pool.

Where does all that water come from? In England, where I live, most homegrown crops are watered by rain. So the water is at least cheap. But remember that a lot of the food consumed in Britain, and all the cotton, is imported. And when the water to grow crops is collected from rivers or pumped from underground, as it is in much of the world, it is increasingly expensive, and its diversion to fields is increasingly likely to deprive someone else of water and to empty rivers and underground water reserves. And when the rivers are running low, it is ever more likely that the water simply will not be there to grow the crops at all.

The water "footprint" of Western countries on the rest of the world deserves to become a serious issue. Whenever you buy a T-shirt made of Pakistani cotton, eat Thai rice, or drink coffee from Central America, you are influencing the hydrology of those regions—taking a share of the Indus River, the Mekong River, or the Costa Rican rains. You may be helping rivers run dry.

Economists call the water involved in the growing and manufacture of products traded around the world "virtual water." In this terminology, every ton of wheat arriving at a dockside carries with it in virtual form the thousand tons of water needed to grow it. The global virtual-water trade is estimated to be around 800 million acre-feet a year, or twenty Nile Rivers. Of that, two thirds is in a huge range of crops, from grains to vegetable oil, sugar to cotton; a quarter is in meat and dairy products; and just a tenth is in industrial products. That means that nearly a tenth of all the water used in raising crops goes into the international virtual-water trade. This trade "moves water in volumes and over distances beyond the wildest imaginings of water engineers," says Tony Allan, of the School of Oriental and African Studies in London, who invented the term "virtual water."

The biggest net exporter of virtual water is the United States. It exports around a third of all the water it withdraws from the natural environment. Much of that is in grains, either directly or via meat. The United States is emptying critical underground water reserves, such as those beneath the High Plains, to grow grain for export. It also exports an amazing 80 million acre-feet of virtual water in beef. Other major exporters of virtual water include Canada (grain), Australia (cotton and sugar), Argentina (beef), and Thailand (rice).

Major importers of virtual water include Japan and the European Union. Few of these countries are short of water, so there are ethical questions about how much they should be doing this. But for other importers, virtual water is a vital lifeline. Iran, Egypt, and Algeria could starve without it; likewise water-stressed Jordan, which effectively imports between 80 and

90 percent of its water in the form of food. "The Middle East ran out of water some years ago. It is the first major region to do so in the history of the world," says Allan. He estimates that more water flows into the Middle East each year as a result of imports of virtual water than flows down the Nile.

While many nations relieve their water shortages by importing virtual water, some exacerbate their problems by exporting it. Israel and arid southern Spain both export water in tomatoes, Ethiopia in coffee. Mexico's virtual-water exports are emptying its largest water body, Lake Chapala, which is the main source of water for its second city, Guadalajara.

Many cotton-growing countries provide a vivid example of this perverse water trade. Cotton grows best in hot lands with year-round sun. Deserts, in other words. Old European colonies and protectorates such as Egypt, Sudan, and Pakistan still empty the Nile and the Indus for cotton-growing, as they did when Britain ruled and Lancashire cotton mills had to be supplied. When Russia transformed the deserts of Central Asia into a vast cotton plantation, it sowed the seeds of the destruction of the Aral Sea. Most of the missing water for the shriveling sea has in effect been exported over the past half-century in the form of virtual water that continues to clothe the Soviet Union.

Some analysts say that globally, the virtual-water trade significantly reduces water demand for growing crops. It enables farmers to grow crops where water requirements are less, they say. But this is mainly because the biggest trade in virtual water is the export of wheat and corn from temperate lands like the United States and Canada to hotter lands where the same crops would require more water. But for many other crops, such as cotton and sugar, the trade in virtual water looks like terribly bad business for the exporters.

Pakistan consumes more than 40 million acre-feet of water a year from the Indus River—almost a third of the river's total flow and enough to prevent any water from reaching the Arabian Sea—in order to grow cotton. How much sense does that make? And what logic is there in the United States pumping out the High Plains aquifer to add to a global grain glut? Whatever the virtues of the global trade in virtual water, the practice lies at the heart of some of the most intractable hydrological crises on the planet.

Taking the Water to the People

By Fred Pearce

It is the world's largest civil engineering project and aims to remake the natural hydrology of the world's most heavily populated nation. But it began rather inauspiciously, one morning in Beijing in April 2003, when the city's vice mayor, Niu Youcheng, accepted a bottle from a visiting local official. The bottle was filled with water from a reservoir on the Yangtze River 800 miles away in the south of the country. Its handover signaled the start of China's south-to-north transfer project, which is intended to be the ultimate solution to the desiccation of the Yellow River and the North China plain.

Some people see the scheme as an exercise in engineering hubris and a disaster in the making. But Chinese leaders say it is a logical extension of the grand schemes of great societies down the ages to remake their hydrology. Ancient Mesopotamia and Egypt both harnessed their rivers to feed their people. The Romans were famous for their aqueducts. Persian empires were built around laboriously excavated tunnels that delivered water from deep underground. But even at their greatest extent, these ancient works were mild modifications to natural drainage patterns. Today's engineers have bigger ambitions, diverting entire rivers onto distant plains. And China's scheme is the most ambitious ever to have got under way. It will, we are told, enable the Middle Kingdom to continue feeding itself as it has done for thousands of years. Maybe.

The south-to-north scheme will divert part of the flow of the Yangtze, the world's fourth biggest river, to replenish the dried-up Yellow River and the tens of millions of people in megacities that rely on it. The price tag is $60 billion, more than twice the cost of even Colonel Qaddafi's fantasy-world Great Manmade River Project. And it aims to deliver twenty times more water than Qaddafi's pipe dream.

Some of the water will come quite soon. In Beijing, people should be drinking Yangtze water regularly in 2007. Certainly it will be there in time to fill the swimming pools and pretty the streets with fountains as Beijing hosts the Olympic Games in 2008. Some of the water will take longer to get there, but within twenty years, say the planners, the project should annually be siphoning north three times as much water as England consumes in a year. The costs may be colossal, but China says the south-to-north project cannot be allowed to fail.

The project is actually three separate diversions. Two of them are already under construction. The first one will enlarge the existing Danjiangkou reservoir on the Han River, a major tributary of the Yangtze, and take its water north. The reservoir is already Asia's widest artificial expanse of water; enlargement will flood another 140 square miles and displace a quarter of a million more people. The canal north will be 200 feet wide and as long as France. As it crosses China's crowded plains, it will span 500 roads and 120 rail lines and tunnel beneath the Yellow River through a giant inverted siphon.

The second will take water from near the Yangtze's mouth across Shandong Province on the North China plain and deliver it to the megacity of Tianjin, which has suffered chronic

es since the 1990s. Part of it will
?ear-old Grand Canal, which was
?est artificial river in preindus-
...s and the first to have lock gates. Today
it is a sump for effluent from China's burgeoning industry, but there are plans to clean it up.

The third, western route is the most ambitious. It alone is expected to cost $36 billion. It
will take water from the Yangtze headwaters
amid the glaciers of Tibet and push it through
tunnels up to 65 miles long into the headwaters
of the Yellow River. There is no firm route yet,
but several tributaries will be tapped, and there
is talk of building the world's highest dam. This
route will be the only one to deliver water directly into the Yellow River. The other two are
intended to relieve pressure on the river by supplying water for cities and farms on the North
China plain that currently take 8 million acre-
feet a year from the river. But altogether the
plan is to send some 36 million acre-feet of water a year from the Yangtze to northern China.

China's leaders love huge projects. Modernism lives on in their souls. With the World Bank
claiming that China has already lost $14 billion
in industrial production from water shortages,
the scheme seems to them like a sound investment. But even as the first earth was dug, fears
were growing about escalating costs. And academics and water planners I met in Beijing in
2004 raised a range of concerns.

The middle route, they said, could cause an
ecological crisis on the Han River, taking a third
of its water and worsening an already serious
pollution problem. Wuhan City, a busy river
port with a population of 3 million, could become a cesspit overnight. What, they wondered,
about the cost of relocating refugees from the
Danjiangkou reservoir? Could the filthy and de-
crepit Grand Canal really be cleared of pollution? Is the engineering intended for Tibet more
than a figment of someone's imagination? And
since China is trying to move to more realistic

pricing for water, won't the transferred water be
far too expensive for the intended recipients
to buy?

China has a vibrant antidam community,
which honed its arguments over the Three
Gorges project. It sees the scheme as another
megalomaniacal folly and wants the billions to
be spent instead on improving Chinese water
efficiency. Ma Jun, a journalist and campaigner
in the mold of Dai Qing, says, "Chinese factories
use ten times more water than most developed
countries to produce the same products. Chinese irrigation uses twice as much." Even
old-fashioned Chinese toilets use much more
water than their Western counterparts. The
United States has been able to grow its economy
for the past thirty years without increasing water use, he says, and so can China. And in the
long run, he argues, it would be easier to shift
the focus of Chinese food production from the
northern plains to the south—where the
water is.

But the antidam contingent lost the war
over Three Gorges, and they seem set to lose
this one too. Already China's scheme is being
taken as a template for an even larger project in
the world's second most populous nation, India.
During 2003, as Chinese earthmovers embarked
on their south-to-north project, politicians in
Delhi were lining up to back plans for what is
known as the River Interlinking Project. It
would redraw the hydrological map of India in a
quite breathtaking way by harnessing the great
monsoon rivers of the north, like the Ganges
and the Brahmaputra, and sending their water
south and west to the parched lands where the
droughts are worst and the underground water
reserves are sinking fastest.

The Indian scheme is far more complex than
the Chinese plan. It would build dozens of
large dams and hundreds of miles of canals to
link fourteen northern rivers that drain the

Himalayas. And it would pump their waters south along 1000 miles of canals, aqueducts, and tunnels and through 300 reservoirs to fill a second network, linking the seventeen major rivers of the country's arid south. These rivers include the Godavari, the Krishna, and the Cauvery, each of which has been diminished by heavy overabstraction for irrigation.

The transfer would involve moving 38 million acre-feet a year, very similar in scale to China's scheme. But with so many more rivers and links, the price tag would be two to three times higher, with official estimates ranging from $112 billion to $200 billion, or around 40 percent of the country's GDP. While the Chinese project sounds doable, whatever the pitfalls, the Indian scheme sounds like a great leap into the unknown.

Even so, the River Interlinking Project did not come out of nowhere. It has a long history. The legendary British engineer Sir Arthur Cotton first conceived of something similar in the mid-nineteenth century as a means of improving the country's transportation by linking rivers with canals. His scheme was dashed when the British decided to build railroads instead. But the fantasy never quite died. For a while it was poetically described as providing India with a "garland of canals." But it took a drought across India in the summer of 2002 to bring the idea back to the fore.

The specter of famine returning to India after more than a decade in which the country has had food to spare was a profound shock. Southern India, like northern China, seems to be on the verge of a hydrological crisis. And with water tables tumbling and the country's population predicted to increase by 50 percent within the next half-century, overtaking China to reach a staggering 1.5 billion people, there is a sense that a hydrological holocaust might not be far away. Surely, say many Indian politicians, the only answer is to replumb the nation.

In 2003, the president and prime minister, most state governments, and the Supreme Court—agencies that in India's complex democratic system spend much of their time in internecine warfare—united to promote the River Interlinking Project. Government scientists said it could provide enough water to increase irrigated farmland by more than 50 percent and to power 34,000 megawatts of hydroelectric capacity. On closer inspection, though, the blueprints show that as much as a third of this power would be needed for pumping water around the scheme's network of canals and tunnels.

Will it happen? There are plenty of objections. The rampant pollution in most northern rivers would result in a grand interchange of sewage down the canals. One estimate holds that an area of land the size of Cyprus would have to be flooded for the various structures, leaving 3 million people homeless. Even engineers in the states that apparently stand to gain the most are skeptical. Karnataka, one of the driest, is also one of the highest—often more than 2000 feet above sea level. Engineers there doubt that the water from the north would ever reach them.

A former head of the national water ministry, Ramaswarmy Iyer, calls the whole idea "technological hubris." India already has half-completed water projects that have cost billions of dollars, which should be finished first. He says that across arid India, three quarters of the monsoon rains still evade dams and wash into the sea. Better to try to collect that rain as it falls onto fields than to try to carry water across the country. "The answer is to harvest our rain better," he says.

Bangladesh objects too. It sits downstream of India on both the Ganges and the Brahmaputra. Bangladesh may fear the rivers' monsoon floods in summer, but it also relies on those rivers to irrigate its crops and recharge underground aquifers. It complained angrily in 1974 when India built the Farakka barrage on the Ganges close to the border, diverting valuable dry-season water flows into Indian irrigation canals. It blames the barrage for dried-up fields, disease, and a salty invasion of seawater into the Sunderbans mangrove swamps in the Ganges delta. In 1996, India promised not to reduce the flow further. Yet now it is talking about doing precisely that.

Like China, India is in a bullish mood at present, with annual economic growth at around 8 percent. Its engineers have always thought big, and now its politicians want to turn their dreams into reality. So it could happen. It is at least possible that within two decades, the two most populous countries in the world—with the two fastest-growing economies—will have spent a quarter of a trillion dollars on redirecting their rivers and remaking their hydrology.

And the urge to build big seems to be spreading. Spain spent 2003 lobbying the European Union to foot most of the $10 billion bill for its own north-to-south project. It wanted to build a 600-mile canal from the Ebro, the biggest river in the wet north of the country, taking as much as three quarters of its water to Murcia and Almería in the country's increasingly arid south. There, it was earmarked to irrigate more than a million acres of desert where spaghetti westerns were once filmed and to water golf courses at new tourist resorts.

The project bit the dust late in 2004, when a general election brought in a new government that had listened to critics of the plan, like Pedro Arrojo-Aguda, an economist from the University of Zaragoza. "It's clearly crazy," he told me just before the plug was pulled. For one thing, he said, it would wreck the Ebro delta. The 12-mile tongue of sandbanks, lagoons, and reed beds protruding into the Mediterranean is one of southern Europe's most important

wetland nature reserves as well as Spain's largest rice-growing area and an important fish nursery. This land of flamingos and paella is already starved of water and silt from the river by upstream dams. The sea is eroding it. The transfer would seal its death warrant, he said. And for what? The golf courses and tourist resorts might be willing to pay for the new water, but the farmers could never pay. "The water will cost more than a dollar for 265 gallons—twice the current cost of the desalination of seawater. By the time it is delivered, few farmers will want it," Arrojo-Aguda said.

For Spaniards like Arrojo-Aguda, the Ebro transfer seems like a return to the bad old days of General Franco, the Fascist dictator who gave Spain more dams than any other similar-sized country. Perhaps that is why, in the heady days of their campaign, angry villagers from valleys in the Pyrenees that would be flooded for new dams joined irate farmers from the Ebro delta, city environmentalists, and political activists in probably the first ever protest to go to Brussels demanding that the EU close its purse. The new government, sworn in in 2004, heard the protests, assessed the economics, and opted to build desalination plants instead. But the project still has powerful backers and is only one general election away from a revival. And the drought that spread across southern Spain in the summer of 2005, reputedly the worst in half a century, brought renewed calls for consideration of the transfer plan.

Europe has other such schemes in the pipeline. The Greek government has a plan to take water out of the country's largest west-flowing river, the Acheloos, and pump it through a tunnel to irrigate tobacco fields on the eastern plains. It would partly destroy the Messolonghi delta, one of the last surviving untouched deltas on the Mediterranean.

In Britain, government agencies have proposed using the eighteenth-century canal system, dug to ship industrial goods around be- fore the age of the railroads, to create a national water grid able to ship water from the wet north and west to the drier south and east. And Lon- don's water engineers have long dreamed of tap- ping the Severn River as it runs out of Wales and through the West Country to pump its wa- ter over the Cotswold hills and into the head- waters of the Thames.

Back in the days of heroic Soviet engineering, there was a plan to tap great north-flowing riv- ers of Siberia like the Ob and the Yenisei and send their water south to refill the canals of the Central Asian cotton industry, and just possibly to help revive the Aral Sea. First proposed by the czars back in the late nineteenth century and revived by Stalin in the 1930s, the idea be- came a serious proposition in the early 1980s. Thousands of scientists and engineers were re- cruited to help bring it about. But in the end it fell foul of a mixture of romantic Russian na- tionalists who did not want to give up their riv- ers to Muslim states far to the south and the reformist pragmatism of Soviet leader Mikhail Gorbachev.

But you cannot keep a bad megaproject down. In 2003, Igor Zonn, the director of Soyu- zvodproject, a Russian government agency in charge of water management and ecology, told me, "We are beginning to revise the old project plans. The old material has to be gathered from more than three hundred institutes." It had won vocal support from ambitious politicians like Moscow's mayor, Yuri Luzhkov, a possible suc- cessor to Vladimir Putin as Russian president. If for no other reason, that link makes it a project to be taken seriously again.

The proposal would be roughly equivalent to irrigating Mexico from the Great Lakes, or Spain from the Danube. It would drive a 650-foot-wide canal southward for some 1500 miles, from where the Ob and the Irtysh meet,

to replenish the Amu Darya and Syr Darya riv- ers near the Aral Sea. The canal, according to blueprints shown to me by Russian scientists, would carry 22 million acre-feet of water a year. Though this is just 7 percent of the Ob's flow, it would be equivalent to half the natural flow of the two Central Asian rivers into the Aral Sea.

Down among the "stans," they have always loved the idea. "Although it seems ambitious, it appears to be the only tangible solution to the ecological and other problems caused by the drying of the Aral Sea," says Abdukhalil Razzakov, of the Tashkent State Economic Uni- versity in Uzbekistan. And early in 2004, Luzh- kov visited Kazakhstan to promote the plan. He said that this time around, there would be no handouts from Moscow. Central Asia would have to pay a realistic price for the water. But behind the scenes, Moscow is starting to see the scheme as one of the water projects that could rebuild its political and economic power in the region.

Madness? Certainly. But as Nikita Glazovsky, a leading Russian geographer and former deputy environment minister under Boris Yeltsin, told me when we met in Moscow in 2001, the region's engineers "still find it easier to divert rivers than to stop inefficient irrigation."

In North America, the parched Western states of America have their eyes on Canada's water. It is not very surprising. Canada has some of the largest rivers in the world. When the spring snowmelt gets going, around a tenth of all the water in all the rivers in the world is gushing through British Columbia and Yukon and the Northwest Territories into the Pacific and Arctic oceans. And the Great Lakes, on the border be- tween the two countries, are one of the largest freshwater reserves on the planet. Meanwhile, only a few hundred miles to the south, the High Plains are parched, the reservoirs in the

Colorado River sit two thirds empty, and California imposes restrictions on its lawn sprinklers.

In 2003, President George W. Bush raised hackles in Canada by calling for talks about U.S. private companies buying some of Canada's water to supply cities in the American West. It could become the ultimate fulfillment of the old maxim that "water flows uphill to money." Exactly how the water would be shifted economically was not made clear. Bush was less interested in the engineering than in establishing that NAFTA, the North American Free Trade Agreement, could cover the continent's water reserves. But for many north of the border, the issue is highly emotional.

The idea also has unpleasant echoes of vast schemes devised in past decades. One would have drained part of the Great Lakes into the Mississippi. Another, dreamed up back in the 1960s by Donald McCord Baker, an official in the Los Angeles water department, would have captured the waters of the Columbia River in the United States and then, in south-to-north order on the map of Canada, the Fraser, the Liard, the Skeena, and finally the might Yukon and Mackenzie rivers.

Its backers, who included Ralph Parsons, the head of one of the world's largest civil-engineering companies, envisaged building dams up to 1800 feet high in the canyons of British Columbia to funnel water into the Rocky Mountain Trench, a natural depression that would have been turned into a 680-million-acre-foot reservoir—that is, one with three times the total capacity of all the manmade reservoirs in the United States today. The project would, the blueprint proposed, carry south 114 million acre-feet of water a year—three times the capacity of China's entire south-to-north project.

That particular plan is dead and buried. But Canadian water officials say the pressure is growing to allow small water exports, especially from the Great Lakes. And they fear that once a precedent has been established, California and Arizona could come calling. Everything has its price under NAFTA. If the current drought in the American West persists, and if climate predictions that there is worse to come prove right, then who knows?

Africa already knows a bit about harnessing great rivers. The Nile today is as dammed as it could be. Its waters power Egypt and supply its irrigators. Barely a drop reaches the sea in most years. But the continent's other great river—the world's second largest river through the world's second largest rainforest—is a new target. The Congo River runs undiminished throughout the year and has ten times the flow of other major sub-Saharan rivers, like the Zambezi. The veteran British colonial water engineer Henry Oliver, who built the Kariba Dam on the Zambezi, called it "one of the greatest single natural sources of hydroelectric power in the world." He would love to have got to grips with it, he told me after he retired to South Africa.

And now his post-apartheid successors say the great river through what Joseph Conrad called the "heart of darkness" could soon be lighting up Africa. South Africa's state-owned utility, Eskom, is leading a five-country project to upgrade a small and largely moribund hydroelectric plant on the river at Inga and turn it into a dynamo that runs a pan-African electricity grid.

At Inga, just downstream of the Congolese capital, Kinshasa, 34 acre-feet of water a second rush down a series of rapids. Eskom's engineers say the force of this staggering volume of water at this point could generate 40,000 megawatts of power. That's twenty times more energy than comes from the Hoover Dam, ten times as much as Africa's current largest hydroelectric dam, the Aswan High Dam on the Nile, and more than twice that of China's Three Gorges

Dam. It is "enough to light up Africa and export to Europe as well," according to the company's adviser on project developments, Ben Munanga.

The proposed $50 billion Grand Inga hydroelectric project would not even require a large dam, because unlike the Nile, the river is guaranteed to run strongly all year round. So there is no need to store water. Most of the money would be spent connecting this vast power source across Africa's jungle, bush, and desert to the continent's main population centers. The first power lines would link it to South Africa via Angola and Namibia, a distance of 1900 miles. Next, pylons would strut across 2500 miles of rainforest and swamp in the Central African Republic and Sudan to Egypt. Nigeria also wants to take Inga power to West Africa. Its power might even straddle the Sahara and enter Europe via Spain.

The plan is backed by South Africa's president, Thabo Mbeki, who hopes that it could become the flagship project of NEPAD, the New Partnership for Africa's Development, which is being promoted by the G8 governments in Europe and North America as a new Marshall Plan for the continent. It could just happen.

There is a surprisingly strong political push too behind another megaproject to harness the Congo. This time the idea is to send the water itself north to irrigate the fringes of the Sahara and refill Lake Chad. In 2002, several governments met in the rainforests of central Africa to sign an agreement on sharing the waters of the Congo. They said they wanted to raise $5 billion for a dam that would barricade one of the river's major arms, the Ubangi River, at a sleepy port

called Palambo in the Central African Republic, and send the water north.

The Lake Chad Basin Commission, representing Nigeria, Niger, Chad, Cameroon, and the Central African Republic, fleshed out the plan in 2004. The dam should, they said, divert 80 million acre-feet of water a year over a narrow watershed into the headwaters of the north-flowing Chari River and down its wide floodplain before ending up 1500 miles away in Lake Chad. The survival of more than 20 million people in the lake basin depends on the Lake Chad Replenishment Project, the commission claimed. It could rehabilitate huge irrigation projects around the lake, such as the South Chad Irrigation Project, which were built in wetter times but are now unused.

"If nothing is done, the lake will disappear," claimed Adamou Namata, the water minister in Niger and the chairman of the commission. But the project would be "an opportunity to rebuild the ecosystem, rehabilitate the lake, reconstitute its biodiversity, and safeguard its people." In late 2004, the Nigerian president, Olusegun Obasanjo, agreed to pay $2.5 million for a feasibility study of the project.

On the Logone and Hadejia rivers, in Cameroon and Nigeria, poor farmers quake at the thought. For them, large engineering projects to remake the rivers have always brought trouble. Wherever the promised water went, it never reached them. Generally they lost water as it was corralled and privatized and sent uphill to money. They want and need very different solutions to their water problems, ones that go with the flow of nature rather than against it.

Discussion Questions

1. What do you perceive as some likely consequences of the global trade in "virtual water?" What are the implications of this water usage for countries that have plentiful water resources, and for those that do not?
2. Does your local community have water supply controversies of its own? What is the source of the controversy, and what are the arguments on both sides of the issue?
3. Civil engineering projects on the scale of the water project proposed in India require massive amounts of capital—an estimated 40% of India's GDP, for example. Do you think this type of investment is warranted? Why or why not? What alternatives might a country such as India have to address its water needs? Do the issues—and possible solutions—for a region such as the American Southwest differ from those found in nations such as India or China?
4. Former president George W. Bush talked about privatization of water resources whereby companies might purchase water from Canada for resale in drought-prone areas of the American West. What reasons would you give to support, or to oppose, such a move?

 Supporting Activities

1. Use the CIA *World Factbook* to compare and contrast the size (population and land mass), demographics, economics (including industries and access to energy resources), communication, and transportation statistics of a developed and a lesser-developed country of your choice (https://www.cia.gov/library/publications/the-world-factbook/index.html).
2. Go to the EPA's "Surf Your Watershed" site (http://cfpub.epa.gov/surf/locate/index.cfm) and locate the watershed area for your home. Identify the water sources that are part of this watershed and which of these sources is "impaired" and why; and find out what citizen-based groups are at work on this watershed.
3. Find the source of your community's drinking water supply. How much water does your community consume daily, on average? Where is your community's sewage treatment plant? If you live rurally and depend on well water, find out how deep your well is and what the flow rate from the well is. If you rely on a localized septic system, learn where it is and what kind of maintenance it requires. Tally how many members of the class rely on municipal or individualized water supplies.

 Additional Resources

1. Review information about other countries of interest on the CIA *World Factbook* (updated bi-weekly): https://www.cia.gov/library/publications/the-world-factbook/index.html.
2. Watch a YouTube documentary about China's controversial Yangtze River hydroelectric project, *The Largest Dam in the World*: https://www.youtube.com/watch?v=b8cCsUBYSkw.
3. For a 2012 analysis of India's ambitious River Linking Project, see: http://www.iwmi.cgiar.org/iwmi-tata/PDFs/2012_Highlight-16.pdf.

Hundreds of Man-Made Chemicals . . .

This article by Gay Daly describes efforts that are being made to document the characteristics and effects of synthetic chemicals, most of which have been developed and introduced within the last half century. These include the synthetic compounds that are used to make plastics, pesticides, herbicides, cosmetics, and dozens of other products. In spite of their relatively recent development, these compounds have become ubiquitous, showing up in thousands of products used every day; traces of these compounds have been found in the soil, water supplies, food, and in the human bloodstream.

There exist a number of federal and state regulatory entities that oversee food, air, and water safety, such as the Food and Drug Administration (FDA) and the Environmental Protection Agency (EPA). However, some individuals erroneously assume that all products undergo rigorous testing by these agencies, and that products that are shown to have harmful effects are regulated and/or removed from the market. In reality, much of the safety testing that is done is carried out by the very companies that stand to gain from development and sale of a product. Furthermore, even when product testing *is* done by independent agencies there may be conflicting evidence, which can lead to stalemates and further delays in regulating harmful substances. The insecticide DDT is an excellent case in point: it first came into widespread use in the United States following World War II and was believed to be a safe, effective way of controlling disease-spreading mosquito populations. The adverse environmental impacts of DDT use became well known following the 1962 publication of the book *Silent Spring* by biologist Rachel Carson. It was not until 1972 that the United States banned sale and use of the compound. Although banned more than 40 years ago, numerous studies have shown that this compound persisted in the soil for decades.

Daly highlighted the work that was done by the late scientist Theo Colborn, whose efforts to catalog the effects of what became termed "endocrine disrupting" chemicals brought together individuals from across the professional spectrum, including physicians, wildlife biologists, anthropologists, toxicologists, and others. The multidisciplinary approach she championed was effective for at least two reasons. First, it allowed pieces of evidence from multiple perspectives to be brought together to achieve a more holistic understanding about the complex nature of the effects of endocrine disrupters. Second, it made it easier for Colborn and her colleagues to amass a body of research whose scope made regulatory action more likely.

Still, doubts about the direct effects of these chemicals remain, and chemical industry representatives and others maintain that many of these compounds are fundamentally safe. This highlights a basic problem with research of this kind: it's difficult to isolate the effects of any one substance when individuals are exposed to so many chemicals throughout their lives, and the task is particularly hard when the effects can manifest over a lifetime or beyond. Thus, identifying any one compound as the direct cause of a problem is very hard to do. Researchers must instead look for a *correlation* between exposure and effects. In the absence of direct causal evidence, adopting policies to regulate substances is often delayed or not pursued at all.

Theo Colborn died in 2014 at the age of 87. In her later years she is reported to have focused her attention on use of endocrine-disrupting compounds in the drilling industry, activity that led gas and oil industry representatives to denigrate her as an activist rather than a scientist (Lofholm, 2014). Author Gay Daly has served as a senior editor at *Discover* magazine, and her work has appeared in *Good Housekeeping, People,* and *Parenting*, among other publications.

Hundreds of Man-Made Chemicals—

In Our Air, Our Water, and Our Food—Could Be Damaging the Most Basic Building Blocks of Human Development

By Gay Daly

Everyone knows that World War II left us, as a legacy, the atomic bomb. Far fewer people are aware that the war also left us a chemical bomb, silently, inexorably ticking away, that may threaten our health, our intelligence, and even our ability to reproduce. It may be exploding as you read.

Before the war, only a few synthetic chemicals—laboratory-made compounds that do not exist in nature—had been invented. With the onset of the war, chemists eager to help their countries achieve victory began inventing plastics, pesticides, solvents, degreasers, insulators, and other materials that could be used to make more effective weapons, increase crop yields, and feed more soldiers. They were, understandably, more focused on success than on safety.

In peacetime, these same labs helped fuel the economic boom of the second half of the twentieth century, formulating new chemicals manufacturers needed to create cheaper, smarter products.

Federal regulation was fragmentary at best, and manufacturers were allowed to provide their own proofs of safety, a situation that remains true today. There are now more than 100,000 synthetic chemicals on the market, and these chemicals are everywhere. They enter our bodies and those of other animals through every possible route of transmission. They are in our food supply, so we eat them. They drift in the air, so we breathe them. (Carried on thermal currents, they have long since reached the Arctic, so polar bears breathe them too.) Present in landfills, they leach into the water supply, so we drink them. Released as effluent into lakes and rivers by factories, they affect the habitat of fish, frogs, and all aquatic life, right down to plankton. Ubiquitous in cosmetics, they are absorbed through our skin. Pregnant women pass them to their fetuses; mothers feed them to their newborns when they breastfeed. A large, uncontrolled scientific experiment has been in progress for the last 60 years, and the question now is: Can we figure out what the results are? And if those results show we are in danger, what we can do about it at this late date?

> For almost two decades after the war, our great faith in the new chemistry went untested. It seemed as if one miracle after another emerged from the labs, providing abundant, cheap food, drugs to cure disease, and technology that made life easier and more pleasurable: televisions, dependable cars, inexpensive, reliable refrigerators to replace the icebox.

Rachel Carson pushed Americans to question these miracles when she published *Silent Spring* in 1962, and legislation was passed to address concerns she and others raised about environmental toxins. By the early 1970s, more warning signs had showed up on the radar. DDT, the pesticide that had saved American soldiers who fought in the South Pacific from malaria and been sprayed on millions of acres of cropland, was fingered as a killer of birds, especially the beloved bald eagle. Eggshells thinned by exposure to the compound meant fewer hatchlings survived. DES, a drug believed to prevent miscarriage, was found to cause cancer in the young women whose mothers took it during pregnancy; emergency hysterectomies saved many of the daughters' lives, but at a terrible cost. PCBs, highly effective lubricants and insulators used in electrical capacitors, transistors, hydraulic fluids, plasticizers, inks, waxes and adhesives, were deforming and killing birds and fish; by 1971, Monsanto had voluntarily stopped making them. Each of these problems was seen as an isolated case: A few rogue chemicals had wreaked havoc, but havoc could be contained. Ban DDT, ban DES, ban PCBs—perhaps we couldn't undo the damage already done, but we thought we could stop it in its tracks and breathe a sigh of relief.

The average person still thinks about chemicals as single entities, and our system of federal regulation still decides on a case-by-case basis whether chemicals are safe enough to circulate in our world. But a paradigm shift is underway among some scientists, who have over the last 30 years quietly begun to wonder: By introducing so many substances that did not evolve along with living organisms over hundreds of millions of years, have we unwittingly initiated changes in our biology that may be damaging it profoundly?

She Went Looking

One of the researchers most responsible for raising this question and pressing to find answers is Theo Colborn, a woman whose career path has been anything but conventional. Colborn got her Ph.D. at 58, an age at which most people are beginning to think about retirement.

By then, she had raised four children while working as a pharmacist, a job that required her to know a great deal about chemistry, biology, and health. In the 1970s she began to see disturbing patterns of illness in the six Colorado communities where she worked as a pharmacist. Eventually, she hypothesized that everybody drank from the local creek or river and each water source had its own unique set of toxins. She went to a number of conferences on water in the Western states and was shocked to find that all anybody talked about was the quantity of water—and who owned it.

Divorced, without a mortgage, her children grown and gone, Colborn decided to go back to school to make herself an expert on the quality of water. A master's degree in freshwater ecology led to a doctorate in zoology, then two years as a Congressional Fellow in the Office of Technology Assessment in Washington.

Then, in 1987, she landed at the Conservation Foundation, where her new boss asked her to take on a survey of research on the impact of pollution in the Great Lakes, a study that

Theo Colborn, 78, has worked for almost 20 years to understand endocrine disruption. "Theo is a Rachel Carson of our day," says Gina Solomon, an expert in the field. "She has none of the trappings of a hero, but she is one."

determined the course of her life's work. A younger scientist would probably have wanted to make her own mark rather than reading over other people's work. There is little glory in this kind of analysis, no tenure. One of Colborn's gifts was that she enjoyed looking for patterns. She was, and is, one of those rare people who can hold thousands of details in her head, shuffling and reshuffling them, able to tolerate the uncertainty of not knowing where they will take her. For six months, she worked seven days a week, reading more than 2,000 research papers and 500 government reports. She developed a primitive filing system: 43 boxes of documents, one for each species that had been studied.

At first, Colborn went looking for increases in cancer, but she found, instead, other problems that disturbed her. Where hundreds of bald eagles had nested on the Great Lakes' shorelines, only 45 pairs remained. Inland, these birds had rebounded in the years since DDT had been banned; near cleaner lakes they also flourished. But on the shores of the Great Lakes, deformed birds were showing up across species with missing eyes, crossed bills, clubfeet. A startling number of gull and tern nests sheltered twice the number of eggs they should, which suggested that females were sharing nests, apparently for lack of a male companion. Many males were not mating or not parenting. Some birds were abandoning their nests altogether. Chicks seemingly born healthy quickly developed a wasting disease and died. Creepy stuff, but what did it mean? She sought out wildlife biologists who told her that they, too, sensed something was wrong, but none of them could put a finger on what it was. Tissue analyses of the animals kept turning up the same chemicals, including DDT, dieldrin, chlordane, lindane, and PCBs. Everyone knew that hundreds of chemicals had been discharged into the lakes, many of them persistent but impossible to measure with methods available at the time.

To tame the data, Colborn made an electronic spreadsheet for species that were most profoundly affected to figure out where the patterns lay. Before long, she realized that something fundamental had to be happening to explain such a wide range of symptoms: reproductive failures, genital deformities, thyroid malfunctions, behavioral abnormalities, and immune suppression. Eventually she decided the most likely probability was endocrine damage.

Her knowledge of endocrinology was sketchy, so she set herself the task of mastering it. Endocrinology is the science of hormones, the chemical signals that, in myriad delicate and subtle ways, manage an organism's most vital functions. Hormones tell the ovaries and testes how to make eggs and sperm, tell the lungs how to breathe, the intestines how to digest, and the heart how to pump; they direct neurons in the brain. The way they do their work is an extraordinarily complicated dance that scientists are still working to comprehend. Estrogens, the female sex hormones, have been accorded the most attention so they are best understood; the male hormones, androgens, run second; and the thyroid, which controls brain development, is a distant third. If hormones cannot do their job properly, the consequences are legion—some subtle, some disastrous. The wrong balance of estrogens and androgens, for instance, can lead to reproductive failure. If a fetus suffers even a small drop in thyroid hormone levels, learning disabilities may be the consequence, IQ points may be lost.

Colborn drew up a list of world-class scientists from different fields—endocrinology, biology, immunology, toxicology, psychiatry, ecology, anthropology—whose work gave them, collectively, the expertise to test her suspicions, and invited them to the Wingspread Conference Center in Racine, Wisconsin, in the summer of 1991. "I was scared to death! There I was, a brand-new Ph.D. who knew only a handful of wildlife biologists." She did her best to set up conditions in which this wary bunch could find common ground. "I kept them working from morning till night so they had to get to know each other," she says. "Thank God there were no cell phones back then." Right away, people began to see surprising connections between their work. They stayed up talking into the small hours.

The term endocrine disruption was coined at the meeting. As the fruit of their work, the group issued a consensus statement that has stood up well to the test of subsequent research. The participants agreed that many man-made chemicals had the potential to disrupt the endocrine system of animals, including humans, by mimicking the activity of a hormone, by blocking it, or through other mechanisms, and that many wildlife populations had already been affected. Even more disturbing, they emphasized that the fetus and newborn are at greatest risk, and that the effects might not be manifested until the animal was mature. Perhaps the greatest bombshell was the statement that "the concentrations of a number of synthetic sex hormone [disruptors] measured in the U.S. human population today are well within the range and dosages at which effects are seen in wildlife populations." Suddenly, this was not about cleaning up a few lakes; the health of all the creatures in our care was at stake—including the health of our unborn children.

Mountains of Data

In the years since that conference, research on endocrine disruption has picked up speed; Colborn and her staff have built a database of 33,000 articles to make that research accessible. Chemical manufacturers have funded many studies that have almost uniformly concluded that endocrine disruption does not occur or, if it does, is not harmful. This is hardly surprising because a great deal of money is at stake. (To offer just one example: In 2002 U.S. companies produced 2.8 million tons of bisphenol A [BPA], a synthetic estrogen used to make baby bottles, plastic water bottles, dental sealants, and resin liners for metal food cans. At 94 cents a pound, this translates to sales of more than $5.3 billion in that year alone.) By contrast, federally funded academic researchers, who have no financial stake in the outcome of their work, have found much compelling evidence that synthetic chemicals, including BPA, do cause endocrine disruption and that the damage can be serious.

One discovery in particular changed the ground of all endocrine disruption research. Frederick vom Saal, a reproductive endocrinologist at the University of Missouri, established in 1997 that significant effects can be seen at extremely low levels of exposure, parts per billion and even per trillion. These levels are present in the blood of humans as well as animals.

The next logical step would be to expose human subjects to these chemicals, but it is considered unethical to subject humans to substances that might damage their endocrine function. So rats and mice have had to stand in for humans, just as they do in cancer research.

Over the last 10 years, vom Saal has studied the effects of BPA on mice, and others have followed his lead. Collaborating with Wade Welshons, a veterinary medical researcher also at the University of Missouri, he established in 1997 that male mice whose mothers were exposed to BPA during gestation routinely developed enlarged prostates. Further research found that BPA has many other impacts. In male offspring, exposure of the mother results in decreased sperm counts, decreased motility of sperm, an increase in malformed sperm, and smaller testes. In females, researchers have observed early onset of puberty, larger uteri, polycystic ovaries, deformed and incomplete vaginal structures and tissues, enlargement of mammary ducts and milk glands in the breast, and an increase in miscarriages. Damage by BPA, vom Saal notes, is not limited to reproductive effects. Structural changes in the brain; immune-system damage; learning problems; hyperaggression; and changes in sexual behavior, social interactions, and play behavior have also been documented.

Chemical manufacturers have worked hard to counter this academic research, hiring chemists to study and discredit the results. Vom Saal and others have had to spend enormous amounts of time and money defending their work, resources better devoted to moving forward onto new ground. Researchers funded by industry, curiously, tend to find that every chemical is safe. In 2004, vom Saal tallied up results of all the studies he could find on BPA. He discovered that of 104 studies done by independent researchers, 94 found adverse effects and 10 found no effects. Of the 11 studies conducted by industry-supported researchers, zero identified adverse effects. Marian Stanley, a spokesperson for the American Chemical Council, which represents the interests of chemical manufacturers, says, "We are unaware of any big discrepancies between the experimental research supported by industry and by others. Animal studies—that is, credible experimental research—from all sectors show basically the same results across the board."

In fact, Colborn observes, academic researchers have been able to demonstrate the effects of chemicals at very low doses, but industry labs have not been able to replicate their work, and use their lack of results to claim that the chemicals are safe. Colborn says that independent researchers have identified possible causes of these discrepancies. Diet is key; animal chow that has more soy, which itself is mildly estrogenic, may skew results. Housing rats in plastic cages or stainless steel may throw things off since some plastics disrupt endocrine levels but metal does not. Intrauterine position can affect results: For instance, a male rat that grew in utero between two female rats will be born with higher levels of estrogen in its blood than one that grew between two male rats. Controlling for all these variables is hard and expensive. The most contentious variable has been breed of rat. Early in the process, researchers determined that the Charles River Sprague Dawley rat was so tough that it barely responded to estrogenic compounds. Many scientists whose work is funded by chemical manufacturers have continued to use this strain, a practice deplored by Colborn and other independent researchers.

Pat Hunt, a geneticist at Washington State University, was shocked when she discovered how great a difference a worn-out plastic cage could make. Suddenly, 40 percent of the healthy control mice in an experiment began to make eggs with grossly abnormal chromosome behavior where she expected to see a rate of 1 to 2 percent. She traced the problem back to BPA they were exposed to when it leached out of their cages and water bottles. She spent five years on the problem, making certain of her results before publishing "because I was going to say exposure to this chemical used in plastics can cause miscarriages." Today, at conferences, Hunt urges fellow scientists to take endocrine disruption seriously. "The mouse is an incredibly robust breeder while we humans are, comparatively, so fragile." She is concerned about delay. "If we wait till we see an increase in chromosomally abnormal [human] miscarriages or a sharp drop in sperm count, by the time that big an effect comes up on the radar screen, we need to ask ourselves if we are going to be reproducing as a species or not."

Research on male sex hormones, or androgens, has shot forward in the past decade, and the man most responsible for this progress is Earl Gray, a toxicologist who works for the Environmental Protection Agency in Research Triangle Park, North Carolina. In 1995, he started by administering very low doses of the fungicide vinclozolin to pregnant rats.

Vinclozolin was widely used until 2002, when the EPA began to restrict it because of its potential health effects. Gray found that the rats' male offspring were born with nipples, malformed scrota and testes, vaginal pouches, and cleft phalluses with hypospadias (urethral openings in the wrong place, along the shaft of the penis or in the scrotum). This finding is particularly resonant for human health, since the rate of hypospadias in human infants doubled for no known reason between 1968 and 1993. The animals in this experiment also displayed delayed puberty, lower sperm counts, and reduced fertility.

Gray went on to examine trenbolone acetate, a synthetic steroid used as a growth promoter in beef cattle in the United States and as a performance-enhancer by athletes who purchase it illegally over the Internet. Trenbolone, excreted in animal waste, shows up in rivers and streams where, Gray believes, it may affect aquatic animals. After experiments on the fathead minnow, Gray concluded that trenbolone was a powerful androgen: Female offspring of mothers exposed to the compound grew tubercles, part of the reproductive system usually seen only in males, and had fewer babies. Observers of wildlife are beginning to report similar effects around the world. Effluents from pulp and paper mills are sufficiently androgenic to sex-reverse female fish in Florida, the Baltic Sea, and New Zealand.

Gray is an extraordinarily productive researcher, at the top of his field. One can only wonder how much more he might discover if he had more resources. Because of a hiring freeze at EPA, Gray's staff of technicians has shrunk from three to one, limiting the number of experiments he can do.

Threats to Our Health

It is extremely difficult to obtain direct evidence that endocrine-disrupting chemicals cause reproductive damage in humans, for reasons beyond the ethical one. For instance, determining the effect of any particular chemical on an individual is nearly impossible because it is so difficult to figure out which chemicals the individual's mother was exposed to during pregnancy. However, Shanna Swan, director of the Center for Reproductive Epidemiology at the University of Rochester School of Medicine and a researcher who is at the forefront of this effort, published last May the first study to link prenatal exposure to phthalates to outcomes in offspring.

She had recruited a group of pregnant women and measured nine phthalate metabolites in their urine. This chemical group had already been shown to disrupt the endocrine system in rodents and is ubiquitous in our world—in plastics, nail polish, perfumes, toothbrushes, pesticides, paint, and the coating on time-release pills. Then Swan asked pediatricians who knew nothing about the maternal exposure levels to measure the distance between the genitals and the anus in the male babies. Then this distance was divided by the infant's weight to establish an anogenital index (AGI), a biomarker animal researchers have long used because it is predictive of the healthy development of the genitals in rodents. Short AGI correlates with smaller penises, smaller, ill-defined scrota, and incomplete testicular descent.

Swan found that a boy born to a mother with a high exposure to dibutyl phthalate (DBP), for example, was 10 times more likely to have a short AGI than a child of a mother with a low exposure to DBP. Swan points out that this was a small study of 85 infants; she has proposed a larger study of 600 families to investigate these effects further. She believes the research is necessary because the mothers of babies with short AGIs had been exposed to levels of phthalates that, according to estimates from the Centers for Disease Control and Prevention, are present in the bodies of one-quarter of all American women.

It is already clear that synthetic chemicals can also powerfully affect the thyroid gland, which is critical to brain development and function, according to Thomas Zoeller, an endocrinologist at the University of Massachusetts Amherst. But work is still in an early stage; much remains to be understood about how the thyroid functions and how that functioning can be disrupted. Zoeller's lab works with PCBs even though they were banned in 1979, largely because the behavior of these chemicals is well understood, which makes it easier both to predict their behavior in the lab and to interpret it. Moreover, although PCB levels dropped at first after the ban, these chemicals have such a long half-life that the rate of decline leveled off in the mid-1990s, which means they will belong to our bodies' burden of toxins for a long time to come.

Zoeller has determined that exposing a fetus to PCBs leads to profound changes in the brain. "The corpus callosum is a big bridge of white matter that connects the two hemispheres, and in our experimental animals, the PCBs cause a reduction in the size of the corpus callosum," he says. This may prove to be a very important finding, he explains, because "a number of neuropsychological diseases in humans have been linked to the development of the corpus callosum—for example, autism and Tourette's." However, he emphasizes that we don't know yet if the link is causative. Zoeller also suspects that disruption of the thyroid may be contributing to the sharp spike in learning disabilities observed over the past two decades, a spike that cannot, he says, be explained away by improvements in diagnosis.

A careful study published in 1996 by Joseph and Sandra Jacobson suggests Zoeller is right to be concerned. Testing children of mothers who ate Great Lakes fish contaminated by PCBs, they found that children whose mother's blood and breast milk, along with umbilical cord blood, showed the highest concentrations of PCBs had lower IQs—on average six points lower—than children of mothers with the lowest concentration. Joe Jacobson points out that what he and his wife documented was a correlation between exposure and a drop in IQs rather than proof that PCBs caused the drop. The children with greatest exposure also exhibited memory and attention deficits and were twice as likely to be at least two years behind kids in the lowest exposure group in reading comprehension. None of these impacts sounds catastrophic, but they could mean more kids who can't sit still in class and are miserable in school. The Jacobsons followed these children only until they were 11 so they do not know how those exposures affected them later in life. But children who have difficulty in school may well grow up less able to read, write, or think clearly.

Two brooding questions have hung over endo-crine-disruption research. One: are the effects of endocrine-disrupting chemicals additive—if you are exposed to many of them, will their effects add up to produce greater changes in hormonal activity? And two: are the effects handed down from one generation to the next? The first attempts to study these questions suggest that the answers are likely to be: yes and yes.

In 2005 Kevin Crofton, a neurotoxicologist who works for the EPA at Research Triangle Park in North Carolina, published a finding that helped to confirm many researchers' worst fears. Crofton gave rats different doses of mixtures of three classes of chemicals—dioxins, PCBs, and dibenzofurans—at concentrations ranging from approximately those that would be found in humans to levels 100 times higher. The chemicals in the mixture were chosen because they are found in foods people eat, from fish to breast milk. The highest dose he used for each chemical was still so low that he had seen no endocrine-disrupting effects for that chemical at that level. At the lower doses, Crofton found that the effect of the mixture was additive and that it significantly reduced the animals' level of thyroxine, the most common thyroid hormone. At higher doses, he observed that the mixtures reduced thyroxine synergistically so that the sum of their effect was slightly greater than simple addition. A fetus must have enough thyroxine for the brain to develop properly; adults need thyroxine to regulate metabolism and heart rate.

This and many other recent studies of mixtures up the ante considerably. They cut right through the endless debates about whether the levels of exposure to a chemical in any given experiment accurately reflect the levels at which humans or animals are actually exposed to that compound in the environment. These studies suggest that we can't solve the problem by taking a handful of the most dangerous chemicals off the market; instead, we will have to consider whether all endocrine disruptors need to go. The European Union has already begun to move in this direction.

The second question, whether effects are handed down from one generation to the next, got an answer almost by accident. Michael Skinner, a molecular and cellular biologist who focuses on reproductive biology at Washington State University, wanted to look at how cells communicate during the development of ovaries and testes. He dosed a group of pregnant rats at mid-gestation with vinclozolin, an anti-androgen (a substance that blocks androgenic hormonal activity), and another group with the pesticide methoxychlor, which is estrogenic, to see if either would alter the development of their offspring. A research fellow in his lab bred that first generation of babies, which was not part of the plan. She apologized, but Skinner told her not to worry, to seize it instead as an opportunity to examine the impact on a second generation. Everyone in his lab was stunned when they found that both chemicals wreaked significant damage. According to Skinner, of those exposed to vinclozolin, "greater than 90 percent of the males developed subfertility with a dramatic increase in developing sperm undergoing cell death" for not one but four generations. Further analysis established that the rats in both experiments had suffered germ-cell defects, the result of a chemical modification of their DNA. Both males and females developed various diseases as they aged. For example, female offspring of the first generation developed a condition equivalent to pre-eclampsia in human mothers, which can result in severe complications for the baby and death for the mother. In humans, incidence of pre-eclampsia has risen sharply over the last 20 years, and no one knows why. Skinner points out that he used a level of toxins higher than what people would be ex-posed to in ordinary circumstances, but he be-lieves that "women in their mid-gestation preg-nancies should be very cautious about their environmental exposures."

We Are Unprotected

Fewer than a thousand of the 100,000 synthetic chemicals have been tested for endocrine dis-ruption by anybody, but even the little we know is alarming. Sadly, the government's effort to mount a response has been checked continually by insufficient funding for research and regula-tion, by the complexity of the science that must be done, and by industry's well-funded efforts to delay the EPA's plans to test chemicals.

After the Wingspread conference, Colborn worked to raise awareness of endocrine disrup-tion in citizens and legislators. With two gifted collaborators, John Peterson Myers and the sci-ence writer Dianne Dumanoski, Colborn wrote *Our Stolen Future*, a book for the lay reader. In 1996, the year it was published, Congress passed ambitious legislation mandating the testing of all synthetic chemicals to determine whether they cause endocrine disruption. The Endocrine

Disruptor Screening and Testing Advisory Com-mittee (EDSTAC) was charged to recommend a testing protocol within two years.

From the start, EDSTAC faced consider-able obstacles. One was its size: 39 members, including chemical company representatives and environmental activists, but only five bench scientists. Gina Solomon, a Harvard-trained physician who had just started work at the Nat-ural Resources Defense Council (NRDC), where she is now a senior scientist, remembers, "It was often hard to get a word in edgewise, let alone talk through anything." She adds, "These were public meetings with audiences of up to 100, held in anonymous airport hotels around the country so there could be local participation and comment, which is a good thing, but it cre-ated a disconnect. The committee was charged to do a very technical scientific task."

Discussions were contentious. Representa-tives of some chemical manufacturers were accompanied by teams of lawyers who had to consult on every issue. At one point, the com-mittee reached a seemingly hopeless impasse on how to define an endocrine disruptor. A com-promise was finally achieved when Colborn sug-gested that they "describe" rather than "define" the term. How to define an adverse effect of an endocrine disruptor also ate up oceans of time. The law required an investigation of estrogenic effects of synthetic chemicals but did not limit the investigation to estrogen alone. Industry wanted to look only at estrogens, while Colborn and others believed all hormones should be studied. Eventually androgens were included, and later thyroid hormones were added as well, but it took months to reach these agreements. (Other hormonal systems that are not yet part of the testing include the pancreas, where malfunction can lead to diabetes or obesity; the pituitary gland; the pineal gland, which controls sleep; and the thymus, critical to the immune system.)

The committee was also divided about whether the goal was to protect human health or the health of wildlife. Colborn considered this a false dichotomy because she does not see animals and humans as two groups with separate fates. If wildlife suffers, so do humans. Yet, while evidence of harm to wildlife was mounting, how to pin down causal connections to human health remained a vexed question. Representatives of industry were quick to exploit the dilemma inherent in the research: They argued that anything less than the gold standard of experiments conducted with human control groups would be "unsound science," experiments that everyone agreed could never be conducted for ethical reasons.

Despite these difficulties, EDSTAC met its deadline: In August 1998, its final report recommended 14 assays, or tests, and a plan for making decisions about how many of these tests a chemical had to pass before it could be deemed safe.

Not even one assay has been approved as we go to press. Before testing can begin, protocols have to be agreed upon for conducting each assay and then each assay has to be validated by running trials in multiple labs to prove that results are reproducible from one lab to the next. Establishing protocols and validating them has proved to be extraordinarily difficult and time-consuming.

But the work is all the more important because the chemical companies themselves will be responsible for conducting these tests. Still, the process of validating the government's battery of assays has eaten up seven years. Colborn says that lack of resources has been the biggest deterrent to progress: "With the lack of funding and the limited staff provided to the EPA, we could not have expected much more." Solomon of the NRDC is cautiously optimistic but warns that validation has seemed within reach several times before, only to be disrupted by unforeseen difficulties. Colborn fears that money and time will be thrown away testing high doses instead of low doses, on adult rats rather than embryos, on Charles River Sprague Dawley rats that won't react.

Gray is, like Colborn, keenly impatient with the delays, but he believes the proposed assays will tell us what we need to know. "We have reliable screening assays for identifying estrogens and anti-estrogens and androgens and anti-androgens that have been used in the scientific community for decades," Gray says. "These assays are reproducible, and they're diagnostic of endocrine effect. They produce valid, interpretable results."

Show Us the Money

Given the strength of the science and the risks in play, it would seem that it is time to spend the money to do the testing and move the regulatory process forward. Unfortunately, the reverse seems to be happening. In 2003, 2004, and 2005, the Bush administration tried to cut all EPA funding for independent scientists who do endocrine-disruptor research. While these efforts failed, the total budget for those three years was still less than $15 million. (By contrast, Japan recently spent $135 million on a research program and has identified some 70 chemicals as endocrine disruptors.)

Spokespeople for chemical companies maintain that the levels at which humans are exposed to endocrine disruptors are not dangerous. Marian Stanley at the American Chemical Council states: "The consensus of the research is clear that there is no evidence that humans have been adversely affected by environmental exposures to endocrine active substances . . . and there is not convincing evidence of a growing human health issue." Still, there are signs that manufacturers have read the handwriting on the wall and are making changes to avoid liability suits down the line. Procter & Gamble has removed dibutyl phthalate (DBP) from all products that it sells around the world. Unilever, Revlon and L'Oréal have pledged to take chemicals banned in Europe out of any products they sell here. Baxter International is developing an alternative to phthalates for its medical bags and tubes. And methoxychlor, one of the pesticides Michael Skinner tested that showed endocrine damage through four generations, quietly disappeared from the U.S. market last year when Drexel Chemical failed to re-register it with the EPA.

Colborn is encouraged by these developments, but she is still extremely worried because these few withdrawals "don't begin to clean up the womb environment." Solomon worries, too, particularly with regard to food production and supply. "Every time a pesticide is re-registered by the EPA, the registration contains a boilerplate statement that there is no evidence that this chemical causes endocrine disruption, but that after tests are approved there may need to be additional testing. In the meantime, that chemical may be affecting the health of hundreds of thousands of farm workers or millions of people who eat the crops that are sprayed with that chemical."

In addition to the chemicals already released into the environment, 2,000 new chemicals go to market every year, and each may have the potential to be another DDT, a DES, a PCB, all of which turned out to be powerful endocrine disruptors. The biggest hurdle to solving the problem is funding. Colborn and others have proposed that those who profit from these chemicals be made financially responsible for determining the environmental safety of their products. Money could be paid by manufacturers into a trust, or directly to the government, so that manufacturers could not influence the outcome of the testing.

Instead of drifting along for years, nibbling away at the problem of how to remove endocrine disruptors from the environment, Colborn hopes we will throw our collective will and enough resources into finishing the job as quickly as possible. "Think of how many billions we've spent on cancer research. If these chemicals threaten our ability to reproduce, then we ought to be spending at least as much money on understanding how they work and whether we need to get them out of our environment," she says. "If we can't reproduce, whether we get cancer or not will be a moot point."

Discussion Questions

1. Daly discusses what she calls a "paradigm shift" in the way some scientists are thinking about the effects of synthetic chemicals on the environment. What is the nature of this paradigm shift, and how does it differ from prior thinking?
2. On the issue of the effects of endocrine disruptors, as with other contentious issues, there are two diametrically opposed points of view: one camp holds that there is no evidence of adverse effects; the other maintains that the evidence is compelling and that more research, and more regulatory oversight, is needed. How is it possible for a society to move forward with responsible policy decisions when there is so little agreement on who is "right" and who is "wrong?" What strategies could be used to overcome this type of stalemate?
3. What do you see as the most important concerns associated with the widespread use of synthetic chemicals? What two to three responses do you think would be most effective for responding to these concerns?

 Supporting Activities

1. Read and discuss the book *Silent Spring* by biologist Rachel Carson, originally published in 1962. This book has long been heralded as a major contributor to the modern environmental movement because it documented direct effects of human impacts on the environment.
2. While DDT has been irrefutably linked to adverse health effects in humans and other species, it remains an effective insecticide. Uncover some global statistics on malaria. If you were a policymaker responsible for reducing malarial deaths in sub-Saharan Africa, what recommendations would you make?
3. View the movie *The Estrogen Effect: Assault on the Male,* which details the search for endocrine-disrupting synthetic chemicals and highlights the work of scientist Theo Colborn and others. The video, first published in 1993, is distributed through Films for the Humanities and Sciences in Princeton, NJ.
4. Go to the web site *Our Stolen Future* (http://www.ourstolenfuture.org/). Select and read one of the research studies presented there, and prepare a one-page summary of the research.

 Additional Resources

1. Visit the web page of The Endocrine Exchange, a nonprofit organization founded by Dr. Theo Colborn and dedicated to compiling and disseminating evidence about chemicals that act as endocrine disruptors: http://www.endocrinedisruption.org/.
2. View the information about toxic substances and pollution prevention laws on the USEPA web site at: http://www2.epa.gov/regulatory-information-topic/toxic-substances.
3. The report *Environmental Threats to Healthy Aging* (2008) by Jill Stein, Ted Schettler, Ben Rohrer, and Maria Valenti summarizes research on the effects of environmental pollutants, among other factors, on overall health, with a particular focus on Alzheimer's and Parkinson's disease. Available at: http://www.agehealthy.org/.

4. For differing points of view about the safety of plastics, particularly its use in food and beverage containers, see the Frequently Asked Questions at a plastics industry information site: http://www.plasticsinfo.org/ and compare this with the article *Pots, pans, and plastics: A shopper's guide to food safety*, which can be found on the WebMD site: http://www.webmd.com/health-ehome-9/plastics-food-safety.
5. Learn more about the chemicals used in cosmetics at the FDA site, under the "Products and Ingredients" tab: http://www.fda.gov/Cosmetics/default.htm.

House Proud *and* Building Materials: What Makes a Product Green?

The idea of creating a prefabricated, environmentally friendly, affordable home is one that has been tried without success before. One of the more interesting and groundbreaking approaches was proposed in the late 1920s by designer and visionary R. Buckminster Fuller. His "Dymaxion House" was designed to be completely self-sufficient, energy efficient, and even recyclable. The house was round, supported by a central mast, and made of aluminum, and Fuller's concept was that the home could be shipped anywhere in the world inside a tube[7]. The idea was definitely ahead of its time, and the Dymaxion House never achieved any kind of commercial acceptance.

More recently architect Michelle Kaufmann, subject of the article by William Booth, attempted to manufacture the Glidehouse, a "green" prefab home. Although the advantages of factory-built over site-built homes are well documented (and briefly described in this article), the modular home concept had yet to break free of its image as a shoddy substitute for the real thing. Although Kaufmann's much-heralded effort at innovative design folded in 2009, a consequence of the financial downturn, in September of that year it was purchased by eco-housing company Blu Homes, with Kaufmann serving as a design consultant. The company today offers seven home designs with a wide range of customizable features.[8]

Consumer demand for products and materials that use less energy and that are less damaging environmentally continues to increase. The aforementioned building standards such as LEED and ENERGY STAR are just two of many attempts to achieve the significant environmental and energy use benefits that are believed to be well within reach through changes in the built environment. As author Alex Wilson pointed out, however, defining what approaches and materials are best is not always a clear-cut process. Some materials are simply "less bad" than others, an achievement that architect William McDonough and his colleague William Braungart would cite as woefully insufficient in the quest for environmentally responsible design.[9] Moreover, because being green is increasingly seen as a good business strategy the prevalence of, and incentives for, "greenwashing" also increase, making it harder for consumers to know whether they are really making the best choices. Nevertheless, Wilson's overview of recent strategies and terminology used in the building industry provides a useful introduction for those interested in creating healthier and more environmentally benign buildings.

House Proud

High Design in a Factory-Made Home? Michelle Kaufmann Believes She Holds the Key

By William Booth

Like the robot maid and the flying car, the perfect prefab house seems like one of those futuristic promises that never quite come true. You know the house: a light and airy, clean and green 3 BR, 2 BA constructed of renewable, energy-efficient materials—delivered to your doorstep. A modern house you can buy the way you buy almost everything else, with a click of the mouse. A modular house that can be assembled in an afternoon and comes complete, right down to the towel racks in the bathroom. Just plug in the utilities.

This is the house that Michelle Kaufmann believes she has designed—a young architect's answer to the challenge of bringing good design to the masses. "We want to create sustainable homes, of high quality, for a reasonable price, for the middle classes," says Kaufmann, 38. And to do that, she says, "you need an assembly line."

Not too long ago, Kaufmann bumped into her old boss, architect and design maestro Frank O. Gehry. "You know," he said, "some pretty smart people have tried this and failed." Indeed, several masters of 20th-century architecture saw the promise of prefab—giants such as Walter Gropius, Charles and Ray Eames and Joseph Eichler—but they could not redeem it.

But where others have failed, Kaufmann sees a way. Gropius or the Eameses could have built the factories to make their prefabricated homes, she says, but they lacked a crucial piece of technology. "The Internet is the key," she says. "A house is not a toothbrush," meaning a one-size-fits-all, perishable good. "You need and want to interface with the customer," to get a sense of how your building might be tailored to individual needs.

But instead of taking a dozen meetings with an architect, pinning down a hundred details, a Kaufmann prefab buyer meets with her once and then communicates with her through a Web site and by e-mail, selecting from a limited menu of options. "If you had to take meetings, you could never have mass production," says Kaufmann, who grew up in Iowa and holds degrees in architecture from Iowa State and Princeton universities. "But with e-mail, we can make the changes, we can tweak in an instant. You can keep the process moving forward."

The prefab house is hot again, at least in the pages of shelter magazines, and Kaufmann's designs are some of the smartest around; she has "definitely answered the question, 'Why prefab?'" wrote Allison Arieff when she was editor of *dwell* magazine. One of them is on view through June 3 at the National Building Museum in Washington, D.C., in an exhibit titled "The Green House: New Directions in Sustainable Architecture and Design." Another one, a demonstration project Kaufmann did with *Sunset* magazine in 2004, went up in a parking lot in Menlo Park, California, and was visited by some 25,000 people over two days. On her own she has designed a third, called mkSolaire, tailored more for urban than suburban lots. Kaufmann's firm's Web site (mkd-arc.com) has received some 15,000 inquiries for information on her modular homes.

How many prefabs has Kaufmann built? A dozen. Which hardly constitutes a revolution—high design, tailored prefab still remains more of an idea than a product line, but Kaufmann vows to change that.

She came to her "eureka" moment through personal experience. In 2002, she and her then-new husband, Kevin Cullen, a carpenter and contractor, began to look for a place to live in the San Francisco Bay Area; they quickly confronted the brutal realities of a real estate market gone bananas. Their choices were as frustrating as they are familiar: pay a gazillion dollars for a tear-down in close-in Oakland (and end up with no money to rebuild) or move to the far reaches of former farmland for a long commute from a soul-sucking tract of mini-mansions.

They looked for six months. "It was really depressing," Kaufmann recalls. "I seriously thought about what kinds of bad decisions had I made in my life to end up in a place where we could not afford a home. We actually went into therapy."

So they decided to build a house themselves. They found a narrow lot in suburban Marin County, and Cullen went to work on a

Kaufmann design with a simple but beguiling floor plan of connected rectangles, just 1,560 square feet, with an easy flow from space to space—a curtain of glass doors under a shed roof covered with solar panels. They called it the Glidehouse. Friends took a look at the plans and said: Make us one too. "This is the thing," Kaufmann says. "They didn't want me to design them another house. They wanted *our* house, the exact same house. And that's when I thought, hmm, could we make this in mass production?"

To hear her preach the prefab gospel, building a home from scratch, on-site—with what she calls "sticks"—makes little sense, while a factory committed to punching out Glidehouses provides nothing but advantages. There is quality control and little waste. Because the house moves down an assembly line, shuttled from station to station with overhead cranes and constructed on a grid with precision cuts, the joinery is plumb, the angles true.

"The factory reuses; the stick builder throws trash in the dumpster. With prefab, you build only what is needed," says Kaufmann. "The wood and other materials are not exposed to rain and the elements. There is also the human element: you know people are going to show up for work. There's no waiting for the subcontractor."

To prove the idea's benefits, Kaufmann performed an experiment in 2003 and 2004. While Cullen built the Glidehouse prototype from scratch on their Marin County lot, she worked with a manufacturer to complete an identical Glidehouse in a factory. The results: the site-built Glidehouse took 21 months to design, engineer and permit, and 14 months to build.

The modular version was built in four months. (Kaufmann thinks she can shave this down to six weeks or less.) The site-built home cost $363,950 to build, or $233 per square foot, while the modular house cost $290,500, or $182 per square foot, including shipping. Both required additional spending for lots, foundations, landscaping, driveways, decks and garages.

After the experiment, Kaufmann dedicated her firm exclusively to prefab construction. "I was just young and naive enough not to know how hard this would be," she says.

Kaufmann soon learned that there were established companies already manufacturing modular structures for oil-field workers or temporary classrooms—decent boxes for temporary shelter, though hardly Glidehouses, with their lightweight paperstone kitchen countertops made of recycled paper, their roofs ready for clip-on solar panels and their clerestory windows. But her efforts to reach them were unavailing—she would discover that they wouldn't even call her back because they considered architects too difficult, and too time-consuming, to work with.

Undeterred, she says, "I basically became a stalker" and got through to a few manufacturers, enough to persuade them that "the future can be much more than what they had been doing." She contracted with them to make 11 Glidehouses and one Breezehouse, but she was still frustrated by the length of time the revolution was taking. So in 2006, she took the plunge and bought her own factory, 25,000 square feet east of Seattle, from a retiring modular house builder. She moved in this past October, with a goal of producing 10,000 prefabs over the next ten years. That's close to the number of post-and-beam houses—still considered jewels of mid-century modernism—that Joseph Eichler built in California between 1949 and 1974.

For Kaufmann, prefab offers something else worth celebrating: a truly green building. "We've already done all the homework to find the most sustainable materials," she says. A client may like a bathroom to be blue or green, but either way it will be lined with recycled glass tiles, finished with nontoxic paint, lit by energy-efficient fluorescent bulbs and equipped with low-flow faucets and a tankless water heater.

"I think about the house like I think about a hybrid car," says Kaufmann, who drives a Toyota Prius. "You can be more efficient, but you don't have to change your life. With the hybrid, you still go to the gas station and fill it up. With the prefab houses, you make it easier to go green."

Her most cherished insight? "You have to stop thinking like an architect and start thinking like a manufacturer," Kaufmann says. "When I started on this, I didn't realize that the way to do it was to do it all."

Building Materials: What Makes a Product Green?

By Alex Wilson

Quite a bit of attention has been focused on the issue of green building materials. What makes a given product "green"? How do you evaluate the relative greenness of different products? How do you find green products? More important, perhaps, manufacturers are asking, "How can we make our products greener?"

There are several directories of green building products available, some national in focus, some regional. In compiling any directory of green building products, the authors have to figure out what qualifies a product for inclusion. That was an exercise the *EBN* editorial staff went through when we began developing the *GreenSpec*® directory, our own entry into the products directory field, in the late 1990s. This article is an attempt to lay out for public examination and discussion our standards for what makes a building product green. Our standards and thresholds have evolved over time, and this article lays out for public examination and discussion our current standards for "what makes a product green." These criteria will continue to change, and as they do, the products included in future editions of *GreenSpec* will also change. We welcome input in this process of determining just what is green.

The Challenges in Defining What Is Green

The Holy Grail of the green building movement would be a database in which the life-cycle environmental impacts of different materials were fully quantified and the impacts weighted so that a designer could easily see which material was better from an environmental standpoint. Though efforts are afoot along these lines we are not even close to realizing that goal. Very often, we are comparing apples to oranges. We are trying to weigh, for example, the resource-extraction impacts of one product with the manufacturing impacts of another, and the indoor-air-quality impacts of a third.

These issues were addressed in an earlier article on material selection (see *EBN* Vol. 6, No. 1), but in that article we were addressing the broader issue of material selection for a given project—not determining which materials should be considered green in general. This distinction is subtle but important. In building a house or office building, a great many materials and products will be used. Even in the greenest of projects it is likely that many products will be used that are not themselves green—but they are used in a manner that helps reduce the overall environmental impacts of the building. A particular window may not be green, but the way it is used maximizes collection of low winter sunlight and blocks the summer sun. So even a relatively conventional window can help make a house green. Creating a green building means matching the products and materials to the specific design and site to minimize the overall environmental impact.

This article examines products in isolation —not how to use a product to make a building green, rather what makes a certain product green. Green products, including virtually all of those found in *GreenSpec*, could be used in dumb ways that result in buildings that are far from environmentally responsible. In a well-thought-out building design, however, substituting green products for conventional products can make the difference between a good building and a great one.

Defining Standards When Feasible

Our tactic with the *GreenSpec* directory is to identify quantifiable, easily verifiable, standards where those could be defined, then base other decisions about what should be included on the collective wisdom of our editorial staff. In a few product categories, such as energy-consuming appliances and VOC-emitting paints, specific thresholds can be established relatively easily. But for many criteria, the lines are much fuzzier and judgment calls are required.

It is important also to note that multiple criteria often apply—in other words, a product may be considered green for more than one reason. Take recycled plastic lumber, for example: it's made from recycled waste, it's highly durable, and it can obviate the need for pesticide treatments. Straw particleboard products are made from agricultural waste materials, and they are free from formaldehyde offgassing. A product with multiple benefits could qualify for *GreenSpec* on the basis of its overall environmental performance, even if it doesn't meet a threshold in any one category alone. Conversely, a product with one or more green attributes might not qualify if it also carries significant environmental burdens. For example, wood treated with toxic preservatives has advantages in terms of durability, but it would not be listed in *GreenSpec* due the health and environmental hazards it represents.

This article reviews the criteria—not listed in any order of priority—used to designate building products as green and therefore suitable for inclusion in our *GreenSpec* directory.

1. Products Made with Salvaged, Recycled, or Agricultural Waste Content

The materials used to produce a building product—and where those materials came from—is a key determinant of green.

1A. SALVAGED PRODUCTS. Whenever we can reuse a product instead of producing a new one from raw materials—even if those raw materials are recycled—we save on resource use and energy. Many salvaged materials used in buildings (bricks, millwork, framing lumber, plumbing fixtures, and period hardware) are sold on a local or regional basis by salvage yards. Fewer salvaged materials are marketed widely, and it is generally only these that are profiled in a national directory such as *GreenSpec*. Local and regional green product directories can really shine when it comes to finding salvaged materials.

1B. PRODUCTS WITH POST-CONSUMER RECYCLED CONTENT. Recycled content is an important feature of many green products. From an environmental standpoint, post-consumer is preferable to pre-consumer recycled content, because post-consumer recycled materials are more likely to be diverted from landfills. For most product categories, there is currently no set standard for the percentage of recycled content required to qualify for inclusion in *GreenSpec*, but such standards will increasingly be developed in the future.

In some cases, products with recycled content are included with caveats regarding where they should be used. Rubber flooring made from recycled automobile tires is a good example—the caveat is that these products should not be used in most fully enclosed indoor spaces due to offgassing concerns.

In certain situations, from a life-cycle perspective, recycling has downsides. For example, energy consumption or pollution may be a concern with some collection programs or recycling processes. Also, closed-loop recycling is generally preferable to downcycling, in which a lower-grade material is produced. As more complete life-cycle information on recycled materials—and the process of recycling—becomes available, we intend to scrutinize recycled products more carefully.

1C. PRODUCTS WITH PRE-CONSUMER RECYCLED CONTENT. Pre-consumer (also called "post-industrial") recycling refers to the use of industrial by-products, as distinguished from material that has been in consumer use. Iron-ore slag used to make mineral wool insulation, fly ash used to make concrete, and PVC scrap from pipe manufacture used to make shingles are examples of post-industrial recycled materials. Usually excluded from this category is the use of scrap within the same manufacturing process from which it was generated—material that would typically have gone back into the manufacturing process anyway. While post-consumer recycled content is better than pre-consumer recycled content, the latter can still qualify a product for inclusion in *GreenSpec* in many product categories—especially those where there are no products available with post-consumer recycled content.

1D. PRODUCTS MADE FROM AGRICULTURAL WASTE MATERIAL. A number of products are included in *GreenSpec* because they are derived from agricultural waste products. Most of these are made from straw—the stems left after harvesting cereal grains. Citrus oil, a waste product from orange and lemon juice extraction, is also used in some green products, but such products usually include other agricultural oils as well and are lumped under 2d–Rapidly renewable products.

2. Products That Conserve Natural Resources

Aside from salvaged or recycled content, there are a number of other ways that products can contribute to the conservation of natural resources. These include products that serve a function using less material than the standard solution, products that are especially durable and therefore won't need replacement as often, products made from FSC-certified wood, and products made from rapidly renewable resources.

2A. PRODUCTS THAT REDUCE MATERIAL USE. Products meeting this criteria may not be distinctly green on their own but are included in *GreenSpec* because of resource efficiency benefits that they make possible. For example, drywall clips allow the elimination of corner studs, engineered stair stringers reduce lumber waste, pier foundation systems minimize concrete use, and concrete pigments can turn concrete slabs into attractive finished floors, eliminating the need for conventional finish flooring.

2B. PRODUCTS WITH EXCEPTIONAL DURABILITY OR LOW MAINTENANCE REQUIREMENTS. These products are environmentally attractive because they need to be replaced less frequently, or their maintenance has very low impact. Sometimes, durability is a contributing factor to the green designation but not enough to distinguish the product as green on its own. This criterion is highly variable by product type. Included in this category are such products as fiber-cement siding, fiberglass windows, slate shingles, and vitrified-clay waste pipe.

2C. CERTIFIED WOOD PRODUCTS. Third-party forest certification, based on standards developed by the Forest Stewardship Council (FSC), is the best way to ensure that wood products come from well-managed forests. Wood products must go through a chain-of-custody certification process to carry an FSC stamp.

Manufactured wood products can meet the FSC certification requirements with less than 100% certified wood content through percentage-based claims. With a few special-case exceptions, any nonsalvaged solid-wood product and most other wood products must be FSC-certified to be included in *GreenSpec*. A few manufactured wood products, including engineered lumber and particleboard or MDF, can be included if they have other environmental advantages—such as absence of formaldehyde binders. Engineered wood products in *GreenSpec* do not qualify by virtue of their resource efficiency benefits alone (for more on this, see *EBN* Vol. 8, No. 11).

2D. RAPIDLY RENEWABLE PRODUCTS. Rapidly renewable materials are distinguished from wood by the shorter harvest rotation—typically 10 years or less. They are biodegradable, often (but not always) low in VOC emissions, and generally produced from agricultural crops. Because sunlight is generally the primary energy input (via photosynthesis), these products may be less energy-intensive to produce—though transportation and processing energy use must be considered. Examples include linoleum, form-release agents made from plant oils, natural paints, geotextile fabrics from coir and jute, cork, and such textiles as organic cotton, wool, and sisal. Note that not all rapidly renewable materials are included in *GreenSpec*—non-organic cotton, for example, is highly pesticide-intensive. In some cases, even though a product qualifies for *GreenSpec* by virtue of its natural raw materials, it may have negatives that render it inappropriate for certain uses—such as high VOC levels that cause problems for people with chemical sensitivities.

3. Products That Avoid Toxic or Other Emissions

Some building products are considered green because they have low manufacturing impacts, because they are alternatives to conventional products made from chemicals considered problematic, or because they facilitate a reduction in polluting emissions from building maintenance. In the *GreenSpec* criteria, a few product components were singled out for avoidance in most cases: substances that deplete stratospheric ozone, and those associated with ecological or health hazards including mercury and halogenated compounds. In a few cases, these substances may be included in a "green" product if that product has significant environmental benefits (for example, low energy or water use).

These substitutes for products made with environmentally hazardous components may not, in themselves, be particularly green (i.e., they may be petrochemical-based or relatively high in VOCs), but relative to the products being replaced they can be considered green. Most of the products satisfying this criterion are in categories that are dominated by the more harmful products—such as foam insulation categories in which most products contain HCFCs. We have created several subcategories here for green products:

3A. NATURAL OR MINIMALLY PROCESSED PRODUCTS. Products that are natural or minimally processed can be green because of low energy use and low risk of chemical releases during manufacture. These can include wood products, agricultural or nonagricultural plant products, and mineral products such as natural stone and slate shingles.

3B. ALTERNATIVES TO OZONE-DEPLETING SUBSTANCES. Included here are categories where the majority of products still contain or use HCFCs: rigid foam insulation and compression-cycle HVAC equipment.

3C. ALTERNATIVES TO HAZARDOUS PRODUCTS. Some materials provide a better alternative in an application dominated by products for which there are concerns about toxic constituents, intermediaries, or by-products. Fluorescent lamps with low mercury levels are included here, along with form release agents that won't contaminate water or soils with toxicants. Also included here are alternatives to products made with chlorinated hydrocarbons such as polyvinyl chloride (PVC) and brominated fire retardants.

3D. PRODUCTS THAT REDUCE OR ELIMINATE PESTICIDE TREATMENTS. Periodic pesticide treatment around buildings can be a significant health and environmental hazard. The use of certain products can obviate the need for pesticide treatments, and such products are therefore considered green. Examples include physical termite barriers, borate-treated building products, and bait systems that eliminate the need for broad-based pesticide application.

3E. PRODUCTS THAT REDUCE STORMWATER POLLUTION. Porous paving products and green (vegetated) roofing systems result in less stormwater runoff and thereby reduce surface water pollution. Stormwater treatment systems reduce pollutant levels in any water that is released.

3F. PRODUCTS THAT REDUCE IMPACTS FROM CONSTRUCTION OR DEMOLITION ACTIVITIES. Included here are various erosion-control products, foundation products that eliminate the need for excavation, and exterior stains that result in lower VOC emissions into the atmosphere. Fluorescent lamp and ballast recyclers and low-mercury fluorescent lamps reduce environmental impacts during demolition (as well as renovation).

3G. PRODUCTS THAT REDUCE POLLUTION OR WASTE FROM OPERATIONS. Alternative wastewater disposal systems reduce groundwater pollution by decomposing organic wastes or removing nutrients more effectively. Masonry fireplaces burn fuel-wood more completely with fewer emissions than conventional fireplaces and wood stoves. Recycling bins and compost systems enable occupants to reduce their solid waste generation.

4. Products That Save Energy or Water

The ongoing environmental impacts that result from energy and water used in operating a building often far outweigh the impacts associated with building it. Many products are included in *GreenSpec* for these benefits. There are several quite distinct subcategories:

4A. BUILDING COMPONENTS THAT REDUCE HEATING AND COOLING LOADS. Examples include structural insulated panels (SIPs), insulated concrete forms (ICFs), autoclaved aerated concrete (AAC) blocks, and high-performance windows and glazings. As these energy-saving products gain market acceptance, our threshold for inclusion in *GreenSpec* may become more stringent. For example, we may begin including only SIPs and ICFs with steady-state R-values above a certain threshold or with other environmental features, such as recycled-content foam insulation. Some products, such as insulation, clearly offer environmental benefits but are so common that they need other environmental features to qualify for *GreenSpec*.

In the case of windows, the base standard for energy performance of windows is an NFRC-rated unit U-factor of 0.25 or lower for at least one product in a listed product line. If the windows are made from an environmentally attractive material (e.g., high recycled content or superb durability), the energy standard is less stringent: U-factor of 0.30 or lower. If the frame material is nongreen, such as PVC (vinyl), the energy standard is more stringent: U-factor of 0.20 or lower. There are a few exceptions to these standards, such as high-recycled-content windows made for unheated buildings.

4B. EQUIPMENT THAT CONSERVES ENERGY AND MANAGES LOADS. With energy-consuming

Sample *GreenSpec* Standards for Selected Equipment

Product Type	GreenSpec *Standard*
Domestic water heaters	Energy Factor = 0.80 or higher
Residential clothes washers	Minimum modified Energy Factor of 1.8 and maximum Water Factor of 5.5 (as defined by the Consortium for Energy Efficiency)
Residential refrigerators	Exceed 2004 National Energy Standards by 20% (full size) or 25% (compact)
Residential dishwashers	Energy Factor = 0.67 or higher
Central AC and heat pumps	Product line must have at least one model with a SEER rating of 16 or greater

equipment, such as water heaters and refrigerators, we have good data on energy consumption and can set clear standards accordingly. In most product categories—e.g., refrigerators, dishwashers, and clothes washers—we set higher thresholds than ENERGY STAR®: for example, exceeding those standards by 10% or 20%. With lighting and lighting control equipment, certain generic products qualify, such as compact fluorescent lamps and occupancy/daylighting controls, while in other categories only a subset of products qualify. (See table for *GreenSpec* standards for certain types of equipment.) In some cases, products that meet the energy efficiency requirements are excluded, because of evidence of poor performance or durability. Microturbines are included here because of the potential for cogeneration (combined heat and power) that they offer. Ice- or chilled-water thermal energy storage (TES) equipment is also included because it helps reduce peak loads, which in turn can reduce energy costs and lower the impact of electricity generation.

4C. RENEWABLE ENERGY AND FUEL CELL EQUIPMENT. Equipment and products that enable us to use renewable energy instead of fossil fuels and conventional electricity are highly beneficial from an environmental standpoint. Examples include solar water heaters, photovoltaic systems, and wind turbines. Fuel cells are also included here, even though fuel cells today nearly always use natural gas or another fossil fuel as the hydrogen source—they are considered green because emissions are lower than combustion-based equipment and because the use of fuel cells will help us eventually move beyond fossil fuel dependence.

4D. FIXTURES AND EQUIPMENT THAT CONSERVE WATER. All toilets and most showerheads today meet the federal water efficiency standards, but not all of these products perform satisfactorily. With toilets and showerheads we include products that meet the federal standards and have dependably good performance. We include in *GreenSpec* only toilets that offer at least 20% water savings, compared with the federal standard of 1.6 gallons per flush (gpf), and we have adopted the Maximum Performance (MaP) standard for the performance of most toilets—requiring a minimum rating of 65 grams of test media removal per liter of flush volume. Some other products, such as rainwater catchment systems, are also included.

5. Products That Contribute to a Safe, Healthy Built Environment

Buildings should be healthy to live or work in and around, and product selection is a significant determinant of indoor environment quality. Green building products that help to ensure a healthy built environment can be separated into several categories:

5A. PRODUCTS THAT DO NOT RELEASE SIGNIFI-CANT POLLUTANTS INTO THE BUILDING. Included here are zero- and low-VOC paints, caulks, and adhesives, as well as products with very low emissions, such as nonformaldehyde manufactured wood products. Just how low the VOC level needs to be for a given product to qualify for inclusion in *GreenSpec* depends on the product category. Ideally those standards should be based not on simple VOC content, but on resultant VOC concentrations in the space after a given period of time—EPA is working on such data for paints (including a way to factor in higher impacts for more toxic VOCs), but this information is not yet available.

5B. PRODUCTS THAT BLOCK THE INTRODUCTION, DEVELOPMENT, OR SPREAD OF INDOOR CONTAM-INANTS. Certain materials and products are green because they prevent the generation or introduction of pollutants—especially biological contaminants—into occupied space. Duct mastic, for example, can block the entry of mold-laden air or insulation fibers into a duct system. "Track-off" systems for entryways help to remove pollutants from the shoes of people entering. Coated ductboard—compared with standard rigid fiberglass ductboard—prevents fiber shedding and helps control mold growth. And linoleum helps to control microbial growth because of the ongoing process of linoleic acid oxidation.

5C. PRODUCTS THAT REMOVE INDOOR POLLU-TANTS. Qualifying for inclusion here are certain ventilation products, filters, radon mitigation equipment, and other equipment and devices that help to remove pollutants or introduce fresh air. Because ventilation equipment is now fairly standard, only products that are particularly efficient or quiet, or that have other environmental benefits are included.

5D. PRODUCTS THAT WARN OCCUPANTS OF HEALTH HAZARDS IN THE BUILDING. Included here are carbon monoxide (CO) detectors, lead paint test kits, and other IAQ test kits. Because CO detectors are so common, other features are needed to qualify such products for *GreenSpec*, such as evidence of superb performance.

5E. PRODUCTS THAT IMPROVE LIGHT QUALITY. There is a growing body of evidence that natural daylight is beneficial to our health and productivity (see *EBN* Vol. 8, No. 9). Products that enable us to bring daylight into a building, including tubular skylights, specialized commercial skylights, and fiber-optic daylighting systems, are included in *GreenSpec*. Some other products, such as full-spectrum lighting systems and highly reflective ceiling panels, could also be included in *GreenSpec* under this criterion.

5F. PRODUCTS THAT HELP CONTROL NOISE. Noise, both from indoor and outside sources, adds to stress and discomfort. A wide range of products are available to help absorb noise, prevent it from spreading, masking it, and even reducing it with sound-cancellation technologies.

5G. PRODUCTS THAT ENHANCE COMMUNITY WELL-BEING. Looking beyond the walls of a building, many products can contribute to safer neighborhoods, increasing walkability and making high-density communities appealing.

Final Thoughts

The primary intent with any green building products directory is to simplify the product selection process. Such directories, including *GreenSpec*, are designed to save you time. For a directory to properly serve your needs, you must be able to trust it—you must have confidence that the process used to select products for inclusion is logical and based on good information and careful analysis. In this article, we have attempted to lay out our process for selecting products for the *GreenSpec* directory.

We are also providing this information so that you can critique it. We print updated copies of *GreenSpec* periodically, and we update the online version every week. That means not just ensuring that we have up-to-date contact information and product descriptions, but also regularly reexamining our standards for what should (and should not) be included. In the next edition of *GreenSpec* certain products will be kicked out—not because they have gotten worse from an environmental standpoint, but because we have reevaluated our standards for inclusion. As more low-VOC paints reach the market, we will likely tighten our standards because we want to include only the very best products. As we consider modifying our standards, we'd like to hear from users of this information. Are our standards too tight in a given area? Are they too lax? What other criteria should we consider adding to our product-evaluation process? We welcome your suggestions and comments by e-mail at: greenspec@BuildingGreen.com.

Finally, we have laid out our standards for *GreenSpec* to advance the development of new, greener products. We want to make it as easy as possible for manufacturers to understand what we consider to be green—so that they can strive to meet those criteria. Doing so will make more green building products available to us all and help to reduce the overall impacts of construction.

Environmental Building News' Checklist for Environmentally Responsible Design and Construction*

Design

- Smaller is better
- Design an energy-efficient building
- Design buildings to use renewable energy
- Optimize material use
- Design water-efficient, low-maintenance landscaping
- Make it easy for occupants to recycle waste
- Look into the feasibility of graywater
- Design for durability
- Design for future reuse and adaptability
- Avoid potential health hazards—radon, mold, pesticides

Land Use and Site Issues

- Renovate older buildings
- Create community
- Encourage in-fill and mixed-use development
- Minimize automobile dependence
- Value site resources
- Locate buildings to minimize impact
- Provide responsible on-site water management
- Situate buildings to benefit from existing vegetation
- Protect trees and topsoil during sitework
- Avoid use of pesticides and other chemicals that may leach into the groundwater

Materials

- Use durable products and materials
- Choose low-maintenance building materials
- Choose building materials with low embodied energy
- Buy locally produced building materials
- Use building products made from recycled materials
- Use salvaged building materials when possible
- Seek responsible wood supplies

From Environmental Building News, 9(1), January 2006. Copyright © 2005 by Building Green Inc. Reprinted by permission.

- Avoid materials that will offgas pollutants
- Minimize use of pressure-treated lumber
- Minimize packaging waste

- Install high-efficiency lights and appliances
- Install water-efficient equipment
- Install mechanical ventilation equipment

Equipment

- Install high-efficiency heating and cooling equipment
- Avoid ozone-depleting chemicals in mechanical equipment and insulation

Business Practices

- Minimize job-site waste
- Make your business operations more environmentally responsible
- Make education a part of your daily practice

Discussion Questions

1. What are the advantages to factory-built homes as compared to conventionally-built homes?
2. The concept of life-cycle assessment of a product or material is increasingly being seen as necessary for understanding the overall impact of that product. What does this mean? What are the challenges of conducting an accurate life-cycle assessment?
3. What do you perceive as obstacles to the use of environmentally responsible building components? What are the incentives for doing so?
4. Which of the product standards cited in the "Green Building Materials" article do you feel are most important—or most feasible—to incorporate in buildings at this time, and why?
5. Besides selecting green building materials, what other strategies do you consider important for creating a home that is truly ecologically sensitive?

 Supporting Activities

1. Take an online tour of the only surviving prototype of Fuller's Dymaxion House and learn more about its history at the Henry Ford Museum web site: http://www.thehenryford.org/exhibits/dymaxion/index.html.
2. Look for examples of greenwashing in television or print advertisements for products. What is the product? Why do you think it represents an example of greenwashing?
3. Review the suggestions provided on the U.S. Department of Energy's Energy Efficiency and Renewable Energy site for how to save energy in your home: http://www.energysavers.gov/your_home/. Conduct an "audit" of your house or apartment, and then make a list of three to five strategies you can/will implement to save energy in your home.
4. View and listen to *Behind the ever-expanding American dream home* (July 4, 2006) on National Public Radio: http://www.npr.org/templates/story/story.php?storyId=5525283.

 Additional Resources

1. The Forest Stewardship Council web site provides more information about certified wood products, sources for green building supplies, and wood use in the paper and printing industry: http://www.fscus.org/.
2. Read about the LEED certification process, buildings that are LEED certified, and the components of the LEED standards at the U.S. Green Building Council web site: http://www.usgbc.org/.
3. Explore various "tiny home" books and web sites. Good bets include *Jay Shafer's DIY Book of Backyard Sheds & Tiny Houses* (2013); *Tiny House Design & Construction Guide* (2012) by Dan Louche; The Tiny Life web site (http://thetinylife.com/); and Tiny House Blog (http://tinyhouseblog.com/).
4. View a variety of building-related topics on the National Association of Home Builders' NAHBTV, accessible via: http://www.youtube.com/nahbtv.

Getting Fossil Fuels Off the Plate

Making a link between energy and food production might not occur to individuals who haven't considered modern agricultural practices. Even Michael Bomford, who holds three degrees in agriculture, admits that it was not until he was well into his PhD program that he made the connection between the two. In this excerpt he details the many points along the industrial food production chain where large energy inputs are required.

During the early nineteenth century, English cleric and scholar Thomas Malthus predicted catastrophic food shortages as world population grew exponentially. Although important for drawing attention to this issue, Malthus' predictions about food supply have failed to play out, in large part due to research and development work over the past century. For example, during the 1960s funding was provided for development of high-yield crops, expansion of irrigation infrastructure, modernization of management techniques, and distribution of synthetic fertilizers and pesticides to farmers, leading to the so-called Green Revolution. These practices led to better nutrition, allowing people to consume more calories and eat more varied diets. As we have seen, however, excessive water use and energy consumption, and pollution caused by use of fertilizers and pesticides, have had negative environmental impacts and are considered unsustainable over the longer term (International Food Policy Research Institute, 2002). The literature on food production today speaks about a new green revolution, one that uses more holistic strategies. For instance, Foley (2014) offered a five-step plan that includes making existing farm land more productive by using organic and "high precision" farming techniques, shifting diets away from meat and dairy-based foods, and reducing food waste (it's estimated that 25% of the world's food calories are lost to waste before they can be consumed).

Like the UNEP and Foley, Bomford promotes the idea of doing more with less. In the case of agriculture, we can decouple crop yields from energy use through a combination of practices such as organic farming (no synthetic fertilizers), promoting greater reliance on local food sources, and extending growing seasons through use of solar-heated greenhouses, among other strategies.

Michael Bomford spent 10 years at Kentucky State University (KSU), where he led research, extension, and teaching programs related to organic and sustainable agriculture, with an emphasis on small farms. Bomford currently teaches at Kwantlen Polytechnic University in Surrey, British Columbia, in the Sustainable Agriculture and Food Systems Program. He holds a PhD in plant and soil science from West Virginia University, a Master of Pest Management degree from Simon Fraser University in Canada, and a bachelor's degree in Plant Science from the University of British Columbia. His research has focused on developing practical solutions for organic farmers, including renewable energy applications for small farms. Bomford has published work in a range of local and internationally recognized journals.

Getting Fossil Fuels Off The Plate

Michael Bomford

MICHAEL BOMFORD is a research scientist and extension specialist at Kentucky State University and an adjunct faculty member in the University of Kentucky Department of Horticulture. His work focuses on organic and sustainable agriculture systems suitable for adoption by small farms operating with limited resources. His projects examine practical ways to reduce food-system energy use and meet farm energy needs using renewable resources produced on the farm. Bomford is a Fellow of Post Carbon Institute.

I learned about photosynthesis early in grade school, but its implications didn't sink in for some time. When they finally did, I got excited.

Suddenly I lived in a magical world filled with plants using energy from the sun to assemble themselves out of thin air. I was among the innumerable living beings interacting with one another on a solar-powered planet shaped by life itself. I could breathe because billions of years of photosynthesis had enriched my planet's atmosphere with oxygen stripped from carbon dioxide molecules. The carbon from those molecules had been reassembled into energy-rich chains that made up the bulk of living things and could be rendered to fuel my body. With every breath I took, my body released a little energy that had once been stored by a plant, reuniting carbon with oxygen to make carbon dioxide. Eating and breathing were photosynthesis in reverse. Without plants, I could do neither.

My grade school years were mostly spent in northern British Columbia, where the growing season is short, but good land is cheap, soils are fertile, and summer days are long. Each spring farmers rushed to plant vast fields of grains and oilseeds as soon as the snow melted. The summer fields turned brilliant yellow with canola flowers and lush green with fast-growing wheat, oats, flax, and barley. By fall the plants were spent, stalks were dry and golden brown, and farmers rushed to collect the energy-rich seeds before the snow returned. The short summer's sunshine could be stored as grain for the long winter ahead. It would feed our animals, so we could have fresh meat, eggs, and milk in the depth of winter. It would feed us, as my dad reminded me with his bumper sticker "Don't complain about farmers with your mouth full."

My parents gardened. Half of our giant backyard was filled with vegetables every summer. The garden filled our plates with fresh produce, and there was plenty left over to fill our freezer and root cellar for the winter ahead. Before we said grace, Mom often proclaimed with delight, "Everything in this meal is from the garden." It all came from photosynthesis.

Agriculture is an important part of the economy in northern British Columbia, but oil is even more so. My grubby little town was full of young men in big trucks and muscle cars who had come north to make their fortunes in the oil fields. During oil booms they kept the bars hopping and the hookers busy, dropping hundred-dollar bills like candy. They didn't have gardens—they seemed to live in a realm separate from sunlight—but somehow they managed to eat and breathe. When the wells ran dry the young men disappeared, shops shuttered their windows, and the town shrank. New oil discoveries brought them back, with all of the gold-rush excitement and disarray that accompanied them. In the seven years I lived there, I saw two cycles of boom and bust.

I left home for university, brimming with idealism and determined to serve humanity. I took a degree in plant science: What could be more fundamental to human existence than plants? There I studied farm management, greenhouse management, weed management, and pest management; fruit production, vegetable production, agronomy, and agro-forestry. I learned about the wonders of the Green Revolution and the promise of genetic engineering. I learned about innovations that allowed fewer farmers to grow more food on less land, to meet the ever-expanding appetite of a growing human population. It all came from photosynthesis.

Or so I thought. I remember the sunny day—well into my PhD work—when I first read that each calorie of energy I got from food required seven to ten calories from fossil fuels to get to my plate. I was stunned. Surely this couldn't be true. I, like other living organisms, got my energy from plants, which got it from the sun. Of course I knew it took some petroleum to farm, process, package, haul, and market food, but I still considered food a renewable resource.

I checked other sources, and found that anybody who took a serious look at the energy balance of an industrialized food system reached a similar conclusion: My food was much more nonrenewable than renewable. The young men in the oil patch were doing more to feed me than the farmers.

I knew how fickle those young men were. The sun would keep shining, but the oil would run out, and they would be gone. I didn't want my food supply to depend on them, and I knew it didn't have to.

For most of human history we, like other animals, got by on renewable energy. We used muscle power for farm tools and food hauling. We ate fresh food when it was available, keeping what we could in root cellars or storing it longer by pickling, salting, fermenting, and drying. We cooked and heated with wood fires. We packaged our food in ceramic jars, wooden boxes, leaves, and paper. Our diets were shaped by where we lived, and changed with the seasons. We lost a lot of food to spoilage.

Only in the past century and a half did we start to invest a lot of fossil energy in our food system. The 1840s brought a diverse array of new factory-made farm machines that made farming easier but demanded that farmers raise enough cash crops to pay for them. The wheel-blade can opener was patented in 1870. A glass-bottle blowing machine made mass production of jars possible in 1903. By 1910 we were beginning to make synthetic nitrogen fertilizer and use gasoline-powered tractors. Frozen foods, fridges, freezers, and refrigerated trucks showed up in the early 1930s and 1940s.

Each ingenious new invention made it easier to get food to the plate—at an energy cost. In 1840 the U.S. food system depended almost entirely on renewable energy sources, including labor from 70 percent (12 million) of the 17 million Americans of the day, more than 2 million of whom were enslaved. By 1900 the population had grown to 76 million, less than 40 percent (30 million) farmed, slavery had finally been abolished, and the food system consumed about 3 quadrillion Btu of fossil fuel.

Today less than 1 percent of the population farms, and those 2 million farmers feed more than 300 million of their fellow citizens. The entire U.S. food system consumes about 10 quadrillion Btu from fossil fuel every year: 1 quadrillion to make farm inputs like fuel, fertilizer, and machinery; 1 quadrillion to farm; 1 quadrillion to haul; 4 quadrillion to process, package, and sell food; and 3 quadrillion to run the fridges, freezers, stoves, and the other appliances that fill our home kitchens. The vast majority of energy used to get food to our plates is used after the food leaves the farm. Our kitchens consume far more energy than our farms.

The past century in America was characterized by rising crop yields that more than kept pace with a growing population, despite a dramatic decline in the number of farms and farmers. It isn't easy to determine how essential fossil-fuel energy inputs were in achieving this remarkable feat. Although the energy used by the American food system increased over the course of the century, the energy used to feed each American declined. Energy consumption by U.S. farms peaked in 1978 and has fallen almost 30 percent since, while yields continue to rise.

There are some obvious ways to further reduce farm energy use. Making nitrogen fertilizer is an energy-intensive process, accounting for most of the indirect energy consumption of U.S. farms. Some give synthetic nitrogen fertilizer the lion's share of the credit for increasing crop yields over the past century, but even without it organic farms today achieve yields comparable to those of conventional farms. Studies that show organic farming to be more energy efficient than conventional often find that most of the difference comes from eschewing synthetic nitrogen.

In places like Kentucky, where I live now, it is possible to grow cold-tolerant winter cover crops that build soil health, protect soil from erosion, and convert atmospheric nitrogen to plant-available forms using energy from photosynthesis. These soil-building crops can be killed in the spring to release plenty of nitrogen for a summer cash crop, eliminating the need for synthetic nitrogen applications. Very few farmers use this energy- and soil-saving strategy in Kentucky today because applying synthetic nitrogen is cheaper and easier than managing a nitrogen-fixing winter cover crop. That changed when the price of nitrogen fertilizer spiked

along with energy prices in 2008, giving the economic advantage to those who had planted a nitrogen-fixing winter cover crop. I fully expect that less nitrogen fertilizer will be applied to U.S. farms as energy prices climb, with conventional farmers adopting techniques used mainly by organic growers today.

In northern British Columbia, the growing season is too short, and the winter too cold, to allow nitrogen-fixing winter cover crops. There, the organic farms have to plant nitrogen-fixing cover crops that grow through the summer, like alfalfa. This precludes production of a grain or oilseed crop on the same land that year, but still generates income for the farmer, who can cut alfalfa hay for sale while the plant's roots add nitrogen to the soil.

Some types of agriculture are much more energy efficient than others. The typical meat-centered diet is an energy-intensive luxury. By the time it reaches the plate, a serving of beef consumes about twenty times more energy than an equivalent serving of bread. Grain farming accounts for most of the energy used for beef but only 10 percent of the energy that goes into bread (the rest is mostly for milling and baking). In fact, very little of the grain grown in the United States is destined for bread, or other human food: It's far more likely to be fed to animals.

This is wasteful. The digestive system of cattle evolved to process grass, not grain. Cattle allowed to graze on grass use less energy than cattle fed on grain. Grass-based cattle operations use more land than grain-based systems, but they are often on marginal land planted to sustainable perennial mixtures. In contrast, confinement-based animal agriculture systems relying on grain are not just energy intensive and cruel, they compete directly and unnecessarily for grain harvests that could feed people. Meat and dairy products from pasture-raised animals tend to be healthier, too: They are leaner and richer in the omega-3 fatty acids often lacking in our diets.

A grain- and vegetable-based diet almost always consumes less energy than a meat-based diet, yet vegetables can be energy hogs too. North America's big vegetable greenhouses—marvels of Dutch technology—are a case in point. Tomato, pepper, cucumber, and lettuce plants flourish in the nearly ideal environments the greenhouses maintain: never too hot or too cold; roots bathed in scientifically perfected nutrient solutions; no wind or rain; air enriched with carbon dioxide; human-reared beneficial insects released constantly to devour pests. It's plant heaven, but it comes at a hellish energy cost. The energy used to get one serving of greenhouse-grown tomatoes to the plate is about the same as for a serving of chicken, or twelve servings of field-grown tomatoes. A local vegetable grown out of season in a heated greenhouse usually uses considerably more energy than its imported field-grown equivalent, trucked or shipped from afar.

It doesn't have to be this way. Innovative farmers around the world are developing low-energy alternatives to the Dutch greenhouse system. Perhaps the simplest is the high tunnel—a low-tech, unheated, plastic-covered structure that extends the growing season for soil-based fruit and vegetable systems. Plants grown in high tunnels lead a more stressful existence than those grown in Dutch-style greenhouses, and they don't yield as well, but the energy savings compensates for the yield reduction many times over. High-tunnel-grown vegetables offer health benefits, too: Beneficial phytochemicals are often more concentrated in plants that have experienced stress than in plants that are pampered.

High tunnels extend the growing season but do not allow winter production of warm-season crops, like tomato, in most of North America. Vegetable farmers in China may have a low-energy solution. Rejecting the Dutch model, Chinese farmers are increasingly constructing low-input solar-heated greenhouses with thick walls of concrete or brick on the north face to absorb solar radiation by day and warm the growing area at night. Before the sun goes down the farmer lowers an insulating blanket of rice straw over the clear plastic cladding to trap daytime heat, then returns at sunrise to roll the blanket up. Using this passive solar system, Chinese farmers keep tomatoes and other warm-season crops growing through winters similar to those in much of North America, without burning fuel for heat.

The Chinese-style greenhouse is probably superior to the Dutch-style greenhouse from an energy efficiency perspective, but paying somebody to roll an insulating blanket up and down every day may be more expensive than paying for heating fuel. Organic farmers may use energy more efficiently than conventional farmers, but they also use more labor—a trade-off that is often justified by premium prices available for organic products. Labor has been one of the most expensive inputs in North American agriculture over the past fifty years, and farmers have responded by developing labor-optimizing systems, capable of producing more and more food with fewer and fewer people. Such systems will stop making sense as energy prices continue their inevitable long-term climb in response to declining fossil-fuel supplies.

I am concerned about the increasing fossil-fuel dependence of American farms that characterized most of the twentieth century, but impressed by the marked reduction in farm energy use that followed the energy price shocks of the 1970s—and confident that many more opportunities exist to reduce farm energy use. Elimination of fossil-fuel consumption by U.S. farms, and replacement with renewable energy sources, appears to be a realistic and achievable goal in the near term.

But farms are just a small part of our industrialized food system. Animal feedlots and heated greenhouses are exceptional examples of farming systems that account for most of the energy used to get food to our plates. Weaning our food system of fossil fuels demands a hard look at the journey food takes after it leaves the farm. Too often, this analysis is limited to an attempt to measure the distance that food travels between farm and fork. The "food mile" has caught the popular imagination as a simple indicator of food-system sustainability. But it is not a very useful one.

How food travels is much more important, from an energy perspective, than how far it travels. Oceangoing freighters are more efficient than trains, which are more efficient than semi-trucks, which are more efficient than small trucks. Air freight would be the worst way to move food, if it weren't for individuals driving big cars to carry small quantities of food. Far less energy is needed to import bananas by boat than to fly fresh fish from the same tropical starting point. A quick jaunt in the SUV to fetch a few of those bananas at the grocery store two miles down the road uses more fuel per banana than the journey of thousands of miles over water that brought them from their tropical home. Taking fewer trips to the grocery store, or getting there by foot, bike, transit, or carpool, has far more impact on food-system energy use than obsessing over paper versus plastic bags. (We should be reusing cloth bags, anyway.)

Food often takes a convoluted route to get from farm to fork, traveling twice as far as the direct distance between the two points. Even so, transporting food accounts for just 10 percent of our food-system energy use. We need to find ways to reduce this energy cost—and we can—but doing so will not wean our food system of fossil-fuel dependency.

Recognizing the relatively small and tremendously variable impact of food miles on food-system energy use is important to avoid fetishizing the "local" instead of conducting rigorous analyses of food-system energy use. It is easy to find gee-whiz renderings of urban skyscrapers filled with plants, increasingly billed as the answer to our food energy woes. These fantastical vertical farms would be obscenely expensive structures, dependent on synthetic fertilizers, heating fuel, electric grow lights, pumps, water purifiers, and computers. Like Dutch-style heated greenhouses, they appear to ignore the energy cost usually incurred when we attempt to replace free ecosystem services with human ingenuity. Although vertical farms can almost certainly produce high yields of hyper-local food, their ecological footprint would far exceed that of field-grown products transported to urban centers from land-based farms that depend on sun, rain, soil, and other gifts of nature.

Food processing, packaging, storage, and preparation account for most of the energy cost of most of our food. If local food economies can reduce the need for these elements of the food system they will succeed in reducing our fossil-fuel dependence dramatically. Whole, unprocessed foods—often promoted for their health benefits—offer tremendous energy benefits too. If we're concerned about food-system energy, it's hard to beat whole grains, protein-rich beans (stored dry), and fresh produce, prepared simply. Yum!

In a society where less than 1 percent of the population grows most of the food for the other 99 percent, it's easy to feel removed from the food system, or disempowered by decisions that appear to be in the hands of others. The reality is that most of the power to wean the food system from fossil fuels rests with eaters, not farmers. The choices that we make in our homes and kitchens matter.

I work with many rural residents of Kentucky who have clear memories of getting their first fridge. Today almost everybody I know has a fridge (or two), and, chances are, it's a lot bigger than the one they had ten years ago. They probably also have a freezer, a microwave, a dishwasher, a food processor, a toaster, a coffee maker, a slow cooker, an electric kettle, a blender, and other electric kitchen appliances. Over the past thirty years our farms have reduced their energy consumption, but our kitchens demand ever more.

All of this kitchen technology should offer energy advantages. Microwaves are much more efficient than ovens; dishwashers can be more efficient than hand-washing; slow cookers and electric kettles can be more efficient than stovetops. Advances in fridge, freezer, and stove technology generally make newer appliances more efficient than similarly sized older appliances. The problem is that we expect our new high-tech kitchens to do much more than replace the functionality of our old kitchens. Using the fridge as an example, we might replace a small, low-efficiency fridge with a bigger high-efficiency fridge, ultimately using more energy despite the efficiency gain. The unexpected result of efficiency gains leading to greater resource consumption is so common it has a name: the Jevons paradox.

Weaning the food system off fossil fuels demands that we simplify our diets and kitchens instead of demanding an endless parade of bigger, better, and faster. It will be a difficult lesson.

Simplification does not mean an end to technological advances. On the contrary, it offers many opportunities for creative problem solving and new ideas. I think back to the freezer in my parents' basement in northern British Columbia. Why were we using energy to keep our food frozen in a heated basement when it was minus 40 degrees outside? Couldn't the freezer be outside of the house, with just an insulated door opening in? As we face the reality of higher energy prices, eaters—like farmers—will invent creative solutions that might have existed all along, but only become obvious when the bills come due.

We need only look to our own backyards—or apartment balconies, or community plots—to find one of the easiest, cheapest, and most enjoyable solutions: the garden. Stepping outside to harvest the evening meal is not only deeply satisfying, it eliminates most of the energy-intensive steps between farm and fork that contribute to our food system's dependence on fossil fuels. Provided that we can avoid the temptation to indulge in synthetic fertilizers, plastics, and pesticides, our gardens allow us to approach the ideal that most other animals realize as a matter of survival. We again become organisms fueled by photosynthesis.

Discussion Questions

1. What technological developments helped to change how we processed and stored food in the late nineteenth and early twentieth centuries?
2. What percentage of the U.S. population is directly involved with food production today? How does this compare to 100 years ago? What are the *implications* of this change in terms of the number of farmers?
3. What does Bomford mean when he states that the "food mile" is not a very useful indicator of food-system sustainability?
4. One of the recommendations made by Bomford and others is that we simplify our diets by moving away from reliance on meat and dairy products for our food calories and nutrition. Discuss the reasons for this recommendation. Do you think it would be difficult to implement personally? As a society?

 Supporting Activities

1. View the National Geographic article by Jonathan Foley on his "Five-Step Plan to Feed the World," at: http://www.nationalgeographic.com/foodfeatures/feeding-9-billion/.
2. Conduct a large or small group discussion on farming. Who knows a farmer? Who gardens? Who preserves food at home? Try to characterize your group with respect to these attributes. Does your group mirror the national statistics?
3. Read the article "No Bar Code" by Michael Pollan, published in *Mother Jones Magazine* in 2006. The article features farmer Joel Salatin and his Polyface Farm in Virginia, considered by many to be a model of sustainable food production (Available: http://www.motherjones.com/environment/2006/05/no-bar-code). You can also find a number of short videos featuring Joel Salatin on YouTube.

 Additional Resources

1. Investigate the resources and services available through your state's Cooperative Extension Service. In North Carolina, the web address is: https://www.ces.ncsu.edu/.
2. Read the book *The Dirty Life: On Farming, Food, and Love* by Kristin Kimball (2010; Scribner) for a first-hand account of a family whose goal was to grow everything needed to feed a community. A related book is Barbara Kingsolver's *Animal, Vegetable, Miracle: A Year of Food Life* (2007; HarperCollins Publishers).

 References

Adler, M. (2006, July 4). *Behind the ever-expanding American dream house.* National Public Radio, All Things Considered. Retrieved from http://www.npr.org/templates/story/story.php?storyId=5525283

Dimick, D. (2014, September 21). As world's population booms, will its resources be enough for us? *National Geographic.* Retrieved from http://news.nationalgeographic.com/news/2014/09/140920-population-11billion-demographics-anthropocene/

Foley, J. (2014, May). A five-step plan to feed the world. *National Geographic, 225*(5), 26–59.

Gillis, J., & Richtel, M. (2015, April 5). Beneath California crops, groundwater crisis grows. *The New York Times.* Retrieved from http://www.nytimes.com/2015/04/06/science/beneath-california-crops-groundwater-crisis-grows.html?_r=0

Goklany, I.M. (2007). Have increases in population, affluence and technology worsened human and environmental well-being? *Electronic Journal of Sustainable Development, 1*(3). Retrieved from http://www.ejsd.co/public/journal_article/11

International Food Policy Research Institute. (2002). *Green revolution: Curse or blessing?* Washington, DC: Author. Retrieved from http://www.ifpri.org/sites/default/files/publications/ib11.pdf

Lofholm, N. (2014, December 18). Revolutionary research scientist Theo Colborn dies at 87 in Paonia. *The Denver Post.* Retrieved from http://www.denverpost.com/obituaries/ci_27159082/revolutionary-research-scientist-theo-colborn-dies-at-87

Podmolik, M.E. (2014, June 2). Average home size hits new record. *Chicago Tribune.* Retrieved from http://articles.chicagotribune.com/2014-06-02/business/chi-average-home-size-sets-new-record-20140603_1_home-size-home-builders-new-record

United Nations Environment Programme. (2011). *Decoupling natural resource use and environmental impacts from economic growth: A Report of the Working Group on Decoupling to the International Resource Panel.* Paris, France: Author.

U.S. Department of Agriculture. (2015). *80 years helping people help the land: A brief history of NCRS.* Retrieved from http://www.nrcs.usda.gov/wps/portal/nrcs/detail/national/about/history/?cid=nrcs143_021392

U.S. Department of Energy. (2015). *Buildings sector energy consumption* (Table 1.1.5). Retrieved from http://buildingsdatabook.eren.doe.gov/TableView.aspx?table=1.1.5

World Food Programme. (2015). *Hunger statistics.* Retrieved from http://www.wfp.org/hunger/stats

World Health Organization and UNICEF. (2014). *Progress on drinking water and sanitation: 2014 update.* Geneva, Switzerland: WHO Press. Retrieved from http://www.wssinfo.org/fileadmin/user_upload/resources/JMP_report_2014_webEng.pdf

Endnotes

1. Watch the world and U.S. population clocks on the U.S. Census Bureau web site: http://www.census.gov/popclock/. Additionally, an excellent explanation of exponential growth as it pertains to resources and population can be found at: http://www.peakprosperity.com/video/85828/playlist/92161/crash-course-chapter-3-exponential-growth, which is just one of a series of videos by Chris Martenson in what he calls his "Crash Course."

2. See, for example, an interview in *The Guardian* with Nigel Lawson, former British energy minister, whose 2008 book *An Appeal to Reason: A Cool Look at Global Warming* is one of several such books in print that challenge the scientific evidence on climate change (http://www.guardian.co.uk/environment/2008/may/03/climatechange.greenpolitics).

3. See, for example, this CNN report on desalination as a response to shortages of fresh water: http://www.cnn.com/2014/05/26/tech/city-tomorrow-desalination/.

4. For more information, visit the Energy Star web site (http://www.energystar.gov/); the U.S. Green Building Council web site (http://www.usgbc.org/); and the growing "tiny homes" movement (e.g., http://www.newyorker.com/magazine/2011/07/25/lets-get-small; http://tinyhouseblog.com/; and many others).

5. To view a series of images of California's largest lakes before and after the current three-year drought, go to: http://www.theatlantic.com/photo/2014/09/dramatic-photos-of-californias-historic-drought/100804/

6. United States Department of Justice. (2007, May 31). *Landmark settlement aims to clean up raw sewage discharges in Allegheny County.* Retrieved from http://www.justice.gov/archive/opa/pr/2007/May/07_enrd_394.html

7. There are numerous sources of information about Fuller's Dymaxion House; two good starting points for more information include the Henry Ford Museum site (http://www.thehenryford.org/exhibits/dymaxion/index.html) and a 2008 critique in *Architectural Digest* (http://archrecord.construction.com/features/critique/0811critique-1.asp).

8. More information about Blu Homes can be found at their web site: http://www.bluhomes.com/.

9. McDonough, W., & Braungart, M. (2002). *Cradle to cradle: Remaking the way we make things.* New York, NY: North Point Press.

Fueling the Technological Revolution

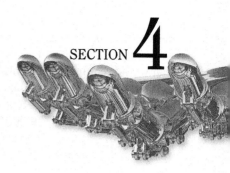

Energy is the most critical ingredient of our existence. The basics of life—food, water, clothing, and shelter—all require the accumulation and expenditure of energy. When your diet includes fresh fruit in winter washed down with imported Perrier, the shirt on your back is made of polyester (a petroleum product), and your 3,000 ft² suburban home is located 15 miles from your work or school, the energy requirement is enormous. You may say you can't live without your cell phone or computer or car, but a seemingly endless supply of cheap energy is really what you can't live without. In fact, as you'll read, access to energy is strongly correlated to "standard of living," a quantity difficult to rigorously define, but whose general meaning is clear enough.

Energy consumption is sometimes used as proxy measure for standard of living, because it suggests that individuals have access to material goods that contribute to comfort, mobility, and health. For example, a report from Lawrence Livermore National Laboratory (Pasternak, 2000) found a correlation between annual per-capita electricity consumption and the United Nations' Human Development Index (HDI), which is a widely referenced quantitative measure of human well-being. The report noted that electricity consumption shows a better correlation with HDI than does total energy consumption, with a sharper threshold. According

to that analysis, HDI reaches its maximum value (0.9) when electricity use is approximately 4,000 kWh per person per year. To put this in perspective, according to International Energy Agency (IEA) data for 1999 (upon which the Lawrence Livermore analysis was based), annual per-capita electricity use in the United States was about 13,000 kWh compared to about 60 kWh in Nepal. The Lawrence Livermore analysis, which included data from the 60 most populous nations at the time representing 90% of both world population and world electricity consumption, found that no country with electricity consumption below 4,000 kWh per person per year had an HDI of 0.9 or greater. Of greatest interest were their findings that above 5,000 kWh per capita, no country had an HDI below 0.9, but as electricity consumption increased there was also no significant increase in HDI. Based on these findings, the researchers calculated how much additional electricity capacity would be needed to get all nations up to the 4,000 kWh threshold and concluded electricity capacity would need to be 2.3 times greater (Pasternak, 2000).

In Europe, some have promoted the concept of the 2,000 Watt Society. The goal of this movement is to achieve worldwide per-capita electricity consumption levels equivalent to the current global per-capita average of 2,000 W. The 2,000 Watt Society would see citizens of

India (at around 1,000 W per capita) and citizens of the United States (at around 12,000 W per capita) consuming at equal levels—a goal that would require fundamental changes on the part of citizens in developed nations but would substantially add to the standard of living in other nations (Kolbert, 2008). This concept recognizes the correlation between electricity consumption and human well-being, but pushes the energy-use envelope far below the 4,000 kWh threshold identified in the Lawrence Livermore report. It's worth noting that Switzerland, the country where the 2,000 Watt Society concept originated in 1998, is currently a 5,000 W society. Achieving the lower threshold without sacrificing well-being will require significant changes in how we build, how we transport people and goods, how we produce food, and how we produce other consumer goods (Huebner, 2009).

To gain a more full understanding of energy consumption, one must also look at the *energy intensity* of a nation. In the simplest terms, energy intensity is a measure of how well energy is converted into income. In other words, is a country getting the maximum benefit out of each unit of energy consumed? Consider the data represented in Figure 1, comparing total energy use per capita across a range of less-developed and more-developed countries. This uses a common measure of energy (kg of oil equivalent) to allow for meaningful cross-country comparisons. Figure 2 looks at the energy intensity of the same countries. In Figure 2, the nations are compared using a different measure, purchasing power parity (PPP). Essentially, the PPP calculates the value of a country's goods and services as if they were being sold at U.S. prices—in other words, it provides a common standard against which to examine, in this case, GDP.

In better understanding our energy landscape, it's also helpful to know the sources for the energy that we rely on to fuel our way of

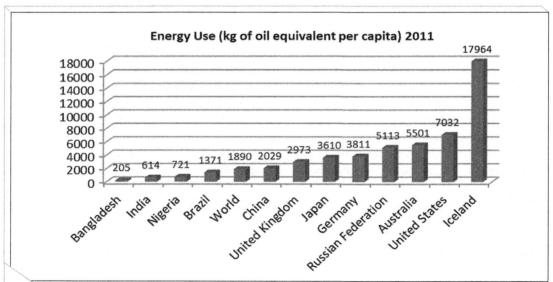

Figure 1. Energy use refers to use of primary energy before transformation to other end-use fuels, minus exports. Conversion to kg of oil equivalents allows by-country comparisons of energy use per capita. Graph created using data from the International Energy Agency and World Bank.

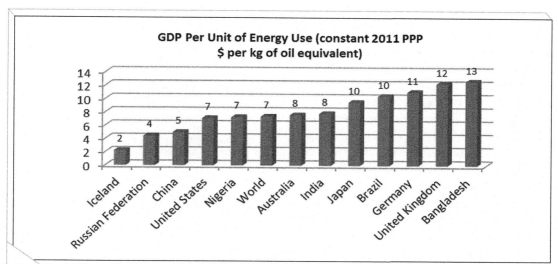

Figure 2. GDP per unit of energy use gives a measure of the energy intensity of a country, or the energy efficiency of a nation's economy. The higher the energy intensity, the higher the cost of converting energy into GDP. PPP is GDP converted to 2011 constant international dollars using purchasing power parity rates. An international dollar has the same purchasing power as a U.S. dollar has in the U.S. Graph created using data from the International Energy Agency and World Bank.

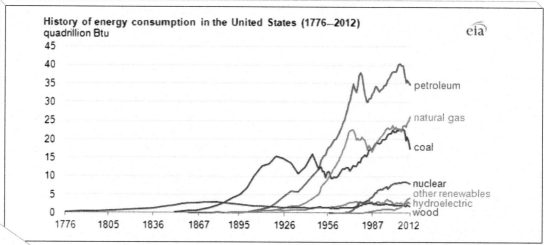

Figure 3. Changes in amount and sources of energy used in the United States between 1776 and 2012 (U.S. Energy Information Administration, 2013).

life. Figure 3 shows how energy sources in the United States have changed over time. For the hundred years following this country's founding, Americans relied almost exclusively on wood. In the mid-nineteenth century, coal became a leading energy resource, fueling transportation and industry and heating buildings. Beginning in the mid-twentieth century, oil and natural gas use became more prominent. Together with coal, these three major fossil fuel resources have dominated the U.S. energy portfolio for over 100 years (U.S. Energy Information Administration, 2015).

Fossil fuels have many beneficial attributes that have led to our heavy reliance on them. Most importantly, they are energy-dense, meaning we get a lot of useful work out of them per unit of volume or mass. They are relatively easy to transport from their source to point of use and can thus provide fuel to any geographic location. Until recently they have been both cheap and abundant, at least in certain locations. Their extraordinary value is undeniable and often taken for granted. As population and energy use have expanded, however, we have begun to understand the dark side of the fossil fuel bargain. Recovery of fossil fuels, whether through mining or drilling (including variations such as hydraulic fracturing), has led to pollution of water, air, and land. We have a better understanding about the availability of these fossil fuels, and rapid depletion of known resources means their future availability is in serious doubt. Burning of fossil fuels, as noted in an earlier section, emits carbon dioxide into the atmosphere, and today there is widespread agreement that global climate change is the result. Some of these issues are illustrated in the readings that follow.

As shown in Figure 4, however, the United States is slowly changing its energy balance. Renewable energy sources today represent approximately 10% of our energy mix, and this percentage is growing domestically as well as globally. According to the International Energy Agency (2015), renewables are the fastest-growing energy source and are a crucial part of the world's overall energy portfolio. The IEA predicts that renewables will provide

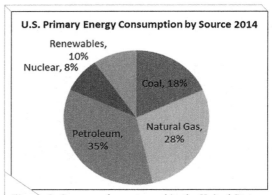

U.S. Primary Energy Consumption by Source 2014

Renewables, 10%
Nuclear, 8%
Coal, 18%
Natural Gas, 28%
Petroleum, 35%

Figure 4. Sources of energy used in the United States in 2014. Graph created using data from the U.S. Energy Information Administration.

25% of the world's gross power generation by 2018 (the U.S. Energy Information Administration puts the date at 2040). Further adoption of renewable energy technologies will be aided by adoption of federal and state incentives or mandates.[1] According to DSIRE, 28 states, the District of Columbia, and three territories have renewable portfolio standard policies in place as of June 2015. The goals range from a low of 10% renewables in a state's energy portfolio (at this time, representing five states) to a high of 40% renewables (the State of Maine, which hopes to achieve this standard by 2017). Nine additional states and one U.S. territory have adopted renewable portfolio goals (Database of State Incentives for Renewables and Efficiency [DSIRE], 2015). Standards provide mandatory targets, while goals are voluntary targets.

The readings contained within this section provide snapshots of just some of the issues that surround the ways we produce and consume energy. You are encouraged to examine the ways you use energy resources personally and to learn more about the larger energy use trends within your state and across the nation.

The Problem of Production

In this excerpt, the first chapter in the influential 1973 book *Small is Beautiful*, E. F. Schumacher introduced the concept of "natural capital," which applies economic terms to a discussion of how we use our mineral resources, most particularly fossil fuels. These resources are irreplaceable; in other words, "once they are gone they are gone for ever." Schumacher believed that Western man, emboldened by spectacular scientific and technological achievements, operates under the mistaken illusion that we can treat mineral resources as "income items" that can continue to yield benefits to humankind. In reality, they are capital items, the use of which we should minimize and do everything possible to conserve. Although the term was not in vogue in the early 1970s, Schumacher advocated for sustainable development, or new patterns of consumption and lifestyles "designed for permanence."

The notion of natural capital, which one could argue is the foundation for the only truly rational approach humanity can take in its use of irreplaceable resources like fossil fuels, has spawned an impressive array of advocates. Among these are Paul Hawken, Amory Lovins, and Hunter Lovins, who coauthored the 1999 book *Natural Capitalism: Creating the Next Industrial Revolution;* the World Forum on Natural Capital; the Natural Capital Project; the Natural Capital Coalition; and many other groups. A basic goal of many of these groups is to measure the value of what are called *ecosystem services;* for example, what is the value of a mangrove swamp, which protects coastal land from erosion? Although the mangrove swamp itself is difficult to put a price tag on, the cost of not having the mangrove swamp in the event of coastal hurricanes could be massive.

Schumacher's writings reflected the growing understanding of the ecosphere in the 1960s and 1970s, and aligned with the tenets of the burgeoning ecological movement. Another influential figure of that time, discussed in an earlier section, was R. Buckminster Fuller, who coined the term "Spaceship Earth" to illustrate the fact that we exist within a closed ecosystem. Decisions made by one group in one place influence the well-being of individuals across the ecosystem. This perspective calls for a radically different view of nature than the prevalent viewpoint characterized by Schumacher in his criticism of Western man for seeking to dominate and conquer nature.

E. F. Schumacher was born in Germany in 1911. Beginning in 1930 he studied in England as a Rhodes Scholar and later in New York City, earning a degree in economics. For two decades (1950–1970) Schumacher was Chief Economic Advisor to Britain's National Coal Board. During this time he wrote about economics for London's *The Times,* and also served as an economic advisor to the governments of India, Zambia, and Burma. His essay "Buddhist Economics" was widely read, but his books *Small is Beautiful: Economics as if People Mattered* and *A Guide for the Perplexed* (1977) garnered worldwide attention and cemented Schumacher's legacy. He is credited as one of the founders of the appropriate technology movement, advocating for smaller-scale or "intermediate" technologies that are environmentally sound, energy-efficient, and that better serve the people and communities in which they are used. Schumacher died in 1977.

The Problem of Production

One of the most fateful errors of our age is the belief that "the problem of production" has been solved. Not only is this belief firmly held by people remote from production and therefore professionally unacquainted with the facts—it is held by virtually all the experts, the captains of industry, the economic managers in the governments of the world, the academic and not-so-academic economists, not to mention the economic journalists. They may disagree on many things but they all agree that the problem of production has been solved; that mankind has at last come of age. For the rich countries, they say, the most important task now is "education for leisure" and, for the poor countries, the "transfer of technology."

That things are not going as well as they ought to be going must be due to human wickedness. We must therefore construct a political system so perfect that human wickedness disappears and everybody behaves well, no matter how much wickedness there may be in him or her. In fact, it is widely held that everybody is born good; if one turns into a criminal or an exploiter, this is the fault of "the system." No doubt "the system" is in many ways bad and must be changed. One of the main reasons why it is bad and why it can still survive in spite of its badness, is this erroneous view that the "problem of production" has been solved. As this error pervades all present-day systems there is at present not much to choose between them.

The arising of this error, so egregious and so firmly rooted, is closely connected with the philosophical, not to say religious, changes during the last three or four centuries in man's attitude to nature. I should perhaps say: Western man's attitude to nature, but since the whole world is now in a process of westernisation, the more generalised statement appears to be justified. Modern man does not experience himself as a part of nature but as an outside force destined to dominate and conquer it. He even talks of a battle with nature, forgetting that, if he won the battle, he would find himself on the losing side. Until quite recently, the battle seemed to go well enough to give him the illusion of unlimited powers, but not so well as to bring the possibility of total victory into view. This has now come into view, and many people, albeit only a minority, are beginning to realise what this means for the continued existence of humanity.

The illusion of unlimited powers, nourished by astonishing scientific and technological achievements, has produced the concurrent illusion of having solved the problem of production. The latter illusion is based on the failure to distinguish between income and capital where this distinction matters most. Every economist and businessman is familiar with the distinction, and applies it conscientiously and with considerable subtlety to all economic affairs—except where it really matters: namely, the irreplaceable capital which man has not made, but simply found, and without which he can do nothing.

A businessman would not consider a firm to have solved its problems of production and to have achieved viability if he saw that it was rap-

Pages 13–22 from *Small Is Beautiful: Economics As If People Mattered* by E.F. Schumacher. Copyright © 1973 by E.F. Schumacher. Published by Hutchinson. Reprinted by permission of HarperCollins Publishers (for U.S. distribution) and The Random House Group Limited (for Canadian distribution).

idly consuming its capital. How, then, could we overlook this vital fact when it comes to that very big firm, the economy of Spaceship Earth and, in particular, the economies of its rich passengers?

One reason for overlooking this vital fact is that we are estranged from reality and inclined to treat as valueless everything that we have not made ourselves. Even the great Dr. Marx fell into this devastating error when he formulated the so-called "labour theory of value." Now we have indeed laboured to make some of the capital which today helps us to produce—a large fund of scientific, technological, and other knowledge; an elaborate physical infrastructure; innumerable types of sophisticated capital equipment, etc.— but all this is but a small part of the total capital we are using. Far larger is the capital provided by nature and not by man—and we do not even recognize it as such. This larger part is now being used up at an alarming rate, and that is why it is an absurd and suicidal error to believe, and act on the belief, that the problem of production has been solved.

Let us take a closer look at this "natural capital." First of all, and most obviously, there are the fossil fuels. No one, I am sure, will deny that we are treating them as income items although they are undeniably capital items. If we treated them as capital items, we should be concerned with conservation; we should do everything in our power to try and minimize their current rate of use; we might be saying, for instance, that the money obtained from the realisation of these assets—these irreplaceable assets—must be placed into a special fund to be devoted exclusively to the evolution of production methods and patterns of living which do not depend on fossil fuels at all or depend on them only to a very slight extent. These and many other things we should be doing if we treated fossil fuels as capital and not as income.

And we do not do any of them, but the exact contrary of every one of them: we are not in the least concerned with conservation; we are maximising, instead of minimising, the current rates of use; and, far from being interested in studying the possibilities of alternative methods of production and patterns of living—so as to get off the collision course on which we are moving with ever-increasing speed—we happily talk of unlimited progress along the beaten track, of "education for leisure" in the rich countries, and of "the transfer of technology" to the poor countries.

The liquidation of these capital assets is proceeding so rapidly that even in the allegedly richest country in the world, the United States of America, there are many worried men, right up to the White House, calling for the massive conversion of coal into oil and gas, demanding ever more gigantic efforts to search for and exploit the remaining treasures of the earth. Look at the figures that are being put forward under the heading "World Fuel Requirements in the Year 2000." If we are now using something like 7000 million tons of coal equivalent, the need in twenty-eight years' time will be three times as large—around 20,000 million tons! What are twenty-eight years? Looking backwards, they take us roughly to the end of World War II, and, of course, since then fuel consumption has trebled; but the trebling involved an increase of less than 5000 million tons of coal equivalent. Now we are calmly talking about an increase three times as large.

People ask: Can it be done? And the answer comes back: It must be done and therefore it shall be done. One might say (with apologies to John Kenneth Galbraith) that it is a case of the bland leading the blind. But why cast aspersions? The question itself is wrong-headed, because it carries the implicit assumption that we are dealing with income and not with capital. What is so special about the year 2000? What about the year 2028, when little children running about today will be planning for their retirement? Another trebling by then? All these questions and answers are seen to be absurd the moment we realise that we are dealing with capital and not with income: fossil fuels are not made by men; they cannot be recycled. Once they are gone they are gone for ever.

But what—it will be asked—about the income fuels? Yes, indeed, what about them? Currently, they contribute (reckoned in calories) less than four per cent to the world total. In the foreseeable future they will have to contribute seventy, eighty, ninety per cent. To do something on a small scale is one thing: to do it on a gigantic scale is quite another, and to make an impact on the world fuel problem, contributions have to be truly gigantic. Who will say that the problem of production has been solved when it comes to income fuels required on a truly gigantic scale?

Fossil fuels are merely a part of the "natural capital" which we steadfastly insist on treating as expendable, as if it were income, and by no means the most important part. If we squander our fossil fuels, we threaten civilisation; but if we squander the capital represented by living nature around us, we threaten life itself. People are waking up to this threat, and they demand that pollution must stop. They think of pollution as a rather nasty habit indulged in by careless or greedy people who, as it were, throw their rubbish over the fence into the neighbour's garden. A more civilised behaviour, they realise, would incur some extra cost, and therefore we need a faster rate of economic growth to be able to pay for it. From now on, they say, we should use at least some of the fruits of our ever-increasing productivity to improve "the quality of life" and not merely to increase the quantity of consumption. All this is fair enough, but it touches only the outer fringe of the problem.

To get to the crux of the matter, we do well to ask why it is that all these terms—pollution, environment, ecology, etc.— have *so suddenly* come into prominence. After all, we have had an industrial system for quite some time, yet only five or ten years ago these words were virtually unknown. Is this a sudden fad, a silly fashion, or perhaps a sudden failure of nerve?

The explanation is not difficult to find. As with fossil fuels, we have indeed been living on the capital of living nature for some time, but at a fairly modest rate. It is only since the end of World War II that we have succeeded in increasing this rate to alarming proportions. In comparison with what is going on now and what has been going on, progressively, during the last quarter of a century, all the industrial activities of mankind up to, and including, World War II are as nothing. The next four or five years are likely to see more industrial production, taking the world as a whole, than all of mankind accomplished up to 1945. In other words, quite recently—so recently that most of us have hardly yet become conscious of it—there has been a unique quantitative jump in industrial production.

Partly as a cause and also as an effect, there has also been a unique qualitative jump. Our scientists and technologists have learned to compound substances unknown to nature. Against many of them, nature is virtually defenceless. There are no natural agents to attack and break them down. It is as if aborigines were suddenly attacked with machine-gun fire: their bows and arrows are of no avail. These substances, unknown to nature, owe their almost magical effectiveness precisely to nature's defencelessness— and that accounts also for their dangerous ecological impact. It is only in the last twenty years or so that they have made their appearance *in bulk*. Because they have no natural enemies, they tend to accumulate, and the long-term consequences of this accumulation are in many cases known to be extremely dangerous, and in other cases totally unpredictable.

In other words, the changes of the last twenty-five years, both in the quantity and in the quality of man's industrial processes, have produced an entirely new situation—a situation resulting not from our failures but from what we thought were our greatest successes. And this has come so suddenly that we hardly noticed the fact that we were very rapidly using up a certain kind of irreplaceable capital asset, namely the *tolerance margins* which benign nature always provides.

Now let me return to the question of "income fuels" with which I had previously dealt in a somewhat cavalier manner. No one is suggesting that the world-wide industrial system which is being envisaged to operate in the year 2000, a generation ahead, would be sustained primarily by water or wind power. No, we are told that we are moving rapidly into the nuclear age. Of course, this has been the story for quite some time, for over twenty years, and yet, the contribution of nuclear energy to man's total fuel and energy requirements is still minute. In 1970, it amounted to 2.7 per cent in Britain; 0.6 per cent in the European Community; and 0.3 per cent in the United States, to mention only the countries that have gone the furthest. Perhaps we can assume that nature's tolerance margins will be able to cope with such small impositions, although there are many people even today who are deeply worried, and Dr. Edward D. David, President Nixon's Science Adviser, talking about the storage of radioactive wastes, says that "one has a queasy feeling about something that has to stay underground and be pretty well sealed off for 25,000 years before it is harmless."

However that may be, the point I am making is a very simple one: the proposition to replace thousands of millions of tons of fossil fuels, every year, by nuclear energy means to "solve" the fuel problem by creating an environmental and ecological problem of such a monstrous magnitude that Dr. David will not be the only one to have "a queasy feeling." It means solving one problem by shifting it to another sphere—there to create an infinitely bigger problem.

Having said this, I am sure that I shall be confronted with another, even more daring proposition: namely, that future scientists and technologists will be able to devise safety rules and precautions of such perfection that the using, transporting, processing and storing of radioactive materials in ever-increasing quantities will be made entirely safe; also that it will be the task of politicians and social scientists to create a world society in which wars or civil disturbances can never happen. Again, it is a proposition to solve one problem simply by shifting it to another sphere, the sphere of everyday human behaviour. And this takes us to the third category of "natural capital" which we are recklessly squandering because we treat it as if it were income: as if it were something we had made ourselves and could easily replace out of our much-vaunted and rapidly rising productivity.

Is it not evident that our current methods of production are already eating into the very substance of industrial man? To many people this is not at all evident. Now that we have solved the problem of production, they say, have we ever had it so good? Are we not better fed, better clothed, and better housed than ever before—and better educated? Of course we are: most, but by no means all, of us: in the rich countries. But this is not what I mean by "substance." The substance of man cannot be measured by Gross National Product. Perhaps it cannot be measured at all, except for certain symptoms of loss. However, this is not the place to go into the statistics of these symptoms, such as crime, drug addiction, vandalism, mental breakdown, rebellion, and so forth. Statistics never prove anything.

I started by saying that one of the most fateful errors of our age is the belief that the problem of production has been solved. This illusion, I suggested, is mainly due to our inability to recognise that the modern industrial system, with all its intellectual sophistication, consumes the very basis on which it has been erected. To use the language of the economist, it lives on irreplaceable capital which it cheerfully treats as income. I specified three categories of such capital: fossil fuels, the tolerance margins of nature, and the human substance. Even if some readers should refuse to accept all three parts of my argument, I suggest that any one of them suffices to make my case.

And what is my case? Simply that our most important task is to get off our present collision course. And who is there to tackle such a task? I think every one of us, whether old or young, powerful or powerless, rich or poor, influential or uninfluential. To talk about the future is useful only if it leads to action *now*. And what can we do *now*, while we are still in the position of "never having had it so good"? To say the least—which is already very much—we must thoroughly understand the problem and begin to see the possibility of evolving a new life-style, with new methods of production and new patterns of consumption: a life-style designed for permanence. To give only three preliminary examples: in agriculture and horticulture, we can interest ourselves in the perfection of production methods which are biologically sound, build up soil fertility, and produce health, beauty and permanence. Productivity will then

look after itself. In industry, we can interest ourselves in the evolution of small-scale technology, relatively nonviolent technology, "technology with a human face," so that people have a chance to enjoy themselves while they are working, instead of working solely for their pay packet and hoping, usually forlornly, for enjoyment solely during their leisure time. In industry, again—and, surely, industry is the pace-setter of modern life—we can interest ourselves in new forms of partnership between management and men, even forms of common ownership.

We often hear it said that we are entering the era of "the Learning Society." Let us hope this is true. We still have to learn how to live peacefully, not only with our fellow men but also with nature and, above all, with those Higher Powers which have made nature and have made us; for, assuredly, we have not come about by accident and certainly have not made ourselves.

The themes which have been merely touched upon in this chapter will have to be further elaborated as we go along. Few people will be easily convinced that the challenge to man's future cannot be met by making marginal adjustments here or there, or, possibly, by changing the political system.

The following chapter is an attempt to look at the whole situation again, from the angle of peace and permanence. Now that man has acquired the physical means of self-obliteration, the question of peace obviously looms larger than ever before in human history. And how could peace be built without some assurance of permanence with regard to our economic life?

Discussion Questions

1. Schumacher claims that it was only in the period following WWII that the "problem of production" reached a magnitude where the rate at which we consumed natural capital reached "alarming proportions." What factors contributed to this "entirely new situation?"
2. What does the notion of "technology with a human face" mean to you? What attributes would such a technology possess?
3. Schumacher states that "to talk about the future is useful only if it leads to action *now*." What types of actions does he advocate for?
4. If humankind has been blinded by the tremendous technological gains we have made into thinking that we can innovate our way through "the problem of production," yet we look to new methods of production to help solve this problem, will we find ourselves continuing to consume our natural capital at unsustainable rates? What circumstances might break this spiral?
5. Schumacher uses the terms "natural capital" and "income fuels" in a business analogy. What is the essence of that business analogy, and how should it impact the way we look at the problem of production and conservation?

 Supporting Activities

1. Visit the web site of the Schumacher Center for a New Economics at: http://www .centerforneweconomics.org/schumacher. Read more of his essays ("Buddhist Economics" is a favorite) and view some of the video clips of lectures by Schumacher.
2. Read the text of the "Natural Capital Declaration," signed by financial institutions from around the world: http://www.naturalcapitaldeclaration.org/the-declaration/. Discuss the feasibility and importance of the recommendations made within the Declaration. Contrast this with the statements made within the 1908 Presidential Address found in Section 3 of this book.
3. Take the quiz "Know Your Power Plant" on the U.S. Department of Energy web site: http:// energy.gov/maps/quiz-know-your-power-plant-0.
4. Use the legislation database provided by the National Council of State Legislatures to find out what recent legislation your state has adopted regarding renewable energy. You can find this up-to-date and user-friendly database at: http://www.ncsl.org/research/energy/energy-environment-legislation-tracking-database.aspx.

 Additional Resources

1. Read the book *Natural Capitalism* by Paul Hawken, Amory Lovins, and L. Hunter Lovins (1999; Little, Brown and Company). Book excerpts and downloadable chapters can be found at: http://www.natcap.org/sitepages/pid5.php.
2. Learn more about valuing ecosystem services at this USDA/Forest Service web site: http://www. fs.fed.us/ecosystemservices/.

Razing Appalachia

The article "Razing Appalachia" highlights the social, environmental, and economic implications of mountaintop removal coal mining in West Virginia. Mountaintop removal (MTR), a particularly devastating form of surface mining, is now the preferred method to mine coal, replacing the more expensive and more dangerous method of underground mining. The reading highlights two sides to the story.

One side is fighting to stop MTR from destroying their generations-old lifestyle. Communities that live in the shadows of these megaprojects are subjected daily to blasting, polluted air and ground water, and the fear of toxic slurry spills. Regionally, the Appalachian people have contended with an ever-growing number of lost mountains and valleys, and are trying to put an end to it. On the other side are coal miners and owners struggling to maintain their generations-old lifestyle, and to satisfy the nation's growing demand for electricity. Increasingly restrictive environmental regulations squeeze their profit margins. Community leaders, desperate for any jobs, tout the economic development of coal mining. Coal miners simply want to feed their families. Coal mine operators say "we're obeying the law," and in most cases they are.

The conflict described in this 1999 article is playing out all over again across Appalachia as the nation pursues a different kind of energy resource, natural gas.[2] The same geological formations that make this region rich in coal also make it rich in oil and gas reserves. Today, landowners in Appalachia are more likely to face developers who want to set up drilling pads to conduct hydraulic fracturing—more commonly known as fracking—on their land. New technological developments that enabled horizontal drilling deep underground combined with a growing demand for oil and natural gas (the "clean" fossil fuel) have resulted in a massive expansion in fracking activity in Appalachia and elsewhere in the United States over the past 10 years. As with coal mining, the associated problems have deeply affected the communities where fracking is prevalent.

Maryanne Vollers is an author and journalist based in Livingston, Montana. She has written and ghostwritten several books. A former editor at *Rolling Stone* magazine, she has published articles in periodicals such as *Time, Esquire,* and *The New York Times Magazine*. She and husband William Campbell founded Homefire Productions to create features and documentaries on social and environmental issues, and their PBS documentary *Wolves in Paradise* won a CINE Golden Eagle award. "Razing Appalachia" was the motivation for the award-winning documentary of the same name released in 2003. It was directed by Sasha Waters for Room 135 Productions and is available through Bullfrog Films.

Razing Appalachia

By Maryanne Vollers

First they dug out the land. Then they strip mined it. Now Big Coal is leveling the mountains themselves–and tearing communities apart.

"Hear that quiet?" Larry Gibson asks as he climbs through the highland cemetery where nearly 300 of his kin lie buried. "You know they're about to set off a shot when they shut down the machines." Gibson, a 53-year-old retired maintenance worker and evangelist of the environmental cause, hunkers down with some visitors to wait for the blast.

Gibson knows the routine by heart. After all, the Princess Beverly Coal Company has been blowing up the hills around his family's 50-acre "homeplace" in West Virginia for more than a decade. When the demolition team is ready down below, the "Ukes"—heavy shovel trucks—back away from a line of high explosives drilled into solid rock. Then the warning horn sounds: two minutes.

The graveyard sits atop Kayford Mountain, a modest, leafy peak that sticks out of the shattered landscape like a fat, green thumb. The view from the edge of the cemetery looks more like the Tunisian outback than a West Virginia mountain range: The ground drops 300 or 400 feet into a dust bowl of raw coal and rubble, crosscut by dirt tracks. In the distance, what used to be forested ridges now resemble flat-topped buttes crusted over with rough grass and a few stunted trees.

West Virginia has been mined since the mid-18th century, but nobody has seen annihilation like this before. In the past 20 years, environmentalists claim, 500 square miles of the state have been stripped and gutted for their coal. In the most apocalyptic form of strip mining, called mountaintop removal, whole peaks are razed to extract layers of relatively clean-burning low-sulfur coal, while the excess rock and earth "overburden" is dumped into the valleys. Hundreds of miles of streams have been buried under these "valley fills," and dozens of mountains have been flattened into synthetic prairies.

Now, an environmental group called the West Virginia Highlands Conservancy and seven coalfield residents are taking state and federal regulators to court for the first time, claiming not only that mountaintop removal devastates the environment, but that existing laws designed to mitigate the damage are not being enforced. Coal companies and their proxies defend the practice as necessary for the economy, and assert that there is no proof it permanently damages the environment. Since last year, both sides have been presenting their cases in a federal court. What's at stake is the future of surface coal mining in West Virginia, the economies of several counties, the way of life of thousands of people, and, environmentalists contend, the ecological health of the northern Appalachian watershed.

Whatever the outcome of the lawsuit, most of Kayford Mountain is destined to be strip-mined one way or another. But Larry Gibson won't let the coal companies take it all. He represents the large extended clan that owns that 50-acre parcel atop Kayford, the remnant of a mountaintop farm dating back to the 18th century. It's one of the rare private holdings in West Virginia's southern highlands, where most land is owned by corporations and leased to coal companies. Millions of dollars in coal lie beneath the picnic ground and vacation cabins, but the family trust won't sell.

"The man from the coal company told me, 'We haven't seen anything we can't buy,'" Gibson recalls. "I said, 'You're not buying this land.' If we sell, we sell our heritage. We have no past after that. Where can we show our family where their roots are?"

As we watch, a huge explosion wallops a coal-streaked bench below the cemetery, flinging up plumes of yellow dust and sending cascades of dirt and shale overburden into the valley. The hillside shudders with the shock wave. "That warn't nothing," observes Gibson's cousin, Carl "Red" Fraker, a 70-year-old retired miner who lives in a half-deserted village along Cabin Creek, below Kayford. "The big ones roll the ground like an earthquake." Fraker was born on Kayford Mountain, and he intends to be buried here some day.

But most of his friends and neighbors have moved on. Aside from the environmental damage caused by mountaintop removal, the practice is killing a way of life in West Virginia's hollows. Explosions shower dust and rocks down on people who live below the mountaintop mines. The foundations of their houses crack and their wells dry up. Whole towns are disappearing as people sell their homes and move away.

Machines do almost all the work in these modern mines; the coal miners and their communities are now an inconvenience. Thousands of people once lived in simple wood-frame houses along Cabin Creek. Now the road that follows the streambed is lined with ghost towns with names like Red Warrior and Acme and White Row, casualties of the conversion from underground mining to strip mining and now mountaintop removal. After the shops and movie theaters were shuttered and shacks were emptied, the bulldozers came. All that remains now are worn patches in the mountainside, and a few stubborn clusters of daffodils planted long ago in now-vanished gardens.

Up above, when the dust clouds settle after the latest blast, the Ukes start chugging up the hill to scrape out the exposed coal. Red Fraker takes another look out at the black wasteland below. "I want to ask, what's gonna happen to West Virginia when all the coal's gone?" he says. "Ain't no timber on it. No dirt left. Nothin'. What's it gonna be?"

That was precisely the question members of Congress were asking when they passed the Surface Mining Control and Reclamation Act, SMCRA (familiarly known as smack-ra), back in 1977. The gist of the law is this: If you mine it, you have to restore the land to the same or better condition than it was in before you got there. The law also provides detailed regulations designed to reduce the environmental impact of such destructive mining. According to SMCRA, strip mines, including mountaintop mines, cannot be allowed within 100 feet of active streams unless it can be shown that the streams won't be damaged. The law further requires "contemporaneous reclamation"—meaning that soil replacement and reseeding must occur soon after the coal is removed. The land must be returned to its "approximate original contour," or AOC. The permit holder can be granted a variance from the AOC rule only after submitting a detailed plan for post-mining flatland development, such as a school, airport, or shopping center that would benefit nearby communities.

West Virginia's Department of Environmental Protection (DEP) is charged with enforcing SMCRA, with the oversight of the federal Office of Surface Mining. Unfortunately, there has been very little regulation by the DEP, whose ranks are filled with former coal-industry employees, and even less supervision from the weak and understaffed federal agency.

When SMCRA was written, mountaintop removal was still an unusual practice. It became more prevalent in the 1980s, when 20-story-tall, rock-eating machines called draglines were brought in to make the technique profitable. Ironically, it was stricter environmental laws that increased the demand for West Virginia's low-sulfur coal. More than 80 percent of America's coal is consumed by coal-burning electric power plants, which in turn provide the nation with 56 percent of its electricity. Following passage of 1990's Clean Air Act, power plants were forced to reduce the sulfur content of smokestack emissions, which react with the atmosphere to cause acid rain. Some of the purest and hottest-burning coal in the nation is found in thin, multiple seams high in West Virginia's southern mountains. Rather than mine this coal out of the mountains, industry accountants found, it's cheaper and faster to take the mountains off the coal.

In recent years, the DEP has kept up with the demand for low-sulfur coal by granting permits for more and bigger surface mines. Since 1995, the agency has approved permits subjecting 27,000 new acres to mountaintop removal. (In contrast, journalist Ken Ward, Jr. discovered while researching a prizewinning series of articles for the *Charleston Gazette*, the state's largest and most influential newspaper, fewer than 10,000 acres were permitted during the 1980s.) Anywhere from a tenth to two-thirds of the mining permits issued in West Virginia in 1997 (the number depends on whether you consult state regulators or the *Gazette's* Ward) are for mountaintop-removal mines, which account for 16 percent of the state's coal output. Environmentalists assert that some mountaintop mining areas are now 10 miles wide, and that the largest will eventually gobble up 20,000 acres.

But it is not just the size of a given mining area that's worrisome; nobody has studied what the cumulative impact of so much disruption will be on the environment of northern Appalachia. "It might be a different story if it was a 200-acre plot here, and 500 acres in another county," says Cindy Rank of the West Virginia Highlands Conservancy. "But mountaintop removal is spreading and connecting all through the areas where there are coal reserves." If permits continue to be approved at the pace set over the past decade, environmentalists say, half the peaks in some southern counties could be lopped off.

Despite assurances from coal companies that the technique is perfectly safe, environmentalists are focused on an array of problems associated with mountaintop removal. They worry about increased acid runoff from these giant gashes, particularly since they estimate that 75 percent of West Virginia's streams and rivers are already polluted by mining and other industries. They fear the loss of groundwater in the land below flattened mountains that were once laced with springs and aquifers. And even though coal-industry technicians insist that the gargantuan valley fills behave "like sponges" and are actually a form of flood control, other experts remain skeptical. "What you see in a lot of these valley fills has no engineering method to it at all," says Rick Eades, a hydrogeologist who used to work in the mining industry and is now an environmental activist. "It's just dirt and rock being pushed over the side of a hill and filling in vertically several hundred feet." Although none of the valley fills has failed since they became a part of West Virginia's landscape 25 years ago, Eades fears a disastrous flood within the next 25. "Nature will cut those valley fills right out of there, given time. And there's no way that the mountains can heal in a way that will resemble the original ability of the land to hold back the water during heavy rains, hold back sediments, and retain groundwater." Such concerns led two West Virginia conservation groups to put the DEP on notice in January of this year of their intent to sue the agency for not assessing the "cumulative hydrological impacts" of mountaintop removal during the permitting process.

Still more problems exist. "Mountaintop removal destroys the beauty of the state, which is somewhat intangible," says William Maxey, West Virginia's former chief forester. "More tangible is the fact that it deforests the state." Maxey says that, as of 1997, 300,000 acres of hardwood forest had been destroyed by mountaintop removal. He characterizes the mining industry's preferred reforestation methods as "bogus," saying they are "totally superficial and will not work." After Maxey failed to convince the DEP to require adequate reforestation of mountaintop mines, he resigned from his job in disgust.

King Coal rules West Virginia like a petulant monarch, one used to getting its way. Coal production accounts for 13 percent of West

Virginia's gross state product, commands an annual payroll of $900 million, and provides more than a third of the state's business-tax revenues. King Coal also finds campaign contributions a good investment, and is famously generous with them. For instance, Gov. Cecil Underwood, a former coal executive, is the recent beneficiary of $250,000 in campaign donations from coal companies. (An additional quarter-million was contributed to cover the cost of his inauguration party.) It was Underwood who pushed a bill through the state legislature last year to make mountaintop-removal mining even easier and more profitable. It allowed companies to obliterate up to 480 acres of the drainage above any stream (up from 250 acres) before paying mitigation costs to the state—of $200,000 per buried acre.

But the blatant coal-industry giveaway backfired—leading to the bill's repeal—when it roused public interest, even outrage. City people started paying more attention to what was going on out of sight, up in the remote coalfields. A 1998 opinion poll showed that 53 percent of West Virginians opposed mountaintop removal, versus 29 percent in favor.

At the same time that Underwood was lobbying for the pro-industry bill in March 1998, the *Charleston Gazette* was employing the Freedom of Information Act to obtain 81 mining permits issued by the DEP, which it then reviewed against federal laws such as SMCRA and the Clean Water Act. The investigation revealed some startling facts: The DEP didn't keep complete records of how many permits it issued, so there was no way to track the cumulative effects of mining. The U.S. Army Corps of Engineers routinely gave general "nationwide" permits for valley fills that should have required more rigorous individual permits. And in almost all cases, mountaintop-removal AOC variances were issued without post-mining development plans. In those cases when plans were

submitted, most of them were for "timberland" or "wildlife habitat"—uses not recognized by SMCRA.

The Office of Surface Mining conducted its own investigation, which essentially confirmed the newspaper's findings. In other words, for 20 years the DEP had been stretching the law to please the coal companies, and the U.S. government had been letting them get away with it.

In response to an increasing public outcry over mountaintop removal, Gov. Underwood appointed a task force to investigate the issue. It came up with recommendations for more studies and increased vigilance by the regulators. But old hands at this game don't believe coal companies can be regulated. Ken Hechler, West Virginia's 84-year-old secretary of state, is a longtime nemesis of the coal industry. As a West Virginia congressman from 1959 to 1977, Hechler tried to abolish strip mining altogether.

"I still feel that it is impossible to have either strip mining or mountaintop removal and have adequate reclamation, which I characterize as putting lipstick on a corpse," he says. He recently appeared at an environmental rally at the capital and sang a song, to the tune of John Denver's "Take Me Home, Country Roads." It began: "Almost level, West Virginia/Scalped-off mountains, dumped into our rivers."

Meanwhile, Arch Coal, the country's second-largest coal company, was trying to push through a 3,100-acre mountaintop-removal permit to expand its giant Dal-Tex mine in Logan County. It would be the largest permit ever granted—amounting to about five square miles of what the DEP calls "total extraction." The Dal-Tex mine had already filled in dozens of hollows on the west side of the Spruce Fork River along state Highway 17. All but 40 of the 200 families that once lived in the hamlet of Blair had already moved away. That was when James Weekley, a 58-year-old grandfather and former miner, began to fear that Arch Coal wanted the rest—including the headwaters of Pigeonroost Branch, in the leafy hollow where he and his family have lived for generations.

In July 1998, Weekley and nine other coalfield residents joined with the West Virginia Highlands Conservancy to sue the Army Corps and the DEP for ignoring SMCRA, the Clean Water Act, and other laws. (Three of the original plaintiffs have since dropped out.) Although no coal companies were specifically sued, the purpose of the lawsuit was to make sure the mines comply with the law.

Pro-coal letter writers to West Virginia newspapers labeled Weekley and the other plaintiffs environmental radicals. "I'm not an environmentalist—I'm a citizen!" says Weekley. "I was born in this hollow and I'm gonna die here. They'll have to bulldoze me out before I go."

Last December, the plaintiffs decided to settle part of the case against the federal government. They agreed that the Army Corps, in conjunction with other federal and state agencies, would conduct a two-year environmental impact study to assess and deal with the cumulative damage caused by mountaintop removal in West Virginia. Meanwhile, new permits, and ones already in the pipeline, would be subjected to closer scrutiny to ensure their compliance with existing regulations and standards. But after Arch Coal, responding to pressure from the U.S. Environmental Protection Agency that was unrelated to the lawsuit, made significant changes in its permit application—including reducing the lifetime of the Dal-Tex expansion mine from 12 to five years and scaling back its proposed valley fills—the federal defendants argued that the Dal-Tex permit should be exempted from new, stricter scrutiny, and that mining should be allowed to begin.

But Weekley and the other plaintiffs balked at exempting the Dal-Tex mine. They asked U.S.

District Chief Judge Charles Haden for a preliminary injunction to delay the permit until the rest of the lawsuit could be resolved in a trial scheduled for this July.

To the astonishment of almost everyone, the conservative Republican judge—who had visited Pigeonroost Hollow and flown over the coalfields—granted the preliminary injunction. In doing so, he cited the "imminent and irreversible" harm that would be done to the Weekleys, and to the stream flowing through Pigeonroost Hollow, if the mining were to proceed, and distinguished it from the "purely temporary economic harms" that Arch would endure from the delay in its operations. The judge then noted that the other legal questions the plaintiffs had raised regarding the conduct of mountaintop removal would be addressed in the future trial. Meanwhile, Arch Coal would have to wait for its permit.

The coal company responded to the ruling by laying off 30 miners at its Dal-Tex mine, and promising to shut down its operation and put 300 more employees out of work by summer. The loss of jobs and tax revenues would poleax the economy of Logan County, one of the poorest counties in a poor state. Less money would be available for schools, police—everything would be affected. The president of the Logan County Commission declared, "It's a war!" and the commission vowed to fight to keep the mine open. Days after the Haden decision, 1,500 miners, along with union and business leaders from Logan County, marched on Charleston to protest.

The United Mine Workers of America (UMWA) found itself in a terrible position. The stark reality of labor in West Virginia is this: At the end of World War II there were more than 100,000 union coal miners in the state. Now, of the fewer than 19,000 who remain, only 40 percent belong to the UMWA. The union's president, Cecil Roberts, perceived as a moderate on the issue of mountaintop removal, had already come out in favor of protecting communities from the technique's excesses. But the imminent loss of one of the biggest union mines in the state was more than he could take. Roberts called for observation of April 2, 1999, as a "memorial day" without pay for the nation's 35,000 union miners to protest the situation in West Virginia. He was hoping that up to 10,000 would attend a rally in Charleston. Perhaps because it was the Easter weekend, only about 500 miners and family members showed up at the Capitol steps.

Roberts, a wiry, bearded, native West Virginian, shouted like a preacher at the modest crowd that day, telling them they'd all been "kicked in the teeth again by the environmental community. We're fed up and we're fired up!" Roberts has been busy leading the union in its fight with the Clinton-Gore administration over U.S. support for the Kyoto treaty on global warming, which he fears will put the nation's coal industry out of business and cost his workers their jobs. He told the crowd, "You can't say 'Don't burn it' in Washington and 'Don't mine it' in West Virginia and say you're not trying to take the jobs of every coal miner in the United States. And I'm here to say no, no, and hell no!"

Some in West Virginia have accused Roberts of stirring up an already volatile situation in the coalfields. Roberts responds that he's been reasonable for the past year, trying to negotiate a solution to the mountaintop-removal problem. "We were working to find a compromise for workers to keep their jobs and at the same time protect the environment. I believe you can do both," he told *Mother Jones*. "We argued that we shouldn't eliminate mountaintop mining at that moment. It wasn't fair to the workers, wasn't fair quite frankly to the companies that had invested literally millions and millions of dollars in West Virginia."

Secretary of State Hechler, who has a long history of supporting the UMWA, is disappointed in Roberts' stance. "Like all wars," he says, "a war against the mountains creates employment. But you don't keep fighting just to supply jobs. In any event, we ought to start diversifying our economy early on instead of making such a heavy dependence on coal, which pollutes the streams, pollutes the politics, and is a finite resource."

The coal hasn't quite run out yet. In fact, the last two years have set new records for West Virginia coal production, with 182 million tons extracted in 1997 alone. Furthermore, most of the mining jobs eliminated over the past half-century were lost to mechanization of the mines and a conversion to surface mining—not a decline in coal production.

But Hechler is right: The coal will run out some day. And the big lie of Big Coal is that West Virginia depends on mining for its prosperity. Skeptics ask: What prosperity? West Virginia is 49th among the 50 states in household income. And in this very poor state, the poorest counties are the ones with the most coal mines.

"No state has given more to the American Dream and gotten less back from it than West Virginia," says Norm Steenstra, director of the West Virginia Citizen Action Group and a former coal operator himself. "The corrupt political system, the dead streams, the severed mountains, the fraud, the dust, the noise, the air pollution—what for? All to supply the voracious American appetite for cheap electricity."

It's a risky business calling up a coal company and saying you're with *Mother Jones*. But David Todd, vice president and spokesman for Arch Coal, is a good sport, and he agrees to a tour of the Hobet 21 mine near Madison, West Virginia. The mine is a cousin of the Dal-Tex operation, 40 miles south of here, and a showcase for mountaintop removal.

We climb into a 4 x 4 truck to have a look at a section that was mined 20 years ago. In fact, the reclaimed parts of Hobet 21 are quite handsome. There are rolling, grassy hills, stands of small trees here and there, a number of ponds where ducks like to nest. To my eyes, it looks more like western Nebraska than West Virginia. But to Todd, and to the regulators who approved this reclamation, this is a fine example of restoring the approximate original contour of the land. "The hills are smaller but with similar rolls as the original mountains," says Todd, sweeping his hand across the pastures to the forested bumps on the horizon. "This is just more manicured-looking." Secretary of the Interior Bruce Babbitt (who oversees the Office of Surface Mining) took a similar tour of the Hobet 21 mine in the summer of 1996. Impressed, he announced that the Hobet mine was "a rebuke to those who say, Jobs or the environment. This landscape shouts out: You can have both!" Babbitt also said something that continues to haunt the foes of mountaintop removal: "The landscape has changed. It is a better landscape in many ways, a different landscape—a savanna of forests coming back, of fields." The local headline read "Landscape improved, Babbitt says." And Arch Coal helpfully provides copies of the story in its press kit.

Before we wrap up the afternoon tour, Todd wants to get something off his chest about the mountaintop-removal controversy and the Dal-Tex permit problem. "If you detect a level of frustration, sometimes even anger, I don't deny it," says Todd, a fair-haired man in a white hard hat. "Because, dammit, we've done everything and more that people have asked us to do throughout the years." He says Arch Coal has bent over backward to get the right permits and keep the mine running, taking a loss of $1 million a month since September 1998 in the process. "All we ask is, tell us what the standard is, how we should comply with the law, the

permits we need, and we will do that!" he says, throwing up his hands. "Meantime, shutting us down and costing 300 jobs at Dal-Tex is unconscionable!"

It's touching to hear a coal executive so concerned about the loss of jobs. In the past year, 900 union miners have been laid off in West Virginia due to reduced domestic demand (after a pair of mild winters) and a general consolidation in the coal industry. Nobody marched on Charleston when those cuts were announced, and no corporate vice presidents expressed their anger and frustration. Most of the coal-mining jobs are moving to the Powder River Basin of Wyoming, where there are no unions, and where seams 75 feet thick lie right below the gentle, rolling surface of the land. Arch Coal recently purchased Atlantic Richfield Company's giant strip mine there and, a few days after Judge Haden's decision, began to dismantle one of its 340-ton coal shovel trucks to ship to Wyoming.

Ricky Light of Sharples, West Virginia, used to drive that truck. Light, 32, who has a wife, three young daughters, and payments to make on a new modular home, was one of the first to be laid off at Dal-Tex. He used to make $55,000 a year; now he receives unemployment income of $1,200 a month, though his bills amount to $1,800, not including groceries. He and his wife, Samantha, may be shutting off the phone soon, and are considering moving in with her mother. "We planned our life around 15 more years of mining," says Light, a slender, dark-haired man in a Nike swoosh cap. "I didn't believe it'd go this far. I thought they'd get the permits."

Light says he has a "few good possibilities" for another job. He's been told he could relocate to Arch's new mine, near Gillette, Wyoming, but Light doesn't want to leave his hometown. Like the business leaders in Logan, Ricky Light doesn't fault Arch Coal or the grim realities of mining for his predicament. He blames the people who brought the lawsuit, some of them his neighbors. "There's a lot of hard feelings here," he says. "It's just getting started. 'Cause you don't take things off people's tables. You don't mess with people's livelihoods."

Pigeonroost Hollow is just a mile or so east of Blair Mountain, which was the site of the biggest union battle in the history of West Virginia. That was in 1921, when a young firebrand named Bill Blizzard—whose great-nephew happens to be UMWA president Cecil Roberts—led 15,000 men on a march to unionize the southern coalfields. Famed organizer Mary Harris "Mother" Jones herself tried to stop the confrontation, but she couldn't turn them back. The union men met the sheriff's private army on the slopes of Blair Mountain. As many as 20 people were killed; nobody knows the exact number. Blizzard ended up in jail. It took another decade and still more blood to organize the West Virginia mines.

Another war is now being fought in the shadow of Blair Mountain. The barriers seem harder to define, and the sons and daughters of those union foot soldiers are dug in on both sides of the line. It's a battle over jobs and the environment, tradition and change—a fight that is going on here in the coalfields, and out in the redwood forests of California, and in the copper mines of Montana, and overseas where the natural resources are running dry.

There used to be a historical marker at the foot of Blair Mountain describing the great union war. But somebody stole it, and the sign was never replaced. Soon the mountain itself will be gone, consumed by the dragline and converted into an artificial pasture big enough for a hundred future Wal-Marts, although there will be hardly anyone left to shop there. There may not even be a marker to commemorate the battle, or the times when Mother Jones walked up the creeks to organize the coal camps because the coal company owned the roads. The creeks themselves will be buried under tons of dirt and rock, buried like the mountain and the memory of a time when the people of the coalfields and their union knew which side they were on.

Discussion Questions

1. What conclusions can you draw from the absence of discussion about global warming, acid rain, and other "hot" environmental topics? Is MTR an "Appalachian" issue? A national issue? An international issue?

2. According to the Department of Energy's Energy Information Administration, the productivity of a U.S. surface miner (in tons mined per worker-hour) is close to four times higher than that of an underground miner. Surface mining accounts for around 100 times fewer mine fatalities per unit of coal than does underground mining. How do you think these statistics should be factored into the MTR debate?

3. One potential solution to the MTR debate is strict enforcement of existing environmental and reclamation laws. Do you think this is an effective approach? Why or why not?

4. How much do you pay per kilowatt-hour for electricity? If you're not sure, then check your electricity bill. Would you support a 10% increase in your electricity bill to subsidize more environmentally benign coal mining in West Virginia? How much of an increase would you pay for electricity to shift away from coal to electricity generated from renewable energy sources?

 Supporting Activities

1. On Google Earth, fly to Logan County, WV and locate a surface mine. Use the measuring tool to estimate the area of the operation.

2. Find out coal consumption levels for your state and for the United States in the last year. The U.S. Department of Energy's Energy Information Administration (www.eia.doe.gov) is a good source for this information. While there, look for information about the projected supply of coal at currently producing mines, at current consumption rates.

3. Where is the nearest coal-fired power plant to where you live? What is the name and generation capacity of this facility?

4. View the movie *Razing Appalachia*. You can learn more about the movie and how to access it on this PBS site: http://www.pbs.org/independentlens/razingappalachia/film.html.

 Additional Resources

1. The regional environmental group Appalachian Voices is dedicated to reducing the impact of coal on the Appalachian region. Learn more about this organization and its work at: www.appvoices.org.

2. The organization Sustainable Williamson (http://sustainablewilliamson.org/) is working to create more resilient and sustainable communities within central Appalachia that do not rely on the coal economy. Their site provides short videos and descriptions of their approach to economic revitalization in the heart of West Virginia coal country.

Light's Out: Approaching the Historic Interval's End

No one disputes that fossil fuels are a finite resource. However, our technological capacity to satisfy global demand for cheap energy has led consumers and policy makers to continue to operate as if we can expect a future with more of the same. As Heinberg points out, low prices in a critical commodity like oil tend to breed complacency. This is an example of misguided "cornucopian" thinking that defies well-accepted science. Fossil fuels will not satisfy global demand forever.

When will we run out of oil? According to author Richard Heinberg, that's really not what matters. How much of this or that fuel is left isn't the important factor, but rather the price. Price, as any economist will tell you, depends on supply and demand. Energy, except for brief exceptions, has been historically cheap because supply has been able to satisfy demand, even as both have risen dramatically. However, evidence suggests that the supply of petroleum will not keep pace with demand for much longer. Oil production, or the rate at which oil is extracted from the ground, has "peaked" and will soon decline, by Heinberg's reckoning. The greater the demand and the greater the rate at which it's extracted the sooner the peak will occur. This peak is predicted to occur (or to have occurred) sometime between the mid-2000s and 2020. At that point prices will invariably rise and, as Heinberg puts it, the party will truly be over. Imagine the downward slope on the production curve, when oil gets increasingly harder and more expensive to retrieve even as demand rises, and you can quickly understand what he means.

Do we have time to act? Can a timely, affordable alternative be found that will simply replace oil without a hitch? The answer is, most likely, no. Historically cheap oil in the United States has resulted in an economy and infrastructure that rely heavily on the automobile and on large quantities of oil. Cheap energy has also discouraged the search for alternatives to fossil fuels, making the transition to alternatives that much slower and more difficult.

In this excerpt, Richard Heinberg presents the scientific case for "peak oil" by explaining the observations and arguments that support the claim. Although not himself a scientist, Heinberg has the ability to readily identify the salient points. Be alerted, however, that he sometimes employs biased language and perhaps occasionally stretches the facts a bit thin. While reading, consider what type of further information you need in order to establish a well-informed position. In the end, Heinberg acknowledges that uncertainties in energy projections always exist, and that new sources and processes can be identified. And he underscores the most fundamental point of all: that the entire economy of every developed nation is completely dependent on energy resources.

Richard Heinberg is a Senior Fellow of the Post Carbon Institute in Sebastopol, California. He has authored numerous articles and essays and is considered one of the world's foremost experts on peak oil. He is the author of twelve books, including the sequel to *The Party's Over*, titled *Powerdown: Options and Actions for a Post-Carbon Future* (2004) and *Afterburn: Society Beyond Fossil Fuels* (2015).

Lights Out: Approaching the Historic Interval's End

By Richard Heinberg

The Ground Giving Way

In nearly every year since 1859, the total amount of oil extracted from the world's ancient and finite underground reserves had grown— from a few thousand barrels a year to 65 million barrels per day by the end of the 20th century, an increase averaging about two percent per annum. Demand had grown just as dramatically, sometimes lagging behind the erratically expanding supply. The great oil crises of the 1970s—the most significant occasions when demand exceeded supply—had been politically-based interruptions in the delivery of crude that was otherwise readily available; there had been no actual physical shortage of the substance then, or at any other time.

In the latter part of the year 2000, as Al Gore and George W. Bush were crisscrossing the nation vying for votes and campaign contributions, the world price of oil rose dramatically from its low point of $10 per barrel in February 1999 to $35 per barrel by mid-September of 2000. Essentially, Venezuela and Mexico had convinced the other members of OPEC to cease cheating on production quotas, and this resulted in a partial closing of the global petroleum spigot. Yet while Saudi Arabia, Iraq, and Russia still had excess production capacity that could have been brought on line to keep prices down, most other oil-producing nations were pumping at, or nearly at, full capacity throughout this period.

Meanwhile, a wave of mergers had swept the industry. Exxon and Mobil had combined into Exxon-Mobil, the world's largest oil company; Chevron had merged with Texaco; Conoco had merged with Phillips; and BP had purchased Amoco-Arco. Small and medium-sized companies—such as Tosco, Valero, and Ultramar Diamond Shamrock Corp—also joined in the mania for mergers, buyouts, and downsizing. Nationally, oil-company mergers, acquisitions, and divestments totaled $82 billion in 1998 and over $50 billion in 1999.

Altogether, the oil industry appeared to be in a mode of consolidation, not one of expansion. As Goldman Sachs put it in an August 1999 report, "The oil companies are not going to keep rigs employed to drill dry holes. They know it but are unable . . . to admit it. The great merger mania is nothing more than a scaling

down of a dying industry in recognition that 90 percent of global conventional oil has already been found."[4]

Meanwhile the Energy Information Agency (EIA) predicted that global *demand* for oil would continue to grow, increasing 60 percent by the year 2020 to roughly 40 billion barrels per year, or nearly 120 million barrels per day.[5]

The dramatic price hikes of 2000 soon triggered a global economic recession. The link between energy prices and the economy was intuitively obvious and had been amply demonstrated by the oil crises and accompanying recessions of the 1970s. Yet, as late as mid-2000, many pundits were insisting that the new "information economy" of the 1990s was impervious to energy-price shocks. This trend of thought was typified in a comment by British Prime Minister Tony Blair, who in January 2000 stated that "[t]wenty years on from the oil shock of the '70s, most economists would agree that oil is no longer the most important commodity in the world economy. Now, that commodity is information."[6] Yet when fuel prices soared in Britain during the last quarter of the year, truckers went on strike, bringing commerce within that nation to a virtual standstill. Though energy resources now *directly* accounted for only a small portion of economic activity in industrialized countries—1.2 percent to 2 percent in the US—all manufacturing and transportation still required fuel. In fact, the *entire* economy in every industrial nation was completely dependent on the continuing availability of energy resources at low and stable prices.

As the world economy slowed, demand for new goods also slowed, and manufacturing and transportation were scaled back. As a result, demand for oil also decreased, falling roughly five percent in the ensuing year. Prices for crude began to soften. Indeed, by late 2001, oil prices had plummeted partly as the result of market-share competition between Russia and Saudi Arabia. Gasoline prices at the pump in California had topped $2 in late 2000, but by early 2002 they had drifted to a mere $1.12 per gallon.

Such low prices tended to breed complacency. The Bush administration warned of future energy shortages, but proposed to solve the problem by promoting exploration and production within the US and by building more nuclear power plants—ideas that few with much knowledge of the energy industry took seriously. Now that gasoline prices were low again, not many citizens contemplated the possible future implications of the price run-ups of 2000. In contrast, industry insiders expressed growing concern that fundamental limits to oil production were within sight.

This concern gained public recognition in 2004, as oil prices again shot upward, this time attaining all-time highs of over $55 per barrel. *National Geographic* proclaimed in its cover story that this was "The End of Cheap Oil"; *Le Monde* announced "The Petro-Apocalypse;" while Paul Erdman, writing for the CBS television magazine *Marketwatch,* proclaimed that "the looming oil crisis will dwarf 1973." In article after article, analysts pointed to dwindling discoveries of new oil, evaporating spare production capacity, and burgeoning global demand for crude. The upshot: world oil production might be near its all-time peak.

If this were indeed the case—that world petroleum production would soon no longer be able to keep up with demand—it would be the most important news item of the dawning century, dwarfing even the atrocities of September 11. Oil was what had made 20th-century industrialism possible; it was the crucial material that had given the US its economic and technological edge during the first two-thirds of the century, enabling it to become the world's superpower. If world production of oil could no

longer expand, the global economy would be structurally imperiled. The implications were staggering.

There was every reason to assume that the Bush administration understood at least the essential outlines of the situation. Not only were many policy makers themselves—including the President, Vice President, and National Security Advisor—former oil industry executives; in addition, Vice President Dick Cheney's chief petroleum-futures guru, Matthew Simmons, had warned his clients of coming energy-supply crises repeatedly. Moreover, for many years the CIA had been monitoring global petroleum supplies; it had, for example, subscribed to the yearly report of Switzerland-based Petroconsultants, published at $35,000 per copy, and was thus surely also aware of another report, also supplied by Petroconsultants, titled "The World's Oil Supply 1995," which predicted that the peak of global oil production would occur during the first decade of the new century.

It would be an understatement to say that the general public was poorly prepared to understand this information or to appreciate its gravity. The *New York Times* had carried the stories of the oil company mergers on its front pages, but offered its readers little analysis of the state of the industry or that of the geological resources on which it depended. Mass-audience magazines *Discover* and *Popular Science* blandly noted, in buried paragraphs or sidebars, that "early in [the new century] . . . half the world's known oil supply will have been used, and oil production will slide into permanent decline"[7] and that "experts predict that production will peak in 2010, and then drop over subsequent years"[8]—but these publications made no attempt to inform readers of the monumental implications of these statements. It would be safe to say that the average person had no clue whatever that the entire world was poised on the brink of an economic cataclysm that was as vast and unprecedented as it was inevitable.

Yet here and there were individuals who did perfectly comprehend the situation. Many were petroleum geologists who had spent their careers searching the globe for oil deposits, honing the theoretical and technical skills that enabled them to assess fairly accurately just how much oil was left in the ground, where it was located, and how easily it could be accessed.

What these people knew about the coming production peak—and how and when they arrived at this knowledge—constitutes a story that centers on the work of one extraordinary scientist.

M. King Hubbert: Energy Visionary

During the 1950s, '60s, and '70s, Marion King Hubbert became one of the best-known geophysicists in the world because of his disturbing prediction, first announced in 1949, that the fossil-fuel era would prove to be very brief.

Of course, the idea that oil would run out eventually was not, in itself, original. Indeed, in the 1920s many geologists had warned that world petroleum supplies would be exhausted in a matter of years. After all, the early wells in Pennsylvania had played out quickly; and extrapolating that initial experience to the limited reserves known in the first two decades of the century yielded an extremely pessimistic forecast for oil's future. However, the huge discoveries of the 1930s in east Texas and the Persian Gulf made such predictions laughable. Each year far more oil was being found than was being extracted. The doomsayers having been proven wrong, most people associated with the industry came to assume that supply and demand could continue to increase far into the future, with no end in sight. Hubbert, armed with better data and methods, doggedly challenged that assumption.

M. King Hubbert had been born in 1903 in central Texas, the hub of world oil exploration during the early 20th century. After showing a childhood fascination with steam engines and telephones, he settled on a career in science. He earned BS, MS, and Ph.D. degrees at the University of Chicago and, during the 1930s, taught geophysics at Columbia University. In the summer months, he worked for the Amerada Petroleum Corporation in Oklahoma, the Illinois State Geological Survey, and the United States Geological Survey (USGS). In 1943, after serving as a senior analyst at the Board of Economic Warfare in Washington, DC, Hubbert joined Shell Oil Company in Houston, where he directed the Shell research laboratory. He retired from Shell in 1964, then joined the USGS as a senior research geophysicist, a position he held until 1976. In his later years, he also taught occasionally at Stanford University, the University of California at Los Angeles, the University of California at Berkeley, the Massachusetts Institute of Technology, and Johns Hopkins University.

During his career, Hubbert made many important contributions to geophysics. In 1937 he resolved a standing paradox regarding the apparent strength of rocks that form the Earth's crust. Despite their evident properties of hardness and brittleness, such rocks often show signs of plastic flow. Hubbert demonstrated mathematically that, because even the hardest of rocks are subject to immense pressures at depth, they can respond in a manner similar to soft muds or clays. In the early 1950s, he showed that underground fluids can become entrapped under circumstances previously not thought possible, a finding that resulted in the redesign of techniques employed to locate oil and natural gas deposits. And by 1959, in collaboration with USGS geologist William W. Rubey, Hubbert also explained some puzzling characteristics of overthrust faults—low-angle fractures in rock formations in which one surface is displaced relative to another by a distance on the order of kilometers.

These scientific achievements would have been sufficient to assure Hubbert a prominent place in the history of geology. However, his greatest recognition came from his studies of petroleum and natural gas reserves—studies he had begun in 1926 while a student at the University of Chicago. In 1949, he used statistical and physical methods to calculate total world oil and natural gas supplies and documented their sharply increasing consumption. Then, in 1956 on the basis of his reserve estimates and his study of the lifetime production profile of typical oil reservoirs, he predicted that the peak of crude-oil production in the United States would occur between 1966 and 1972. At the time most economists, oil companies, and government agencies (including the USGS) dismissed the prediction. The actual peak of US oil production occurred in 1970, though this was not apparent until 1971.[9]

Let us trace just how Hubbert arrived at his prediction. First, he noted the production from a typical reservoir or province does not begin, increase to some stable level, continue at that level for a long period, and then suddenly drop

off to nothing after all of the oil is gone. Rather, production tends to follow bell-shaped curve. The first exploratory well that punctures a reservoir is capable of extracting only a limited amount; but once the reservoir has been mapped more wells can be drilled.

During this early phase, production increases rapidly as the easiest-accessed oil is drained first. However, beyond a certain point, whatever remains is harder to get at. Production begins to decline, even if more wells are still being drilled. Typically, the production peak will occur when about half of the total oil in the reservoir has been extracted. Even after production has tapered off, some oil will still be left in the ground: it is economically impractical—and physically impossible—to remove every last drop. Indeed, for some reservoirs only a few percent of the existing oil may be recoverable (the average is between 30 and 50 percent).

Hubbert also examined the history of discovery in the lower-48 United States. More oil had been found in the 1930s than in any decade before or since—and this despite the fact that investment in exploration had increased dramatically in succeeding decades. Thus discovery also appeared to follow a bell-shaped curve. Once the history of discovery had been charted, Hubbert was able to estimate the total ultimately recoverable reserves (URR) for the entire lower-48 region. He arrived at two figures: the most pessimistic reasonable amount (150 billion barrels) and the most optimistic reasonable amount (200 billion barrels). Using these two estimates, he calculated future production rates. If the total URR in the lower-48 US amounted to 150 billion barrels, half would be gone—and production would peak—in 1966; if the figure were closer to 200 billion barrels, the peak would come in 1972.

These early calculations involved a certain amount of guesswork. For example, Hubbert chose to chart production rates on a logistic

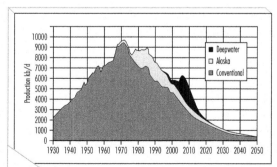

Figure 1. US oil production, history and projection, including lower 48, Alaska and Gulf of Mexico (deep water).

Source: ASPO.

curve, whereas he might have employed a better-fitting Gaussian curve.[10] Even today, according to Princeton University geophysicist Kenneth S. Deffeyes, author of *Hubbert's Peak: The Impending World Oil Shortage*, the "numerical methods that Hubbert used to make his prediction are not crystal clear."[11] Despite many conversations with Hubbert and ensuing years spent attempting to reconstruct those original calculations, Deffeyes finds aspects of Hubbert's process obscure and "messy." Nevertheless, Hubbert did succeed in obtaining important, useful findings.

Following his prediction of the US production peak, Hubbert devoted his efforts to forecasting the global production peak. With the figures then available for the likely total recoverable world petroleum reserves, he estimated that the peak would come between the years 1990 and 2000. This forecast would prove too pessimistic, partly because of inadequate data and partly because of minor flaws in Hubbert's method. Nevertheless as we will see shortly, other researchers would later refine both input data and method in order to arrive at more reliable predictions—ones that would vary only about a decade from Hubbert's.

Hubbert immediately grasped the vast economic and social implications of this information. He understood the role of fossil fuels in the creation of the modern industrial world, and thus foresaw the wrenching transition that would likely occur following the peak in global extraction rates. In lectures and articles, starting in the 1950s, Hubbert outlined how society needed to change in order to prepare for a post-petroleum regime. The following passage, part of a summary by Hubbert of one of his own lectures, conveys some of the breadth and flavor of his macrosocial thinking:

> The world's present industrial civilization is handicapped by the coexistence of two universal, overlapping, and incompatible intellectual

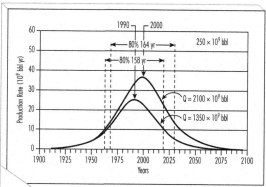

Figure 2. M. King Hubbert's projected cycles for world crude production for the extreme values of the estimated total resource.

Source: M. K. Hubbert, *Resources and Man.*

> systems: the accumulated knowledge of the last four centuries of the properties and interrelationships of matter and energy; and the associated monetary culture which has evolved from folkways of prehistoric origin.
>
> The first of these two systems has been responsible for the spectacular rise, principally during the last two centuries, of the present industrial system and is essential for its continuance. The second, an inheritance from the prescientific past, operates by rules of its own having little in common with those of the matter-energy system. Nevertheless, the monetary system, by means of a loose coupling, exercises a general control over the matter-energy system upon which it is superimposed.
>
> Despite their inherent incompatibilities, these two systems during the last two centuries have had one fundamental characteristic in common, namely exponential growth, which has made a reasonably stable coexistence possible. But, for various reasons, it is impossible for the matter-energy system to sustain exponential growth for more than a few tens of doublings, and this phase is by now almost over. The monetary system has no such constraints, and, according to one of its most fundamental rules, it must continue to grow by compound interest.[12]

Hubbert thus believed that society, if it is to avoid chaos during the energy decline, must give up its antiquated, debt-and-interest-based monetary system and adopt a system of accounts based on matter-energy—an inherently ecological system that would acknowledge the finite nature of essential resources.

Hubbert was quoted as saying that we are in a "crisis in the evolution of human society. It's unique to both human and geologic history. It has never happened before and it can't possibly happen again. You can only use oil once. You can only use metals once. Soon all the oil is going to be burned and all the metals mined and scattered."[13]

Statements like this one gave Hubbert the popular image of a doomsayer. Yet he was not a pessimist; indeed, on occasion he could assume the role of utopian seer. We have, he believed, the necessary know-how; all we need do is overhaul our culture and find an alternative to money. If society were to develop solar-energy technologies, reduce its population and its demands on resources, and develop a steady-state economy to replace the present one based on unending growth, our species' future could be rosy indeed. "We are not starting from zero," he emphasized. "We have an enormous amount of existing technical knowledge. It's just a matter of putting it all together. We still have great flexibility but our maneuverability will diminish with time."[14]

Reading Hubbert's few published works—for example, his statement before the House of Representatives Subcommittee on the Environment on June 6, 1974—one is struck by his ability to follow the implications of his findings on oil depletion through the domains of economics and ecology.[15] He was a holistic and interdisciplinary thinker who deserves, if anyone does, to be called a prophet of the coming era.

Hubbert died in 1989, a few years before his predicted date for the global production peak.

That all-important forecast date was incorrect, as the rate of world oil production continued to increase through the first months of 2005. But by how far did he miss the mark? It would be up to his followers to find out.

Zeroing in on the Date of the Peak

As a growing community of scientists applies itself to the task of determining exactly when the world's oil production will begin to decline, four principle methods for doing so are emerging.

1. Estimate the total ultimately recoverable resource (URR) and calculate when half will have been extracted. This is the original method developed and used by Hubbert himself, beginning in the 1950s. As we have seen, Hubbert noted that for a typical oil-producing region, a graph of extraction over time tends to take on a bell-shaped curve: the more cheaply and easily accessed portion of the resource is depleted first, so that when about half is gone the rate at which extraction can proceed tends to diminish.

The method is relatively simple, and it worked well for predicting the U.S. production peak. However, it relies on the availability of accurate discovery and reserve data so that URR can be accurately estimated, and on accurate extraction data as well. For the US, these figures were not problematic, but for some other important oil-producing regions this is not the case: reserve data for Saudi Arabia, for example, are controversial.

Moreover, there is no natural law stating that the extraction curve must be precisely bell-shaped or symmetrical. Indeed, political, economic, and technological factors can deform the curve in an infinite number of ways. In reality the actual production curves from producing nations never conform to a simple mathematical curve, and are characterized by bumps, plateaus, valleys, and peaks of differing sizes and durations. A war, a recession, the application of a new recovery technology, or the decision by a government to restrain extraction can reshape the curve arbitrarily.

Nevertheless, what comes up must come down: for every oil-producing region, extraction starts at zero, increases to a maximum, and declines, regardless of the tortuous bumps in between. And, in general, the latter half of the resource will require more effort and time to extract than the first half. Moreover, experience shows that if actual production strays far from the predicted curve because of political or economic factors, it will tend to return to it once the influence of those factors subsides.

The Hubbert model is therefore a good way of providing a first-order approximation: it gives us a general overview of the depletion process, and (depending on the accuracy of the available reserve and production data) yields a likely peak year, with a window of uncertainty. However, it cannot be used to forecast actual production for the next month or even the next decade.

Using this method (with various refinements), Kenneth Deffeyes, in his book *Hubbert's Curve,* arrives at a peak date of 2005. Other researchers, such as Jean Laherrère, using more optimistic reserve estimates, place the peak further out, up to 2020.

2. Count the number of years from peak of discovery. Hubbert realized that, when graphed over time, the *discovery* of oil within any given region tends to peak and decline, just as production does. Understandably, discovery always peaks first—since it is necessary to find oil before it can be extracted.

In the US, discoveries of oil peaked in the early 1930s with the stupendous finds in east Texas; production peaked almost exactly 40 years later. Are we likely to find a similar time lag for other oil producing regions? If so, this could provide a basis for predicting the timing of the global production peak.

The duration of the lag between discovery and production peaks depends on a number of factors: the geological conditions (some fields can be depleted more quickly than others); the extraction technology being used (new recovery methods can deplete a reservoir more quickly and efficiently, but can also increase the total amount recoverable and thus extend the life of the field); and whether the resource is being extracted at maximum possible rate (as already noted, economic or political events can intervene to reduce production rates).

The North Sea provides an example of a relatively brief lag between discovery and extraction peaks: there, discoveries peaked in the early 1970s, while production peaked only 30 years later, at the turn of the new century. The latest exploration and extraction technologies were applied, and the resource base was drawn down at virtually the maximum possible rate because North Sea oil was in high demand throughout this period.

Iraq provides a counterexample: there, two principal periods of major discovery occurred—in the early 1950s and the mid-1970s. For that country, political and economic events have constrained production to a very significant degree: first, the Iran-Iraq war of the 1980s, then the US-led embargo of the 1990s, and finally the turmoil surrounding the US invasion and occupation have reduced extraction rates well below levels that would otherwise have been achieved. Consequently, Iraqi oil production may not peak until 2015 at the earliest, though more likely a decade or so later, yielding a discovery-to-production-peak lag of 45 to 60 years.

Will other discovery-to-production-peak lag times tend to more closely match those of the North Sea countries, or that of Iraq? Chances are that, as individual anomalies cancel each other out, lag times are on average likely to cluster around that of the US—roughly 40 years.

Global oil discoveries peaked in 1963. This is not a controversial fact: both the oil industry and the US Department of Energy acknowledge that this is the case.

Given this, we might expect that the global peak in the rate of oil extraction would occur roughly 40 years later—i.e., in 2003.

However, we must take into account intervening economic and political events that might have tended to reduce extraction rates below their potential, and thus increase the time lag. The principal such events were the Arab OPEC embargo of the early 1970s, the fall of the Shah of Iran, and the subsequent Iran-Iraq war a few years later. The consequent oil price spikes reduced demand for oil, and led to a decline in extraction rates. The effect may have been to add up to ten years to the global discovery-to-production-peak time lag, yielding a likely peak date window of 2005 to 2013.

3. Track the reserve and production data of individual countries. For the past few years, both Colin Campbell (Association for the Study of Peak Oil) and Richard C. Duncan (Institute on Energy and Man) have been keeping close track of production data for individual producing nations.

Campbell's detailed discussions of oil statistics nation by nation are available in the archived newsletters of the Association for the Study of Peak Oil (www.asponews.org), and in his book, *The Essence of Oil & Gas Depletion* (MultiScience, 2003).

Duncan uses a "graphical-heuristic-iterative (GHI)" method to forecast world oil production, repeating the entire modeling and forecasting process annually to give a series of consistent but unique world oil forecasts. According to Duncan, *heuristic* means "a method of computer programming in which the modeler and machine proceed along empirical lines, using data,

other information, and rules of thumb to find solutions or answers." *Iterative* means "repetitious; repeating or repeated." The *Graphical Input Device* (used in system dynamics programs such as Stella) enables the modeler "to quickly create and/or edit an oil production forecast of a nation just before each trial run (iteration) of the model." The *Scatter Graph* (system dynamics) is used to depict "the forecasted peak year of oil production (x-axis) *versus* the forecasted peak production rate (y-axis) of our ongoing series of world oil forecasts." Duncan describes this as a work in progress "that will eventually converge on Peak Oil—whether the Peak is near at hand or far in the future."[24]

Many countries are now clearly past their individual all-time extraction peaks. The list includes not only the US, but also Indonesia, Gabon, Great Britain, and Norway. Altogether, according to Duncan, of 45 significant oil-producing countries, 25 are past-peak (*BP Statistical Review of World Energy* currently estimates the latter number at 18, indicating that there is some uncertainty on this point, but also that oil companies are keenly aware of the peaking phenomenon and are keeping score).[25]

Some of the pre-peak nations are major producers with huge reserves (e.g., Iraq and Saudi Arabia). Thus it would be unwise to assume that the global peak will occur when exactly half of all producing nations have undergone their individual peaks. Clearly, more complex calculations are necessary, and this is the work that Duncan and Campbell are undertaking.

The countries in decline account for about 30 percent of the world's total oil production. Further, according to *Oil & Gas Journal,* as demand for oil expanded and prices rose during 2004, all of the added supply came from Russia and a few OPEC nations. Evidently, all of the nations outside of Russia and OPEC, when taken together, have already peaked in production (though there are individual exceptions, such as Brazil).

By examining the geology, history, and economic-political circumstances of each oil-producing country, it is possible to encircle the remaining uncertainties and pick away at them. How much oil has been discovered in each given nation? How long ago did discoveries peak? Are significant future discoveries likely? What kinds of recovery methods are being used?

Duncan summarizes his method as follows:

I make a separate computer-based model to forecast the oil production for each of the major oil-producing nations in the world; 2) The latest oil data and related information on each nation are gathered from journals, the internet, and colleagues just before each national model is run; 3) Then both a Low oil forecast and a Medium oil forecast are made for each nation; 4) Next all of the Medium oil forecasts are combined (added up) to give the world oil forecast; 5) This process is repeated annually as soon as new oil data and related information become available; 6) A Scatter Graph indicates that the eight world oil forecasts that we've completed so far seem to be converging on Peak Oil in 2006 or 2007; 7) One new forecast (point) will be added to the Scatter Graph each year until Peak Oil is confirmed.

Campbell's analysis of likely future oil production by individual producing nations yields a global peak date of 2008.

4. Compare the amount of new production capacity likely to be available over the coming years with the amount of production capacity needed to offset decline rates from existing fields. The global oil industry needs to develop new production capacity yearly, in order to meet new demand and offset declines in production rates from individual wells and producing regions already past their all-time peaks. Currently, the world produces about 83 million

barrels per day of all petroleum liquids combined (conventional oil plus oil from tar sands, natural gas liquids, and so on). The IEA estimates that in 2005 the world will need another 1.5 million barrels per day of new production capacity in order to meet new demand, plus another 4 mb/d to offset declines from existing fields—a total of about 5.5 mb/d. In 2006, a slightly greater new quantity will be needed, and in 2007, more still. In the five years from 2005 to 2010 a total of over 35 mb/d of new production capacity will need to come online. (These figures are agreed upon by both industry and various governmental agencies.) A substantial effort is necessary, to say the least.

But where will all this new production capacity come from?

In general, new production capacity arises from three sources: the discovery of new resources; the development of previously discovered resources (including reserve growth and infill drilling); or the development of unconventional resources (which sometimes depends on the invention and implementation of new technologies).

It takes time and investment to develop new production capacity. Thus it is possible—though no simple matter!—to gather the necessary data, analyze it, and project how much new production capacity is likely to emerge over the next five years, given current rates of investment, the available technology, and the discoveries in place. (Even if a huge new discovery were to be made next year, it would probably be impossible to bring the oil from it into production before 2010.) Chris Skrebowski, editor of *Petroleum Review,* has done just that in his 2004 report, "Oil Field Megaprojects," sponsored by the Oil Depletion Analysis Centre (ODAC).

Skrebowski compiles and regularly updates the details of planned major production projects, as reported by the oil companies. The list contains data on all announced fields with at least 500 million barrels of estimated reserves, and on projects with the claimed potential to produce 100,000 barrels a day or more.

Skrebowski and ODAC analyzed 68 production projects with announced start-up dates ranging from 2004 through 2010, and found that they are likely to add about 12.5 million barrels per day of new production capacity. In a press release, he stated: "This new production would almost certainly not be sufficient to offset diminishing supplies from existing sources and still meet growing global demand," and that "even with relatively low demand growth, our study indicates a seemingly unbridgeable supply-demand gap opening up after 2007."[27]

"It is disturbing to see such a dramatic fall-off of new project commitments after 2007, and not more than a handful of tentative projects into the next decade," Skrebowski said. "This could very well be a signal that world oil production is rapidly approaching its peak, as a growing number of analysts now forecast, especially in view of the diminishing prospects for major new oil discoveries."

At the end of the day, there are still uncertainties. Major new oil discoveries are always possible, though increasingly unlikely. Probably the greatest uncertainty with respect to the timing of the global oil production peak is future demand. If the global economy fares well, then demand will increase and the peak will come sooner; if the economy falters, then the peak will come later. If the world stumbles into a full-fledged depression, the peak could be delayed significantly, and the effects of the phenomenon could be masked by other events.

Nevertheless, as we have seen, the results of the possible forecasting methods tend to converge. We are within only a few years of the all-time global oil production peak. We are virtually at the summit now, with almost no time left for maneuvering before the event itself is upon us.

Author Citations

4. Goldman Sachs, *Energy Weekly*, 11 August 1999.
5. EIA Annual Energy Outlook 2000 with Projections to 2020; current report available online at www.eia.doe.gov/oiaf/aeo/.
6. Blair made these comments on January 28, 2000, at Davos, Switzerland. See, for example, http://Singapore.emc/com/news/in_depth_archive/01032001_year_info.jsp.
7. Eric Haseltine, "Twenty Things That Will Be Obsolete in Twenty Years," *Discover*, Vol. 21, No. 10, October, 2000, p. 85.
8. William G. Phillips, "Are We Really Running Out of Oil?", *Popular Science*, May 2000, p. 56.
9. Hubbert was fortunate to deal with the US lower-48, where a simple bell-shaped curve could be derived from production statistics. Adding production data from Alaska changes the curve, revealing two cycles. Further, between 1960 and 1980 supply was almost never constrained by demand—because of mandatory quotas on oil imports instituted by Eisenhower in 1959. Without these quotas, US production would have been less since foreign oil was cheaper. Thus reduced demand for more expensive oil would have delayed the peak.
10. Kenneth S. Deffeyes, *Hubbert's Peak: The Impending World Oil Shortage* (Princeton University Press, 2001), pp. 134–49.
11. Kenneth S. Deffeyes, *Hubbert's Peak*, p. 135.
12. "Two Intellectual Systems: matter-energy and the Monetary Culture." Summary, by M. King Hubbert, of a seminar he taught at MIT Energy Laboratory, 30 September 1981, at www.hubbertpeak.com/hubbert/monetary.htm.
13. See www.hubbertpeak.com/hubbert/hubecon.htm.
14. See www.hubbertpeak.com/hubecon.htm.
15. See www.technocracy.com/articles/hubbert-econ.html.
24. From a personal communication with the author.
25. See www.bp.com/subsection.do?categoryId=95&contentId=2006480.
26. From a personal communication with the author.
27. See www.odac-info.org.

Discussion Questions

1. If only half of the world's oil reserves have been consumed when "peak oil" occurs, why is the peak a big deal?
2. Summarize the four methods for predicting peak oil.
3. In another chapter of *The Party's Over*, Heinberg discusses the concept of "Energy Returned over Energy Invested" (EROEI). This is essentially a measure of how hard it is to produce a fuel (in other words, to find, extract, and process the fuel). If a fuel's EROEI is less than one, the fuel delivers less energy than was consumed in its production. Discuss peak oil in the context of EROEI.
4. Heinberg claims that in the early twentieth century, a "threshold" was crossed that forever changed humanity's relationship to energy. What was that threshold, and what is its significance?

 Supporting Activities

1. Find three independent predictions about when peak oil will occur. Record the year, the group or individual making the prediction, and, if possible, information about the methodology that was used to make the prediction.
2. Find one source that refutes the notion of peak oil. Record the source and summarize the argument made.
3. Investigate what a barrel of crude oil sells for *today* as well as a year ago. How volatile has the price been over the past year? If possible, find out what the current price per barrel represents in 1960, 1970, or 1980 dollars.
4. Consider what you would do if the price of gasoline suddenly increased tenfold. How would your daily routine change? Would you be able to bear this increased cost?

 Additional Resources

1. Visit Richard Heinberg's website (http://richardheinberg.com/), which includes information about his recent books and articles addressing life after oil.
2. Watch the 2004 movie *End of Suburbia* (http://www.endofsuburbia.com/). A shorter version of this video is available on YouTube (https://www.youtube.com/watch?v=Q3uvzcY2Xug).
3. Anti-peak oil voices can be readily found. For example, this article in *Forbes* magazine (http://www.forbes.com/sites/davidblackmon/2013/05/13/the-illogic-and-folly-of-peak-oil-or-is-it-peak-gas-alarmism/) and this book review in *Technology Review* (http://www.technologyreview.com/news/425509/peak-oil-debunked/) both challenge the concept. For a more comprehensive critique of peak oil and examination of the future of energy, read Daniel Yergin's book *The Quest: Energy, Security, and the Remaking of the Modern World* (2011, The Penguin Press).
4. Visit Chris Martenson's Peak Prosperity web site (http://www.peakprosperity.com/crashcourse) and watch Chapters 19–24 of the "Crash Course" for a clear and thorough explanation of how peak oil and other limited finite resources affect energy and the economy.

Energy End-Use Efficiency

Energy efficiency, or providing more desired goods and services per unit of energy consumed, has received an increasing amount of attention in recent years, but as Amory Lovins noted in this report the potential for energy efficiency has tremendous room for growth across all end-use sectors. Lovins' excerpt is one of the more technical readings contained in this book and it details some important concepts that will help readers gain a better understanding of both energy use and energy efficiency. He emphasized that energy efficiency should not be confused with simply doing less or doing without some goods or services, but focused on providing desired levels of service—often in better ways—using less energy than before. Additionally, this report focused primarily on technological improvements that can lead to greater efficiency, rather than on behavioral changes or policy tools.

Two ideas explained in this excerpt deserve special attention here. The first is that the overall efficiency of a technical system is the product of efficiencies applied along the whole chain of energy conversions that occur to deliver the good or service. Even small improvements in efficiency along that conversion chain can multiply to yield large overall gains in efficiency. Lovins uses the analogy of a lobster to illustrate this: we cannot just focus on the big chunks of meat in the lobster's tail, but must also look for the "tasty morsels hidden in crevices." Second, he alludes to one of humankind's most powerful means for averting the negative consequences of technology: simply saying no, or not using the technology. Even energy-efficient lamps, for example, save the most energy when they're turned off, and if we want to achieve the greatest efficiency in personal transport, we should live close to the places we wish to be! Among all of the ways we can reduce the impacts of technology, saying no is perhaps the most often ignored option.

Lovins, who has long been a proponent of the importance of energy efficiency, coined the term "negawatts" to refer to the energy saved through efficiency measures. Although some challenge the levels of energy savings that Lovins says are possible, his message is nevertheless of critical importance. Energy not consumed wastefully is in effect an important "source" of energy because it displaces the need for energy. Taking steps toward greater efficiency also enhances the resiliency of our energy supply by making us less dependent on volatile fossil fuel resources.

Amory Lovins was cofounder, with his then-wife L. Hunter Lovins, of the Rocky Mountain Institute (RMI) in Snowmass, Colorado in 1982. He currently serves as Chief Scientist and CEO Emeritus of RMI. Trained as an experimental physicist, for over 40 years he has served as a consultant on energy, energy efficiency, and related topics in more than 50 countries. Winner of numerous awards, Lovins and his colleagues at RMI have continued to promote the potential for energy efficiency in influential ways. Lovins' 2011 book *Reinventing Fire* provides a blueprint for a transformed energy economy that relies almost completely on efficiency (negawatts) and renewable energy technologies. The InterAcademy Council (IAC) is a multinational organization of science academies that was created to provide knowledge and advice to governments about critical issues facing the world, including energy.

Energy End-Use Efficiency

Amory B. Lovins, CEO, Rocky Mountain Institute

1. Importance

Increasing energy end-use efficiency—technologically providing more desired service per unit
of delivered energy consumed—is generally the
largest, least expensive, most benign, most
quickly deployable, least visible, least understood, and most neglected way to provide energy services. The 46% drop in U.S. energy intensity (primary energy consumption per dollar
of real GDP) during 1975–2005 represented by
2005 an effective energy "source" 2.1× as big as
U.S. oil consumption, 3.4× net oil imports, 6×
domestic oil output or net oil imports from
OPEC countries, and 13× net imports from Persian Gulf countries. U.S. energy intensity has
lately fallen by ~2.5% per year, apparently due
much more to improved efficiency than to
changes in behavior or in the mix of goods and
services provided, and outpacing the growth of
any fossil or nuclear source. Yet energy efficiency has gained little attention or respect. Indeed, since official statistics focus ~99% on
physical energy supply, only the fifth of the
1996–2005 increase in U.S. energy services that
came from supply was visible to investors and
policymakers; the four-fifths saved was not. The
last time this incomplete picture led to strongly
supply-boosting national policies, in the early
1980s, it caused a trainwreck within a few
years—glutted markets, crashed prices, bankrupt suppliers—because the market had meanwhile invisibly produced a gusher of efficiency.
Savings were deployed faster than the big, slow,
lumpy supply expansions, whose forecast
revenues disappeared. Today we have *two* fast
competitors: efficiency and micropower.

Physical scientists find that despite energy
efficiency's leading role in providing new energy
services today, it has barely begun to tap its
profitable potential. In contrast, many engineers tend to be limited by adherence to past
practice, and most economists by their assumption that any profitable savings must already
have occurred. The potential of energy efficiency is also increasing faster through innovative designs, technologies, policies, and marketing methods than it is being used up through
gradual implementation. The uncaptured "efficiency resource" is becoming bigger and
cheaper even faster than oil reserves have lately
done through stunning advances in exploration
and production. The expansion of the "efficiency
resource" is also accelerating, as designers realize that whole-system design integration
(Part 4) can often make very large (one- or
two-order-of-magnitude) energy savings cost
less than small or no savings, and as energy-saving technologies evolve discontinuously rather
than incrementally. Moreover, similarly rapid
evolution and enormous potential apply also to
marketing and delivering energy-saving technologies and designs; R&D can accelerate both.

A. Terminology

"Efficiency" means different things to the two
professions most engaged in achieving it. To
engineers, "efficiency" means a physical output/
input ratio. To economists, "efficiency" means a

"Energy and end-use efficiency" by Amory Lovins. In Transitions to Sustainable Systems, Volume 19, 2005. Copyright ©
2005 by Interacademy Council. Reprinted by permission.

monetary output/input ratio (though for practical purposes many use a monetary output/physical input ratio)— and also, confusingly, "efficiency" may refer to the economic optimality of a market transaction or process. This paper uses only physical output/input ratios, but the common use of monetary ratios confuses policymakers accustomed to economic jargon.

Wringing more work from energy via smarter technologies is often, and sometimes deliberately, confused with a pejorative usage of the ambiguous term "energy conservation." Energy *efficiency* means doing more (and often better) with less—the opposite of simply doing less or worse or without. This confusion unfortunately makes the honorable and traditional term "energy conservation" no longer useful in certain societies, notably the United States, and underlies much of their decades-long neglect or suppression of energy efficiency.

However, deliberately reducing the amount or quality of *energy services* remains a legitimate, though completely separate, option for those who prefer it or are forced by emergency to accept it. The 2000–01 California electricity crisis ended abruptly when customers, exhorted to curtail their use of electricity, cut their peak load per dollar of weather-adjusted real GDP by 14% in the first half of 2001. Most of that dramatic reduction, undoing the previous 5–10 years' demand growth, was temporary and behavioral, but later became permanent and technological. Even absent crises, some people do not consider an ever-growing volume of energy services to be a worthy end in itself, but seek to live more simply—with elegant frugality rather than involuntary penury—and to meet nonmaterial needs by nonmaterial means. (Trying to do otherwise is ultimately futile.) Such choices can save even more energy than technical improvement alone, though they are often considered beyond the scope of energy efficiency.

Several other terminological distinctions are also important:

- At least five different kinds of energy efficiency can be measured in at least five different stages of energy conversion chains (Part 1B), but this paper is only on *end-use* efficiency.
- Technical improvements in energy efficiency can be applied only to new buildings and equipment, or installable in existing ones ("retrofitted"), or addable during minor or routine maintenance ("slip-streamed"), or conveniently added when making major renovations or expansions for other reasons ("piggybacked").
- *Efficiency* saves energy whenever an energy service is being delivered, whereas *load management* (sometimes called *demand response* to emphasize reliance on customer choice) only changes the *time when* that energy is used—either by shifting the timing of the service delivery or by, for example, storing heat or coolth so energy consumption and service delivery can occur at different times. In the context chiefly of electricity, *demand-side management*, a term coined by the [U.S.] Electric Power Research Institute, comprises both these options, plus others that may even increase the use of electricity. Most efficiency options yield comparable or greater savings in peak loads; both kinds of savings are valuable, and both kinds of value should be counted. They also have important but seldom-recognized linkages: for example, because most U.S. peak electric loads are met by extremely inefficient simple-cycle gas-fired combustion turbines, saving 1% of U.S. electricity, including peak hours, reduces total natural-gas consumption by 2% and cuts its price by 3–4% (Lovins, Datta, et al. 2004).
- Conflating three different things—*technological* improvements in energy efficiency (such as thermal insulation), *behavioral* changes

(such as resetting thermostats), and the *price* or *policy tools* used to induce or reward those changes—causes endless confusion.

- The theoretical potential for efficiency gains (up to the maximum permitted by the laws of physics) exceeds the technical potential, which exceeds the economic potential based on social value, which exceeds the economic potential based on private internal value, which exceeds the actual uptake not blocked by market failures, which exceeds what happens spontaneously if no effort is made to accelerate efficiency gains deliberately; yet these six quantities are often not clearly distinguished.
- Energy statistics are traditionally organized by the economic sector of apparent consumption, not by the physical end-uses provided or services sought. End-uses were first seriously analyzed in 1976, rarely appear in official statistics even three decades later, and can be hard to estimate accurately. But end-use analysis can be valuable because matching energy supplies in quality and scale, as well as in quantity, to end-use needs can save much energy and money. Supplying energy of superfluous quality, not just quantity, for the task is wasteful and expensive. For example, the U.S. now provides about twice as much electricity as the fraction of end-uses that economically justify this special, costly, high-quality form of energy—yet during 1975–2000, 45% of the total growth in primary energy consumption came from increased conversion and grid losses in the expanding, very costly, and heavily subsidized electricity system. Much of the electric growth, in turn, provided low-temperature heat—a physically and economically wasteful use of electricity, an extremely high-quality and costly carrier.

Many subtleties of defining and measuring energy efficiency merit but seldom get rigorous treatment, such as:

- distribution losses downstream of end-use devices (an efficient furnace feeding leaky ducts or poorly distributing the heated air yields costlier delivered comfort);
- undesired or useless services, such as leaving equipment on all the time (as many factories do) even when it serves no useful purpose;
- misused services, such as space-conditioning rooms that are open to the outdoors;
- conflicting services, such as heating and cooling the same space simultaneously (wasteful even if both services are provided efficiently);
- parasitic loads, as when the inefficiencies of a central cooling system reappear as additional fed-back cooling loads that make the system less efficient than the sum of its parts;
- misplaced efficiency, such as doing with energy-using equipment, however efficiently, a task that doesn't need the equipment—such as cooling with a mechanical chiller when groundwater or ambient conditions can more cheaply do the same thing; and
- incorrect metrics, such as measuring lighting by raw quantity (lux) unadjusted for its visual effectiveness (Equivalent Sphere Illuminance), which may actually decrease if greater illuminance is improperly delivered, causing veiling reflections and uncomfortable glare.

To forestall a few other semantic quibbles:

- Physicists (including the author) know that energy is not "consumed," as economists' term "consumption" implies, nor "lost," as engineers refer to unwanted conversions into less useful forms. Energy is only converted from one form to another; yet the common metaphors are clear, common, and adopted here. Thus an 80%-efficient motor converts its electricity input into 80% torque and 20% heat, noise, vibration, and stray electromagnetic fields; the total equals 100% of the electricity input, or roughly 30% of the fuel input at a classical thermal power station. (Note that this definition of efficiency combines engineering metrics with human preference. The motor's efficiency may change, with no change in the motor, if changing *intention* alters which of the outputs are desired and which are unwanted: the definition of "waste" is as much social or contextual as physical. An incandescent floodlamp used to keep plates of food warm in a restaurant may be effective for that purpose even though it is an inefficient source of visible light.)

- More productive use of energy is not, strictly speaking, a physical "source" of energy but is only a way to displace physical sources. This distinction is rhetorical, since the displacement or substitution is real and makes supply fully fungible with efficiency.
- Energy/GDP ratios are a very rough, aggregated, and sometimes misleading metric, because they combine changes in technical efficiency, human behavior, and the composition of GDP (a metric that problematically conflates goods and services with bads and nuisances, counts only monetized activities, and is an increasingly perverse measure of well-being). Yet the 46% drop in U.S. energy intensity and the 52% drop in oil intensity during 1975–2004 reflect mainly better technical efficiency. Joseph Romm has also shown that an important compositional shift of U.S. GDP—the information economy emerging in the late 1990s—has significantly decreased energy and probably electrical energy intensity, as bytes substituted for (or increased the capacity utilization of) travel, freight transport, lit and conditioned floorspace, paper, and other energy-intensive goods and services.

The aim here is not to get mired in word games, but to offer a clear overview of what kinds of energy efficiency are available, what they can do, and how best to consider and adopt them.

B. Efficiency along energy conversion chains

The technical efficiency of using energy is the product of efficiencies successively applied along the chain of energy conversions: the conversion efficiency of primary into secondary energy, times the distribution efficiency of delivering that secondary energy from the point of conversion to the point of end-use, times the end-use efficiency of converting the delivered secondary energy into such desired energy services as hot showers and cold beer. Some analysts add another term at the upstream end—the extractive efficiency of converting fuel in the ground, wind or sun in the atmosphere, etc. into the primary energy fed into the initial conversion device—and another term at the downstream end—the hedonic efficiency of converting delivered energy services into human welfare. (Delivering junk mail with high technical efficiency is futile if the recipients didn't want it.)

Counting all five efficiencies permits comparing ultimate means—primary energy tapped—with ultimate ends—happiness or economic welfare created. Focusing only on intermediate means and ends loses sight of what human purposes an energy system is to serve. Most societies pay attention to only three kinds of energy efficiency: extraction (because of its cost, not because the extracted fuels are assigned any intrinsic or depletion value), conversion, and perhaps distribution. End-use and hedonic efficiency are left to customers, are least exploited, and hence hold the biggest potential gains.

They also offer the greatest potential leverage. Since successive efficiencies along the conversion chain all multiply, they are often assumed to be equally important. Yet downstream savings—those nearest the customer—are the most important. Fig. 1 shows schematically the successive energy conversions and losses that require about ten units of fuel to be fed into a conventional thermal power station in order to deliver one unit of flow in a pipe. But conversely, every unit of flow (or friction) saved in the pipe will save approximately ten units of fuel, cost, pollution, and "global weirding" at the power station. It will also make the pump's motor (for example) nearly two and a half units smaller, hence cheaper. To save the most primary energy and the most capital cost, therefore, efficiency efforts should start all the way downstream (Part 4B), by asking: How little flow can actually deliver the desired service? How small can the piping friction become? How small, well-matched to the flow regime, and efficient can the pump be made? Its coupling? Its motor? Its controls and electrical supplies?

Analyses of energy use should, but seldom do, start with the desired services or changes in well-being, then work back upstream to primary supplies. This maximizes the extra value of downstream efficiency gains and the capital-cost savings from smaller, simpler, cheaper upstream equipment. Similarly, most energy policy analysts analyze how much energy could be supplied before asking how much is optimally needed and at what quality and scale it could be optimally provided. This backwards direction (upstream to downstream) and supply orienta-

tion lie at the root of many if not most energy policy problems.

Even modest improvements in efficiency at each step of the conversion chain can multiply to large collective values. For example, suppose that during 2000–50, world population and economic growth increased economic activity by 6–8×, in line with conventional projections. But meanwhile, the carbon intensity of primary fuel, following a two-century trend, is likely to fall by at least 2–4× as coal gives way to gas, renewables, and carbon offsets or sequestration. Conversion efficiency is likely to increase by at least 1.5× with modernized, better-run, combined-cycle, and cogenerating power stations. Distribution efficiency should improve modestly. End-use efficiency could improve by 4–6× if the intensity reductions sustained by many industrial countries when they were paying attention were sustained for 50 years (*e.g.*, the U.S. decreased its primary energy/GDP intensity at an average rate of 3.4%/y during 1979–86 and 3.0%/y during 1996–2001). And the least-understood term, hedonic efficiency, might remain constant or might perhaps double as better business models and customer choice systematically improve the quality of services delivered and their match to what customers want. On these plausible assumptions, global carbon emissions from burning fossil fuel could decrease by 1.5–12× despite the assumed 6–8× grosser World Product. The most important assumption is sustained success with end-use efficiency, but the decarbonization and conversion-efficiency terms also appear able to take up some slack if needed.

C. Service redefinition

Some major opportunities to save energy redefine the service being provided. This is often a cultural variable. A Japanese person, asked why the house isn't heated in winter, might reply, "Why should I? Is the house cold?" In Japanese culture, the traditional goal is to keep the *person* comfortable, not to heat or cool empty space. Thus a modern Japanese room air conditioner may contain a sensor array and swiveling louvers that detect and blow air toward people's locations in the room, rather than wastefully cooling the entire space. Western office workers, too, can save energy (and can often see better, feel less tired, and improve aesthetics) by properly adjusting Venetian blinds, bouncing glare-free daylight up onto the ceiling, and turning off the lights. As Jørgen Nørgård remarks, "Energy-efficient lamps save the most energy when they are turned off"; yet many Westerners automatically turn on every light when entering a room.

This example also illustrates that energy efficiency may be hard to distinguish from energy supply that comes from natural energy flows. All houses are already ~98% solar-heated, because if there were no Sun (which provides 99.8% of the Earth's heat), the temperature of the Earth's surface would average approximately −272.6°C rather than +15°C. Thus, strictly speaking, engineered heating systems provide only the last 1–2% of the total heating required.

Service redefinition becomes complex in personal transport. Its efficiency is not just about vehicular fuel economy, people per car, or public transport alternatives. Rather, the underlying service should often be defined as access, not mobility. Typically the best way to gain access to a place is to be there already, so one needn't go somewhere else. This is the realm of spatial planning—no novelty in the U.S., where it's officially shunned yet practiced (zoning laws mandate *dispersion* of location and function, real-estate practices segregate housing by income, and other market distortions maximize unneeded and often unwanted travel). Obviously sprawl would decrease if not mandated and

subsidized. Another way to gain access is virtually—moving just the electrons while leaving the heavy nuclei behind—via telecommunications, soon including realistic "virtual presence." Sometimes that's a realistic alternative to physically moving flesh. And if such movement is really necessary, it merits real competition, at honest prices, between all modes: personal or collective, motorized or human-powered, conventional or innovative. Creative policy tools can enhance that choice in ways that enhance property value, saved time, quality of life, and public amenity and security. Efficient cars can be an important part of efficient personal mobility, and (importantly) are vehicles for emotions as well as for bodies, but also reducing the need to drive can save even more energy and yield greater total benefit.

D. Historic summaries of potential

People have been saving energy for centuries, even millennia; this is the essence of engineering. Most savings were initially in conversion and end-use: pre-industrial households often used more primary energy than modern ones do, because fuelwood-to-charcoal conversion, inefficient open fires, and crude stoves burned much fuel to deliver sparse cooking and warmth. Lighting, materials processing, and transport end-uses were also very inefficient. Billions of human beings still suffer such primitive conditions today. Developing countries' primary energy/GDP intensities *average* ~3× those of industrialized countries. Corrected for purchasing power, China's energy intensity is ~3× that of the U.S., ~5× of the E.U., and ~9× of Japan. Fast-growing economies like China's have the greatest *need* and the greatest *opportunity* to leapfrog to efficiency. But even the most energy-efficient societies still have enormous and expanding room for further efficiency gains. Less than one-fourth of the energy delivered to a typical European cookstove ends up in food; less than one percent of the fuel delivered to a standard car actually moves the driver; U.S. power plants discard waste heat equivalent to 1.2× Japan's total energy use; and even Japan's economy doesn't approach one-tenth the efficiency that the laws of physics permit. Nor is energy efficiency the end of the story: *e.g.,* not only are Chinese shaft kilns an extremely energy-wasteful way to make cement, but the cement is of such poor and uncertain quality that manyfold more of it must be used to make each m^3 of concrete with a certain strength, so the energy leverage of a modern cement plant is these terms' *product*—and the carbon leverage is then multiplied by switching to any no- or low-carbon fuel.

Detailed and exhaustively documented engineering analyses of the scope for improving energy efficiency, especially in end-use devices, have been published for many industrial and some developing countries. By the early 1980s, those analyses had compellingly shown that most of the energy currently used was being wasted—*i.e.,* that the same or better services could be provided using several-fold less primary energy by fully installing, wherever practical and profitable, the most efficient conversion and end-use technologies then available. Such impressive efficiency gains cost considerably less than the long-run, and often even the short-run, marginal private internal cost of supplying more energy. Most policymakers ignore both these analyses, well-known to specialists, and the less-well-known findings showing even bigger and cheaper savings from whole-system design integration (Part 4). Despite much higher E.U. energy consciousness, policymakers still greatly underestimate efficiency's potential, while in the U.S., national policymakers in the past 20 years have forgotten more than they learned in the previous 20 years, leaving efficiency to

be advanced instead by private-sector, local, and state choices.

Many published engineering analyses show a smaller saving potential because of major conservatisms, often deliberate (because the real figures seem too good to be true), or because they assume only partial adoption over a short period rather than examining the ultimate potential for complete practical adoption. For example, the American Council for an Energy-Efficient Economy estimates that just reasonable adoption of the top five conventional U.S. opportunities—industrial improvements, 4.88 L/100 km light-vehicle standards, cogeneration, better building codes, and a 30%-better central-air-conditioning standard—could save 530 million T/y of oil-equivalent—respectively equivalent to the total 2000 primary energy use of Australia, Mexico, Spain, Austria, and Ireland. But the full long-term efficiency potential is far larger, much of it in many small terms. Saving energy is like eating an Atlantic lobster: there are big, obvious chunks of meat in the tail and the front claws, but there's also a similar total quantity of tasty morsels hidden in crevices and requiring some skill and persistence to extract.

The whole-lobster potential is best, though still not fully, seen in bottom-up technological analyses comparing the quantity of potential energy savings with their marginal cost. That cost is typically calculated using the Lawrence Berkeley National Laboratory methodology, which divides the marginal cost of buying, installing, and maintaining the more efficient device by its discounted stream of lifetime energy savings. The levelized cost in dollars of saving, say, 1 kW-h then equals $Ci/S[1-(1+i)^{-n})]$, where C is installed capital cost ($), i is annual real discount rate (assumed here to be 0.05), S is energy saved by the device (kW-h/y), and n is operating life (y). Thus a $10 device that saved 100 kW-h/y and lasted 20 y would have a levelized "cost of saved energy" (CSE) of 0.8¢/kW-h.

Against a 5¢/kW-h electricity price, a 20-y device with a 1-y simple payback would have CSE = 0.4¢/kW-h. It is then conventional for engineering-oriented analysts to represent efficiency "resources" as a supply curve, rather than as shifts along a demand curve (the convention among economists). CSE is methodologically equivalent to the cost of supplied energy (*e.g.*, from a power station and grid): the price of the energy saved is not part of the calculation. Whether the saving is cost-effective depends on comparing the cost of achieving it with the avoided cost of the energy saved. (As Part 2 notes, this conventional engineering-economic approach materially understates the benefits of energy efficiency.)

On this basis, the author's analyses in the late 1980s found, from measured cost and performance data for more than 1,000 electricity-saving end-use technologies, that their full practical retrofit could save about three-fourths of U.S. electricity at an average CSE~0.9¢/kWh (2004 $)—roughly consistent with a 1990 Electric Power Research Institute analysis whose differences were mainly methodological rather than substantive. So many key technologies, now in Asian mass production, are now far cheaper yet more effective that today's potential is even larger and cheaper. (The analyses explicitly excluded the small financing and transaction costs. A huge literature accurately predicts and rigorously measures the empirical size, speed, and cost of efficiency improvements delivered by actual utility and government programs.)

Such findings are broadly consistent with equally or more detailed ones by European analysts: for example, that late-1980s technologies could save three-fourths of Danish buildings' electricity or half of all Swedish electricity at $0.024/kW-h (2004 $), or four-fifths of German home electricity (including minor fuel-switching)

with a ~40%/y aftertax return on investment. Such findings with ever greater sophistication have been published worldwide since 1979, but are generally rejected by nontechnological economic theorists who argue that if such cost-effective opportunities existed, they'd already have been captured in the marketplace, even in planned economies with no marketplace or mixed economies with a distorted one. This mental model— "Don't bother to bend over and pick up that banknote lying on the ground, because if it were real, someone would have picked it up already"— often dominates government policy. It seems ever less defensible as more is learned about the reality of pervasive market failures (Part 5) and the astonishing size and cheapness of the energy savings empirically achieved by diverse enterprises (Part 3). But by now, the debate has become theological (Part 3)— about whether existing markets are essentially perfect, as most economic modelers assume for comfort and convenience, or whether market failures are at least as important as market function and lie at the heart of business and policy opportunity. This seems a testable empirical question.

It may soon be tested in the transport sector. The author's team's uncontested analysis in the Pentagon-cosponsored independent study *Winning the Oil Endgame*, published in September 2004, found that 52% of the officially forecast U.S. 2025 oil use could be saved (half by then, half later as vehicle stocks turn over), at an average cost of just $12/bbl (2000 $). The remaining oil use could be displaced by saved natural gas and advanced biofuels at an average cost of $18/bbl. Thus, by the 2040s, the U.S. could use *no* oil and revitalize its economy, led by business for profit, and encouraged by public policies not requiring mandates, fuel taxes, subsidies, or new national laws. Rather, the transition would be driven by competitive strategy in the car, truck, plane, and oil industries, plus military needs. These findings surprised many, yet a year later, remain unchallenged. Early sectoral progress with implementation has been encouraging.

E. Discontinuous technological progress

This engineering/economics divergence about the potential to save energy also reflects a tacit assumption that technological evolution is smooth and incremental, as mathematical modelers prefer. In fact, while much progress is as incremental as technology diffusion, discontinuous technological leaps, more like "punctuated equilibrium" in evolutionary biology, can propel innovation and speed its adoption, as perhaps with Hypercar® vehicles (Part 4A).

Technological discontinuities can even burst the traditional boundaries of possibility by redefining the design space:

- Generations of engineers learned that big supercritical-steam power plants were as efficient as possible—40-odd percent from fuel in to electricity out. But through sloppy learning or teaching, they'd overlooked the possibility of stacking two Carnot cycles atop each other. Such combined-cycle (gas-then-steam) turbines, based on mass-produced jet engines, can exceed 60% efficiency and are cheaper and faster to build, so in the 1990s, they quickly displaced the big steam plants. Fuel cells, the next innovation, avoid Carnot limits altogether by being an electrochemical device, not a heat engine. Combining both may soon achieve 80–90% fuel-to-electric efficiency. Even inefficient distributed generators can already exceed 90% system efficiency by artfully using recaptured heat.
- Pumps, fans, and other turbomachinery (the main uses of electricity) seemed a ma-

ture art until a novel biomimetic rotor (www.paxscientific.com), using laminar vortex flow instead of turbulent flow, proved substantially more efficient.

- The canonical theoretical efficiency limit for converting sunlight into electricity using single-layer photovoltaic (PV) cells is normally stated as 33%–50+% using multicolor stacked layers, *vs.* lab values around 24% and 39% (lower in volume production). That's because semiconductor bandgaps were believed too big to capture any but the high-energy wavelengths of sunlight. But those standard data are wrong. A Russian-based team suspected in 2001, and Lawrence Berkeley National Laboratory proved in 2002, that indium nitride's bandgap is only 0.7 eV, matching near-infrared (1.77 μm) light and hence able to harvest almost the whole solar spectrum. This may raise the theoretical limit to 50% for two-layer and to ~70% for many-layer thin-film PVs. Perhaps optical-dimension lithographed antenna arrays or quantum-dot PVs can do even better.

Caution is likewise vital when interpreting Second Law efficiency (the ratio of the least available work that could have done the job to the actual available work used to do the job). In the macroscopic world, the laws of thermodynamics are normally considered ineluctable—but the definition of the desired change of state can be finessed. Ernie Robertson notes that when turning limestone into a structural material, one is not confined to the conventional possibilities of cutting it into blocks or calcining it at ~1,250°C into Portland cement. One can instead grind it up and feed it to chickens, whose ambient-temperature technology turns it into eggshell stronger than Portland cement. Were we as smart as chickens, we would have mastered this life-friendly technology. Extraordinary new opportunities to harness 3.8 billion years of biological design experience, as described by Janine Benyus in Biomimicry, can often make heat-beat-and-treat industrial processes unnecessary. So, in principle, can the emerging techniques of nanotechnology using molecular-scale self-assembly, as pioneered by Eric Drexler.

More conventional innovations can also bypass energy-intensive industrial processes. Making artifacts that last longer, use materials more frugally, and are designed and deployed to be repaired, reused, remanufactured, and recycled can save much or most of the energy traditionally needed to produce and assemble their materials (and can increase welfare while reducing GDP, which perversely swells when ephemeral goods are quickly discarded and replaced). Microfluidics can even shrink a big chemical plant to the size of a watermelon: millimeter-scale flow in channels etched into silicon wafers can control time, temperature, pressure, stoichiometry, and catalysis so exactly that a narrow product spectrum is produced, without the side-reactions that normally need most of the chemical plant to separate undesired from desired products.

Such "end-run" solutions—rather like the previous example of substituting sensible land-use for better vehicles, or better still, combining both—can greatly expand the range of possibilities beyond simply improving the narrowly defined efficiency of industrial equipment, processes, and controls. By combining many such options, it is now realistic to contemplate a long-run advanced industrial society that provides unprecedented levels of material prosperity with far less energy, cost, and impact than today's best practice. Part 4A, drawn from Paul Hawken et al.'s synthesis in *Natural Capitalism* and Ernst von Weizsäcker *et al.*'s earlier *Factor Four*, further illustrates recent breakthroughs

in integrative design that can make very large energy savings cost less than small ones; and Part 6 summarizes similarly important discontinuities in policy innovation.

In light of all these possibilities, why does energy efficiency, in most countries and at most times, command so little attention and such lackadaisical pursuit? Several explanations come to mind. Saved energy is invisible. Energy-saving technologies may look and outwardly act just like inefficient ones, so they're invisible too. They're also highly dispersed—unlike central supply technologies that are among the most impressive human creations, inspiring pride and attracting ribbon-cutters and rent- and bribe-seekers. Many users believe energy efficiency is binary—you either have it or lack it—and that they already did it in the 1970s, so they can't do it again. Energy efficiency has relatively weak and scattered constituencies. And major energy efficiency opportunities are disdained or disbelieved by policymakers indoctrinated in a theoretical economic paradigm that claims big untapped opportunities simply cannot exist.

2. Benefits

Energy efficiency avoids the direct economic costs and the direct environmental, security, and other costs of the energy supply and delivery that it displaces. Yet most literature neglects several key side-benefits (economists call them "joint products") of saving energy.

A. Indirect benefits from qualitatively superior services

Improved energy efficiency, especially end-use efficiency, often delivers better services. Efficient houses are more comfortable; efficient lighting systems can look better and help you see better; efficient motors can be more quiet, reliable, and controllable; efficient refrigerators can keep food fresher for longer; efficient clean-rooms can improve the yield, flexibility, throughput, and setup time of microchip fabrication plants; aerodynamically efficient chemical fume hoods can improve safety; airtight houses with constant controlled ventilation (typically through heat exchangers to recover warmth or coolth) have more healthful air than leaky houses that are ventilated only when wind or some other forcing function fortuitously blows air through cracks; efficient supermarkets can improve food safety and merchandising; retail sales pressure can rise 40% in well-daylit stores; students' test scores imply ~20–26% faster learning in well-daylit schools. Such side-benefits can be one or even two more orders of magnitude more valuable than the energy directly saved. For example, careful measurements show that in efficient buildings—where workers can see what they're doing, hear themselves think, breathe cleaner air, and feel more comfortable—labor productivity typically rises by about 6–16%. Since office workers in industrialized countries cost ~100× more than office energy, a 1% increase in labor productivity has the same bottom-line effect as *eliminating* the energy bill—and the actual gain in labor productivity is ~6–16× bigger than that. Practitioners can market these attributes without ever mentioning lower energy bills.

B. Leverage in global fuel markets

Much has been written about the increasing pricing power of major oil-exporting countries, especially Saudi Arabia with its important swing production capacity. Yet the market power of the United States—the Saudi Arabia of energy waste—is even greater on the demand side. The U.S. can save oil faster than OPEC can conveniently sell less oil. This was illustrated during 1977–85, when U.S. GDP rose 27% while total U.S. oil use fell 17%, oil imports fell 50%, and imports from the Persian Gulf fell 87%. OPEC's exports fell 48% (one-fourth of this fall was due to U.S. action), breaking its pricing power for a decade. The most important single cause of the U.S. 5.2%/y gain in oil productivity was more-efficient cars, each driving 1% fewer km on 20% less gasoline—a 7-mi/USgal gain in six years for new American-made cars—and 96% of those savings came from smarter design, only 4% from smaller size.

C. Buying time

Energy efficiency buys time. Time is the more precious asset in energy policy, because it permits the fuller and more graceful development and deployment of still better techniques for energy efficiency and supply. This pushes supply curves down towards the lower right (larger quantities at lower prices), postpones economic depletion, and buys even more time. The more time is available, the more information will emerge to support wiser and more robust choices, and the more fruitfully new technologies and policy options can meld and breed new ones. Conversely, hasty choices driven by supply exigencies almost always turn out badly, waste resources, and foreclose important options. Of course, once bought, time should be used wisely. Instead, the decade of respite bought by the U.S. efficiency spurt of 1977–85 was almost entirely wasted as attention waned, efficiency and alternative-supply efforts stalled, R&D teams were disbanded, and political problems festered. We all pay today the heavy price of that stagnation.

D. Integrating efficiency with supply

To first order, energy efficiency makes supply cheaper. But second-order effects reinforce this first-order benefit, most obviously when efficiency is combined with onsite renewable supplies, making them nonlinearly smaller, simpler, and cheaper. For example:

- A hot-water-saving house can achieve a very high solar-water-heat fraction (*e.g.*, 99% in the author's home high in the Rocky Mountains) with only a small collector, so it needs little or no backup, partly because collector efficiency increases as stratified-tank storage temperature decreases.
- An electricity-saving house (the author's saves ~90%, using only ~110–120 average W for 372 m2) needs only a few m^2 of PVs and a simple balance-of-system (storage, inverter, etc.). This can cost less than connecting to the grid a few meters away.
- A passive-solar, daylit building needs little electricity, and can pay for even costly forms of onsite generation (such as PVs) by eliminating or downsizing mechanical systems.
- Such mutually reinforcing options can be bundled: *e.g.*, 1.18 peak MW of photovoltaics retrofitted onto the Santa Rita Jail in Alameda County, California, was combined with efficiency and load management, so at peak periods when the power was most valuable, less was used by the jail and more sold back to the grid. This bundling yielded an internal rate of return over 10% including state subsidies, and a present-valued customer benefit/cost ratio of 1.7 without or 3.8 with those subsidies.

E. Gaps in engineering economics

Both engineers and economists conventionally calculate the cost of supplying or saving energy using a rough-and-ready toolkit called "engineering economics." Its methods are easy-to-use but flawed, ignoring such basic tenets of

financial economics as risk-adjusted discount rates. Indeed, engineering economics omits 207 economic and engineering considerations that together increase the value of decentralized electrical resources by typically an order of magnitude. Many of these "distributed benefits," compiled in the author's team's *Small Is Profitable*, apply as much to end-use efficiency as to decentralized generation. Most of the literature on the cost of energy alternatives is based solely on accounting costs and engineering economics that greatly understate efficiency's value. Properly counting its benefits will yield far sounder investments.

End-use efficiency is also the most effective way to make energy supply systems more resilient against mishap or malice, because it increases the duration of buffer stocks, buying time to mend damage or arrange new supplies, and it increases the share of service that curtailed or improvised supplies can deliver. Efficiency's high "bounce per buck" makes it the cornerstone of any energy system design for secure service provision in a dangerous world.

6. Old and new ways to accelerate energy efficiency

A. Old but good methods

In the 1980s and 1990s, practitioners and policymakers greatly expanded their toolkits for implementing energy efficiency. During 1973–86, the U.S. doubled its new-car efficiency, and during 1977–85, cut national oil intensity 5.2%/y. In 1983–85, ten million people served by Southern California Edison Company were cutting its decade-ahead forecast of peak load by 8½%/y, at ~1% the long-run marginal cost of supply. In 1990, New England Electric System signed up 90% of a pilot market for small-business retrofits in two months. In the same year, Pacific Gas and Electric Company marketers captured a fourth of the new-commercial-construction market for design improvements in three months, so in 1991, PG&E raised the target—and got it all in the first nine days of January.

Such impressive achievements resulted from nearly two decades' refinement of program structures and marketing methods. At first, utilities and governments wanting to help customers save energy offered general, then targeted, information, and sometimes loans or grants. Demonstration programs proved feasibility and streamlined delivery. Standards knocked the worst equipment off the market. (Congress did this for household appliances without a single dissenting vote, because so many appliances are bought by landlords, developers, or public housing authorities—a manifest split incentive with the householders who'll later pay the energy bills.) Just refrigerator standards cut new U.S. units' electricity usage by fourfold during 1975–2001— 5%/y—saving 40 GW of electric supply. In Canada, labeling initially did nearly as well. Utilities began to offer rebates—targeted, then generic—to customers, then to other value-chain participants—for adopting energy-saving equipment, or scrapping inefficient equipment, or both. Some rebate structures proved potent, such as paying a shop assistant a bonus for selling an energy-efficient refrigerator but nothing for selling an inefficient one. So did leasing (20¢ per compact fluorescent lamp per month, so you pay for it over time just like a power plant . . . but the lamp is far cheaper), paying for better design, and rewarding buyers for beating minimum standards. Energy-saving companies, independent or utility-owned, provided turnkey design and installation to reduce hassle. Sweden aggregated technology procurement to offer "golden carrot" rewards to manufacturers bringing innovations to market; once these new products

were introduced, competition quickly eliminated their modest price premia.

These engineered-service-delivery models worked well, often spectacularly well. Steve Nadel's 1990 review of 237 programs at 38 U.S. utilities found many costing <1¢/kWh (1988 $). During 1991–94, the entire demand-side-management portfolio of California's three major investor-owned utilities saved electricity at an average program cost that fell from about 2.8 to 1.9 current ¢/kW-h (1.2¢ for the cheapest), saving society over $2 billion more than the effort cost.

B. New and better methods

Since the late 1980s, another model has been emerging that promises even better results: not just marketing negawatts (saved watts)— maximizing how many customers save and how much—but also making markets *in* negawatts—thus maximizing competition in who saves and how, so as to drive quantity and quality up and cost down. Competitive bidding processes let saved and produced energy compete fairly. Savings can be made fungible in time and space, transferred between customers, utilities, and jurisdictions, and procured by "bounty-hunters." Spot, futures, and options markets can be expanded from just megawatts to embrace negawatts too, permitting arbitrage between them. Property owners can commit never to use more than x MW, then trade those commitments in a secondary market that values reduced demand and reduced uncertainty of demand. Efficiency can be cross-marketed between electric and gas distributors, each rewarded for saving *either* form of energy. Revenue-neutral "feebates" for connecting new buildings to public energy supplies—fees for inefficiency, rebates for efficiency— can reward continuous improvement. Standardized measurement and reporting of energy savings lets them be aggregated and securitized like home mortgages, sold promptly into liquid secondary markets, and hence financed easily and cheaply (www.ipmvp.org). Efficiency techniques can be conveniently bundled and translated to "vernacular" forms—easily chosen, purchased, and installed. Novel real-estate value propositions emerge from integrating efficiency with onsite renewable supply (part of the revolutionary shift now underway to distributed resources) so as to eliminate all wires and pipes, the trenches carrying them, and the remote infrastructure they connect to. Performance-based design fees, targeted mass retrofits, greater purchasing aggregation, and systematic barrier-busting all show immense promise. And aggressively scrapping inefficient devices—paying bounties to destroy them instead of reselling them—could both solve many domestic problems (*e.g.,* oil, air, and climate in the case of inefficient vehicles) and boost global development by reversing "negative technology transfer."

Winning the Oil Endgame offers a similarly novel policy menu for saving oil. Revenue-and size-neutral "feebates" for widening the price spread between more and less efficient light vehicles in each size class—thus arbitraging the discount-rate spread between car-buyers and society—are far more effective than fuel taxes or efficiency standards, and can yield both consumer and producer surpluses. Tripled-efficiency heavy trucks and planes can be elicited, respectively, by "demand pull" from big customers (once they're informed of what's possible, as began to occur in 2005) and by innovative financing for insolvent airlines (on condition of scrapping inefficient parked planes). The first 25% fuel saving for trucks and 20% for planes (in Boeing's 787 Dreamliner) is *free*; the rest of the tripling of efficiency has very high returns.

A key player may be the military, which needs superefficient platforms for agile deployment and to cut the huge cost and risk of fuel logistics. Speeding ultralight, ultrastrong materials fabrication processes to market could transform civilian vehicle industries as profoundly as military R&D did to create the Internet, GPS, jet engines, and chips. Only this time, that transformation could lead countries like the U.S. off oil, making oil no longer worth fighting over.

Altogether, the conventional agenda for promoting energy efficiency—prices and taxes, plus regulation or deregulation—ignores nearly all the most effective, attractive, trans-ideological, and quickly spreadable methods. And it ignores many of the new marketing "hooks" just starting to be exploited: security (national, community, and individual), economic development and balance of trade, avoiding price volatility and costly supply overshoot, profitable integration and bundling with renewables, and expressing individual values.

Consider, for example, a good compact fluorescent lamp. It emits the same light as an incandescent lamp but uses 4–5× less electricity and lasts 8–13× longer, saving tens of dollars more than it costs. It avoids putting a ton of carbon dioxide and other pollutants into the air. But it does far more. In suitable volume—about a billion are now made each year—it can cut by a fifth the evening peak load that causes blackouts in overloaded Mumbai, can boost poor American chicken farmers' profits by a fourth, or can raise destitute Haitian households' disposable cash income by up to a third. As mentioned above, making the lamp requires 99.97% less capital than does expanding the supply of electricity, thus freeing investment for other tasks. The lamp cuts power needs to levels that make solar-generated power affordable, so girls in rural huts can learn to read at night, advancing the role of women. One light bulb does all that. You can buy it at the supermarket and install it yourself. One light bulb at a time, we can make the world safer. "In short," concludes Jørgen Nørgård, by pursuing the entire efficiency potential systematically and comprehensively, "it is possible in the course of half a century to offer everybody on Earth a joyful and materially decent life with a per capita energy consumption of only a small fraction of today's consumption in the industrialized countries...."

C. De-emphasizing traditionally narrow price-centric perspectives

These burgeoning opportunities suggest that price may well become less important to the uptake of energy efficiency. Price remains important and should be correct, but is only one of many ways to get attention and influence choice; ability to respond to price can be far more important. End-use efficiency may increasingly be marketed and bought mainly for its qualitatively improved services, just as distributed and renewable supply-side resources may be marketed and bought mainly for their distributed benefits. Outcomes would then become decreasingly predictable from economic experience or using economic tools.

Meanwhile, disruptive technologies and integrative design methods are clearly inducing dramatic shifts *of*, not just along, demand curves, and are even making them less relevant by driving customer choice through non-price variables. Ultralight-hybrid Hypercar® vehicles,

for example, would do an end-run around two decades of trench warfare in the U.S. Congress (raising efficiency standards *vs*. gasoline taxes). They would also defy the standard assumption that efficient cars must trade off other desirable attributes (size, performance, price, safety), requiring government intervention to induce customers to buy the compromised vehicles. If, as now seems incontrovertible, light vehicles can achieve 3–5× fuel savings as a byproduct of breakthrough design integration, yet remain uncompromised and competitively priced, then the energy-price-driven "tradeoff" paradigm becomes irrelevant. People will prefer such vehicles because they're *better*, not because they're clean and efficient, much as most people now buy digital media rather than vinyl phonograph records: they're a superior product that redefines market expectations. This implies a world where energy price and regulation become far less influential than today, displaced by imaginative, holistic, integrative engineering and marketing.

In the world of consumer electronics—ever better, faster, smaller, cheaper—that world is upon us. In the wider world of energy efficiency, the master key to so many of the world's most vexing problems, it is coming rapidly over the horizon. We need only understand it and do it. And as inventor Edwin Land said, "People who seem to have had a new idea have often only stopped having an old idea." To think truly "outside the barrel," in the apt phrase of Rijkman Groenink (Chairman of ABN Amro's supervisory board), we all have much to unlearn.

BIBLIOGRAPHY

American Institute of Physics (1975). *Efficient Use of Energy, AIP Conf. Procs.* #25. AIP, New York.

Benyus, J.M. (1997). *Biomimicry: Innovation Inspired by Nature*. William Morrow, New York.

Brohard, G.J., Brown, M.W., Cavanagh, R., Elberling, L.E., Hernandez, G.R., Lovins, A., and Rosenfeld, A.H. (1998). "Advanced Customer Technology Test for Maximum Energy Efficiency (ACT²) Project: The Final Report." Procs. *Summer Study on Energy-Efficient Buildings*. American Council for an Energy-Efficient Economy, Washington, DC.

Daly, H.E. (1996) *Beyond Growth—The Economics of Sustainable Development*, Beacon Press, Boston. Drexler, K.E. (1992). *Nanosystems: Molecular Machinery, Manufacturing, and Computation*. John Wiley and Sons, New York.

E SOURCE (2002). *Technology Atlas series* (6 vols.) and *Electronic Encyclopedia* CD-ROM. E SOURCE, Boulder, Colorado, www.esource.com.

Fiberforge, Inc. (Glenwood Springs, Colorado), advanced-composites manufacturing process information at www.fiberforge.com.

Fickett, A.P., Gellings, C.W., and Lovins, A.B. (1990). "Efficient Use of Electricity." *Sci. Amer.* 263(3):64–74 (September).

Hawken, P.G., Lovins, A.B. and L.H. (1999). *Natural Capitalism: Creating the Next Industrial Revolution*. Little Brown, New York, www.natcap.org.

IPSEP (1989–99). *Energy Policy in the Greenhouse.* Report to Dutch Ministry of Environment, International Project for Sustainable Energy Paths, El Cerrito CA 94530, www.ipsep.org.

Johansson, T.B., Bodlund, B., and Williams, R.H., eds. 1989: *Electricity*. Lund University Press, Lund, Sweden, particularly Bodlund et al.'s chapter "The Challenge of Choices."

Koplow, D., "Energy Subsidy Links Pages," Earthtrack (Washington DC), 2005, http://earthtrack.net/earthtrack/index.asp?page_id=177&catid=66

Krause, F., Baer, P., and DeCanio, S. (2001). "Cutting Carbon Emissions at a Profit: Opportunities for the U.S." IPSEP, El Cerrito, California, www.ipsep.org/latestpubs.html.

Lovins, A.B. (1992). *Energy-Efficient Buildings: Institutional Barriers and Opportunities*. Strategic Issues Paper II. E SOURCE, Boulder, Colorado, www.esource.com.

Lovins, A.B. (1994). "Apples, Oranges, and Horned Toads." *Electricity J.* 7(4):29–49.

Lovins, A.B. (1995). "The Super-Efficient Passive Building Frontier." *ASHRAE J.* 37(6):79–81, June; RMI Publication #E95-28, Rocky Mountain Institute, Snowmass, Colorado, www.rmi.org.

Lovins, A.B. (2003). "Twenty Hydrogen Myths," www.rmi.org/sitepages/pid171.php\#20H2Myths.

Lovins, A.B. (2004). "Energy efficiency, taxonomic overview," *Encyc. of Energy* 2:382–401, Elsevier, free download at www.rmi.org/images/other/Energy/E04-02_EnergyEffTax.pdf.

Lovins, A.B. (2005). "More Profit With Less Carbon," *Sci. Amer.* 293:74–82, Sept., www.rmi.org/sitepages/pid171.php#E05-05.

Lovins, A.B. (2005a). "Nuclear economics and climate-protection potential," Rocky Mountain Institute, 11 Sept. 2005, free download at www.rmi.org/sitepages/pid171.php#E05-08.

Lovins, A.B. and Cramer, D.R. (2003). Hypercars®, Hydrogen, and the Automotive Transition. *Intl. J. Veh.* Design, 35(1/2):50–85, www.rmi.org/images/other/Trans/T04-01_HypercarH2AutoTrans.pdf.

Lovins, A.B., Datta, E.K., Feiler, T., Rábago, K.R., Swisher, J.N., Lehmann, A., and Wicker, K. (2002). *Small Is Profitable: The Hidden Economic Benefits of Making Electrical Resources the Right Size*. Rocky Mountain Institute, Snowmass, Colorado, www.smallisprofitable.org.

Lovins, A.B., and Gadgil, A. (1991). "The Negawatt Revolution: Electric Efficiency and Asian Development." RMI Publication #E91-23. Rocky Mountain Institute, Snowmass, Colorado.

Lovins, A.B., Datta, E.K., Bustnes, O.-E., Koomey, J.G., and Glasgow, N. (2004). *Winning the Oil Endgame*, Rocky Mountain Institute, Snowmass, Colorado, www.oilendgame.com.

Lovins, A.B. & L.H. (1991). "Least-Cost Climatic Stabilization." *Annual Review of Energy and the Environment* 16:433–531.

Lovins, A.B. & L.H. (1996). "Negawatts: Twelve Transitions, Eight Improvements, and One Distraction." Energy Policy 24(4):331–344, www.rmi.org/images/other/E-Negawatts12-8-1.pdf.

Lovins, A.B. & L.H. (1997). "Climate: Making Sense *and* Making Money." Rocky Mountain Institute, Snowmass, Colorado, www.rmi.org/images/other/C-ClimateMSMM.pdf.

Lovins, A.B. & L.H. (2001). "Fool's Gold in Alaska." *Foreign Affairs* 80(4):72–85, July/August; annotated at www.rmi.org/images/other/E-FoolsGoldAnnotated.pdf.

Lovins, A.B. & L.H., Krause, F., and Bach, W. (1982). *Least-Cost Energy: Solving the CO_2 Problem*. Brick House, Andover, Massachusetts. Reprinted 1989 by Rocky Mountain Institute, Snowmass, Colorado.

Lovins, A.B., and Williams. B.D. (1999). "A Strategy for the Hydrogen Transition." *Procs. 10th Ann. Hydrogen Mtg.*, 8 April, National Hydrogen Assn., Washington, DC, www.rmi.org/images/other/HC-StrategyHCTrans.pdf.

Nadel. S. (1990). *Lessons Learned*. Report #90–08. New York State Energy R&D Authority (Albany), with N.Y. State Energy Office and Niagara

Mohawk Power Corp. American Council for an Energy-Efficient Economy, Washington, DC.

Nørgård, Jørgen S. (2002). "Energy Efficiency and the Switch to Renewable Energy Sources. Natural Resource System Challenge II: Climate Change. Human Systems and Policy" (ed. A. Yotova), *UN-ESCO Encyclopedia of Life Support Systems*, EOLSS Publisher Co., Oxford, UK.

Reddy, A.K.N., Williams, R.H., and Johansson, T.B. (1997). *Energy After Rio: Prospects and Challenges.* United Nations Development Program, New York.

Repetto, R., & Austin, D. (1997). "The Costs of Climate Protection: A Guide to the Perplexed." World Resources Institute, Washington, DC, www.wri.org/wri/climate/.

Romm, J.J., Rosenfeld, A.H., and Herrmann, S. (1999). "The Internet Economy and Global Warming: A Scenario of the Impact of E-Commerce on Energy and the Environment." Center for Energy and Climate Solutions, Washington, DC, www.cool-companies.org.

Romm, J.J., and Browning, W.D. (1994). "Greening the Building and the Bottom Line: Increasing

Productivity Through Energy-Efficient Design." Rocky Mountain Institute, Snowmass, Colorado, www.rmi.org/sitepages/pid174.php.

Swisher, J.N. (2002). "The New Business Climate." Rocky Mountain Institute, Snowmass, Colorado, www.rmi.org/store/p385pid2421.php.

Swisher, J.N., Jannuzzi, G., and Redlinger, R. (1998). *Tools and Methods for Integrated Resource Planning: Improving Energy Efficiency and Protecting the Environment*, UNEP Collaborating Centre on Energy and Environment, Denmark, http://www.uccee.org/IRPManual/index.htm.

von Weizs\du\acker, E.U., Lovins, A.B. & L.H. (1995/97). *Factor Four: Doubling Wealth, Halving Resource Use.* Earthscan, London.

Wilson, A., Uncapher, J., McManigal, L., Lovins, L.H., Cureton, M., and Browning, W. (1998). *Green Development: Integrating Ecology and Real Estate.* John Wiley & Sons, New York; Green Developments CD-ROM (2002), Rocky Mountain Institute, Snowmass, Colorado.

Discussion Questions

1. Lovins identifies different categories of inefficiency that he says often get overlooked, such as distribution losses downstream from production, useless or misused services, parasitic loads, and misplaced efficiency. What does each of these refer to, and how can each contribute to reduced efficiency?
2. Which of the key side benefits of saving energy highlighted by Lovins do you think are most important? Why?
3. Lovins is careful to distinguish between *efficiency* and *conservation*. What is his rationale for doing this?
4. If you were responsible for setting U.S. energy policy, what energy efficiency policies would you promote? Give a brief rationale for your choices.

 Supporting Activities

1. Have each member of your class read and report on a blog entry from the Rocky Mountain Institute blog site: http://blog.rmi.org/.
2. How much electricity did you and/or your family consume last month in your home? Get a copy of an electric bill and figure out the kilowatt-hour (kWh) consumption overall and on a per-person basis for your household. In many areas, it's also possible to monitor your household's daily consumption online. See what the effect of making changes in your energy use make in your daily consumption.
3. Look at the resources contained on Appalachian State University's Office of Sustainability web site. These include a *Sustainable Living Guide* for students and a plethora of information about sustainability topics and initiatives. Visit: http://sustain.appstate.edu/.
4. Learn more about how the Department of Defense is integrating energy efficiency measures and renewable energy systems into the operations of all military branches at: http://www.defense.gov/home/features/2010/1010_energy/.

Additional Resources

1. The Lovins report was one of several commissioned by the IAC that provided "essential building blocks" for a 2007 report by the IAC, titled *Lighting the Way: Toward a Sustainable Energy Future*. You can find the full text of the 2007 report at: http://www.interacademycouncil.net/.
2. The National Academy of Engineering has a downloadable report and an overview of the potential for energy efficiency; both are available at: https://www.nae.edu/Publications/Bridge/EnergyEfficiency14874/ThePotentialofEnergyEfficiencyAnOverview.aspx.

The New Oil Landscape

The Appalachian region of the United States is certainly not the only area being impacted by energy-related mining and drilling activity. North Dakota's Bakken formation has led that state to become one of the largest oil-producing states in the country, second only to Texas. This article by Edwin Dobb about recent oil development in North Dakota serves to highlight key points made in earlier readings in this section; it also illustrates some additional important aspects of drilling activity, particularly fracking.

For example, virtually every energy-producing state in the country has experienced the so-called boom/bust cycles, with rapid population growth and development when people flock to the region to find one of the plentiful and well-paying jobs. Once the resource is tapped, or when there is a downturn in energy prices, those same job-seekers leave just as quickly, deeply impacting the local economy. Hydraulic fracturing—what Dobbs labels "a skeleton key that can be used to open other fossil fuel treasure chests"—requires vast amounts of water which, when mixed with fracking chemicals and pumped into the ground, comes back out as heavily polluted wastewater (known in the industry as "produced water"). In the absence of pipelines, all of this water, as well as the oil or gas that is pumped out, must be trucked on and off the site. By one estimate cited in this article, every single new well requires about 2,000 truck trips, or about six 18-wheelers into and out of the well site daily. And even when there is laid pipeline available to reduce the amount of truck hauling, environmental catastrophes can result when these inevitably leak, particularly when the material being pumped through them is caustic.

North Dakota provides yet another poignant example of how difficult it can be to agree on the value of ecosystem services and natural capital. Dobbs writes of the "inestimable values of the prairie—silence, solitude, serenity," three characteristics that are surely broken by fracking activity but on which it would be extraordinarily difficult to put a price tag. And, just as in West Virginia and Pennsylvania and many other states, we see that many residents of North Dakota are in favor of the economic boost provided by mining and drilling and believe it is beneficial to their region, so accept the trade-off it presents to such ecosystem services.

Edwin Dobb was a contributing writer at *Harper's* magazine from 1998 to 2007, and for the past several years has been writing for *National Geographic* magazine. He has also published regularly in the *High Country News*, a nonprofit media organization based in Paonia, Colorado that covers issues defining the American West. He was cowriter and coproducer of the documentary "Butte, America," which aired in 2009. Dobb has been a lecturer in the UC Berkeley Graduate School of Journalism since 2000, where he teaches reported narrative writing, literary nonfiction, and environmental journalism.

When Susan Connell arrives at the first oil well of the day, she tosses her stylish black-rimmed glasses onto the dashboard of her 18-wheeler, climbs down from the cab, and pulls the zipper on her fire-resistant coveralls up to her neck. It's early July, about 7 a.m. We're on the Fort Berthold Reservation, in western North Dakota. Connell, 39, the mother of two young girls and one of the few female big-rig drivers in the oil patch, is hauling water. Produced water, as it's officially known. The drivers call it dirty water. During the early days of pumping at a new well, oil is accompanied by fluids and other substances used during drilling, along with salt water, which is abundant above the sub-terranean layers of rock where the coveted sweet crude is found. Eventually the man-made additives diminish, leaving mostly salt water. Five

Edwin Dobb/National Geographic Creative.

of the three-story-high tanks in front of us contain oil; the sixth, everything else. That's what Connell is here to transfer to a waste-disposal well.

"Just don't pass out on me," Connell says, half in jest. We've scaled a steep stairway to a narrow steel catwalk 30 feet above the ground, but she's not referring to the height. She says that one of the first times she opened the hatch atop a dirty water tank, she was overcome by fumes. "I fell to my knees." No one had warned her about the dozens of chemicals in the water, including hydrogen sulfide, H_2S, its rotten-egg odor created by bacteria growing inside wells. In high enough concentrations it can be poisonous, even lethal.

Ironically, the gas poses the greatest risk when it deadens your sense of smell, another safety lesson Connell had to learn on her own. Eventually someone gave her an H_2S detector, which she clipped to her collar whenever she approached a well that had turned "sour" enough to be hazardous. Once she was pumping dirty water from her tanker truck when the detector sounded. She scrambled away, thinking she'd escaped harm. But hours later she felt stabbing pains in her stomach, the prelude to a weeklong bout of vomiting. Her next purchase was a gas mask.

Connell tells me to stand upwind, then gingerly lifts the hatch. No fumes. It's what she expected, having often hauled water from this well, but, she says, you never know when a routine activity will be interrupted by a nasty surprise. She unwinds a measuring tape into the tank. For a moment, from the vantage of the catwalk, I'm granted a bird's-eye view of the surrounding country. Just outside the coral-colored gravel of the well site are patches of flax and sunflowers, then sealike fields of wheat, alfalfa, and canola, and beyond them, heavily eroded badlands through which the Missouri

River has cut a wide, sweeping bend. The understated glory of the northern plains.

But my pastoral interlude is cut short. Connell has descended the stairs and is removing a 20-foot hose—like a fire hose, only heavier—from the side of the truck. Though only five feet six inches tall and weighing just a hundred pounds, she moves quickly, leaning forward to get traction as she drags the thick hose along the ground. She attaches one end to the rear of the truck tank, the other to an outlet at the base of the storage tank. She then pulls a long metal handle, opening the storage valve. If you don't look closely, you might miss the brunette pigtails that fall to Connell's shoulders, the blue eyes in the shadow cast by her well-worn baseball cap.

A half hour later we're back in the cab, a hundred barrels heavier, rolling away. Connell doesn't use the clutch much. "Just like a pro," she says with a mischievous smile, before admitting it took months to master shifting gears at stoplights.

Truck driving is the most common job in the oil patch, an area about the size of West

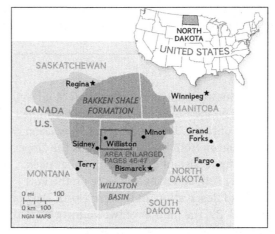

Edwin Dobb covered a controversial mine in Alaska in December 2010. Eugene Richards portrayed the emptying of North Dakota in January 2008.

Virginia where advances in drilling and extraction technology have made it possible to remove oil from deep, widely dispersed deposits. Since early 2006, production from what's known as the Bakken formation has increased nearly 150-fold, to more than 660,000 barrels a day, moving North Dakota into second place among domestic suppliers, behind Texas and ahead of Alaska.

No one but a handful of industry insiders saw that coming. Now some optimistic oilmen predict that the state's daily output could eventually close in on Texas'—at two million barrels. The number of wells could increase from the roughly 8,000 operating today to between 40,000 and 50,000. By the time the frenzy ends, perhaps 20 years from now, as many as 14 billion barrels of high-quality crude may have been removed. Until more pipelines are built in this landlocked rural region, most of the oil and water will be transported by truck. So will everything else needed for swift, large-scale development: gravel, construction materials, tools, machinery. The prairie is being industrialized. If the transformation needs an emblem, there's no better candidate than Connell's 18-wheeler.

Change of such scope and intensity is bound to raise questions. Thousands of people are converging on the area, looking for work, looking for redemption, looking for trouble. And jobs are plentiful. In Williston, in the heart of the oil patch, the unemployment rate is less than one percent. But how does a region of farms and small towns weather the human onslaught? Another risk is environmental damage. Most attention has focused on hydraulic fracturing, or fracking, by which large amounts of fresh water combined with sand and other substances, some toxic, are driven under high pressure down wells drilled into deep layers of shale, creating cracks through which bubbles of trapped oil and natural gas can escape into

the well. Where will all the clean water come from? How will the dirty water that's pumped out be prevented from contaminating groundwater, as has happened in other parts of the country? Stepping back for a broader view, can the inestimable values of the prairie—silence, solitude, serenity—be preserved in the face of full-throttle, regionwide development, of extracting as much oil as possible as fast as possible?

The implications are already reverberating far beyond North Dakota. Bakken-like shale formations occur across the U.S., indeed, across the world. The extraction technology refined in the Bakken is in effect a skeleton key that can be used to open other fossil fuel treasure chests.

That technology, stunning enough in itself, coupled with shifts in the marketplace that favor exploiting deposits that are harder, and therefore more expensive, to tap has convinced some experts that the carbon-based economy can continue much longer than they'd imagined. Billionaire oilman and Bakken pioneer Harold Hamm argues that the assumption we're running out of oil and gas is false. America, in his view, needs a national policy based on abundance, one that doesn't favor developing renewable sources of energy. Either way, you're not likely to hear anyone in the oil patch mention what's ultimately at stake if we keep burning fossil fuels with abandon.

"Climate change?" Connell says. "We don't talk about that here."

North Dakota has boomed before, in the 1950s and '80s. But besides being much larger and likely to last much longer, the current boom differs from earlier ones because it has coincided with an economic malaise. For refugees from the recession, the Bakken is a chance—often the last chance—to escape ruin.

So it was for Susan Connell. While we head for the disposal site on a two-lane highway chewed up by truck traffic, she describes how she came to be behind the wheel of a Kenworth Anteater. The trouble started in 2009, when she and her husband could no longer find construction work in southwestern Montana, where they live. By the fall they were three months behind on their house payments. The bank sent threatening letters. Then Connell heard that truckers were needed in North Dakota. The Delaware native had driven a commercial bus between Philadelphia and Atlantic City, also an airport transit bus in Portland, Oregon. How much harder could an 18-wheeler be? But to qualify she would have to upgrade her license, and for that she would need to attend a special training program. Cost: $4,000. At a time when Connell and her husband could scarcely buy groceries for their kids, they charged the fee to a credit card. "It was a big gamble," she says, referring less to the likely availability of work than to the reception she would almost certainly get in what she calls the "testosterone cloud."

When she was a teenager, Connell did stand-up comedy in cafés in Philadelphia. HBO and *Saturday Night Live* expressed interest, but her abiding love was art—painting, filmmaking, and especially writing stories *(Continued on page 44)* and acting them out, sometimes with props,

(Continued on page 44)

before audiences. She was the lead singer in a rock band for six years. All that experience bred in her a cheerful, disarming fearlessness. Now she was auditioning for a demanding new role.

On a frigid day in mid-December, Connell fixed pancakes for her daughters, fought back tears as she said goodbye, then made the seven-hour trip from southwestern Montana to the Montana–North Dakota border. With the temperature dropping at night to well below zero, she alternated between sleeping in her car and staying in shabby motels while applying at more than a dozen trucking companies. All turned her down. Several managers said women didn't belong in the oil patch. One guy in Tioga told her it was a sacrilege that she wasn't home tending to her children. She was angry. "They were messing with my livelihood," she says.

When the first offer came, after the holidays, it was to haul grain, not water or oil, and for considerably less pay, over a territory covering most of western North Dakota as well as eastern Montana and southern Saskatchewan. To make matters worse, the winter of 2010–2011 was unusually severe. This was no place to be piloting an 18-wheeler for the first time—and alone. "I was so nervous I thought I was going to die," Connell says of her inaugural trip. Everywhere she drove, the roads were iced over. "I chained up all the time," she says. After much trial and error, occasionally featuring a cursing farmer, she learned how to back up an 18-wheeler across snow-laden fields, then to unload silos while standing atop the trailer in 20-below weather, often in the dark, sleet and grain dust pelting her face. She did her own truck maintenance, including oiling hubs and greasing bearings.

During the first months of 2011, Connell continued to apply for oil jobs. The odds were improving because the need for semi operators was increasing rapidly. Since the 1990s fracking had been combined with directional drilling—excavating horizontally from the bottom of the vertical portion of a well into thin layers of oil- and gas-bearing rock. In the Bakken, Harold Hamm's Continental Resources and other nimble companies had refined that technology by extending the lateral leg as far as two miles and altering the fracking-solution recipe. In 2004 Continental had brought in the first commercially viable well in the state. Two years later an EOG Resources well produced oil under so much pressure that the company had to shut down the well until a second one could be drilled to reduce the pressure.

"That created huge excitement," recalls Lynn Helms, director of the North Dakota Department of Mineral Resources. Anticipation was building. The turning point came at the end of 2009, when Brigham Oil & Gas split the single lateral leg of a well south of Williston into 25 legs, each of which was fracked separately, making it possible to reach more oil— hundreds of barrels a day. Helms calculated that the first year of every new well, from drilling to fracking to early production, would entail 2,000 truck trips. This didn't include the hauling out of huge amounts of oil and salt water during the remainder of a well's life. State officials were already thinking in terms of tens of thousands of new wells, most of which would be located in only four counties bordering the Missouri River—Williams, Mountrail, McKenzie, and Dunn. The implications were staggering. "A flag went up," Helms says. Much more of everything—manpower, highways, railroads, electricity lines, patience—would be needed.

This is a full-scale mining operation," says Brent Sanford, mayor of Watford City, a McKenzie County community that's been transformed by the boom. "And I'm all for it." The 40-year-old, fourth-generation native sits in front of a computer monitor in his office at S & S Motors, which his grandfather started in 1946 and he took over when he moved back home nine years ago. While scanning for bargains on a car-auc-

tion website, he explains his enthusiasm. "My town was dying," he says. Watford City was one of dozens facing the same plight, which once prompted geographers to propose that the region be turned over to the buffalo again, a notion you don't want to bring up with Sanford or any of his neighbors unless you're itching for a fight. Every year western North Dakota was becoming emptier—of promise as well as people. The fracking boom has reversed the decline. "Now we can get back to work," Sanford says.

To appreciate the nature of the work, I visited a well northeast of Williston. A leak had developed at the bottom of the vertical leg, about two miles underground. To bring the pipe to the surface, a derricklike structure, similar to a drill rig but smaller, had been erected. On a deck about 30 feet up the rig, four roughnecks were removing the entire 10,750 feet of pipe, one 32-foot, 500-pound segment at a time, a task both tedious and highly dangerous. A device underneath the deck held each segment in place as it emerged, to prevent the pressure of the oil from sending all two miles of pipe, some 84 tons of steel, rocketing into the sky. As if to remind us of that possibility, a fountain of oil suddenly burst from the hole, covering the men, their hard hats, faces, everything. The odor of gas permeated the air. More fountains followed. Here were guys who knew what they were doing, who were exposed to constant peril, who were paid well, and who, because of all that, had ample reason to be proud. It was skilled manual labor in perilous circumstances, which in our age of high-tech jockeys and private-equity sharks seemed exotic, almost heroic.

Sanford isn't blind to the trauma Watford City is undergoing. A population that in the past two years has soared from about 1,700 to at least 6,000 and, Sanford estimates, perhaps as many as 10,000. A housing shortage so acute that men—and it's still mostly men—are forced to sleep in their trucks or in overpriced motels;

pay "gougezone" fees to park their campers, RVs, and house trailers; or live in one of the expensive prefab, dormlike "man camps" that serve as instant but sterile bedroom communities for towns and work sites. Streets clotted with noisy, exhaust-belching tanker trucks, gravel trucks, flatbeds, dump trucks, service trucks, and—the personal vehicle of choice in the oil patch—oversize, gas-gorging pickups. More crime, more highway accidents, more medical emergencies. People on fixed incomes forced to move because they can't afford steep rent hikes. Overtaxed water and sewer systems. Prostitution. Registered sex offenders at large in the community.

But Sanford, a former CPA, believes the media have overemphasized the negative side of the ledger. Not only will Watford City survive intact, he insists, but the eventual benefits will far outweigh the costs. Regarding housing, "our greatest problem," he says the difficulties should be seen as part of an evolution from temporary lodging like RVs and man camps to "rooftops"— new apartment buildings and, eventually, single-family homes. Already the elementary school has been expanded. A new recreation center, a public housing and daycare complex, and a hospital will soon be built. Roads are being repaired, upgraded, widened. All across town old businesses—including S & S Motors—are flourishing, and new ones are opening their doors.

Trucking is one of the most lucrative enterprises. Seven years ago Power Fuels, a Watford City—based company that specializes in transporting oil, water, and other fluids, had a staff of 50. Today it has 1,200 employees in four different towns and is building eleven 42-unit apartment . . .

One night in early April 2011, waiting out the "umpteenth blizzard" of the season with two dozen oil and water drivers at a Cenex gas sta-

tion in Parshall, Connell insinuated herself into conversations, inquiring about jobs and collecting phone numbers of trucking firms. Someone asked her where her rig had slid into the ditch. Turns out that Connell, the only female driver in the room, was also the only driver who hadn't gone off the road during the storm.

The following day, she got up at 5 a.m., shoveled out her snowbound 18-wheeler, and was the first of the stranded drivers back on the road. That didn't escape the notice of her newfound admirers, including one of the guys Connell had talked to the night before—the owner of a small water-hauling company based in Killdeer, who had one truck and wanted someone to help him drive. Soon afterward he called and offered her a job. Her pay jumped from $600 a week to $2,000. There would be no more worrisome letters from the bank. She'd saved the family house.

In western North Dakota stories like this are commonplace—among drivers, construction workers, and roughnecks; service providers and equipment suppliers; geologists, engineers, and drilling specialists. But viewed at close range, the apparent robustness of the Bakken boom sometimes looks like a collection of fragile mini-booms. Within six months of Connell's lucky layover in Parshall, for instance, her new boss didn't have enough work to keep her on.

Of everything that's happening here today—of all the change and growth—what will last? Will the enduring things be the most desirable things? These questions haunt Dan Kalil, chairman of the Williams County Board of Commissioners. "Oil is a rental business," he says, meaning that it doesn't stay in one place, doesn't owe any allegiance to the traditional farming and ranching way of life, which Kalil's family has been doing west of Williston, the county seat, for more than a hundred years. Perhaps nothing better symbolizes the contrast than the two most iconic structures on this part

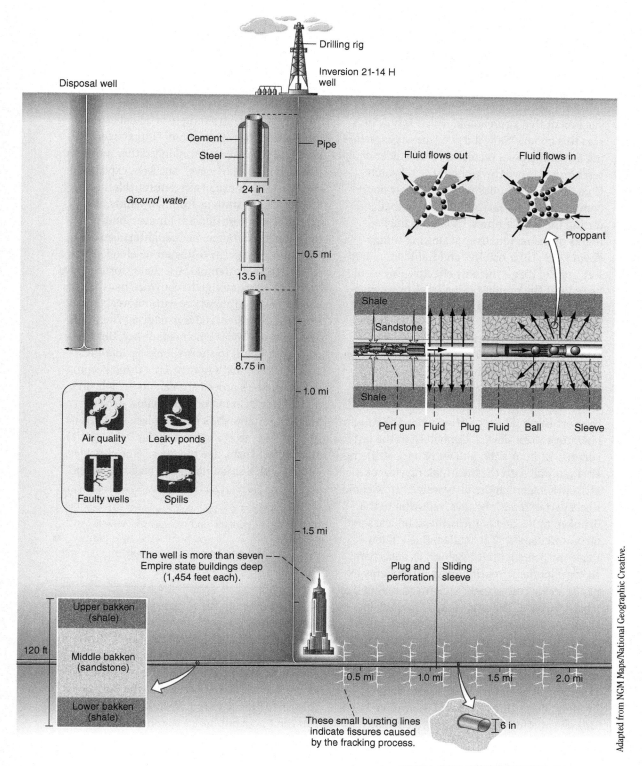

Drilling rig

Inversion 21-14 H well

Disposal well

Cement

Steel

Pipe

24 in

Ground water

0.5 mi

13.5 in

8.75 in

1.0 mi

Air quality

Leaky ponds

Faulty wells

Spills

1.5 mi

The well is more than seven Empire state buildings deep (1,454 feet each).

Fluid flows out

Fluid flows in

Proppant

Shale

Sandstone

Shale

Perf gun   Fluid   Plug   Fluid   Ball   Sleeve

Plug and perforation | Sliding sleeve

0.5 mi   1.0 mi   1.5 mi   2.0 mi

120 ft

Upper bakken (shale)

Middle bakken (sandstone)

Lower bakken (shale)

These small bursting lines indicate fissures caused by the fracking process.

6 in

Adapted from NGM Maps/National Geographic Creative.

of the prairie—the itinerant drill rig and the steadfast grain silo. "When the industry goes south, and it will go south," Kalil says, "they just walk away."

Kalil doesn't oppose development, only development that's run amok, which is how he sees this boom. "Slow it down," he urges, echoing a sentiment—a recurring, ever louder counterchorus—heard throughout the oil patch. Contain it before it destroys the closely bound communities and easygoing lifestyle that, during the best of times, have been the hallmarks of the region. Even if slowing things down were still possible—and Kalil has all but lost hope of that—the only effective way would be to limit the number of drill rigs or well permits, and state officials have no appetite for either.

"It breaks my heart," Kalil says.

I put the blessing-or-curse question to Connell, who's gone from boom to bust and back again several times, including finding steady work with a large trucking company based on the Fort Berthold Reservation when the Killdeer operator's work slowed. Connell is on the last run of a 12-hour shift, and we're back at the reservation well with the breathtaking view of the Missouri, loading more dirty water. "How could I be a part of this?" she says, referring to the drunken fights and homelessness, oil leaks and dirty-water spills. "I struggled. But I finally made my peace with it." Behind us a gas flare, its ten-foot flame roaring upward, suddenly expands and becomes more violent, sounding like a blast furnace. There are few gathering pipelines in the Bakken, so at least a third of the natural gas that comes up with the crude is burned off, a waste all regret and the state hopes to end soon. At night in some areas the prairie is ablaze with giant candles, a sight both wondrous and unsettling. "During the winter," Connell says wistfully, as if recalling a cherished childhood memory, "we'd park next to the flares to stay warm."

She writes down the amount of water she's removed from the storage tank: another hundred barrels. "There's good and bad in everything," she says, straining to articulate something that defies explanation. "I just accept it." Which isn't to say she wouldn't rather move on. "I've been trying to leave," she says, explaining that the work is exhausting, unreliable, and lonely. The separations from her family have been getting more difficult for everyone; every time she leaves home, her daughters beg her not to go. And in the testosterone cloud, physical threats and attempts at sexual extortion have occurred often enough to convince her that she should never go anywhere without weapons. Brandishing a steel rod is usually all she needs to discourage those who menace her. But well-paid work is still in short supply back home, and, she says, that's not the only thing keeping her here. She's proved she can do the job, and do it better than many of her fellow drivers. Most important, she's made a place for herself in life. "After working hard all day," she says, "I start to feel feisty, like the guys." She chuckles, adding with a sly smile, "I'm a badass trucker."

> The owner of a small water-hauling company, who had one truck and wanted someone to help him drive, offered Susan Connell a job. Her pay jumped from $600 a week to $2,000.

The day I drove to the Jorgensons' place, in the northwest corner of Mountrail County, was the day I fell under the spell of the prairie. North of Tioga I turned off Route 40, heading east. On both sides of the gravel road, fields of wheat, alfalfa, and sunflowers spread to the horizon. In this part of the country, if you're not in a hurry, you can't help but notice the sound. There's so little of it, for one thing, and it's orchestrated mostly by the wind, howling, thrumming, or, as on that morning, whispering, as it sifted through the still-green crops. I continued for eight miles on a road without bends in a land without contours, none of which prepared me for my destination—the White Earth Valley, a wide, grassy basin whose subtle charm owes much to the flatness of the area surrounding it. Here, on a bluff above the valley, Richard and Brenda Jorgenson, both 59, have lived for more than 30 years.

While Richard drove a swather in a nearby field, cutting pungent alfalfa for cattle feed, Brenda gave me a tour on an ATV with two of her grandchildren, seven-year-old Ashley, sitting on her lap, and five-year-old daredevil Kyle, riding hands free next to me in the back. We headed north of the house, skirting patches of virgin prairie—home to coneflowers, blue-eyed grass, and blanket flowers—and coulees, where ash trees and Juneberry bushes were abundant.

Brenda was still in college when Richard first showed her the valley. "It was instant love," she says. Making a go of it, however, has never been easy. Eight years passed before they were able to build a house, which they did themselves, moving in on Easter weekend in 1980. Farming in this part of the country rarely provides enough income to support a family, and like most landowners I met in the oil patch, Richard held a second job, not retiring until 2006. Brenda worked part-time.

We arrived at a spot that afforded a view of the White Earth River, a narrow stream that winds through the Jorgensons' best farmland. The valley floor is where a company called Alliance Pipeline plans to locate a 12-inch, high-pressure gas conduit that would connect an existing gas-processing plant in Tioga to its main line some 80 miles away. Today is supposed to be the last day company surveyors will traipse around the ranch. The Jorgensons and several of their neighbors vehemently oppose the project. "I don't want a bomb in my backyard," Richard says, meaning a possible gas explosion. But Alliance has gone to court, threatening to use eminent domain, the controversial process by which private property can be seized in the name of a larger public good, in this instance, providing energy the U.S. demands.

Catastrophic well-casing failures can happen at any time. The EPA is now investigating a 2011 blowout during fracking in a well near Killdeer that pierced the aquifer the town relies on.

While the Jorgensons fight to retain control of their bottomland, they're already living with the intrusive consequences of drilling. Eight hundred feet from their house a Petro-Hunt pump jack runs day and night, with the attendant noise, traffic, and contamination risks. They had no say. North Dakota allows landowners to separate surface rights from mineral rights, and during hard times some have been tempted to sell or trade the latter—for, say, needed equipment, like a new tractor. Richard's father had purchased a thousand acres from someone who didn't tell him he had sold the mineral rights—in five-acre parcels—to people all over the country. Further complicating the picture, the rights have since been bequeathed many times. After poring over records at the county courthouse, Brenda discovered to her horror that 110 strangers owned the minerals beneath the 40 acres surrounding her house. If a petroleum company can persuade 51 percent of mineral rights owners to agree—and given that they will make money, perhaps lots of it, without taking any risk, they usually do—it can drill on land that doesn't belong to them.

Perhaps farsighted action on the part of the state legislature could have corrected this bizarre arrangement, but now the minerals leasing and exploration phase is largely over in western North Dakota, giving people who don't live and work on the land the power to dictate the fate of many who do. This predicament bears out a larger truth: Benefits from the oil boom are being widely dispersed. To be sure, local landowners who have retained mineral rights can earn a great deal of money from leasing. But much more wealth is leaving the region. Truck drivers like Connell and other temporary workers are paying down debts in their home states. Profits are flowing to oil company executives living in Canada, Texas, and Oklahoma, as well as to shareholders everywhere. The costs, by contrast, are localized. Taking the bad with the good may indeed be inescapable, even if the good isn't good for long and the "public good" often favors private interests. But in western North Dakota the bad must be borne largely by the long-term residents. They have the most to lose, and any fair calculation of risk would make their interests paramount.

Last August, Connell spent a day hauling oil pipe on an 18-wheel flatbed. She relished the chance to try something new. A "huge guy" at the storage yard held her by the waist while showing her the proper way to tie down a load. "He was awesome," she says. Becoming a badass pipe hauler would be a prudent move, because the next stage of development in the Bakken will include replacing a large portion of the oil and water fleet with a regionwide network of gathering pipes. Governor Jack Dalrymple, hoping to reduce the negative effects of truck hauling and to lower oil transportation costs, has urged pipeline companies to build the network as fast as possible. He and other state officials envision 6,000 to 8,000 miles of feeder line being constructed for each of the four well products—flow back, which is the mix of fluids both natural and man-made that's used in fracking; sweet crude; natural gas; and salt water. That's enough pipe crisscrossing western North Dakota to encircle the planet.

The boom's permanent legacy will also include several large pipelines for conveying oil out of the region, as many as 50,000 two-mile-deep oil wells, hundreds of waste-disposal wells, and an unknown number of waste-reprocessing and storage facilities. The depth of the shale formations and the intervening rock layers make it unlikely fracking fluids will migrate upward far enough to contaminate shallow aquifers. But no one knows for sure. This is the first time fracking has been used under these geologic circumstances. The more we experiment with underground drilling, the more we discover that "impermeable" layers can be surprisingly permeable and fractures in the rock can be interlinked in unexpected ways.

Of special concern are the hundreds of fracking components, some of which contain chemicals known to be or suspected of being carcinogenic or otherwise toxic. Increasing the likelihood of unwanted environmental effects is the so-called Halliburton loophole, named after the company that patented an early version of hydraulic fracturing. Passed during the Bush-Cheney Administration, the loophole exempts the oil and gas industry from the requirements of the Safe Drinking Water Act. What's more, manufacturers and operators are not required to disclose all their ingredients, on the principle that trade secrets might be revealed. Even George P. Mitchell, the Texas wildcatter who pioneered the use of fracking, has called for more transparency and tighter regulation. In the absence of well-defined federal oversight, states are starting to assert control. In 2011 the North Dakota legislature passed a bill that said, in effect, fracking is safe, end of discussion.

Looking further ahead, it's uncertain how long oil well casings and plugs will last. A recent

U.S. Geological Survey study of decades-old wells in eastern Montana found plumes of salt water migrating into aquifers and private wells, rendering the water from them unfit for drinking. And catastrophic casing failures can happen at any time. The EPA is now investigating a 2011 blowout during fracking in a well near Killdeer that pierced the aquifer the town relies on. As for the thousands of miles of gathering pipelines, they're another immense experiment. Many different companies, some less careful than others, will be involved, but even well-built pipes leak and rupture. The state lacks the resources to oversee a construction project of this magnitude, and once a line is approved, decisions as to where the pipes will be located and how they'll be monitored during their decades-long life span will be left to the landowners, or most likely the landowners' descendants, and the pipeline company, assuming it's still in business.

If the Bakken oil boom is a classic Greek drama, the second act is starting now, and the prairie chorus is once again issuing a warning.

Warming tied to extremes" read the headline in the July 11, 2012, issue of the *Minot Daily News*, a conservative paper in a conservative town on the eastern edge of the oil patch. Warming, meaning man-made climate change, and weather extremes, meaning events such as a recent record heat wave in Texas, part of a severe drought that afflicted much of the West and Midwest last year. So far western North Dakota has been spared drought, but agriculture survives there only because farmers and ranchers have strictly husbanded fresh water, of which there is precious little. Local landowners now worry that the oil industry will deplete their aquifers. They argue that the Missouri River, not groundwater, should be the primary source of water used in fracking. However that controversy is resolved, an oil boom is under

way in a region that may yet suffer drought for decades—prolonged and intensified, according to recent studies, by the burning of fossil fuels. If the cliché that there's no free lunch is true, then what's the price of an all-you-can-eat buffet?

North Dakota is still in a position to parlay the boom into something lastingly beneficial. Of every dollar the oil industry earns, the state takes 11.5 cents, which produced revenues of more than two billion dollars from July 2011 to October 2012. One-third of that has been deposited in a permanent fund, the interest on which cannot be touched until 2017. The rest is to be divided between the state and local jurisdictions. How the money will be spent remains uncertain, although plans are in the works to send some of it back to the oil patch for new roads, power lines, and municipal services like firefighting and law enforcement, and to help build schools, hospitals, and recreation facilities.

Another opportunity is at hand. Narayana Kocherlakota, an influential economist and president of the Federal Reserve Bank that oversees the district that includes North Dakota, told reporters in Williston last August that the boom is a onetime windfall that should be invested in long-range social programs and sustainable economic development. "How do we want western North Dakota to look in 20 years?" he asked.

To believe the old lifestyle will survive intact is to ignore the wrenching changes that have already reshaped this corner of the prairie. Even so, the state could use its oil bonanza to finally free itself from its boom-bust history by taking advantage of a natural resource both abundant and inexhaustible—the ever present wind. North Dakota's wind resource is ranked sixth in the country, according to the American Wind Energy Association, which helps explain why in 2010 Google chose the state for its first investment in commercial-scale wind farms.

Meanwhile, for a generation to come, and maybe longer, plenty of jobs will be available for roughnecks, construction workers, and truck drivers. To someone like Susan Connell, riding a roller coaster of mini-booms is better than the alternative. Besides the money, even though it fluctuates greatly, and the pride she takes in what she does, she says there are intangibles she's come to value. "I'm on a well, it's night, I'm alone." Stars overhead, gas flares in the distance, maybe the far-off cry of a coyote. Connell's standing on the catwalk, high above the ground, opening the hatch on a tank of clear salt water that came from thousands of feet beneath the surface, in the middle of the continent. She leans forward and breathes deeply. "It smells just like the ocean," she says.

Discussion Questions

1. What is the estimated life span of the Bakken formation? In other words, for how much longer is it estimated that oil will be readily recovered from this region? What are the implications of this for the region and for the country? Do these estimates change the way you think about oil drilling activity?

2. Consider the position of Susan Connell, the trucker featured in this article. What are the pros and cons of working in the oil field for this individual? If you were in her position, would you have made a different decision about your employment?

3. Discuss the social, environmental, and economic effects of oil and gas development in the Bakken on the North Dakota communities in the region.

4. What are the implications of allowing the sale of mineral rights that are separate from the ownership of the land under which the minerals lie?

 Supporting Activities

1. Oil and gas developer Harold Hamm, listed by *Forbes* magazine as the richest man in Oklahoma, is cited in the article as favoring a national energy policy based on "abundance," one that does not include developing renewable energy technologies. Read a recent bio about Harold Hamm published in Forbes magazine: http://www.forbes.com/sites/christopherhelman/2015/03/09/welcome-to-cowboyistan-fracking-king-harold-hamms-plan-for-u-s-domination-of-global-oil/.

2. Watch a 90-second, no-words video illustrating the effects of climate change: http://350.org/resources/videos/the-350-movement-90-seconds-no-words/. A variety of other climate-change related videos are available on the 350.org web site: http://350.org/.

 Additional Resources

1. See an article reported by Reuters in 2013 about the sometimes unexpected ways that landowners learn they don't own the mineral rights below their land: http://www.reuters.com/article/2013/10/09/us-usa-fracking-rights-specialreport-idUSBRE9980AZ20131009 .

2. Articles assessing the safety of fracking can be found in *Scientific American* (http://www.scientificamerican.com/article/can-fracking-be-done-without-impacting-water/) and on the Environment Yale web site (http://environment.yale.edu/envy/stories/fracking-outpaces-science-on-its-impact).

3. The higher than normal number of earthquakes in some areas, such as Oklahoma, has been in the news in recent months. Learn what the U.S. Geological Survey (USGS) has to say about "induced" seismic activity: http://earthquake.usgs.gov/research/induced/.

4. In June 2015, the USEPA issued a report on the effects of fracking on drinking water supplies. Read about it here: http://www2.epa.gov/hfstudy.

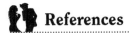 References

Database of State Incentives for Renewables and Efficiency (DSIRE). (2015). *Renewable portfolio standards detailed summary map.* Retrieved from http://www.dsireusa.org/resources/detailed-summary-maps/

Huebner, K. (2009). *2,000 watt society.* United Nations University. Retrieved from http://ourworld.unu.edu/en/2000-watt-society

International Energy Agency (IEA). (2015). *About renewable energy.* Retrieved from http://www.iea.org/topics/renewables/

Kolbert, E. (2008). The island in the wind. *The New Yorker, 84*(20), 68–77.

Pasternak, A. D. (2000). *Global energy futures and human development: A framework for analysis.* U.S. Department of Energy, Lawrence Livermore National Laboratory. Retrieved from www.llnl.gov/tid/lof/documents/pdf/239193.pdf

U.S. Energy Information Administration. (2013). *Energy sources have changed throughout the history of the United States.* Retrieved from http://www.eia.gov/todayinenergy/detail.cfm?id=11951

 Endnotes

1. The legislation database provided by the National Council of State Legislatures to find out what recent legislation your state has adopted regarding renewable energy. You can find this up-to-date and user-friendly database at: http://www.ncsl.org/research/energy/energy-environment-legislation-tracking-database.aspx. You can also find a comprehensive interactive listing of state incentives and policies on the DSIRE web site at: http://www.dsireusa.org/.

2. There is a growing amount of information available about fracking, as you'll find if you do a simple Internet search of the term. Two resources that highlight the impact of fracking on individuals and communities are *The Shale Rebellion* (http://storyscapes.prospect.org/shale-rebellion/) and the movie *Gasland* (http://www.gaslandthemovie.com/home), along with the final article in this section ("The New Oil Landscape").

Perspectives on Transportation Technologies

Getting around: all animals must do it to find food and shelter. We are no different from other animals in that respect, and the trails we have forged are as natural as the trails that deer etch in the forest floor. Indeed, many of the earliest human paths follow the trails of game. However, as is the wont of the human animal we seek to make those trails more permanent and resilient. Constructed roads are as old as civilization itself, from the Inca Highway of South America to the Appian Way of the Romans. Moreover, as the Appian Way demonstrates, the civilization with the best roads usually dominates other cultures militaristically, because roads create "the line of supply" that keeps a distant army functioning. As the name of the Act establishing the U.S. Interstate Highway System implies, the legislation was justified in part through military reasoning. The *National Interstate and Defense Highways Act* was enacted on June 29, 1956.[1] At that time, it was the largest public works project in U.S. history.

Roads are a critical aspect of a civilization's technological infrastructure. Tribes in Waziristan, Afghanistan hope for just a single road to alleviate the hardships of their nomadic lifestyle and to help bring down their tragically high rate of infant mortality. In more technologically developed countries such as the United States, roads can take on an almost mythical status, such as the "Mother Road," Route 66,

the first highway that crossed the United States (from Chicago to LA), or the "Iron Road" (the railroad), which was the symbol of the Industrial Revolution and Western expansion. It has been suggested that the final spike driven into the rail to complete the U.S. transcontinental railroad, in 1869, was also the metaphorical final nail in the coffin of the indigenous culture of the stone-age people who had inhabited North America (Angevine, 2004; Swonitzer, 2003).

We treasure perhaps more than any other technologies the conveyances that carry us over these roads. Those in the United States have had an ongoing romance with the automobile and the freedom it represents ever since the first Model T rolled off Henry Ford's assembly line (Kay, 1997). Strategically, international policy since WWII has been centered on procuring and securing the fuel—petroleum—that makes these automobiles and our transportation system go. The first article in this section, from the U.S. Energy Information Administration (EIA) shows just how dependent the U.S. transportation sector is on oil. Even though the population of the United States is only 350 million, compared to the 1.6 billion population of China, our consumption of oil (18 million barrels per day) is almost twice that of China, the second largest global consumer of oil. However, even as we pollute our air to the point where in some cities there are days one is advised not go outside, we cannot envision a world without our personal automobiles. It seems at times that we would rather choke to death in a greenhouse than give up our cars. Indeed, in a perfect example of what James Burke (1977), in his video series *Connections*, calls a "technology trap," we could not give up our cars even if we wanted to because our lives are so entwined with this technology. In the second article in this section, Lewis Mumford (1963) explores this question of why the United States is so uniquely dependent on the automobile. He postulates it is the product of a mentality that does not tackle the basic question of transportation in a holistic way:

> *The purpose of transportation is to bring people and goods to places where they are needed, and to concentrate the greatest variety of goods and people within a limited area, in order to widen the possibility of choice without making it necessary to travel. (p. 93)*

Historically, the U.S. national policy has been to build more roads. Mumford (1963) foresaw many of the problems, such as congestion and splintering of urban space, that plague our cities. However, it is not just poor planning or negligence that has put the United States in this unique situation, it is also circumstance. The United States is the only industrial civilization that went through its primary developmental stage during the era of cheap fossil fuels. Europe developed its city structure long before the Industrial Revolution. Wayt Gibbs, in *Transportation's Perennial Problems* (1997), points out that cars and cheap oil sparked explosive suburban growth in the United States, with 86% of U.S. population growth between 1970 and 1997 occurring in suburbs. By contrast, European cities typically have four times the density of U.S. urban centers, and Europeans make nearly half of all trips by walking or biking and about

10% by public transit, whereas in the United States 87% of trips are by car and only 3% via public transit (Gibbs, 1997). The era of cheap oil led the United States to abandon its rail systems in favor of the more convenient automobile, while Europe kept its well-established rail systems. Countries developing in the current era of high oil prices, like China, have focused on rail development as well as on roads. The result is that the United States is the only advanced industrial country without high-speed rail.

As promoted by the Congress for the New Urbanism (1996), public transportation and redesign of cities are often touted as ways to reduce our dependence on the personal vehicle, yet public transportation seldom meets the needs of those in rural areas. Therefore, individuals living in low-density rural areas are by necessity dependent on automobiles. Indeed, the pick-up truck is as much a symbol of the contemporary American West as the cowboy on horseback used to be. Many promote the electric vehicle as the solution to our oil dependence and to pollution problems created by the automobile. However, if the United States were to replace all the BTUs of oil used to drive about with BTUs of energy to generate electricity, it would put an incredible burden on its already technologically compromised electric grid. It would also undoubtedly increase the combustion of other fossil fuels like coal and natural gas, because renewable energy in the foreseeable future will only provide a small percentage of the electricity generated. Bayless, Neelakantan, and Guan (2014), in *Connected Vehicle Assessment: Vehicle Electrification and the Smart Grid,* explore the technological implications of electric vehicles. Their report points out that 72% of U.S. oil consumption is in the transportation sector; thus, transitioning transportation from a petroleum-based to an electricity-based system has the potential to greatly reduce both oil demand and pollution. Nevertheless, such a transition creates infrastructure challenges, such as a reduction in gas tax revenue, which is the current mechanism used to maintain roads. The large increase in electricity demand created by a transition to electric vehicles could also present challenges for the current grid and power generation infrastructure. But the report also points out that it would create opportunities to improve the grid by making it smarter, allowing vehicles to communicate with electric utilities as well as to provide a source of electrical storage, which will become even more important as renewable energy systems contribute ever-larger percentages of grid capacity. They claim the most significant current constraints on electric vehicles are battery capacity, driving range, and costs.

Another important question surrounds the infrastructure to permit battery charging for electric vehicles. There are currently gas stations in so many locations that one seldom is concerned about not being able to find a station when one is low on gas. However, such an extensive system of filling stations took decades to develop, and perhaps an even more extensive system of charging stations (due to the current limited range of electric vehicles) will be needed for electric vehicles. This also highlights another current problem with electric vehicles: charging a battery pack takes much longer than filling your gas tank, which would not be acceptable for most long-distance travelers. Like all technological systems, it is not just a matter of making *one* part that works (like the electric vehicle), but developing all the parts that support the system. This highlights why it is not easy to quickly change technological infrastructures, even when the will and technology exist, because it takes time and money (often a *lot* of money).

As important as roads have been throughout history, perhaps an even more significant impact was the development of travel by water, which led to the ability to carry large amounts of cargo more quickly and economically than over land. Buckminster Fuller and Kiyoshi Kuromiya, in the book *Critical Path* (1981), discuss the primary importance of water travel in the development and dominance of particular civilizations, claiming that the Roman Empire owed its dominance more to the development of its ships and the overseas lines of supply that transported and supplied its legions than to its famous road system.

Historically, the technology and speed of transportation remained more or less the same for thousands of years. Eugen Weber (1989), in his video series *The Western Tradition*, points out that Napoleon's armies in 1815 did not travel much faster than Julius Caesar's did nearly 2000 years earlier. However, by the end of the nineteenth century, ordinary people could travel across Europe within a few days. The Industrial Revolution was the driver of this change in transportation technology. The steam engine is often seen as the symbol of the Industrial Revolution, but it was more the devices that used the steam engine for locomotion, the locomotive and the steam ship, that truly represent the change and pace of civilization created by the Industrial Revolution. As Susskind (1973) writes in *Understanding Technology*:

> The railroad became far and away the greatest user of iron (and hence of coal, which is used in smelting iron ore), creating the first large-scale capital-goods industry in country after country, beginning in Britain, where a rail network was elaborated soonest. . . . Most of the railroads in North and South America and a good part of those on the continent were financed by British capital. . . . They could haul passengers and goods in unprecedented quantities, at speeds that represented the first substantial increase in 2000 years, opening up entire continents and linking sites of raw materials with ports. . . . By 1850,

British investors had sunk 240 million pounds in domestic railways alone—and had brought industrialization to maturity. (p. 9)

Once those goods transported by rail reached the ports, steam-powered ships took over, protected by gunships, which Weber (1989) claims was the beginning of gunship and oil diplomacy that continues to this day, as illustrated by the ever-present U.S. fleet in the Persian Gulf:

The warship of the late 19th century was as much the symbol of the Industrial Revolution as was the textile mill or the coal mine. It was a masterpiece of modern engineering. It burned the coal, later the oil, that fueled the industry . . . it protected and advanced European trade. It made sure that the goods went out from the producers to the consumers, and that the raw materials came in from every part of the world. And it impressed the "lesser breeds" without the law and kept them in their place which was of course now firmly under the sway of Europe. . . . It was the gunboat that symbolized that Europe ruled the world, economically, politically, [and] militarily. (Weber, 1989)

Our current era of economic globalization could not be possible without the newly developed massive diesel engines that drive the giant cargo ships of today, capabilities that we did not possess a mere 20 years ago. Moreover, the modern era of shuttle diplomacy and international business would not be possible without the use of airplanes. So many people use our airways that just the shutting of a single major hub such as Chicago due to inclement weather sends shockwaves throughout the country and the economy. Modern industrial civilization is based on rapid and prolific modes of transportation dependent on oil. Which leads one to wonder: as the supply of oil dwindles, what will happen to the current structure and quality of civilization so dependent on these significant modes of transportation?

Transportation Sector Energy Demand

This excerpt provides straightforward facts about current energy use in the U.S. transportation sector. The data from the EIA show that our personal vehicles are the greatest energy consumers in the transportation sector, and that even though energy efficiency has improved in these vehicles the amount of miles driven has also increased. Nevertheless, the EIA does not predict any increase in energy use by the U.S. transportation sector through 2040 due to more stringent Corporate Average Fuel Economy (CAFE) standards.

The Department of Energy Organization Act of 1977 established The U.S. Energy Information Administration (EIA), part of the U.S. Department of Energy, as the principal agency of the U.S. Federal Statistical System responsible for collecting, analyzing, and disseminating energy information. EIA programs cover data on coal, petroleum, natural gas, electric, renewable, and nuclear energy. It had 370 federal employees and a budget of $117 million in fiscal year 2015.

Transportation Sector Energy Demand

Nonmanufacturing Efficiency Gains are Slowed by Rising Energy Intensity in the Mining Industry

From 2011 to 2040, total energy consumption in the non-energy-intensive manufacturing and nonmanufacturing industrial subsectors increases by 18 percent (1.4 quadrillion Btu) in the Low Economic Growth case, 36 percent (2.8 quadrillion Btu) in the Reference case, and 58 percent (4.6 quadrillion Btu) in the High Economic Growth case (Figure 1).

The nonmanufacturing subsector (construction, agriculture, and mining) accounts for roughly 57 percent of the energy consumed in the non-energy-intensive industries but only 31 percent of the total shipments in 2040. The nonmanufacturing industries are more energy-intensive than the manufacturing industries, and there is no significant decline in energy intensity for the nonmanufacturing industries over the projection period. Construction and agriculture show annual declines in energy

intensity from 2011 to 2040 (1.0 percent and 0.9 percent per year, respectively), whereas the energy intensity of the mining industry increased by 0.7 percent from 2011 to 2040 in the *AEO2013* Reference case. Within the nonmanufacturing sector, the mining industry accounts for 17.3 percent of shipments in 2040 and

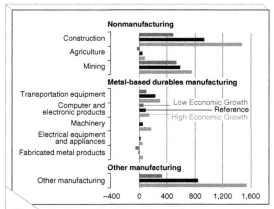

Figure 1. Change in delivered energy consumption for non-energy-intensive industries in three cases, 2011–2040 (trillion Btu).

This material is excerpted from: U.S. Energy Information Administration. (2013). *Annual energy outlook 2013*, pp. 68-70

roughly 43.2 percent of the energy consumed, as the energy intensity of mining activity increases with resource depletion over time.

In comparison, the non-energy-intensive manufacturing industries—such as plastics, computers, and transportation equipment—show a 33-percent decline in energy intensity from 2011 to 2040, or an average decline of about 1.4 percent per year. For the transportation equipment industry, which accounts for 19 percent of the increase in energy use but roughly 29 percent of the increase in shipments, energy intensity declines by 1.5 percent per year on average in the Reference case.

Growth in Transportation Energy Consumption Flat across Projection

The transportation sector consumes 27.1 quadrillion Btu of energy in 2040, the same as the level of energy demand in 2011 (Figure 2). The projection of no growth in transportation energy demand differs markedly from the historical trend, which saw 1.1-percent average annual growth from 1975 to 2011 [126]. No growth in transportation energy demand is the result of declining energy use for LDVs, which offsets increased energy use for heavy-duty vehicles (HDVs), aircraft, marine, rail, and pipelines.

Energy demand for LDVs declines from 16.1 quadrillion Btu in 2011 to 13.0 quadrillion Btu in 2040, in contrast to 0.9-percent average annual growth from 1975 to 2011. Higher fuel economy for LDVs more than offsets modest growth in vehicle miles traveled (VMT) per driver.

Energy demand for HDVs (including tractor trailers, buses, vocational vehicles, and heavy-duty pickups and vans) increases the fastest among transportation modes, from 5.2 quadrillion Btu in 2011 to 7.6 quadrillion Btu in 2040, as a result of increased travel as economic output grows. The increase in energy demand for HDVs is tempered by standards for HDV fuel efficiency and greenhouse gas (GHG) emissions starting in 2014.

Energy demand for aircraft increases from 2.5 quadrillion Btu in 2011 to 2.9 quadrillion Btu in 2040. Increases in personal air travel are offset by gains in aircraft fuel efficiency, while air freight movement grows with higher exports. Energy consumption for marine and rail travel increases as industrial output rises, and pipeline energy use rises moderately as increasing volumes of natural gas are produced closer to end-use markets.

CAFE and Greenhouse Gas Emissions Standards Boost Light-Duty Vehicle Fuel Economy

The 1978 introduction of corporate average fuel economy (CAFE) standards for LDVs increased their average fuel economy from 19.9 mpg in 1978 to 26.2 mpg in 1987. Despite technological improvement, fuel economy fell to between 24 and 27 mpg over the next two decades, as sales

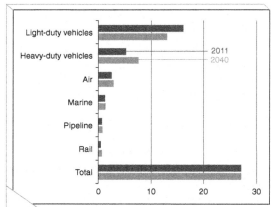

Figure 2. Delivered energy consumption for transportation by mode, 2011 and 2040 (quadrillion Btu).

of light trucks increased from 18 percent of new LDV sales in 1980 to 55 percent in 2004 [127]. The subsequent rise in fuel prices, reduction in sales of light trucks, and more stringent CAFE standards for light-duty trucks starting in model year (MY) 2008 and for passenger cars in MY 2011, resulted in a rise in estimated LDV fuel economy to 29.0 mpg in 2011 [128].

The National Highway Traffic Safety Administration (NHTSA) and the U.S. Environmental Protection Agency have jointly announced new GHG emissions and CAFE standards for MY 2012 through MY 2025 [129, 130], which are included in AEO2013. As a result, the fuel economy of new LDVs, measured in terms of their compliance values in CAFE testing [131], rises from 32.5 mpg in 2012 to 47.3 mpg in 2025 (Figure 3). The GHG emissions and CAFE standards are held roughly constant after 2025, but fuel economy continues to rise, to 49.0 mpg in 2040, as new fuel-saving technologies are adopted. In 2040, passenger car fuel economy averages 56.1 mpg and light-duty truck fuel economy averages 40.5 mpg.

Travel Demand for Personal Vehicles Continues to Grow, but more Slowly than in the Past

Personal vehicle travel demand, measured as annual VMT per licensed driver, grew at an average annual rate of 1 percent from 1970 to 2007, from about 8,700 miles per driver in 1970 to 12,800 miles in 2007. Since peaking in 2007, travel per licensed driver has declined because of rapidly increasing fuel prices and the economic recession.

Demographic changes moderate projected growth in VMT per licensed driver, which grows by an average of 0.3 percent per year, remaining below the 2007 level until 2029 and then growing to 13,300 miles in 2040 (Figure 4). Although vehicle sales rise through 2040, the number of vehicles per licensed driver declines from the all-time peak of 1.12 in 2007 to 1.01 in 2040. Further, unemployment remains above prerecession levels until around 2020, tempering the growth in demand for personal travel.

From 2011 to 2040, the price of motor gasoline increases by 26 percent (on a Btu basis),

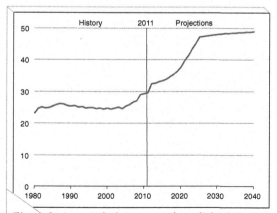

Figure 3. Average fuel economy of new light-duty vehicles, 1980–2040 (miles per gallon, CAFE compliance values).

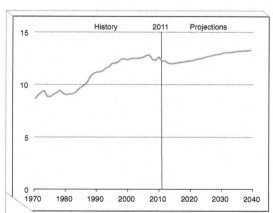

Figure 4. Vehicle miles traveled per licensed driver, 1970–2040 (thousand miles).

while real disposable personal income grows by 95 percent. Faster growth in income than fuel price lowers the percentage of income spent on fuel, boosting travel demand. In addition, the increase in fuel costs is more than offset by a 50-percent improvement in new vehicle fuel economy. Implementation of the new GHG and CAFE standards for LDVs lowers the cost of driving per mile and leads to growth in personal travel demand. Personal vehicle travel demand could vary, however, depending on several uncertainties, including the impact of changing demographics on travel behavior, the intensity of mass transit use, and other factors discussed above, such as fuel prices. The implications of a possible longterm decline in VMT per licensed driver are considered in the "Issues in focus" section of this report (see "Petroleum import dependence in a range of cases").

Sales of Alternative Fuel, Fuel Flexible, and Hybrid Vehicles Sales Rise

LDVs that use diesel, other alternative fuels, hybrid-electric, or all-electric systems play a significant role in meeting more stringent GHG emissions and CAFE standards over the projection period. Sales of such vehicles increase from 20 percent of all new LDV sales in 2011 to 49 percent in 2040 in the *AEO2013* Reference case.

Micro hybrid vehicles, defined here as conventional gasoline vehicles with micro hybrid systems that manage engine operation at idle, represent 28 percent of new LDV sales in 2040, the largest share among vehicles using diesel, alternative fuels, hybrid-electric, or all-electric systems.

Flex-fuel vehicles (FFVs), which can use blends of ethanol up to 85 percent, represent the second largest share of these vehicle types in 2040, at 7 percent of all new LDV sales. Current incentives for manufacturers selling FFVs, which are available in the form of fuel economy

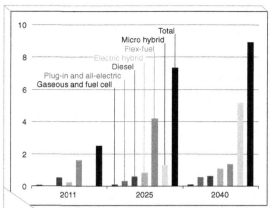

Figure 5. Sales of light-duty vehicles using nongasoline technologies by type, 2011, 2025, and 2040 (million vehicles sold).

credits earned for CAFE compliance, expire in 2019. As a result, the FFV share of LDV sales rises over the next decade and then declines.

Sales of hybrid electric and all-electric vehicles that use stored electric energy for motive power grow considerably in the Reference case (Figure 5). Gasoline- and diesel-electric hybrid vehicles account for 6 percent of total LDV sales in 2040; and plug-in hybrid and all-electric vehicles account for 3 percent of total LDV sales, or 6 percent of sales of vehicles using diesel, alternative fuels, hybrid, or all-electric systems.

The diesel vehicle share of total sales remains constant over the projection period at about 4 percent of total LDV sales. Light-duty gaseous and fuel cell vehicles account for less than 1 percent of new vehicle sales throughout the projection period because of limited fueling infrastructure and high incremental vehicle costs.

Heavy-duty Vehicles Dominate Natural Gas Consumption in the Transportation Sector

Natural gas, as compressed natural gas (CNG) and liquefied natural gas (LNG), is the fastest-growing fuel in the transportation sector,

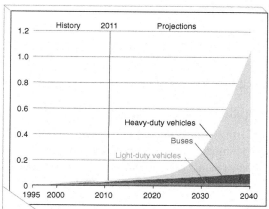

Figure 6. Natural gas consumption in the transportation sector, 1995–2040 (quadrillion Btu).

with an average annual growth rate of 11.9 percent from 2011 to 2040 (Figure 6). HDVs—which include tractor trailers, vocational vehicles, buses, and heavy-duty pickups and vans with a gross vehicle weight rating (GVWR) of 10,001 pounds or more—lead the growth in natural gas demand throughout the projection period. Natural gas fuel consumption by HDVs increases from almost zero in 2011 to more

than 1 quadrillion Btu in 2040, at an average annual growth rate of 14.6 percent.

Although HDVs fueled by natural gas have significant incremental costs in comparison with their diesel-powered counterparts, the increase in natural gas consumption for HDVs is spurred by low prices of natural gas compared with diesel fuel, as well as purchases of natural gas vehicles for relatively high-VMT applications, such as tractor trailers.

The total number of miles traveled annually by HDVs grows by 82 percent in the Reference case, from 240 billion miles in 2011 to 438 billion miles in 2040, for an average annual increase of 2.1 percent. HDVs, those with a GVWR greater than 26,000 pounds (primarily tractor trailers), account for about three-fourths of truck VMT and 91 percent of natural gas consumption by all HDVs in 2040. The rise in VMT is supported by rising economic output over the projection period and an increase in the number of trucks on the road, from 9.0 million in 2011 to 13.7 million in 2040.

Discussion Questions

1. How many trips per week do you make by any mode of transportation *other than* a personal petroleum-fueled vehicle? Count the bus, but don't count a recreational bicycle ride. How many businesses that you regularly frequent are within a reasonable walk from your apartment or house?

2. Refer to the Intelligent Transportation Society of America website (http://www.itsa.org/) and the Rocky Mountain Institute website (http://www.rmi.org/project_get_ready) for information on electric vehicles and infrastructure. Consider the impacts that a transition from gasoline-powered personal automobiles to electric vehicles would have. What current resource and environmental problems would this transition help to solve? What problems would not be solved?

3. Using the same resources referred to in Discussion Question #2 above, reflect on what you think would be the biggest technical challenges in transitioning to electric vehicles, and how do you think these might be solved in the long run? Do you think such a transition is a realistic option in the United States and, if so, on what time scale?

4. Estimate the daily savings in gasoline in million barrels per day if the average commuting distance of U.S. workers was cut in half. It's easy to find the necessary data (average commuting distance, number of workers, and gallons per barrel of oil): try Googling the U.S. Census for starters. What percentage of total petroleum consumption would this savings represent?

 Supporting Activities

1. Look on the Energy Information Administration's web site and find the amount of petroleum consumed by the United States and the world (in million barrels per day).

2. Use an online "commuting cost calculator" such as http://www.commuterpage.com/Userweb/CostCommuting/CostCommuting.htm to determine your own commuting costs.

3. Investigate recent public transit bonds that have been passed by voters in Massachusetts, California, New York, and Maine, among other states. What was the outcome of these votes? Briefly describe what projects were funded.

4. For 1 week, record the number of trips you make in your (or your friend's) car. For the next week, consciously try to reduce the number of trips. Record your data in a spreadsheet. How did you do?

5. Visit your local car dealership and ask to test drive an electric vehicle.

 Additional Resources

1. The Intelligent Transportation Society of America (ITS America) was established in 1991 as a not-for-profit organization. It is the nation's largest organization dedicated to advancing the research, development, and deployment of Intelligent Transportation Systems (ITS) to improve the nation's surface transportation system, and it also sponsors an annual meeting and expo. ITS

America's membership includes more than 450 public agencies, private sector companies, and academic and research institutions. ITS America's 27 state chapters are represented across 40 states and include more than 1200 member organizations. Its website is: http://www.itsa.org/.

2. The Rocky Mountain Institute has a webpage dedicated to promoting electric vehicle readiness (http://www.rmi.org/project_get_ready). Rocky Mountain Institute (RMI) is an independent, non-partisan nonprofit co-founded in 1982 by Amory Lovins. RMI advances market-based solutions, engaging businesses, communities, and institutions to cost-effectively shift to energy efficiency and renewables.

3. A good current review of the electric vehicles can be found at: Fairley, P. (2011). Will electric vehicles finally succeed? *Technology Review, 114* (1), 58-63.

4. A good interactive webpage on hydrogen fuel cells and the hydrogen economy is: http://www.afdc.energy.gov/vehicles/fuel_cell.html.

5. An interactive look at the smart grid is: Briefing: The smart grid. (2011). *Technology Review, 114*(1), 65-73.

6. Joel K. Bourne's October 2007 *National Geographic* article on biofuels is available online at: http://ngm.nationalgeographic.com/2007/10/biofuels/biofuels-text, along with a photo gallery and an interactive biofuels calculator.

7. A review of U.S. federal transportation policy can be found at: http://www.brookings.edu/reports/2003/12metropolitanpolicy_beimborn.aspx.

8. A history of the growth and demise of rail in the United States is by Goddard, S. B. (1994). *Getting there: The epic struggle between road and rail in the American century*. Chicago, IL: University of Chicago Press.

9. A documentary about the end of light rail in the United States is the video *Taken for a Ride* by New Day Films (http://www.newday.com/film/taken-ride).

10. A full series of video on demand lectures by Eugen Weber, *The Western Tradition,* is available on the Annenberg Learner web site: https://www.learner.org/resources/series58.html.

The Highway and the City

In the essay *The Highway and the City*, excerpted from his 1968 book *The Urban Prospect*, Mumford predicted the suburban sprawl that marked the development of the United States in the last half of the twentieth century. Mumford correctly ascertained that America's love affair with the car would take away from it the one thing that makes the car so attractive: the ability to escape the city. Perhaps even more presciently, he predicted that the money required to feed this sprawling, inefficient system would deprive schools, libraries, and other societal institutions of sufficient funds that would have to be diverted toward roads.

He stated that we actually crippled the motorcar "by placing on this single means of transportation the burden of every kind of travel." Alternatively, he suggested that each type of transportation has its special use and that transportation policy should think of those purposes in the development of a *system* to enhance the use and efficiency of each form of transportation. But instead, he claimed, we came to think of transportation policy as simply how to build more roads and where to put them.

Mumford examined road structure and planning from an architectural, engineering, and need perspective. He suggested, for instance, that it would probably be more sensible to provide ample free parking on the outskirts of cities and encourage the use of public transportation within the city so that city centers do not become unworkable and uninhabitable. It is only now that some major cities like New York are actually starting to consider such ideas as viable options as the congestion and splintering of urban space that Mumford predicted in 1968 has come to pass in most major cities.

This article illustrates that we must plan technological development from an overall systems perspective. The *system* must be developed, not the individual pieces of the system that one then hopes somehow come together in some kind of sufficient fashion. They seldom do. As Mumford wrote, "chaos does not have to be planned" (p. 96).

Even in 1968 Mumford was calling for electric cars. Some insightful thinkers can see the consequences of present-day actions far into the future, but the rest of society often does not see the consequences until they start to happen, and then we wonder why we did not heed the advice of those who grasped the situation early on. The problem, of course, is that we do not know who has the correct vision of the future. However, when we do find writings from the past that accurately predicted our present-day situation, we are well advised to consult those works for their opinions on what should have been done instead.

Mumford thought that every urban plan should put the pedestrian at the center of its proposals, because that is the most efficient way to move people and to facilitate better use of vehicles. He cited the example of the London Bridge, which could accommodate 50,000 people per hour on foot, but only 4,000–5,000 cars. However, to make walking efficient we would need to eliminate single-use zoning that makes large areas suitable for just one type of development, often separating people from the fundamental services they need. Again, this illustrates how just a single solution, like putting more walkways or public transportation in urban areas, will not necessarily facilitate walking if the structure or *system* of the city itself does not change. These kinds of changes, however, are starting to occur, finally, in our major cities as the problems of traffic congestion and inner city decay have become endemic. "The first lesson we have to learn," wrote Mumford, "is that the city exists, not for the facile passage of motorcars, but for the care and culture of men" (p. 98).

Lewis Mumford never graduated from college and held no university position, yet he was internationally renowned for his writings on cities, architecture, technology, literature, and modern life, and was considered one of the most original voices of the twentieth century. He was architectural critic for *The New Yorker* magazine for over 30 years, and his 1961 book, *The City in History*, received the National Book Award. In 1923 Mumford was a cofounder, with Clarence Stein, Benton MacKaye, Henry Wright and others, of the Regional Planning Association of America, which advocated limited-scale development and the region as significant for city planning. In 1964, Mumford received the Presidential Medal of Freedom and in 1975 Mumford was made an honorary Knight Commander of the Order of the British Empire (KBE). In 1986, he was awarded the National Medal of Arts. He passed away at the age of 94 at his home in Amenia, New York on January 26, 1990. Nine years later it was listed on the National Register of Historic Places.

The Highway and the City

Lewis Mumford

When the American people, through their Congress, voted last year for a twenty-six-billion-dollar highway program, the most charitable thing to assume about this action is that they hadn't the faintest notion of what they were doing. Within the next fifteen years they will doubtless find out; but by that time it will be too late to correct all the damage to our cities and our countryside, to say nothing of the efficient organization of industry and transportation, that this ill-conceived and absurdly unbalanced program will have wrought.

Yet if someone had foretold these consequences before this vast sum of money was pushed through Congress, under the specious guise of a national defense measure, it is doubtful whether our countrymen would have listened long enough to understand; or would even have been able to change their minds if they did understand. For the current American way of life is founded not just on motor transportation but on the religion of the motorcar, and the sacrifices that people are prepared to make for this religion stand outside the realm of rational criticism. Perhaps the only thing that could bring Americans to their senses would be a clear demonstration of the fact that their highway program will, eventually, wipe out the very area of freedom that the private motorcar promised to retain for them.

As long as motorcars were few in number, he who had one was a king: he could go where he pleased and halt where he pleased; and this machine itself appeared as a compensatory device for enlarging an ego which had been shrunken by our very success in mechanization. That sense of freedom and power remains a fact today only in low-density areas, in the open country; the popularity of this method of escape has ruined the promise it once held forth. In using the car to flee from the metropolis the motorist finds that he has merely transferred congestion to the highway; and when he reaches his destination, in a distant suburb, he finds that the countryside he sought has disappeared: beyond him, thanks to the motorway, lies only another suburb, just as dull as his own. To have a minimum amount of communication and sociability in this spreadout life, his wife becomes a taxi driver by daily occupation, and the amount of money it costs to keep this whole system running leaves him with shamefully overcrowded, understaffed schools, inadequate police, poorly serviced hospitals, underspaced recreation areas, ill-supported libraries.

In short, the American has sacrificed his life as a whole to the motorcar, like someone who, demented with passion, wrecks his home in order to lavish his income on a capricious mistress who promises delights he can only occasionally enjoy.

For most Americans, progress means accepting what is new because it is new, and discarding what is old because it is old. This may be good for a rapid turnover in business, but it is bad for continuity and stability in life. Progress, in an organic sense, should be cumulative, and though a certain amount of rubbish-clearing is always necessary, we lose part of the gain offered by a new invention if we automatically discard all the still valuable inventions that preceded it. In transportation, unfortunately, the old-fashioned linear notion of progress prevails. Now that motorcars are becoming universal, many people take for granted that pedestrian movement will disappear and that the railroad system will in time be abandoned; in fact, many of the proponents of highway building talk as if that day were already here, or if not, they have every intention of making it dawn quickly. The result is that we have actually crippled the motorcar, by placing on this single means of transportation the burden for every kind of travel. Neither our cars nor our highways can take such a load. This overconcentration, moreover, is rapidly destroying our cities, without leaving anything half as good in their place.

What's transportation for? This is a question that highway engineers apparently never ask themselves: probably because they take for granted the belief that transportation exists for the purpose of providing suitable outlets for the motorcar industry. To increase the number of cars, to enable motorists to go longer distances, to more places, at higher speeds has become an end in itself. Does this overemployment of the motorcar not consume ever larger quantities of gas, oil, concrete, rubber, and steel, and so provide the very groundwork for an expanding economy? Certainly, but none of these make up the essential purpose of transportation, which is to bring people or goods to places where they are needed, and to concentrate the greatest variety of goods and people within a limited area, in order to widen the possibility of choice without making it necessary to travel. A good

transportation system minimizes unnecessary transportation; and in any event, it offers a change of speed and mode to fit a diversity of human purposes.

Diffusion and concentration are the two poles of transportation: the first demands a closely articulated network of roads—ranging from a footpath to a six-lane expressway and a transcontinental railroad system. The second demands a city. Our major highway systems are conceived, in the interests of speed, as linear organizations, that is to say, as arteries. That conception would be a sound one, provided the major arteries were not overdeveloped to the exclusion of all the minor elements of transportation. Highway planners have yet to realize that these arteries must not be thrust into the delicate tissue of our cities; the blood they circulate must, rather, enter through an elaborate network of minor blood vessels and capillaries.

In many ways, our highways are not merely masterpieces of engineering, but consummate works of art: a few of them, like the Taconic State Parkway in New York, stand on a par with our highest creations in other fields. Not every highway, it is true, runs through country that offers such superb opportunities to an imaginative highway builder as this does; but then not every engineer rises to his opportunities as the planners of this highway did, routing the well-separated roads along the ridgeways, following the contours, and thus, by this single stratagem, both avoiding towns and villages and opening up great views across country, enhanced by a lavish planting of flowering bushes along the borders. If this standard of comeliness and beauty were kept generally in view, highway engineers would not so often lapse into the brutal assaults against the landscape and against urban order that they actually give way to when they aim solely at speed and volume of traffic, and bulldoze and blast their way across country to shorten their route by a few miles without making the total journey any less depressing.

Perhaps our age will be known to the future historian as the age of the bulldozer and the exterminator; and in many parts of the country the building of a highway has about the same result upon vegetation and human structures as the passage of a tornado or the blast of an atom bomb. Nowhere is this bulldozing habit of mind so disastrous as in the approach to the city. Since the engineer regards his own work as more important than the other human functions it serves, he does not hesitate to lay waste to woods, streams, parks, and human neighborhoods in order to carry his roads straight to their supposed destination. As a consequence the 'cloverleaf' has become our national flower and 'wall-to-wall concrete' the ridiculous symbol of national affluence and technological status.

The fatal mistake we have been making is to sacrifice every other form of transportation to the private motorcar—and to offer as the only long-distance alternative the airplane. But the fact is that each type of transportation has its special use; and a good transportation policy must seek to improve each type and make the most of it. This cannot be achieved by aiming at high speed or continuous flow alone. If you wish casual opportunities for meeting your neighbors, and for profiting by chance contacts with acquaintances and colleagues, a stroll at two miles an hour in a relatively concentrated area, free from vehicles, will alone meet your need. But if you wish to rush a surgeon to a patient a thousand miles away, the fastest motorway is too slow. And again, if you wish to be sure to keep a lecture engagement in winter, railroad transportation offers surer speed and better insurance against being held up than the airplane. There is no one ideal mode or speed: human purpose should govern the choice of the means of transportation. That is why we need a

better transportation *system*, not just more highways. The projectors of our national highway program plainly had little interest in transportation. In their fanatical zeal to expand our highways, the very allocation of funds indicates that they are ready to liquidate all other forms of land and water transportation.

In order to overcome the fatal stagnation of traffic in and around our cities, our highway engineers have come up with a remedy that actually expands the evil it is meant to overcome. They create new expressways to serve cities that are already overcrowded within, thus tempting people who had been using public transportation to reach the urban centers to use these new private facilities. Almost before the first day's tolls on these expressways have been counted, the new roads themselves are overcrowded. So a clamor arises to create other similar arteries and to provide more parking garages in the center of our metropolises; and the generous provision of these facilities expands the cycle of congestion, without any promise of relief until that terminal point when all the business and industry that originally gave rise to the congestion move out of the city, to escape strangulation, leaving a waste of expressways and garages behind them. This is pyramid building with a vengeance: a tomb of concrete roads and ramps covering the dead corpse of a city.

But before our cities reach this terminal point, they will suffer, as they now do, from a continued erosion of their social facilities: an erosion that might have been avoided if engineers had understood MacKaye's point that a motorway, properly planned, is another form of railroad for private use. Unfortunately, highway engineers, if one is to judge by their usual performance, lack both historic insight and social memory: accordingly, they have been repeating, with the audacity of confident ignorance, all the mistakes in urban planning committed by their predecessors who designed our railroads. The wide swathes of land devoted to cloverleaves and expressways, to parking lots and parking garages, in the very heart of the city, butcher up precious urban space in exactly the same way that freight yards and marshalling yards did when the railroads dumped their passengers and freight inside the city. These new arteries choke off the natural routes of circulation and limit the use of abutting properties, while at the points where they disgorge their traffic they create inevitable clots of congestion, which effectively cancel out such speed as they achieve in approaching these bottlenecks.

Today the highway engineers have no excuse for invading the city with their regional and transcontinental trunk systems: the change from the major artery to the local artery can now be achieved without breaking the bulk of goods or replacing the vehicle: that is precisely the advantage of the motorcar. Arterial roads, ideally speaking, should engirdle the metropolitan area and define where its greenbelt begins; and since American cities are still too impoverished and too improvident to acquire greenbelts, they should be planned to go through the zone where relatively high-density building gives way to low-density building. On this perimeter through traffic will bypass the city, while cars that are headed for the center will drop off at the point closest to their destination.

Since I don't know a city whose highways have been planned on this basis, let me give as an exact parallel the new semicircular railroad line, with its suburban stations, that bypasses Amsterdam. That is good railroad planning, and it would be good highway planning, too, as the Dutch architect H. Th. Wijdeveld long ago pointed out. It is on relatively cheap land, on the edge of the city, that we should be building parking areas and garages: with free parking privileges, to tempt the commuter to leave his

car and finish his daily journey on the public transportation system. The public officials who have been planning our highway system on just the opposite principle are likewise planning to make the central areas of our cities unworkable and uninhabitable.

Now, as noted before, the theory of the insulated, highspeed motorway, detached from local street and road systems, immune to the clutter of roadside 'developments,' was first worked out, not by highway engineers, but by Benton MacKaye, the regional planner who conceived the Appalachian Trail. He not merely put together its essential features, but identified its principal characteristic: the fact that to achieve speed it must bypass towns. He called it, in fact, the Townless Highway. (See 'The New Republic,' March 30, 1930.) Long before the highway engineers came through with Route 128, MacKaye pointed out the necessity for a motor bypass around the ring of suburbs that encircle Boston, in order to make every part of the metropolitan area accessible, and yet to provide a swift alternative route for through traffic.

MacKaye, not being a one-eyed specialist, visualized this circuit in all its potential dimensions and developments: he conceived, accordingly, a metropolitan recreation belt with a northbound motor road forming an arc on the inner flank and a southbound road on the outer flank—the two roads separated by a wide band of usable parkland, with footpaths and bicycle paths for recreation. In reducing MacKaye's conception to Route 128, without the greenbelt and without public control of the areas adjacent to the highway, the 'experts' shrank the multi-purpose Bay Circuit into the typical 'successful' expressway: so successful in attracting industry and business from the center of the city that it already ceases to perform even its own limited functions of fast transportation, except during hours of the day when ordinary highways would serve almost as well. This, in contrast to MacKaye's scheme, is a classic example of how not to do it.

Just as highway engineers know too little about city planning to correct the mistakes made in introducing the early railroad systems into our cities, so, too, they have curiously forgotten our experience with the elevated railroad—and, unfortunately, most municipal authorities have been equally forgetful. In the middle of the nineteenth century the elevated seemed the most facile and up-to-date method of introducing a new kind of rapid transportation system into the city; and in America, New York led the way in creating four such lines on Manhattan Island alone. The noise of the trains and the overshadowing of the structure lowered the value of the abutting properties even for commercial purposes; and the supporting columns constituted a dangerous obstacle to surface transportation. So unsatisfactory was elevated transportation even in cities like Berlin, where the structures were, in contrast to New York, Philadelphia, and Chicago, rather handsome works of engineering, that by popular consent subway building replaced elevated railroad building in all big cities, even though no one could pretend that riding in a tunnel was nearly as pleasant to the rider as was travel in the open air. The destruction of the old elevated railroads in New York was, ironically, hailed as a triumph of progress precisely at the moment that a new series of elevated highways were being built, to repeat on a more colossal scale the same errors.

Like the railroad, again, the motorway has repeatedly taken possession of the most valuable recreation space the city possesses, not merely by thieving land once dedicated to park uses, but by cutting off easy access to the waterfront parks, and lowering their value for refreshment and repose by introducing the roar of traffic and the bad odor of exhausts, though both noise and gasoline exhaust are inimical to health. Witness the shocking spoilage of the Charles River Basin parks in Boston, the arterial blocking off of the Lake Front in Chicago (after the removal of the original usurpers, the railroads), the barbarous sacrifice of large areas of Fairmount Park in Philadelphia, the insistent official efforts, despite public disapproval, to deface the San Francisco waterfront.[1]

One may match all these social crimes with a hundred other examples of barefaced highway robbery in every other metropolitan area. Even when the people who submit to these annexations and spoliations are dimly aware of what they are losing, they submit without more than a murmur of protest.

What they do not understand is that they are trading a permanent good for a very temporary advantage, since until we subordinate highway expansion to the more permanent requirements of regional planning, the flood of motor traffic will clog new channels. What they further fail to realize is that the vast sums of money that go into such enterprises drain necessary public monies from other functions of the city, and make it socially if not financially bankrupt.

Neither the highway engineer nor the urban planner can, beyond a certain point, plan his facilities to accommodate an expanding population. On the over-all problem of population pressure, regional and national policies must be developed for throwing open, within our country, new regions of settlement, if this pressure, which appeared so suddenly, does not in fact abate just as unexpectedly and just as suddenly. But there can be no sound planning anywhere until we understand the necessity for erecting norms, or ideal limits, for density of population. Most of our congested metropolises need a lower density of population, with more parks and open spaces, if they are to be attractive enough physically to retain even a portion of their population for day-and-night living; but most of our suburban and exurban communities must replan large areas at perhaps double their present densities in order to have the social, educational, recreational, and industrial facilities they need closer at hand. Both suburb and metropolis need a regional form of government, working in private organizations as well as public forms, to decentralize their strangled resources and facilities, so as to benefit the whole area.

To say this is to say that both metropolitan congestion and suburban scattering are obsolete. This means that good planning must work to produce a radically new pattern for urban growth. On this matter, public policy in the United States is both contradictory and self-defeating. Instead of lowering central area densities, most urban renewal schemes, not least those aimed at housing the groups that must be subsidized, either maintain old levels of congestion, or create higher levels than existed in the slums they replaced. But the Home Loan agencies, on the other hand, have been subsidizing the wasteful, ill-planned, single-family house, on cheap land, ever remoter from the center of our cities; a policy that has done as much to promote the suburban drift as the ubiquitous motorcar.

In order to cement these errors in the most solid way possible, our highway policy maximizes congestion at the center and expands the area of suburban dispersion—what one might call the metropolitan 'fall-out.' The three public agencies concerned have no official connections with each other: but the total result of their efforts proves, once again, that chaos does not have to be planned.

Motorcar manufacturers look forward confidently to the time when every family will have two, if not three, cars. I would not deny them that hope, though I remember that it was first voiced in 1929, just before the fatal crash of our economic system, too enamored of high profits even to save itself by temporarily lowering prices. But if they don't want the motorcar to paralyze urban life, they must abandon their fantastic commitment to the indecently tumescent chariots they have been putting on the market. For long-distance travel, the big car, of course, has many advantages; but for town use, let us insist upon a car that fits the city's needs: it is absurd to make over the city to fit the swollen imaginations of Detroit. The Isetta and the Gogomobil have already pointed the way; but what we need is a less cramped but still compact vehicle, powered by electricity, delivered by a powerful storage cell, yet to be invented: the exact opposite of our insolent chariots.[2] Maneuverability and parkability are the prime urban virtues in cars; and the simplest way to achieve this is by designing smaller cars. These virtues are lacking in all but one of our current American models. But why should our cities be destroyed just so that Detroit's infantile fantasies should remain unchallenged and unchanged?

If we want to make the most of our national highway program, we must keep most of the proposed expressways in abeyance until we have done two other things. We must replan the inner city for pedestrian circulation, and we must rebuild and extend our public forms of mass transportation. In our entrancement with the motorcar, we have forgotten how much more efficient and how much more flexible the footgoer is. Before there was any public transportation in London, something like fifty thousand people an hour used to pass over London Bridge on their way to work: a single artery. Mass public transportation can bring from forty to sixty thousand people per hour, along a single route, whereas our best expressways, using far more space, cannot move more than four to six thousand cars, and even if the average occupancy were more than one and a half passengers, as at present, this is obviously the most costly and inefficient means of handling the peak hours of traffic.

As for the pedestrian, one could move a hundred thousand people, by using all the existing streets, from, say, downtown Boston to the Common, in something like half an hour, and find plenty of room for them to stand. But how many weary hours would it take to move them in cars over these same streets? And what would one do with the cars after they had reached the Common? Or where, for that matter, could one assemble these cars in the first place? For open spaces, long distances, and low densities, the car is now essential; for urban space, short distances, and high densities, the pedestrian.

Every urban transportation plan should, accordingly, put the pedestrian at the center of all its proposals, if only to facilitate wheeled traffic. But to bring the pedestrian back into the picture, one must treat him with the respect and honor we now accord only to the automobile: we should provide him with pleasant walks, insulated from traffic, to take him to his destination, once he enters a business precinct or residential quarter. Every city should heed the example of Rotterdam in creating the Lijnbaan, or of Coventry in creating its new shopping area. It is nonsense to say that this cannot be done in America, because no one wants to walk.

Where walking is exciting and visually stimulating, whether it is in a Detroit shopping center or along Fifth Avenue, Americans are perfectly ready to walk. The legs will come into their own again, as the ideal means of neighborhood transportation, once some provision is made for their exercise, as Philadelphia is now doing, both in its Independence Hall area and in Penn Center. But if we are to make walking attractive, we must not only provide trees and wide pavements and benches, beds of flowers and outdoor cafés, as they do in Zurich: we

must also scrap the monotonous uniformities of American zoning practice, which turns vast areas, too spread out for pedestrian movement, into single-district zones, for commerce, industry, or residential purposes. (As a result, only the mixed zones are architecturally interesting today despite their often frowzy disorder.)

Why should anyone have to take a car or a taxi and drive miles to get domestic conveniences needed every day, as one must often do in a suburb? Why, on the other hand, should a growing minority of people not be able again to walk to work, by living in the interior of the city, or, for that matter, be able to walk home from the theater or the concert hall? Where urban facilities are compact, walking still delights the American: does he not travel many thousands of miles just to enjoy this privilege in the historic urban cores of Europe? And do not people now travel for miles, of an evening, from the outskirts of Pittsburgh, just for the pleasure of a stroll in Mellon Square? Nothing would do more to give life back to our blighted urban cores than to reinstate the pedestrian, in malls and pleasances designed to make circulation a delight. And what an opportunity for architecture!

While federal funds and subsidies pour without stint into highway improvements, the two most important modes of transportation for cities—the railroad for long distances and mass transportation, and the subway for shorter journeys—are permitted to languish and even to disappear. This is very much like what has happened to our postal system. While the time needed to deliver a letter across the continent has been reduced, the time needed for local delivery has been multiplied. What used to take two hours now sometimes takes two days. As a whole, our postal system has been degraded to a level that would have been regarded as intolerable even thirty years ago. In both cases, an efficient system has been sacrificed to a new industry, motorcars, telephones, airplanes; whereas, if the integrity of the system itself had been respected, each of these new inventions could have added enormously to the efficiency of the existing network.

If we could overcome the irrational drives that are now at work, promoting shortsighted decisions, the rational case for rebuilding the mass transportation system in our cities would be overwhelming. The current objection to mass transportation comes chiefly from the fact that it has been allowed to decay: this lapse itself reflects the general blight of the central areas. In order to maintain profits, or in many cases to reduce deficits, rates have been raised, services have decreased, and equipment has become obsolete, without being replaced and improved. Yet mass transportation, with far less acreage in roadbeds and rights of way, can deliver at least ten times more people per hour than the private motorcar. This means that if such means were allowed to lapse in our metropolitan centers—as the interurban electric trolley system, that beautiful and efficient network, was allowed to disappear in the nineteen-twenties—we should require probably five to ten times the existing number of arterial highways to bring the present number of commuters into the city, and at least ten times the existing parking space to accommodate them. In that tangled mass of highways, interchanges, and parking lots, the city would be nowhere: a mechanized nonentity ground under an endless procession of wheels. Witness Los Angeles, Detroit, Boston—indeed, every city whose municipal officials still stubbornly equate expressways, highrise buildings, and parking facilities with urban progress.

That plain fact reduces a one-dimensional transportation system, by motorcar alone, to a calamitous absurdity, as far as urban development goes, even if the number of vehicles and

the population count were not increasing year by year. Now it happens that the population of the core of our big cities has remained stable in recent years: in many cases, the decline which set in as early as 1910 in New York seems to have ceased. This means that it is now possible to set an upper limit for the daily inflow of workers, and to work out a permanent mass transportation system that will get them in and out again as pleasantly and efficiently as possible.

In time, if urban renewal projects become sufficient in number to permit the design of a system of minor urban throughways, at ground level, that will bypass the neighborhood, even circulation by motorcar may play a valuable part in the total scheme—provided, of course, that minuscule-size town cars take the place of the long-tailed dinosaurs that now lumber about our metropolitan swamps. But the notion that the private motorcar can be substituted for mass transportation should be put forward only by those who desire to see the city itself disappear, and with it the complex, many-sided civilization that the city makes possible.

There is no purely engineering solution to the problems of transportation in our age: nothing like a stable solution is possible without giving due weight to all the necessary elements in transportation—private motorcars, railroads, airplanes and helicopters, mass transportation services by trolley and bus, even ferryboats, and finally, not least, the pedestrian. To achieve the necessary over-all pattern, not merely must there be effective city and regional planning, before new routes or services are planned; we also need eventually—and the sooner the better—an adequate system of federated metropolitan government. Until these necessary tools of control have been created, most of our planning will be empirical and blundering; and the more we do, on our present premises, the more disastrous will be the results. What is needed is more thinking on the lines that Robert Mitchell, Edmund Bacon, and Colin Buchanan have been following, and less action, until this thinking has been embodied in a new conception of the needs and possibilities of contemporary urban life. We cannot have an efficient form for our transportation system until we can envisage a better permanent structure for our cities. And the first lesson we have to learn is that the city exists, not for the facile passage of motorcars, but for the care and culture of men.

Notes

1. The fact that the aroused citizens of San Francisco not only halted the engirdlement of the Bay but now also demand that the present structure be torn down may prove a turning point in the local community's relations with an entrenched and high-handed bureaucracy. An encouraging example to all other cities similarly threatened. In November 1967 the New York 'Times' headlined the happy news: "U.S. Road Plans Periled by Rising Urban Hostility."
2. Both the cell and the car are now, a decade later, on the way.

Discussion Questions

1. How "pedestrian friendly" is your town? Consider the availability of sidewalks, signage, busses, and bike racks. What are the *disincentives* to pedestrian traffic?
2. Which of Mumford's predictions seem to have come true? Can you list three consequences that you think have occurred, and three that you do not think have become a problem?
3. What are some of the reasons Mumford offered for why we have not developed public transportation systems, and instead focused on the automobile? Which points do you agree with and which do you not, and why?
4. What do you think would be the ideal transportation *system*? Do you think that it is realistically achievable? Why or why not? What are some of the obstacles that would stand in its way, and what kind of policies would have to be developed to make it a reality?

 Supporting Activities

1. Explore the public transportation options in your area and try to develop a schedule that could depend on them rather than on a personal vehicle. Is it possible? Write down a daily schedule (for the week) that relies solely on the public transportation in your area.
2. Drive into a major city and try to observe the phenomenon that Mumford describes. Do you see any of the solutions he proposed being implemented? (Keep your eyes on the road, of course, unless you are taking a train into town.)
3. For goodness' sake, take another walk! And time how long it takes you to get to key destinations such as the grocery store, work, or school.

 Additional Resources

1. The New Urbanist movement promotes many of the ideas Mumford discussed. Two examples of New Urbanist movement web sites are: http://www.newurbanism.org/ and http://www.cnu.org/.
2. A commentary on the car and urban planning is: Kunstler, J.H. (1993). *The geography of nowhere: The rise and decline of America's man-made landscape.* New York, NY: Simon & Schuster.
3. A sampling of books on New Urbanism includes:
   - Katz, P. (1993). *The new urbanism: Toward an architecture of community.* McGraw-Hill.
   - Haas, T. (Ed.). (2008). *New urbanism and beyond: Designing cities for the future.* Rizzoli.
   - Leinberger, C. B. (2007). *The option of urbanism: Investing in a new American dream.* Island Press.
   - Hall, K.B., & Porterfield, G. A. (2001). *Community by design: New urbanism for suburbs and small communities.* McGraw-Hill Professional.

 References

Angevine, R. G. (2004). *The railroad and the state: War, politics, and technology in nine-teenth-century America.* Stanford, CA: Stanford University Press.

Bayless, S.H., Neelakantan, R., & Guan, A. (2014). *Connected vehicle assessment: Vehicle electrification and the smart grid.* Washington, DC: The Intelligent Transportation Society of America.

Burke, J. (Writer), & Jackson, M. (Director). (1978). *Connections: An alternative view of change.* In M. Jackson (Producer). London, UK: BBC.

Congress for the New Urbanism. (1996). *Charter of the new urbanism.* New York, NY: Mc-Graw-Hill, Inc.

Fuller, R. B., & Kuromiya, K. (1981). *Critical path.* New York, NY: St. Martin's Press.

Gibbs, W. W. (1997). Transportation's perennial problems. *Scientific American. 277*(4), 54–57.

Kay, J. H. (1997). *Asphalt nation: How the automobile took over America and how we can take it back.* Berkeley, CA: University of California Press.

Susskind, C. (1973). *Understanding technology.* Baltimore, MD: Johns Hopkins University Press.

Swonitzer, M. (Writer), & Chin, M., & Swonitzer, M. (Director). (2003). *The America experience: The transcontinental railroad.* In M. Swonitzer (Producer). Boston, Mass.: Hidden Hill Productions, WGBH.

Weber, E. (1989). *The Western tradition.* Boston, MA: WGBH.

 Endnotes

1. The Interstate Highway System celebrates its 50th birthday this year. For a wealth of historical information about this system view the Federal Highway Administration web site: http://www.fhwa.dot.gov/interstate/history.cfm.

Communication Technologies

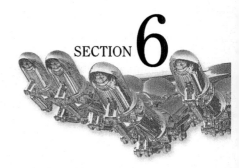

Humans communicate in many ways, but usually when we think of communication we think of either vocalizations (the spoken word) or symbols (the written word). However, do these two fall within the purview of technology? Is the spoken word a technology? It is a debatable subject within the field of technological studies. At first, it may be difficult to think about language in this way. If we define technology as all the constructs created by our hands or minds, then our natural instinctual vocalizations (e.g., language) would not be considered technology. Other animals vocalize; who is to say they do not have a language, although incomprehensible to us? Most definitions of technology do, however, include human-devised, nonphysical systems or hierarchies. In that case, perhaps the organizing of our grunts into a formalized system of grammar *is* technology. Indeed, Lewis Mumford, one of the twentieth century's foremost philosophers of technology, stated in his 1965 essay *Technics and the Nature of Man* that rather than any physical tool, language is the most significant technology ever developed by humans:

> From the beginning, the creation of significant modes of symbolic expression, rather than more effective tools, was the basis of the further development of Homo sapiens. . . The invention of language—a culmination of man's more elementary forms of expressing and transmitting meaning—was incomparably more important to further human development than the chipping of a mountain of hand axes . . . for only when knowledge and practice could be stored in symbolic forms, and passed on by word of mouth from generation to generation, was it possible to keep each fresh cultural acquisition from dissolving with the passing moment or the dying generation. Then, and then only, did the domestication of plants and animals become possible. (p. 925)

Mumford opined that "the struggle for existence, though sometimes severe, did not engross the energy and vitality of early man" (p. 926), but the central need of early humans, and one could suppose of ourselves, was to bring order and meaning into every part of their lives. Throughout the centuries artists, poets, and philosophers have used the spoken and written word to try to explain our place in the world. And despite all of our great technological achievements it is often those artists and thinkers whom history holds in highest esteem, and whom societies promote as evidence of their greatness, from Homer, to Confucius, Aristotle, Shakespeare, Gandhi, Maya Angelou, and countless others the world over.

Perhaps of equal significance but seldom recognized is how the construct of language itself dictates our perception and understanding of the world. Langdon Winner (1986), in his essay *Technologies as Forms of Life*, observed that technology creates the structures in which we must live: "Technologies are not merely aids to human activity, but also powerful forces acting to reshape that activity and its meaning" (p. 6). Robert Pirsig (1974) struggled with the concept of creating real change in our technological society, or "the system." In *Zen and the Art of Motorcycle Maintenance*, he wrote "the true system, the real system, is our present construction of systematic thought itself, rationality itself" (p. 100). It is language and how we use it that creates this rational structure, a product of the human mind. Combining these two ideas, one might go so far as to say that language, rather than just reflecting our view of the world, actually helps create it. Before dismissing the above as an overly esoteric concept that does not have a significant impact on our day-to-day lives, it would be wise to reflect on the "newspeak" of George Orwell's (1949) dystopian future in his novel *Nineteen Eighty-Four*. In the book, newspeak is a simplistic language created by the State to control the thoughts of its citizens and to limit their ability to communicate complex thoughts that might pose a threat to the State's authoritarian control.

If Mumford claims that the technology of language created the first great revolution in the advancement of humanity, then perhaps an even stronger claim could be made for the invention of the written word. Even more powerfully than spoken language, the written word preserves the knowledge and practice of previous generations. In *A Short History of Technology: From the Earliest Times to A.D. 1900*, authors Derry and Williams (1961) speculate that it may have been the burning of the library in Alexandria (one of the largest libraries of the ancient world) by Julius Caesar in 48 BC that precipitated Europe's descent into the Dark Ages.

Examples of writing first appeared about 12,000 years ago in the Mideast (Turkey and Iran) in the form of clay tokens. Each token was a separate unit of meaning used together in an order to create a syntax. 5,000 years ago they started using impressions of the tokens on clay, which led to cuneiform, using a web shaped stylus to quickly write pictograms in clay. There were over 2,000 symbols, and the mastery of these signs took many years of training. Only a select few, the scribes, could do it. The Sumerian scribal school of the third millennium BC was a driving force behind society and generated a small literate elite. Echoing the thoughts of Pirsig (1974), Burke and Ornstein (1995), in the *Axemaker's Gift*, claimed that writing led to conformity in public thought and behavior on a scale not imaginable before. Oral commands could be distorted but writing was permanent and codified. With the written word came the beginning of law in Mesopotamia. The oldest known legal code was written 4,500 years ago in the city of Nippur by King Ur-Nammu, founder of the third Ur dynasty. About 3,600 years ago the alphabet appeared. It first appeared in the Sinai Peninsula, in mines run by the Canaanites. Buckminster Fuller and Kiyoshi Kuromiya (1981), in *Critical Path*, suggest that the alphabet may have originated with the Phoenicians. Different groups began to use syllabaries, but still in the form of pictographs. Canaanites reduced the syllabaries to single letters indicating unique sounds so they could do business with members of different linguistic groups. This *Phoenician* alphabet became the precursor of most Western script. When script reached Greece it triggered the beginning of modern thought (Burke & Ornstein, 1995).

As mentioned above, however, literacy was the province of a select few. The great mass of humanity was illiterate, a new condition created by the technology of written script. All that was due to change, however, with a new technological revolution—the development of moveable metal type and the printing press by German

Johann Gutenburg in 1455. In 1455 there were no printed books in Europe, but by 1500 there were 20 million. According to Burke and Ornstein (1995), this technological innovation changed the map of Europe, reduced the power of the Catholic Church, and drove all Europe from a monolithic, backward-looking culture to a dynamic and complex world power. *De Revolutionubus,* which advanced the idea that the sun was the center of the solar system and that the planets, including the earth, revolved around it, was published in 1543 after the author Copernicus' death and, according to Lynn White Jr. (1967), marked the beginning of modern science. An explosion of scientific inquiry followed in the Renaissance that led to the Age of Enlightenment, from which sprang the Industrial Revolution, democracies, and our modern industrial world.

In *Understanding Media: The Extensions of Man*, author Marshall McLuhan (1964) (he of the famous quote "the medium is the message"), suggested that modern society has entered a postliterate society, a return to an "electronic tribe." Certainly, we in industrial societies live awash in electronic communication, so much so that our marriage to the Internet seems almost irreversible and its intrusion into our personal lives almost unavoidable. Disconnection from the network appears no longer an option. We, as individuals and especially as a society, are plugged in and cannot unplug even if we wanted to. As the control systems of our physical infrastructures that generate power, deliver electricity and water, clean our sewage, and direct public transportation become more and more integrated into the Internet and more reliant on computer automation, we become more vulnerable to system collapse or malicious manipulation, and yet more and more incapable of disconnecting our dependence from this system of control. It is another example of what James Burke (1978), in his BBC series *Connections*, famously called a "technology trap." Andy Greenberg (2007) points out in *America's Hackable Backbone* that SCADA [supervisory control and data acquisition] systems that are used to control all types of technological infrastructure throughout the United States are increasingly connected to the Internet, which makes them susceptible to hacking. One example he highlights is a nuclear power plant that they challenged a hacker to break into. The plant's security officials were sure their system was impenetrable and secure, but the hacker, a researcher for IBM's Internet Security Systems, found it disturbingly easy to hack into and control the plant's operations:

> *"It turned out to be one of the easiest penetration tests I'd ever done," he says. "By the first day, we had penetrated the network. Within a week, we were controlling a nuclear power plant. I thought, 'Gosh. This is a big problem.'"* (para. 2)

Is it really true, however, that we in industrial societies cannot disconnect even if we want to? Do we as individuals have no control over our own fate? These questions revisit the never-ending quandary in technological studies about the autonomy of technology. Do we have control over the technology that creates our "forms of life" (Winner, 1986), or are we just corks adrift in a sea of technology? Are we simply carried away by the deluge? What are the implications of being so wired? The Arab Spring, the recent popular uprisings against authoritarian regimes in the Middle East, has often been credited to young people's access to social media. Cell phones and wireless Internet technology have brought isolated cultures across the world rapidly into the world community. In places like Nepal and Central America, young people who grew up in mud huts with no plumbing and electricity, with little education or knowledge of the outside world, have suddenly become connected to the rest of the world and its information. This connectivity created by wireless and satellite communication is an infrastructure development that would have taken decades to occur, if at all, with land-line communication. So we are becoming more connected in one way at the same time we may be becoming more disconnected in another way, as in the shallow "friends" of Facebook. Has our ability to communicate been increased or diminished as we "tweet" about this and that? Are we voluntarily entering the age of newspeak that Orwell (1949) warned us about? Such are the themes explored in this section's first excerpt by author Sherry Turkle, from her 2011 book *Alone Together: Why We Expect More from Technology and Less from Each Other.*

Has electronic connectedness, then, finally brought us to the age of "Big Brother" envisioned by George Orwell? According to Farmer and Mann (2003) in *Surveillance Nation*, the second excerpt in this section, it has at least become a technological possibility. Indeed, the revelations of Edward Snowden, a former system administrator for the CIA, about the National Security Agency's (NSA) electronic surveillance program, delivered to the world by the journalist Glenn Greenwald and most recently dramatically illustrated in the Academy Award-winning documentary *Citizenfour,* seem to indicate we may be well on our way. *Inside the Matrix* by James Bamford (2012), about the Utah Data Center being built for the NSA, reinforces this impression. The heavily-fortified $2 billion center is under construction by contractors with top-secret clearances:

> *Flowing through its servers and routers and stored in near-bottomless databases will be all forms of communication, including the complete contents of private e-mails, cell phone calls, and Google searches, as well as all sorts of personal data trails—parking receipts, travel itineraries, bookstore purchases, and other digital "pocket litter." It is, in some measure, the realization of the "total information awareness" program created during the first term of the Bush administration—an effort that was killed by Congress in 2003 after it caused an outcry over its potential for invading Americans' privacy. (p. 80)*

What is the future of electronic communication? Will our existence in the "cloud" be as ephemeral as the name suggests? Will all the knowledge and imagination of our civilization be wiped out in an instant through an electromagnetic pulse, akin to the burning of the Library of Alexandria? Do these things matter? The Dead Sea Scrolls persisted for thousands of years to be discovered and read by generations long hence of their creation. Can the same be expected of our thoughts stored on so many thumb drives or servers? As Cohen and Rosenzweig (1998) write in *Digital History: A Guide to Gathering, Preserving, and Presenting the Past on the Web*:

> *If only digital preservation were as easy as changing the quality of the paper we print on, as publishers and archivists have done by using high-grade acid-free paper for documents deemed sufficiently important for long-term preservation. Electronic resources are profoundly unstable, far more unstable than such paper records. . . . We have gleaned information from letters and photographs discolored by exposure to decades of sunlight, from hieroglyphs worn away by centuries of wind-blown sand, and from papyri partially eaten by ancient insects. In contrast, a stray static charge or wayward magnetic field can wreak havoc on the media used to store "digital objects" that we might want to look at in the future. Occasionally the accidental corruption of a few bits out of the millions or billions of bits that comprise a digital file renders that file unreadable or unusable. ("The Fragility of Digital Materials," para. 1 and 2)*

What is a server? Do you know how the communication system upon which our civilization has become so dependent works? How much energy does it take to maintain? And, indeed, where is it? How are we archiving the knowledge of our civilization? Are we being responsible stewards of our civilization's knowledge, or are we simply being swept downstream without a rudder?

To those entrusted with the maintenance of society's institutions these are not merely academic questions. They are at the core of our humanity. Indeed, if language and the passing on of knowledge are as critical and integral to the nature of humanity and civilization as Mumford (1965) suggests, then these questions of communication and retention of collective knowledge are primary questions confronting our civilization.

Connectivity and its Discontents *and* Growing Up Tethered

In these excerpts from her book *Alone Together: Why We Expect More from Technology and Less from Each Other*, Sherry Turkle discusses the potential psychological effects on the current generation of young people who are growing up fully tethered to the Internet, social media, and smart phones. She states that the rules of personal engagement have changed; technology has increased both the speed and brevity of social interactions. Through numerous interviews she explores whether these effects are ultimately beneficial or detrimental, or a little of both. No matter what, the reality of these changes to our social environments is undeniable. Most children are given cell phones between the ages of 9 to 13, with the implied agreement that they are now tethered to the parent. According to Turkle, this allows children to engage in social activities they may not have been allowed to do without the phone, but she wonders what the effect is of losing that rite of passage, when children confront the world alone for the first time, on their own and responsible for themselves.

Turkle draws from hundreds of interviews she has conducted with children and adults, exploring their relationship to technology and its impact on their personal lives, to get their reactions to these changed conditions, and finds mixed reactions of relying on this connectivity and yet feeling a perceived lack of privacy and independence, particularly when it comes to parental expectations of being tethered by the cell phone. It also affects the parents, who may react negatively and fearfully when texts or calls are not returned. We are more connected, but the connection, rather than enhancing our sense of security, can raise feelings of anxiety and being trapped. Turkle expresses concern that, even among a young person's peers, the constant connectivity and the ease of responding emotionally without tempering one's feelings may hinder the development of the independent self, "capable of having a feeling, considering it, and deciding whether to share it." Turkle worries that such connectivity may ultimately harm intimacy rather than enhance it.

Turkle speaks of the "collaborative self" that seeks constant affirmation from others to confirm emotional self-truths. Although people have always sought affirmation from others, Turkle states that the ubiquitous cell phone has made this tendency even more pronounced. A narcissist is not so much a person infatuated with himself or herself, but a personality so fragile it needs constant support. Turkle also invokes the concept of the "avatar," the presentation that we make of ourselves through social media, which is by necessity limiting and stereotypical. She relates numerous anecdotes from young people about the pressures of maintaining those images; the online presence is a source of stress, even as it helps them feel more connected. Of course, relationships have always been a source of stress. Turkle writes, "none of these conflicts about self-presentation are new to adolescence or to Facebook. What is new is living them out in public, sharing every mistake and false step" (p. 186). As Turkle points out, what once may have seemed unnatural or strange is now perfectly normal for those who have grown up tethered.

Sherry Turkle is Abby Rockefeller Mauzé Professor of the Social Studies of Science and Technology in the Program in Science, Technology, and Society at MIT and the founder (2001) and current director of the MIT Initiative on Technology and Self. She has a joint doctorate in sociology and personality psychology from Harvard University and is a licensed clinical psychologist. She was named "woman of the year" by *Ms.* Magazine and *Boston Magazine* named her one of Boston's top "visionaries, idealists, and thinkers" as part of their 2014 profile of "the power of ideas."

Connectivity and its Discontents

Online connections were first conceived as a substitute for face-to-face contact, when the latter was for some reason impractical: Don't have time to make a phone call? Shoot off a text message. But very quickly, the text message became the connection of choice. We discovered the network—the world of connectivity—to be uniquely suited to the overworked and overscheduled life it makes possible. And now we look to the network to defend us against loneliness even as we use it to control the intensity of our connections. Technology makes it easy to communicate when we wish and to disengage at will.

A few years ago at a dinner party in Paris, I met Ellen, an ambitious, elegant young woman in her early thirties, thrilled to be working at her dream job in advertising. Once a week, she would call her grandmother in Philadelphia using Skype, an Internet service that functions as a telephone with a Web camera. Before Skype, Ellen's calls to her grandmother were costly and brief. With Skype, the calls are free and give the compelling sense that the other person is present—Skype is an almost real-time video link. Ellen could now call more frequently: "Twice a week and I stay on the call for an hour," she told me. It should have been rewarding; instead, when I met her, Ellen was unhappy. She knew that her grandmother was unaware that Skype allows surreptitious multitasking. Her grandmother could see Ellen's face on the screen but not her hands. Ellen admitted to me, "I do my e-mail during the calls. I'm not really paying attention to our conversation."

Ellen's multitasking removed her to another place. She felt her grandmother was talking to someone who was not really there. During their Skype conversations, Ellen and her grandmother were more connected than they had ever been before, but at the same time, each was alone. Ellen felt guilty and confused: she knew that her grandmother was happy, even if their intimacy was now, for Ellen, another task among multitasks.

I have often observed this distinctive confusion: these days, whether you are online or not, it is easy for people to end up unsure if they are closer together or further apart. I remember my own sense of disorientation the first time I realized that I was "alone together." I had traveled an exhausting thirty-six hours to attend a conference on advanced robotic technology held in central Japan. The packed grand ballroom was Wi-Fi enabled: the speaker was using the Web for his presentation, laptops were open throughout the audience, fingers were flying, and there was a sense of great concentration and intensity. But not many in the audience were attending to the speaker. Most people seemed to be doing their e-mail, downloading files, and surfing the Net. The man next to me was searching for a *New Yorker* cartoon to illustrate his upcoming presentation. Every once in a while, audience members gave the speaker some attention, lowering their laptop screens in a kind of curtsy, a gesture of courtesy.

Outside, in the hallways, the people milling around me were looking past me to virtual others. They were on their laptops and their phones, connecting to colleagues at the conference going on around them and to others around the globe. There but not there. Of

Republished with permission of *Basic Books, from Alone Together* by Sherry Turkle, 2011; permission conveyed through Copyright Clearance Center, Inc.

course, clusters of people chatted with each other, making dinner plans, "networking" in that old sense of the word, the one that implies having a coffee or sharing a meal. But at this conference, it was clear that what people mostly want from public space is to be alone with their personal networks. It is good to come together physically, but it is more important to stay tethered to our devices. I thought of how Sigmund Freud considered the power of communities both to shape and to subvert us, and a psychoanalytic pun came to mind: "connectivity and its discontents."

The phrase comes back to me months later as I interview management consultants who seem to have lost touch with their best instincts for what makes them competitive. They complain about the BlackBerry revolution, yet accept it as inevitable while decrying it as corrosive. They say they used to talk to each other as they waited to give presentations or took taxis to the airport; now they spend that time doing e-mail. Some tell me they are making better use of their "downtime," but they argue without conviction. The time that they once used to talk as they waited for appointments or drove to the airport was never downtime. It was the time when far-flung global teams solidified relationships and refined ideas.

In corporations, among friends, and within academic departments, people readily admit that they would rather leave a voicemail or send an e-mail than talk face-to-face. Some who say "I live my life on my BlackBerry" are forthright about avoiding the "real-time" commitment of a phone call. The new technologies allow us to "dial down" human contact, to titrate its nature and extent. I recently overheard a conversation in a restaurant between two women. "No one answers the phone in our house anymore," the first woman proclaimed with some consternation. "It used to be that the kids would race to pick up the phone. Now they are up in their rooms, knowing no one is going to call them, and texting and going on Facebook or whatever instead." Parents with teenage children will be nodding at this very familiar story in recognition and perhaps a sense of wonderment that this has happened, and so quickly. And teenagers will simply be saying, "Well, what's your point?"

A thirteen-year-old tells me she "hates the phone and never listens to voice-mail." Texting offers just the right amount of access, just the right amount of control. She is a modern Goldilocks: for her, texting puts people not too close, not too far, but at just the right distance. The world is now full of modern Goldilockses, people who take comfort in being in touch with a lot of people whom they also keep at bay. A twenty-one-year-old college student reflects on the new balance: "I don't use my phone for calls any more. I don't have the time to just go on and on. I like texting, Twitter, looking at someone's Facebook wall. I learn what I need to know."

Randy, twenty-seven, has a younger sister—a Goldilocks who got her distances wrong. Randy is an American lawyer now working in California. His family lives in New York, and he flies to the East Coast to see them three or four times a year. When I meet Randy, his sister Nora, twenty-four, had just announced her engagement and wedding date via e-mail to a list of friends and family. "That," Randy says to me bitterly, "is how I got the news." He doesn't know if he is more angry or hurt. "It doesn't feel right that she didn't call," he says. "I was getting ready for a trip home. Couldn't she have told me then? She's my sister, but I didn't have a private moment when she told me in person. Or at least a call, just the two of us. When I told her I was upset, she sort of understood, but laughed and said that she and her fiancé just wanted to do things simply, as simply as possible. I feel very far away from her."

Nora did not mean to offend her brother. She saw e-mail as efficient and did not see beyond. We have long turned to technology to make us more efficient in work; now Nora illustrates how we want it to make us more efficient in our private lives. But when technology engineers intimacy, relationships can be reduced to mere connections. And then, easy connection becomes redefined as intimacy. Put otherwise, cyberintimacies slide into cybersolitudes.

And with constant connection comes new anxieties of disconnection, a kind of panic. Even Randy, who longs for a phone call from Nora on such an important matter as her wedding, is never without his BlackBerry. He holds it in his hands during our entire conversation. Once, he puts it in his pocket. A few moments later, it comes out, fingered like a talisman. In interviews with young and old, I find people genuinely terrified of being cut off from the "grid." People say that the loss of a cell phone can "feel like a death." One television producer in her mid-forties tells me that without her smartphone, "I felt like I had lost my mind." Whether or not our devices are in use, without them we feel disconnected, adrift. A danger even to ourselves, we insist on our right to send text messages while driving our cars and object to rules that would limit the practice.

Only a decade ago, I would have been mystified that fifteen-year-olds in my urban neighborhood, a neighborhood of parks and shopping malls, of front stoops and coffee shops, would feel the need to send and receive close to six thousand messages a month via portable digital devices or that best friends would assume that when they visited, it would usually be on the virtual real estate of Facebook. It might have seemed intrusive, if not illegal, that my mobile phone would tell me the location of all my acquaintances within a ten-mile radius. But these days we are accustomed to all this. Life in a media bubble has come to seem natural. So has the end of a certain public etiquette: on the street, we speak into the invisible microphones on our

mobile phones and appear to be talking to ourselves. We share intimacies with the air as though unconcerned about who can hear us or the details of our physical surroundings.

I once described the computer as a second self, a mirror of mind. Now the metaphor no longer goes far enough. Our new devices provide space for the emergence of a new state of the self, itself, split between the screen and the physical real, wired into existence through technology.

Teenagers tell me they sleep with their cell phone, and even when it isn't on their person, when it has been banished to the school locker, for instance, they know when their phone is vibrating. The technology has become like a phantom limb, it is so much a part of them. These young people are among the first to grow up with an expectation of continuous connection: always on, and always on them. And they are among the first to grow up not necessarily thinking of simulation as second best. All of this makes them fluent with technology but brings a set of new insecurities. They nurture friendships on social-networking sites and then wonder if they are among friends. They are connected all day but are not sure if they have communicated. They become confused about companionship. Can they find it in their lives on the screen? Could they find it with a robot? Their digitized friendships—played out with emoticon emotions, so often predicated on rapid response rather than reflection—may prepare them, at times through nothing more than their superficiality, for relationships that could bring superficiality to a higher power, that is, for relationships with the inanimate. They come to accept lower expectations for connection and, finally, the idea that robot friendships could be sufficient unto the day.

Overwhelmed by the volume and velocity of our lives, we turn to technology to help us find time. But technology makes us busier than ever and ever more in search of retreat. Gradually, we come to see our online life as life itself. We come to see what robots offer as relationship. The simplification of relationship is no longer a source of complaint. It becomes what we want. These seem the gathering clouds of a perfect storm.

Technology reshapes the landscape of our emotional lives, but is it offering us the lives we want to lead? Many roboticists are enthusiastic about having robots tend to our children and our aging parents, for instance. Are these psychologically, socially, and ethically acceptable propositions? What are our responsibilities here? And are we comfortable with virtual environments that propose themselves not as places for recreation but as new worlds to live in? What do we have, now that we have what we say we want—now that we have what technology makes easy?" This is the time to begin these conversations, together. It is too late to leave the future to the futurists.

Romancing the Machine: two Stories

I tell two stories in *Alone Together*: today's story of the network, with its promise to give us more control over human relationships, and tomorrow's story of sociable robots, which promise relationships where we will be in control, even if that means not being in relationships at all. I do not tell tomorrow's story to up his books and laptop so he can find a quiet place to set himself to the task. As he says good-bye, he adds, not speaking particularly to me but more to himself as an afterthought to the conversation we have just had, "I can't imagine doing this when I get older." And then, more quietly, "How long do I have to continue doing this?"

Growing Up Tethered

Roman, eighteen, admits that he texts while driving and he is not going to stop. "I know I should, but it's not going to happen. If I get a Facebook message or something posted on my wall. . . I have to see it. I have to." I am speaking with him and ten of his senior classmates at the Cranston School, a private urban coeducational high school in Connecticut. His friends admonish him, but then several admit to the same behavior. Why do they text while driving? Their reasons are not reasons; they simply express a need to connect. "I interrupt a call even if the new call says 'unknown' as an identifier—I just have to know who it is. So I'll cut off a friend for an 'unknown,'" says Maury. "I need to know who wanted to connect. . . . And if I hear my phone, I have to answer it. I don't have a choice. I have to know who it is, what they are calling for." Marilyn adds, "I keep the sound on when I drive. When a text comes in, I have to look. No matter what. Fortunately, my phone shows me the text as a pop up right up front. . . so I don't have to do too much looking while I'm driving." These young people live in a state of waiting for connection. And they are willing to take risks, to put themselves on the line. Several admit that tethered to their phones, they get into accidents when walking. One chipped a front tooth. Another shows a recent bruise on his arm. "I went right into the handle of the refrigerator."

I ask the group a question: "When was the last time you felt that you didn't want to be interrupted?" I expect to hear many stories. There are none. Silence. "I'm waiting to be interrupted right now," one says. For him, what I would term "interruption" is the beginning of a connection.

Today's young people have grown up with robot pets and on the network in a fully tethered life. In their views of robots, they are pioneers, the first generation that does not necessarily take simulation to be second best. As for online life, they see its power—they are, after all risking their lives to check their messages they also view it as one might the weather: to be taken for granted, enjoyed, and sometimes endured. They've gotten used to this weather but there are signs of weather fatigue. There are so many performances; it takes energy to keep things up; and it takes time, a lot of time. "Sometimes you don't have time for your friends except if they're online," is a common complaint. And then there are the compulsions of the networked life—the ones that lead to dangerous driving and chipped teeth.

Today's adolescents have no less need than those of previous generations to learn empathic skills, to think about their values and identity, and to manage and express feelings. They need time to discover themselves, time to think. But technology, put in the service of always-on communication and telegraphic speed and brevity, has changed the rules of engagement with all of this. When is downtime, when is stillness? The text-driven world of rapid response does not make self-reflection impossible but does little to cultivate it. When interchanges are reformatted for the small screen and reduced to the emotional shorthand of emoticons, there are necessary simplifications. And what of adolescents' need for secrets, for marking out what is theirs alone?

I wonder about this as I watch cell phones passed around high school cafeterias. Photos and messages are being shared and compared. I cannot help but identify with the people who sent the messages to these wandering phones. Do they all assume that their words and photographs are on public display? Perhaps. Traditionally, the development of intimacy required privacy. Intimacy without privacy reinvents what intimacy means. Separation, too, is being reinvented. Tethered children know they have a parent on tap—a text or a call away.

Degrees of Separation

Mark Twain mythologized the adolescent's search for identity in the Huck Finn story, the on-the-Mississippi moment, a time of escape from an adult world. Of couse, the time on the river is emblematic not of a moment but of an ongoing process through which children separate from their parents. That rite of passage is now transformed by technology. In the traditional variant, the child internalizes the adults in his or her world before crossing the threshold of independence. In the modern, technologically tethered variant, parents can be brought along in an intermediate space, such as that created by the cell phone, where everyone important is on speed dial. In this sense, the generations sail down the river together, and adolescents don't face the same pressure to develop the independence we have associated with moving forward into young adulthood.

When parents give children cell phones— most of the teenagers I spoke with were given a phone between the ages of nine and thirteen— the gift typically comes with a contract: children are expected to answer their parents' calls. This arrangement makes it possible for the child to engage in activities—see friends, attend movies, go shopping, spend time at the beach—that would not be permitted without the phone. Yet, the tethered child does not have the experience of being alone with only him- or herself to count on. For example, there used to be a point for an urban child, an important moment, when there was a first time to navigate the city alone. It was a rite of passage that communicated to children that they were on their own and responsible. If they were frightened, they had to experience those feelings. The cell phone buffers this moment.

Parents want their children to answer their phones, but adolescents need to separate. With a group of seniors at Fillmore, a boys' preparatory school in New York City, the topic of parents and cell phones elicits strong emotions. The young men consider, "If it is always possible to be in touch, when does one have the right to be alone?"

Some of the boys are defiant. For one, "It should be my decision about whether I pick up the phone. People can call me, but I don't have to talk to them." For another, "To stay free from parents, I don't take my cell. Then they can't reach me. My mother tells me to take my cell, but I just don't." Some appeal to history to justify ignoring parents' calls. Harlan, a distinguished student and athlete, thinks he has earned the right to greater independence. He talks about older siblings who grew up before cell phones and enjoyed greater freedom: "My mother makes me take my phone, but I never answer it when my parents call, and they get mad at me. I don't feel I should have to. Cell phones are recent. In the last ten years, everyone started getting them. Before, you couldn't just call someone whenever. I don't see why I have to answer when my mom calls me. My older sisters didn't have to do that." Harlan's mother, unmoved by this argument from precedent, checks that he has his phone when he leaves for school in the morning; Harlan does not answer her calls. Things are at an unhappy stalemate.

Several boys refer to the "mistake" of having taught their parents how to text and send instant messages (IMs), which they now equate with letting the genie out of the bottle. For one, "I made the mistake of teaching my parents how to text-message recently, so now if I don't call them when they ask me to call, I get an urgent text message." For another, "I taught my parents to IM. They didn't know how. It was the stupidest thing I could do. Now my parents IM me all the time. It is really annoying. My parents are upsetting me. I feel trapped and less independent."

Teenagers argue that they should be allowed time when they are not "on call." Parents say that they, too, feel trapped. For if you know your child is carrying a cell phone, it is frightening to call or text and get no response.

"I didn't ask for this new worry," says the mother of two high school girls. Another, a mother of three teenagers, "tries not to call them if it's not important." But if she calls and get no response, she panics:

I've sent a text. Nothing back. And I know they have their phones. Intellectually, I know there is little reason to worry. But there is something about this unanswered text. Sometimes, it made me a bit nutty. One time, I kept sending texts, over and over. I envy my mother. We left for school in the morning. We came home. She worked. She came back, say at six. She didn't worry. I end up imploring my children to answer my every message. Not because I feel I have a right to their instant response. Just out of compassion.

Adolescent autonomy is not just about separation from parents. Adolescents also need to separate from each other. They experience their friendships as both sustaining and constraining. Connectivity brings complications. Online life provides plenty of room for individual experimentation, but it can be hard to escape from new group demands. It is common for friends to expect that their friends will stay available—a technology-enabled social contract demands continual peer presence. And the tethered self becomes accustomed to its support.

Traditional views of adolescent development take autonomy and strong personal boundaries as reliable signs of a successfully maturing self. In this view of development, we work toward an independent self capable of having a feeling, considering it, and deciding whether to share it. Sharing a feeling is a deliberate act, a movement toward intimacy. This description was always a fiction in several ways. For one thing, the "gold standard" of autonomy validated a style that was culturally "male." Women (and indeed, many men) have an emotional style that defines itself not by boundaries but through relationships. Furthermore, adolescent conversations are by nature exploratory, and this in healthy ways. Just as some writers learn what they think by looking at what they write, the years of identity formation can be a time of learning what you think by hearing what you say to others. But given these caveats, when we think about maturation, the notion of a bounded self has its virtues, if only as a metaphor. It suggests, sensibly, that before we forge successful life partnerships, it is helpful to have a sense of who we are.

But the gold standard tarnishes if a phone is always in hand. You touch a screen and reach someone presumed ready to respond, someone who also has a phone in hand. Now, technology makes it easy to express emotions while they are being formed. It supports an emotional style in which feelings are not fully experienced until they are communicated. Put otherwise, there is every opportunity to form a thought by sending out for comments.

The Collaborative Self

Julia, sixteen, a sophomore at Branscomb, an urban public high school in New Jersey, turns texting into a kind of polling. Julia has an outgoing and warm presence, with smiling, always-alert eyes. When a feeling bubbles up, Julia texts it. Where things go next is guided by what she hears next. Julia says,

> If I'm upset, right as I feel upset, I text a couple of my friends . . . just because I know that they'll be there and they can comfort me. If something exciting happens, I know that they'll be there to be excited with me, and stuff like that. So I definitely feel emotions when I'm texting, as I'm texting. . . . Even before I get upset and I know that I have that feeling that I'm gonna start crying, yeah, I'll pull up my friend . . . uh, my phone . . . and say like . . . I'll tell them what I'm feeling, and, like, I need to talk to them, or see them.

"I'll pull up my friend . . . uh, my phone." Julia's language slips tellingly. When Julia thinks about strong feelings, her thoughts go both to her phone and her friends. She mixes together "pulling up" a friend's name on her phone and "pulling out" her phone, but she does not really correct herself so much as imply that the phone is her friend and that friends take on identities through her phone.

After Julia sends out a text, she is uncomfortable until she gets one back: "I am always looking for a text that says, 'Oh, I'm sorry,' or 'Oh, that's great.'" Without this feedback, she says, "It's hard to calm down." Julia describes how painful it is to text about "feelings" and get no response: "I get mad. Even if I e-mail someone, I want the response, like, right away. I want them to be, like, right there answering me. And sometimes I'm like, 'Uh! Why can't you just answer me?. . . I wait, like, depending on what it is, I wait like an hour if they don't answer me, and I'll text them again. 'Are you mad? Are you there? Is everything okay?'" Her anxiety is palpable. Julia must have a response. She says of those she texts, "You want them there, because you need them." When they are not there, she moves on with her nascent feelings, but she does not move on alone: "I got to another friend and tell them."

Claudia, seventeen, a junior at Cranston, describes a similar progression. "I start to have some happy feelings as soon as I start to text." As with Julia, things move from "I have a feeling, I want to make a call" to "I want to have a feeling, I need to make a call," or in her case, send a text. What is not being cultivated here is the ability to be alone and reflect on one's emotions in private. On the contrary, teenagers report discomfort when they are without their cell phones. They need to be connected in order to feel like themselves. Put in a more positive way, both Claudia and Julia share feelings as part of discovering them. They cultivate a collaborative self.

Estranged from her father, Julia has lost her close attachments to his relatives and was traumatized by being unable to reach her mother during the day of the September 11 attacks on the Twin Towers. Her story illustrates how digital connectively—particularly texting—can be used to manage specific anxieties about loss and separation. But what Julia does—her continual texting, her way of feelings only as she shares them—is not unusual. The particularities of every individual case express personal history, but Julia's individual "symptom" comes close to being a generational style.

Sociologist David Riesman, writing in the mid-1950s, remarked on the American turn from an inner- to an other-directed sense of self. Without a firm inner sense of purpose, people looked to their neighbors for validation. Today, cell phone in hand, other-directedness is raised to a higher power. At the moment of beginning to have a thought or feeling, we can have it validated, almost prevalidated. Exchanges may be brief, but more is not necessarily desired. The necessity is to have someone be there.

Ricki, fifteen, a freshman at Richelieu, a private high school for girls in New York City, describes that necessity: "I have a lot of people on my contact list. If one friend doesn't 'get it,' I call another." This marks a turn to a hyper-other-directedness. This young woman's contact or buddy list has become something like a list of "spare parts" for her fragile adolescent self. When she uses the expression "get it," I think she means "pick up the phone." I check with her if I have gotten this right. She says, "'Get it,' yeah, 'pick up,' but also 'get it,' 'get *me*.'" Ricki counts on her friends to finish her thoughts. Technology does not cause but encourages a sensibility in which the validation of a feeling becomes part of establishing it, even part of the feeling itself.

I have said that in the psychoanalytic tradition, one speaks about narcissism not to indicate people who love themselves, but a personality so fragile that it needs constant support. It cannot tolerate the complex demands of other people but tries to relate to them by distorting who they are and splitting off what it needs, what it can use. So, the narcissistic self gets on with others by dealing only with their made-to-measure representations. These representations (some analytic traditions refer to them as "part objects," others as "self-objects") are all that the fragile self can handle. We can easily imagine the utility of inanimate companions to such a self because a robot or a computational agent can be sculpted to meet one's needs. But a fragile person can also be supported by selected and limited contact with people (say, the people on a cell phone "favorites" list). In a life of texting and messaging, those on that contact list can be made to appear almost on demand. You can take what you need and move on. And, if not gratified, you can try someone else.

Again, technology, on its own, does not cause this new way of relating to our emotions and other people. But it does make it easy. Over time, a new style of being with each other becomes socially sanctioned. In every era, certain ways of relating come to feel natural. In our time, if we can be continually in touch, needing to be continually in touch does not seem a problem or a pathology but an accommodation to what technology affords. It becomes the norm.

The history of what we think of as psychopathology is dynamic. If in a particular time and place, certain behaviors seem disruptive, they are labeled pathological. In the nineteenth century, for example, sexual repression was considered a good and moral thing, but when women lost sensation or the ability to speak, these troubling symptoms were considered a disease, hysteria. With more outlets for women's sexuality, hysterical symptoms declined, and others took their place. So, the much-prescribed tranquilizers of the 1950s spoke to women's new anxieties when marginalized in the home after a fuller civic participation during World War II.

Now, we have symptoms born of fears of isolation and abandonment. In my study of growing up in the networked culture, I meet many children and teenagers who feel cast off. Some have parents with good intentions who simply work several jobs and have little time for their children. Some have endured divorce—sometimes multiple divorces—and float from one parent to another, not confident of their true home. Those lucky children who have intact families with stable incomes can experience other forms of abandonment. Busy parents are preoccupied, often by what is on their cell phones. When children come home, it is often to a house that is empty until a parent returns from work.

For young people in all of these circumstances, computers and mobile devices offer communities when families are absent. In this context, it is not surprising to find troubling patterns of connection and disconnection: teenagers who will only "speak" online, who rigorously avoid face-to-face encounters, who are in text contact with their parents fifteen or twenty times a day, who deem even a telephone call "too much" exposure and say that they will "text, not talk." But are we to think of these as pathologies? For as social mores change, what once seemed "ill" can come to seem normal. Twenty years ago, as a practicing clinical psychologist, if I had met a college junior who called her mother fifteen times a day, checking in about what shoes to buy and what dress to wear, extolling a new kind of decaffeinated tea, and complaining about the difficulty of a physics problem set, I would have thought her behavior problematic. I would have encouraged her to explore difficulties with separation. I would have assumed that these had to be addressed for her to proceed to successful adulthood. But these days, a college student who texts home fifteen times a day is not unusual.

High school and college students are always texting—while waiting in line at the cafeteria, while eating, while waiting for the campus shuttle. Not surprisingly many of these texts are to parents. What once we might have seen as a problem becomes how we do things. But a behavior that has become typical may still express the problems that once caused us to see it as pathological. Even a typical behavior may not be in an adolescent's developmental interest.

Consider Leo, a college sophomore far from home, who feels crippling loneliness He tells me that he "handles" this problem by texting and calling his mother up to twenty times a day. He remarks that this behavior does not make him stand out; everyone he knows is on a phone all day. But even if invisible, he considers his behavior a symptom all the same.

These days, our relationship to the idea of psychological autonomy is evolving. I have said that central to Erik Erikson's thinking about adolescents is the idea that they need a moratorium, a "time out," a relatively consequence-free space for experimentation. But in Erikson's thinking, the self, once mature, is relatively stable. Though embedded in relationships, in the end it is bounded and autonomous. One of Erikson's students, psychiatrist Robert Jay Lifton, has an alternative vision of the mature self. He calls it *protean* and emphasizes its multiple aspects. Thinking of the self as protean accents connection and reinvention. This self, as Lifton puts it, "fluid and many-sided," can embrace and modify ideas and ideologies. It flourishes when provided with things diverse, disconnected, and global.

Publicly, Erikson expressed approval for Lifton's work, but after Erikson's death in 1994, Lifton asked the Erikson family if he might have the books he had personally inscribed and presented to his teacher. The family agreed; the books were returned. In his personal copy of

Lifton's *The Protean Self*, Erikson had written extensive marginal notes. When he came to the phrase "protean man," Erikson had scrawled "protean boy?" Erikson could not accept that successful maturation would not result in something solid. By Erikson's standards, the selves formed in the cacophony of online spaces are not protean but juvenile. Now I suggest that the culture in which they develop tempts them into narcissistic ways of relating to the world.

The Avatar Of Me

Erikson said that identity play is the work of adolescence. And these days adolescents use the rich materials of online life to do that work. For example, in a game such as The Sims Online (think of this as a very junior version of Second Life), you can create an avatar that expresses aspects of yourself, build a house, and furnish it to your taste. Thus provisioned, you can set about reworking in the virtual aspects of life that may not have gone so well in the real.

Trish, a timid and anxious thirteen-year-old, has been harshly beaten by her alcoholic father. She creates an abusive family on The Sims Online, but in the game her character, also thirteen, is physically and emotionally strong. In simulation, she plays and replays the experience of fighting off her aggressor. A sexually experienced girl of sixteen, Katherine, creates an online innocent. "I want to have a rest," she says. Beyond rest, Katherine tells me she can get "practice at being a different kind of person. That's what Sims is for me. Practice."

Katherine "practices" on the game at breakfast, during school recess, and after dinner. She says she feels comforted by her virtual life. I ask her if her activities in the game have led her to do anything differently in her life away from it. She replies, "Not really," but then goes on to describe how her life is in fact beginning to change: "I'm thinking about breaking up with my boyfriend. I don't want to have sex anymore, but I would like to have a boyfriend. My character on Sims has boyfriends but doesn't have sex. They [the boyfriends of her Sims avatar] help her with her job. I think to start fresh I would have to break up with my boyfriend." Katherine does not completely identify with her online character and refers to her avatar in the third person. Yet, The Sims Online is a place where she can see her life anew.

This kind of identity work can take place wherever you create an avatar. And it can take place on social-networking sites as well, where one's profile becomes an avatar of sorts, a statement not only about who you are but who you want to be. Teenagers make it clear that games, worlds, and social networking (on the surface, rather different) have much in common. They all ask you to compose and project an identity. Audrey, sixteen, a junior at Roosevelt, a suburban public high school near New York City, is explicit about the connection between avatars and profiles. She calls her Facebook profile "my Internet twin" and "the avatar of me."

Mona, a freshman at Roosevelt, has recently joined Facebook. Her parents made her wait until her fourteenth birthday, and I meet her shortly after this long-awaited day. Mona tells me that as soon as she got on the site, "Immediately, I felt power." I ask her what she means. She says, "The first thing I thought was, 'I am going to broadcast the real me.'" But when Mona sat down to write her profile, things were not so straightforward. Whenever one has time to write, edit, and delete, there is room for performance. The "real me" turns out to be elusive. Mona wrote and rewrote her profile. She put it away for two days and tweaked it again. Which pictures to add? Which facts to include? How much of her personal life to reveal? Should she give any sign that things at home were troubled? Or was this a place to look good?

Mona worries that she does not have enough of a social life to make herself sound interesting: "What kind of personal life should I *say* I have?" Similar questions plague other young women in her class. They are starting to have boyfriends. Should they list themselves as single if they are just starting to date someone new? What if they consider themselves in a relationship, but their boyfriends do not? Mona tells me that "it's common sense" to check with a boy before listing yourself as connected to him, but "that could be a very awkward conversation." So there are misunderstandings and recriminations. Facebook at fourteen can be a tearful place. For many, it remains tearful well through college and graduate school. Much that might seem straightforward is fraught. For example, when asked by Facebook to confirm someone as a friend or ignore the request, Helen, a Roosevelt senior, says, "I always feel a bit of panic . . . . Who should I friend? . . . I really want to only have my cool friends listed, but I'm nice to a lot of other kids at school. So I include the more unpopular ones, but then I'm unhappy." It is not how she wants to be seen.

In the Victorian era, one controlled whom one saw and to whom one was connected through the ritual of calling cards. Visitors came to call and, not necessarily expecting to be received, left a card. A card left at your home in return meant that the relationship might grow. In its own way, friending on Facebook is reminiscent of this tradition. On Facebook, you send a request to be a friend. The recipient of the request has the option to ignore or friend you. As was the case in the Victorian era, there is an intent to screen. But the Victorians followed socially accepted rules. For example, it was understood that one was most open to people of similar social standing. Facebook is more democratic—which leaves members to make up their own rules, not necessarily understood by those who contact them. Some people make a

request to be a Facebook friend in the spirit of "I'm a fan" and are accepted on that basis. Other people friend only people they know. Others friend any friend of a friend, using Facebook as a tool to expand their acquaintanceships. All of this can be exciting or stressful—often both at the same time, because friending has consequences. It means that someone can see what you say about yourself on your profile, the pictures you post, and your friends' postings on your "wall," the shared communication space for you and your friends. Friending someone gives that person implicit permission to try to friend your friends. In fact, the system constantly proposes that they do so.

Early in this project, I was at a conference dinner, sitting next to an author whose publisher insisted that she use Facebook as a way to promote her new book. The idea was to use the site to tell people where she would be speaking and to share the themes of her book with an ever-expanding potential readership. Her publisher hoped this strategy would make her book "go viral." She had expected the Facebook project to feel like business, but instead she described complicated anxieties about not having enough friends, and about envy of her husband, also a writer, who had more friends than she. It also felt wrong to use the word "friends" for all of those she had "friended," since so many of the friended were there for professional reasons alone. She left me with this thought: "This thing took me right back to high school."

I promised her that when I joined Facebook I would record my first feelings, while the site was still new to me. My very first feelings now seem banal: I had to decide between "friending" plan A (this will be a place for people I actually know) and plan B (I will include people who contact me because they say they appreciate my work). I tried several weeks on plan A and then switched to the more inclusive Plan B, flattered by the attention of strangers, justifying my decision in professional terms.

But now that I had invited strangers into my life, would I invite myself into the lives of strangers? I would have anticipated not, until I did that very thing. I saw that one of my favorite authors was a Facebook friend of a friend. Seized by the idea that I might be this writer's friend, I made my request, and he accepted me. The image of a cafeteria came to mind, and I had a seat at his virtual table. But I felt like a gatecrasher. I decided realistically that I was taking this way too seriously. Facebook is a world in which fans are "friends." But of course, they are not friends. They have been "friended." That makes all the difference in the world, and I couldn't get high school out of my mind.

Presentation Anxiety

What are the truth claims in a Facebook profile? How much can you lie? And what is at stake if you do? Nancy, an eighteen-year-old senior at Roosevelt, answers this question. "On the one hand, low stakes, because no one is really checking Then, with a grimace, she says, "No, high stakes. Everyone is checking A few minutes later, Nancy comes back to the question: "Only my best friends will know if I lie a little bit, and they will totally understand." Then she laughs. "All of this, it is, I guess, a bit of stress."

At Cranston, a group of seniors describe that stress. One says, "Thirteen to eighteen are the years of profile writing." The years of identity construction are recast in terms of profile production. These private school students had to write one profile for their applications to middle school, another to get into high school, and then another for Facebook. Now they are beginning to construct personae for college applications. And here, says Tom, "You have to have a slightly different persona for the different colleges to which you are applying: one for

Dartmouth, a different one, say, for Wesleyan." For this aficionado of profile writing, every application needs a different approach. "By the time you get to the questions for the college application, you are a professional profile writer," he says. His classmate Stan describes his online profiles in great detail. Each serves a different purpose, but they must overlap, or questions of authenticity will arise. Creating the illusion of authenticity demands virtuosity. Presenting a self in these circumstances, with multiple media and multiple goals, is not easy work. The trick, says Stan, is in "weaving profiles together . . . so that people can see you are not too crazy . . . What I learned in high school was profiles, profiles, profiles, how to make a me."

Early in my study, a college senior warned me not to be fooled by "anyone you interview who tells you that his Facebook page is 'the real me.' It's like being in a play. You make a character." Eric, a college-bound senior at Hadley, a boys' preparatory school in rural New Jersey, describes himself as savvy about how you can "mold a Facebook page." Yet, even he is shocked when he finds evidence of girls using "shrinking" software to appear thinner on their profile photographs. "You can't see that they do it when you look at the little version of the picture, but when you look at a big picture, you can see how the background is distorted." By eighteen, he has become an identity detective. The Facebook profile is a particular source of stress because it is so important to high school social life. Some students feel so in its thrall that they drop out of Facebook, if only for a while, to collect themselves.

Brad, eighteen, a senior at Hadley, is about to take a gap year to do community service before attending a small liberal arts college in the Midwest. His parents are architects; his passion is biology and swimming. Brad wants to be part of the social scene at Hadley, but he doesn't like texting or instant messaging. He is careful to make sure I know he is "no Luddite." He has plenty of good things to say about the Net. He is sure that it makes it easier for insecure people to function. Sometimes the ability to compose his thoughts online "can be reassuring," he says, because there is a chance to "think through, calculate, edit, and make sure you're as clear and concise as possible." But as our conversation continues, Brad switches gears. Even as some are able to better function beause they feel in control, online communication also offers an opportunity to ignore other people's feelings. You can avoid eye contact. You can elect not to here how "hurt or angry they sound in their voice." He says, "Online, people miss your body language, tone of voice. You are not really you." And worst of all, online life has led him to mistrust his friends. He has had his instant messages "recorded" without his knowledge and forwarded on "in a cut-and-paste world."

In fact, when I meet Brad in the spring of his senior year, he tells me he has "dropped out" of online life. "I'm off the Net," he says, "at least for the summer, maybe for my year off until I go to college." He explains that it is hard to drop out because all his friends are on Facebook. A few weeks before our conversation, he had made a step toward rejoining but immediately he felt that he was not doing enough to satisfy its demands. He says that within a day he felt "rude" and couldn't keep up. He felt guilty because he didn't have the time to answer all the people who wrote to him. He says that he couldn't find a way to be "a little bit" on Facebook—it does not easily tolerate a partial buy-in. Just doing the minimum was "pure exhaustion."

In the world of Facebook, Brad says, "your minute movie preferences matter. And what groups you join. Are they the right ones?" Everything is a token, a marker for who you are:

When you have to represent yourself on Facebook to convey to anyone who doesn't know you
what and who you are, it leads to a kind of obsession about minute details about yourself. Like, "Oh, if I like the band State Radio and the band Spoon, what does it mean if I put State Radio first or Spoon first on my list of favorite musical artists? What will people think about me?" I know for girls, trying to figure out, "Oh, is this picture too revealing to put? Is it prudish if I don't put it?" You have to think carefully for good reason, given how much people will look at your profile and obsess over it. You have to know that everything you put up will be perused very carefully. And that makes it necessary for you to obsess over what you do put up and how you portray yourself. . . . And when you have to think that much about what you come across as, that's just another way that . . . you're thinking of yourself in a bad way.

For Brad, "thinking of yourself in a bad way" means thinking of yourself in reduced terms, in "short smoke signals" that are easy to read. To me, the smoke signals suggest a kind of reduction and betrayal. Social media ask us to represent ourselves in simplified ways. And then, faced with an audience, we feel pressure to conform to these simplifications. On Facebook, Brad represents himself as cool and in the know—both qualities are certainly part of who he is. But he hesitates to show people online other parts of himself (like how much he likes Harry Potter). He spends more and more time perfecting his online Mr. Cool. And he feels pressure to perform him all the time because that is who he is on Facebook.

At first Brad thought that both his Facebook profile and his college essays had gotten him into this "bad way" of thinking, in which he reduces himself to fit a stereotype. Writing his Facebook profile felt to him like assembling cultural references to shape how others would see him. The college essay demanded a victory narrative and seemed equally unhelpful: he had to brag, and he wasn't happy. But Brad had a change of heart about the value of writing his college essays. "In the end I learned a lot about how I write and think—what I know how to think about and some things, you know, I really can't think about them well at all." I ask him if Facebook might offer these kinds of opportunities. He is adamant that it does not: "You get reduced to a list of favorite things. 'List your favorite music'—that gives you no liberty at all about how to say it." Brad says that "in a conversation, it might be interesting that on a trip to Europe with my parents, I got interested in the political mural art in Belfast. But on a Facebook page, this is too much information. It would be the kiss of death. Too much, too soon, too weird. And yet . . . it is part of who I am, isn't it? . . . You are asked to make a lot of lists. You have to worry that you put down the 'right' band or that you *don't* put down some Polish novel that nobody's read." And in the end, for Brad, it is too easy to lose track of what is important:

> *What does it matter to anyone that I prefer the band Spoon over State Radio? Or State Radio over Cake? But things like Facebook . . . make you think that it really does matter . . . I look at someone's profile and I say, "Oh, they like these bands." I'm like, "Oh, they're a poser," or "they're really deep, and they're into good music." We all do that, I think. And then I think it doesn't matter, but . . . the thing is, in the world of Facebook it does matter. Those minute details do matter.*

Brad, like many of his peers, worries that if he is modest and doesn't put down all of his interests and accomplishments, he will be passed over. But he also fears that to talk about his strengths will be unseemly. None of these conflicts about self presentation are new to adolescence or to Facebook. What is new is living them out in public, sharing every mistake and false step. Brad, attractive and accomplished sums it up with the same word Nancy uses: "Stress. That's what it comes down to for me. It's just worry and stressing out about it." Now Brad only wants to see friends in person or talk to them on the telephone. "I can just act how I want to act, and it's a much freer way." But who will answer the phone?

Discussion Questions

1. If it is true that communication technologies go beyond just helping us to communicate to actually changing the ways that we think and interact, in what ways do you think the Internet and social media have changed us? Do you see this change as positive or negative, or a mix of both? Explain.
2. Some young people have expressed difficulties in controlling their Internet or smart phone usage. Is this, or has this ever been, true for you? Has this created problems in your personal or professional life? In what ways?
3. Do you agree with Turkle's conclusions about growing up tethered? Which of the effects that she describes do you think are legitimate concerns, and which ones are not? Do they apply to everyone? Do you feel any of the effects she mentions apply to your own life?
4. Increasingly, sites like Facebook utilize "customization of content" so that busy readers can see only the news and content that is of interest. What are the larger societal implications of this trend?

 Supporting Activities

1. In a small group, determine what your average smart phone/Internet use per day is (or, alternatively, calculate the average number of hours per week per individual). Among members of your group, what are the most popular uses or apps?
2. For fun, watch the movie *Her* (2013), a dramatic comedy with Joaquin Phoenix and Scarlett Johansson, about a man who falls in love with his computer's operating system.

 Additional Resources

1. Watch Sherry Turkle's TED talk on *Alone Together*: http://www.ted.com/talks/sherry_turkle_alone_together?language=
2. For an academic discussion of online privacy, see: Joinson, A. N., & Paine, C. B. (2007). Self disclosure, privacy and the Internet. In *The Oxford Handbook of Internet Psychology* (Chapter 16; pp. 237–251). Oxford University Press.
3. The following website has many links to resources on cyberbullying: http://www.safekids.com/bullying-cyberbullying-resources/

Surveillance Nation

This article provides a good overview of some of the common uses of surveillance in the United States and abroad. These surveillance tools range from the seemingly helpful—things like "nanny-cams" so that anxious parents can monitor the child care their preschool children are receiving—to the more disturbing—such as monitors used in employee restrooms to prevent theft. As Farmer and Mann note, the world is fast becoming a place where "unmonitored public space will effectively cease to exist."

Why is the surveillance industry one of the fastest growing areas of communication technology? Partly because the tools exist: cameras, monitors, electronic identification tags, drones, and other computer tools needed to monitor activity are affordable and easy to use. The uses to which surveillance tools have been put are surprisingly diverse and sometimes just downright surprising. For example, you can get a sub-dermal computer chip implanted in your dog so that, if he becomes lost, your contact information can be readily retrieved. Numerous products now have radio frequency identification (RFID) tags so that their progress through the supply chain can be tracked from manufacture to sale and beyond. In some cases these technologies have been adopted with little fanfare, so lots of people are not aware that their locations can be tracked via their cell phones; that chances are good that their employer is monitoring them electronically; or that their purchases at the local supermarket are being tracked. In some cases the surveillance tool was just a matter of built-in functionality that was deemed useful. If your instructor in this course uses a courseware program like Blackboard, for example, he or she can monitor when and for how long you access course materials on the site.

Charles C. Mann has written extensively on the intersection of science, technology, and commerce for publications such as *Science, Wired, The Atlantic Monthly,* and *Fortune*. The author of several books, his recent effort *1491* won the U.S. National Academy of Sciences' Keck Award for best book of the year in 2006. He is a three-time "National Magazine Award" finalist and a recipient of writing awards from the American Bar Association, the American Institute of Physics, the Alfred P. Sloan Foundation, and the Lannan Foundation. Dan Farmer is a software engineer and web security expert known for creating the Security Administrator's Tool for Analyzing Networks (SATAN), which is a program for investigating the vulnerabilities of remote systems. He served as head of security at EarthLink and cofounded and served as chief technology officer at Elemental Security. Farmer coauthored the book *Forensic Discovery* (2005). He was recognized as a technology visionary by InfoWorld Magazine and named as an "innovator to watch in 2006."

Surveillance Nation

By Dan Farmer and Charles C. Mann

Route 9 is an old two-lane highway that cuts across Massachusetts from Boston in the east to Pittsfield in the west. Near the small city of Northampton, the highway crosses the wide Connecticut River. The Calvin Coolidge Memorial Bridge, named after the president who once served as Northampton's mayor, is a major regional traffic link. When the state began a long-delayed and still ongoing reconstruction of the bridge in the summer of 2001, traffic jams stretched for kilometers into the bucolic New England countryside.

In a project aimed at alleviating drivers' frustration, the University of Massachusetts Transportation Center, located in nearby Amherst, installed eight shoe-size digital surveillance cameras along the roads leading to the bridge. Six are mounted on utility poles and the roofs of local businesses. Made by Axis Communications in Sweden, they are connected to dial-up modems and transmit images of the roadway before them to a Web page, which commuters can check for congestion before tackling the road. According to Dan Dulaski, the system's technical manager, running the entire webcam system—power, phone, and Internet fees—costs just $600 a month.

The other two cameras in the Coolidge Bridge project are a little less routine. Built by Computer Recognition Systems in Wokingham, England, with high-quality lenses and fast shutter speeds (1/10,000 second), they are designed to photograph every car and truck that passes by. Located eight kilometers apart, at the ends of the zone of maximum traffic congestion, the two cameras send vehicle images to attached computers, which use special character-recognition software to decipher vehicle license plates. The license data go to a server at the company's U.S. office in Cambridge, MA, about 130 kilometers away. As each license plate passes the second camera, the server ascertains the time difference between the two readings. The average of the travel durations of all successfully matched vehicles defines the likely travel time for crossing the bridge at any given moment, and that information is posted on the traffic watch Web page.

To local residents, the traffic data are helpful, even vital: police use the information to plan emergency routes. But as the computers calculate traffic flow, they are also making a record of all cars that cross the bridge—when they do so, their average speed, and (depending on lighting and weather conditions) how many people are in each car.

Trying to avoid provoking privacy fears, Keith Fallon, a Computer Recognition Systems project engineer, says, "we're not saving any of the information we capture. Everything is deleted immediately." But the company could change its mind and start saving the data at any time. No one on the road would know.

The Coolidge Bridge is just one of thousands of locations around the planet where citizens are crossing—willingly, more often than not—into a world of networked, highly computerized surveillance. According to a January report by J.P. Freeman, a security market-research firm in Newtown, CT, 26 million surveillance cameras have already been installed worldwide, and more than 11 million of them are in the United States. In heavily monitored London, England, Hull University criminologist Clive Norris has estimated, the average person is filmed by more than 300 cameras each *day*.

The $150 million-a-year remote digital-surveillance-camera market will grow, according to Freeman, at an annual clip of 40 to 50 percent for the next 10 years. But astonishingly, other, nonvideo forms of monitoring will increase even faster. In a process that mirrors the unplanned growth of the Internet itself, thousands of personal, commercial, medical, police, and government databases and monitoring systems will intersect and entwine. Ultimately, surveillance will become so ubiquitous, networked, and searchable that unmonitored public space will effectively cease to exist.

This prospect—what science fiction writer David Brin calls "the transparent society"—may sound too distant to be worth thinking about. But even the farsighted Brin underestimated how quickly technological advances—more powerful microprocessors, faster network transmissions, larger hard drives, cheaper electronics, and more sophisticated and powerful software—would make universal surveillance possible.

It's not all about Big Brother or Big Business, either. Widespread electronic scrutiny is usually denounced as a creation of political tyranny or corporate greed. But the rise of omnipresent surveillance will be driven as much by ordinary citizens' understandable—even laudatory—desires for security, control, and comfort as by the imperatives of business and government. "Nanny cams," global-positioning locators, police and home security networks, traffic jam monitors, medical-device radio-frequency tags, small-business webcams: the list of monitoring devices employed by and for average Americans is already long, and it will only become longer. Extensive surveillance, in short, is coming into being because people like and want it.

"Almost all of the pieces for a surveillance society are already here," says Gene Spafford, director of Purdue University's Center for Education and Research in Information Assurance and Security. "It's just a matter of assembling them." Unfortunately, he says, ubiquitous surveillance faces intractable social and technological problems that could well reduce its usefulness or even make it dangerous. As a result, each type of monitoring may be beneficial in itself, at least for the people who put it in place, but the collective result could be calamitous.

To begin with, surveillance data from multiple sources are being combined into large databases. For example, businesses track employees' car, computer, and telephone use to evaluate their job performance; similarly, the U.S. Defense Department's experimental Total Information Awareness project has announced plans to sift through information about millions of people to find data that identify criminals and terrorists.

But many of these merged pools of data are less reliable than small-scale, localized monitoring efforts; big databases are harder to comb for bad entries, and their conclusions are far more difficult to verify. In addition, the inescapable nature of surveillance can itself create alarm, even among its beneficiaries. "Your little camera network may seem like a good idea to you," Spafford says. "Living with everyone else's could be a nightmare."

The Surveillance Ad-Hocracy

Last October deadly snipers terrorized Washington, DC, and the surrounding suburbs, killing 10 people. For three long weeks, law enforcement agents seemed helpless to stop the murderers, who struck at random and then vanished into the area's snarl of highways. Ultimately, two alleged killers were arrested, but only because their taunting messages to the authorities had inadvertently provided clues to their identification.

In the not-too-distant future, according to advocates of policing technologies, such unstoppable rampages may become next to impossible, at least in populous areas. By combining police cameras with private camera networks like that on Route 9, video coverage will become so complete that any snipers who waged an attack—and all the people near the crime scene—would be trackable from camera to camera until they could be stopped and interrogated.

The unquestionable usefulness and sheer affordability of these extensive video-surveillance systems suggest that they will propagate rapidly. But despite the relentlessly increasing capabilities of such systems, video monitoring is still but a tiny part—less than 1 percent—of surveillance overall, says Carl Botan, a Purdue center researcher who has studied this technology for 15 years.

Examples are legion. By 2006, for instance, law will require that every U.S. cell phone be designed to report its precise location during a 911 call; wireless carriers plan to use the same technology to offer 24-hour location-based services, including tracking of people and vehicles. To prevent children from wittingly or unwittingly calling up porn sites, the Seattle company N2H2 provides Web filtering and monitoring services for 2,500 schools serving 16 million students. More than a third of all large corporations electronically review the computer files used by their employees, according to a recent American Management Association survey. Seven of the 10 biggest supermarket chains use discount cards to monitor customers' shopping habits: tailoring product offerings to customers' wishes is key to survival in that brutally competitive business. And as part of a new, federally mandated tracking system, the three major U.S. automobile manufacturers plan to put special radio transponders known as radio frequency identification tags in every tire sold in the nation. Far exceeding congressional requirements, according to a leader of the Automotive Industry Action Group, an industry think tank, the tags can be read on vehicles going as fast as 160 kilometers per hour from a distance of 4.5 meters.

Many if not most of today's surveillance networks were set up by government and big business, but in years to come individuals and small organizations will set the pace of growth. Future sales of Net-enabled surveillance cameras, in the view of Fredrik Nilsson, Axis Communications' director of business development, will be driven by organizations that buy more than eight but fewer than 30 cameras—condo associations, church groups, convenience store owners, parent-teacher associations, and anyone else who might like to check what is happening in one place while he is sitting in another.

A dozen companies already help working parents monitor their children's nannies and day-care centers from the office; scores more let them watch backyards, school buses, playgrounds, and their own living rooms. Two new startups—Wherify Wireless in Redwood Shores, CA, and Peace of Mind at Light Speed in Westport, CT—are introducing bracelets and other portable devices that continuously beam locating signals to satellites so that worried moms and dads can always find their children.

As thousands of ordinary people buy monitoring devices and services, the unplanned result will be an immense, overlapping grid of surveillance systems, created unintentionally by the same ad-hocracy that caused the Internet to explode. Meanwhile, the computer networks on which monitoring data are stored and manipulated continue to grow faster, cheaper, smarter, and able to store information in greater volume for longer times. Ubiquitous digital surveillance will marry widespread computational power—with startling results.

The factors driving the growth of computing potential are well known. Moore's law—which roughly equates to the doubling of processor speed every 18 months—seems likely to continue its famous march. Hard drive capacity is rising even faster. It has doubled every year for more than a decade, and this should go on "as far as the eye can see," according to Robert M. Wise, director of product marketing for the desktop product group at Maxtor, a hard drive manufacturer. Similarly, according to a 2001 study by a pair of AT&T Labs researchers, network transmission capacity has more than doubled annually for the last dozen years, a tendency that should continue for at least another decade and will keep those powerful processors and hard drives well fed with fresh data.

Today a company or agency with a $10 million hardware budget can buy processing power equivalent to 2,000 workstations, two petabytes of hard drive space (two million gigabytes, or 50,000 standard 40-gigabyte hard drives like those found on today's PCs), and a two gigabit Internet connection (more than 2,000 times the capacity of a typical home broadband connection). If current trends continue, simple arithmetic predicts that in 20 years the same purchasing power will buy the processing capability of 10 million of today's workstations, 200 exabytes (200 million gigabytes) of storage capacity, and 200 exabits (200 million megabits) of bandwidth. Another way of saying this is that by 2023 large organizations will be able to devote the equivalent of a contemporary PC to monitoring every single one of the 330 million people who will then be living in the United States.

One of the first applications for this combination of surveillance and computational power, says Raghu Ramakrishnan, a database researcher at the University of Wisconsin-Madison, will be continuous intensive monitoring of buildings, offices, and stores: the spaces where middle-class people spend most of their lives. Surveillance in the workplace is common now: in 2001, according to the American Management Association survey, 77.7 percent of major U.S. corporations electronically monitored their employees, and that statistic had more than doubled since 1997 (see "Eye on Employees," p. 194). But much more is on the way. Companies like Johnson Controls and Siemens, Ramakrishnan says, are already "doing simplistic kinds of 'asset tracking,' as they call it." They use radio frequency identification tags to monitor the locations of people as well as inventory. In January, Gillette began attaching such tags to 500 million of its Mach 3 Turbo razors. Special "smart shelves" at Wal-Mart stores will record the removal of razors by shoppers, thereby alerting stock clerks whenever shelves need to be refilled—and effectively transforming Gillette customers into walking radio beacons. In the future, such tags will be used by hospitals to ensure that patients and staff maintain quarantines, by law offices to keep visitors from straying into rooms containing clients' confidential papers, and in kindergartens to track toddlers.

By employing multiple, overlapping types of monitoring, Ramakrishnan says, managers will be able to "keep track of people, objects, and environmental levels throughout a whole complex." Initially, these networks will be installed for "such mundane things as trying to figure out when to replace the carpets or which areas of lawn get the most traffic so you need to spread some grass seed preventively." But as computers and monitoring equipment become cheaper and more powerful, managers will use surveillance data to construct complex, multidimensional records of how spaces are used. The models will be analyzed to improve efficiency and security—and they will be sold to other businesses or governments. Over time, the thousands of individual monitoring schemes inevitably will merge together and feed their data into large commercial and state-owned networks. When surveillance databases can describe or depict what every individual is doing at a particular time, Ramakrishnan says, they will be providing humankind with the digital equivalent of an ancient dream: being "present, in effect, almost anywhere and anytime."

Garbage In, Gragbea Otu

In 1974 Francis Ford Coppola wrote and directed *The Conversation*, which starred Gene Hackman as Harry Caul, a socially maladroit surveillance expert. In this remarkably prescient movie, a mysterious organization hires Caul to record a quiet discussion that will take place in the middle of a crowd in San Francisco's Union Square. Caul deploys three microphones: one in a bag carried by a confederate and two directional mikes installed on buildings overlooking the area. Afterward Caul discovers that each of the three recordings is plagued by background noise and distortions, but by combining the different sources, he is able to piece together the conversation. Or, rather, he thinks he has pieced it together. Later, to his horror, Caul learns that he misinterpreted a crucial line, a discovery that leads directly to the movie's chilling denouement.

The Conversation illustrates a central dilemma for tomorrow's surveillance society. Although much of the explosive growth in monitoring is being driven by consumer demand, that growth has not yet been accompanied by solutions to the classic difficulties computer systems have integrating disparate sources of information and arriving at valid conclusions. Data quality problems that cause little inconvenience on a local scale—when Wal-Mart's smart shelves misread a razor's radio frequency identification tag—have much larger consequences when organizations assemble big databases from many sources and attempt to draw conclusions about, say, someone's capacity for criminal action. Such problems, in the long run, will play a large role in determining both the technical and social impact of surveillance.

The experimental and controversial Total Information Awareness program of the Defense Advanced Research Projects Agency exemplifies these issues. By merging records from corporate, medical, retail, educational, travel, telephone, and even veterinary sources, as well as such "biometric" data as fingerprints, iris and retina scans, DNA tests, and facial-characteristic measurements, the program is intended to create an unprecedented repository of information about both U.S. citizens and foreigners with U.S. contacts. Program director John M. Poindexter has explained that analysts will use custom data-mining techniques to sift through the mass of information, attempting to "detect, classify, and identify foreign terrorists" in order

to "preempt and defeat terrorist acts"—a virtual Eye of Sauron, in critics' view, constructed from telephone bills and shopping preference cards.

In February Congress required the Pentagon to obtain its specific approval before implementing Total Information Awareness in the United States (though certain actions are allowed on foreign soil). But President George W. Bush had already announced that he was creating an apparently similar effort, the Terrorist Threat Integration Center, to be led by the Central Intelligence Agency. Regardless of the fate of these two programs, other equally sweeping attempts to pool monitoring data are proceeding apace. Among these initiatives is Regulatory DataCorp, a for-profit consortium of 19 top financial institutions worldwide. The consortium, which was formed last July, combines members' customer data in an effort to combat "money laundering, fraud, terrorist financing, organized crime, and corruption." By constantly poring through more than 20,000 sources of public information about potential wrongdoings— from newspaper articles and Interpol warrants to disciplinary actions by the U.S. Securities and Exchange Commission—the consortium's Global Regulatory Information Database will, according to its owner, help clients "know their customers."

Equally important in the long run are the databases that will be created by the nearly spontaneous aggregation of scores or hundreds of smaller databases. "What seem to be small-scale, discrete systems end up being combined into large databases," says Marc Rotenberg, executive director of the Electronic Privacy Information Center, a nonprofit research organization in Washington, DC. He points to the recent, voluntary efforts of merchants in Washington's affluent Georgetown district. They are integrating their in-store closed-circuit television networks and making the combined results available to city police. In Rotenberg's view, the

Eye on Employees

Percentage of major U.S. employers that record and review their workers' activities

Surveillance Activity	1997	1998	1999	2000	2001
Recording telephone conversations	10.4	11.2	10.6	11.5	11.9
Monitoring telephone usage	34.4	40.2	38.6	44.0	43.3
Storing and reviewing voice mail	5.3	5.3	5.8	6.8	7.8
Storing and reviewing computer files	13.7	19.6	21.4	30.8	36.1
Storing and reviewing e-mail	14.9	20.2	27.0	38.1	46.5
Monitoring Internet connections	NA[1]	NA[1]	NA[1]	54.1	62.8
Clocking overall computer use	16.1	15.9	15.2	19.4	18.9
Video recording of employee performance	15.7	15.6	16.1	14.6	15.2
Video surveillance for security	33.7	32.7	32.8	35.3	37.7
Any active electronic monitoring	35.3	42.7	45.1	73.5[2]	77.7[2]

[1] Not available.
[2] Includes Internet monitoring, which was not measured prior to 2000

collection and consolidation of individual surveillance networks into big government and industry programs "is a strange mix of public and private, and it's not something that the legal system has encountered much before."

Managing the sheer size of these aggregate surveillance databases, surprisingly, will not pose insurmountable technical difficulties. Most personal data are either very compact or easily compressible. Financial, medical, and shopping records can be represented as strings of text that are easily stored and transmitted; as a general rule, the records do not grow substantially over time.

Even biometric records are no strain on computing systems. To identify people, genetic-testing firms typically need stretches of DNA that can be represented in just one kilobyte—the size of a short email message. Fingerprints, iris scans, and other types of biometric data consume little more. Other forms of data can be preprocessed in much the way that the cameras on Route 9 transform multimegabyte images of cars into short strings of text with license plate numbers and times. (For investigators, having a video of suspects driving down a road usually is not as important as simply knowing that they were there at a given time.) To create a digital dossier for every individual in the United States—as programs like Total Information Awareness would require—only "a couple terabytes of well-defined information" would be needed, says Jeffrey Ullman, a former Stanford University database researcher. "I don't think that's really stressing the capacity of [even today's] databases."

Instead, argues Rajeev Motwani, another member of Stanford's database group, the real challenge for large surveillance databases will be the seemingly simple task of gathering valid data. Computer scientists use the term GIGO—garbage in, garbage out—to describe situations in which erroneous input creates erroneous output. Whether people are building bombs or buying bagels, governments and corporations try to predict their behavior by integrating data from sources as disparate as electronic toll-collection sensors, library records, restaurant credit-card receipts, and grocery store customer cards—to say nothing of the Internet, surely the world's largest repository of personal information.

Unfortunately, all these sources are full of errors, as are financial and medical records. Names are misspelled and digits transposed; address and e-mail records become outdated when people move and switch Internet service providers; and formatting differences among databases cause information loss and distortion when they are merged. "It is routine to find in large customer databases defective records—records with at least one major error or omission—at rates of at least 20 to 35 percent," says Larry English of Information Impact, a database consulting company in Brentwood, TN.

Unfortunately, says Motwani, "data cleaning is a major open problem in the research community. We are still struggling to get a formal technical definition of the problem." Even when the original data are correct, he argues, merging them can introduce errors where none had existed before. Worse, none of these worries about the garbage going into the system even begin to address the still larger problems with the garbage going out.

The Dissolution of Privacy

Almost every computer-science student takes a course in algorithms. Algorithms are sets of specified, repeatable rules or procedures for accomplishing tasks such as sorting numbers; they are, so to speak, the engines that make programs run. Unfortunately, innovations in algorithms are not subject to Moore's law, and progress in the field is notoriously sporadic. "There are certain areas in algorithms we basically can't do better and others where creative work will have to be done," Ullman says. Sifting through large surveillance databases for information, he says, will essentially be "a problem in research in algorithms. We need to exploit some of the stuff that's been done in the data-mining community recently and do it much, much better."

Working with databases requires users to have two mental models. One is a model of the data. Teasing out answers to questions from the popular search engine Google, for example, is easier if users grasp the varieties and types of data on the Internet—Web pages with words and pictures, whole documents in a multiplicity of formats, downloadable software and media files—and how they are stored. In exactly the same way, extracting information from surveillance databases will depend on a user's knowledge of the system. "It's a chess game," Ullman says. "An unusually smart analyst will get things that a not-so-smart one will not."

Second, and more important according to Spafford, effective use of big surveillance databases will depend on having a model of what one is looking for. This factor is especially crucial, he says, when trying to predict the future, a goal of many commercial and government projects. For this reason, what might be called *reactive* searches that scan recorded data for specific patterns are generally much more likely to obtain useful answers than *proactive* searches that seek to get ahead of things. If, for instance, police in the Washington sniper investigation had been able to tap into a pervasive network of surveillance cameras, they could have tracked people seen near the crime scenes until they could be stopped and questioned: a reactive process. But it is unlikely that police would have been helped by proactively asking surveillance databases for the names of people in the Washington area with the requisite characteristics (family difficulties, perhaps, or military training and a recent penchant for drinking) to become snipers.

In many cases, invalid answers are harmless. If Victoria's Secret mistakenly mails 1 percent of its spring catalogs to people with no interest in lingerie, the price paid by all parties is small. But if a national terrorist-tracking system has the same 1 percent error rate, it will produce millions of false alarms, wasting huge amounts of investigators' time and, worse, labeling many innocent U.S. citizens as suspects. "A 99 percent hit rate is great for advertising," Spafford says, "but terrible for spotting terrorism."

Because no system can have a success rate of 100 percent, analysts can try to decrease the likelihood that surveillance databases will identify blameless people as possible terrorists. By making the criteria for flagging suspects more stringent, officials can raise the bar, and fewer ordinary citizens will be wrongly fingered. Inevitably, however, that will mean also that the "borderline" terrorists—those who don't match all the search criteria but still have lethal intentions—might be overlooked as well. For both types of error, the potential consequences are alarming.

Yet none of these concerns will stop the growth of surveillance, says Ben Shneiderman, a computer scientist at the University of Maryland. Its potential benefits are simply too large. An example is what Shneiderman, in his recent book *Leonardo's Laptop: Human Needs and the New Computing Technologies*, calls the World Wide Med: a global, unified database that makes every patient's complete medical history instantly available to doctors through the Internet, replacing today's scattered sheaves of paper records (see "Paperless Medicine" in *TR*, April 2003, p. 58). "The idea," he says, "is that if you're brought to an ER anywhere in the world, your medical records pop up in 30 seconds." Similar programs are already coming into existence. Backed by the Centers for Disease Control and Prevention, a team based at Harvard Medical School is planning to monitor the records of 20 million walk-in hospital patients throughout the United States for clusters of symptoms associated with bioterror agents. Given the huge number of lost or confused medical records, the benefits of such plans are clear. But because doctors would be continually adding information to medical histories, the system would be monitoring patients' most intimate personal data. The network, therefore, threatens to violate patient confidentiality on a global scale.

In Shneiderman's view, such tradeoffs are inherent to surveillance. The collective by-product of thousands of unexceptionable, even praiseworthy efforts to gather data could be something nobody wants: the demise of privacy. "These networks are growing much faster than people realize," he says. "We need to pay attention to what we're doing right now."

In *The Conversation*, surveillance expert Harry Caul is forced to confront the trade-offs of his profession directly. The conversation in Union Square provides information that he uses to try to stop a murder. Unfortunately, his faulty interpretation of its meaning prevents him from averting tragedy. Worse still, we see in scene after scene that even the expert snoop is unable to avoid being monitored and recorded. At the movie's intense, almost wordless climax, Caul rips his home apart in a futile effort to find the electronic bugs that are hounding him.

The Conversation foreshadowed a view now taken by many experts: surveillance cannot be stopped. There is no possibility of "opting out." The question instead is how to use technology, policy, and shared societal values to guide the spread of surveillance—by the government, by corporations, and perhaps most of all by our own unwitting and enthusiastic participation—while limiting its downside.

Discussion Questions

1. Which of the examples provided in the article by Farmer and Mann do you believe represent useful and appropriate uses of surveillance technology? Which do not? Support your opinion with reasoning.

2. Events such as the terrorist attacks on the World Trade Towers and the Pentagon in 2001 are often used as a justification for expanded use of surveillance. Do you believe that this expanded surveillance achieves the goal of making us safer as a society? Are there reasons why, or situations when, we should resist expanded uses of surveillance?

3. An important issue that emerges in the field of surveillance is the "garbage in/garbage out" syndrome. What does this mean, in this context? Why is it a major concern with regard to surveillance?

4. The authors suggest that it's not possible to "opt out" of the surveillance society. Do you think this is true? Why or why not? Under what conditions do you think it might be possible to opt out?

5. Eric Snowden is a famous whistleblower who leaked classified information about the surveillance programs at the U.S. National Security Agency (NSA) in 2013. Since that time he has lived abroad seeking asylum from U.S. prosecution, unable to return to the United States. What are your feelings about Snowden's actions? Is he a hero or a criminal? Did his revelations affect the passage of the recently-enacted U.S. Freedom Act that modified the U.S. Patriot Act? How should the U.S. treat whistleblowers like Snowden?

 Supporting Activities

1. Watch and discuss (or write a review of) the movies *Gattica* (1997) or *Minority Report* (2002), both of which imagine a science-fiction world of the future in which biometric identifiers are used to track the movement of individuals.

2. Watch *Citizenfour* (2014) a documentary film directed by Laura Poitras concerning Edward Snowden and the NSA spying scandal. It won the Academy Award for Best Documentary Feature at the 2015 Oscars.

3. Find a surveillance camera in your community that provides real-time video footage of a public space. Can you locate information about why the camera was installed? For example, you can view streaming video of Times Square (NY) from any of a number of different video cameras at: http://www.earthcam.com/usa/newyork/timessquare/.

4. As a group, try to compile a listing of all of the ways that your activity is monitored on a day-to-day basis. Which of these do you think is useful or appropriate? Which, if any, do you object to?

 Additional Resources

1. A summary of HR 3162, the USA PATRIOT Act, developed by the Congressional Research Service of the Library of Congress, can be found at: http://www.fas.org/irp/crs/RS21203.pdf. The full text of the bill can be read on the Electronic Privacy Information Center (EPIC) site: http://epic.org/privacy/terrorism/hr3162.html. The full text of the USA FREEDOM Act that modified

the PATRIOT Act in response to the United States Court of Appeals for the Second Circuit ruling that the bulk collection of Americans' phone metadata by the NSA wasn't authorized by section 215 of the PATRIOT Act can be seen at: https://www.congress.gov/bill/114th-congress/house-bill/2048/text.

2. The American Civil Liberties Union (ACLU) is an organization devoted to protecting civil rights. See what they have to say about privacy and surveillance at: https://www.aclu.org/issues/privacy-technology.

3. For a very readable description of how RFID tags work, visit the How Stuff Works site: http://electronics.howstuffworks.com/rfid.htm.

4. View the materials on the National Geographic site about the so-called War on Terror. Go to: http://www.nationalgeographic.com/ and use the search function to find the "high tech war on terror" page, which includes photos and video.

5. For an interesting look at the intersection between news and surveillance, read the article "Having Won a Pulitzer for Exposing Data Mining, *Times* Now Eager to Do Its Own Data Mining" by Keach Hagey, available on *The Village Voice* (http://www.villagevoice.com/) web site. Once at the site, type in the search phrase "data mining." On that same page notice the article "Citizenfour's Laura Poitras Explains Why Edward Snowden Did It."

 # References

Bamford, J. (2012, April). Inside the matrix. *Wired, 3*, 78–85.

Burke, J. (Writer), & Jackson, M. (Director). (1978). *Connections: An alternative view of change.* London, UK: BBC.

Burke, J., & Ornstein, R. (1995). *The axemaker's gift: A double-edged history of human culture.* New York, NY: Putnam Adult.

Cohen, D. J., & Rosenzweig, R. (1998). The fragility of digital materials. In *Digital history: A guide to gathering, preserving, and presenting the past on the Web* ("Preserving Digital History"). Retrieved from http://chnm.gmu.edu/digitalhistory/preserving/1.php

Derry, T. K., & Williams, T. I. (1961). *A short history of technology: From the earliest times to A.D. 1900.* New York, NY: Dover Publications, Inc.

Fuller, R. B., & Kuromiya, K. (1981). *Critical path.* New York, NY: St. Martin's Press.

Greenburg, A. (2007). America's hackable backbone. *Forbes.* Retrieved from http://www.forbes.com/2007/08/22/scada-hackers-infrastructure-tech-security-cx_ag_0822hack.html

McLuhan, M. (1964). *Understanding media: The extensions of man.* New York, NY: McGraw-Hill, Inc.

Mumford, L. (1965). Technics and the nature of man. *Nature, 208* (5014), 923–928.

Orwell, G. (1949). *Nineteen eighty-four.* London: Secker and Warburg.

Pirsig, R. (1974). *Zen and the art of motorcycle maintenance: An inquiry into values.* New York, NY: William Morrow and Company, Inc.

White, L. Jr. (1967). The historical roots of our ecological crisis. *Science,155* (3767), 1203–1207.

Winner, L. (1986). Technologies as forms of life. In *The whale and the reactor: A search for limits in an age of high technology* (pp. 3–18). Chicago, IL: The University of Chicago Press.

Perspectives on Biological and Medical Technologies

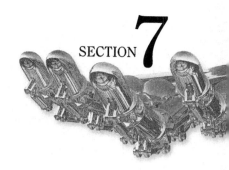

Developments within the field of medical technologies, perhaps more than any other area, are ones we might agree have been predominantly beneficial to humankind. These include medicines such as antibiotics, pain relievers, and drug therapies; diagnostic tools such as MRIs, ultrasound, and even the lowly stethoscope; and life-extending machines such as oxygen tanks, life-support equipment, and kidney dialysis. All of these technologies and scientific breakthroughs have allowed humans to live longer and to survive accidents or illnesses that at one time would have meant certain death. Furthermore, emerging fields such as genetic therapy and advanced neuroscience mean that even intractable illnesses or infirmities may become a thing of the past.

Why, then, would anyone raise concerns about advances in medical technology? Because, as with every other category of technological development, we can identify both positive and negative outcomes. In other words, the effects of medical technologies, although substantially positive, have also created dilemmas related to costs, access, and the ways that medicine is practiced. There will also be a growing number of ethical dilemmas to grapple with if, as many envision, medical technologies advance to the point where humans and technology converge.

The debate about access to health care that has been waged in the United States for many years centers around one essential issue: in spite of recent federal legislation known as the Affordable Care Act, which expanded access to health insurance and ended some exclusions to coverage, a number of Americans still cannot afford to cover their health care costs and do not qualify for public assistance for medical care. As health-care costs continue to rise[1], currently representing over 17% of the U.S. GDP for total national spending of over $2.9 trillion, this means that millions of Americans simply cannot afford health care, preventative or otherwise[2]. Developments in new medical technologies have contributed greatly to the rising cost of health care, yet their availability has not necessarily translated into better overall care. Because health care is necessary for all yet represents one of the single biggest categories of spending in the United States, we must come to terms with the need to identify ways of making it both more accessible and more affordable.

In addition to access issues, some new medical technologies have fundamentally challenged our concept of what is meant by "health care." Should some things be ethically off limits? For example, should cloning technology be pursued to provide replacement organs (as portrayed in the popular movie *The Island*)? Should a couple know the full genetic details of their unborn child, perhaps causing them to terminate a pregnancy? Should embryos harvested for in-vitro fertilization be used for stem cell research? These questions, by definition, cannot be resolved through technology, but rather must be answered by members of a society who are both technologically literate and ethically engaged. In the arena of health care the "slippery slope" phenomenon is particularly prominent. For example, reproductive technologies that even 10 years ago would have been ethically controversial are today part of the accepted standard of care. Today, the web sites of medical centers that perform in-vitro fertilization (IVF) contain very matter-of-fact discussions about the process called preimplantation genetic diagnosis. Twenty years ago this may have been considered "playing God," but as IVF technology has grown incrementally more sophisticated, such diagnostic tools gradually become best practice. Why *wouldn't* you choose diagnostic prescreening?

One reason individuals might not choose more advanced technological procedures is that most medical procedures carry some risks. Generally speaking, the more intrusive the procedure, the greater the likelihood of complications, which in some cases turn out to be more damaging than the original condition. The statistics on iatrogenic (treatment-induced) illness and death are sobering. By one recent estimate, between 210,000 and 400,000 premature deaths per year are attributed to preventable harm to patients in hospitals in the United States (James, 2013). Another study calculated the annual cost of measurable medical errors in the United States at $985 million in 2008 and over $1 billion in 2009 (David, Gunnarsson, Waters, Horblyuk, & Kaplan, 2013). This problem is not confined to the United States alone, and is certainly not always a result of high-tech medical care. Nevertheless, medical consumers are cautioned to actively oversee their health care, and to question the necessity of prescribed medicines and procedures (Moser, 2002).

Another key point regarding the cultural effects of medical technologies is the way this technologically mediated approach to health care has influenced our relationships with our own health. There is less incentive to follow good judgment with regard to nutrition, exercise, adequate rest, and exposure to illness, when we believe that there will be treatments for whatever ill health may result. For example, according to the National Institutes of Health (NIH) over 68% of American adults and 30% of children are estimated to be overweight or obese, and as a nation we spend tens of billions of dollars annually on weight loss products and services[3]. A technological approach to medical care also may make us less likely to seek out and/or to accept complementary and alternative treatments, some of which may be superior to riskier or more costly modern approaches[4]. (And even if we do seek out some alternative treatments, our insurance may not cover them!)

There are also concerns associated with the convergence of medical and information technologies. If you have visited a physician lately, it's likely that he or she carried a laptop into which detailed notes about your visit were typed as you and the physician conversed. Medical billing, medical records, information about medicines, insurance claims: all of these are now stored in electronic databases that carry the same vulnerabilities as other digital data, presenting significant privacy concerns.

In the end, we must consider how we want our medical technologies to serve us, and how we can best assure (and afford) the health and well-being of all citizens. It is worth noting that the United States is the only industrialized nation in the world that does not provide comprehensive health care coverage to its entire population (Physicians for a National Health Program, 2015). In spite of a mandate within the 2010 Affordable Care Act that requires individuals not already covered through a health plan to purchase private insurance, the United States still has a long way to go before more affordable care is universally available to its citizens.

Medicine's New Toolbox

Among the holy grails for modern medicine is the ability to use stem cells for a range of diagnostic and medical treatments. Once believed to be only available from embryonic tissue, researchers are now perfecting the practice described in this article: the reprogramming of adult cells to act like embryonic stem cells through a process that creates what are known as induced pluripotent stem (iPS) cells. As Gravitz describes, there is a great deal of interest in iPS as a means of unraveling the structure and trajectory of diseases, and using that information to develop more effective treatments.

The article also spends time examining the business model of iPS technology—in other words, how to turn this development into a profit. To be sure, health care is big business (as the statistics provided in the Endnotes bear out) and extraordinarily profitable to many who work in the industry. Consider some of these numbers, and then think about what they mean in the context of human health in the United States: according to an article in *Business Insider*, more than 60% of all personal bankruptcies in the United States are the result of medical bills; moreover, three-fourths of those who have had to declare bankruptcy due to unpaid medical bills actually had health insurance. American hospitals are estimated to overcharge patients by some $10 billion annually. The hospital charges for insured Americans are often adjusted through negotiations by the insurance company, whereas uninsured patients are charged the full cost. Health insurance premiums for small companies increased by 180% in the 10-year span from 1999–2009; in 2009 alone, U.S. health insurance company profits rose by 56% (Business Insider, 2011). Thus, our enthusiasm about remarkable new technologies like iPS must be tempered by the understanding that access to such treatments is by no means assured.

Lauren Gravitz is a freelance writer and editor based in Los Angeles, California. A former scientist, Gravitz is a journalist whose work focuses on science, medicine, and the environment. She has contributed nearly a hundred articles to *Technology Review*, and has written for *Discover, The Economist, The Oprah Magazine,* and several other publications.

An Alternative Way to Make Stem Cells Could Open a Window on Human Disease.

By Lauren Gravitz

On the second floor of a building in one of South San Francisco's numerous business parks, a new biotech company has set up shop. The walls sport a fresh coat of white paint, and the bench tops are shiny and bare. The tile floors are still glossy, and an expensive new cell-sorting machine sits, untouched, on the loading dock downstairs.

The building's new inhabitant, iZumi Bio, is pursuing a technology as new and full of promise as the lab itself—a technology that's moving faster than the company can fill its empty space. It revolves around induced pluripotent stem (iPS) cells: adult cells genetically reprogrammed to act like embryonic stem cells, which can turn into just about any type of cell in the human body.

Scientists have been talking about the medical promise of stem cells for more than a decade, even before human embryonic stem cells were successfully isolated in 1998. Most of the public attention has focused on their regenerative power: since stem cells can renew themselves and differentiate into specialized cell types, they could potentially be used to build replacement organs, heal spinal-cord injuries, or repair damaged brain tissue. But the research world has also pursued another, even broader-reaching goal: using the cells of patients with various illnesses to derive pluripotent stem cells, which can give rise not just to the specialized cells in a particular organ or tissue but to virtually any cell type. Those cells could be used to create laboratory models of disease. For example, a cell from a Parkinson's patient could be turned into a neuron, which would exhibit the progressive molecular changes at work in the neurodegenerative disorder. This type of tool could capture the details of human disease with unprecedented accuracy, and it could revolutionize the way researchers search for new treatments.

Studying human disease in the lab is an enormously challenging task. It's difficult to obtain brain tissue from a living Alzheimer's patient, for example, and impossible to study how that tissue changes as the disease progresses. Animal models can offer only rough approximations of a human illness, capturing at best a few of its symptoms or causes. But iPS cells could yield a much more comprehensive picture. Because each cell line comes from a human patient, the cells reflect the complex array of factors that led to the patient's disease: the genetic mutations, the effects of environmental history. And because those cells can be prodded to

develop into a variety of tissue types, scientists can watch the disease unfold in a petri dish. They can observe, for example, the subtle molecular changes that take place in the neurons of a patient with Alzheimer's long before the telltale signs of the disease, such as amyloid plaques, can be seen in the brain. It's the difference between trying to piece together the details of a plane crash from photos of the wreckage and watching a video of the crash from every angle, with the ability to stop, zoom in, and rewind at will.

"The past two years have been nothing short of a revolution," says John Dimos, a senior scientist at iZumi. "These cells didn't really exist two years ago. This is all brand-new technology, and it's opening up the potential for brand-new science." The company plans to take advantage of that potential by developing a bank of iPS cells from patients with various diseases and using the cells to screen candidates for drug development.

Thousands of other labs are jumping at the chance to use iPS cells as well—whether to create new disease models, to study tissue development, or even to figure out how to build tissue for transplantation. Biologists say the field is charged with a kind of energy not seen since soon after the structure of DNA was discovered. "This is a really rare phenomenon in the biological research community." says Sheng Ding, a chemist at the Scripps Research Institute in La Jolla, CA. "It's a sensation, really. Everyone, more or less, is working on using iPS-cell technology for their specific research interest."

STEM CELLS 2.0

Scientists have been searching for ways to directly reprogram adult cells for decades. That hunt has been pushed forward by the desire to develop an alternative to human embryonic stem cells, which are fraught with both technical and ethical issues. The cells are usually derived from four- or five-day-old embryos that would otherwise be discarded from in vitro fertilization clinics (although sometimes embryos have been created expressly for research purposes). Using this technique to create a robust cell line is tricky and highly inefficient. Not only are the embryos themselves hard to obtain, but the cells are delicate and difficult to grow.

Another technique, human therapeutic cloning, is even more controversial, and both technically and practically challenging. Scientists transfer the nucleus of an adult cell into the hollowed-out shell of an unfertilized egg cell—which can then develop into an embryo, yielding stem cells that are genetic clones of the adult cells. But the lack of human eggs for research has proved a huge hurdle, and scientists have yet to generate cloned human cell lines.

But three years ago Shinya Yamanaka, of Kyoto University in Japan, figured out how to return adult mouse cells to an embryonic-like state in a process that never involved an actual embryo. He found that using a virus to deliver genes for just four specific proteins to the nucleus of an adult cell could give it the ability to differentiate into a wide variety of cell types, just like the stem cells derived from embryos. Those proteins, typically found in developing embryos, appear to turn other genes on and off in a pattern characteristic of embryonic rather than adult cells. A year after Yamanaka's discovery, his group and two others reported that they could induce human cells to do the same thing.

As a physician and venture capitalist closely following stem-cell research, Beth Seidenberg saw the potential almost immediately. Seidenberg, a partner at Kleiner Perkins Caufield and Byers, teamed up with another venture capital firm, Highland Capital Partners, to found iZumi in 2007, funding the company with $20 million. After 20 years in pharmaceutical research,

Seidenberg has had a lot of time to think about what the industry is doing right and where it's going wrong. She says, "I became really intrigued by the idea of starting with a patient who had a disease and working backwards, which is exactly the opposite of how we pursue new therapies for treatment of disease today."

To illustrate the role iPS cells could play in drug discovery, John Dimos points to amyotrophic lateral sclerosis (ALS), a neurodegenerative disease he has studied for years. About 2 percent of all cases have a known genetic cause—a mutation in a gene called *SOD1*. Nearly all the work in animal models has focused on this rare form of the disease, because researchers know how to use the gene to trigger it in mice. With the new technology, however, scientists can use a skin biopsy to generate pluripotent stem cells from any patient with ALS. The genetics and other possible factors underlying the disease are captured in the cells, even if no one knows explicitly what those factors are. The same holds true for Alzheimer's, diabetes, autism, heart disease, and myriad other conditions whose complex origins have proved difficult to identify.

As a postdoc at Harvard, Dimos built a cellular model of ALS, making it possible to study a neurodegenerative disease outside an animal for the first time. He and his colleagues collected skin cells from an 82-year-old woman with ALS, reprogrammed them into iPS cells, and directed the cells to differentiate into motor neurons that were genetically identical to the donor's defective cells. "It was the first paper to show that you can use a stem cell to see disease pathology in a petri dish," says Douglas Melton, codirector of the Harvard Stem Cell Institute. "That means you can now study diseases in petri dishes and not in people. That's huge."

Because they are derived from human patients with documented medical histories, iPS cells are accompanied by reams of previously inaccessible information. "You can see from their medical history the progression of the disease, how they responded to different drugs, exactly what symptoms they experienced, and when," says Dimos. Certain drugs may be more or less effective depending on a patient's genetic makeup; some people, for instance, respond well to the breast-cancer medication taxol, while others may have no response at all. If scientists knew that specific medications worked for certain people or, conversely, caused them to suffer severe side effects, they could use their cells to try to figure out why—and use that information to develop better therapies.

So far, Harvard Stem Cell Institute scientists and their colleagues have used iPS-cell technology to create more than 20 disease-specific stem-cell lines designed to help them study conditions including Parkinson's and type 1 diabetes. While the field is still in its early stages, researchers have begun to see evidence that they can replicate certain aspects of human disease in a dish.

The first goal for iZumi is to establish its own bank of reprogrammed cells. To start, the bank will be stocked with cells derived from patients with various neurodegenerative diseases—ALS, spinal muscular atrophy, and Parkinson's—as well as a cardiovascular disorder known as calcific aortic valve disease, which they're studying in conjunction with collaborators at the Gladstone Institute at the University of California, San Francisco. By creating complex systems of cells that incorporate the different cell types affected in each disease, such as motor neurons and skeletal muscle cells, they can watch precisely how ALS and the other conditions develop.

The company wants to develop drugs, focusing on therapies for neurodegenerative diseases. It will also work with other pharmaceutical companies to find treatments for other diseases. "We believe that we'll have our own proprietary therapeutics in development in the fifth year—by 2012," says CEO John Walker.

A BUMPY ROAD

If iPS-cell scientists have learned anything from the saga of embryonic-stem-cell research, it's that potential doesn't always translate into profit or success: despite the vast promise of embryonic stem cells, building a business model around their therapeutic use has been a challenge. Some of the blame can be laid on President George W. Bush. In 2001—citing ethical objections to the process used to obtain the cells, which destroys a days-old embryo— he restricted federal research funding for the technology to a small number of stem-cell lines already in existence. The controversy, the lack of federal investment, and some uncertainty surrounding the science itself made some researchers reluctant to study embryonic stem cells, and many venture capitalists were hesitant to back efforts to commercialize them.

Barack Obama ordered the limits on federal funding removed early in his presidency, but his predecessor's policies probably set the field back many years. And embryonic stem cells are so finicky and unpredictable that developing treatments based on them has been difficult even apart from the funding obstacles. Only this year,

Other iPS Companies

Company	Strategy
Fate Therapeutics La Jolla, CA	Using iPS cells to search for drugs that trigger growth of adult stem cells
Cellular Dynamics Madison, WI	Turning iPS cells into colonies of heart, immune, kidney, and other cells for drug screening
GlaxoSmithKline Worldwide (HQ in the U.K.)	$25 million collaboration with the Harvard Stem Cell Institute

more than a decade after human embryonic stem cells were first isolated, will they finally make it into clinical trials. The first therapy, a treatment for acute spinal-cord injury developed by biotech startup Geron, is headed for trials later this year.

"It's kind of a 'good news, bad news' scenario," says Daniel Omstead, CEO of Hambrecht and Quist Capital Management. "Every quarter or year, you see new developments that make you very excited about the future but more circumspect about . . . being able to make money in the near term for investment in technology that will cure disease." He's not yet sure whether iPS-cell technology will prove to be the stem-cell field's home run, and neither are his fellow venture capitalists. "I think many companies will come out of the stem-cell area, but I don't know that they'll be focused on iPS cells necessarily," says Amir Nashat of Polaris Venture Partners, which has funded a company partly based on the technology *(see table above)*.

Stem cells might be easier to commercialize as tools for drug development, an area in which the new technology seems especially promising. But iPS cells still hold many unknowns: they are not as well studied as embryonic stem cells, and there is not yet any standard by which they can be measured. That is one reason no one is yet willing to claim that iPS cells will make embryonic stem cells obsolete; indeed, the inconsistency of iPS cells is one of the biggest research hang-ups at the moment. Researchers don't quite understand why, but even cells from the same batch can behave very differently. Some are easy to turn into other tissues; some are stubborn. And the rapidly growing repertoire of methods for making iPS cells is adding to the variability.

Only a year ago, researchers had to use a virus to insert the four proteins required to turn an adult cell into an iPS cell. The virus also inserted little bits of itself into the cell's genome, an invasion that not only prevents therapeutic use but makes lab studies much less reliable. Newer methods use proteins or chemicals, while some techniques still use viruses. Before they can use the cells generated in all these different ways, scientists need to study and document their characteristics. "We just finished initial characterization of a group of 12 lines we made. And then we made some more," says Jeanne Loring, director of the Center of Regenerative Medicine at Scripps. "So we're suffering from the same thing everyone else is." In other words: "Oh my God, we have more lines than we know what to do with."

But Harvard's Melton, for one, thinks these problems are only temporary. "This is all solvable in the short term—in the next year or so," he says. After that, the trick will be figuring out how to prompt the cells to differentiate in the desired ways. There are more than 200 different kinds of cells in the body, and although iPS cells have the *potential* to turn into any of them, actually getting them to do so is a different story. "How do you tell a cell to become a pancreatic beta cell? How do you tell it to become a four-grain basal cell or a motor neuron?" he says. Scientists have already figured out how to make some neurons and blood cells, to name a few. But they cannot yet efficiently make such important types as pancreatic beta cells, the insulin producers that are destroyed in diabetes. Still, says Melton, "we're getting closer."

Though it seems a long way off, scientists still hold out the possibility that iPS-cell technology could one day be used for treatment. "The near-term value for iPS cells is in disease modeling, pathway identification, and drug screening and development," says George Daley, a stem-cell biologist at Harvard University and Children's Hospital in Boston. "But I don't give up hope that we will generate cells that will have therapeutic relevance."

For now, though, iZumi and other companies are focusing sharply on what they think will be the most immediate use of iPS cells: as tools for understanding some of our most devastating diseases and finding better ways to treat them. The new technology, they hope, will fundamentally change the repetitive, variations-on-a-theme approach to drug development that has hindered pharmaceutical progress in recent years. The discoveries it makes possible could one day transform medicine into something we're only just beginning to imagine.

Discussion Questions

1. In describing the bumpy road being traveled by iPS-cell scientists, Gravitz writes: "potential doesn't always translate into profit or success: despite the vast promise of embryonic stem cells, building a business model around their therapeutic use has been a challenge." Does characterization of any medical treatment in terms of its "business model" disturb you in any way? Why or why not?
2. What are some of the challenges surrounding use of iPS cells as tools for development of new drug therapies?
3. In what ways does iPS technology have the potential to "transform medicine into something we're only just beginning to imagine"? Is there reason for caution?

 Supporting Activities

1. Compare U.S. health care statistics with those of other industrialized nations. Your search could include statistics such as total health care spending, infant mortality rates, incidence of specific surgical procedures per 1,000 people, and so on. If differences are observed (as they are likely to), to what do you think these differences can be attributed? The web sites of the U.S. Center for Disease Control and Prevention and of the World Health Organization are both good bets for locating this type of information.
2. One way to deal with the rising costs of health care is to require all citizens to carry insurance, as is mandated in the Affordable Care Act. Select another country, either industrialized or non-industrialized, and learn more about how that country handles insurance and access to health care. How does this contrast to the situation in the United States?
3. Read and discuss the article "The cost conundrum: What a Texas town can teach us about health care" by Atul Gawande in the June 1, 2009 issue of *The New Yorker* (available online at: http://www.newyorker.com/reporting/2009/06/01/090601fa_fact_gawande?yrail).
4. Visit "WebMD" (http://www.webmd.com/) and look up a condition that you or a close friend or family member has had in the past few years. Compare the information provided there with the information you were given by your physician or caregiver. Pay particular attention to the diagnostic tests recommended for the condition. Are web-based information sites like this one helpful? Potentially dangerous? Support your response.

 Additional Resources

1. Read an article in *The Guardian* about some of the first uses of stem cell therapy and the concerns surrounding its use: http://www.theguardian.com/science/2012/jun/04/stem-cell-first-human-trials.
2. Visit the Human Genome Research Institute web site (http://www.genome.gov/) to learn more about genome research and the future of DNA testing and therapy. See also the work that has been done on genomics by the U.S. Department of Energy (http://genomics.energy.gov/).
3. Read this NPR article about iatrogenic deaths: http://www.npr.org/sections/health-shots/2013/09/20/224507654/how-many-die-from-medical-mistakes-in-u-s-hospitals

Defending Human Dignity

In this excerpt Kass offers an excellent outline of the various aspects of human dignity that are affected by biotechnological advances. He acknowledges that dignity is a contested idea and that preserving dignity in the same ways that we profess to support freedom or justice is not a goal shared by all. Dignity may be seen as something too private or vague upon which to base public policy. He also suggests, however, that struggles against slavery, segregation, and sweatshop labor were at their core battles for human dignity. In the face of "gathering powers to intervene in human bodies and minds in ways that will affect our very humanity," Kass argues, "we neglect human dignity at our peril."

The challenges posed by biotechnologies threaten human dignity in a variety of ways, according to Kass: there is, for example, the dignity of procreation, threatened by the prospect of turning childbearing into little more than a form of manufacture; the dignity of human activity, with reliance on performance-enhancing drugs threatening what it means to display excellence; the dignity of the human life cycle, with efforts to conquer both aging and dying threatening the arc of life as we know it. Beyond our more traditional concerns within medical bioethics—respect, beneficence, and justice—and concerns about the safety and efficacy of treatments, the emerging biotechnological advances will require "a more robust notion of human dignity." As social theorists such as Fukuyama (2003) contemplate a so-called "posthuman future" involving the redesign of humans and the advent of human-machine hybrids, we clearly face a whole host of ethical questions about what it means to be human, and what human dignity represents.

The Presidential Commission for the Study of Bioethical Issues (the 2001–2009 version of this body was called the President's Council on Bioethics) is an advisory panel of leaders in medicine, science, ethics, religion, law, and engineering. The Bioethics Commission advises the President on issues arising from advances in biomedicine and related areas of technology and science.

Leon R. Kass is Addie Clark Harding Professor in the Committee on Social Thought and the College at the University of Chicago and Hertog Fellow in Social Thought at the American Enterprise Institute. Kass was a member of the President's Council on Bioethics until 2007, and served as chairman of the Council from 2002 to 2005. He earned an M.D. degree at the University of Chicago and a PhD in bio-chemistry at Harvard. For more than 35 years he has been engaged with the ethical, philosophical, and cultural issues surrounding biomedical advances, and is the author of many articles and books, including *The Ethics of Human Cloning* (1998) and *Life, Liberty, and the Defense of Dignity: The Challenge for Bioethics* (2002).

Defending Human Dignity

Leon R. Kass

It is difficult to define what human dignity is. It is not an organ to be discovered in our body, it is not an empirical notion, but without it we would be unable to answer the simple question: what is wrong with slavery?
-Leszek Kolakowski[1]

In American discussions of bioethical matters, human dignity, where it is not neglected altogether, is a problematic notion. There are disagreements about its importance relative to other human goods, such as freedom or justice. There are differences of opinion about exactly what it means and what it rests on, a difficulty painfully evident when appeals to "human dignity" are invoked on opposite sides of an ethical debate, for example, about whether permitting assisted suicide for patients suffering from degrading illnesses would serve or violate their human dignity. There are also disagreements about the extent to which considerations of human dignity should count in determining public policy.

We friends of human dignity must acknowledge these difficulties, both for practice and for thought. In contrast to continental Europe and even Canada, human dignity has not been a powerful idea in American public discourse, devoted as we are instead to the language of rights and the pursuit of equality. Among us, the very idea of "dignity" smacks too much of aristocracy for egalitarians and too much of religion for secularists and libertarians. Moreover, it seems to be too private and vague a matter to be the basis for legislation or public policy.

Yet, that said, we Americans actually care a great deal about human dignity, even if the term comes not easily to our lips. In times past, our successful battles against slavery, sweatshops, and segregation, although fought in the name of civil rights, were at bottom campaigns for human dignity-for treating human beings as they deserve to be treated, *solely because of their humanity*. Likewise, our taboos against incest, bestiality, and cannibalism, as well as our condemnations of prostitution, drug addiction, and self-mutilation- having little to do with defending liberty and equality-all seek to defend human dignity against (voluntary) acts of *self*-degradation. Today, human dignity is of paramount importance especially in matters bioethical. As we become more and more immersed in a world of biotechnology, we increasingly sense that we neglect human dignity at our peril, especially in light of gathering powers to intervene in human bodies and minds in ways that will affect our very humanity, likely threatening things that everyone, whatever their view of human dignity, holds dear. Truth to tell, it is beneath our human dignity to be indifferent to it.

As part of its effort to develop and promote a "richer" bioethics, the President's Council on Bioethics, in its previously published works, has paid considerable attention to various aspects of human dignity that are at risk in our biotechnological age: the dignity of human procreation, threatened by cloning-to-produce-children and other projected forms of "manufacture"; the dignity of nascent human life, threatened by treating embryonic human beings as mere raw material for exploitation and use in research and commerce; the dignity of the human difference, threatened by research that would produce man-animal or man-machine hybrids; the dignity of bodily integrity, threatened by trafficking in human body parts; the dignity of psychic integrity, threatened by chemical interventions that would erase memories, create factitious moods, and transform personal identity; the dignity of human self-command, threatened by methods of behavior modification that bypass human agency; the dignity of human activity and human excellence, threatened by reliance on performance-enhancing or performance-transforming drugs; the dignity of living deliberately and self-consciously, mindful of the human life cycle and our finitude, threatened by efforts to deny or eliminate aging and to conquer mortality; the dignity of dying well (or of living well while dying), threatened by excessive medical intervention at the end of life; and the dignity of human being as such, threatened by the prospect of euthanasia and other "technical solutions" for the miseries that often accompany the human condition.[2] Beyond these practical issues, the Council has also tried to call attention to the dignity of proper human self-understanding, threatened by shallow "scientistic" thinking about human phenomena-for example, views of human life that see organisms as mere means for the replication of their genes, the human body as a lifeless machine, or human love and moral choice as mere neurochemical events.[3] In my own personal writings on biology and human affairs, spanning over thirty-five years, I have dealt with many of the same aspects of human dignity and the dangers they face from the new biology, both to our practice and to our thought.[4]

Yet neither the Council nor I have tried to articulate a full theoretical account of human dignity; neither have we tried to reconcile some of the competing views that are held by the various members, all bidding fair to gain our assent. This essay is offered as a contribution toward the development of such a conceptual account. Specifically, it aims to do three things: to defend a robust role in bioethics for the idea of human dignity; to make clearer what human dignity is and what it rests on; and to try to show the relationship between two equally important but sometimes competing ideas of human dignity: the *basic* dignity of human *being* and the *full* dignity of being (actively) *human*, of human *flourishing*.[i]

Why Bioethics Must Care About Human Dignity: Old and New Concerns

Attention to human dignity is important in nearly all arenas of bioethical concern: clinical medicine; research using human subjects; uses of novel biotechnologies "beyond therapy" (especially for so-called "enhancement" purposes); and "transhumanist" activities aimed at altering and transcending human nature. But because the central ethical concerns in these domains differ, *each realm of bioethics gives special salience to a different aspect of human dignity*.

In clinical medicine, a primary ethical focus is on the need to respect the equal worth and dignity of each patient at every stage of his or her life-regardless of race, class or gender, condition of body and mind, severity of illness, nearness to death, or ability to pay for services rendered. Defenders of human dignity rightly insist that every patient deserves-from every physician, nurse, or hospital-equal respect in speech and deed and equal consideration regarding the selection of appropriate treatment. Moreover, they also rightly insist that no life is to be deemed worthier than another and that under no circumstances should we look upon a fellow human being as if he or she has a "life unworthy of life" and deserves to be made dead. The ground of these opinions, and of the respect for human dignity they betoken, lies not in the patient's autonomy or any other of his personal qualities or excellences, but rather in the patient's very being and vitality. Doctors should always respect the life the patient has, all the more because he has entrusted it to their care in the belief that they will indeed respect it to the very last.

Regarding research with human subjects, the major ethical issues concern not only safeguarding the subject's life and health but also respecting the subject's humanity, even as he is being treated as an experimental animal. Concern for human dignity focuses on enlisting the human subject as a knowing and willing co-partner in the research enterprise. Soliciting voluntary informed consent pays tribute to the humanity of the human subject, even as that humanity will be largely overlooked in the research protocol. Bioethicists usually believe that respecting human dignity here means respecting subject autonomy-the freedom of the subject's will-and so it does; but there is more to it. It involves respecting also the subject's courage in accepting risks and discomforts, his philanthropic desire to contribute to a worthy cause, and his generosity of time and trouble in embracing activities from which he will receive no direct benefit.

In these domains of clinical medicine and research involving human subjects, appeals to human dignity, while tacitly employing an ideal of proper treatment and respect, function explicitly and mainly as bulwarks against abuse: patients should not be reduced to "thing-hood" or treated as mere bodies; research subjects should not be utilized as mere means or treated only as experimental animals. This "negative" function of the concept of human dignity in these domains makes perfect sense, inasmuch as it is intended-and needed-to restrain the strong in their dealings with the weak. It makes even more sense once we remember the origins of modern biomedical ethics: a concern for human dignity hovers over all of modern biomedical ethics owing to the world's horror at the Nazi atrocities, atrocities in which German scientists and German doctors were deeply implicated. They more than lent a hand with eugenic sterilization, barbaric human experimentation, and mass extermination of the "unfit"-all undertaken, mind you, in order to produce "a more perfect human." The rise to prominence of the idea of "human dignity" in post-World-War-II Europe, expressed in the laws of many nations and especially in the United Nations' *Universal Declaration of Human Rights,* was surely intended to ensure that no human beings should ever again be so abused, degraded, and dehumanized-and, of course, annihilated.

But a more robust notion of human dignity is needed when we turn from these traditional domains of medical ethics to the moral challenges raised by new biotechnological powers and the novel purposes to which they are being put, and when we turn from concerns with abuse of power that the strong inflict upon the weak to concerns with ethically dubious uses of powers that the strong-indeed, most of us-will choose to exercise for and on ourselves. Our desires for a better life do not end with health, and the uses of biotechnology are not limited to therapy. Its powers to alter the workings of body and mind are attractive not only to the sick and suffering, but to everyone who desires to look younger, perform better, feel happier, or become more "perfect."

We have already entered the age of biotechnical enhancement: growth hormone to make children taller; pre-implantation genetic screening to facilitate eugenic choice (now to rule out defects, soon to rule in assets); Ritalin and other stimulants to control behavior or boost performance on exams; Prozac and other drugs to brighten moods and alter temperaments-not to mention Botox, Viagra, and anabolic steroids. Looking ahead, other invitations are already visible on the horizon: Drugs to erase painful or shameful memories or to simulate falling in love. Genes to increase the size and strength of muscles. Nano-mechanical implants to enhance sensation or motor skills. Techniques to slow biological aging and increase the maximum human lifespan. Thanks to these and other innovations, venerable human desires-for better children, superior performance, ageless bodies, and happy souls-may increasingly be satisfied with the aid of biotechnology. A new field of "transhumanist" science is rallying thought and research for wholesale redesign of human nature, employing genetic and neurological engineering and man-machine hybrids, en route to what has been blithely called a "posthuman future."

Neither the familiar principles of contemporary bioethics-respect for persons, beneficence (or "non-maleficence"), and justice- nor our habitual concerns for safety, efficacy, autonomy, and equal access will enable us to assess the true promise and peril of the biotechnology revolution. Our hopes for self-improvement and our disquiet about a "posthuman" future are much more profound. At stake are the kind of human being and the sort of society we will be creating in the coming age of biotechnology. At stake are the dignity of the human being-including the dignity or worth of human activity, human relationships, and human society-and the nature of human flourishing.

To be sure, the biotechnological revolution may, as the optimists believe, serve to enhance human dignity. It may enable more and more people to realize the American dream of liberty, prosperity, and justice for all. It may enable many more human beings-biologically better-equipped, aided by performance-enhancers, liberated from the constraints of nature and fortune-to live lives of achievement, contentment, and high self-esteem, come what may.

But there are reasons to wonder whether life will really be better if we turn to biotechnology to fulfill our deepest human desires. There is an old expression: to a man armed with a hammer, everything looks like a nail. To a society armed with biotechnology, the activities of human life may come to be seen in purely technical terms, and more amenable to improvement than they really are. We may get more easily what we asked for only to realize it is vastly less than what we really wanted. Worse, we may get exactly what we ask for and *fail* to recognize what it cost us *in coin of our humanity* .

We might get better children, but only by turning procreation into manufacture or by altering their brains to gain them an edge over their peers. We might perform better in the activities of life, but only by becoming mere creatures of our chemists or by turning ourselves into bionic tools designed to win and achieve in inhuman ways. We might get longer lives, but only at the cost of living carelessly with diminished aspiration for living well or becoming people so obsessed with our own longevity that we care little about the next generations. We might get to be "happy," but only by means of a drug that gives us happy feelings without the real loves, attachments, and achievements that are essential for true human flourishing. As Aldous Huxley prophetically warned us, in his dystopian novel *Brave New World* , the unbridled yet well-meaning pursuit of the mastery of human nature and human troubles through technology can issue in a world peopled by creatures of human shape but of shrunken humanity-engaged in trivial pursuits; lacking science, art, religion, and self-government; missing love, friendship, or any true human attachments; and getting their jollies from high-tech amusements and a bottle of soma.

This is not the place to argue whether we have more to fear than to hope from biotechnological enhancement or the pursuit of a posthuman future. I happen to share Huxley's worries, and I surely see no reason to adopt the optimism of the transhumanists-especially because they cannot provide a plausible picture of "the new posthuman being," and, worse, can offer no standards for judging whether their new "creature" will be *better* than *Homo sapiens* . But for present purposes, my point is simply this: we cannot evaluate *any* proposed enhancements or alterations of our humanity unless we have some idea of human dignity, some notion of what is estimable and worthy and excellent about being human. In order to know whether change is progress rather than degradation, we need a standard of the *un* degraded and the admirable. We need to understand the nature and worth of human flourishing in order to recognize both the true promise of self-improvement and the hazards of self-degradation; we need to understand the nature and worth of human agency and human activity in order to recognize both enhancement and corruption of our ways of encountering the world and one another; we need to understand the nature and worth of human aspiration and human fulfillment in order to assess not only the means but also the ends that we will be pursuing in the coming age of biotechnology, both for ourselves as individuals and for our society. We need, in short, wisdom about human dignity and what sustains and enhances it- and what destroys it.

Concerns for human dignity in bioethical matters take mainly two forms: concerns for the dignity of life around the edges (the "life and death" issues) and concerns for the dignity of life in its fullness and flourishing (the "good life" and "dehumanization" issues; the "Brave New World" issues). In the former case are questions regarding what we owe to nascent life (including fetal and embryonic life, *in vivo* and *in vitro*) that has yet to attain full development of human powers, and what we owe to fading or dying human life, life not only past its prime but, in many cases, life with the most human of our powers dwindling to near-nothingness. Especially poignant are those cases in which-often thanks to previous medical successes, and the ease of combating potentially lethal infections-individuals are sustained, often for years, in greatly degraded conditions, incapable of living dignifiedly while dying or having a timely end to their life. In the latter case are questions regarding what makes for true human flourishing and how to keep human life human, in the face of the soul-flattening and dehumanizing dangers of a Brave New World. Especially difficult here will be discerning which proposed enhancements of body or mind actually conduce to human dignity and to living well and which do not-and which, tragically, at once improve and degrade.

Depending on which of the two dangers most trouble us, defenders of human dignity will emphasize either the basic dignity of human *being* or the full dignity of being (flourishingly) *human*.[ii] If one believes that the greatest threat we face comes in the form of death and destruction-say, in the practices of euthanasia and assisted suicide, embryo research, or even just denial of treatment to the less than fully fit-then one will be primarily concerned to uphold the equal dignity of every still-living human being, regardless of condition. If, conversely, one thinks that the greatest threat we face comes *not* from killing the creature made in God's image but either from trying to redesign him after our own fantasies or from *self* -abasement owing to shrunken views of human well-being (à la Nietzsche's "last man"), then one will be primarily concerned to uphold the full dignity of human excellence and rich human flourishing.

The two aspects of human dignity do not always have the same defenders, especially when concerns for equality and life seem to be at odds with concerns for excellence and living well. Indeed, defenders of one aspect of dignity sometimes ignore the claims made on behalf of the other. Certain pro-lifers appear to care little whether babies are cloned or even "born" in bottles, so long as no embryo dies in the process; and others insist that life must be sustained come what may, even if it means being complicit in prolonging the degradation and misery of loved ones. Conversely, certain advocates of so-called "death with dignity" appear to care little whether the weak and the unwanted will be deemed unworthy of life and swept off the stage, so long as *they* get to exercise control over how *their own* life ends; and patrons of excellence through biotechnological enhancement often have little patience with the need to care, here and now, for those whose days of excellence are long gone. Meanwhile, those who dream of posthuman supermen appear to care not a fig either for the dignity of human being or for the dignity of being human, since they esteem not at all the dignity of us ordinary mortals, never mind those of us who are even less than merely ordinary.

Yet there is no reason why friends of human dignity cannot be- and, indeed, should not be-defenders of *all* aspects of human dignity, both the dignity of "the low" and the dignity of "the high." Yes, there will be times when there will be tensions between them, demanding prudent and loving attention lest we make major mistakes. Yes, each aspect if emphasized single-mindedly may appear to threaten the other: concern for the dignity of human flour-ishing may appear to look down invidiously on the less than excellent; concern for the dignity of ("mere") human aliveness may appear willing to level all higher human possibilities. But precisely to avoid the dangers of myopic single-mindedness, we can, and must, defend both the dignity of human *being* and the dignity of being *human* . In fact, as I will suggest at the end, when properly understood, the two notions are much more intertwined than they are opposed. But first, we need to look at each more closely, beginning with the dignity of being human-the dignity of human flourishing, the dignity of living well.

Footnotes

i. Application to specific bioethical topics and debates of any conceptual clarifications found in this essay must await subsequent exploration. The purpose of this paper is entirely philosophical; and it intends no immediate or direct implications for public policy in any substantive field of bioethics.

ii. The justification and meaning of the names given here will be made clearer in sections two and three of this paper. Another set of terms I considered using were " *human* dignity" and "human *dignity* ," the former to stress the horizontal dimension of universal "human-all-too-human"-ness, carried by the term "human," the latter to stress the vertical dimension of excellence or worthiness, carried by the term "dignity." Once again, the discussion below should clarify matters beyond such attempts at finding the right shorthand phrases.

Endnotes

1. Leszek Kolakowski, "What Is Left of Socialism," First Things 126 (October 2002): 42-46.

2. See, among other places, *Human Cloning and Human Dignity: An Ethical Inquiry* (2002), especially chapter 5, "The Ethics of Cloning-to-Produce-Children," and chapter 6, "The Ethics of Cloning-for-Biomedical-Research"; *Monitoring Stem Cell Research* (2004), especially chapter 3,

"Recent Developments in the Ethical and Policy Debates"; *Beyond Therapy: Biotechnology and the Pursuit of Happiness* (2004), all chapters, and especially the discussion of "The Dignity of Human Activity" in chapter 3, "Superior Performance"; *Reproduction and Responsibility: The Regulation of New Biotechnologies* (2005), especially the section on "The Character and Significance of Human Procreation" in (the introductory) chapter 1, chapter 6 on "Commerce," and the section on "Targeted Legislative Measures" in chapter 10, "Recommendations"; *Being Human: Readings from the President's Council on Bioethics* (2004), especially chapter 10, "Human Dignity"; and *Taking Care: Ethical Caregiving in Our Aging Society* (2005), especially chapters 3 and 4, "The Ethics of Caregiving: General Principles," and "The Ethics of Caregiving: Principle and Prudence in Hard Cases." All of these books except for *Being Human* are available online at www.bioethics.gov.

3. The readings in *Being Human* were collected and offered to provide the humanistic wherewithal for thinking about and responding to these and other inadequate views of our humanity. See especially the chapters on "The Pursuit of Perfection," "Are We Our Bodies," "Among the Generations," "Why Not Immortality," "The Meaning of Suffering," "Living Immediately," and, of course, "Human Dignity." This anthology has been republished by W. W. Norton, under the title *Being Human: Core Readings in the Humanities* (2004).

4. See, among other places, *Life, Liberty and the Defense of Dignity: The Challenge for Bioethics* (San Francisco, California: Encounter Books, 2002), especially the Introduction, the discussion of the "Profundity of Sex" in chapter 5, "Cloning and the Post Human Future," chapter 6, "Organs for Sale: Propriety, Property, and the Price of Progress," chapter 8, "Death with Dignity and the Sanctity of Life," and chapter 9, " *L'Chaim* and Its Limits: Why Not Immortality"; *Toward a More Natural Science: Biology and Human Affairs* (New York: The Free Press, 1984), especially chapters 2, 3, and 4 on reproductive technologies and genetic screening, chapter 10, "Thinking About the Body," and most especially chapter 13, "Looking Good: Nature and Nobility"; an essay on "The Right to Life and Human Dignity," in *The New Atlantis* 16 (Spring 2007), pp. 23-40; *The Hungry Soul: Eating and the Perfecting of Our Nature* (New York: The Free Press, 1994; Chicago: University of Chicago Press, 1998), especially chapter 2, "The Human Form: Omnivorosus Erectus"; and *The Beginning of Wisdom: Reading Genesis* (New York: The Free Press, 2003; Chicago: University of Chicago Press, 2006), especially chapters 2 and 3 on the anthropology of the Garden of Eden story and chapter 6 on the Noahide Law and its foundations.

Discussion Questions

1. Among the various aspects of human dignity at risk due to biotechnological advances, introduced early in this excerpt, which do you find of most concern? Which most surprised you—in the sense that you hadn't considered it before?

2. Explain what you think Kass means by distinguishing between the basic dignity of human *being* and the full dignity of being *human*.

3. If, as a society, we truly supported the ethical focus of clinical medicine on the equal worth of every patient, regardless of his or her social, racial, or economic status, and that every patient deserves equal respect in speech and deed, what would the implications of this support look like in practice? How would you imagine the U.S. health care would differ from the way it is currently structured?

4. Kass writes, "To a society armed with biotechnology, the activities of human life may come to be seen in purely technical terms. . . . We may get more easily what we asked for only to realize it is vastly less than what we wanted. Worse, we may get exactly what we ask for and *fail* to recognize what it cost us *in coin of our humanity*. What does Kass mean by this? Which of the two scenarios he offers do you think is more likely to occur, and why?

 Supporting Activities

1. Have each member of the class select a blog entry from the Presidential Commission for the Study of Bioethical Issues (http://blog.bioethics.gov/) and report back to the class on what he or she learned.

2. To learn more about how access to health care and insurance differs by age group, location, employment status, and other factors, view the "interactive tool" on the Kaiser Foundation web site: http://kff.org/interactive/the-uninsured-an-interactive-tool/.

 Additional Resources

1. Read the book *Our posthuman future: Consequences of the biotechnology revolution* (2002) by Francis Fukuyama. (Listed below in the references section.)

2. Another good book that explores the possibilities of a posthuman future is Bill McKibben's *Enough: Staying human in an engineered age* (2003). New York, NY: Henry Holt and Company, LLC.

3. To read from the perspective of someone who fully embraces the posthuman future, see: Kurzweil, R. (2005). *The singularity is near.* New York, NY: Penguin Group. See also the movie that was made about Ray Kurzweil and the Singularity, titled *Transcendent Man* (http://transcendentman.com/).

4. Popular novels that explore a near-future where human–machine interface (transhumanism) is commonplace are *Neuromancer* (1984) by William Gibson (considered the father of the cyberpunk genre), and *Do Androids Dream of Electric Sheep* (1968) by Philip K. Dick, which became the basis for the classic sci-fi film *Blade Runner* (1982).

5. For an outrageous take on a near-future transhumanist culture that explores the impact on human dignity read the graphic novel series *The Transmetropolitan* (1997–2002).

 References

Business Insider. (2011). *18 ridiculous statistics about the health care industry that will make you tear your hair out*. Retrieved from http://www.businessinsider.com/statistics-about-the-health-care-industry-2011-2

David, G., Gunnarsson, C. L., Waters, H. C., Horblyuk, R., & Kaplan, H. S. (2013). Economic measure of medical errors using a hospital claims database. *Value Health, 16*(2), 305–310. doi: 10.1016/j.jval.2012.11.010.

Fukuyama, F. (2002). *Our posthuman future: Consequences of the biotechnology revolution.* New York, NY: Picador.

James, J. T. (2013). A new, evidence-based estimate of patient harms associated with hospital care. *Journal of Patient Safety, 9*(3), 122–128. doi: 10.1097/PTS.0b013e3182948a69

Moser, M. (2002). The patient as a consumer. In B. L. Zaret, M. Moser, & L. S. Cohen (Eds.), *Yale University School of Medicine Heart Book*, (pp. 359–362). New York: William Morrow and Company, Inc.

Physicians for a National Health Program (PNHP). (2015). *Single-payer national health insurance*. Retrieved from http://www.pnhp.org/facts/single-payer-resources

 Endnotes

1. According to the National Coalition on Health Care, total national health expenditures in 2010 represented 17% of GDP and are projected to be more than 40% of GDP by 2040. The CDC notes that in 2013, per capita health expenditures were $9,255, for a total national health expenditure rate of $2.9 trillion. Although the year-to-year growth rate in health care expenditures slowed in 2012 and 2013 compared to previous years, to 4.0% and 3.6% growth, respectively, the share of the economy devoted to health spending has remained steady. See: http://www.cdc.gov/nchs/hus/healthexpenditures.htm.

2. The passage of the Affordable Care Act (a.k.a. "Obamacare") in 2013 has led to significant reductions in the number of uninsured American adults. According to Health and Human Services Department data, the uninsured rate dropped from 20.3% in 2012 to 13.2% in the first quarter of 2015, with over 14 million more Americans covered this year than in 2012 (See: http://aspe.hhs.gov/health/reports/2015/uninsured_change/ib_uninsured_change.pdf).

3. View ABC News 20/20 program titled "Losing It: The Big Fat Trap" at: http://abcnews.go.com/2020/video/losing-big-fat-trap-16331564?tab=9482930&section=1206863&playlist=16332677

4. Learn how the U.S. National Institutes of Health treats "alternative" medicines at the National Center for Complementary and Alternative Medicine website (http://www.nccam.nih.gov/).

Perspectives on Military and Security Technologies

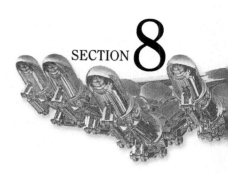

In the opening to the film *2001: A Space Odyssey* (Stanley Kubrick's 1968 opus on the relationship of humanity to technology), we see an early hominid competing with feral pigs for food and predated by panthers, "discover" the first tool. The tool is the femur of a pig that the hominid uses to increase the force of his blows, ushering in, according to Kubrick, the age of weapons, hunting, war, murder, and human dominance over the natural world. The hominid, as portrayed by Kubrick, had an intrinsic, fundamental impulse to develop weapons in order to secure food, resources and himself. We modern humans still refer to our weapons as "arms," as if they are an extension of our existing appendages as fundamental to our existence as the natural appendages themselves.

Our history is one of weaponry. The names we give the different epochs of humanity (e.g., Stone Age, Bronze Age, and Iron Age) refer primarily to the materials used to make weapons. The military establishment is often the first major client for mines, smelters, and forges. The first bronze artifact discovered was a dagger and the first iron and steel implements were spears and swords. Jared Diamond, the Pulitzer Prize-winning author of *Guns, Germs and Steel* (1999) demonstrated that it is the civilizations with the greatest weapons that prevail. It is not a moral equation, but rather a technological one predicated on weaponry, that dictates the establishment of the dominant culture. Mao Tse-tung (1971), the leader of the communist revolution in China, famously observed, "political power comes from the barrel of a gun" (para. 5). Either cultures adopt the gun (or more advanced weaponry such as nuclear weapons) or they perish. Yet, particularly with cases such as nuclear or biological weapons, our existential savior can become our existential threat.

As mentioned in previous chapters, technological determinists tend to believe that technology controls our destiny and that we have only limited, if any, control over its direction or adoption. Others, like the scholar Lynn White, Jr. (1962), disagree: "Technology merely opens a door, it does not compel one to enter" (p. 28). Nevertheless, as Witold Rybczynski (1983) points out in *Taming the Tiger: The Struggle to Control Technology*:

> If all technological devices open a door, weapons do so in a most provocative way. There is an urgency to war that accelerates the making of decisions; the effect of choosing to use, or not to use, a particular weapon is usually obvious and swift. War often makes the film of technological change look as it were being run at double speed. (p. 166)

Many technological developments have been spurred by military needs: the mining of ores led to developments in hydraulics and mechanics, gunnery advanced the science of mathematics, and naval warfare prompted advancements in navigation. Armies required large numbers of standardized products, which led to the standardization of products and mass production. Portsmouth, England in 1808 was the first example of large-scale mass production with modern methods. Specialized preset machines were used with which just 10 workmen could produce 130,000 wooden pulley blocks per year for the British navy. In the United States, inventor and manufacturer Eli Whitney was financed by the military to produce muskets and popularized the concept of standardized interchangeable parts. German processes for creating nitrogen for explosives during WWI lead to the creation of artificial fertilizer, which spawned the Green Revolution that made it possible to feed the world's ever-expanding human population. Even the federal legislation that led to the interstate highway system was justified by security concerns; it is officially known as the Dwight D. Eisenhower National System of Interstate and Defense Highways. Most significantly, the space program and race to the moon were largely spurred by the United States' concern about Soviet military dominance in space due to the fact that Sputnik, the first-ever satellite, was deployed by the Soviet Union. Having Sputnik orbiting overhead stoked fear within the American psyche. Moreover, the basis for the U.S. rocket program that eventually resulted in the Saturn rocket used in the Apollo moon landing had its genesis in Germany during WWII. German scientists from the Society for Space Travel received research funds from the militaristic Nazi regime because of the regime's desire to develop the V-2 rocket as a weapon. All of the above led eventually to intercontinental ballistic missiles (ICBMs) armed with nuclear warheads that have the potential to annihilate the human race.

As these examples show, often the *potential* of a technology's use as a weapon is what determines which technologies are developed. Rybczynski (1983) uses the example of the airship to make this point. The incongruent mast on top of the Empire State Building was not built for King Kong to grab onto, but rather it was designed as a mooring for the Graf Zeppelin to help usher in the coming Age of the Airship. In 1929, the Graf Zeppelin completed a 21,000 mile round-the-world journey in three weeks, with only three refueling stops! It was also used in WWI to bomb London. Raids were conducted at night to prevent airplane attacks and the use of rudimentary anti-aircraft defenses. However, to counter this weapon the British invented phosphorus-coated incendiary bullets to ignite the lighter-than-air hydrogen that kept the zeppelins afloat. The only defense for the zeppelins was to fly higher (over 20,000 ft), but at such heights they became ineffective. Ultimately, the Germans decided not to pursue further development of the airship. It is often assumed that the famous fiery crash of the Hindenburg prevented more widespread use of the airship. However, that was the first accident that an airship had ever had, and only 35 people died, while 61 survived. As Rybczynski points out, the tragic sinking of the Titanic did not stop the use of transatlantic ships. In addition, nonreactive helium was destined to replace hydrogen. The real reason the zeppelin was not developed, according to Rybczynski, was that the Nazis had no interest in it as a weapon. In effect, the faster and more agile warplane caused the death of blimps; even though at the time blimps were far better for passenger transport than commercial planes, their demise was due to their failure as a weapon. Rybczynski quotes Hugo Eckener, the director of the Zeppelin Company:

"What good is the airship to the contemporary politician or State which is following a policy of

ruthless pursuit of power and national safety, when the airship, considered from a military point of view, has become completely worthless? Every penny which a State spends nowadays in promoting aviation is lavished on airplanes, which can be weapons of the greatest value." (1983, p. 194)

In conclusion, Rybczynski muses, "it is ironic that just as the door to the development of the airship was opened by its perceived, and real, ability to wreak violence, so it was finally closed because it was not violent enough" (p. 194).

Similarly, after WWII the United States' development of nuclear energy for electrification was dependent on uranium-based reactors, similar to the ones used to produce nuclear material for atomic bombs. However, it is also possible to use thorium for nuclear reactors and Oak Ridge National Laboratory successfully operated such a reactor from 1965 to 1969. Science writer Richard Martin (2009) states, in his article "Uranium Is So Last Century–Enter Thorium, the New Green Nuke," that nuclear physicist and Oak Ridge Director Alvin Weinberg, who was primarily responsible for the new reactor, lost his job as director because he championed development of the safer thorium reactors. Weinberg's unwillingness to sacrifice potentially safe nuclear power for the benefit of military uses forced him to retire:

> *Weinberg realized that you could use thorium in an entirely new kind of reactor, one that would have zero risk of meltdown. . . . His team built a working reactor . . . . and he spent the rest of his 18-year tenure trying to make thorium the heart of the nation's atomic power effort. He failed. Uranium reactors had already been established, and Hyman Rickover, de facto head of the US nuclear program, wanted the plutonium from uranium-powered nuclear plants to make bombs. Increasingly shunted aside, Weinberg was finally forced out in 1973. (Martin, 2009, para. 16)*

Our world is paying for such decisions. Any state that claims it wants to develop nuclear energy for peaceful purposes, like Iran currently, is suspected—and has the real potential—of developing nuclear weapons. Understanding such issues of technology becomes vital for societies, especially when they threaten to go to war over potential nuclear development, as the United States and Israel have threatened to do against Iran. Perhaps it would be better to redouble our research efforts on thorium-based reactors, rather than risk war. For a working democracy, such technological knowledge is essential for its citizens to make reasoned decisions about policies that could so drastically affect their lives.

However, weapons are so ingrained in the existential question of survival that many people neither question nor doubt the validity of their society's development of weapon technology. If our weaponry, our "arms," are not superior, then we shall perish, and so believes the rest of humanity and therein lays potential disaster. Humanity's fundamental feelings of insecurity, highlighted by Kubrick in *2001: A Space Odyssey,* have not changed, but our technological ability to violently maximize our so-called "security" has increased tremendously. In this section's first excerpt, Clarke and Knake (2010) explore the "battlespace," which in this instance means the Internet. Modern industrial society has entered a completely new realm of warfare with cyber war. And as Clarke and Knake make clear, cyber war has the potential to do real physical harm out in the "real" world, due to the connectedness of all our infrastructure systems (as highlighted in the introduction to Section 6). This again illustrates the amount of ignorance most of us have about crucial technologies we are dependent on, yet which have the potential to do us great harm and may threaten our security rather than protect it.

Clarke and Knake do their best in this piece to explain the workings of the Internet and how it can be used to wage a very real war. In the section's second excerpt Fred Kaplan, in *The World as Free-Fire Zone,* explores the ramifications of the newly developed remotely controlled and potentially automatous drone technology that may bring something much more destructive than just Amazon's latest product to your very doorstep.

Perhaps in no other area does the autonomy of technology become a more important question. If we do not control our weapons, and weapons determine the course of civilization, can we consider ourselves to be truly in control of our own destiny?

The Battlespace

In the section on communication technologies we pondered whether people really know what a computer server is, or how the Internet, which so many of us depend on, actually works. This excerpt from Clarke and Knake's book *Cyber War* gives a brief yet detailed explanation of exactly how it all works as they explain how these tools can be controlled in a malicious way to be used as weapons.

Cyberspace, as they explain, is not just the Internet, but all the peripheral hardware, systems, and networks connected to it. Unfortunately, all those things can be and have been used maliciously to do things like blow up generators, crash financial systems, and derail trains, among other destructive acts. Few of us realize how connected our objects are to the Internet, encompassing everything from elevators to photocopiers to computers, and if they are reporting to the Internet that means that someone can control them remotely. The people who can control them know how to manipulate the computer code that connects things to the Internet. When these hackers go somewhere they are not authorized to go, they are known as cyber criminals; when they do it under the aegis of governments, they are known as cyber warriors.

Clarke and Knake outline and explain in some detail the three basic elements that make cyber war possible: (1) flaws in Internet design, (2) flaws in hardware and software, and (3) the move to put an increasing number of critical systems online. The authors systematically go through each of these items, and by the time you are done reading you will probably know more than 95% of the population about how the Internet actually works. And you will start to recognize both how vulnerable our systems are and the kinds of steps that we will need to take to make them secure.

Richard Clarke is the former National Coordinator for Security, Infrastructure Protection, and Counter-terrorism, the chief counter-terrorism adviser on the National Security Council. He served in the White House for presidents Ronald Reagan, George H.W. Bush, Bill Clinton, and George W. Bush. He currently teaches at Harvard's Kennedy School of Government, consults for ABC News, and is chairman of Good Harbor Consulting. Robert Knake is a technical expert on cyber security. He was an international affairs fellow at the Council on Foreign Relations and holds a master's degree in international security studies from Harvard's Kennedy School of Government.

THE BATTLESPACE

Cyberspace. It sounds like another dimension, perhaps with green lighting and columns of numbers and symbols flashing in midair, as in the movie The Matrix. Cyberspace is actually much more mundane. It's the laptop you or your kid carries to school, the desktop computer at work. It's a drab windowless building downtown and a pipe under the street. It's everywhere, everywhere there's a computer, or a processor, or a cable connecting to one. And now it's a war zone, where many of the decisive battles in the twenty-first century will play out. To understand why, we need to answer some prior questions, like: What is cyberspace? How does it work? How can militaries fight in it?

How and why Cyber War is Possible

Cyberspace is all of the computer networks in the world and everything they connect and control. It's not just the Internet. Let's be clear about the difference. The Internet is an open network of networks. From any network on the Internet, you should be able to communicate with any computer connected to any of the Internet's networks. Cyberspace includes the Internet plus lots of other networks of computers that are not supposed to be accessible from the Internet. Some of those private networks look just like the Internet, but they are, theoretically at least, separate. Other parts of cyberspace are transactional networks that do things like send data about money flows, stock market trades, and credit card transactions. Some networks are control systems that just allow machines to speak to other machines, like control panels talking to pumps, elevators, and generators.

What makes these networks a place where militaries can fight? In the broadest terms, cyber warriors can get into these networks and control or crash them. If they take over a network, cyber warriors could steal all of its information or send out instructions that move money, spill oil, vent gas, blow up generators, derail trains, crash airplanes, send a platoon into an ambush, or cause a missile to detonate in the wrong place. If cyber warriors crash networks, wipe out data, and turn computers into doorstops, then a financial system could collapse, a supply chain could halt, a satellite could spin out of orbit into space, an airline could be grounded. These are not hypotheticals. Things like this have already happened, sometimes experimentally, sometimes by mistake, and sometimes as a result of cyber crime or cyber war. As Admiral Mike McConnell has noted, "information managed by computer networks—which run our utilities, our transportation, our banking and communications—can be exploited or attacked in seconds from a remote location overseas. No flotilla of ships or intercontinental missiles or standing armies can defend against such remote attacks located not only well beyond our borders, but beyond physical space, in the digital ether of cyberspace."

Why, then, do we run sophisticated computer networks that allow unauthorized access or unauthorized commands? Aren't there security measures? The design of computer networks, the software and hardware that make them work, and the way in which they were architected, create thousands of ways that cyber warriors can get around security defenses. People write software and people make mistakes, or get sloppy, and that creates opportunities. Networks that aren't supposed to be connected to the public Internet very often actually are, sometimes without their owners even knowing. Let's look at some things in your daily life as a way of explaining how cyber war can happen. Do you think your condominium association knows that the elevator in your building is, like ET in the movie of the same name, "phoning home"? Your elevator is talking over the Internet to the people who made it. Did you know that the photocopier in your office is probably doing the same thing? Julia Roberts's character in the recent movie Duplicity knew that many copying machines are connected to the Internet and can be hacked, but most people don't know that their copier could even be online. Even fewer think about the latest trick, shredders that image. Just before all those sensitive documents pass through the knives that cut them into little pieces, they go by a camera that photographs them. Later, the cleaning crew guy will take his new collection of pictures away to whoever hired him.

Your elevator and copier "phoning home" is supposed to be happening, the software is working properly. But what if your competitor has a computer programmer who wrote a few lines of code and slipped them into the processor that runs your photocopier? Let's say those few lines of computer code instruct the copier to store an image of everything it copies and put them into a compressed data (or zip) file. Then, once a day, the copier accesses the Internet and—ping!—it shoots that zip file across the country to your competitor. Even worse, on the day before your company has to submit a competitive bid for a big contract—ping!—the photocopier catches fire, causing the sprinklers to turn on, the office to get soaked, and your company to be unable to get its bid done in time. The competitor wins, you lose.

Using an Internet connection you did not know existed, someone wrote software and downloaded it onto your photocopier, which you did not even know had an onboard processor big enough to be a computer. Then that someone used the software to make the photocopier do something it wouldn't otherwise do, short-circuit or jam and overheat. They knew the result would be a fire. They probably experimented with a copier just like yours. The result is your office is flooded by the sprinkler system and you think it was an accident. Somebody reached out from cyberspace and made your physical space a mess. That someone is a hacker. Originally "hacker" meant just somebody who could write instructions in the code that is the language of computers to get them to do new things. When they do something like going where they are not authorized, hackers become cyber criminals. When they work for the U.S. military, we call them cyber warriors.

In this scenario, the cyber criminal used the Internet as his avenue of attack, first to get information and then to do damage. His weapon was a few lines of software, which he inserted into the computer in the copier. Or you may think about it this way: he used software to turn your copier into the weapon.

He succeeded because the software program that ran the copier was written to allow people to add commands and give those commands remotely. The designers of the copier never thought anyone would make it a weapon, so they never wrote their software in a manner that would make that difficult or impossible to do. The same is true of the designers of the electric power grid and other systems. They didn't think about people hacking them and turning their systems into weapons. Your office manager didn't pay attention when the sales-person said the copier would have a remote diagnostics capability to download improvements, fix problems, and dispatch a repairman with the right replacement parts. Hackers paid attention, or maybe they were just exploring their cyberspace neighborhood and found an address that identified itself as "Xeonera Copier 2000, serial number 20-003488, at Your Company, Inc."

If you doubt that copiers are part of cyber-space, read Image Source Magazine:

> Historically, remote diagnostics required dial up modems. The methodology at that time was somewhat of an inconvenience to the customer and very expensive for the dealer who had to install phone jacks near each device and switch boxes to be compatible with their client's phone systems. But those barriers have now been eliminated with the introduction of the web and wireless networks. Now that all networked de-vices have an address, a diagnostic error report can be transmitted in real time via the web and technicians can be dispatched by the device itself, sometimes before the customer knows there is a problem. Today, there is no excuse for any service organization to ignore the cost sav-ings and value of remote diagnostics. Virtually every printer manufacturer either has their own remote diagnostic tool (i.e. Ricoh's Remote, Kyocera Admin, Sharp's Admin, Xerox's DRM) or have partnered with third party companies like Imaging Portals or Print Fleet.

While mundane, this hypothetical scenario is helpful because it shows the three things involved in cyberspace that make cyber war possible: (1) flaws in the design of the Internet; (2) flaws in hardware and software; and (3) the move to put more and more critical systems online. Let's look at each.

Vulnerabilities of the Internet

There are at least five major vulnerabilities in the design of the Internet itself. The first of these is the addressing system that finds out where to go on the Internet for a specific address.

ISPs are sometimes called "carriers," because they are the companies that carry the Internet's traffic. Other companies make the computer terminals, the routers, the servers, the software, but it is the ISPs that link them all together. All ISPs are not created equal. For our discussion, let's divide them into two categories. There are the national ISPs that own and operate thousands of miles of fiber-optic cable running from coast to coast, connecting all the big cities. There are six of these big ISPs in the United States (Verizon, AT&T, Qwest, Sprint, Level 3, and Global Crossing). Because their big fiber-optic cable pipes form the spine of the Internet in the U.S., they are called the "backbone providers," or, more technically, the Tier 1 ISPs. Once they get the backbone into your city, they connect up with lots of smaller ISPs that run service to local businesses and to your house. Your local ISP is probably the phone company or the cable TV company. (If it's the phone company, it may be that you have one of the Tier 1 ISPs also providing your local service.) Their wires run from your house down the street to the world.

To see how this works, and to discover some of the vulnerabilities of the Internet addressing system, follow what happens when I connect to the Internet. I open a "browser" on my laptop. Just by opening the browser, I am requesting that it go out onto the Internet and bring back "my homepage." Let's say that "homepage" is that of the consulting firm where I work. So, sitting in my home office in Rappahannock County, Virginia, in the foothills of the Blue Ridge Mountains, I click and my browser goes to www.mycompany.com. Since computers can't understand words like "mycompany," the address needs to be translated into 1's and 0's that computers can read. To do that, my browser uses the Domain Name System. Think of it as the 411 information operator. You say a name, you get a number.

My consulting firm is headquartered seventy-five miles away from my home in Virginia, but its webpage is hosted on a remote server in Minneapolis with the Internet address of, let's say, 123.45.678.90. That is a lot of numbers to memorize. Luckily I don't have to. The browser uses the Domain Name System to look up the address. The browser sends a message to a database kept on a server computer, part of an elaborate hierarchy of such computers that together form the Domain Name System. For cyber warriors, the Domain Name System is a target. It was designed with little thought to security, so hackers can change its information and misdirect you to a phony webpage.

When I open up the browser it sends a request to the server hosting the page. The request is broken down into a series of packets that are each sent individually. Let's trace just one packet along its way from my computer to the website. The first hop is from my computer to the wi-fi card in my computer, where the packets are translated into radio waves and sent out over the air to the wi-fi router in my house. If that router is improperly secured, hackers can get into the computer over the wi-fi connection. The wi-fi router turns the signal back from a radio wave into an electronic signal passed to my local ISP in the booming megalopolis of Culpepper, Virginia.

If you know it, you may think that Culpepper is lovely, but not necessarily near the heart of cyberspace. Because it's just beyond the blast radius if a nuclear weapon were to go off in Washington, the government and the financial community have all sorts of databases nearby. So, there is an AT&T node there, at 13456 Lovers Lane. (Really.) My ISP has a line running across town to the AT&T facility, where the electrons of my request for the webpage get converted into photons so they can hop on AT&T's fiber-optic network. Once on the fiber, the packet first hits a router in Morristown, New Jersey, is passed to another AT&T router in Washington, D.C., and then back to New Jersey, this time to a router in Middletown.

At Middletown, the router passes the packet to another Tier 1 company, Level 3. Once on the Level 3 backbone, the packet is routed through three different nodes in Washington, D.C. At this point, the packet has traveled over radio waves, copper wires, and high-speed bundles of fiber-optic cables for more than 800 miles, but is only about 75 miles from where I first sent it off. The last Level 3 router, in Washington, sends it speeding toward Chicago (now we are getting somewhere), where it descends through two more Level 3 routers before being sent to Minneapolis. What goes to Minneapolis, though, does not necessarily stay in Minneapolis. Instead of handing off to our web hosting provider, the packet goes another 741 miles to another Level 3 router in the company's headquarters in Broomfield, Colorado, which then routes the packet back to our company's ISP, in Minneapolis, and on to our web server. To travel the 900 miles to Minneapolis, the packet went about 2,000 miles out of its way, but the whole process took a few seconds. It also provided several opportunities for cyber warriors.

If cyber warriors had wanted to send those packets to the wrong place, or to prevent them from going anywhere, they had at least two opportunities. First, as noted earlier, they could have attacked that Internet 411, the Domain Name System, and sent me to the wrong page, perhaps to a phony look-alike webpage, where I would enter my account number and password. Rather than hacking the Domain Name System to hijack a webpage request, however, cyber warriors could attack the system itself. This is just what happened in February 2007, when six of the thirteen top-level worldwide domain servers were targeted in a DDOS attack. Similar to the botnets that hit Estonia and Georgia, the attack flooded the domain name servers with thousands of requests per second. Two of the servers targeted were taken down, including one that handles traffic for the Department of Defense. The other four were able to manage the attack by shifting requests to other servers not targeted in the attack. The attack was traced back to the Pacific region and lasted only eight hours. The attackers stopped it either because they were afraid continuing it would allow investigators to trace it back to them or, more likely, because they were just testing to see if they could do it.

In 2008, the hacker Dan Kaminsky showed how a sophisticated adversary could hack the system. Kaminsky released a software tool that could quietly access the Domain Name System computers and corrupt the database of name addresses and their related numbered addresses. The system would then literally give you a wrong number. Just misdirecting traffic could cause havoc with the Internet. One cyber security company found twenty-five different ways it could hack the Domain Name System to cause disruption or data theft.

The second vulnerability of the Internet is routing among ISPs, a system known as the Border Gateway Protocol. Another opportunity for a cyber warrior in the one-second, 2,000-mile trip of packets from my home came when they jumped onto the AT&T network. AT&T runs the most secure and reliable Internet service in the world, but it is as vulnerable as anyone else to the way the Internet works. When the packets got on the backbone, they found that AT&T does not connect directly to my company. So who does? The packets checked a database that all of the major ISPs contribute to. There they found a posting from Level 3 that said, in effect, "If you want to connect to mycompany.com, come to us." This routing system regulates traffic at the points where the ISPs come together, where one starts and the other stops, at their borders.

BGP is the main system used to route packets across the Internet. The packets have labels with a "to" and "from" address, and BGP is the postal worker that decides what sorting station the packet goes to next. BGP also does the job of establishing "peer" relationships between two routers on two different networks. To go from AT&T to Level 3 requires that an AT&T router and a Level 3 router have a BGP connection. To quote from a report from Internet Society, a nonprofit organization dedicated to developing Internet-related standards and policies, "There are no mechanisms internal to BGP that protect against attacks that modify, delete, forge, or replay data, any of which has the potential to disrupt overall network routing behavior." What that means is that when Level 3 said, "If you want to get to mycompany.com, come to me," nobody checked to see if that was an authentic message. The BGP system works on trust, not, to borrow Ronald Reagan's favorite phrase, on "trust but verify." If a rogue insider working for one of the big ISPs wanted to cause the Internet to seize up, he could do it by hacking into the BGP tables. Or someone could hack in from outside. If you spoof enough BGP

instructions, Internet traffic will get lost and not reach its destination.

Everyone involved in network management for the big ISPs knows about the vulnerabilities of the Domain Name System and the BGP. People like Steve Kent of BBN Labs in Cambridge, Massachusetts, have even developed ways of eliminating those vulnerabilities, but the Federal Communications Commission has not required the ISPs to do so. Parts of the U.S. government are deploying a secure Domain Name System, but the practice is almost nonexistent in the commercial infrastructure. Decisions on the Domain Name System are made by a nongovernmental international organization called ICANN (pronounced "eye-can"), which is unable ("eye-cannot") to get agreement on a secure system. The result is that the Internet itself could easily be a target for cyber warriors, but most cyber security experts think that unlikely because the Internet is so useful for attacking other things.

ICANN demonstrates the second vulnerability of the Internet, which is governance, or lack thereof. No one is really in charge. In the early days of the Internet, ARPA (DoD's Advanced Research Project filled the function of network administrator, but nobody does now. There are technical bodies, but few authorities. ICANN, the Internet Corporation for Assigned Names and Numbers, is the closest that any organization has come to being responsible for the management of even one part of the Internet system. ICANN ensures that web addresses are unique. Computers are logical devices, and they don't deal well with ambiguity. If there were two different computers on the Internet each with the same address, routers would not know what to do. ICANN solves that problem by working internationally to assign addresses. ICANN solves one of the problems of Internet governance, but not a host of other issues. More than a dozen intergovernmental and nongovernmental organizations play some role in Internet governance, but no authority provides overall administrative guidance or control.

The third vulnerability of the Internet is the fact that almost everything that makes it work is open, unencrypted. When you are crawling around the web, most of the information is sent "in the clear," meaning that it is unencrypted. It's like your local FM classic rock station broadcasting Pink Floyd and Def Leppard "in the clear" so that anyone tuned to that channel can receive the signal and rock along rolling down the highway. A radio scanner purchased at Radio Shack can listen in on the two-way communications between truckers, and in most cities, between police personnel. In some cities, however, the police will "scramble" the signal so that criminal gangs cannot monitor police comms. Only someone with a radio that can unencrypt the traffic can hear what is being said. To everyone else, it just sounds like static.

The Internet generally works the same way. Most communication is openly broadcast, and only a fraction of the traffic is encrypted. The only difference is that it is a little more difficult to tune in to someone else's Internet traffic. ISPs have access (and can give it to the government), and mail-service providers like Google's Gmail have access (even if they say they don't). In both those cases, by using their services you are more or less agreeing that they may be able to see your web traffic or e-mails. For a third party to get access, they need to do what security folks call "snoop" and use a "packet sniffer" to pick up the traffic. A packet sniffer is basically a wiretap device for Internet traffic and can be installed on any operating system and used to steal other people's traffic on a local area network. When plugged into a local or an Ethernet network, any user on the system can use a sniffer to pull in all the other traffic. The standard Ethernet protocol tells your computer to ignore everything that is not addressed to it, but

that doesn't mean it has to. An advanced packet sniffer on an Ethernet network can look at all the traffic. Your neighbors could sniff everything on the Internet on your street. More advanced sniffers can trick the network in what is known as a "man-in-the-middle" attack. The sniffer appears to the router as the user's computer. All information is sent to the sniffer, which then copies the information before passing it on to the real addressee.

Many (but not most) websites now use a secure, encrypted connection when you log on so that your password is not sent in the clear for anyone sniffing around to pick up. Due to cost and speed, most then drop the connection back into an unsecure mode after the password transmission is made. When sniffing the transmission isn't possible, or when the data being sent is unreadable, that doesn't mean you are safe. A keystroke logger, a small hidden piece of malicious code installed surreptitiously on your computer, can capture everything you type and then transmit it secretly. Of course, this type of keystroke logger does require you to do something stupid in order for it to be installed on your computer, such as visiting a website that has been infected or downloading a file from an e-mail that is not really from someone you trust. In October 2008 the BBC reported that "computer scientists at the Security and Cryptography Laboratory at the Swiss Ecole Polytechnique Fédérale de Lausanne have demonstrated that criminals could use a radio antenna to 'fully or partially recover keystrokes' by spotting the electromagnetic radiation emitted when keys were pressed."

A fourth vulnerability of the Internet is its ability to propagate intentionally malicious traffic designed to attack computers, malware. Viruses, worms, and phishing scams are collectively known as "malware." They take advantage of both flaws in software and user errors like going to infected websites or opening attachments. Viruses are programs passed from user to user (over the Internet or via a portable format like a flash drive) that carry some form of payload to either disrupt a computer's normal operation, provide a hidden access point to the system, or copy and steal private information. Worms do not require a user to pass the program on to another user; they can copy themselves by taking advantage of known vulnerabilities and "worm" their way across the Internet. Phishing scams try to trick an Internet user into providing information such as bank account numbers and access codes by creating e-mail messages and phony websites that pretend to be related to legitimate businesses, such as your bank.

All this traffic is allowed to flow across the Internet with few, if any, checks on it. For the most part, you as an Internet user are responsible for providing your own protection. Most ISPs do not take even the most basic steps to keep bad traffic from getting to your computer, in part because it is expensive and can slow down the traffic, and also because of privacy concerns.

The fifth Internet vulnerability is the fact that it is one big network with a decentralized design. The designers of the Internet did not want it to be controlled by governments, either singly or collectively, and so they designed a system that placed a higher priority on decentralization than on security. The basic idea of the Internet began to form in the early 1960s, and the Internet as we know it today is deeply imbued with the sensibilities and campus politics of that era. While many regard the Internet as an invention of the military, it is really the product of now aging hippies on the campuses of MIT, Stanford, and Berkeley. They had funding through DARPA, the Defense Department's Advanced Research Project Agency, but the ARPANET, the Advanced Research Project Agency's Network, was not created just for the De-

fense Department to communicate. It initially connected four computers: at UCLA, Stanford, UC Santa Barbara, and, oddly, the University of Utah.

After building the ARPANET, the Internet's pioneers quickly moved on to figuring out how to connect the ARPANET to other networks under development. In order to do that, they developed the basic transmission protocol still used today. Robert Kahn, one of the ten or so people generally regarded as having created the Internet, laid out four principles for how these exchanges would take place. They are worth noting here now:

- Each distinct network should have to stand on its own, and no internal changes should be required to any such network to connect it to the Internet.
- Communications should be on a best-effort basis. If a packet didn't make it to the final destination, it should be retransmitted shortly from the source.
- Black boxes would be used to connect the networks; these would later be called gateways and routers. There should be no information retained by the gateways about the individual packets passing through them, thereby keeping them simple and avoiding complicated adaptation and recovery from various failure modes.
- There should be no global control at the operations level.

While the protocols that were developed based on these rules allowed for the massive growth in networking and the creation of the Internet as we know it today, they also sowed the seeds for the security problems. The writers of these ground rules did not imagine that anyone other than well-meaning academics and government scientists would use the Internet. It was for research purposes, for the exchange of ideas, not for commerce, where money would change hands, or for the purposes of controlling critical systems. Thus, it could be one network of networks, rather than separate networks for government, financial activity, etc. It was designed for thousands of researchers, not billions of users who did not know and trust each other.

Up to and through the 1990s, the Internet was almost universally seen as a force for good. Few of the Internet's boosters were willing to admit that the Internet was a neutral medium. It could easily be used to facilitate the free flow of communication between scientists and the creation of legitimate e-commerce, but could also allow terrorists to provide training tips to new recruits and to transmit the latest beheading out of Anbar Province on a web video. The Internet, much like the tribal areas of Pakistan or the tri-border region in South America, is not under the control of anyone and is therefore a place to which the lawless will gravitate.

Larry Roberts, who wrote the code for the first versions of the transmission protocol, realized that the protocols created an unsecure system, but he did not want to slow down the development of the new network and take the time to fix the software before deploying it. He had a simple answer for the concern. It was a small network. Rather than trying to write secure software to control the dissemination of information on the network, Roberts concluded that it would be far easier to secure the transmission lines by encrypting the links between each computer on the network. After all, the early routers were all in secure locations in government agencies and academic laboratories. If the information was secure as it traveled between two points on the network, that was all that really mattered. The problem was that the solution did not envision the expansion of the technology beyond the handful of sixty-odd computers that then made up the network. Trusted people ran all those sixty computers. A precondition for joining the network was that

you were a known entity committed to promoting scientific advancement. And with so few people, if anything bad got on the network, it would not be hard to get it off and to identify who had put it there.

Then Vint Cerf left ARPA and joined MCI. Vint is a friend, a friend with whom I fundamentally disagree about how the Internet should be secured. But Vint is one of those handful of people who can legitimately be called "a father of the Internet," so what he thinks on Internet issues usually counts for a lot more than what I say. Besides, Vint, who always wears a bow tie, is a charming guy, and he now works for Google, which urges us all not to be evil.

MCI (now part of AT&T) was the first major telecommunications company to lay down a piece of the Internet backbone and to take the technology out of the small network of government scientists and academics, offering it to corporations and even, through ISPs, to home users. Vint took the transmission protocol with him, introducing the security problem to a far larger audience and to a network that could not be secured through encrypting the links. No one really knew who was connecting to the MCI network.

There are bound to be vulnerabilities in anything so large. Today, it has grown so extensive that the Internet is running out of addresses. When the Internet was cobbled together, the inventors came up with a numbering system to identify every device that would connect to the network. They decided that all addresses had to be a 32-bit number, a number so large that it would allow for 4.29 billion addresses. Never did they imagine that we would need more than that.

As of last count, there are nearly 6.8 billion people living on the planet. On the current standard, that's more than one address for every two people. And today, that is not enough. As the West grows more dependent on the Internet, and as the Second and Third worlds expand their use, 4.29 billion addresses cannot possibly satisfy all the possible people and devices that will want to connect to the web. That the Internet is running out of addresses on its own may be a manageable problem. If we move quickly to converting to the IPv6 address standard, by the time we run out of IPv4 addresses, in about two years, most devices should be able to operate on the new standard. But step back for a moment and a cause for concern begins to emerge.

The Pentagon envisions a near-future scenario in which every soldier on the battlefield will be a hub in a network, and as many as a dozen devices carried by that soldier will be plugged into the network and require their own addresses. If you stroll through the appliance aisle at a high-end home-goods store, you will notice that many of the washing machines, dryers, dishwashers, stoves, and refrigerators are advertising that they can be controlled through the Internet. If you are at work and want the oven to be preheated to 425 degrees when you arrive home, you could log onto a webpage, access your oven, and set it to the right temperature from your desktop.

What all this means is that as we move beyond 4.29 billion internal web addresses, the degree to which our society will be dependent on the Internet, for everything from controlling our thermostats to defending our nation, is set to explode, and with it the security problem is only going to get worse. What this could mean in a real-world conflict is something that until recently most policy makers in the Pentagon were loath to think about. It means that if you can hack into things on the Internet, you might not just be able to steal money. You might be able to cause some real damage, including damage to our military. So exactly how is it that you can hack into things, and why is that possible?

Software and Hardware

Of the three things about cyberspace that make cyber war possible, the most important may be the flaws in the software and hardware. All of those devices on the Internet we just discussed (the computer terminals and laptops, the routers and switches, the e-mail and webpage servers, the data files) are made by a large number of companies. Often, separate companies make the software that run devices. In the U.S. market, most laptops are made by Dell, HP, and Apple. (A Chinese company, Lenovo, is making a dent after having bought IBM's laptop computer unit.) Most big routers are made by Cisco and Juniper, and now the Chinese company Huawei. Servers are made by HP, Dell, IBM, and a large number of others, depending upon their purpose. The software they run is written mainly by Microsoft, Oracle, IBM, and Apple, but also by many other companies. Although these are all U.S. corporations, the machines (and sometimes the code that runs on them) come from many places.

In *The World Is Flat,* Thomas Friedman traces the production of his Dell Inspiron 600m notebook from the phone order he places with a customer-service representative in India to its delivery at his front door in suburban Maryland. His computer was assembled at a factory in Penang, Malaysia. It was "co-designed" by a team of Dell engineers in Austin and notebook designers in Taiwan. Most of the hard work, the design of the motherboard, was done by the Taiwanese team. For the rest of the thirty key components, Dell used a string of different suppliers. Its Intel processor might have been made in the Philippines, Costa Rica, Malaysia, or China. Its memory might have been made in Korea by Samsung, or by lesser-known companies in Germany or Japan. Its graphic card came from one of two factories in China. The motherboard, while designed in Taiwan, could have been made at a factory there, but probably came from one of two plants in Mainland China. The keyboard came from one of three factories in China, two of them owned by Taiwanese companies. The wireless card was made either by an American-owned company in China or by a Chinese-owned company in Malaysia or in Taiwan. The hard drive was probably made by the American company Seagate at a factory in Singapore, or by Hitachi or Fujitsu in Thailand, or by Toshiba in the Philippines.

After all these parts were assembled at the factory in Malaysia, a digital image of the Windows XP operating system (and probably Windows Office) was burned onto the hard drive. The code for that software, amounting to more than 40 million lines for XP alone, was written at a dozen or more locations worldwide. After the system was imprinted with the software, the computer was packaged up, placed on a pallet with 150 similar computers, and flown on a 747 to Nashville. From there, the laptop was picked up by UPS and shipped to Friedman. All told, Friedman proudly reports that "the total supply chain for my computer, including suppliers of suppliers, involved about four hundred companies in North America, Europe, and primarily Asia."

Why does Friedman spend six pages in a book about geopolitics documenting the supply chain for the computer he wrote the book on? Because he believes that the supply chain that built his computer knits together the countries that were part of that process in a way that makes interstate conflicts of the sort we saw in the twentieth century less likely. Friedman admits this is an update of his "Golden Arches Theory of Conflict Prevention" from his previous book, which argued that two states that both had a McDonald's would not go to war with each other. This time, Friedman's tongue-in-cheek argument has a little more meat to it

than the hamburger theory. The supply chain is a microeconomic example of the trade that many theorists of international relations believe is so beneficial to the countries involved that even threatening war would not be worth the potential economic loss. Friedman looks at the averted crisis in 2004, when Taiwanese politicians running on a pro-independence platform were voted out of office. In his cute bumper-sticker-slogan way, Friedman observed that "Motherboards won over motherland," concluding that the status quo economic relationship was more valuable than independence to the Taiwanese voters.

Or maybe the Taiwanese voters just didn't want to end up dead after China invaded, which is what China more or less said it would do if Taiwan declared its independence. What Friedman sees as a force that makes conflict less likely, the supply chain for producing computers, may in fact make cyber warfare more likely, or at least make it more likely that the Chinese would win in any conflict. At any point in the supply chain that put together Friedman's computer (or your computer, or the Apple MacBook Pro that I am writing this book on), vulnerabilities were introduced, most accidentally, but probably some intentionally, that can make it both a target and a weapon in a cyber war.

Software is used as an intermediary between human and machine, to translate the human intention to find movie times online or read a blog, into something that a machine can understand. Computers really are just evolved electronic calculators. Early computer scientists realized that timed electrical pulses could be used to represent 1's and that the absence of a pulse could be used to represent 0's, like long and short bursts in Morse code. The base-10 numbers that humans use, because we have ten fingers, could be translated into this binary code that a machine could understand so that when, for instance, the 5 key on an early electronic calculator was depressed, it would close circuits that would send a pulse followed by a pause followed by another pulse in quick succession to represent the 1, 0, and 1 that make up the number 5 in a binary logic system.

All computers today are just evolutions of that same basic process. A simple e-mail message is converted into electric pulses that can be carried over copper wires and fiber-optic cables and then retranslated into a message readable to a human eye. To make that happen someone needed to provide instructions that a computer could understand. Those instructions are written in programming languages as computer code, and most people who write code make mistakes. The obvious ones get fixed, or else the computer program does not function as intended; but the less-obvious ones are often left in the code and can be exploited later to gain access. As computer systems have gotten faster, computer programs have grown more complex to take advantage of all the new speed and power. Windows 95 had less than 10 million lines of code. Windows XP, 40 million. Windows Vista, more than 50 million. In a little over a decade, the number of lines of code has grown by a factor of five, and with it the number of coding errors. Many of those coding errors allow hackers to make the software do something it was not supposed to, like let them in.

In order to manipulate popular software to do the wrong thing, like let you assume system administrator status, hackers design small applications, "applets," that are focused on specific software design or system configuration weaknesses and mistakes. Because computer crime is a big business, and getting ready to conduct cyber war is even well-funded, criminal hackers and cyber warriors are constantly generating new ways to trick systems. These hacker applications are called malware. On average in 2009, a new type or variant of malware was entering cyberspace every 2.2 seconds. Do the math. The

three or four big antivirus software companies have sophisticated networks to look for the new malware, but they find and issue a "fix" for about one in every ten pieces of malware. The fix is a piece of software designed to block the malware. By the time the fix gets to the antivirus company's customers, often days, and sometimes weeks, have gone by. During that time, companies, government departments, and home users are entirely vulnerable to the new malware. They won't even know if they have been hit by it.

Frequently the malware is sitting on innocent websites, waiting for you. Let's say you surf to the website of a Washington think tank to read their latest analysis of some important public policy issue. Think tanks are notorious for not having enough money and not giving enough attention to creating secure and safe websites. So, as you are reading about the latest machinations over health care or human rights in China, a little piece of malware is downloading itself onto your computer. You have no way of knowing, but now your new friend in Belarus is logging your every keystroke. What happens when you log into your bank account or to the Virtual Private Network of your employer, the Really Big Defense Company? You can probably guess.

The most common software error for years, and one of the easiest to explain, is something called "buffer overflow." Code for a webpage is supposed to be written in such a way that when a user comes to that webpage, the user can only enter a certain amount of data, like a user name and password. It's supposed to be like Twitter, a program where you can enter, say, no more than 140 characters. But if the code writer forgets to put in the symbols that limit the number of characters, then a user can put in more. Instead of just putting in a user name or password, you could enter entire lines of instruction code. Maybe you enter instructions to allow you to add an account. Think about those instructions overflowing the limited area where a public user is supposed to be able to add information and then those instructions falling into the application. The instruction code reads as if a systems administrator had entered it and—ping!—you are inside.

Software errors are not easily discovered. Even experts cannot usually visually identify coding errors or intentional vulnerabilities in a few lines of code, let alone in millions. There is now software that checks software, but it is far from able to catch all the glitches in millions of lines. Each line of that code had to be written by a computer programmer, and each additional line of code increased the number of bugs introduced into the software. In some cases, programmers actually put those bugs in intentionally. The most famous case, and one that illustrates a larger phenomenon, occurred when somebody at Microsoft dumped an entire airplane-simulation program inside the Excel 97 database software. Microsoft only discovered it when people started thanking the company for it. Programmers may do it for fun, for profit, or in the service of a competing company or foreign intelligence service; but whatever their motive, it is a nearly impossible task to ensure that a few lines of code allowing for unauthorized access through a "trapdoor" are kept out of such massive programs. The original Trojan Horse had hidden commandos; today we have hidden commands of malicious code. In the case of the Excel spreadsheet, you began by opening a new blank document, pressing F5, and when a reference box opened, you typed in "X97:L97" and pressed enter, then pressed tab. This took you to cell M97 on the spreadsheet. Then if you clicked on the chart wizard button while holding down the control and shift keys—ping!—you activated a flight-simulator program, which popped right up.

Sometimes developers of code leave behind secret trapdoors so they can get back into the code easily later on to update it. Sometimes, unknown to their company, they do it for less reputable reasons. And sometimes other people, like hackers and cyber warriors, do it so they can get into parts of a network where they are not authorized. Thus, when someone hacks into a software product under development (or later), they may not just be stealing a copy, they may be adding to it. Intentional trapdoors, as well as others that occur because of mistakes in code writing, sometimes allow a hacker to gain what is called "root." Hackers trade or sell each other "root kits." If you have "root access" to a software program or a network, you have all the permissions and authorities of the software's creator or the network's administrator. You can add software. You can add user accounts. You can do anything. And, importantly, you can erase any evidence that you were ever there. Think of that as a burglar who wipes away his fingerprints and then drags a broom behind him to the door, erasing his footprints.

Code developers may go one step further than just leaving an access point and insert a "logic bomb." The term encompasses a spectrum of software applications, but the idea is simple. In addition to leaving behind a trapdoor in a network so you can get back in easily, without setting off alarms and without needing an account, cyber warriors often leave behind a logic bomb so they don't have to take the time to upload it later on when they need to use it. A logic bomb in its most basic form is simply an eraser, it erases all the software on a computer, leaving it a useless hunk of metal. More advanced logic bombs could first order hardware to do something to damage itself, like ordering an electric grid to produce a surge that fries circuits in transformers, or causing an aircraft's control surfaces to go into the dive position. Then it erases everything, including itself.

America's national security agencies are now getting worried about logic bombs, since they seem to have found them all over our electric grid. There is a certain irony here, in that the U.S. military invented this form of warfare. One of the first logic bombs, and possibly the first incidence of cyber war, occurred before there even really was much of an Internet. In the early 1980s, the Soviet leadership gave their intelligence agency, the KGB, a shopping list of Western technologies they wanted their spies to steal for them. A KGB agent who had access to the list decided he would rather spend the rest of his days sipping wine in a Paris café than freezing in Stalingrad, so he turned the list over to the French intelligence service in exchange for a new life in France. France, which was part of the Western alliance, gave it to the U.S. Unaware that Western intelligence had the list, the KGB kept working its way down, stealing technologies from a host of foreign companies. Once the French gave the list to the CIA, President Reagan gave it the okay to help the Soviets with their technology needs, with a catch. The CIA started a massive program to ensure that the Soviets were able to steal the technologies they needed, but the CIA introduced a series of minor errors into the designs for things like stealth fighters and space weapons.

Weapons designs, however, were not at the top of the KGB's wish list. What Russia really needed was commercial and industrial technology, particularly for its oil and gas industry. In order to get the product from the massive reserves in Siberia to Russian and Western consumers, oil and gas had to be piped over thousands of miles. Russia lacked the technology for the automated pump and valve controls crucial to managing a pipeline thousands of miles long. They tried to buy it from U.S. companies, were refused, and so set their sights on stealing it from a Canadian firm. With the complicity of our northern neighbors, the CIA inserted malicious code into the software of the Canadian firm. When the Russians stole the code and used it to operate their pipeline, it worked just fine, at least initially. After a while, the new control software started to malfunction. In one segment of the pipeline, the software caused the pump on one end to pump at its maximum rate and the valve at the other end to close. The pressure buildup resulted in the most massive non-nuclear explosion ever recorded, over three kilotons.

If the Cold War with Russia heats up again, or if we were to go to war with China, this time it might be our adversaries who have the upper hand in cyber war. The United States' sophisticated arsenal of space-age weapons could be turned against us to devastating effect. Our air, land, and sea forces rely on networked technologies that are vulnerable to cyber weapons that China and other near peer adversaries have developed with the intention of eliminating our conventional superiority. The U.S. military is no more capable of operating without the Internet than Amazon.com would be. Logistics, command and control, fleet positioning, everything down to targeting, all rely on software and other Internet-related technologies. And all of it is just as insecure as your home computer, because it is all based on the same flawed underlying technologies and uses the same insecure software and hardware.

With the growth of outsourcing to countries like India and China that Friedman got so excited about, the likelihood that our peer competitors have been able to penetrate major software and hardware companies and insert such code into the software we rely on has only increased. In the world of computer science and networking, experts long thought that the two most ubiquitous operating-system codes (software that tells hardware what to do) were also the most badly written, or "buggy," computer code. They were Microsoft's Windows operating system for desktop and laptop computers, and Cisco's for large Internet routers. Both systems were proprietary, meaning not publicly available. You could buy the software as a finished product, but you could not get the underlying code. There were, however, several known instances in which Microsoft's security was compromised and the code stolen, giving the recipient the opportunity to identify the software errors and ways to exploit them.

I mentioned above (in chapter 2) that China had essentially blackmailed Microsoft into cooperating with it. China had announced that it would develop its own system based on Linux, called Red Flag, and said it would require that it be used instead of Microsoft. Soon Microsoft was bargaining with the Chinese government at the highest level, helped along by its consultant, Henry Kissinger. Microsoft dropped its price, gave the Chinese its secret code, and established a software research lab in Beijing (the lab is directly wired into Microsoft's U.S. headquarters). A deal was struck. It must have been a good deal: the President of China then visited Bill Gates at his home near Seattle. The Chinese government now uses Microsoft, but it is that special variation with a Chinese government encryption module. One former U.S. intelligence officer told us, "This may mean that no one can hack Windows easily to spy on China. It certainly does not mean that China is less able to hack Windows to spy on others."

What can be done to millions of lines of code can also be done with millions of circuits imprinted on computer chips inside computers, routers, and servers. Chips are the guts of a computer, like software in silicon. They can be customized, just like software. Most experts cannot look at a complicated computer chip and determine whether there is an extra piece here or there, a physical trapdoor. Computer chips were originally made in the U.S., although now they are mostly manufactured in Asia. The U.S.

government once had its own chip factory, called a "fab" (short for "fabrication facility"); however, the facility has not kept pace with technology and cannot manufacture the chips required for modern systems. Recently the world's second-largest chip manufacturer, AMD, announced its intentions to build the most advanced fab in the world in upstate New York. It will be partially government funded, but not by the U.S. government: AMD got a big investment from the United Arab Emirates.

It is not that the U.S. government is unaware of the problem of software and hardware being made globally. In fact, in his last year in office, President George W. Bush signed PDD-54, a secret document that outlines steps to be taken to defend the government better from cyber war. One of those programs is reported to be a "Supply Chain Security" initiative, but it will be difficult for the U.S. government to purchase only software and hardware made in the U.S. under secure conditions. Currently, it would be difficult to find any.

Machines Controlled from Cyberspace

Neither the vulnerabilities of Internet design nor the flaws in software and hardware quite explain how cyber warriors could make computers attack. How is it that some destructive hand can reach out from cyberspace into the real world and cause serious damage?

The answer stems from the rapid adoption of the Internet and cyberspace by industries in the U.S. in the 1990s. During that decade evangelical information-technology companies showed other corporations how they could save vast amounts of money by taking advantage of computer systems that could do things deep into their operations. Far beyond e-mail or word processing, these business practices involved automated controls, inventory monitoring, just-in-time delivery, database analytics, and limited applications of artificial-intelligence programs. One Silicon Valley CEO told me enthusiastically in the late 1990s how he had applied these techniques to his own firm. "Somebody wants to buy something, they go online to our site. They customize the product they want and hit BUY. Our system notifies the parts makers, plans to ship the parts to the assembly plant, and schedules assembly and delivery. At the assembly plant, robotic devices put the product together and put it in a box with a delivery label on it. We don't own the computer server that took the order, the parts plants, the assembly plant, or the delivery aircraft and trucks. It's all outsourced and it's all just-in-time delivery." What he owned was the research department, the design team, and some corporate overhead. At companies like his, and in the U.S. economy in general, profitability soared.

What made all of that possible was the deep penetration in the 1990s of information-technology systems into companies, into every department. In many industries, controls that were once manually activated were converted to digital processors. Picture the factory or plant of the twentieth century where some guy in a hard hat got a call from his supervisor telling him to go over and crank some round valve or change some setting. I can see it vividly, my father worked in a place like that. Today, in almost every industry, fewer people are required. Digital control systems monitor activity and send commands to engines, valves, switches, robotic arms, lights, cameras, doors, elevators, trains, and aircraft. Intelligent inventory systems monitor sales in real time and send out the orders to make and ship replacements, often without a human in the loop.

The conversion to digital control systems and computer-managed operations was quick and thorough. By the turn of the century, most of the old systems were retired, even from the role of "backup." Like Cortés burning his ships

after arriving in the New World, U.S. companies and government agencies built a new world in which there were only computer-based systems. When the computers fail, employees stand around doing nothing or go home. Try to find a typewriter and you will get the picture of this new reality.

Just as the Internet, and cyberspace in general, is replete with software and hardware problems and configuration shortcomings, so are the computer networks that run major corporations, from utilities to transportation to manufacturing. Computer networks are essential for companies or government agencies to operate. "Essential" is a word chosen with care, because it conveys the fact that we are dependent upon computer systems. Without them, nothing works. If they get erroneous data, systems may work, but they will do the wrong things.

Despite all the money spent on computer security systems, it is still very possible to insert erroneous data into networks. It can mean that systems shut down, or damage themselves, or damage something else, or send things or people to the wrong places. At 3:28 p.m. on June 11, 1999, a pipeline burst in Bellingham, Washington. Gasoline began spilling out into the creek below. The gas quickly extended well over a mile along the creek. Then it caught fire. Two ten-year-old boys playing along the stream were killed, as was an eighteen-year-old farther up the creek. The nearby municipal water-treatment plant was severely damaged by the fire. When the U.S. National Transportation Safety Board examined why the pipeline burst, it focused on "the performance and security of the supervisory control and data acquisition (SCADA) system." In other words, the software failed. The report does not conclude that in this case the explosion was intentionally caused by a hacker, but it is obvious from the analysis that pipelines like the one in Bellingham can be manipulated destructively from cyberspace.

The clearest example of the dependency and the vulnerability brought on by computer controls also happens to be the one system that everything else depends upon: the electric power grid.

As a result of deregulation in the 1990s, electric power companies were divided up into generating firms and transmission companies. They were also allowed to buy and sell power to each other anywhere within one of the three big power grids in North America. At the same time, they were, like every other company, inserting computer controls deep into their operations. Computer controls were also installed to manage the buying and selling, generation, and transmission. A SCADA system was already running each electric company's substations, transformers, and generators. That Supervisory Control and Data Acquisition system got and sent signals out to all of the thousands of devices on the company's grid. SCADAs are software programs, and most electric companies use one of a half dozen commercially available products.

These control programs send signals to devices to regulate the electric load in various locations. The signals are most often sent via internal computer network and sometimes by radio. Unfortunately, many of the devices also have other connections, multiple connections. One survey found that a fifth of the devices on the electric grid had wireless or radio access, 40 percent had connections to the company's internal computer network, and almost half had direct connections to the Internet. Many of the Internet connections were put in place to permit their manufacturers to do remote diagnostics.

Another survey found that at one very large electric company, 80 percent of the devices were connected to the corporate intranet, and there were, of course, connections from the intranet out to the public Internet. What that means is that if you can hack from the Internet to the intranet, you can give orders to devices on the electric grid, perhaps from some nice cyber café on the other side of the planet. Numerous audits of electric power companies by well-respected cyber security experts have found that this is all very doable. What sort of things might you do with controls to the grid?

In 2003, the so-called Slammer worm (big, successful computer malware attacks get their own names) got into and slowed controls on the power grid. A software glitch in a widely used SCADA system also contributed to the slowed controls. So when a falling tree created a surge in a line in Ohio, the devices that should have stopped a cascading effect did not do so until the blackout got to somewhere in southern New Jersey. The result was that eight states, two Canadian provinces, and 50 million people were without electricity, and without everything that needs electricity (such as the water system in Cleveland). The tree was the initiator, but the same effects could have been achieved by a command given over the control system by a hacker. In fact, in 2007 CIA expert Tom Donahue was authorized to tell a public audience of experts that the Agency was aware of instances when hackers had done exactly that. Although Tom didn't say where hackers had caused a blackout as part of a criminal scheme, it was later revealed that the incident took place in Brazil.

The 2003 blackout lasted a few long hours for most people, but even without anyone trying to prolong the effect it lasted four days in some places. In Auckland, New Zealand, in 1998 the damage from overloading power lines triggered a blackout and kept the city in the dark for five weeks. If a control system sends too much power down a high-tension line, the line itself can be destroyed and initiate a fire. In the process, however, the surge of power can overwhelm home and office surge protectors and fry electronic devices, computers to televisions to refrigerators, as happened recently in my rural county during a lightning storm.

The best example, however, of how computer commands can cause things to destroy themselves may be electric generators. Generators make electricity by spinning, and the number of times they spin per minute creates power in units expressed in a measurement called Hertz. In the United States and Canada, the generators on most subgrids spin at 60 Megahertz. When a generator is started, it is kept off the grid until it gets up to 60 MHz. If it is connected to the grid at another speed, or if its speed changes very much while on the grid, the power from all of the other generators on the grid spinning at 60 MHz will flow into the slower generator, possibly ripping off its turbine blades.

To test whether a cyber warrior could destroy a generator, a federal government lab in Idaho set up a standard control network and hooked it up to a generator. In the experiment, code-named Aurora, the test's hackers made it into the control network from the Internet and found the program that sends rotation speeds to the generator. Another keystroke and the generator could have severely damaged itself. Like so much else, the enormous generators that power the United States are manufactured when they are ordered, on the just-in-time delivery principle. They are not sitting around, waiting to be sold. If a big generator is badly damaged or destroyed, it is unlikely to be replaced for months.

Fortunately, the Federal Electric Regulatory Agency in 2008 finally required electric companies to adopt some specific cyber security measures and warned that it would fine companies for noncompliance up to one million dollars a day. No one has been fined yet. The companies have until sometime in 2010 to comply. Then the commission promises it will begin to inspect some facilities to determine if they are compliant. Unfortunately, President Obama's "Smart Grid" initiative will cause the electric grid to become even more wired, even more dependent upon computer network technology.

The same way that a hand can reach out from cyberspace and destroy an electric transmission line or generator, computer commands can derail a train or send freight cars to the wrong place, or cause a gas pipeline to burst. Computer commands to a weapon system may cause it to malfunction or shut off. What a cyber warrior can do, then, is to reach out from cyberspace, causing things to shut down or blow up, things like the power grid, or a thousand other critical systems, things like an opponent's weapons.

The design of the Internet, flaws in software and hardware, and allowing critical machines to be controlled from cyberspace, together, these three things make cyber war possible. But why haven't we fixed these problems by now?

Discussion Questions

1. Do you think that the threat of cyber war is real? Based on examples from the reading do you feel the threat is exaggerated or do you think that average people should be more concerned about it?

2. Have you yourself or anyone you know ever been a victim of a cyber attack? Think carefully about this. You may have been and not been aware of it. What are all the kind of attacks the authors discuss?

3. Based on the reading, do you think there is any way to make us safe from cyber attacks? Is the only safe option disconnecting critical systems? Before the Internet, all these systems functioned, so why couldn't we just do it that way again? Is it possible to take steps backward in technological development? Can you think of any examples?

4. The authors discuss Thomas Friedman's belief that the supply chains that knit the production of our computer hardware and software together reduce the possibility of conflict between nations; however, the authors believe that the supply chain may make cyber warfare *more* likely. Why do they conclude that? Which position do you feel is correct (perhaps they both are in different ways)? Why or why not?

5. Why do the authors say that the rapid adoption of the Internet by industries in the U.S. is the main thing that makes cyber warfare possible? Why did the industries do that? What benefits do they, and we, derive from it? Do the benefits outweigh the negatives?

 Supporting Activities

1. Watch the movie *The Interview* (2014) with James Franco and Seth Rogan. Having watched this movie, are you now worried that agents from North Korea might mess with your life? Investigate what happened before this movie was released and the consequences.

2. Explore the security options on your computer and on social media platforms like Facebook. Do you know how to find and adjust them?

3. Investigate and report on three major cyber attacks that have happened in the last 5 years.

 Additional Resources

1. View a timeline and history of the Internet at the web site of the Computer History Museum of Mountain View, California (http://www.computerhistory.org/internet_history/).

The World as Free-Fire Zone

In this article Fred Kaplan points out how the use of drone technology for targeted assassinations by the United States has become a topic of great controversy and debate, and a source of policy dispute within the government. However, before we develop new policies Kaplan cautions that we should understand the issues as well as possible. He sets out to puncture myths and to tease out the real issues from misinformed and misleading information.

Kaplan reviews the history of drone technology and shows how these tools came to be used by the military in their current capacity. Originally designed as an anti-tank weapon for Cold War applications against the Soviet Union, in 2001 the Predator drone was first equipped with a Hellfire missile and introduced into the new War on Terror. By 2009, the U.S. Air Force was training more drone-joystick pilots than airplane-cockpit pilots, the beginning of a new era.

The real controversy began when drones started hunting and killing people in countries in which the United States was not officially at war. Is this an act of war against those countries? The question is debatable and there are varying opinions about the effectiveness of drone warfare strategy. Some contend it is the most effective and safest way to bring terrorists to justice without large amounts of collateral damage or civilian casualties, while others say the anger in the countries where our drones are used generates more terrorists than it eliminates.

Fred M. Kaplan is an American author and Pulitzer Prize-winning journalist. His weekly "War Stories" column for *Slate* magazine covers international relations and U.S. foreign policy. He received a Ph.D. in political science from the Massachusetts Institute of Technology, and from 1978 to 1980 was a foreign and defense policy adviser to U.S. Congressman Les Aspin (D, Wisconsin). Prior to writing for *Slate*, Kaplan was a correspondent at the *Boston Globe*. He has also written for other publications, including *The New York Times*, *The Atlantic*, *The New Yorker*, and *Scientific American*. His 1983 book *The Wizards of Armageddon* won the Washington Monthly Political Book of the Year award.

The World as Free-Fire Zone

How drones made it easy for Americans to kill a particular person anywhere on the planet.

By Fred Kaplan on June 7, 2013

Editor's Note: This story relies upon anonymous sources who could not have spoken on the record without prosecution or other serious repercussions. The author revealed their identities to MIT Technology Review.

The unmanned aerial vehicle—the "drone," the very emblem of American high-tech weaponry—started out as a toy, the fusion of a model airplane and a lawn-mower engine. While its original purpose was to bust up Soviet tanks in the first volleys of World War III, it has evolved into the favored technology for targeted assassinations in the global war on terror. Its use has sparked a great debate—at first within the most secret parts of the government, but in recent months among the general public—over the tactics, strategy, and morality not only of drone warfare but of modern warfare in general.

But before this debate can go much further—before Congress or other branches of government can lay down meaningful standards or ask pertinent questions—distinctions must be drawn, myths punctured, real issues teased out from misinformed or misleading distractions.

A little history is helpful. The drone as we know it today was the brainchild of John Stuart Foster Jr., a nuclear physicist, former head of the Lawrence Livermore National Laboratory (then called the Lawrence Radiation Laboratory), and—in 1971, when the idea occurred to him—the director of defense research and engineering, the top scientific post in the Pentagon. Foster was a longtime model-airplane enthusiast, and one day he realized that his hobby could make for a new kind of weapon. His idea: take an unmanned, remote-controlled airplane, strap a camera to its belly, and fly it over enemy targets to snap pictures or shoot film; if possible, load it with a bomb and destroy the targets, too.

Two years later, the Defense Advanced Research Projects Agency (DARPA) built two prototypes based on Foster's concept, dubbed Praeire and Calere. Weighing 75 pounds and powered by a modified lawn-mower engine, each vehicle could stay aloft for two hours while hoisting a 28-pound payload.

Pentagon agencies design lots of prototypes; most of them never get off the drawing board. Foster's idea became a real weapon because it converged with a new defense doctrine. In the early-to-mid 1970s, the Soviet Union was beefing up its conventional military forces along the border between East and West Germany.

A decade earlier, U.S. policy was to deter an invasion of Western Europe by threatening to retaliate with nuclear weapons. But now, the Soviets had amassed their own sizable nuclear arsenal. If we nuked them, they could nuke us back. So DARPA commissioned a study to identify new technologies that might give the president "a variety of response options" in the event of a Soviet invasion, including "alternatives to massive nuclear destruction."

By the fall of 2009, the Air Force was training more drone-joystick pilots than airplane pilots. It was the start of a new era.

The study was led by Albert Wohlstetter, a former strategist at the RAND Corporation, who in the 1950s and '60s wrote highly influential briefings and articles on the nuclear balance of power. He pored over various projects that DARPA had on its books and figured that Foster's unmanned airplanes might fit the bill. In the previous few years, the U.S. military had developed a number of "precision-guided munitions"—products of the microprocessor revolution—that could land within a few meters of a target. Wohlstetter proposed putting the munitions on Foster's pilotless planes and using them to hit targets deep behind enemy lines— Soviet tank echelons, air bases, ports. In the past, these sorts of targets could have been destroyed only by nuclear weapons, but a small bomb that hits within a few feet of its target can do as much damage as a very large bomb (even a low-yield nuclear bomb) that misses its target by a few thousand feet.

By the end of the 1970s, DARPA and the U.S. Army had begun testing a new weapon called Assault Breaker, which was directly inspired by Wohlstetter's study. Soon, a slew of super-accurate weapons —guided by laser beams, radar emissions, millimeter waves, or, later (and more accurately), the signals of global positioning satellites—poured into the U.S. arsenal. The Army's

Assault Breaker was propelled by an artillery rocket; the first Air Force and Navy versions, called Joint Direct Attack Munitions (JDAMs), were carried under the wings, and launched from the cockpits, of manned fighter jets.

Something close to Foster's vision finally materialized in the mid-1990s, during NATO's air war over the Balkans, with an unmanned aerial vehicle (UAV) called the Predator. It could loiter for 24 hours at an altitude of 25,000 feet, carrying a 450-pound payload. In its first incarnation, it was packed only with video and communications gear. The digital images taken by the camera were beamed to a satellite and then transmitted to a ground station thousands of miles away, where operators controlled the drone's flight path with a joystick while watching its real-time video stream on a monitor.

In February 2001, the Pentagon and CIA conducted the first test of a modified Predator, which carried not only a camera but also a laser-guided Hellfire missile. The Air Force mission statement for this armed UAV noted that it would be ideal for hitting "fleeting and perishable" targets. In an earlier era, this phrase would have meant destroying tanks on a battlefield. In the opening phase of America's new war on terror, it meant hunting and killing jihadists, especially Osama bin Laden and his lieutenants in al-Qaeda.

And so a weapon designed at the height of the Cold War to impede a Soviet armor assault on the plains of Europe evolved into a device for killing bands of stateless terrorists—or even an individual terrorist—in the craggy mountains of South Asia. In this sense, drones have hovered over U.S. military policy for more than three decades, the weapons and the policy shifting in tandem over time.

A War without Boundaries

How this came about is another far-from-inevitable story. The rise of the drone met serious resistance from one powerful quarter: the senior officer corps of the United States Air Force, the same organization that developed the weapon. The dominant culture in each of the armed services—the traits that are valued, the kinds of officers who get promoted—is shaped by its big-ticket weapons systems. Thus, from 1947 to 1981, every Air Force chief of staff rose through the ranks as a nuclear bombardier in Strategic Air Command. For the next quarter-century, as spending on conventional forces soared, every chief of staff had been a fighter pilot in Tactical Air Command.

That's where things stood in 2003, when President George W. Bush ordered the invasion of Iraq. As liberation became an occupation, which sparked an insurgency and then a sectarian civil war, U.S. commanders on the ground requested support from those shiny new Predator drones. The most lethal threat to American soldiers and Marines was the improvised explosive device, or roadside bomb. A drone's camera in the sky could see an insurgent planting the IED and follow him back to his hideout. But drones (slow, unmanned hovering planes) were anathema to the dominant Air Force culture (which cherished fast, manned jet fighters). So the Air Force generals turned down or ignored the Army and Marine commanders' pleas for more drones.

The most common criticism is that drones often wind up killing civilians. This is true, but it's hardly unique to drones.

All this changed in 2006, when Bush named Robert Gates to replace Donald Rumsfeld as secretary of defense. Gates came into the Pentagon with one goal: to clean up the mess in Iraq. He was shocked that the generals in the three big services cared more about high-tech weapons for the wars of the future than the needs of the war they were fighting. He was particularly appalled by the Air Force generals' hostility toward drones. Gates boosted production; the generals slowed down delivery. He accelerated delivery; they held up deployment. He fired the Air Force chief of staff, General T. Michael Moseley (ostensibly for some other act of malfeasance but really because of his resistance to UAVs), and appointed in his place General Norton Schwartz, who had risen as a gunship and cargo-transport pilot in special operations forces. Just before his promotion, Schwartz had been head of the U.S. Transportation Command—that is, he was in charge of rushing supplies to soldiers and Marines. As the new chief, Schwartz placed high priority on shipping drones to the troops in Iraq—and over the next few years, he turned the drone-joystick pilots into an elite cadre of the Air Force.

By the fall of 2009, toward the end of Barack Obama's first year as president, the Air Force was training more drone-joystick pilots than airplane-cockpit pilots. It was the start of a new era, not only for Air Force culture but also for the American way of war.

That year, 2009, saw not just a surge in U.S. drone strikes—in part because more drones were available and the institutional resistance to them had evaporated—but also a shift in where those strikes took place. There was nothing politically provocative about drones in Iraq or Afghanistan. They were weapons of war, used mainly for close air support of U.S. ground troops in countries where those troops were fighting wars. The controversy—which persists today—began when drones started hunting and killing specific people in countries where the United States was not officially at war.

These strikes took place mainly in Pakistan and Yemen. Pakistan was serving as a sanctuary for Taliban fighters in neighboring Afghanistan; Yemen was emerging as the center of a new wing of al-Qaeda in the Arabian Peninsula. Bush had ordered a few strikes in those countries: in fact, the first drone strike outside a formal war zone took place in Yemen, on November 3, 2002, against an al-Qaeda leader who a few years earlier had helped plan the attack on the USS *Cole*. Bush also launched 48 drone strikes in the Waziristan region of Pakistan, along the mountainous border with Afghanistan—36 of them during his last year in office.

Obama, who had pledged during the 2008 presidential campaign to get out of Iraq and deeper into Afghanistan, accelerated this trend, launching 52 drone strikes on Pakistani territory just in his first year. In 2010 he more than doubled the number of these strikes, to 122. Then, the next year, the number fell off, to 73. In 2012 it declined further, to 48—which still equaled the total number of strikes in all eight years of Bush's presidency. In a contrary shift, 2012 was also the year when the number of drone strikes soared in Yemen, from a mere handful to 54.

These strikes have provoked violent protest in those countries, alienating even those who'd previously felt no affection for jihadists and, in some cases, provided some support for the United States. At home, a political and legal debate rages over the wisdom and propriety of drone strikes as a tool in the war on terror.

Heightening the controversy is the fact that everything about these strikes outside war zones—including, until recently, their occurrence—is secret. Drone strikes in Iraq and Afghanistan, like all other military operations, have been conducted by the Defense Department. But drone strikes elsewhere are covert operations conducted by the Central Intelligence Agency, which operates in the dark (even congressional oversight is limited to the members of the select intelligence committees) and under a different, more permissive legal authority (Title 50 of the U.S. Code, not the Defense Department's Title 10).

Discussion Questions

1. Do you feel that the use of drones and other robots in warfare is ethical? Why or why not?
2. Do you think the use of drones by the U.S. in countries where we are not at war represents an act of war? Why or why not? How is it different than flying our manned airplanes into another country's airspace? How would you feel if Mexico used drones in Texas to hunt down drug cartel criminals? How is that different than the United States using drones in Yemen to assassinate terrorists?
3. Do you think that the use of robots in warfare will increase in the future? What would be the implications to the nature of warfare? How will the situation be impacted when other countries acquire drone technology? In the past, what happened as additional countries developed nuclear weapons? How does that example differ from the example of drones?
4. What do you think might be the effect on soldiers trained to kill using remote robots? How would you feel about using such technology if you were in the military?

 Supporting Activities

1. Watch the movie *Good Kill* (2014) starring Ethan Hawke. Write a short review of the film, commenting on its themes and messages. Is it an effective film? Why or why not?
2. Watch the video *Future Combat Systems* on YouTube: https://www.youtube.com/watch?v=YjsychklJBg.
3. To see many current and future uses of drones visit the *Popular Mechanics* website: http://www.popularmechanics.com/the-future-of-drones/.

 Additional Resources

1. See the full text of the 9-11 Commission Report (available: http://www.9-11commission.gov/report/911Report.pdf).
2. Check out these two on-line articles, *The Coming Robot Army* (http://www.wesjones.com/robot.htm#Title) and *The Drones Come Home* (http://ngm.nationalgeographic.com/2013/03/unmanned-flight/horgan-text).
3. Watch the popular movie *Fat Man and Little Boy* (1989), a fictionalized account of the development of the first atomic bomb via the Manhattan Project. For a detailed account of the Manhattan Project, view the U.S. Department of Energy Office of History and Heritage Resources web site (https://www.osti.gov/opennet/manhattan-project-history/index.htm).
4. Visit the Stockholm International Peace Research Institute for comprehensive analyses of worldwide military expenditures, the various categories of military weapons, and the development of nonproliferation agreements (http://www.sipri.org/).
5. The phrase "military industrial complex" is most often associated with the farewell speech of President Dwight D. Eisenhower on January 17, 1961. View footage of this powerful message on YouTube at: http://www.youtube.com/watch?v=8y06NSBBRtY.
6. See the history of military spending at: http://www.globalissues.org/print/article/75#WorldMilitarySpending.

References

Diamond, J. (1999). *Guns, germs and steel: The fate of human societies*. New York, NY: W. W. Norton & Company, Inc.

Kubrick, S. (Producer), & Kubrick, S. (Director). (1968). 2001: *A Space Odyssey* [Motion picture]. UK: MGM.

Martin, R. (2009). Uranium is so last century—enter thorium, the new green nuke. *Wired*. Retrieved from http://www.wired.com/2009/12/ff_new_nukes/

Rybczynski, W. (1983) Taming the tiger: *The struggle to control technology*. New York, NY: Viking Press.

Tse-tung, M. (1971). *Selected works of Mao Tse-tung: Talks with responsible comrades at various places during provincial tour*. Retrieved from https://www.marxists.org/reference/archive/mao/selected-works/volume-9/mswv9_88.htm

White, L. Jr. (1962). Medieval technology and social change. Oxford: Oxford University Press.

Perspectives on Workplace and Leisure Technologies

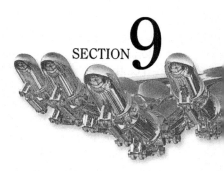

Ahhhh…. the dream of all hard-working people everywhere: a job where you don't have to work hard and still make a lot of money. This has, perhaps, been the dream of all people since the advent of what Lewis Mumford (1965), in his essay *Technics and the Nature of Man*, called the Megamachine, the hierarchical specialized society created by the first major human civilizations. In these first civilizations, the development of a permanent nonworking elite was created for the first time. In hunter-gatherer societies all members of the society share the work (although the roles tend to be gender divided, with the males hunting and the females gathering). It is the conventional wisdom, expressed by authors like Jared Diamond (1999) in his Pulitzer-prize winning polemic on the origins of technology *Guns, Germs and Steel*, that it is only when a society develops advanced agriculture, thereby creating a food surplus, that work specialization can occur. Since not all members need be involved in the production and/or gathering of food, a society can develop a leisure class, a permanent priesthood, and a ruling class that is free from labor, such as the Pharaohs of ancient Egypt. Ever since that time, work, for the vast majority of humanity, has been for the lesser classes and the value of work has been demeaned.

Mills (1951), in *White Collar: The American Middle Class*, writes that ancient Greeks believed that mechanical labor "brutalized the mind and made man unfit for virtuous pursuits" (p.1). Hence, such labor was only suitable for "slaves and other menials" (p.1). To this day manual labor is seen as a demeaning profession, something suitable for only the uneducated or for marginalized members of society such as migrant workers and other "untouchable" castes. How often have we heard in the debate over the need for farm laborers in agriculture that "Americans" will not do *that* type of work? Frederick Winslow Taylor, the creator of Scientific Management—the dominant management paradigm of the twentieth century that replaced artisans and artisan knowledge on the factory floor with unskilled laborers who did menial tasks derived from the analysis of artisan knowledge by management—famously wrote in *The Principles of Scientific Management*:

> Now one of the very first requirements for a man who is fit to handle pig iron as a regular occupation is that he shall be so stupid and so phlegmatic that he more nearly resembles in his mental make-up the ox than any other type. The man who is mentally alert and intelligent is for this very reason entirely unsuited to what would, for him, be the grinding monotony of work of this character. Therefore, the workman who is best suited to handling pig iron is unable to understand the real science of doing this class of work. (Taylor, 1997[1911], p. 59)

Modern technology was heralded as a means of freeing all of us from such grinding monotony. No longer would we have to haul pig iron or wash clothes—a machine would do that for us. During the nineteenth century the development of agricultural machinery eliminated the need for slaves, and a machine defeated and made obsolete the likes of John Henry, the legendary steel-driving railroad worker. Automated technology, it was thought, would free people to pursue more artistic and erudite pursuits, thus ushering in a golden age of humanity, full of leisure and contemplation, just as the Greeks had imagined. And yet, in spite of ever more sophisticated tools to perform labor for us, we seem busier than ever. In the most technologically developed countries, people complain of sleep deprivation, and complain that there is no longer time for family meals. Microwave ovens cannot seem to cook our food fast enough. Indeed, many people eschew cooking entirely because they simply do not have the time, and instead resort to "fast" food.

If machines were supposed to free us from manual drudgery (which they have to a large extent), then where has all the time gone? As Volti (2009) pointed out in his book *Society and Technological Change,* the Kung hunter-gatherers have a great deal of leisure time, which they devote to play and ritual. Mumford (1965) also noted the rich ritualistic and spiritual life of hunter-gatherer societies. So the apparent contradiction is created that the more technologically advanced societies, with automation to reduce human labor, paradoxically seem to have less time for play and ritual than do the less technologically advanced hunter-gatherer societies. Nevertheless, at the same time, it is estimated that the average American watches up to five hours of television a day (Nielsen Company, 2014). So perhaps we do have the time, but as Marshall McLuhan (1964) pointed out in *Understanding Media: The Extensions of Man,* the

flickering magic of the TV mesmerizes us into inactivity, essentially sucking time out of our day, so that at the end we wonder again, where has all the time gone? And where have all the jobs gone? Surprisingly, the automation that was supposed to free us from the drudgery of work is now implicated in freeing us from our jobs, which most of us still need to make a living. David Rottman (2013), an editor of MIT *Technology Review*, in *How Technology is Destroying Jobs* (the first article in this section), points out that throughout U.S. history increases in productivity led to a comparable increase in the number of jobs. Yet starting in 2000 those two trends started to diverge, so that by 2012 there was economic growth with no parallel increase in employment.

Historically, workers have reacted against automation replacing their jobs. Machine-breaking has been a tradition among artisans since the middle ages. Some believe the word sabotage itself derives from the Netherlands of the fifteenth century, when workers would throw their sabots (wooden shoes) into the wooden gears of the textile looms to break the cogs. This revolt against automation reached its apex during the beginning of the Industrial Revolution in the early nineteenth century, with the ascension of the Luddite rebellion in the English midlands. Named after the mythical "General Ludd," Luddites were mobs of textile workers who attacked and destroyed the automated machinery of the rapidly evolving textile industry (such as the spinning jenny, a wool-spinning machine that textile workers saw as a threat to their jobs). To this day, "Luddite" is a name given to people opposed to technological development.

Despite Rottman's assertion that machines are replacing workers, there are counter examples. Volti (2009) points out that in Japan, the country with the most developed automated production technologies, many firms have taken out their machines and brought back people. People are more available, able to learn faster, take up less space, and are less expensive than running a completely automated production facility. Another development from Japan in the 1970s, when the Japanese began to out-compete European and American companies, was the concept of Total Quality Management (TQM), which was to replace the dominant paradigm of Scientific Management. In Kaoru Ishikawa's *What Is Total Quality Control? The Japanese Way* (1981), he pointed out that the way to ensure quality in manufacturing was to have all workers understand and be invested in the entire process, directly opposed to Taylor's belief that workers need only know the minor tasks that management assigns them. The second reading in this section, *From Ford to Dell: Mass Production to Mass Customization* by Roger Alcaly, explores how some major companies have historically dealt with this intersection of workers and technology. Both these readings explore this basic question of how the technology we create to help us do our work affects the definition and quality of work, as well as the value of the individual.

How Technology is Destroying Jobs

The basic premise put forth in this article is one expressed by Erik Brynjolsson, a professor at the MIT Sloan School of Management, and his associate Andrew McAfee. They believe that rapid technological change, in the form of robots and computerized automation, has been destroying jobs faster than it has been creating them. In the past in the United States, there had always been a positive correlation between increased productivity, employment, and rising incomes. Since the turn of the twenty-first century, this has not been true.

However, as with all theories, not all agree. Other economists are not convinced that such a connection can be made, nor even that there has been a great increase in productivity, because the science of economics is notorious for having a various number of disputed indices for monitoring economic trends. Many simply think the lack of job and wage growth is due to an overall sluggish economy and that there is not nearly enough solid evidence to link it conclusively to a cause and effect relationship between automation and job loss. Autor and Dorn (2014) cite another phenomenon which they attribute to technology: the hollowing-out of the middle class, because technology has taken over many of the middle management jobs associated with clerical and accounting services, leaving only high-end very technical jobs, or lower-end service type jobs (like janitors). So the total number of jobs is not being affected, but the kind of jobs available is. Throughout history new technologies have always caused shifts in the workplace, and these usually start with a loss of obsolete jobs, but the loss is temporary as new jobs created by the new technologies emerge. The question is whether this current technological manifestation is somehow fundamentally different.

To explore this question Rotman reviews many of the new automation technologies and how they interact with the workers and businesses that utilize them. There are a number of competing factors, not the least of which is that automation helps some companies survive that would otherwise fail without the automated help, preserving the jobs those companies do provide.

Ultimately, the divergent views seem to agree on one thing, that whatever the cause, the current economic transition is causing a good deal of pain to a large number of people. "It's one of the dirty secrets of economics: technological progress does grow the economy and create wealth, but there is no economic law that says everyone will benefit."

David Rotman is the editor of *MIT Technology Review*. He supervises editorial content for both the print magazine and the web site. A science and business journalist, he has written extensively on chemistry, biotechnology, materials science, and environmental issues. He joined *MIT Technology Review* in January 1998 as a senior editor covering nanotechnology. Before joining *Technology Review*, Rotman was managing senior editor at *Chemical Week* magazine in New York City, where he supervised coverage of technology, research, and environmental issues. He has a BS degree from the University of Massachusetts in Amherst.

How Technology Is Destroying Jobs

Given his calm and reasoned academic demeanor, it is easy to miss just how provocative Erik Brynjolfsson's contention really is. Brynjolfsson, a professor at the MIT Sloan School of Management, and his collaborator and coauthor Andrew McAfee have been arguing for the last year and a half that impressive advances in computer technology—from improved industrial robotics to automated translation services—are largely behind the sluggish employment growth of the last 10 to 15 years. Even more ominous for workers, the MIT academics foresee dismal prospects for many types of jobs as these powerful new technologies are increasingly adopted not only in manufacturing, clerical, and retail work but in professions such as law, financial services, education, and medicine.

That robots, automation, and software can replace people might seem obvious to anyone who's worked in automotive manufacturing or as a travel agent. But Brynjolfsson and McAfee's claim is more troubling and controversial. They believe that rapid technological change has been destroying jobs faster than it is creating them, contributing to the stagnation of median income and the growth of inequality in the United States. And, they suspect, something similar is happening in other technologically advanced countries.

Perhaps the most damning piece of evidence, according to Brynjolfsson, is a chart that only an economist could love. In economics, productivity—the amount of economic value created for a given unit of input, such as an hour of labor—is a crucial indicator of growth and wealth creation. It is a measure of progress. On the chart Brynjolfsson likes to show, separate lines represent productivity and total employment in the United States. For years after World War II, the two lines closely tracked each other, with increases in jobs corresponding to increases in productivity. The pattern is clear: as businesses generated more value from their workers, the country as a whole became richer, which fueled more economic activity and created even more jobs. Then, beginning in 2000, the lines diverge; productivity continues to rise robustly, but employment suddenly wilts.

By 2011, a significant gap appears between the two lines, showing economic growth with no parallel increase in job creation. Brynjolfsson and McAfee call it the "great decoupling." And Brynjolfsson says he is confident that technology is behind both the healthy growth in productivity and the weak growth in jobs.

It's a startling assertion because it threatens the faith that many economists place in technological progress. Brynjolfsson and McAfee still believe that technology boosts productivity and makes societies wealthier, but they think that it can also have a dark side: technological progress is eliminating the need for many types of jobs and leaving the typical worker worse off than before. Brynjolfsson can point to a second chart indicating that median income is failing to rise even as the gross domestic product soars. "It's the great paradox of our era," he says. "Productivity is at record levels, innovation has never been faster, and yet at the same time, we have a falling median income and we have fewer jobs. People are falling behind because technology is advancing so fast and our skills and organizations aren't keeping up."

Brynjolfsson and McAfee are not Luddites. Indeed, they are sometimes accused of being too optimistic about the extent and speed of recent digital advances. Brynjolfsson says they began writing *Race Against the Machine*, the 2011 book in which they laid out much of their argument, because they wanted to explain the economic benefits of these new technologies (Brynjolfsson spent much of the 1990s sniffing out evidence that information technology was boosting rates of productivity). But it became clear to them that the same technologies making many jobs safer, easier, and more productive were also reducing the demand for many types of human workers.

Anecdotal evidence that digital technologies threaten jobs is, of course, everywhere.

Robots and advanced automation have been common in many types of manufacturing for decades. In the United States and China, the world's manufacturing powerhouses, fewer people work in manufacturing today than in 1997, thanks at least in part to automation. Modern automotive plants, many of which were transformed by industrial robotics in the 1980s, routinely use machines that autonomously weld and paint body parts—tasks that were once handled by humans. Most recently, industrial robots like Rethink Robotics' Baxter (see "The Blue-Collar Robot," May/June 2013), more flexible and far cheaper than their predecessors, have been introduced to perform simple jobs for small manufacturers in a variety of sectors. The website of a Silicon Valley startup called Industrial Perception features a video of the robot it has designed for use in warehouses picking up and throwing boxes like a bored elephant. And such sensations as Google's driverless car suggest what automation might be able to accomplish someday soon.

A less dramatic change, but one with a potentially far larger impact on employment, is taking place in clerical work and professional services. Technologies like the Web, artificial intelligence, big data, and improved analytics—all made possible by the ever increasing availability of cheap computing power and storage capacity—are automating many routine tasks. Countless traditional white-collar jobs, such as many in the post office and in customer service, have disappeared. W. Brian Arthur, a visiting researcher at the Xerox Palo Alto Research Center's intelligence systems lab and a former economics professor at Stanford University, calls it the "autonomous economy." It's far more subtle than the idea of robots and automation doing human jobs, he says: it involves "digital processes talking to other digital processes and creating new processes," enabling us to do

many things with fewer people and making yet other human jobs obsolete.

It is this onslaught of digital processes, says Arthur, that primarily explains how productivity has grown without a significant increase in human labor. And, he says, "digital versions of human intelligence" are increasingly replacing even those jobs once thought to require people. "It will change every profession in ways we have barely seen yet," he warns.

McAfee, associate director of the MIT Center for Digital Business at the Sloan School of Management, speaks rapidly and with a certain awe as he describes advances such as Google's driverless car. Still, despite his obvious enthusiasm for the technologies, he doesn't see the recently vanished jobs coming back. The pressure on employment and the resulting inequality will only get worse, he suggests, as digital technologies—fueled with "enough computing power, data, and geeks"— continue their exponential advances over the next several decades. "I would like to be wrong," he says, "but when all these science-fiction technologies are deployed, what will we need all the people for?"

New Economy?

But are these new technologies really responsible for a decade of lackluster job growth? Many labor economists say the data are, at best, far from conclusive. Several other plausible explanations, including events related to global trade and the financial crises of the early and late 2000s, could account for the relative slowness of job creation since the turn of the century. "No one really knows," says Richard Freeman, a labor economist at Harvard University. That's because it's very difficult to "extricate" the effects of technology from other macroeconomic effects, he says. But he's skeptical that technology would change a wide range of business sectors fast enough to explain recent job numbers.

Employment trends have polarized the workforce and hollowed out the middle class.

David Autor, an economist at MIT who has extensively studied the connections between jobs and technology, also doubts that technology could account for such an abrupt change in total employment. "There was a great sag in employment beginning in 2000. Something did change," he says. "But no one knows the cause." Moreover, he doubts that productivity has, in fact, risen robustly in the United States in the past decade (economists can disagree about that statistic because there are different ways of measuring and weighing economic inputs and outputs). If he's right, it raises the possibility that poor job growth could be simply a result of a sluggish economy. The sudden slowdown in job creation "is a big puzzle," he says, "but there's not a lot of evidence it's linked to computers."

To be sure, Autor says, computer technologies are changing the types of jobs available, and those changes "are not always for the good." At least since the 1980s, he says, computers have increasingly taken over such tasks as bookkeeping, clerical work, and repetitive production jobs in manufacturing—all of which typically provided middle-class pay. At the same time, higher-paying jobs requiring creativity and problem-solving skills, often aided by computers, have proliferated. So have low-skill jobs: demand has increased for restaurant workers, janitors, home health aides, and others doing service work that is nearly impossible to automate. The result, says Autor, has been a "polarization" of the workforce and a "hollowing out" of the middle class—something that has been happening in numerous industrialized countries for the last several decades. But "that is very different from saying technology is affecting the total number of jobs," he adds. "Jobs can change a lot without

there being huge changes in employment rates."

What's more, even if today's digital technologies are holding down job creation, history suggests that it is most likely a temporary, albeit painful, shock; as workers adjust their skills and entrepreneurs create opportunities based on the new technologies, the number of jobs will rebound. That, at least, has always been the pattern. The question, then, is whether today's computing technologies will be different, creating long-term involuntary unemployment.

At least since the Industrial Revolution began in the 1700s, improvements in technology have changed the nature of work and destroyed some types of jobs in the process. In 1900, 41 percent of Americans worked in agriculture; by 2000, it was only 2 percent. Likewise, the proportion of Americans employed in manufacturing has dropped from 30 percent in the post—World War II years to around 10 percent today—partly because of increasing automation, especially during the 1980s.

While such changes can be painful for workers whose skills no longer match the needs of employers, Lawrence Katz, a Harvard economist, says that no historical pattern shows these shifts leading to a net decrease in jobs over an extended period. Katz has done extensive research on how technological advances have affected jobs over the last few centuries—describing, for example, how highly skilled artisans in the mid-19th century were displaced by lower-skilled workers in factories. While it can take decades for workers to acquire the expertise needed for new types of employment, he says, "we never have run out of jobs. There is no long-term trend of eliminating work for people. Over the long term, employment rates are fairly stable. People have always been able to create new jobs. People come up with new things to do."

Still, Katz doesn't dismiss the notion that there is something different about today's digital technologies—something that could affect an even broader range of work. The question, he says, is whether economic history will serve as a useful guide. Will the job disruptions caused by technology be temporary as the workforce adapts, or will we see a science-fiction scenario in which automated processes and robots with superhuman skills take over a broad swath of human tasks? Though Katz expects the historical pattern to hold, it is "genuinely a question," he says. "If technology disrupts enough, who knows what will happen?"

Dr. Watson

To get some insight into Katz's question, it is worth looking at how today's most advanced technologies are being deployed in industry. Though these technologies have undoubtedly taken over some human jobs, finding evidence of workers being displaced by machines on a large scale is not all that easy. One reason it is difficult to pinpoint the net impact on jobs is that automation is often used to make human workers more efficient, not necessarily to replace them. Rising productivity means businesses can do the same work with fewer employees, but it can also enable the businesses to expand production with their existing workers, and even to enter new markets.

Take the bright-orange Kiva robot, a boon to fledgling e-commerce companies. Created and sold by Kiva Systems, a startup that was founded in 2002 and bought by Amazon for $775 million in 2012, the robots are designed to scurry across large warehouses, fetching racks of ordered goods and delivering the products to humans who package the orders. In Kiva's large demonstration warehouse and assembly facility at its headquarters outside Boston, fleets of robots move about with seemingly endless energy:

some newly assembled machines perform tests to prove they're ready to be shipped to customers around the world, while others wait to demonstrate to a visitor how they can almost instantly respond to an electronic order and bring the desired product to a worker's station.

A warehouse equipped with Kiva robots can handle up to four times as many orders as a similar unautomated warehouse, where workers might spend as much as 70 percent of their time walking about to retrieve goods. (Coincidentally or not, Amazon bought Kiva soon after a press report revealed that workers at one of the retailer's giant warehouses often walked more than 10 miles a day.)

Despite the labor-saving potential of the robots, Mick Mountz, Kiva's founder and CEO, says he doubts the machines have put many people out of work or will do so in the future. For one thing, he says, most of Kiva's customers are e-commerce retailers, some of them growing so rapidly they can't hire people fast enough. By making distribution operations cheaper and more efficient, the robotic technology has helped many of these retailers survive and even expand. Before founding Kiva, Mountz worked at Webvan, an online grocery delivery company that was one of the 1990s dot-com era's most infamous flameouts. He likes to show the numbers demonstrating that Webvan was doomed from the start; a $100 order cost the company $120 to ship. Mountz's point is clear: something as mundane as the cost of materials handling can consign a new business to an early death. Automation can solve that problem.

Meanwhile, Kiva itself is hiring. Orange balloons—the same color as the robots—hover over multiple cubicles in its sprawling office, signaling that the occupants arrived within the last month. Most of these new employees are software engineers: while the robots are the company's poster boys, its lesser-known innovations lie in the complex algorithms that guide the robots' movements and determine where in the warehouse products are stored. These algorithms help make the system adaptable. It can learn, for example, that a certain product is seldom ordered, so it should be stored in a remote area.

Though advances like these suggest how some aspects of work could be subject to automation, they also illustrate that humans still excel at certain tasks—for example, packaging various items together. Many of the traditional problems in robotics—such as how to teach a machine to recognize an object as, say, a chair—remain largely intractable and are especially difficult to solve when the robots are free to move about a relatively unstructured environment like a factory or office.

Techniques using vast amounts of computational power have gone a long way toward helping robots understand their surroundings, but John Leonard, a professor of engineering at MIT and a member of its Computer Science and Artificial Intelligence Laboratory (CSAIL), says many familiar difficulties remain. "Part of me sees accelerating progress; the other part of me sees the same old problems," he says. "I see how hard it is to do anything with robots. The big challenge is uncertainty." In other words, people are still far better at dealing with changes in their environment and reacting to unexpected events.

For that reason, Leonard says, it is easier to see how robots could work *with* humans than on their own in many applications. "People and robots working together can happen much more quickly than robots simply replacing humans," he says. "That's not going to happen in my lifetime at a massive scale. The semiautonomous taxi will still have a driver."

One of the friendlier, more flexible robots meant to work with humans is Rethink's Baxter. The creation of Rodney Brooks, the company's founder, Baxter needs minimal training to perform simple tasks like picking up objects and moving them to a box. It's meant for use in relatively small manufacturing facilities where conventional industrial robots would cost too much and pose too much danger to workers. The idea, says Brooks, is to have the robots take care of dull, repetitive jobs that no one wants to do.

It's hard not to instantly like Baxter, in part because it seems so eager to please. The "eyebrows" on its display rise quizzically when it's puzzled; its arms submissively and gently retreat when bumped. Asked about the claim that such advanced industrial robots could eliminate jobs, Brooks answers simply that he doesn't see it that way. Robots, he says, can be to factory workers as electric drills are to construction workers: "It makes them more productive and efficient, but it doesn't take jobs."

The machines created at Kiva and Rethink have been cleverly designed and built to work with people, taking over the tasks that the humans often don't want to do or aren't especially good at. They are specifically designed to enhance these workers' productivity. And it's hard to see how even these increasingly sophisticated robots will replace humans in most manufacturing and industrial jobs anytime soon. But clerical and some professional jobs could be more vulnerable. That's because the marriage of artificial intelligence and big data is beginning to give machines a more humanlike ability to reason and to solve many new types of problems.

Even if the economy is only going through a transition, it is an extremely painful one for many.

In the tony northern suburbs of New York City, IBM Research is pushing super-smart computing into the realms of such professions as medicine, finance, and customer service. IBM's efforts have resulted in Watson, a computer system best known for beating human champions on the game show *Jeopardy!* in 2011. That version of Watson now sits in a corner of a large data center at the research facility in Yorktown Heights, marked with a glowing plaque commemorating its glory days. Meanwhile, researchers there are already testing new generations of Watson in medicine, where the technology could help physicians diagnose diseases like cancer, evaluate patients, and prescribe treatments.

IBM likes to call it cognitive computing. Essentially, Watson uses artificial-intelligence techniques, advanced natural-language processing and analytics, and massive amounts of data drawn from sources specific to a given application (in the case of health care, that means medical journals, textbooks, and information collected from the physicians or hospitals using the system). Thanks to these innovative techniques and huge amounts of computing power, it can quickly come up with "advice"—for example, the most recent and relevant information to guide a doctor's diagnosis and treatment decisions.

Despite the system's remarkable ability to make sense of all that data, it's still early days for Dr. Watson. While it has rudimentary abilities to "learn" from specific patterns and evaluate different possibilities, it is far from having the type of judgment and intuition a physician often needs. But IBM has also announced it will begin selling Watson's services to customer-support call centers, which rarely require human judgment that's quite so sophisticated. IBM says companies will rent an updated version of Watson for use as a "customer service agent" that responds to questions from consumers; it has already signed on several banks. Automation is nothing new in call centers, of course, but Watson's improved capacity for natural-language processing and its ability to tap into a large amount of data suggest that this system could speak plainly with callers, offering them

specific advice on even technical and complex questions. It's easy to see it replacing many human holdouts in its new field.

Digital Losers

The contention that automation and digital technologies are partly responsible for today's lack of jobs has obviously touched a raw nerve for many worried about their own employment. But this is only one consequence of what Brynjolfsson and McAfee see as a broader trend. The rapid acceleration of technological progress, they say, has greatly widened the gap between economic winners and losers—the income inequalities that many economists have worried about for decades. Digital technologies tend to favor "superstars," they point out. For example, someone who creates a computer program to automate tax preparation might earn millions or billions of dollars while eliminating the need for countless accountants.

New technologies are "encroaching into human skills in a way that is completely unprecedented," McAfee says, and many middle-class jobs are right in the bull's-eye; even relatively high-skill work in education, medicine, and law is affected. "The middle seems to be going away," he adds. "The top and bottom are clearly getting farther apart." While technology might be only one factor, says McAfee, it has been an "underappreciated" one, and it is likely to become increasingly significant.

Not everyone agrees with Brynjolfsson and McAfee's conclusions—particularly the contention that the impact of recent technological change could be different from anything seen before. But it's hard to ignore their warning that technology is widening the income gap between the tech-savvy and everyone else. And even if the economy is only going through a transition similar to those it's endured before, it is an extremely painful one for many workers, and that will have to be addressed somehow. Harvard's Katz has shown that the United States prospered in the early 1900s in part because secondary education became accessible to many people at a time when employment in agriculture was drying up. The result, at least through the 1980s, was an increase in educated workers who found jobs in the industrial sectors, boosting incomes and reducing inequality. Katz's lesson: painful long-term consequences for the labor force do not follow inevitably from technological changes.

Brynjolfsson himself says he's not ready to conclude that economic progress and employment have diverged for good. "I don't know whether we can recover, but I hope we can," he says. But that, he suggests, will depend on recognizing the problem and taking steps such as investing more in the training and education of workers.

"We were lucky and steadily rising productivity raised all boats for much of the 20th century," he says. "Many people, especially economists, jumped to the conclusion that was just the way the world worked. I used to say that if we took care of productivity, everything else would take care of itself; it was the single most important economic statistic. But that's no longer true." He adds, "It's one of the dirty secrets of economics: technology progress does grow the economy and create wealth, but there is no economic law that says everyone will benefit." In other words, in the race against the machine, some are likely to win while many others lose.

Discussion Questions

1. Do you agree with the premise of this article, that automation is increasing productivity while causing job loss and wage suppression? Why or why not? Can you think of examples from the article or your own personal experience to support your position?
2. If the premise is true, does society have an obligation to help people get through the transition? If so, what types of policies might be appropriate?
3. Which do you believe in more, that this is a temporary situation and as previously in history the economy will adjust to these new technologies and incomes will once again rise with increased employment in new jobs created; or that this is a unique historical situation that will lead to a radical change in the nature of our economy, where automated processes and robots take over a wide swath of human tasks, leaving many unemployed? Support your answer.
4. If automation and robots are having a permanent detrimental effect on our economy, is there anything we can do to stop it? Is a Luddite approach reasonable? If not, what might be reasonable, or must we simply adjust to the new technological situation?

 Supporting Activities

1. Visit local businesses and observe and take notes of how much automation there is and what kind of jobs the automated systems are doing.
2. Interview local business owners about the role automation plays in their business and how they think it is affecting employment and the overall economy.
3. Break into groups and within each group share personal stories about how changes in workplace technologies have positively or negatively affected your life or workplace experience. Does anyone feel like they have lost a job to a machine, or that their job has been fundamentally changed due to a machine?
4. Find and briefly summarize one article, book excerpt, or web page dealing with the historical reaction to the introduction of automation into the workplace.

 Additional Resources

1. An excellent historical explanation of the Luddite movement can be found at the *Smithsonian Magazine* site: http://www.smithsonianmag.com/history/what-the-luddites-really-fought-against-264412/?no-ist.
2. This is a fun site that lists many different instances within popular media where robots are depicted as displacing humans in their jobs. It lists many movies, books, TV shows, and so on that you can watch to see how this theme is dealt with in the popular media. Which ones ring true to you? See: http://tvtropes.org/pmwiki/pmwiki.php/Main/JobStealingRobot.

From Ford to Dell: Mass Production to Mass Customization

The following excerpt from Roger Alcaly's book *The New Economy* considers how technology historically and currently is radically transforming the way business is conducted. Case studies of two companies are presented: Ford Motor Company and Dell Computer. Both businesses leveraged the cutting-edge technology of their time to become powerhouses. Ford pioneered the use of automated assembly lines, and Dell pioneered the use of real-time information technology.

However, there are significant differences in how Ford and Dell applied their new technologies. Ford pursued a highly centralized structure in which the company itself controlled the technology. The decision to move parts and materials suppliers, machinists, and car distributers in-house was believed to simplify the manufacturing process and therefore result in cost savings. Ford also strived to reduce costs per unit by pursuing standardization. Dell, in sharp contrast, is using IT to outsource virtually all noncore aspects of its business and prides itself on built-to-order products.

Alcaly is particularly interested in whether the IT revolution and outsourcing, as implemented by Dell, can be applied to a "blue chip" company like Ford. Is a build-to-order model possible, or perhaps necessary, for such companies to survive? What would it mean for the businesses and consumers?

Roger Alcaly, who formerly taught economics at Columbia University, is a principal and director of Mount Lucas Management Corporation, an investment firm in Princeton, New Jersey. He is a regular contributor to *The New York Review of Books* and author of the 2003 book *The New Economy*. Dr. Alcaly was active in leveraged acquisitions, merger arbitrage, and value-oriented equity investing, first as a Partner at Kellner DiLeo & Co. and KD Equities, and then at Riverside Capital, a company he formed. He served as an Assistant Director of the Council on Wage and Price Stability and as a Senior Economist at the Federal Reserve Bank of New York. He holds a B.A. from Amherst College and a Ph.D. in Economics from Princeton University.

From Ford to Dell: Mass Production to Mass Customization

By Roger Alcaly

Henry Ford developed mass production, the manufacturing model that held sway for most of the twentieth century, but the term "mass production" was apparently coined by an editor of the *Encyclopaedia Britannica* who in 1925 asked Ford to write an article for a three-volume supplement he was preparing. The piece first appeared as a feature story in a Sunday edition of *The New York Times* titled "Henry Ford Expounds Mass Production: Calls It the Focussing of the Principles of Power, Economy, Continuity, and Speed." Although the article was attributed to Ford, it was written by his spokesman, William Cameron, who later said that he "should be very much surprised to learn that [Henry Ford had] read it."[1]

Mass production originated as a new approach to making automobiles, but its influence was far more pervasive, demonstrating to all manufacturers how to produce efficiently for a broad market. As the *Britannica* article suggests, Ford was not shy about publicizing his innovative methods, and they spread rapidly throughout the economy, shifting attention to larger-scale production and spurring growth and productivity. "The Ford Motor Company," the historian David Hounshell writes, "educated the American technical community in the ways of mass production." Unlike other turn-of the-century automakers who used skilled craftsmen to produce small quantities of expensive cars tailored to their customers' needs, Ford concentrated on producing large quantities of standardized products at low cost, and his success initially elicited caustic responses. In 1912, for example, an English automotive journal commented:

> It is highly to the credit of our English makers that they choose rather to maintain their reputation for high grade work than cheapen that reputation by the use of the inferior material and workmanship they would be obliged to employ to compete with American manufacturers of cheap cars.

A year later, Ford introduced his first moving assembly line at his Highland Park plant in Detroit and by 1914 was probably producing more cars than all English manufacturers combined. By the early 1920s mass-production techniques had spread throughout the U.S. automobile industry, tripling its annual output to more than 3 million cars, with Ford accounting for about two-thirds of the total. These methods also began to be used in producing electrically powered consumer durables such as washing machines, refrigerators, vacuum cleaners, and radios, as well as farm equipment and other products whose potential sales were large enough to justify the necessary investments in new factories and equipment.[2]

The key to mass production, Ford believed, was the "simplicity" of its constituent operations, a consequence of dividing the production process into a finely specified sequence of steps that could be carried out by unskilled or semiskilled workers using specially designed limited-purpose equipment. Beyond repeatedly performing their specific tasks, assembly-line workers had no role in the operation. Thinking about issues such as product design, how the factories should be laid out, what each assembler should do, or scheduling deliveries of materials and shipments of finished products was done by professionals: designers, industrial engineers, production engineers, and so on. Workers were discouraged from offering suggestions for making their own jobs more efficient. Even chores such as cleaning work areas, repairing equipment, or checking product quality were done by specialists, including housekeeping workers, equipment repairmen, and quality inspectors. And because production was geared to meet anticipated demand—that is, goods were "built-to-forecast" rather than to meet firm orders—and equipment could not readily be stopped and started, companies tended to accumulate massive inventories of final goods, materials, and work in progress.[3]

Carrying out the simple individual tasks of Fordist production required standardized parts of uniformly high quality that could be fit together easily without interrupting the assembly process, a need that few others recognized but one that Ford pursued with "near-religious zeal." Aided by improved machine tools that could work with hardened metals that would hold their shape, Ford-produced parts became increasingly homogeneous and easy to assemble, enabling the company to progressively routinize workers' tasks and speed the flow of work. It helped that Ford cars were designed to be easy to manufacture as well as easy to operate and repair, especially the Model T, which was introduced in 1908, the nineteenth model Henry Ford had built since the original Model A in 1903.

Before 1908 Ford cars had been assembled at a single station, frequently by one or two assemblers who worked an average of almost nine hours on each set of tasks, such as attaching the wheels, springs, motor, transmission, and generator to the chassis, before performing the same operations on another car. In this early setup, assemblers had to collect the parts needed for each phase of their work and file and smooth them so that they fit together. However, by the end of 1912, the last year before Ford began using the moving assembly line to carry the car in progress from worker to worker, the assembly process had been streamlined and the individual steps pared down so much that workers were spending less than 2.5 minutes on each set of tasks for which they were responsible. The moving assembly line cut the average "task cycle" in half, to about 1.2 minutes, and the time required to form an almost finished vehicle fell even more, from twelve and a half hours to about an hour and a half.

Ford's development of the moving assembly line to improve productivity in his plants illustrates a critical difference between his approach and that of Frederick Taylor, with whose scientific management it is often linked. Like Taylor, Ford and his engineers constantly sought to establish precise procedures and standards for performing most efficiently the tasks involved in producing automobiles. Indeed, Ford and other Detroit-based companies may have adopted many of the core principles of "Taylorism" before Taylor did. But, more fundamental, "the Ford approach was to eliminate labor by machinery," Hounshell concluded, "not, as the Taylorites customarily did, to take a given production process and improve the efficiency of the workers through time and motion study and a differential piecerate system of payment." In other words, "Ford engineers mechanized work processes and found workers to feed and tend their machines"; as a consequence, "the machine ultimately set the pace of work at Ford, not a piecerate or an established standard

for a 'fair day's work.' This was the essence of the assembly line and all the machinery that fed it."[4]

By boosting productivity, assembly-line production allowed Ford to keep prices low, thus increasing sales and, because mass-production techniques were so effective in capturing economies of large-scale production, enabling it to reduce prices further as more cars were produced and unit costs fell. Between 1908, when the first Model Ts were produced, and the early 1920s, when more than 2 million were made, the Model T's price fell by almost 70 percent after inflation. The assembly line was introduced at Ford's Highland Park plant in mid-1913 but was resisted at first by the workers. For the year as a whole, employment averaged 13,623, but only because nearly 65,000 workers were hired, enough to make up for more than 50,000 who left the company in frustration, out of boredom, or because they couldn't keep up with the pace of the line. The turnover rate averaged 370 percent for the year but was much higher in the months after the assembly line was installed. "So great was labor's distaste for the new machine system," a Ford biographer wrote, "that toward the close of 1913 every time the company wanted to add 100 men to its factory personnel, it was necessary to hire 963."[5]

Although Detroit was not yet a union town, the threat of unionization and work stoppages may have concerned Ford more than high turnover. High fixed costs and dedicated machinery made mass-production plants particularly vulnerable to strikes and disruptions, and the Wobblies—the Industrial Workers of the World, or IWW—had been active in Detroit in the spring of 1913, briefly stopping production at Studebaker. Whether reducing turnover or staving off the Wobblies and other unions was the main factor, Ford moved quickly to stabilize relations with his workers, establishing his famous "five-dollar day" in January 1914. Under the plan, workers would continue to earn a base wage of $2.34 per day, which had been set just three months earlier, but they could also qualify for supplements, boosting their daily pay to $5 or more. These bonuses were called "profit-sharing" payments, but they were based on a worker's "character" rather than his effectiveness. To determine who was worthy, the company established its intrusive Sociological Department, whose members visited workers every six months to ensure that they were leading "clean, sober, and industrious" lives, in "well lighted and ventilated" homes, located outside "congested and slum areas of the city," making it unlikely that they would waste the money in "riotous living."

The five-dollar day generated favorable publicity for the company, burnished Henry Ford's image as an industrial statesman, and, by raising workers' incomes, increased their buying power and thus their demand for other goods and services if not for cars. Business leaders initially denounced Ford as a utopian, a socialist, and "a traitor to his class," but by the 1920s many had come to appreciate the benefits of higher wages and profit sharing in raising morale, productivity, and aggregate demand and in gaining labor peace. High wages were an integral part of the philosophy of "welfare capitalism" that many leading companies adopted after World War I, and even though he eschewed general wage increases after 1919 and fought viciously against unionization of his company, Henry Ford continued to celebrate the advantages of greater pay, maintaining, for example, in *Today and Tomorrow,* which was published in 1926, that the "wage motive" was "the fundamental motive of our company." But higher wages only were justified, he believed, if they stimulated workers and managers to boost productivity and lower prices. "It is this thought of enlarging buying power by paying high wages and selling at low prices which is behind the prosperity of this country," he wrote. "If we set ourselves to the payment of wages, then we can find methods of manufacturing which will make high wages the cheapest of wages."[6]

Ford's obsessive quest to control production costs by mechanizing, standardizing, and simplifying the work process extended beyond his search for better ways to manufacture automobiles. He also sought to integrate assembly operations with many of the other steps involved in making and distributing cars, including producing the necessary steel, glass, and tires and transporting the raw materials and finished products to and from the Ford facilities. This vision was embodied in the mammoth Rouge production complex, built shortly after World War I on a two-thousand-acre piece of land along the Rouge River in Dearborn, just outside Detroit. Rouge was the largest industrial complex in the world, an "industrial colossus" that employed almost 100,000 workers at its peak. Extreme and striking, a facility in which raw materials "came in one gate, while finished cars went out the other gate . . . completely eliminating the need for outside assistance," Rouge symbolized the possibilities of "vertical integration" that other companies sought to emulate. Ford even tried to add raw materials to the mix, maintaining a rubber plantation in Brazil and iron mines in Minnesota. He also had fleets of ships, railroad cars, and airplanes for carrying resources, equipment, and finished cars.[7]

Ford was motivated to integrate in this way because he was much more efficient than his suppliers and thus could profit from doing more things internally, but he also distrusted others and seemed to need to control everything himself. Whatever the benefits in the short term, the managerial difficulties of coordinating such large and diverse operations were equally great, especially for somebody who could not bear delegating authority. In addition, Ford's obsession with manufacturing may have caused him to neglect marketing and design. For almost twenty years, the company concentrated almost exclusively on the Model T, leaving it vulnerable to competition from General Motors, which had adopted Ford's production methods but also had created a far broader product line with annual model changes. In 1927 Ford was forced to stop producing the Model T and closed the Rouge complex for almost a year in order to develop new products. Fittingly, because it was so representative of its patriarch's strengths and weaknesses, Rouge was the setting for a bloody labor battle about a decade later in which the United Automobile Workers won the right to represent Ford workers, the last of the Big Three's employees to be organized.[8]

If Ford and Rouge are emblematic of the old business system, Dell Computer, which Michael Dell describes as *virtually* integrated," is representative of the new one. What he means, beyond the clever wordplay, is that Dell has succeeded by "focusing on delivering solutions and systems to customers" and "stitching together a business with partners that are treated *as if* they're inside the company," rather than by following Ford's example and trying to do everything itself. In other words, the company, which sells directly to its customers the computers that they specify, is largely a middleman, coordinating its selling and assembly of computers with the activities of outside suppliers, service technicians, and delivery firms such as Airborne Express and UPS. Virtual integration would not be possible without sophisticated information and communications technology. With it, Dell has been able to expand its direct-to-customer business model and become in less than twenty years the world's leading computer maker, with 2001 sales of approximately $30 billion and a market value, even at its low point on September 21, 2001, of more than $40 billion. It employs fewer than twenty thousand people directly but four or five times as many through the business it commits to its partners. Dell's superior efficiency was especially apparent during the 2000–2002 economic slump, when it slashed prices aggressively and gained market share, a strategy that may have helped drive Compaq and Hewlett-Packard, the second- and fourth-ranking computer manufacturers, to merge.[9]

To better appreciate how the system works, consider Dell's relationships with some of its vendors and big customers. Sony produces monitors for Dell's computers, and they are so reliable that Dell doesn't feel it has to test them or carry any buffer stocks. It doesn't even have to take delivery of the monitors. Instead, Michael Dell recounted, "we went to Sony and said, 'Hey, we're going to buy two or three million of these monitors this year. Why don't we just pick them up every day as we need them?'" What actually happens is that Dell instructs "Airborne Express or UPS to come to Austin and pick up 10,000 computers a day and go over to the Sony factory in Mexico and pick up the corresponding number of monitors. Then while we're all sleeping, they match up the computers and the monitors, and deliver them to the customer." For Sony, the relationship with Dell is a large source of demand, and because Dell builds computers only in response to firm customer orders, its needs are relatively predictable, at least in the short term. Moreover, Dell's advanced data-sharing systems allow it to communicate this information to its suppliers, in some cases reporting its inventory levels, replacement needs, and delivery schedules hourly.

Similarly, because Dell maintains electronic records of customer orders, including the exact specifications of their computers and workstations, its technicians can pinpoint problems much more easily and precisely when complaints arise. And for large customers such as Boeing and Eastman Chemical, it often provides special services. Boeing has more than 100,000 Dell PCs, and to service its needs, Dell stationed roughly thirty people at the company who "look like Boeing's PC department" but are not employed by Boeing and probably are not even employed directly by Dell. Eastman Chemical, on the other hand, has developed unique software packages for its workstations, and Dell maintains in its factory a high-speed network and massive server loaded with the relevant software components, enabling it to equip

Eastman's new computers during the assembly process with the particular software mix that each requires, saving the company roughly three hundred dollars per machine.[10]

One of the most obvious advantages of the Dell build-to-order system is that it substantially reduces the need for inventories, and some of the clearest evidence that companies have adopted such new operating methods can be seen in the decline in inventories throughout the economy over the last twenty years. Relative to sales, inventories in the goods-producing sectors of the economy have fallen by about 20 percent since the early 1980s, driven largely by the fall among durable-goods producers such as Dell and Ford, whose inventory-to-sales ratios dropped roughly 30 percent during this period. Curtailing inventories lowers businesses' operating costs, but it also appears to have helped reduce the volatility of economic growth and inflation, reinforcing the benefits of better monetary policy that has aided the economy since Paul Volcker became chairman of the Federal Reserve System in August 1979. Better inventory controls increase profits because less money is tied up in carrying inventories and because firms with lower inventories tend to link them to product lines that are selling well, making it likely that fewer items will become obsolete or have to be discounted or written off. For the U.S. durable-goods sector, the capital freed up by carrying fewer inventories is on the order of $500 billion, saving roughly $25 billion in annual carrying costs if financing rates are around 5 percent and more if they are higher.[11]

Progress in controlling inventories and managing supply chains has encouraged automakers and other businesses to think about capturing the even bigger payoffs that may be possible by further emulating Dell's methods. For example, automobile inventories are now about $100 billion, and McKinsey & Company consultants estimate they would be 60–80 percent lower if cars were built to order rather than in anticipation of future sales. According to Nissan, the resulting savings could be as much as thirty-six hundred dollars per car. The problem for the automakers, however, is that most auto plants do not make money unless they operate at 80 percent of capacity or higher. As a result, the potential advantages of building to order are likely to be eaten away by inefficiently small production runs unless demand can be spread out appropriately or production methods made flexible enough to accommodate lower volumes more effectively.[12]

In fact, Dell not only builds its computers solely in response to firm orders; it also encourages buyers to customize them to fit their own needs. (An ad that ran widely in the fall of 2000, for example, featured a typical teenager dressed in baggy pants and sneakers and slouched before his computer, telling readers, "Everyone at school bought these shoes and got this haircut, but my computer is 100% me.") Even if they don't customize their computers, however, Dell customers pay for them when they place their orders, giving the company free use of the money until it must pay its workers and suppliers for producing the machines. In the first few months of 2000, Dell's average float—prepayments that are temporarily available to the company—was about $1.5 billion, roughly two-thirds of its monthly sales. Assuming Dell earns 5 percent on the money, float of this magnitude contributes close to $100 million to its annual earnings, a further attraction to automakers and others not yet engaged in mass customization or able to get customers to prepay.

Dell is able to produce customized computers for a mass market because they can be built from a limited number of modular components that can be assembled quickly in response to customer specifications. And while automobile suppliers have been working closely with car companies to design and produce complete units for the manufacturers to assemble, including systems for braking, climate control, and car interiors, there may be limits to how far they can go, particularly since the United Automobile Workers remains strongly opposed to modularization because it would reduce even further the work done under their contracts with the Big Three automakers. The attractions are so great, however, that automakers are unlikely to stop trying to become more like Dell, transforming themselves into virtually integrated "brand owners" that simply design, engineer, and market cars, while outsourcing everything else. A Finnish engineering company currently makes Porsche Boxters, and even once-proud Rouge, which now houses only three thousand workers producing eight hundred Mustangs a day, is heading in that direction, undergoing a $2 billion face-lift designed to turn it into a flexible assembly plant of the future.[13]

Author Citations

1. David A. Hounshell, *From the American System to Mass Production, 1800–1932: The Development of Manufacturing Technology in the United States* (Baltimore: Johns Hopkins University Press, 1984), p. 1.
2. Ibid., pp. 260–261; and David C. Mowery and Nathan Rosenberg, *Paths of Innovation* (New York: Cambridge University Press, 1999); pp. 48–55, which quotes the magazine *Autocar*.
3. The discussion of mass production in the next few pages relies on James P. Womack, Daniel T. Jones, and Daniel Roos, *The Machine That Changed the World: The Story of Lean Production* (New York: Harper-Perennial, 1991), pp. 26–29.
4. Hounshell, *From the American System to Mass Production*, pp. 250–53.
5. Daniel M. G. Raff, "Wage Determination Theory and Five-Dollar Day at Ford," *Journal of Economic History* (June 1988), pp. 388–91; Hounshell, *From the American System to Mass Production*, pp. 256–59; and Irving Bernstein, *The Lean Years: A History of the American Worker, 1920–1933* (Boston: Houghton Mifflin, 1960), pp. 179–80. The Ford biographer is Keith Sward, *The Legend of Henry Ford*, who is quoted by Hounshell, p. 257.
6. See Henry Ford (in collaboration with Samuel Crowther), *Today and Tomorrow* (New York: Doubleday, Page & Company, 1926), pp. 8–10; Raff, "Wage Determination Theory," pp. 387–99; Hounshell, *From the American System to Mass Production*, pp. 258–59; Bernstein, *Lean Years*, pp. 179–81; and Stuart D. Brandes, *American Welfare Capitalism, 1880–1940* (Chicago: University of Chicago Press, 1976), pp. 88–89. According to Raff, Joseph Galamb, chief designer of the Model T and one of Henry Ford's close associates, recalled Ford saying he established the five-dollar day to ward off the Wobblies.
7. Womack, Jones, and Roos, *The Machine That Changed the World*, pp. 33–35, 38–39; and Hounshell, *From the American System to Mass Production*, pp. 267–68. The term "industrial colossus," which is from Allan Nevins and Frank Ernest Hill, *Ford: Expansion and Challenge, 1915–1933* (New York: Scribner, 1957), is quoted on p. 267 of Hounshell's book.
8. Mowery and Rosenberg, Paths of Innovation, pp. 54–55; and Irving Bernstein, *Turbulent Years: A History of the American Worker, 1933–1941* (Boston: Houghton Mifflin, 1969), pp. 734–51.
9. Joan Magretta, "The Power of Virtual Integration: An Interview with Dell Computer's Michael Dell," *Harvard Business Review* (March-April 1998), pp. 74–76; and John Swartz, "Dell Computer is in the Catbird Seat, for Now," *New York Times* (Sept. 11, 2001). The emphasis has been added to Michael Dell's remarks.
10. All the quoted remarks in this paragraph, as in the prior one, are Michael Dell's and are from the Margretta interview, pp. 76–79.
11. James Kahn, Margaret M. McConnell, and Gabriel Perez-Quiros, "On the Causes of the Increased Stability of the U.S. Economy," *Economic Policy Review*, Federal Reserve Bank of New York (May 2002), esp. pp. 184–87 and chart 3.
12. Mani Agrawal, T. V. Kumaresh, and Glenn A. Mercer, "The False Promise of Mass Communication," *McKinsey Quarterly* (2001); and "Mass Customization: A Long March," *Economist* (July 14, 2001), pp. 63–65.
13. "Incredible Shrinking Plants," *Economist* (Feb. 23, 2002); "All Yours," *Economist* (Arpil 1, 2000), pp. 57–58; and Fred Andrews, "Dell, It Turns Out, Has a Better Idea," *New York Times* (Jan 26, 2000).

Discussion Questions

1. Explain the difference between "vertical" and "virtual" integration. How has technology made possible both of these business models?

2. The economic landscape has changed considerably since the publication of *The New Economy* in 2003. Do you see Dell's 2003 business model as more or less relevant now compared to then, and why? (See supporting activity number 4 below.)

3. One of Alcaly's main points is that the Dell build-to-order approach reduces inventories. What does he say are the benefits of reducing inventories? Is reduction of inventories a trend in manufacturing? Why does he say this approach may be difficult with automobile production? How does that relate to what Tesla Motor company is doing? (See supporting activity number 3 below.) What do you see as major obstacles to this transition? Major benefits?

4. Toyota in Japan developed the just-in-time (JIT) manufacturing concept during the 1960s just as TQM was being developed. How does this approach compare to the processes Alcaly discusses? Do you think that the manufacturing process developed in Japan during the 1960s has become the main paradigm for industrial manufacturing? Has it replaced Taylorism? Outline the reasons for your conclusions.

5. Alcaly points out that business leaders initially denounced Henry Ford as a socialist and "traitor to his class" but that they eventually recognized the benefits of higher wages and profit sharing. How do these circumstances and sentiments apply to today's economy?

 Supporting Activities

1. Research Frederick Winslow Taylor and his theory of Scientific Management. How is Scientific Management similar to, and different from, Ford's assembly line model?

2. The adoption of technology in the workplace, whether through automation or IT, has its critics. Research some of the objections raised to each of these technologies, and some of the benefits. Form small discussion groups with one side arguing for automation and the other against it. Develop a group consensus and formulate a policy statement about the correct role of automation and IT in the workplace. Have the different groups present their statements and have the whole class vote on which one is the best.

3. Tesla Motors is a company combining the techniques of both Ford and Dell by allowing customers to directly customize and order cars through their web site. Visit http://www.teslamotors.com/ and go through the process of ordering a car (you don't actually have to buy one). You will be allowed to customize the car to your own liking and see what it will look like. This approach bypasses car dealerships and some companies are seeking legal action against Tesla. Research the reasoning behind these objections. Do you think they have merit? Do you see the business model of Tesla as the future of automobile manufacturing? Why or why not?

4. Visit the Dell website (http://www.dell.com/). Go through the process of ordering a computer. Alcaly claims that Dell has succeeded by focusing on delivering solutions and systems to customers and a build-to-order approach. Does the experience seem different than other online ordering? How does it compare to Tesla?

Additional Resources

1. For a detailed analysis of the effects of IT on business, read: Atkinson, R.D., & McKay, A.S. (2007). *Digital prosperity: Understanding the benefits of the information technology revolution*. The Information Technology and Innovation Foundation.

 ## References

Autor, D., & Dorn, D. (2013, August 24). How technology wrecks the middle class. *The New York Times*. Retrieved from http://opinionator.blogs.nytimes.com/2013/08/24/how-technology-wrecks-the-middle-class/?_r=0

Diamond, J. (1999). *Guns, germs and steel: The fate of human societies*. New York, NY: W. W. Norton & Company, Inc.

Ishikawa, K. (1981). *What is total quality control? The Japanese way*. New Jersey: Prentice Hall.

McLuhan, M. (1964). *Understanding media: The extensions of man*. New York, NY: McGraw-Hill, Inc.

Mills, C. W. (1951). *White collar: The American middle class*. Oxford: Oxford University Press.

Mumford, L. (1965). Technics and the nature of man. *Nature, 208* (5014), 923–928.

Nielsen Company. (2014). *Shifts in viewing: The cross platform report* (Q2 2014). New York, NY: Nielsen Holdings N.V.

Taylor, F. W. (1997). *The principles of scientific management*. Mineola, NY: Dover. (Original work published 1911).

Volti, R. (2009). *Society and technological change* (6th ed.). New York, NY: Worth.

Wild Promises: Anticipating Our Technological Future

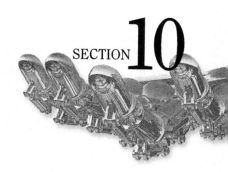

In the previous nine sections, we have explored the role technology plays in every facet of our lives. Hopefully, you have gained an appreciation for the impacts technology has on us, individually and collectively. Conversely, you have seen the role that people play in the process of technological development and adoption, and may more fully recognize the responsibility we all share to become technologically literate citizens and voters.

This last section examines some emerging technological developments and future scenarios that have the potential to radically transform society as we know it. How can we anticipate what technologies the future will hold and what their impacts will be? People who study such things have been labeled futurists. Forecasting future events and developments is no easy task, and a variety of methods have been developed for doing so. One widely used method is to *extrapolate* into the future based on trends observed in historical data. Another method, known as the *Delphi technique,* solicits the opinions of experts in a variety of fields and seeks a consensus opinion, often with multiple blind iterations. Arriving at a consensus is often quite difficult, but the technique has proven to be worthwhile. Simulations, including mathematical, physical, or conceptual modeling, have also been employed. Scenario development, typically including best, worst, and most-likely cases, is helpful in framing the range of future possibilities. Sometimes a combination of methods is used. These and other methods all have their strengths and weaknesses. The nature of forecasts and their interpretations will also be dependent on the kind of world view one brings to the table. For example, someone with a cornucopian view will likely reject predictions like the ones made in the second reading in this section as being far too pessimistic about the coming years.

Knowing what the future holds is a desire that humans have always had, and our tools for predicting the future have recently become more sophisticated. For example, Loveridge (2009) promotes the idea of applying systems thinking that considers the holistic context of social, technological, economic, ecological, political, and value/norm (STEEPV) events to effectively gain foresight about the future. De Chant (2014) recognizes the potential of analytical tools that can be used to mine vast amounts of data to uncover meaningful relationships between events. With the convergence of powerful computers, social media, mathematical modeling tools, and expanding quantities of stored digital data, De Chant says that predicting the future becomes "inevitable," not to mention more accurate than ever before possible.

Beyond mere curiosity, is it actually important to be able to predict our technological future? Many would say that this type of anticipatory thinking (an idea championed by Buckminster Fuller) is critical for achieving the kind of future we want. Computer scientist Alan Kay, who at the time was a Fellow at Apple Computer, wrote in 1989:

> Look, the best way to predict the future is to invent it. This is the century in which you can be proactive about the future; you don't have to be reactive. The whole idea of having scientists and technology is that those things you can envision and describe can actually be built. (Kay, 1989)

If we can apply holistic, STEEPV-oriented analysis to the design and development of our future technologies, surely we have a better chance of optimizing these systems to reflect our larger societal goals. The real challenge then, is to identify and reach consensus on what those larger societal goals are. Will we be more mindful of human dignity, and what it means to be human? Will we learn to value those ecosystems that sustain life on earth? Will we apply informed decision-making to the design and adoption of technologies that are appropriate for the setting and the users? We hope that in your journey through this book you have gained greater insights into the kind of technological future you wish to see, and how to effect it.

The Future: What is the Problem?

Susan Greenfield acknowledges that for the past 100 years, society has greatly benefited from scientific and technological advances. In her book *Tomorrow's People* she tries to predict what science and technology have in store for us over the next 100 years. Can we simply extrapolate the rapid pace of technological change from the past and expect more of the same? What types of unpredictable technological developments should we anticipate? Will technologies of the future carry the same levels of benefits and risks that prior technologies did?

Following the lead of Bill Joy, a prominent computer scientist and futurist, Greenfield highlights three broad and important categories of technologies: biotech, infotech, and nanotech. These mirror the categories identified by Joy (genetics, robotics, and nanotechnology) in his thought-provoking and influential article in *Wired* magazine, titled "Why the Future Doesn't Need Us" (Joy, 2000). There have been tremendous accomplishments in these areas to date, and all three are poised for an explosion of scientific breakthroughs and technological advances that cannot be predicted based on past innovation. These emerging technological fields are expected to dramatically increase in power and scope, and may very well interact in synergistic ways beyond our contemporary understanding. The questions should be asked: Knowing at least some of the potential risks, is it advisable to pursue these technologies? Do the benefits outweigh the risks? The technological optimist would obviously say yes.

Greenfield uses pop culture to make her point. For example, consider the evolution of Hollywood robotics, from HAL in *2001: A Space Odyssey* (1968) to the *Terminator* Series (1984, 1991, 2003, and 2009) and the more recent *Chappie* and *Ex Machina* (2015). Early on, Hollywood predicted robots would be smarter and more powerful in 2001, and perhaps evil, but not substantially different from technology of the day and still in rather dull boxes. Later, Hollywood writers anticipated that robotics would have potential well beyond current technology, and the Terminator was born. Interestingly, the time lapse between HAL and the first Terminator (16 years) was considerably shorter than the (current) duration of the Terminator franchise (now over 30 years). The two more recent movies mentioned above highlight the emotional intelligence and "humanity" of the robots in question.

Hollywood and Susan Greenfield are in agreement that future technological advances can't be predicted from past performance. What we'll likely get in the future is not simply a smaller, faster, more advanced version of what we have now, but something perhaps radically different, with unknowable, unintended consequences. Perhaps the phrase "technological revolution" may not be hyperbole after all. This makes forecasting the future a very tricky endeavor indeed.

Susan Adele Greenfield (Baroness Greenfield) is a British scientist, writer, and member of the House of Lords. Her field of expertise is the physiology of the brain, and her research has focused on the impact of twenty-first-century technologies on the mind and novel approaches to neurodegenerative diseases such as Alzheimer's. Greenfield has written several books, including *Mind Change: How Digital Technologies are Leaving Their Mark On Our Brains* (2014) and *The Private Life of the Brain* (2000). She started the biotech company Neuro-bio Ltd. in 2013, and serves as its Chief Scientific Officer. Baroness Greenfield is currently Senior Research Fellow at Lincoln College, Oxford University.

The Future: What Is the Problem?

By Susan Greenfield

Look through an old album of sepia photographs from the early 1900s. There they are, our forebears, most usually posed in front of some cardboard Arcadian scene, doomed to manual or social drudgery and a rigid code of conduct and thought. Those placid, distant faces stare into a world, invisible and unknowable to us, of toothache, outside privies, stale sweat and certainty. 'The past is a foreign country,' mused L. P. Hartley in *The Go-Between*, 'they do things differently there.' Yet the mid-20th-century British prime minister Harold Macmillan, looking back over a long life to his Victorian childhood, once reminisced that the great watchword of the turn of the century was 'progress'. Progress—social, economic and above all scientific—was perceived as just that, the forward march of the human intellect, from which we would reap only benefits. And progress came from science.

In the 1950s the scientist knew everything. He (always he) was characterized in television advertisements as the white-coated authority, condescending to endorse 'scientifically' the latest washing powder. The very fact that there was television at all transformed not only people's lives but also the way they viewed the world beyond the confines of their own community. The chirpy, capped, short-trousered schoolboy of that era, voraciously swotting up endless facts that 'every schoolboy knows', was fascinated by the technological marvels of the Festival of Britain and the new world that science was making possible. Meanwhile penicillin was rescuing many from misery and early death, whilst the contraceptive pill, no longer just a pipe dream, was about to revolutionize the outlook of, and for, women.

But the 20th century has surely taught us, among much else, that everything comes with a price; every schoolchild now knows that scientific and technological advances have colossal potential for both good and evil. Although the public have been aware, ever since Hiroshima, of the need to try to understand the implications of new scientific discoveries, it has only been in the last few decades of the previous century that the alarm bells have grown deafening. GM foods, mad cow disease and brain-scrambling mobile phones have compelled the most ostrich-like technophobe to question what might be happening in the remote and rarefied stratosphere of the laboratory. For science is increasingly not just on our minds but at the heart of our lives, encroaching upon everything that we hold dear: nutrition, reproduction, the climate, communication and education . . . The impact of science and technology on our existence, in the future, is no longer a whimsical excursion into science fiction.

Those sci-fi images of yesteryear now have an enchantingly amateurish glow. The Daleks in pursuit of Dr. Who, the politically correct crew in *Star Trek*—even that ultimate icon, from Stanley Kubrick's film *2001*, the psychopathic computer, HAL—are as far-fetched and unthreatening as the tin-foil outfits and staccato jerks of the marionettes in *Thunderbirds*. The human and humanoid characters, in most cases, think and act like we do. They have similar sets of values and expectations, and the bulk of the appeal depends on a good guys/bad guys plot. And that is how most people used to see the future—not chasing bandits around the galaxy so much as still being human in a world of souped-up, high-tech gadgetry—a gadgetry perhaps of interest to some anorak-kitted nerds, but for the majority of us reasonable everyday folk to be taken in our stride.

But now we face a future where science could actually change everyday life any day soon; many think such transformations are already under way. Yet there are some—let's dub them, without much originality, The Cynics—who do not see any point in dusting down the crystal ball. The chances are, glancing at the track records of our predecessors, that pretty much any prediction anyone makes now will be either impractical or uninspired.

Moreover, just because a technology is up and running doesn't mean to say it will become central to the daily grind. One late-19th-century prediction of the future, for example, was that everyone would travel around in hot-air balloons. And on the other hand, unknown, unimaginable technology can catch us unawares: a picture of a domestic scene 'in the future' drawn back in the 1950s shows all manner of gleaming appliances, but no computers, let alone anyone surfing the web. Even a glimmer of the priming technology just wasn't part of normal existence; it would have been a fairly impressive intellectual leap to conceptualize our 50-emails-a-day lifestyle from the standing start of clunky, expensive and essentially mechanical computers whirring and churning in their remote rarity in custom-made rooms of their own. And I remember a summer afternoon in the 1970s, lounging after a heavy lunch on a lawn with friends, when someone, a physicist, first mentioned the microchip—he prophesied that 'it will change all our lives'. The rest of us hadn't the vaguest idea what he was talking about.

The problem with thinking about the future, shrug The Cynics complacently, is that it is impossible to predict the big new scientific advances that underpin serious technological progress; meanwhile, how easy to be distracted by high-tech toys, the latest variation on an existing theme, amusing enough for escapist science fiction but not sufficiently innovative to restructure our entire existence and our seemingly impregnable mindset. Yet, as physicist Michio Kaku points out, the problem with extrapolating the future in the past—as with the hot-air balloon mass transport system—is that it hasn't been the scientists themselves making the predictions. Now they are in a very strong position to do so.

However, The Cynics have long placed a trip wire on the track of human progress, even when scientists have indulged in flights of fancy. They laughed at Christopher Columbus, derided Galileo, scoffed at Darwin and sneered at Freud. A curious feature of The Cynic's attitude is that he (and again it usually is he) thinks that science is on his side, backing up his sane voice of reason against the fantastic. In 1903 a *New York Times* editorial glibly wrote off Langley's attempts at flight: 'We hope that Professor Langley will not put his substantial greatness as a scientist in further peril by continuing to waste his time, and the money involved, in further airship experiments. Life is short, and he is capable of services to humanity incomparably greater than can be expected to result from trying to fly . . .' And a few decades later, in 1936, when technology had become much more part of life, Charles Lindbergh wrote to Harry Guggenheim of Robert Goddard's rocket research: 'I would much prefer to have Goddard interested in real scientific development than to have him primarily interested in more spectacular achievements which are of less real value.'

Even now one of the most popular quotes for after-dinner speeches has to be the famous prediction of Thomas Watson, Chairman of IBM, in 1943: 'I think there is a world market for maybe five computers.' And if you had suggested to our 1950s schoolboy that one day his, or her, 21st-century counterpart would have no idea what a slide rule was, or what log tables were all about, they would have thought you utterly crazy.

But it still does not follow that *this* time, *this* century should be any different, in terms of the revolutions in science and technology that come and go. Yes, as we shall see, we may well have the technology for a disease-free, hunger-free and even work-free existence. But then, too, the values, fears and hopes engendered in a chilly, smelly cottage on a bleak hillside would have produced an outlook very different from one based on a 20th-century upbringing in a centrally heated suburbia shimmering with shiny, chrome appliances and unforgiving neon lights. Yet we still have the same human brains as our very early ancestors, who stumbled uncomprehendingly around on the savannah some 100,000 years ago.

For the first time, however, our brains and bodies might be directly modified by electronic interfaces. For a second group, The Technophiles, such a prospect is welcome. The electrical engineer Kevin Warwick, for one, would welcome the prospect of heightened senses, sensations and muscle power that being a cyborg might bring—as we will see later. And cyber-guru Ray Kurzweil is gung-ho for the intimate embrace of silicon:

> There is a clear incentive to go down this path. Given a choice, people will prefer to keep their bones from crumbling, their skin supple, their life systems strong and vital. Improving our lives through neural implants on the mental level, and nanotechnology-enhanced bodies on the physical level, will be popular and compelling. It is another one of those slippery slopes—

> there is no obvious place to stop this progression until the human race has largely replaced the brains and bodies that evolution first provided.

Both Warwick and Kurzweil, not to mention other intellectual luminaries such as Marvin Minsky and Igor Aleksander, along with various futurologists such as Ian Pearson and Hans Moravec, all take it as read that another feature of future life will be conscious machines. Kurzweil's message is that our only future as a species will be to merge intimately with our technology: if you can't beat the robots, join them. So imagine a spectrum of beings, from pure carbon-based (as we humans are now) through the cyborg silicon-carbon hybrids that we could become to the ultimate—the vastly superior thinking silicon systems that will be Masters (and again they will have to be male) of the Universe.

It was actually because he was eavesdropping on a discussion between Kurzweil and the philosopher John Searle, concerning the very question of computer consciousness, that the co-founder and Chief Scientist of Sun Microsystems, Bill Joy, began to feel anxious about the direction in which future technology was heading. As an undisputed techno-mandarin, Joy created an enormous stir when he wrote of his urgent concern in the magazine *Wired*, in April 2000, in an article titled 'Why the future doesn't need us':

> The 21st-century technologies—genetics, nanotechnology, and robotics—are so powerful that they can spawn whole new classes of accidents and abuses. Most dangerously, for the first time, these accidents and abuses are widely within the reach of individuals and small groups. They will not require large facilities or rare raw materials. Knowledge alone will enable the use of them.

True, a critical difference between the technology of the 21st-century genetics, nanotechnology and robotics and that of the previous 100 years—darkening as they were with nuclear, biological and chemical doom—is that now it is no longer necessary to take over large facilities or access rare raw materials. Yet an even bigger change in the technology of the future, compared to that of the past, is that a nuclear bomb, though hideous in its potential, cannot self-replicate; but something that might—nanorobots—could soon be taking over the planet.

Just browse a few websites that are devoted to 'problems of preserving our civilization'. One worry, you will read, is that the manipulation of matter at the level of atoms, the nanotechnology that promises to be 'the manufacturing industry of the 21st century', will bring a new enemy—robots scaled down to the billionth of a metre that the nanolevel mandates, minuscule serfs who are focused on assembling copies of themselves. What might happen, one website asks, if such prolific yet single-minded operatives fell into the hands of even a lone terrorist? But then, of course, intelligent robots do not have to be small to be evil—just much cleverer than us. Common-or-garden human-sized machines might also soon be able to self-assemble, and, more importantly, to think autonomously.

Bill Joy had never thought of machines heretofore as having the ability to 'think'; now he is worried that they will, and in so doing lead us into a technology that may replace our species. He worries that humans will become so dependent on machines that we will let machines make decisions. And because these machines will be so much better than humans at working out the best course of action, soon we will capitulate entirely. Joy argues that, in any case, the problems will soon be so complex that humans will be incapable of grasping them. Considering that, in addition to greater mental

prowess, these silicon masterminds will have no need to sleep in, nor to hang out in bars, they will soon be way ahead of us, treating us as a lower species destined, as one website warns, to be 'used as domestic animals' or even 'kept in zoos'.

Kevin Warwick's predictions are similarly ominous: 'With intelligent machines we will not get a second chance. Once the first powerful machine, with an intelligence similar to that of a human, is switched on, we will most likely not get the opportunity to switch it back off again. We will have started a time bomb ticking on the human race, and we will be unable to switch it off.'

Equally nightmarish would be an elite minority of humans commanding large systems of machines, whilst the masses languish redundant. Either the elite will simply destroy this useless press of humanity or, in a more benign mood, generously brainwash them so that they give up reproducing and eventually make themselves extinct—it would be kindest to ensure that at all times the masses are universally content. They will be happy, but not free. It is a disturbing thought that these are the views of the Unabomber, Theodore Kaczynski; though he was obviously criminally insane, and no one would for a moment condone his actions, still Joy felt compelled to confront the sentiment that 'as we are downloaded into our own technology, our humanity will be lost'.

The coming Age of IT, then, offers a raft of possibilities from conscious automata to self-assembling autocrats to carbon-silicon hybrids. Extreme though such possibilities might seem, especially to The Cynics, it is very likely that a more modest version of carbon-silicon interfacing will feature in 21st-century life before too long. Soon computers will be invisible and ubiquitous—if not actually inside our bodies and brains then sprinkled throughout our clothes, in our spectacles and watches, and converting the most unlikely inanimate objects into 'smart' interactive gadgets.

The real problem is not what is technically feasible but the extent to which what is technically feasible can change our values. The gadgets of applied technology are the direct consequences of the big scientific breakthroughs of the previous century, and promise any day now to influence, with unprecedented intimacy, the previously independent, isolated inner world of the human mind. Yet this widespread availability of modern technology is, for some, a loud enough wake-up call for us to re-evaluate our priorities as a society. Bill Joy again: 'I think it is no exaggeration to say that we are on the cusp of the further perfection of extreme evil, an evil whose possibility spreads well beyond that which weapons of mass destruction bequeathed to the nation-states, on to a surprising and terrible empowerment of extreme individuals.'

But of course not all of this third group, The Technophobes, are scientists. Not surprisingly, and indeed more typically, non-scientists' fears are usually grounded in a more romantic view of life, but the fears are there nonetheless. In his Reith Lecture in 2000 Prince Charles summed up the worries of many: 'If literally nothing is held sacred anymore . . . what is there to prevent us treating our entire world as some 'great laboratory of life', with potentially disastrous long-term consequences?'

It may be a little unfair, and certainly incautious, to write off this type of view as simply that of latter-day Luddites, striving in vain to hold back progress with a misconceived vision of some golden bygone age when humans adhered to a Rousseau-like natural nobility, and no one died in childbirth, suffered poor housing, worked at mind-numbing manual tasks or froze to death . . . It's just that for many there is a very real fear that science, and the technology that it has spawned, have outpaced the checks

and balances we need for society to survive—indeed for life as we know it to continue at all.

In our growing knowledge of life, in biology, the trend for science to be slipping out of control appears already to be gaining an ever faster pace. The rigid hierarchy of a society segregated by biochemical and genetic manipulation, from intellectual 'alphas' down to 'epsilons' who operate the lifts, portrayed by Aldous Huxley in *Brave New World,* is now seen as a real future threat by many. Predictably, a morass of websites express serious concerns over genetics, for example: 'The path is open, by-passing the natural evolution, to design unusual creatures—from fairly useful to imagination-striking monsters.'

And we might well end up with 'designer' babies, potential geniuses or highly obedient and tough soldiers. But manipulation of genes allows further possibilities too; offset against the benefits of gene therapy and new types of medication and diagnostics, there are clones, artificial genes, germ-line engineering, and the tricky relationship of genetic profiling to insurance premiums and job applications. In any event, for The Technophobes, the question of basic survival seems far from certain; according to Bill Joy, the philosopher John Leslie puts the risk of human extinction at 30 per cent at the least. And the astronomer Martin Rees, in his latest book, *Our Final Century*, rates the chance as no better than odds on that civilization will avoid a catastrophic setback.

No one could really disagree with Aristotle that 'All men by nature desire to know'; the human brain has evolved to ask questions, and to survive by answering them. Science is simply the formal realization of our natural curiosity. Yet no one could fool themselves any longer that, as we stand on the cusp of this new century, we are travelling the simple path of 'progress'. Sure, for several generations now we have strived to balance the pay-off between 'unnatural' mechanization and a pain-free, hunger-free, longer-lasting existence; but now we face a future of interactive and highly personalized information technology, an intrusive but invisible nanotechnology, not to mention a sophisticated and powerful biotechnology, that could all conspire together to challenge how we think, what kind of individuals we are, and even whether each of us stays an individual at all.

For The Cynics the implications that this prospect poses, in all its horror and excitement, will be sensationalist hype at best and scaremongering at worst. They won't believe that science will ever be able to produce new types of fundamentally life-transforming technologies, and even if it were, they feel that humans are sufficiently wise and have an inbuilt sanity check to deal with any ethical, cultural or intellectual choices that might ensue. This attitude is not only questionable—in the light of the far more modest precedents that we have witnessed in technology over the last half century—but also chillingly complacent. Can we really afford to assume that humanity will be able to muddle through? And even if we did survive as the unique personalities we are now, in a world bristling with biotech, infotech and nanotech, can we still be sure that such passivity, just letting it all happen, will be the best way to optimize the benefits and reduce any ensuing risks?

Perhaps both Technophiles and Technophobes would agree on one very important issue that sets them aside from The Cynics: we must be proactive and set the agenda for what we want and need from such rapid technical advances; only then shall we, our children and our grandchildren come to have the best life possible. So first we need to evaluate the 21st-century technologies, and then unflinchingly open our minds to all possibilities . . .

Discussion Questions

1. Briefly describe the Cynic, the Technophile, and the Technophobe's view of the role of technology in the future. In which camp do you place yourself? These categories should sound familiar—versions of them were presented in Section One. Has your answer to this question changed as a result of participation in this course?

2. Support or refute Bill Joy's contention, echoed by Greenfield, that robotics, nanotechnology, and genetics pose a fundamentally greater risk to humanity than do the previous generation's "big three" technological fears: biological, chemical, and nuclear.

3. Based on your knowledge of the emerging technologies highlighted in this article, which of these three technologies do you think will have the greatest impact on humanity as a whole? Do you see this impact as positive or negative? Explain your answer.

4. In your opinion, which aspect of humanity is in greatest need of a technological revolution?

 Supporting Activities

1. Listen to any of the segments in a 2013 *TED Talk Radio Hour* episode focused on predicting the future, available at: http://www.npr.org/2013/08/26/215826949/predicting-the-future.

2. Identify an emerging technology that you think holds the greatest promise for humanity and learn more about it. At what stage of development is the technology? How soon is the technology expected to be "ready for prime time?"

3. Watch two short video clips from 1964, in which science fiction writer Sir Arthur C. Clarke (best known for his novel *2001: A Space Odyssey*) predicts what the world will look like 50 years later (in other words, in 2014): http://mentalfloss.com/article/57157/arthur-c-clarke-predicts-future-1964.

4. Find prior forecasts about the future and see if they came true. This article on the BBC News web site lists predictions that came true: http://www.bbc.com/news/magazine-16444966. This article in *Scientific American* identifies the "worst tech predictions of all time:" http://www.scientificamerican.com/article/pogue-all-time-worst-tech-predictions/ .

5. Conduct the following simple group futuring activity:
    a. Identify a technology from one of the readings in this book.
    b. Determine a "preferred future" (or where you would like your country to be with regard to technology policy in this area) for the year 2025.
    c. Identify (brainstorm) a variety of means, or policy options, for reaching that preferred future. Write down all ideas.
    d. After group discussion, select two of these policy options that you believe hold the most promise. Consider the feasibility of the options selected.
    e. Identify potential outcomes (both positive and negative) of implementing these two policies, including economic, environmental, moral/ethical, social, political and cultural outcomes.

6. Describe some hypothetical events that might disrupt the historic trends of technological development from the present day and continuing into the future. For example, what type of

event might disrupt the trend of greater numbers of personal automobiles worldwide? Think of a particular technological context described in this book, examine current trends with regard to that technology, and then consider and describe the effects of disruptive events.

7. Watch a movie in which a robot is an important figure. Write a 1-page report that includes a brief summary but that primarily focuses on the issues raised in the movie with regard to robotic technology.

Additional Resources

1. See Susan Greenfield's web site (http://www.susangreenfield.com/) for more information about this writer, scientist, and policy maker and her work.

2. Read the full text of Tim De Chant's article "The Inevitability of Predicting the Future," available at: http://www.pbs.org/wgbh/nova/next/tech/predicting-the-future/.

3. Visit the website of the International Institute of Forecasters (www.forecasters.org).

4. Watch the classic movie that really put Sci-Fi on the map: *2001: A Space Odyssey* (1967). The film won an Academy Award and has been deemed "culturally, historically, or aesthetically significant" by the Library of Congress.

5. Watch the movies in the Terminator series and look for ways that the robots depicted change over time: *The Terminator* (1984; recognized by the Library of Congress as "culturally, historically, or aesthetically significant"); *Terminator 2: Judgment Day* (1991; winner of four Academy Awards); *Terminator 3: Rise of the Machines* (2003); and *Terminator Genisys* (2015).

6. Watch the James Burke series *Connections* (1978), *Connections²* (1994), *Connections³* (1997) and *The Day the Universe Changed* (1985) for an exploration of the forces that created technological change in the past to gain insights into how technology and society may change in the future.

Sleepwalking into the Future

Someone had to do it—address the prospect of the end of cheap oil head-on, that is. We've read technical analyses about peak oil, learned about the potential for energy efficiency, and seen how oil development is impacting communities in North Dakota. None of those readings took the next step to imagine what the world really will look like when oil becomes too difficult or too expensive to acquire. Kunstler takes a hard look at a post-oil world, and the forecast that results isn't a happy one. As the author observes, "throughout history, even the most important and self-evident trends are often completely ignored because the changes they foreshadow are simply unthinkable." Interestingly, a future of unlimited oil supplies might also be unthinkable, as writer Charles Mann (2013) suggests in his article "What if We Never Run Out of Oil?" Increasing worldwide development of oil fields through advanced recovery methods like fracking can lead to political instability and corruption. Most critically, continuing reliance on fossil fuels means any hope of curbing carbon emissions is lost.

When one considers the history of oil dependency in the United States, what's remarkable is how relatively short-lived the era of oil has been. The first oil wells in the United States were drilled in Pennsylvania in 1859. As we saw in Section Four, it was almost 1950 before oil surpassed coal as the dominant fuel source. Access to oil has enabled all of the trappings of modernity—automobiles, skyscrapers, a wide array of material goods—but one doesn't have to look too far into our past to find a time when Americans survived quite adequately without access to oil. Therein lays the silver lining to the dark cloud of the Long Emergency described by Kunstler. Will the transition be as traumatic as he predicts? The answer to that question is as difficult as most other predictions. But the act of spinning out the scenario helps us to understand what the issues, challenges, and realities will be, and forces us to consider these possibilities, rather than "sleepwalking into the future."

James Howard Kunstler is the author of a number of books, both fiction and nonfiction. The latter include *The Geography of Nowhere* (1993), a critique of suburban development, and *Too Much Magic: Wishful Thinking, Technology, and the Fate of the Nation* (2012). In 2014 Kunstler published the third book in his *World Made by Hand* trilogy, a fictional account of a town in upstate New York existing in a post-oil era. Kunstler publishes a weekly Monday blog, in which he comments on a wide range of cultural issues and events.

Sleepwalking into the Future

Carl Jung, one of the fathers of psychology, famously remarked that "people cannot stand too much reality." What you're about to read may challenge your assumptions about the kind of world we live in, and especially the kind of world into which time and events are propelling us. We are in for a rough ride through uncharted territory.

It has been very hard for Americans—lost in dark raptures of nonstop infotainment, recreational shopping, and compulsive motoring—to make sense of the gathering forces that will fundamentally alter the terms of everyday life in technological society. Even after the terrorist attacks of September 11, 2001, that collapsed the twin towers of the World Trade Center and sliced through the Pentagon, America is still sleepwalking into the future. We have walked out of our burning house and we are now headed off the edge of a cliff. Beyond that cliff is an abyss of economic and political disorder on a scale that no one has ever seen before. I call this coming time the Long Emergency.

What follows is a harsh view of the decades ahead and what will happen in the United States. Throughout this book I will concern myself with what I believe *is* happening, what *will* happen, or what *is likely* to happen, not what I hope or wish will happen. This is an important distinction. It is my view, for instance, that in the decades to come the national government will prove to be so impotent and ineffective in managing the enormous vicissitudes we face that the United States may not survive as a nation in any meaningful sense but rather will devolve into a set of autonomous regions. I do not welcome a crack-up of our nation but I think it is a plausible outcome that we ought to be prepared to face. I have published several books critical of the suburban living arrangement, which I regard as deeply pernicious to our society. While I believe we will be better off living differently, I don't welcome the tremendous personal hardship that will result as the infrastructure of that life loses its value and utility. I predict that we are entering an era of titanic international military strife over resources, but I certainly don't relish the prospect of war.

If I hope for anything in this book, it is that the American public will wake up from its sleepwalk and act to defend the project of civilization. Even in the face of epochal discontinuity, there is a lot we can do to assure the refashioning of daily life around authentic local communities based on balanced local economies, purposeful activity, and a culture of ideas consistent with reality. It is imperative for citizens to be able to imagine a hopeful future, especially in times of maximum stress and change. I will spell out these strategies later in this book.

Our war against militant Islamic fundamentalism is only one element among an array of events already under way that will alter our relations with the rest of the world, and compel us to live differently at home—sooner rather than later—whether we like it or not. What's more, these world-altering forces, events, and changes will interact synergistically, mutually amplifying each other to accelerate and exacerbate the emergence of meta-problems. Americans are woefully unprepared for the Long Emergency.

Your Reality Check Is in the Mail

Above all, and most immediately, we face the end of the cheap fossil fuel era. It is no exaggeration to state that reliable supplies of cheap oil and natural gas underlie everything we identify as a benefit of modern life. All the necessities, comforts, luxuries, and miracles of our time—central heating, air conditioning, cars, airplanes, electric lighting, cheap clothing, recorded music, movies, supermarkets, power tools, hip replacement surgery, the national defense, you name it—owe their origins or continued existence in one way or another to cheap fossil fuel. Even our nuclear power plants ultimately depend on cheap oil and gas for all the procedures of construction, maintenance, and extracting and processing nuclear fuels. The blandishments of cheap oil and gas were so seductive, and induced such transports of mesmerizing contentment, that we ceased paying attention to the essential nature of these miraculous gifts from the earth: that they exist in finite, nonrenewable supplies, unevenly distributed around the world. To aggravate matters, the wonders of steady technological progress under the reign of oil have tricked us into a kind of "Jiminy Cricket syndrome," leading many Americans to believe that anything we wish for hard enough can come true. These days, even people in our culture who ought to know better are wishing ardently that a smooth, seamless transition from fossil fuels to their putative replacements—hydrogen, solar power, whatever—lies just a few years ahead. I will try to demonstrate that this is a dangerous fantasy. The true best-case scenario may be that some of these technologies will take decades to develop—meaning that we can expect an extremely turbulent interval between the end of cheap oil and whatever comes next. A more likely scenario is that new fuels and technologies may *never* replace fossil fuels at the scale, rate, and manner at which the world currently consumes them.

What is generally not comprehended about this predicament is that the developed world will begin to suffer long before the oil and gas actually run out. The American way of life—which is now virtually synonymous with suburbia—can run only on reliable supplies of dependably cheap oil and gas. Even mild to moderate deviations in either price or supply will crush our economy and make the logistics of daily life impossible. Fossil fuel reserves are not scattered equitably around the world. They tend to be concentrated in places where the native peoples don't like the West in general or America in particular, places physically very remote, places where we realistically can exercise little control (even if we wish to). For reasons I will spell out, we can be certain that the price and supplies of fossil fuels will suffer oscillations and disruptions in the period ahead that I am calling the Long Emergency.

The decline of fossil fuels is certain to ignite chronic strife between nations contesting the remaining supplies. These resource wars have already begun. There will be more of them. They are very likely to grind on and on for decades. They will only aggravate a situation that, in and of itself, could bring down civilizations.

The extent of suffering in our country will certainly depend on how tenaciously we attempt to cling to obsolete habits, customs, and assumptions—for instance, how fiercely Americans decide to fight to maintain suburban lifestyles that simply cannot be rationalized any longer.

The public discussion of this issue has been amazingly lame in the face of America's post-9/11 exposure to the new global realities. As of this writing, no one in the upper echelon of the federal government has even ventured to state that we face fossil fuel depletion by mid-century and severe market disruptions long before that. The subject is too fraught with scary implications for our collective national behavior, most particularly the not-incidental fact that our economy these days is hopelessly tied to the creation and servicing of suburban sprawl.

Within the context of this feeble public discussion over our energy future, some wildly differing positions stand out. One faction of so-called "cornucopians" asserts that humankind's demonstrated technical ingenuity will overcome the facts of geology. (This would seem to be the default point of view of the majority of Americans, when they reflect on these issues at all.) Some cornucopians believe that oil is not fossilized, liquefied organic matter but rather a naturally occurring mineral substance that exists in endless abundance at the earth's deep interior like the creamy nougat center of a bonbon. Most of the public simply can't entertain the possibility that industrial civilization will not be rescued by technological innovation. The human saga has indeed been amazing. We have overcome tremendous obstacles. Our late-twentieth-century experience has been especially rich in technologic achievement (though the insidious diminishing returns are far less apparent). How could a nation that put men on the moon feel anything but a nearly godlike confidence in its ability to overcome difficulties?

The computer at which I am sitting would surely have been regarded as an astounding magical wonder by someone from an earlier period of American history, say Benjamin Franklin, who helped advance the early understanding of electricity. The sequence of discoveries and developments since 1780 that made computers possible is incredibly long and complex and includes concepts that we may take for granted, starting with no-volt alternating house current that is always available. But what would Ben Franklin have made of video? Or software? Or broadband? Or plastic? By extension, one would have to admit the possibility that scientific marvels await in the future that would be difficult for people of our time to imagine. Humankind may indeed come up with some fantastic method for running civilization on seawater, or molecular organic nanomachines, or harnessing the *dark matter* of the universe. But I'd argue that such miracles may lie on the far shore of the Long Emergency, or may never happen at all. It is possible that the fossil fuel efflorescence was a one-shot deal for the human race.

A coherent, if extremely severe, view along these lines, and in opposition to the cornucopians, is embodied by the "die-off" crowd.[1] They believe that the carrying capacity of the planet has already exceeded "overshoot" and that we have entered an apocalyptic age presaging the imminent extinction of the human race. They lend zero credence to the cornucopian belief in humankind's godlike ingenuity at overcoming problems. They espouse an economics of net entropy. They view the end of oil as the end of everything. Their worldview is terminal and tragic.

The view I offer places me somewhere between these two camps, but probably a few degrees off center and closer to the die-off crowd. I believe that we face a dire and unprecedented period of difficulty in the twenty-first century, but that humankind will survive and continue further into the future—though not without taking some severe losses in the meantime, in population, in life expectancies, in standards of living, in the retention of knowledge and technology, and in decent behavior. I believe we will see a dramatic die-back, but not a die-off. It seems to me that the pattern of human existence involves long cycles of expansion and contraction, success and failure, light and darkness, brilliance and stupidity, and that it is grandiose to assert that our time is so special as to be the end of all cycles (though it would also be consistent with the narcissism of baby-boomer intellectuals to imagine ourselves to be so special). So I have to leave room for the possibility that we humans will manage to carry on, even if we must go through this dark passage to do it. We've been there before.

The Groaning Multitudes

It has been estimated that the world human population stood at about one billion around the early 1800s, which was roughly about when the industrial adventure began to gain traction.[2] It has been inferred from this that a billion people is about the limit that the planet Earth can support when it is run on a nonindustrial basis. World population is now past six and a half billion, having more than doubled since my childhood in the 1950s. The mid-twentieth century was a time of rising anxiety over the "population

1. *www.dieoff.com*, an Internet site started by Jay Hanson, popularizing the ideas of many who believe that the Industrial Age is a terminal condition of humankind.

2. Historian Paul Johnson's notion of "the Modern" commencing around the end of the Napoleonic Wars is a good benchmark. See Johnson, *The Birth of the Modern*, New York: Harper, 1991.

explosion." The marvelous technological victory over food shortages, including the "green revolution" in crop yields, accelerated that already robust leap in world population that had begun with modernity. Dramatic improvements in sanitation and medicine extended lives. Industry sopped up expanding populations and reassigned them from rural lands to work in the burgeoning cities. The perceived ability of the world to accommodate these newcomers and latecomers in a wholly new disposition of social and economic arrangements seemed be the final nail in the coffin of Thomas Robert Malthus, the much-abused author of the 1798 "An Essay on the Principle of Population as It Affects the Future Improvement of Society."

Malthus (1766–1834), an English country clergyman educated at Cambridge, has been the whipping boy of idealists and techno-optimists for two hundred years. His famous essay proposed that human population, if unconstrained, would grow exponentially while food supplies grew only arithmetically, and that therefore population growth faced strict and inevitable natural limits. Most commentators, however, took the math at face value and overlooked the part about constraints. These "checks" on population come in the form of famine, pestilence, war, and "moral restraint," i.e., the will to postpone marriage or forgo parenthood (from a perhaps antiquated notion that the ability to support a family might enter into anyone's plans for forming one, or even that society could influence such choices). Malthus's essay has been mostly misconstrued to mean that the human race was doomed at a certain arbitrary set point, and the pejorative "Malthusian" is attached to any idea that suggests that human ingenuity cannot make accommodation for more human beings to join the party on Spaceship Earth.

Interestingly, Malthus's essay was aimed at the reigning Enlightenment idealists of his own youth, the period of the American and French Revolutions, in particular the seminal figures of William Godwin and the Marquis de Condorcet. Both held that mankind was infinitely improvable and that a golden age of social justice, political harmony, equality, abundance, brotherhood, happiness, and altruism loomed imminently. Although sympathetic to social improvement, Malthus deemed these claims untenable and thought it necessary to debunk them.

In recent times, population pessimists such as Paul Ehrlich, author of *The Population Bomb* (1968), Lester Brown of the Worldwatch Institute, and other commentators who predicted dire consequences of overpopulation by 1980, were supposedly shown up by the failure of dire events to occur; this led a new generation of idealists (including cornucopians such as economist Julian Simon) to proclaim that hypergrowth was a positive benefit to society because the enlarged pool of social capital and intellect would inevitably lead to fantastic new technological discoveries that would in turn permit the earth to support a greater number of humans—including social or medical innovations that would aid eventually in establishing a permanently stabilized optimum human population.

I would offer a different view. Malthus was certainly correct, but cheap oil has skewed the equation over the past hundred years while the human race has enjoyed an unprecedented orgy of nonrenewable condensed solar energy accumulated over eons of prehistory. The "green revolution" in boosting crop yields was minimally about scientific innovation in crop genetics and mostly about dumping massive amounts of fertilizers and pesticides made out of fossil fuels onto crops, as well as employing irrigation at a fantastic scale made possible by abundant oil and gas. The cheap oil age created an artificial bubble of plenitude for a period not much longer than a human lifetime, a hundred years.

Within that comfortable bubble the idea took hold that only grouches, spoilsports, and godless maniacs considered population hypergrowth a problem, and that to even raise the issue was indecent. So, I hazard to assert that as oil ceases to be cheap and the world reserves arc toward depletion, we will indeed suddenly be left with an enormous surplus population—with apologies to both Charles Dickens and Jonathan Swift—that the ecology of the earth will not support. No political program of birth control will avail. The people are already here. The journey back to non-oil population homeostasis will not be pretty. We will discover the hard way that population hypergrowth was simply a side effect of the oil age. It was a condition, not a problem with a solution. That is what happened and we are stuck with it.

Trashed Planet

We are already experiencing huge cost externalities from population hypergrowth and profligate fossil fuel use in the form of environmental devastation. Of the earth's estimated 10 million species, 300,000 have vanished in the past fifty years. Each year, 3,000 to 30,000 species become extinct, an all-time high for the last 65 million years. Within one hundred years, between one-third and two-thirds of all birds, animals, plants, and other species will be lost. Nearly 25 percent of the 4,630 known mammal species are now threatened with extinction, along with 34 percent of fish, 25 percent of amphibians, 20 percent of reptiles, and 11 percent of birds. Even more species are having population declines.[3] Environmental scientists speak of an "omega point" at which the vast interconnected networks of Earth's ecologies are so weakened that human existence is no longer

possible. This is a variant of the die-off theme that I consider unlikely, but it does raise grave questions about the ongoing project of civilization. How long might the Long Emergency last? A generation? Ten generations? A millennium? Ten millennia? Take your choice. Of course, after a while, an emergency becomes the norm and is no longer an emergency.

Global warming is no longer a theory being disputed by political interests, but an established scientific consensus.[4] The possible effects range from events as drastic as a hydrothermal shutdown of the Gulf Stream—meaning a much colder Europe with much reduced agriculture—to desertification of major world crop-growing areas, to the invasion of temperate regions by diseases formerly limited to the tropics, to the loss of harbor cities all over the world. Whether the cause of global warming is human activity and "greenhouse emissions," a result of naturally occurring cycles, or a combination of the two, this does not alter the fact that it is having swift and tremendous impacts on civilization and that its effects will contribute greatly to the Long Emergency.

Global warming projections by the Intergovernmental Panel on Climate Change (IPCC) show a widespread increase in the risk of flooding for tens of millions of people due to increased storms and sea-level rise. Climate change is projected to aggravate water scarcity in many regions where it is already a problem. It will increase the number of people exposed to

---

3. *World Watch*, Jan./Feb. 1997, p. 7.

4. Authorities who agree that global warming and climate change are real and serious problems include the National Academy of Sciences, the UN-sponsored World Meteorological Association's Intergovernmental Panel on Climate Change (IPCC), the National Oceanic and Atmospheric Administration, the U.S. Environmental Protection Agency, the U.S. Department of Energy, NASA's Goddard Institute, the Union of Concerned Scientists, the World Resources Institute, and many others.

vector-borne disease (e.g., malaria and dengue fever) and waterborne disease (e.g., cholera). It will obviate the triumphs of the green revolution and bring on famines. It will prompt movements of populations fleeing devastated and depleted lands and provoke armed conflicts over places that are better endowed.

Global warming will add a layer of further desperation to the political turmoil ensuing from contests over dwindling oil supplies. It will aggravate the environmental destruction in China, where massive desertification and freshwater depletion are already at crisis levels, in a nation grossly overpopulated and attempting to industrialize just as the means for industrializing worldwide are diminishing. Global warming will contribute to conditions that will shut down the global economy.

Revenge of the Rain Forest and Other Tiny Destroyers

The high tide of the cheap oil age also happened to be a moment in history when human ingenuity gained an upper hand against the age-old scourges of disease. We have enjoyed the great benefits of antibiotic medicine for roughly a half-century. Penicillin, sulfa drugs, and their descendants briefly gave mankind the notion that diseases caused by microorganisms could, and indeed would, be systematically vanquished. Or, at least, this was the popular view. Doctors and scientists knew better. The discoverer of penicillin, Alexander Fleming, himself warned that antibiotic misuse could result in resistant strains of bacteria.

The recognition is now growing that the victory over microbes was short-lived. They are back in force, including familiar old enemies such as tuberculosis and staphylococcus in new drug-resistant strains. Other old diseases are on the march into new territories, as a response to climate change brought on by global warming. In response to unprecedented habitat destruction by

humans, and the invasion of wilderness, the earth itself seems to be sending forth new and much more lethal diseases, as though it had a kind of protective immune system with antibody-like agents aimed with remarkable precision at the source of the problem: *Homo sapiens*. Human immunodeficiency virus (HIV), the precursor of AIDS, may be the revenge of the rain forest. In the twentieth century, a critical mass of humans encountered organisms long hidden in tropical backwaters, presenting ripe targets for opportunistic mutant strains of immunodeficiency virus jumping species. Once infected, these humans are able to travel out of the rain forest, courtesy of motor vehicles, and reenter the social mainstream with a newly acquired ability to infect others. One theory holds that HIV first developed in the 1940s from the simian immunodeficiency virus (SIV), which has long infected green monkeys, mangabeys, and baboons in Africa. The human immunodeficiency viruses HIV-2 and HIV-O both bear similarities to SIV. The virus may have jumped to humans through the consumption of monkeys as so-called "bush meat," or through monkey bites. The virus may have infected human hosts, where it then mutated into its current lethal form. HIV probably first infected rural areas of Africa, slowly moving into the cities and around the world until it hit homosexual communities, where conditions were sufficient for rapid transmission of the disease via blood and, incidentally, other body fluids. AIDS also enjoyed the advantage of having a long incubation period so that in the initial stage of the epidemic, few if any carriers had any idea that they harbored a vicious disease, allowing them to unwittingly spread the disease further.

In any case, AIDS is now a growing menace—despite the illusion in wealthy nations such as the United States that it is a manageable chronic illness—with its cases doubling every two years around the world. Having exploded across sub-Saharan Africa, it is now marching with in-

creasing lethality into the most heavily populated parts of the world: India and China. The
virus mutates continually and there may be vari-
ants too numerous to count. It has been transmitted through homosexual and heterosexual
acts, by needle sharing among intravenous drug
addicts, and lately in China among commercial
blood harvesters reusing needles. The virus
could hardly have exhausted its ability to mutate
into new modes of transmission, and while that
ought to be a big worry for all human societies,
there is probably little that can be done about it.
A deadly emergent system has been set in motion and it has not finished emerging. All other
human problems may pale in comparison to the
AIDS epidemic in another ten years if infection
rates continue along their current arc.

At the same time, the world is overdue for
an extreme influenza epidemic. The last major
outbreak was the 1918 Spanish influenza, which
killed 50 million people worldwide and changed
the course of history. That flu, which seems to
have originated on a Kansas pig farm, affected
the outcome of World War I, toppled three dy-
nasties (the Hohenzollerns in Germany, the
Hapsburgs of Austria, and the Romanovs of Russia), and set the course of the world toward fas-
cism, communism, and the Second World War.

Disease will certainly play a larger role in
the Long Emergency than many can now imagine. An epidemic could paralyze social and economic systems, interrupt global trade, and
bring down governments. Regimes overwhelmed with population pressures—at a time
of crashing worldwide oil supplies and a melting
global economic system—might be tempted to
deploy "designer" viruses against their own
masses, inoculating beforehand an elite of select
survivors. Disease would provide a convenient
moral cover for an act of political desperation.
The medical technology is certainly available. If
this sounds too fantastic, imagine how outland-
ish the liquidation of European Jewry might

have seemed to civilized Berliners in 1933. Yet
it happened. The machinery of the Holocaust
employed all the latest state-of-the-art industrial technology, and it was carried out by the
statistically best-educated nation in Europe.

At the very least, the Long Emergency will
be a time of diminished life spans for many of
us, as well as reduced standards of living—at
least as understood within the current social
context. Fossil fuels had the effect of temporarily raising the carrying capacity of the earth.
Our ability to resist the environmental corrective of disease will probably prove to have been
another temporary boon of the cheap-oil age,
like air conditioning and lobsters flown daily
from Maine to the buffets of Las Vegas. So much
of what we construe to be among our entitlements to perpetual progress may prove to have
been a strange, marvelous, and anomalous moment in the planet's history.

Adios Globalism

The so-called global economy was not a permanent institution, as some seem to believe it was,
but a set of transient circumstances peculiar to
a certain time: the Indian summer of the fossil
fuel era. The primary enabling mechanism was
a world-scaled oil market allocation system able
to operate in an extraordinary sustained period
of relative world peace. Cheap oil, available everywhere, along with ubiquitous machines for
making other machines, neutralized many former comparative advantages, especially of geography, while radically creating new ones—
hypercheap labor, for instance. It no longer
mattered if a nation was halfway around the
globe, or had no prior experience with manufacturing. Cheap oil brought electricity to distant
parts of the world where ancient traditional
societies had previously depended on renewables such as wood and dung, mainly for cooking, as many of these places were tropical and

heating was not an issue. Factories could be started up in Sri Lanka and Malaysia, where swollen populations furnished trainable workers willing to labor for much less than those back in the United States or Europe. Products then moved around the globe in a highly rationalized system, not unlike the oil allocation system, using immense vessels, automated port facilities, and truck-scaled shipping containers at a minuscule cost-per-unit of whatever was made and transported. Shirts or coffeemakers manufactured 12,000 miles away could be shipped to Wal-Marts all over America and sold cheaply.

The ability to globalize industrial manufacturing this way stimulated a worldwide movement to relax trade barriers that had existed previously to fortify earlier comparative advantages, which were now deemed obsolete. The idea was that a rising tide of increased world trade would lift all boats. The period (roughly 1980–2001) during which these international treaties relaxing trade barriers were made—the General Agreements on Tariffs and Trade (GATT)— coincided with a steep and persistent drop in world oil and gas prices that occurred precisely because the oil crises of the 1970s had stimulated so much frantic drilling and extraction that a twenty-year oil glut ensued. The glut, in turn, allowed world leaders to forget that the globalism they were engineering depended wholly on nonrenewable fossil fuels and the fragile political arrangements that allowed their distribution. The silly idea took hold among the free, civilized people of the West, and their leaders, that the 1970s oil crises had been fake emergencies, and that oil was now actually superabundant. This was a misunderstanding of the simple fact that the North Sea and Alaskan North Slope oil fields had temporarily saved the industrial West when they came online in the early 1980s, and postponed the fossil fuel depletion reckoning toward which the world has been inexorably moving.

Meanwhile, among economists and government figures, globalism developed the sexy glow of an intellectual fad. Globalism allowed them to believe that burgeoning wealth in the developed countries, and the spread of industrial activity to formerly primitive regions, was based on the potency of their own ideas and policies rather than on cheap oil. Margaret Thatcher's apparent success in turning around England's sclerotic economy was an advertisement for these policies, which included a heavy dose of privatization and deregulation. Overlooked is that Thatcher's success in reviving England coincided with a fantastic new revenue stream from North Sea oil, as quaint old Britannia became energy self-sufficient and a net energy-exporting nation for the first time since the heyday of coal. Globalism then infected America when Ronald Reagan came on the scene in 1981. Reagan's "supply-side" economic advisors retailed a set of fiscal ideas that neatly accessorized the new notions about free trade and deregulation, chiefly that massively reducing taxes would actually result in greater revenues as the greater aggregate of business activity generated a greater aggregate of taxes even at lower rates. (What it actually generated was huge government deficits.)

By the mid-1980s deregulated markets and unbridled business were regarded as magic bullets to cure the ills of senile smokestack industrialism. Greed was good. Young college graduates marched into MBA programs in hordes, hoping to emerge as corporate ninja warriors. It was precisely the entrepreneurial zest of brilliant young corporate innovators that produced the wizardry of the computer industry. The rise of computers, in turn, promoted the fantasy that commerce in sheer information would be the long-sought replacement for all the played-out activities of the smokestack economy. A country like America, it was now thought, no longer needed steelmaking or tire factories or other harsh, dirty, troublesome enterprises. Let the poor masses of Asia and South America have them and lift themselves up from agricultural peonage. America would outsource all this old economy stuff and use computers to orchestrate the movement of parts and the assembly of products from distant quarters of the world, and then sell the stuff in our own Kmarts and Wal-Marts, which would become global juggernauts of retailing. Computers, it was believed, would stupendously increase productivity all the way down the line. The jettisoned occupational niches in industry would be replaced by roles in the service economy that went hand in hand with the information economy. We would become a nation of hair stylists, masseurs, croupiers, restaurant owners, and show business agents, catering to one another's needs. Who wanted to work in a rolling mill?

Finally, the disgrace of Soviet communism in the early 1990s resolved any lingering philosophical complaints among the educated classes about the morality of business per se and of the institutions needed to run it. The Soviet fiasco had proven that a state without property laws or banking was just another kind of scaled-up social Ponzi scheme running on cheap oil and slave labor.[5]

5. Charles K. Ponzi (1888–1949), an Italian-born swindler who emigrated first to Canada, in 1903, where he served a prison term for forgery, came to the United States in 1920 and devised an investment fraud based on the same "pyramid" principles as a chain letter. Early investors in the postal coupon scam, which Ponzi ran out of Boston, were paid with money from later investors. Within six months, Ponzi was in the hands of federal prosecutors. He was sentenced to five years on a single plea-bargained count of mail fraud. He later engaged in Florida land swindles. He spent the 1930s in and out of state and federal penitentiaries. He was eventually deported back to Italy, moved to Brazil before World War II, and died in the charity ward of a Rio de Janeiro hospital in 1949, leaving an estate of $75 to cover funeral expenses.

In the short term, finance also benefited hugely from the removal of legal barriers to trade in currencies and investment instruments between nations. Computers enabled money to move around the planet at the speed of light. Investors in Luxembourg could just as easily invest in American securities, or in China's, as in their own. Other players benefited from trading in world currencies, securities, commodities, and interest rates at minute differentials that existed because, since the 1970s, all monies and fungible financial instruments pegged to money floated on a collective hallucination of relative value, rather than being pegged to a fixed medium of value, such as gold. This aggravated the tendency, in a financial climate of extreme relativism, to create increasingly abstract vehicles of investment that were pegged to little more than wishes. These so-called derivatives ended up far removed from the actual purpose of investment, which is to pay for new or expanded enterprise in return for earnings and dividends, and instead simply became an end in themselves: bets within global finance casinos. Eventually, this speculative trade was carried on by firms and individuals at such huge increments that whole national currencies and economies could be undermined, as when financier George Soros devalued the British pound in a single currency trade gamble, or when the Long-Term Capital Management firm, operating out of a luxury boiler room in suburban Connecticut, nearly destabilized the entire world finance system in a skein of fantastically huge and complex hedged derivatives trades—i.e., wild bets.

Finance under globalism, or turbo-capitalism (Edward Luttwak's term), or neoliberal economics (John Gray's term) took on the characteristics of a worldwide pyramid racket, played against the background of a geopolitical game of musical chairs.[6] In this case, the profits of a generation of speculators would be converted into costs passed along to future generations in the form of lost jobs, squandered equity, and reduced living standards. It was also like a convoluted liquidation sale of the accrued wealth of two hundred years of industrial society for the benefit of a handful of financial buccaneers, with the great masses relegated to a race to the bottom as the economic assets are dismantled and sold off, and their livelihoods are closed down. Both Luttwak and Gray make the case that millennial economics produced ever-greater disparities between winners and losers, between the wealthy and the poor, and that these deformities of economic behavior have the power to wreck societies.

I have argued in previous books that capitalism is not strictly speaking an "ism," in the sense that it is not so much a set of beliefs as a set of laws describing the behavior of money as it relates to accumulated real wealth or resources. This wealth can be directed toward the project of creating more wealth, which we call investment, and the process can be rationally organized within a body of contract and property law. Within that system are many subsets of rules and laws that describe the way money in motion operates, much as the laws of physics describe the behavior of objects in motion. Concepts such as interest, credit, revenue, profit, and default don't require a belief in capitalism in order to operate. Compound interest has worked equally well for communists and Wall Street financiers, whatever they personally thought about the social effects of wealth and poverty. People of widely differing beliefs are also equally subject to the law of gravity.

6. Edward Luttwak, *Turbo Capitalism: Winners and Losers in the Global Economy*, New York: HarperCollins, 1999; John Gray, *False Dawn: The Delusions of Global Capitalism,* New York: New Press, 1998.

It is therefore not a matter of whether people believe in capitalism (hyper, turbo, neoliberal, or anything else you might call it), but of the choices they make as individuals, and in the aggregate as communities and nations, that determine their destiny. I am going to argue in later chapters that Americans in particular among the so-called "advanced" nations made some especially bad choices as to how they would behave in the twilight of the fossil fuel age. For instance, conditions over the past two decades made possible the consolidation of retail trade by a handful of predatory, opportunistic corporations, of which Wal-Mart is arguably the epitome. That this development was uniformly greeted as a public good by the vast majority of Americans, at the same time that their local economies were being destroyed—and with them, myriad social and civic benefits—is one of the greater enigmas of recent social history. In effect, Americans threw away their communities in order to save a few dollars on hair dryers and plastic food storage tubs, never stopping to reflect on what they were destroying. The necessary restoration of local networks of economic interdependence, and the communities that rely on them, will be a major theme later in this book.

I will also propose that globalism as we have known it is in the process of ending. Its demise will coincide with the end of the cheap-oil age. For better or worse, many of the circumstances we associate with globalism will be reversed. Markets will close as political turbulence and military mischief interrupt trade relations. As markets close, societies will turn increasingly to import replacement for sheer economic survival. The cost of transport will no longer be negligible in a post-cheap-oil age. Many of our agricultural products will have to be produced closer to home, and probably by more intensive hand labor as oil and natural gas supplies become increasingly unstable. The world will stop shrinking and become larger again. Virtually all of the economic relationships among persons, nations, institutions, and things that we have taken for granted as permanent will be radically changed during the Long Emergency. Life will become intensely and increasingly local.

The End of the Drive-In Utopia

America finds itself nearing the end of the cheap-oil age having invested its national wealth in a living arrangement—suburban sprawl—that has no future. When media commentators cast about struggling to explain what has happened in our country economically, they uniformly overlook the colossal misinvestment that suburbia represents—a prodigious, unparalleled misallocation of resources. This is quite apart from its social, spiritual, and ecological deficiencies as an everyday environment. We constructed an armature for daily living that simply won't work without liberal supplies of cheap oil, and very soon we will be without both the oil needed to run it and the wealth needed to replace it. Nor are we likely to come up with a miraculous energy replacement for oil that will allow us to run all this everyday infrastructure even remotely the same way. I will go into detail about the mirage of alternative fuels later, in Chapter Four.

In any case, the tragic truth is that much of suburbia is unreformable. It does not lend itself to being retrofitted into the kind of mixed-use, smaller-scaled, more fine-grained walkable environments we will need to carry on daily life in the coming age of greatly reduced motoring. Nor is a Jolly Green Giant going to come and pick up the millions of suburban houses on their half-acre lots on cul-de-sac streets in the far-flung subdivisions and set them back down closer together to make more civic environments. Instead, this suburban real estate,

including the chipboard and vinyl McHouses, the strip malls, the office parks, and all the other components, will enter a phase of rapid and cruel devaluation. Many of the suburban subdivisions will become the slums of the future.

Overall, I view the period ahead as one of generalized and chronic contraction. In the final chapter I will discuss comprehensively what this means in terms of how we may have to live. I refer to this process as the downscaling of America—rescaling or rightsizing might be other ways to say it. All of our accustomed modes of activity are going to have to change in the direction of smaller, fewer, and better. The crisis in agriculture will be one of the defining conditions of the Long Emergency. We will simply have to grow more of our food locally. The crisis will present itself when industrial farming, dependent on massive oil and gas "inputs" at gigantic scales of operation, can no longer be carried on economically. The implications for how we use our land are tremendous, and the unavoidable change is likely to be accompanied by severe social turbulence, not to mention hunger and hardship. Well into the Long Emergency, food production at the local level may become the focus of the American economy. The fact that it will almost certainly require a lot of human labor has further implications of its own.

We'll have to live in geographically more circumscribed surroundings. As the suburbs disintegrate, we will be lucky if we can reconstitute our existing traditional towns and cities brick by brick and street by street, painfully by hand. Our bigger cities will be in trouble, and some of them may not remain habitable, especially if the natural gas supply problem proves to be as dire as it now appears and electric power generation that depends on it becomes erratic. Skyscrapers will prove to be more experimental than we had come to think. In general, we will probably have to return to a settlement pattern of towns and small cities surrounded by intensively cultivated agricultural hinterlands. When that happens, we will be a far less affluent society and the amount, scale, and increment of new building will seem very modest in years ahead by current standards. We will have access to far fewer, if any, modular building systems. Construction will be much more dependent on traditional masonry, carpentry, and other journeyman skills using simple, easily obtainable, regionally determined materials. Our building and zoning codes will be increasingly ignored. If we return to a human scale of building, there's a good chance that our new urban quarters will be more humane, which is to say beautiful. The automobile era proved that people easily tolerated ugly, utilitarian buildings and horrible streetscapes as long as they were compensated by being able to quickly escape the vicinity in cars luxuriously appointed with the finest digital stereo sound, air conditioning, and cup holders for iced beverages. This will change radically. There will be far less motoring. The future will be much more about staying where you are than traveling incessantly from place to place, as we do now.

The state-of-the-art mega-suburbs of recent decades have produced horrendous levels of alienation, loneliness, anomie, anxiety, and depression, and we may well be better off without them. Note, by the way, that we have been the only nation among the so-called advanced ones to sacrifice our traditional cities and towns so remorselessly to suburbia. Elsewhere, in Europe, Asia, and South America, whatever else their problems may be, cities and towns still exist intact in a more distinct relationship with nearby rural lands. The restoration job in America will be more difficult.

But since I believe that the human race will carry on for many generations after the end of the cheap-oil era, and that civilization of some

form can continue with it, then I would have to suppose that the seasons of civilization will continue with the great cycles of contraction and expansion, and at some point in the future, who knows how many years distant, some of these cities in a land once called America may be robust and cosmopolitan in ways that we can't imagine now, anymore than a Roman of A.D. 38 might have been able to imagine the future London of the Beatles.

In the Long Emergency, some regions of the United States will do better than others and some will suffer deeply. Places that benefited disproportionately during the cheap-oil blowout will find themselves steeply challenged when those benefits, and the entitlement psychology that grew out of them, are withdrawn in the face of new, austere circumstances. The so-called Sunbelt presents extraordinary problems. This is not a good time to begin thinking about moving to Phoenix or Las Vegas. Parts of the Southwest may be significantly depopulated, starved for energy and thirsting for water that depended on cheap energy. Other parts may become contested territory with Mexico. The prospects for disorder in the southeastern states is especially high, given the extremes of religiosity, hyper-individualism, and a cultural disinhibition regarding violence. The social glue holding communities and regions together will be severely strained by the loss of amenities presumed to be normal.

I view the period of history we have lived through as a narrative episode in a greater saga of human history. The industrial story has a beginning, a middle, and an end. It begins in the mid-eighteenth century with coal and the first steam engines, proceeds to a robust second act climaxing in the years before World War I, and moves toward a third act resolution now that we can anticipate with some precision the depletion of the resources that made the industrial episode possible. As the industrial story ends, the greater saga of mankind will move on into a new episode, the Long Emergency. This is perhaps a self-evident point, but throughout history, even the most important and self-evident trends are often completely ignored because the changes they foreshadow are simply unthinkable. That process is sometimes referred to as an "outside context problem," something so far beyond the ordinary experience of those dwelling in a certain time and place that they cannot make sense of available information. The collective mental static preventing comprehension is also sometimes referred to as "cognitive dissonance," a term borrowed from developmental psychology. It helps explain why the American public has been sleepwalking into the future.

The Long Emergency is going to be a tremendous trauma for the human race. It is likely to entail political turbulence every bit as extreme as the economic conditions that prompt it. We will not believe that this is happening to us, that two hundred years of modernity can be brought to its knees by a worldwide power shortage. The prospect will be so grim that some individuals and perhaps even groups (as in nations) may develop all the symptoms of suicidal depression. Self-genocide has certainly been within the means of mankind since the 1950s.

The survivors will have to cultivate a religion of hope, that is, a deep and comprehensive belief that humanity is worth carrying on. I say this as someone who has not followed any kind of lifelong organized religion. But I don't doubt that the hardships of the future will draw even the most secular spirits into an emergent spiritual practice of some kind. There is an excellent chance that this will go way too far, as Christianity and other belief systems have done at various times, in various ways.

If it happens that the human race doesn't make it, then the fact that we were here once will not be altered, that once upon a time we peopled this astonishing blue planet, and wondered intelligently at everything about it and the other things who lived here with us on it, and that we celebrated the beauty of it in music and art, architecture, literature, and dance, and that there were times when we approached something godlike in our abilities and aspirations. We emerged out of depthless mystery, and back into mystery we returned, and in the end the mystery is all there is.

Discussion Questions

1. Kunstler suggests that the cornucopian point of view about resources is "the default point of view of the majority of Americans." Do you agree with this statement? What evidence is there to the contrary?

2. In the Long Emergency, Kunstler says that everyday life in our technological society will be fundamentally altered. What kind of changes does he, and do you, anticipate being required in this scenario?

3. Kunstler speaks about globalism as "the Indian Summer of the fossil fuel era" because he views it as a "set of transient circumstances" particular to (and dependent on) the era of cheap oil. What examples support this idea? What is the logical outcome of the end of globalism?

4. The picture painted of the period Kunstler calls the Long Emergency is a fairly doomsday image of the future. Do you think there is value in presenting this image? Why or why not?

5. In popular fiction there are many dystopian views of a future without oil, such as the George Miller Road Warrior movies (*Mad Max* [1979], *Mad Max 2: The Road Warrior* [1981], *Mad Max Beyond Thunderdrome* [1985], and *Mad Max: Fury Road* [2015]). The web site http://www.futurescenarios.org/content/view/44/60/ explores a number of post-oil futures that are not as dystopian. Which vision of the future do you think is most likely, and why? What actions, if any, are possible to avoid the post-oil dystopian future vision?

6. Do you believe that we really are running out of oil? Why or why not? If we are running out, how long do you think it will take and when will we start feeling the effects on our society?

 Supporting Activities

1. Kunstler writes that the United States is the only developed nation that has adopted a suburban mode of development rather than a majority of its citizens living in towns and cities. Try to discover the factors that led to widespread suburban development in the United States.

2. Visit James Howard Kunstler's web site and view his meanderings on architecture, technology, history, and "other stuff" (http://kunstler.com/).

3. In small groups, investigate various predictions about how much oil is left. What are the longest, and shortest, estimates given? How much consistency is there across the different predictions? How would you characterize those sources of information that reflect more pessimistic, and more optimistic, predictions about the amount of oil left?

 Additional Resources

1. Read the books in Kunstler's trilogy: *World Made by Hand* (2009), *The Witch of Hebron* (2011), and *A History of the Future* (2014).

2. Learn more about one of the more hidden effects of population growth and fossil fuel use: the extinction of species. Visit the Center for Biological Diversity web site (http://www.biologicaldiversity.org/index.html); read this 2014 BBC report on species loss (http://www.bbc.com/news/science-environment-29418983); and read a *New Yorker* article by writer Elizabeth Kolbert on the

so-called "Sixth Extinction" (http://www.newyorker.com/magazine/2009/05/25/the-sixth-extinction).

3. Read the article "What if We Never Run Out of Oil?" by Charles C. Mann, listed in the Reference section below.

 References

De Chant, T. (2014, March 26). The inevitability of predicting the future. *NovaNext.* PBS. Retrieved from http://www.pbs.org/wgbh/nova/next/tech/predicting-the-future/

Joy, B. (2000). Why the future doesn't need us. *Wired,* 8(4), 238–262. Available: www.wired.com/wired/archive/8.04/joy.html.

Kay, A. C. (1989). Predicting the future. *Stanford Engineering, 1*(1), 1–6. Retrieved from http://www.ecotopia.com/webpress/futures.htm

Loveridge, D. (2009). *Foresight: The art and science of anticipation.* New York, NY: Routledge.

Mann, C. C. (2013). What if we never run out of oil? *The Atlantic, 311*(4), 48–63.